"The *fundamentals* of the Philippine economy, allege our economic managers, remain strong. If this were so, why the poverty? This important volume shows the lack of economic imagination that bedevils Philippine policymakers. And it offers a stark warning: more of the same policies means more of the same results."

Lisandro E. Claudio, *Associate Professor, Department of South and Southeast Asian Studies, and Chair, Center for Southeast Asia Studies, Berkeley University, USA*

"The Philippines has been left behind over the last few decades relative to its close East Asian neighbors as a result of a flawed economic development strategy. The government, under constant pressure from multilateral agencies such as the IMF to pursue fiscal austerity, has failed to pursue a high productivity industrial strategy based on manufacturing. Instead, it has overseen a burgeoning service sector which has resulted in low-paid and low productivity employment. Part of this problem has been the dominance of orthodox macroeconomic thinking that has constrained the government's capacity to use fiscal policy to build public goods and infrastructure that would crowd in productive private investment. The Philippines suffers from massive underinvestment because of the unwillingness to use fiscal deficits to promote growth. This book is a very valuable contribution because it correctly frames the problems that the nation faces and provides viable and sensible solutions to take the Philippines forward. It is a rare voice in an environment where the orthodox macroeconomic consensus creates a cone of silence and a climate of denial."

William Mitchell, *Professor of Economics, Centre of Full Employment and Equity University of Newcastle, Australia*

"Unlike South Korea, the Philippines failed to implement a successful land reform capable of making meritocracy credible, nor did it pursue a coordinated strategy of human resource development aligned with export-oriented industrialization. This book examines the Philippines' disappointing economic performance since the mid-1970s, characterized by modest growth with limited structural transformation, and explores how the country can address innovation, coordination, and governance challenges going forward. It is essential reading for those interested in the Philippines and in comparative Asian development."

Wonhyuk Lim, *Professor, KDI School of Public Policy and Management, Korea*

THE PHILIPPINE ECONOMY TOWARD 2050

Economic Structure and Monetary Reality

This book provides a rigorous analysis of the factors underlying the Philippines' relative economic stagnation compared with its Southeast Asian neighbors despite sustained optimistic government rhetoric.

Three critical factors are identified: failure to industrialize and undergo a complete economic transformation, resulting in an underdeveloped agricultural sector and an economy dependent on low-productivity services; ineffective reforms that differ markedly from successful regional models; and self-defeating fiscal conservatism that has prevented adequate investment in essential public goods and industrial policy. Using two innovative economic models—a macroeconometric model and an employment–education forecasting model—the book offers forecasts of the Philippines' income per capita, poverty, or economic structure, through 2050. The researchers warn that unless the country's economic policy focuses on the transformation of the economy (with emphasis on the modernization of agriculture and the development of the manufacturing sector) and the government adopts a more active role, the Philippines will experience *more of the same* (MOTS) during the next decades.

An accessible resource for scholars, students, journalists, officials, and business professionals as an introduction to Philippine history, politics, and economy, the book will also be useful for development practitioners with its insights on structural transformation and on fiscal and monetary policy.

Jesus Felipe is Distinguished Full Professor, Research Fellow, and Dr. Liu Ta-Jen Distinguished Professorial Chair in Business and Economics at the Carlos L. Tiu School of Economics, De La Salle University, Philippines.

Mariel Monica Sauler is Associate Professor at the Carlos L. Tiu School of Economics, De La Salle University, Philippines.

Christopher Cabuay is Associate Professor at the Carlos L. Tiu School of Economics, De La Salle University, Philippines.

Alellie Sobreviñas is Associate Professor at the Carlos L. Tiu School of Economics, De La Salle University, Philippines.

Susan Kurdli is Assistant Professor at the Department of Political Science and Development Studies, De La Salle University, Philippines.

Julián Pérez is Professor at the Department of Applied Economics, Universidad Autónoma de Madrid, Spain.

Eva Marie Aragones is Research Assistant and PhD student at the Carlos L. Tiu School of Economics, De La Salle University, Philippines.

Gerardo Largoza is Associate Professor at the Carlos L. Tiu School of Economics, De La Salle University, Philippines.

THE PHILIPPINE ECONOMY TOWARD 2050

Economic Structure and Monetary Reality

Jesus Felipe, Mariel Monica Sauler, Christopher Cabuay, Alellie Sobreviñas, Susan Kurdli, Julián Pérez, Eva Marie Aragones, and Gerardo Largoza

Routledge
Taylor & Francis Group
LONDON AND NEW YORK

Designed cover image: Getty Images

First published 2026
by Routledge
4 Park Square, Milton Park, Abingdon, Oxon OX14 4RN

and by Routledge
605 Third Avenue, New York, NY 10158

Routledge is an imprint of the Taylor & Francis Group, an informa business

British Library Cataloguing-in-Publication Data
A catalogue record for this book is available from the British Library

Library of Congress Cataloging-in-Publication Data
A catalog record for this book has been requested

ISBN: 978-1-041-21726-8 (hbk)
ISBN: 978-1-041-21725-1 (pbk)
ISBN: 978-1-003-72871-9 (ebk)

DOI: 10.4324/9781003728719

Typeset in Optima
by Apex CoVantage, LLC

We dedicate this book to the future generations, in the hope that they do not have to endure MOTS.

The authors

Manila, November 2025

CONTENTS

Foreword by Arlene Inocencio *xi*
Foreword by Raul Fabella *xv*
Preface and Acknowledgments *xxiv*

1 Introduction and Overview of the Book 1

2 A Brief Overview of the Economic History of the Philippines 16

3 A Primer on Growth: Facts, Constraints, and Engines 43

4 The Structure of the Philippine Economy 71

5 Philippine Development Plans: Development Misunderstandings 121

6 Why Has Philippine Progress Been Slow? I: Incomplete Land Reforms, the Role of Government, and a Weak State with a Rent-Seeking Private Sector 146

7 Why Has Philippine Progress Been Slow? II: Failed Industrialization Programs 162

8 Innovation, Firms, Capabilities, and Modern Industrial Policy 199

9 Why Is the Philippine State Weak?: Spatial and Temporal Fragmentation Obstructing Structural Transformation 213

10 Employment and Education in the Philippines: Misconceptions and Realities 227

11 The Fiscal Deficit, the National Debt, and Monetary Reality: Old Habits Die Hard 249

12 The Philippine Economy Toward 2050: Aspirations and Reality 280

13 Forecasting Employment and Educational Needs 301

14 Poverty and the Cost of a Decent Basket: Who Can Afford It? 332

15 Final Thoughts 349

References *355*
Index *371*

FOREWORD

In 2022, a group of researchers at De La Salle University (DLSU) launched a research program on the future of the Philippine economy. The objective was to seriously examine how far the economy could progress by 2050. This required confronting difficult but necessary issues, including the country's prospects for reaching high-income status, the likely structure of the economy, and the extent to which poverty could be substantially reduced.

The Philippines missed the development train in the 1980s, precisely when other East Asian economies were accelerating. Today, the Philippines has a lower per capita income than several countries that were poorer than it only relatively recently. While many factors are often cited, the fundamental explanation is straightforward: These economies grew faster and eventually overtook us. Despite this, the country's long-run underperformance of its economy has been touted as a "mystery."

This book argues that there is, in fact, no mystery behind the country's weak economic performance since the late 1970s. In essence, the Philippines did not do what its neighbors did—and what historically all successful economies have done. They industrialized by building sizable manufacturing sectors that absorbed labor from agriculture and competed in export markets. These processes generated a virtuous cycle of productivity growth and rising incomes. Over time, their export baskets became more sophisticated, and foreign exchange earnings helped ease balance of payments constraints.

While industrialization featured prominently in the agenda of the first Philippine administrations after independence and an incipient manufacturing sector did emerge, this objective largely faded after President Marcos Sr. left office in 1986.

Over the past four decades, the country has searched for alternative sources of growth outside manufacturing. Services became the default strategy. However, services have not delivered the sustained growth rates that manufacturing generated in neighboring economies. Economic performance over the past two decades has been acceptable—characterized by positive growth up to 2020—but insufficient to close the gap. The Philippines grew, but so did its neighbors. As a result, South Korea, Thailand, Indonesia, China, and Vietnam now all have higher per capita incomes. As of the completion of this book in late 2025, the Philippines remains a lower-middle-income country, with GNI per capita below USD 4,500.

In 2022, President Marcos Jr. won the presidential election, and shortly thereafter, his administration adopted an ambitious Philippine Development Plan for 2022–2028. The plan targeted annual growth rates of 6.5–8.0% for most of his term. These targets have not been realized, and there are structural reasons why.

As the DLSU research team began work on this book, it quickly became apparent that the administration's growth targets were out of reach. Careful analysis of the economy's growth potential suggests that a rate closer to 6% is the realistic upper bound. The explanation lies in the structure of the economy, particularly employment. A large share of Filipino workers remains in agriculture and low-productivity services. While the Philippines does have a manufacturing sector, it employs relatively few workers. From an output perspective, manufacturing remains weakly competitive internationally. There is little mystery, then, as to why growth cannot be significantly higher.

The book advances a second fundamental argument: The Philippines suffers from chronic underinvestment resulting from insufficient deficit spending—that is, government spending exceeding tax revenues. This underspending reflects a widespread belief that the government must first collect taxes before it can spend, much like a household. This view is incorrect and inconsistent with how modern governments operate. Governments spend by coordinating payments through the treasury and central bank, crediting bank accounts in the private sector. This process creates money. Taxes play an important role in the economy, but they do not finance government spending. Rather, taxes return money to the central bank, effectively reducing the money supply. While this may seem counterintuitive, it reflects standard monetary operations.

This understanding implies that the government can financially afford the goods and services the country urgently needs, particularly in infrastructure, education, and health. The authors are careful to emphasize that this description of government finance does not imply that the state can or should spend without restraint. It simply means that pesos—the national currency—are not a scarce resource, despite often being treated as such in policy discussions. In economic terms, *scarcity* refers to real resources: labor, materials, technology, and institutional capacity. While the economy may face real constraints, such as shortages of construction inputs or skilled workers, pesos themselves cannot be scarce. Accordingly, there is little doubt that the government can financially afford essential public services.

Most of these services—including infrastructure, health, education, and efforts to eradicate malnutrition—are paid for in pesos.

Misunderstanding the country's monetary reality has fueled misplaced concerns about fiscal deficits and national debt denominated in pesos. Fiscal deficits are, in fact, necessary to prevent the private sector from running financial deficits, particularly in an economy that consistently runs current account deficits. The administration's emphasis on deficit reduction is therefore misguided. National debt, largely in the form of treasury bills, represents private sector wealth peso for peso and plays a stabilizing role in the financial system. Fiscal responsibility should not be defined by matching spending with tax revenues but by ensuring that the government provides the services the economy and society require.

With these two foundations, the research team asked how far the Philippine economy can realistically progress by 2050. To address this question, the authors developed the ANIMO econometric model of the Philippine economy. Their conclusion is sobering. Under current structural dynamics, the economy will continue to grow, but not at a pace meaningfully different from recent experience. The result is what the authors describe as "more of the same" (MOTS). Per capita income will rise and poverty will decline, but the Philippines will not approach the income levels of South Korea, much less Singapore.

Achieving faster and sustained growth will require a different economic structure—one anchored in manufacturing and exports, and therefore active participation in global markets. At present, most employment generation occurs in low-productivity services, such as retail and delivery. The authors rightly note that the Philippines cannot industrialize today in the same way South Korea did in the 1970s. Nonetheless, they argue that it is essential to identify competitive niches among the wide range of manufactured products produced globally. This process would also support the modernization of agriculture, which still employs more than 20% of Filipino workers at low productivity and low wages. High-income status will remain unattainable as long as this sector remains large and underproductive.

The critical question is whether Philippine firms possess the capabilities to compete, not only in domestic markets, but also globally. The uncomfortable reality is that many firms lack the organizational and technological capacity required to produce high-quality goods at scale.

Recent political developments and corruption scandals have weakened confidence and weighed on growth. While these challenges are likely to be resolved and growth may recover, the administration's original growth targets will remain difficult to achieve. At the same time, this moment presents an opportunity to rethink the country's development strategy. The greater risk, as the authors emphasize, is prolonged stagnation—additional decades of MOTS.

On behalf of the DLSU community, I congratulate the authors for their sustained effort over the past three years to deepen understanding of the Philippine economy and to produce realistic projections through 2050. Their work stands in contrast to the optimistic but simplistic extrapolations that often dominate public discourse. I urge policymakers to engage seriously with these findings and to reconsider a development narrative that has, for too long, left the Philippines trailing its East Asian peers.

Arlene Inocencio
Professor and Dean
Carlos L. Tiu School of Economics
De La Salle University

FOREWORD

By 2025, the evidence that the economic model the Philippines has chosen for itself since the 1980s has led to economic mediocrity, if not ultimately to bankruptcy, has become obvious. This book makes this clear. The volume makes a good case for why that could be so but also suggests alternatives that may serve the economy better as we approach 2050.

First and most glaring is how the Philippines has failed to keep up with its Asian neighbors in per capita income and income distribution. From being one of the envied economies in the region, made manifest by in-migration from neighboring economies—from China in the 1950s to students from Thailand, Indonesia, and Malaysia in the 1960s—we have moved to the bottom of the original ASEAN-6 pile and have been forced to eat the dust of neighbors who were our virtual tutees in business services, accounting, banking, and capital raising (stock market). Vietnam has also overtaken us in income per capita.

The problem started much before the 1980s, but I emphasize the 1980s because it represented a rare opportunity for a reset not just politically but also economically. Instead, we ended the 1980s by instituting the 1987 Constitution, which doubled down on the nationalistic and domestic market-oriented structure following the 1937 Constitution while emphasizing provisions that ensured the non-recurrence of the authoritarian regime. Other episodes in history such as the aftermath of the Asian Financial Crisis of 1998 also opened the opportunity for a reset but seemed never to have been taken.

It became clear by the late 1980s that export promotion and its twin, the incentivizing of the tradable goods sector, has exhibited an undeniable superiority over import substitution and its twin, the incentivizing of the non-traded goods sector. The volume shows this clearly through the comparative cross-country GNI per capita trajectories. Why did this come to pass? The disproportionate influence of the leftist ideology among the cabinet of President Corazon Aquino saw to it that the economy tilted away from greater openness and leaned in favor of doubling down on the familiar home-market orientation. Although the openness rhetoric was present and championed by former NEDA secretary Gerardo Sicat, it never became a serious consideration. Instead, it was served with what this volume correctly calls *palliative economics*, policies that carried the rhetoric but not the substance of a real pivot. The great Japanese factory export to the ASEAN did not materialize in the Philippines primarily because of the political turmoil (coup d'état rumors and risks) and also because of the massive overvaluation of the peso in the wake of the central bank intervention via the so-called *Jobo bills* that forced the peso to return to its pre-crisis levels via very high interest rates. The resulting post–Jobo bills exchange rate level mismatched greatly with the post-crisis economic capacity. It was not unlike the forcing of the peso to its pre-WWII value (2 pesos per US dollar) that mismatched enormously with the devastated economic capacity due to WWII.

The Philippines never abandoned industrialization as a goal, but it decided to pursue it through non-traded goods industrialization. It was convenient since non-traded goods industrialization thrives on currency overvaluation even as it throttles traded goods industrialization. Moreover, non-traded goods do not compete with its global counterparts. There even was a rhetoric that manufacturing was no longer the way to modern industrialization, a thesis that Vietnam has proved false.

What was not clear immediately post–EDSA revolution was that democracy had become demonstrably superior to autocracy as a way to steer the economy to better performance. That Acemoglu and Robinson (2019) had to argue the case for *liberty* as superior to autocracy in the long-run growth 50 years later showed the ambiguity of the thesis at that time. Our acclaimed, better-performing neighbors, such as Singapore, South Korea, and Taiwan, had some form or another of autocracy. Lee Kuan Yew made the "politically democratic on paper" Philippines as a running spectacle to terrorize the Singapore polity away from the allure of democratic ideals. General Park Chung Hee chased out democracy with Syngman Rhee, and Taiwan was under the spell of the Chiang Kai-Shek and Kuomintang Party martial law to guide their faithful journeys. The Philippines and Indonesia also tried to make the tradeoff between political space and economic space (less of the first, more of the second). Marcos (1971) showed part of this rhetoric but failed to replicate the emerging economic miracles. This remains a challenge to the social sciences even to this day: Why did autocracy succeed spectacularly in some but not in others? Less political space but even less, and not more, economic space in the latter was the outcome. This was the Omega question to many economists. Why did the rents made available by strong industrial policy in the first case become the propulsion needed to attain escape velocity from underdevelopment and poverty but became the deadweight burden in the case of the second? Import substitution was clearly a strong industrial policy with large rents that potentially privatized. The fact of the matter is that almost all developing countries started their modernization journey prompted by the big push theory with import substitution.

Rosenstein-Rodan's "big push" idea got its most enthusiastic affirmation with the signal success of the US Marshall Plan, which bankrolled the post-WWII reconstruction of war-ravaged Europe. Rosenstein-Rodan argued that indivisibilities and market failures abounded in the aftermath, especially in infrastructure, and restoring them with a *big push* was the fastest and most efficient way to resolve these problems. The capital gap was clear: Europe did not have the wherewithal to restore its collapsed infrastructure, and capital-abundant America came to the rescue to almost miraculous harvest. The so-called "30 Glorious Years" of Western European growth followed (see, for example, Fabella, 2011).

It was child's play to infer that leapfrogging, similar indivisibilities, and market failures, which also mar post-WWII underdeveloped economies, would produce the same magic. This big push idea, it was argued, will give rise to increasing returns and external economies in various interdependent sectors that will be self-sustaining. Nurkse's (1953) clarion call for a balance growth among the various economic organs growing pari passu to support each other also supported Rosenstein-Rodan's view. The unspoken premise behind the generous Marshall Plan was the growing geopolitical challenge of the socialist bloc led by the fast-recovering Soviet Union. The generosity of America to Western Europe was America's answer to the growing stature of the socialist challenge. The response of the Western capitalist bloc to the financing gap problem in the third world in the form of aid was also partly explained by the socialist challenge that was increasingly attractive to newly independent countries. Leibenstein (1957) corroborated the big push with his proposal of the "critical minimum effort"—low-level equilibria seen marring the development landscape like so many sinkholes on the ground. The consensus hardened with W. W. Rostow's stage of economic development with the "takeoff" as "when the scale of productivity reaches critical level and produces transformations." Gerschenkron (1962) corroborated it. This led to import substitution as the embodiment of the big push/great spurt/minimum critical effort for takeoff. Meanwhile, Domar (1946) proposed a growth model where the GDP was a fixed proportion of the share in investment in GDP. This came to be known as the *Harrod–Domar growth model*. The Harrod–Domar model found its further articulation in the *Lewis–Ranis–Fei dualistic model*, which saw surplus labor in the agricultural sector as the lynchpin for economic transformation. The demand was there in the form of imports helped along by aid, and the supply was there in the form of surplus labor wedded to available mature technology but that had to be afforded. Aid was a first path to affordance of technology. These thinkers coalesced tightly around capital deficit as the main bottleneck and foreign aid as the response. Meanwhile, the Prebisch–Singer thesis (Prebisch, 1950/1962; Singer, 1950) proclaimed the unequal trade between the center and the periphery: The terms of trade between the exports of the periphery, which exported primary commodities, and the center, which exported finished goods made from those primary products, will always be falling against the periphery. It was not a good idea to be a supplier of primary products to the West.

By the 1970s, it was becoming clear that while sustained growth was becoming a reality in some parts of East Asia, it was not yet patent everywhere. The petrodollar loans superabundant in the aftermath of the Arab–Israeli war greatly eased the capital deficit, but the development outlook for many countries did not improve. Instead, sustained growth and poverty reduction concentrated in the so-called East Asian corridor to form the so-called East Asian miracle economies. Everywhere else, it translated only into massive foreign indebtedness, the solutions to which engaged many bright minds, culminating in the Washington Consensus I ("get prices right") and followed by the Washington Consensus II ("get institutions right"). Capital deficit was not the principal constraint to development as was originally thought. Indeed, the discussion switched to whether foreign aid as remedy to capital deficit helped development along with the consensus being ultimately divided (Burnside and Dollar, 2000). People and their motivation mattered.

Recent scholarship has focused specifically on people and motivation, with emphasis on the strength and quality of institutions as the explanations for differential performance. This was first given impetus and a concrete theoretical underpinning by North (1990). North proposed that institutions or the way societies govern their interactions (rules of the game) matter to how societies deploy their assets to create economic surplus. It will be productive if property rights are protected and contracts are enforced. Contracts allow markets to deepen vertically and thrive in the same way that Smithian trade allows market to deepen and thrive horizontally. This is not new. As Nicolo Machiavelli (1984) counselled in *The Prince*:

> Again a prince should show himself a patron of merit and should honor those who excel in every art. He ought accordingly to encourage his subjects by enabling them to pursue their callings whether mercantile, agricultural . . . in security so that this man shall not be deterred from beautifying his possessions from the apprehension that they may be taken away from him, or that other refrain from opening a trade through fear of taxes and he should provide rewards for those who desire to employ themselves . . . to the greatness of his State or City.

In the Middle Ages, the borders were contestable so that if you *screw up*, your neighboring principality will aspire to move borders in their favor and eat your lunch; subjects will switch allegiance, and you will lose the "end which justifies the means," for example, state sovereignty.

We perhaps lack the stories (*fictions* à la Juval Noah Harari, *Sapiens*) that drive the rule of law as natural order of things. One such story is that of the emperor of Prussia and the miller of Sanssouci. Historian Franz Kugler recorded that Frederick the Great, who was disturbed by the clangor of the mill sails at nighttime, had offered to buy the mill. The owner, Johann William Gravenitz, demurred, which angered the emperor, who, in turn, threatened, "Does he not know that I can take the mill away from him by virtue of my royal power without paying one groschen for it?" The miller's answer: "Of course, Your Majesty could easily do that if—begging your pardon—if it were not for the Supreme Court in Berlin." The emperor was struck by this reply because, indeed, there was such a court of last resort whose authority came from the emperor himself. Subsequent retelling of the story had it that the emperor etched the miller's response at the top of the entrance of his palace gate as a reminder. The emperor had chosen to abide by that authority and showed that there was rule of law over and above the royal prerogative. Prussia, which as a latecomer was trailing England and the Netherlands in industrial might, closed the gap in that century of perceived rule of law.

Without the rule of law, defined minimally as the protection of property rights and the enforcement of contracts, nations fail in the long run. It is the rule of law which allows societies to align member preferences toward the common good, be these the nation's visions or, more concretely, public infrastructure. This, in turn, fires up the animal spirits toward investments which sustain growth.

Societies in general consist at the start of many distinct tribes, each with its own separate worldviews. But a common goal among these views may be survival under the common threat of separate tribes. That feature of common survival under one overarching threat among different tribes could keep the tribes entangled with each other. But only if there is an overarching authority that all tribes trust to lead the common endeavor. If they persist as many distinct tribes, the collective action problem (of overcoming tribal centrifugal tendencies) stands in the way of coherence toward a common goal. Members of different tribes will refuse to cooperate with members of other tribes if the system of contribution and payoffs is viewed as "unfair." It is good institutions that ensure that the system is fair. Incoherence is the hallmark of tribal societies. The post–Josip Broz Tito Yugoslavia exemplified the case of tribal exclusion taking over tribal inclusion and spilling over to violence among previously peacefully coexistent tribes. The death of the iron-fisted leader Josip Broz Tito took away the credible overarching external constraint against intertribal enmity.

There is a popular view that a "nation" is an "imagined community" (Anderson, 1991, p. 6). As he put it:

> A nation is imagined because the members of even the smallest nation will never know most of their fellow members, much less meet them or even hear of them; yet in the minds of each lives the image of their communion.

The currency of this communion is trust. The compass of trust is elastic and at first bordered by the tribe; this compass can potentially in-compass a much larger polity with many tribes. By our categories, a "community" is a group whose members maintain an imputation with one another, $(g, g') \rightarrow 1$, where g is A's imputation that *B* is a "friend," while *g*′ is *B*'s imputation that *A* is a "friend." Thus, (g, g') is the entanglement index between *A* and *B*. The closer to 1 (g, g') is, the easier to unlock the bounty of collective action problems. The phrase "in the minds of each lives the image of their communion" fits squarely with the definition of imputation $(g, g') \rightarrow 1$, which, though purely a mental construct, is no less binding than the hardest steel. Cooperative successes in dilemma games are therefore the more likely outcome for "nations" as "imagined community" than for a mere agglomeration of tribes. The concept "imagined community" operationalized as $(g, g') \rightarrow 1$ immediately translates into increased likelihood of success in collective action problems and in competition with outside groups.

An Incoherent Society

An incoherent society, in contrast, is one that cannot iron out the goal and means differences of its members to come to a unified course of action. (g, g') is far removed from "1." When Philippine National Artist F. Sionil Jose lamented that "[t]he Philippines became a state before it became a nation," he likely meant that we have not sufficiently overcome our tribal origins and our tendency to free ride on others, and this underlies our failure to successfully implement meaningful national projects. A *state* is an arbitrary political category; it need not consist of mutually entangled groups and their members. Absent a nation, the state regularly fails at collective action problems. The Kaliwa Dam, planned over decades to alleviate water and power shortages in Metro Manila, does not get delivered. Other flood control projects get delivered as ghosts. "Nations," by contrast, consist of groups that are highly group-entangled: (g, g') close to one. They readily succeed at collective action problems: The Three Gorges Dam gets delivered in good order and in good time despite the withering skepticism from the West.

The overarching question in the Philippine state still remains: "What's in it for me and my immediate family?" rather than "What's in it for us, the Filipino nation?" The Philippines, by this reckoning, remains an "incoherent society." When a gold-and-copper mining project in Tampakan, Bukidnon, is blocked by a mere ordinance from the provincial *sanggunian* despite having passed all national requirements, this incoherence is made manifest. Incoherence is manifest by the incapacity to iron out the differences. When NAIA Terminal 3 was mothballed for a decade from 2002 to 2012 because the parties could not agree on ownership of the facility and the authorities could not smooth out the differences to benefit the nation, that incoherence was manifest. The *universal domain axiom*, which allows every imaginable preference ordering but provides no way to cobble them together, seems echoed in this very local Bukidnon, Philippines, impasse.

To return to the original question we started with: Why did some of our East Asian neighbors manage a complete reset from import substitution to export promotion while others did not? The Philippines failed to completely outgrow its import substitution roots, which, in time, became an emphasis on the non-traded goods sector still insulated from global competition. This may be a question of *path dependence*. But the question still begs: Why were we unable to turn our backs on our legacy of nationalist Filipino-first development, while the Asian miracle economies who confronted with similar path dependence succeeded?

South Korea and Taiwan were frontline states in the bipolar conflict between capitalism and socialism. Like the city-states counselled by Machiavelli, they had barbarians directly knocking at their gates. Taiwan existed in the shadow of bombardment from communist China. I recall growing up in Bacolod City as a primary grader listening to radio broadcasts of this bombardment over Quemoy and profoundly dreading the imminent invasion by the Red Chinese horde. How much more was this fear in the hearts of Taiwanese? Seoul, on the other hand, was only a long-range howitzer fire from the demilitarized zone, where the two armies from both sides faced each other. I recall visiting South Korea as late as the 1970s, when the military, in or out of uniform, were in every corner. It felt like a garrison state. War, it seemed, was imminent, and the Seoul–Busan expressway, which was along our sightseeing route, manifested this paranoia: It suddenly and inexplicably widened to eight times the normal width. When queried why, our guide explained that this segment of the highway was meant as an emergency airport to handle planes and logistics in case of an invasion from the North. This was "eminent threat" made manifest ("eminent" for *massive* and means one that cleared the table of other concerns while being as well "imminent"), a fear you could cut with scissors. War was imminent, and import substitution strategy was not earning enough to sustain a shooting war. You needed hard currency (dollars) for that. Add to that the anxiety that the USA may not be there forever to support the side in case of war. The vent-for-the-dollar made the turn to export promotion an easier and logical policy pivot. They overcame the Prebisch–Singer pessimism for exports. I call this "eminent threat" imperative that made every member of society a critical "decision-maker"—one who, by virtue of the social milieu, makes the players discount the free riding problem (maximizing the fitness "I") of the Nash dilemma game in favor of maximizing the fitness of the "we" (maximizing utilitarian fitness of the "we"). It was eminent threat, among others, that overcame the commitment of these polities to path dependence with import substitution and hastened the switch to export promotion. Besides, the tendency in the capitalist world to switch from "aid to trade" meant that they were willing to incur trade deficit if it meant lessening the aid burden. The frontline states learned to earn resources by trade as a sustainable strategy. I recall talking to an old Binondo, Manila, old-timer who related that in the late 1950s they started receiving letters from Taiwanese relatives inquiring about what may be good products to export to the Philippines. He said that his family (they were in the hardware business) sent them samples of Western door locks, which they (the relatives) started to copy. He said they were of very poor quality at the start but were also of very low price (helped along by the drastic devaluation of the New Taiwan dollar), and poor Filipino households bought them. Thus, there were geopolitical economy reasons behind the switch to export promotion.

Acemoglu (2024) further elaborated on the North thesis and showed that there exists a causal relation (not just a correlation) running from institutions to economic performance (Acemoglu and Robinson, 2012). Acemoglu and Robinson (2019) claim that liberty is not the natural order of things. The natural order of things is one dominated by the free riding problem in dilemma games, and collective failures rule the land. The natural order is in fact a collective action failure born of the dominance of the free riding problem. The natural order in the landscape is, by natural order, entropic (disordered). Society is most productive when it attains the *cooperative nirvana* of collective action games, where every participant chooses to align toward the common good and, more importantly, sustains it. And the most sustainable cooperative nirvana is one attained under liberty (free rather than forced agency); its attainment under duress is possible but fragile. What the frontline states first attained was a cooperative nirvana under duress—the agency of eminent threat being very visible. But when the polity gradually became group-entangled by continued success, cooperation became increasingly normative: It became the dominant option of a people under liberty.

The second major explanation in the volume for our nation's economic situation is that our policymakers incorrectly think that the finances of the economy are like those of a household with a binding budget constraint. This makes policymakers think that the government must raise taxes or borrow in order to spend. The authors argue that this is not how modern sovereign governments (that issue their own currency) operate—what they call the monetary reality. They argue that discussions cannot start under the premise that "resources are scarce" when the term "resources" refers to pesos. These are not a resource and, henceforth, not scarce. The Philippine (central) government is not financially constrained to the extent that it uses its own currency. The authors also elaborate on how the Philippine government (like all governments today) makes payments by simply crediting bank accounts through electronic transfers. Put together, these arguments imply, according to the authors, that the Philippines can afford the infrastructure, education, and health that all Filipinos deserve. The authors emphasize that this realistic description of government finances does not imply that the state should not be mindful about what it spends.

Let me add a comment on this. A country loses monetary sovereignty by tying itself, in varying intensity, to the thought collective. The extreme case of this is a currency fixed to a major currency like the euro. But a weaker version is that you tie yourself by a law (such as the BSP law) to a currency, such as the impossible trinity collective that says it is impossible to have three things at the same time—a fixed exchange range, a free capital mobility, and an independent monetary authority. This is the Mundell–Fleming thesis, which claims that maintaining the three together runs the economy into a crisis sooner or later. But who says that you have to have all three—in particular, that you have to have free capital mobility? Robert Mundell, one of the principal authors himself, agreed to defend the yuan undervaluation through its capital controls in the early 2000s as China's right to reduce by what was then its sizeable poverty load. This capital controls allowed China to maintain an undervalued yuan by up to, some claim, 25%. This earned China the epithet of currency manipulator. It turns out that the epithet implies the effort to divorce from the impossible trinity thought collective, which has proved fruitful for many currency manipulators.

Our own tying of ourselves to this collective via a freely floating exchange rate, and full capital mobility, came from our fear of the capture of the monetary policy by the fiscal authorities. Story has it that a legitimate money printing machine was located in Malacañang itself with knowledge authorization of our monetary authorities. It was the lack of a backbone of our monetary authorities that precipitated this tying of ourselves down. The authors do not dispute the standard interpretation of the impossible trinity. What they do is to add a fiscal stance. Hence, they seem to favor a regime with a floating exchange rate with monetary sovereignty. Since the government cannot "run out" of its own currency, monetary policy independence is preserved. Implicit in their narrative is the fact that the trilemma does not constrain what governments *can* afford; it constrains what they *promise* to do. Crises occur when countries promise what they cannot guarantee. They claim that the current fiscal and monetary system would not allow us to end up like in the 1980s. Of course, under floats, fiscal deficits affect inflation and the exchange rate, but not solvency.

Being in this thought collective means that monetary policies become outsourced to the Federal Reserve Board (FRB) of the USA, which pursues ends not in consonance with our own. The FRB may want to keep the interest rate high to support the US dollar, which keeps the subordinate currencies (peso) appreciated when they need its currency low. The lever for control is through capital movement (you don't want to be too far removed from the accustomed uncovered interest parity differential, since capital movement will move to punish you).

On the whole, this is a very informative exercise by the De La Salle group under Professor Jesus Felipe. Hoping that it will also move the policy levers in consonant directions as we move to 2050.

Raul Fabella
Emeritus Professor, University of the Philippines
National Scientist

PREFACE AND ACKNOWLEDGMENTS

This book is a long-gestated idea. For years, we have been driven by a professional desire to understand why the Philippines has progressed at a slow pace for decades and what can be done about it. Between independence in 1946 and the early 1970s, the Philippines was progressing. These were complex years for most Asian countries. The Philippines was no exception, as it faced social, political, and economic problems, but it was moving forward. The setback of the mid-1970s, during the second part of the Marcos Sr. administration (1972–1986), took a big toll on the nation. It took a long time for the country to recover. Things have improved in recent times (until COVID-19 in 2020), but not enough to make up for the lost decades. We think that the country is progressing (it is growing), but we do not see the type of transformation and the changes that other East Asian nations experienced. The result is that its income per capita is just above USD 4,400 in 2025, with almost 2 million workers abroad sending remittances. Countries in the region that not long ago were poorer than the Philippines (e.g., China, Indonesia, Thailand, and Vietnam) are now richer.

In 2022, we started a research program, "The Future of the Philippine Economy," although some of us had been thinking about these issues for many years, and wondered where the Philippine economy would be 25 years from now, or about 100 years after independence (attained in 1946). We opened several research lines and developed several quantitative models of the Philippine economy. We have also talked to many people and reflected on the state of the nation. As a matter of principle, we always argue in presentations that we are cautiously optimistic about the Philippine economy. We mean it. Yet we are also disappointed when we look through the window and we still see significant poverty and many people performing menial jobs. This means low productivity, low wages, and, consequently, low per capita income. This implies that whatever the country has done in the past and accumulated until today has yielded very little.

Other nations, especially in our region, are also corrupt, have poor institutions, and have all sorts of problems. The Philippines is not that exceptional in this sense. Yet these other nations are moving forward faster and have overtaken us. They must have done something we have not done.

Our first thesis is that over the last few decades, going back to the 20th century, other nations understood that the key was to change the structure of the economy, particularly the employment structure, and that industrialization was the engine of growth. Also, governments played a significant role. Other factors were either secondary or a function of these (i.e., growth was the result of industrialization and not just of building roads . . . for the sake of building roads). This understanding also existed in the Philippines after independence, yet it was slowly lost, and by the 1970s and the 1980s, the country took a more neoliberal route with a "soft state," using the language of Nobel Prize winner Gunnar Myrdal. It became a non-developmental state and focused on implementing piecemeal reforms that have delivered much less progress.

The facts speak for themselves: Most Filipino workers are employed in agriculture and services, both of very low productivity (in the case of services, many workers are domestic helpers, security guards, low-paid masseuses, or delivery persons). Unless this changes substantially, progress will continue to be slow.

Our second thesis is that Filipino governments believe that they "do not have resources" to provide *even* the most basic public goods that are badly needed to construct an egalitarian society. These include, at the very least, the elimination of malnutrition and dire poverty, high-quality infrastructure, a robust public health system, public housing, and education. These are the rights of all Filipino citizens. Pesos, the Philippine currency, is not a *resource* (as they are often referred to), because it can never be scarce in a sovereign country like the Philippines. The Philippines can financially afford the provision of these essential public goods. It is a matter of will.

The fact that the Philippines has not done as well as its East and Southeast Asian neighbors did in recent decades is not a "puzzle" or a "conundrum," as is often referred to (e.g., Pritchett, 2003; Severino and Salazar, 2007). In fact, given the country's development model summarized earlier, the result could not be other than a high agricultural employment share, significant poverty, almost 2 million overseas foreign workers, and the per capita income mentioned previously.

The book was conceived as a single volume and not as an edited volume with independent chapters, with two themes running through it, namely, the need to change the structure of the economy and the fact that a sovereign nation can spend in its own currency because its government does not have a putative budget constraint. These two distinct themes, together with the modeling exercises on the Philippine economy that enable us to generate forecasts up to 2050 and conduct simulations, make this publication different from other books on the Philippine economy.[1] We also stress that our (econometric) models avoid optimistic extrapolations that are bound to be wrong. Many of the great economic forecasting errors of the past half century stemmed from excessive extrapolation of performance in the recent past and treating a country's growth rate as a permanent characteristic rather than a transient condition. Realism is of the utmost importance in our work. We want to avoid the "Asiaphoria" sin (unjustified overoptimism).

This is not a book of anecdotes, references to personalities, storytelling, or the *politics* of the Philippines—we nevertheless touch upon political issues when these are directly related to the main arguments. It is about the economics of why the Philippines is still a relatively poor economy and why its neighbors have performed better. It is also about what we can expect during the next two and a half decades, when the country will celebrate 100 years of independence.

We sincerely hope the book becomes a useful resource for people across the whole spectrum interested in the Philippine economy, including students, colleagues in academia (for their own interest as well as for teaching), journalists, the government at large, and professionals in the private sector. Ultimately, we hope it contributes to changing economic policy in the Philippines. We have concluded that the level of awareness about the reality of the nation, both in the government and in the private sector, is low. To refer to the possibility that things may not change appreciably in the country over the next 25 years, we have created the acronym MOTS, meaning "more of the same." As the book contains some chapters on Philippine history and its politics, it can also be recommended as an introductory source. Finally, the book can be a reference for development scholars and practitioners in general, as it covers topics such as structural transformation and monetary and fiscal policy.

We have benefited from conversations on different parts of the book with Raymond Tan (Vice President for Research and Innovation, DLSU), Arlene Inocencio (Dean of the Carlos L. Tiu School of Economics, DLSU), William Mitchell (University of Newcastle, Australia), Wonhyuk Lim (Korea Development Institute, Korea), Chaly Koh (UrbanMetrics, Malaysia), Raul Fabella (Emeritus, University of the Philippines, and National Scientist), Noel De Dios (Emeritus, University of the Philippines), Bart Verspagen (University of Maastricht), Nanditha Mathew (University of Maastricht), Leloy Claudio (Berkeley University), and Scott Fullwiler. Without any implication, we acknowledge the very useful conversations we have had over the last few years in the Philippines with Rosemarie Edillon, Bong Consing, Ramon del Rosario, Ed Chua, Lubin Nepomuceno, Nestor Tan, Bobby Batungbacal, Carlos Garcia, Ramon Garcia, Calixto Chikiamko, Jeffrey Ng, Eric Werker, and Pedro Pascual. We also received comments from more than 150 participants from Congress, Bangko Sentral ng Pilipinas, Department of Finance, Department of Budget Management, Department of Trade and Industry, Senate Economic Planning Office, National Economic and Development Authority, Bureau of Treasury, and the Philippine Institute for Development Studies (among others). They participated in the workshop "Pathways to Progress: Transforming the Philippine Economy" held at the Philippine

House of Representatives (organized by the Congressional Policy Budget Research Department), on January 21–22, 2025. We also presented material on the government and central bank finances at the Bangko Sentral ng Pilipinas (BSP) in 2020. Finally, we have also presented parts of the material and ideas at events organized by the Entrepreneurs' Organization, Ayala Group, PHINMA Corporation, Petron Corporation, Holcim Philippines, BusinessWorld, and SteelAsia Corporation, between 2022 and 2025, where we had the opportunity to interact with the Philippine private sector and hear its views about the economy. Jacobe Joaquin Sevilla (BS-MS economics student, DLSU) provided excellent research assistance. The usual disclaimer applies, and any errors are solely the authors' responsibility.

We are indebted to De La Salle University (DLSU) for encouraging us to pursue this project with absolute freedom. We are also grateful to the DLSU Angelo King Institute for Business and Economic Studies, and to the DLSU Carlos L. Tiu School of Economics, for financial assistance.

Note

1 Our reference list of papers and books on the Philippines is extensive. We just mention here a few books for comparison with ours: Vos and Yap (1996), Canlas and Fujisaki (2001), Balisacan and Hill (2003), Severino and Salazar (2007), Clarete et al. (2018), and Hill et al. (2022). It is important to note that (1) other than Hill et al. (2022) and Clarete et al. (2018), the others are somewhat outdated by now. The first one of these two focuses on poverty and agriculture, and the second one was written with a very optimistic tone a couple of years before the COVID-19 pandemic; (2) except Vos and Yap (1996), the others are edited volumes, which makes drawing conclusions and recommendations a difficult exercise, and Hill et al.'s (2022) study contains analyses on other countries; (3) with the exception of Vos and Yap (1996), none of the others uses models like ours; and (4) Canlas and Fujisaki (2001) and Severino and Salazar (2007) tried to infer the future of the Philippines in the 21st century, but they lack models to enlighten the reader. The other volumes do not have a clear, forward-looking (predictions) intention like ours.

1

INTRODUCTION AND OVERVIEW OF THE BOOK

1.1 Introduction

Between 1900 and 1930, the Philippines had one of the highest GDP per capita in Asia (Hooley, 2005, Table 5). Then income per capita declined until after the end of WWII and then recovered. Yet it did not grow at the same pace as did other Asian nations, especially after the 1960s. While the Philippines attained very high growth rates for a few years right after the war (between 1946 and 1950), growth declined afterward (see Chapter 3), more so in per capita terms as a result of its high population growth rate.

This is not to say that the Philippines did not progress after the war. Like many other new nations at that time, especially in Asia, it was slowly climbing the ladder. Still, by the 1960s, the Philippines ranked among Asia's highest in per capita income, trailing only Japan, Hong Kong, Malaysia, and Singapore.[1] Until about the mid-1970s, Philippine performance was no different from that of many other developing nations, including those within the region. In fact, it achieved lower-middle-income status (measured in purchasing power parity) in 1975 (Felipe et al., 2017) before Thailand, Indonesia, and China (attained by these countries in 1976, 1986, and 1992, respectively). Then, it entered a long downward spiral in the mid-1970s after the declaration of martial law, with Ferdinand Marcos Sr. as president. This period culminated with a severe economic and political crisis in the mid-1980s. Its repercussions lasted for almost three decades (spanning the administrations of Corazon Aquino, Fidel Ramos, and Joseph Estrada). During this time, average GDP growth was very low. It slowly recovered and managed to register positive growth since the early 2000s—the exception being 2020—but this has not been enough to make up for the long reversal. Moreover, though positive, Philippine growth over the last two decades has not matched that of the most successful East Asian economies, for example, Hong Kong, Singapore,

DOI: 10.4324/9781003728719-1

South Korea, and Taiwan (not even the performance of Indonesia, Malaysia, and Thailand), between the 1970s and the mid-1990s. And certainly not that of China between 2000 and 2020. Thailand, Indonesia, and China are already upper-middle-income economies. As of this writing in 2025, the Philippines remains a lower-middle-income economy.

In this book, we provide two central explanations for why the Philippines has not done better and draw implications for the next 25 years.

Although the country had its share of social and political problems during the first part of the 20th century (when it was still a colony), these were no different from those that afflicted other developing nations. As we documented earlier, growth for 25 years after 1946 was quite high. The setback came in the 1970s and the 1980s. The economic and political mismanagement of the autocratic phase of the Marcos Sr. regime (1972–1986) left the country in a precarious situation, characterized by a very poor countryside, an industrial sector that never managed to attain East Asian levels, and a group of familial dynasties that controlled the political system. As a consequence, the Philippines was referred to for some time as "the sick man of Asia." The explanations of this outcome cover the whole spectrum of historical (e.g., colonialism), economic (e.g., wrong policies), and political (e.g., corruption, elite interests) explanations. The edited volumes by Severino and Salazar (2007), Clarete et al. (2018), and Hill et al. (2022) contain very useful analyses. The knock-down of the 1980s was severe, and its impact lasted for years. The problem was that the medicine applied (i.e., the Philippine development model of the last decades) has been akin to *palliative economics*, focused on easing the symptoms rather than on curing the disease. Whatever the country has done during the last decades has not been consequential and has had a rather small impact: Poverty is declining, albeit slowly; wages are increasing, but they are still low; and per capita income is rising, but we remain a lower-middle-income country.

The hard reality is that the Philippines is still a rather poor economy. Figure 1.1 shows income per capita in 2024, slightly above USD 4,400.

Many of our neighbors, poorer than the Philippines a few decades ago (China, Indonesia, South Korea, and Thailand), overtook us years ago. Vietnam did it in 2018. See Figures 1.2 and 1.3.

Pritchett (2022) compared the GDP per capita of many developing countries in 2018 to that of leading economies at different times in the past. He showed that today, there are 29 countries with per capita incomes below that of the world leaders in 1700. There are likewise 19 countries with per capita incomes below that of the world leaders in 1870, 17 countries with per capita incomes below that of the world leaders in 1918, 24 countries with per capita incomes below that of the world leaders in 1950, and 23 countries with per capita incomes below that of the world leaders in 1968. Pritchett's estimates show that, in 2018, the Philippines' per capita income was below that of the leading economies in 1918.

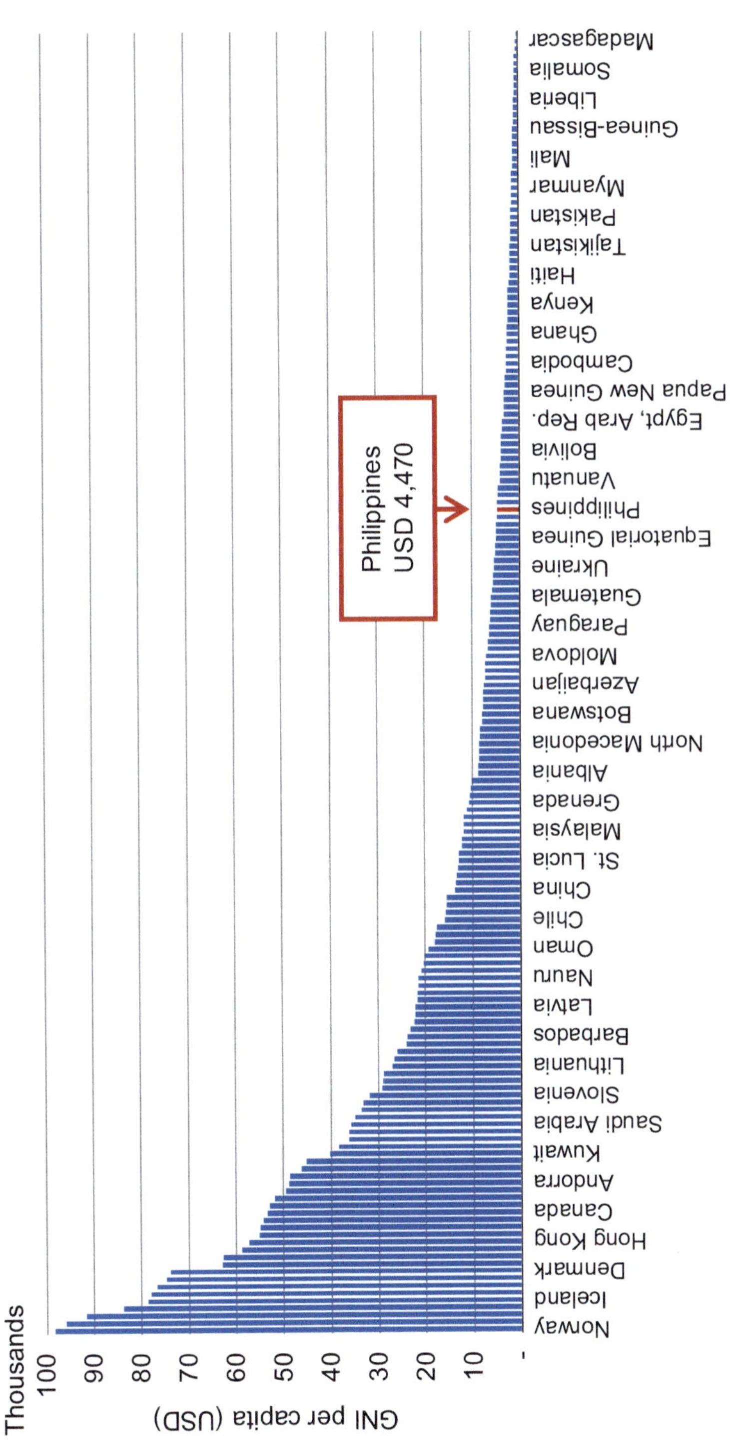

FIGURE 1.1 GNI per Capita, Atlas Method (Current USD), 2024

Source: The World Bank: World Development Indicators (https://data.worldbank.org/indicator/NY.GNP.PCAP.CD)

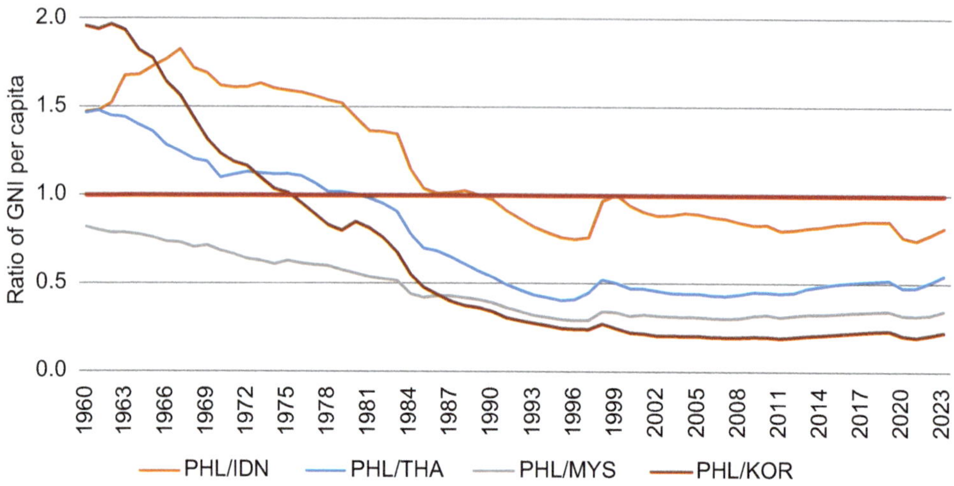

FIGURE 1.2 Ratio of Philippine GNI per Capita to Indonesia, South Korea, Malaysia, and Thailand, 1960–2023

Note: These ratios are calculated by using GNI per capita (2023 PPP, international dollars).

Source: Authors' calculations based on data from The World Bank: World Development Indicators (https://data.worldbank.org)

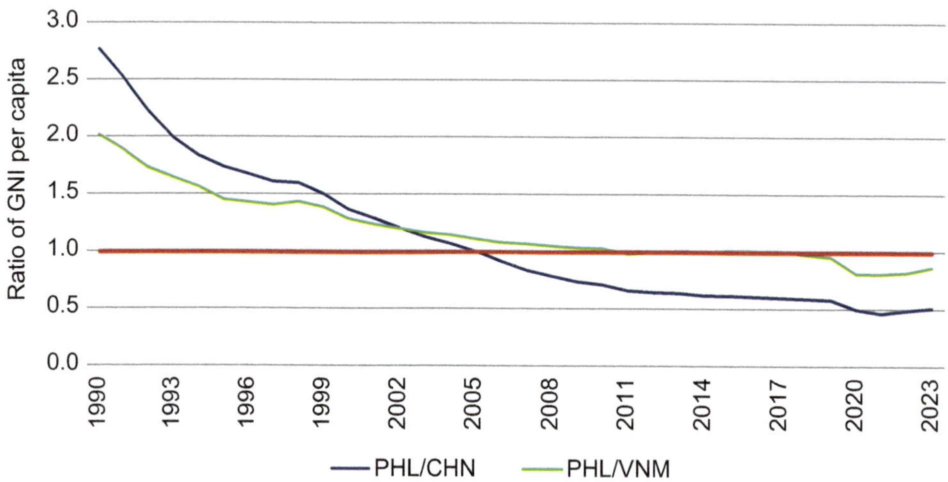

FIGURE 1.3 Ratio of Philippine GNI per Capita to China and Vietnam, 1990–2023

Note: These ratios are calculated by using GNI per capita (2023 PPP, international dollars).

Source: Authors' calculations based on data from The World Bank: World Development Indicators (https://data.worldbank.org)

The Philippine growth path vis-à-vis that of its Asian neighbors has been characterized since the 1970s by a shift away from manufacturing toward services at a persistently low level of per capita income. To describe this (i.e., a developing economy wherein services prematurely overtake industry as the major contributor to GDP), eminent Philippine economist and national scientist Raul Fabella coined the term "development progeria." Meanwhile, the country's neighbors embarked on export-led growth and industrialization strategies that delivered very high growth rates sustained over decades (Felipe, McCombie, et al., 2025). The Plaza Accord in 1985 contributed decisively to this industrialization drive, when Japanese firms sought to restore their competitive advantage by developing a regionally integrated supply chain of component and assembly plants. This impetus, along with the competitive response of European and American firms, led countries in East and Southeast Asia to develop particular niches within their manufacturing sectors according to their own comparative advantages. Thailand was a major recipient of Japanese investments and became a prime location for automotive manufacturing. South Korea and Taiwan became hubs of electronic and semiconductor production. Malaysia was able to boost its information technology industry, whereas Vietnam gained foreign attention as a promising new economy for low-cost, labor-intensive manufacturing.

The Philippines, in contrast, failed to partake in this industrial renaissance, not only losing ground in manufacturing for much of the latter part of the 20th century, but also doing so at a comparatively rapid rate. By the 1990s, the income gap with its neighbors became so significant that the country was not included by the World Bank Group (1993) in its *East Asian Miracle Report* as one of successful Asian economies.

Over the past three to four decades, the country has undergone significant structural reforms that were thought to improve its development prospects. Successive administrations have come to power with promises of rapid growth and poverty reduction. Encouraging macroeconomic trends in recent years brought the Philippine economy closer to the dynamism of its East Asian neighbors. Between 2010 and 2019, the country's GDP growth averaged a very respectable 6.4% annually. Despite this, the Philippines' gross national income per capita (GNI) remains in the lower-middle-income group, just above USD 4,400 in 2025.[2] It was also during the last three decades of significant reforms that China, Indonesia, Thailand, and more recently, Vietnam overtook the Philippines in per capita income. Malaysia, of course, has always been way ahead, and Singapore is in a different league.

Since the early 2000s, the performance of the Philippines has been quite acceptable: The economy has demonstrated resilience and adaptability; growth has remained robust; poverty has declined; macroeconomic fundamentals are sound, with inflation now within target; and the labor market continues to strengthen. Yet as stressed earlier, this has not been enough to close the gap with our neighbors, especially with the most advanced. Felipe et al. (2022) documented how Philippine growth started picking up in the early 2000s, and certainly after 2010. Indeed, before the COVID-19 pandemic of 2020–2021, the country was one of the best performers in East Asia. This good performance raised the possibility of the Philippines finally entering an era of relatively high growth that could be maintained for a significant period (Clarete et al., 2018). Unfortunately, the pandemic derailed these prospects and plunged the country into a deep crisis, with negative growth of almost 10% in 2020. In what has been described as the world's longest lockdown, many workers had to retreat to the countryside, and many companies shut down, wiping out years of positive growth.

Pritchett (2003), Severino and Salazar (2007), and recently, Punongbayan and De Dios (2025) referred to the Philippines' weak economic performance as a "puzzle." Yet their arguments are not convincing. Pritchett, for example, admits that excessive exchange rate appreciation, excessive budget deficits, economic or natural shocks (earthquakes, volcanic eruptions, typhoons), and/or low human and physical capital accumulation do not explain the Philippines' economic performance. His preferred explanation is institutional uncertainty, which increased after democracy was restored in 1986. Certainly, the Philippines went through a period of turmoil after 1986, which may account for the low growth rate for a few years. However, all countries go through periods of uncertainty. The reality is that, over the last few decades, Thailand, Indonesia, and China, each of which experienced episodes of political and social turmoil, have overtaken the Philippines in terms of per capita income. Recently, Vietnam, the other country analyzed by Pritchett (at the time Pritchett's paper was written in 2003, Vietnam was poorer than the Philippines), has also overtaken it.

The thesis we develop in this book is that during the last four decades, the Philippine development model has failed on two crucial aspects: First, it abandoned industrialization, and second, the government believes it has a budget constraint that forces it to behave like a household. Both remain present in the administration of President Marcos Jr. (2022–2028), who initially set on attaining a 6–7% growth rate in 2023 (actual growth ended up being 5.5%), 6–8% in 2024 (actual growth was 5.7%), and 6.5–8% annual growth for 2025–2028.[3] These are very high growth targets that we doubt will be attained—they have not been so far. The 2023 and 2024 growth rates were significantly below what many experts and the government itself predicted. Even reaching a 6% growth rate is proving to be an uphill battle for the Philippine economy.

The international environment has not helped either. Since 2023, the IMF has predicted world growth of about 3% for the coming years. Second, international political uncertainty is still high with, among others, the Russia–Ukraine war and the Israel–Hamas conflict in Gaza. Third, right after US president Donald Trump regained his mandate, he imposed import tariffs on the rest of the world on the grounds that the United States runs a trade deficit, and he sees this (together with issues of a completely different nature, like migration) as the cause of "America's problems." Many countries threatened to retaliate, although the reality is that most did not follow through in the final negotiations, and country after country succumbed to American political pressure. The result is that foreign products will pay tariffs upon entering the United States (starting August 7, 2025), but American products will pay zero tariffs when entering other countries. In the case of the Philippines, its products will be subject to a tariff rate of 19% when they reach the United States, though a significant number of products, electronic components in particular, will be duty-exempt (as of this writing). American products, on the other hand, will pay zero tariff rate when entering the Philippines. It is difficult to assess the overall impact on each country and on the overall economy, also taking into account that tariffs will ultimately be paid by the American consumers.

Besides the aforementioned, over the last few decades, the Philippines has achieved what Fukuyama (2014) referred to as "modernization without development," a situation in which social change occurs more due to the push of rural poverty than through the pull of new industrial employment. Under this setting, people from rural areas move to urban areas, but they retain much of their rural social organization and values and subsist under extremely marginal economic conditions. Megacities like Manila emerge, but in the absence of a vibrant industrial economy. Consequently, the Philippines does not have a large group of middle-class individuals with a high educational level, and neither does it have a strong industrial working class.[4] The Philippines also democratized before creating a modern state with a competent civil service, needed by merchants and industrialists who require increasingly complex services expected to be provided by the government. This has created a substantial amount of patronage and clientelism, with poorly educated voters rewarded with individual benefits such as public-sector jobs, handouts, or political favors.

Under these circumstances, how can the Philippine economy attain and maintain the high growth rates targeted by the Marcos Jr. administration and carry them beyond 2028? Moreover, if the creation of appropriate rules or institutions is crucial for development, as argued by Acemoglu and Robinson (2012) and by Fukuyama (2014), and yet these develop slowly, is there any way for the Philippines to accelerate growth and development?

The problem the Philippines faces is that accelerating and maintaining growth rates similar to those attained by the East Asian miracle countries decades ago will be very difficult today. Targeting growth rates approaching 7–8% per annum amounts to committing the "Asiaphoria" sin (paraphrasing Pritchett and Summers, 2014), that is, the belief that growth rates persist over time and that per capita growth rates above 6% can be maintained indefinitely. The Philippine development model (a myriad of reforms, emphasis on services, and a hands-off government) will not deliver growth rates this high.

1.2 The Book's Arguments

In this book, we argue that the lackluster performance of the Philippine economy during the last few decades is not a puzzle or the result of bad luck. The country's poor performance for decades is the result of two failures. First, it is the result of a development model that has caused it to miss the industrialization and export-led growth train since around the 1970s. While the country implemented industrialization strategies using industrial policies for three decades after independence, these ultimately failed while the country still had a low income per capita. With this came the rise of (low-productivity) services. Today, the manufacturing sector is an important pillar of the nation in terms of its contribution to GDP, but it is a small employer. Second, the Philippine government thinks that its finances are like those of a family and that it faces a similar budget constraint. This is incorrect.

The book revolves around these two failures. They provide a sound explanation of why the country has not advanced faster. We argue that we need to address them if we want to see progress (interpreted as faster and sustained growth) in the coming decades. As a corollary, we will argue that the Philippines needs to grapple with two issues. One is the source of growth: Can services do for the Philippines what manufacturing did in other nations in the 20th century? The second question concerns the role of government: Can it actively coordinate the economy and engineer a *big push*, or should it stay out of the way and let the private sector lead?

1.2.1 The Need to Transform the Economy

The first theme of the book is that the key to Philippine development—that is, becoming an upper-middle-income and, eventually, a high-income nation—lies in transforming its economy. This means that the share of agricultural employment has to decline significantly (the sector's employment share is still above 20%), and those of manufacturing and advanced services must increase. Likewise, exports have to become more complex. The result will be higher productivity and wages. The second theme is that we need an active government that understands its own finances and abandons old ideas about the negative effects of deficit spending. The following paragraphs elaborate both.

The first argument (industrialization, structural transformation) is not new. What is new is our emphasis on it today, when most people have given up on it and think that the future is services, for example, IT-BPOs, tourism. While these activities do contribute to our economy, our argument is that either we move up in the industrialization ladder or the slope to become a high-income economy will continue being very steep. To this we add that the government needs to learn how to guide the economy and undertake a modern industrial policy. The second argument, about the government's finances, is completely novel in a country where most economists and policymakers are orthodox when it comes to the government's finances. The following paragraphs elaborate these two central points.

Philippine economic policies need to focus on transforming the economy in order to increase productivity (recognized in the Philippine Constitution, Article XII, Section 1, as a mechanism to enhance the quality of life). With some simplification, Philippine development since the 20th century has had three distinct phases. The first one corresponds to the 50-year American colonization period. Like in other Asian countries, the Philippines managed to start developing an incipient manufacturing sector during this period. These years saw the rise of a group of Philippine economists who thought about industrialization, independence (nationalism), and the creation of a central bank (finally created in 1949).

The second phase came with independence in 1946 and lasted until the early 1980s. Under Presidents Roxas (1946–1948), Quirino (1948–1953), Magsaysay (1953–1957), and Garcia (1957–1961), the Philippines undertook import substitution industrialization through the allocation of foreign exchange. With President Macapagal (1961–1965), there was a significant philosophical shift in policymaking (minimal government intervention, liberal management of the economy, free enterprise), yet the country continued promoting industrialization, though now through tariff protection. During the first two decades of independence, policymakers understood the importance of industrialization, though this was difficult as a result of the conditions imposed by the United States. Despite this, the Philippines implemented import substitution industrialization strategies until the 1970s, already under President Marcos Sr. The Philippines shifted to an export-oriented regime in the mid-1970s, although high import tariffs remained in place until the late 1980s. Even during the early 1980s, President Ferdinand Marcos Sr. attempted an aggressive industrialization strategy. It failed. As a result came the rise of services and the third phase of development, in place until today. Serious industrialization efforts were abandoned, and since then, there has been an emphasis on the belief that "free trade" and "freedom of enterprise, trade, and investment" (the efficacy of the marketplace allocating resources), combined with a small government, would foster the most advantageous path of economic development. All the country needs to develop is a healthy dose of investment and foreign aid. Policymakers, then, ought to focus on eliminating burdensome regulations. Industrial policy, as commonly understood, is neither necessary nor beneficial. The idea is to "go liberal" and bet on free markets and limited government. As a consequence, the Philippine development model shows aversion toward government spending, deficits, and debt. It has not worked. We insist: The country's slow progress is not a puzzle. It can be explained.

Crucial to productivity growth are manufacturing, exporting (diversification and upgrading), and understanding that firms are at the center of both. We will argue that "development happens in firms" and that today we do not have the firms that will allow the Philippines to achieve high-income status in the coming decades. This is a major constraint on the transformation of the economy. While these themes are included in the Philippine Development Plan (PDP) 2023–2028 (NEDA, 2023a), they are buried underneath a myriad of other priorities that obscure their relevance. Unfortunately, productivity is low in the sectors that employ most workers, and very few firms produce high-quality manufacturing products that compete in export markets. Many of the reforms that successive Philippine governments have implemented over the last few decades, including the current one, do not address what the country really needs. According to Hausmann et al. (2005), evidence indicates that countries that have implemented well-targeted reforms to remove the most severe binding constraints, such as China in 1978 and India in 1980, display better growth performance than those countries that undertook comprehensive economic reforms, such as Latin American countries. We add the Philippines to this group.

The transformation of the economy also faces political economy constraints. We use the conceptual framework proposed by Pritchett and Werker (2012), Sen and Tyce (2019), and Pritchett et al. (2018), which is derived from Khan's (2010) political settlement theory. We refer to it as the Khan–Pritchett–Sen–Werker (KPSW) framework. We use it to analyze the relationship between the political environment, the country's approach to deals, and the sources of firm revenues. We will also argue that the country suffers from spatial and temporal fragmentation.

We will link the need to transform the economy to the macroeconomic constraint on growth that the Philippines faces, namely, the balance of payments, specifically the need to avoid persistent current account deficits. We will develop Thirlwall's (1979) concept of the balance of payments–constrained growth rate.

More structural and policy reforms in areas that impact private investment, infrastructure, and human capital development will not do the job without focusing on productivity and changing the structure of the economy.[5] Contrary to what some members of the current Cabinet have claimed, a more diversified economy out on consumption will not drive higher-quality job creation and accelerate poverty reduction. The employment structure of the country is ultimately determined by what its firms produce, and many are engaged in low-productivity services. Poverty reduction will result from sending workers out of agriculture, but only if this is matched by creating employment in activities that pay higher wages. There is no relevant example of a nation that has progressed without the pull of the manufacturing sector. We repeat: It is about productivity, manufacturing, exports, and firms.

1.2.2 Misunderstood Government Finances

The second main theme of the book concerns finance. It can be considered independent of the previous argument, but both are connected. It will be very difficult for the Philippines to transform its economy without a government that provides, at the very least, all the essential public goods a nation needs to function properly: infrastructure, education, health, and so forth. In fact, we will argue that the government has to do much more than the minimum—for example, by implementing a serious industrial policy.

Unfortunately, the Philippine government believes that it operates under a financial budget constraint, namely, that its spending is paid for with taxes, and that taxes have to be collected in advance. Because tax collection is low, the government cannot afford to spend. To do so, it has to borrow from the private sector, but then the debt increases.

We will show that this argument is flawed, as it does not accurately reflect the reality of how a modern and sovereign government operates. We urge the Department of Finance, Bangko Sentral ng Pilipinas, the Department of Budget and Management, and the Treasury to recognize the *monetary reality* of a sovereign nation like the Philippines, which naturally uses fiat money.[6] This reality implies that (1) the Philippines does not have a budget constraint like a family, (2) the currency in which all prices are denominated, the peso, is not a scarce resource, (3) government payments are made by electronically crediting bank accounts, and (4) terms such as "deficit" (fiscal deficit) and "debt" (national debt) are misleading because they only represent one side of the double-entry accounting inherent in all payments.

Deficits and debts are someone else's surplus and wealth. We are certain the average Filipino does not owe PHP 130,000 from the national debt. This widespread idea is demonstrably false. We shall argue that these four important points on public finance mentioned earlier imply that the government can pay for the infrastructure, health, education, children's nutrition, pensions, and other social programs that the country urgently needs. "We do not have money" or "We need to borrow" are fallacious statements. Worse, this misunderstanding has long put the country at a costly disadvantage.

Certainly, the imperative to transform the economy and the need to understand the government's finances transcend the Marcos Jr. administration. They were present before 2022 and will remain after 2028. All we hope is that this administration and successive ones understand these constraints and set economic policies with the goal of relaxing them.

1.2.3 The Future

Looking ahead, we take a long-term perspective on the Philippine economy and forecast where it will be and what it will look like in 2050, about 100 years as an independent nation. Will the Philippines be a rich nation? Will poverty be eliminated? To do so, we developed the DLSU ANIMO econometric model of the Philippine economy, with over 800 variables and populated with data since the year 2000. The key feature of this model is that the structures of employment and output drive productivity, which drives wages and, consequently, per capita income. The advantage of having such a model is that its statistical solutions provide us with a coherent view of the economy. We generate forecasts for variables such as growth, income per capita, the structure of the economy (both output and employment), and poverty, among others. We also discuss Philippine firms, employment and education, poverty and the cost of a so-called "decent basket," and the role of the budget and national debt as development tools, all in the context of the Philippine Development Plan (PDP) 2023–2028 and *Ambisyon Natin* 2040.

We believe that our two key themes, along with the forecasts we provide, make this a unique book. We end by noting that we are cautiously optimistic about the future of the country, but it is important to qualify this statement and understand how far the Philippines can realistically go and what the real constraints are. This is what the book is about.

1.3 The Book's Structure

The rest of the book is structured into 14 (additional) chapters. The material is organized as a discussion of a variety of issues, with the aforementioned two themes (the structure of the economy and the monetary reality) as the unifying lines. This analysis provides us with a clear picture of where the Philippine economy is today. Then, we use it to assess how far the Philippine economy can realistically go until 2050. Except when we discuss history, the material is not organized following time. We also note that we consciously repeat some important arguments throughout the book. We hope this does not annoy the reader. The following provides a brief overview of each chapter:

- Chapter 2 ("A Brief Overview of the Economic History of the Philippines") provides a summary of the economic history of the Philippines, going back to the 400-year-long colonial period (which marked the Philippine economy until today) and the first decades after decolonization, when very important debates took place: fiscal and monetary policies, exchange rate, austerity, industrialization, import substitution, and "Filipino First."
- Chapter 3 ("A Primer on Growth: Facts, Constraints, and Engines") discusses the concepts of potential and balance of payments–constrained growth rates and estimates them for the Philippines. We conclude that both are about 6%. This is the maximum the Philippine economy can grow on a sustained basis without running into macroeconomic problems. The chapter also discusses the determinants of growth—economic transformation (the shift of workers out of agriculture), exports (the autonomous category of demand), and manufacturing (Kaldor's engine of growth)—and applies the Khan–Pritchett–Sen–Werker political economy framework to analyze growth.
- Chapter 4 ("The Structure of the Philippine Economy") offers an analysis of how the structure of the Philippine economy has changed during the last 20 years. The chapter highlights that the largest employers today are agriculture and wholesale and retail trade, both sectors of low productivity. This is fundamental in our analysis to understand how far, realistically, the Philippine economy can evolve between now and 2050. The analysis also shows that the Philippine manufacturing sector is important as a driver of growth but it is small in terms of employment, and that Philippine exports remain globally uncompetitive.
- Chapter 5 ("Philippine Development Plans: Development Misunderstandings") analyzes the Philippine Development Plan (PDP) 2023–2028 of the current Marcos Jr. administration and contrasts the Plan's targets with our forecasts until 2028. These are based on the DLSU ANIMO econometric model of the Philippine economy that we developed. Most targets will be missed by a few years. The chapter also analyzes Philippine development plans since the mid-1980s and provides a comparison with the planning documents of Malaysia and Vietnam. We conclude that Philippine development plans are not useful guides for policy because they fail to prioritize.

- Chapters 6 ("Why Has Philippine Progress Been Slow? I: Incomplete Land Reforms, the Role of Government, and a Weak State with a Rent-Seeking Private Sector") and 7 ("Why Has Philippine Progress Been Slow? II: Failed Industrialization Programs") deal with causes of slow progress: the agrarian situation, a weak state, a rent-seeking private sector, and failed industrialization programs. Finally, we discuss the government's initiatives today and argue that they do not represent a coherent industrial policy program, as well as the business environment.
- Chapter 8 ("Innovation, Firms, Capabilities, and Modern Industrial Policy") completes the analysis of industrial policy with what we believe industrial policy should be today, that is, a modern industrial policy, as well as with a discussion of innovation, firms, and capabilities.
- Chapter 9 ("Why Is the Philippine State Weak? Spatial and Temporal Fragmentation Obstructing Structural Transformation") links the Philippines' weak state and low capacity to lead transformation of the economy to temporal (the role of political parties) and spatial (national and local governments) fragmentation and discusses how these two have made economic transformation difficult.
- Chapter 10 ("Employment and Education in the Philippines: Misconceptions and Realities") provides an in-depth discussion of the structure of employment and education, the latter a much-discussed and controversial issue. The chapter argues that while education is important for a nation, it is subject to two important misconceptions: (1) A better-educated workforce leads to overall higher employment and wages overall, and (2) the Philippine workforce is not educated enough, and education is a key constraint to the growth of the Philippine economy. Based on these misconceptions, the government's policy is to further enhance skills accumulation. We argue that standard supply-side interventions will not translate into wage increases.
- Chapter 11 ("The Fiscal Deficit, the National Debt, and Monetary Reality: Old Habits Die Hard") deals with the second fundamental theme in this book, namely, that a sovereign government that makes payments in its own currency (pesos in the case of the Philippines) is not *financially* constrained. It may have real constraints, but not financial. We explain how the key economic departments (budget, treasury, central bank) operate in modern economies, including the Philippines.
- Chapters 12 ("The Philippine Economy Toward 2050: Aspirations and Reality") and 13 ("Forecasting Employment and Educational Needs") provide extensive forecasts of the Philippine economy, until 2050, based on the current situation as analyzed in previous chapters. Forecasts are based on the DLSU ANIMO econometric model (see Chapter 5) and on a model that allows us to jointly forecast very disaggregated employment and educational requirements (see Chapter 10). Our analysis indicates that the Philippine economy will certainly progress (e.g., poverty will decline, per capita income will increase), but by less than many think. Under our baseline scenario until 2050, the economy

will not transform into one like that of today's advanced economies. This is a call for action.

- Chapter 14 ("Poverty and the Cost of a Decent Basket: Who Can Afford It?") closes the analysis of the Philippine economy and how far it can go until 2050 with a novel analysis of poverty. We do so by designing what we call a "decent basket" and by estimating the number of Filipinos who can afford it. We estimate that the proportion of Philippine families with income below our estimated *living income* is above 80%.
- Chapter 15 ("Final Thoughts") provides conclusions. Either we change direction and industrialize (to the extent that this is possible today), with the government becoming much more active, or the next decades will bring *more of the same* (MOTS).

We are aware that the future of the Philippines depends on other factors that we do not address in this book, such as environment, climate change, energy, inequalities (regional and personal), or urbanization. We do not have either a specific discussion of the Asian economies, with the exception of South Korea's industrialization in Chapter 7. It has not been possible to cover everything, so we leave room for another book in the future, or for a second edition. Also, many people, including economists, blame institutions for the country's problems. We are not convinced. It is true, though, that we discuss institutions in Chapter 3. But it not the focus of our book. As we show in Chapter 4, there is great variation in productivity across provinces and cities in the country, with the same key institutions and laws. If productivity and income per capita in all cities/provinces were like that of Makati, the Philippines would have been a high-income economy. So yes, institutions probably matter, but they are not the center of our story.

We believe that the two key themes of this book, the need to transform the economy out of agriculture and low-productivity services and the need for the government to understand that it can spend in its own currency to provide basic public services, are the foundations to generate the progress that we have sought for decades.

Notes

1 However, income per capita at that time was very low. We also note that the Philippines was one of the countries cited in Gunnar Myrdal's (1968) *Asian Drama*.

2 In April 2025, the government hinted that upper-middle-income status would not be attained until 2026 or 2027. This was confirmed in July, when the World Bank released its annual classification of countries and income per capita thresholds. On August 1, Secretary Balisacan (Department of Economy, Planning, and Development) recognized that growth is not enough to achieve the country's income targets. More time is needed.

3 We were told by some government officials that the growth "targets" are, in reality, "assumptions" made to calculate debt payments. We are not sure what the difference is.

Whether targets or assumptions, 6–8% is unrealistic. In any case, it was revised downward in 2025.

4 Due to limited opportunities for high-quality employment domestically, many Filipinos seek work abroad to support their families by becoming overseas Filipino workers (OFWs). Typically, they are employed in health care, maritime, construction, and domestic work. Their contributions to the Philippine economy come via remittances, which serve as a vital source of income for many households. However, it is important to note that for those who have a high level of education, migration leads to "brain drain," as the country loses talent and human capital that could otherwise contribute to domestic development.

5 See Landingin and Medalla (2019) for an analysis of reforms.

6 We use this term to differentiate from the administrative/legal reality—conditioned by history, culture, and practice, and self-imposed fiscal rules (e.g., rules about when and how government payments can be made). All this is overwhelmingly influenced by economic theory and interactions with multilateral and rating agencies. The administrative processes that result constrain the government in many ways.

2

A BRIEF OVERVIEW OF THE ECONOMIC HISTORY OF THE PHILIPPINES

2.1 Introduction

This chapter provides a succinct account of Philippine economic history since it was colonized in the 16th century.[1] We focus on those factors that, as a result of being colonized for over 400 years, have conditioned Philippine development until today: agrarian problems (the causes of poverty and inequality), an underdeveloped manufacturing sector, and an excessively thrifty government. This is because development is a path-dependent process. These three issues are widely discussed throughout the book. We start with the colonization period (first by Spain, then by the United States), then decolonization and independence after World War II. This is followed by a discussion of the American influence and how this has shaped the Philippine development thinking.

2.2 Colonization by Spain (1521–1898)

Spain's colonization of the Philippines (1521–1898) was somewhat different from that of the other Western powers in Asia.[2] The reason was that the propagation of the Christian faith played a more important role. Opposition to this was strong in the southern islands. Secondly, the number of Spaniards in the Philippines amounted to no more than a few thousand. Maddison (2001, p. 70) noted that there were 2,000 Spaniards and 10,000 Chinese living in Manila at the end of the 16th century.[3] Thirdly, the Philippines had commodities of interest to regional traders and was integrated into Asian trade networks but did not have luxury goods like spices (like the Moluccas in Indonesia) or silk.

When Magellan and his men arrived in central Philippines, they met a Malay population (people who had come from neighboring Indonesia and Malaysia) organized in small colonies under chiefs called *datus*. Their communities, relatively isolated from each other, were called *barangays* (they held communal

DOI: 10.4324/9781003728719-2

lands—there was no private land ownership). The people who came from Indonesia and Malaysia brought Islam (brought to them by Arab traders), and this spread throughout Mindanao. When the Spanish arrived in Manila Bay in 1569, they found a small Muslim community, under a datu, in a place they called Maynila. The Spanish conquest pushed back Islam, which was confined to the southern islands.

There is evidence that prior to the arrival of Magellan, there was trade with Chinese, Arab, and Indian traders, and the Philippines was already connected to Asian maritime trade routes, with various goods and resources, including gold, beeswax, resin, aromatics, pearls and shells, forest products, foodstuffs, and like in many other parts of the region, slaves (Clemente, 2012), traded with neighboring regions. Spain did exploit the Philippines' resources and strategic position, but not in the same way other colonial powers exploited resource-rich colonies, such as those producing spices or precious metals on a large scale (e.g., the Netherlands in Indonesia or Spain itself in Latin America). The Philippines did not have gold and silver like the American colonies did.

Shortly after the arrival of the conquistadores, religious orders set foot in the countryside and took over the authority of the *datus*. The Spanish divided the land into large areas of jurisdiction, combining several villages whose inhabitants were commended to the Crown by the *encomendadores* (the *encomienda system*). Huge tracts of land were distributed to various religious orders and certain favored individuals. The latter's job was to protect the locals and help them learn the Christian faith. In return for this, the *encomendadores* had the right to levy tribute and require labor. This way, the colony would not be a financial burden to the home government. This system of administration led to the *hacienda*-based export economy and the friar domination of the provincial areas that stultified Philippine economic development.

During the colonial period, commercial links were closer to the Spanish possessions in the Americas than to those in East Asia. Trade through the Manila–Acapulco galleon was the main source of income for the colony during its early years. The service was inaugurated in 1565 and continued until 1815, just before the secession of the American colonies from Spain. The galleon trade brought silver from New Spain (present-day Mexico), which was used to purchase Asian goods, such as silk from China, spices from the Moluccas, lacquerware from Japan, and cotton textiles from the Philippines. These goods were then exported to New Spain, and ultimately Europe, by way of Manila (merely as a transshipment port). Thus, the Philippines earned its income through the trade of the Manila–Acapulco galleon. The galleon would return from Mexico with a 100–300% profit in Mexican silver. All this resulted in cultural and commercial exchanges between Asia and the Americas, leading to the introduction of new crops and animals to the Philippines, such as corn, potatoes, tomatoes, cotton, and tobacco, which gave the colony its first real income. But because of the galleon trade's rapid returns, Spain lacked interest in developing the Philippine economy.

It is also worth noting that Spain's golden period was the 16th century. Afterward, it was rivaled and overpowered by the British, Dutch, and French and eventually declined. The flow of bullion (gold and silver) from America allowed Spain to expand its empire. However, Spain was bogged down in wars that it paid with taxes and the gold and silver from Latin America. Spain did not benefit from this, and it failed to progress. It declined as an imperial power during the 17th and 18th centuries (Reinert, 2019, chapter 3). By the 19th century, Spain was a second-rate imperial player. This had an impact on the colonies, including the Philippines, where corruption was rampant. Moreover, Spain was not benefitting from having the Philippines as a colony.

The governmental system of the colony was organized around the galleon trade as the primary source of income and the major economic activity, as well as the religious orders that controlled and governed the provincial areas. The friars dominated social, political, and economic life, and Filipinos were forced to follow. Overall, Spanish colonialism molded the existing Malay culture and society, and this provided the basis for a more complex political unit. At the same time, the Spanish rule established a highly inegalitarian social structure and economic system. It divided society and impeded modernization.

King Charles III (reigned between 1759 and 1788) tried to remedy the situation. He appointed a reformist as governor-general, Jose Basco y Vargas. His objective was to overhaul institutions in the Philippines, cut red tape in the administration, and make it more efficient. His task was also to improve the galleon trade. Basco drafted a program of reforms for the Philippines in 1779. Its implementation was not easy as a result of renegade barangays, corruption, and a refusal to accept the reforms. In fact, between the middle of the 18th century and the beginning of the 19th, Spain considered abandoning the colony. The year 1782 marks the birth of the *Compañia General de Tabaco de Filipinas*. This revived the Philippine economy. The other important event that saved the Philippines was the shift of trade to cash crops in the 19th century. As a result, the Philippines experienced progress during this century. It was inserted into the global economy and saw the fruits of the Industrial Revolution. Manila became an international port in 1835.

In time, Spanish policies generated pressures that the colonial government could not accommodate. By the 19th century, Christianity had united the Philippines, and friar educational institutions had produced a number of educated Filipinos. Yet the end of the Galleon trade in 1815 created the need for new sources of revenue. Spanish authorities also faced pressure from rapidly evolving Asian economies. The British Empire in particular had established its hegemony over trade a century before. Admitting failure to develop the colony on its own initiative, the Spanish authorities decided to enhance trade with other ports in Southeast Asia. To do so, they developed several ports across the Philippines. Friars and tax agents were sent to collect from peasants and tenants. By the end of the 19th century, conditions for a revolution and for independence were present. In 1898, war broke out between Spain and the United States. By that time, Spain had only two colonies, Cuba and the Philippines. Spain lost both to the United States. The Philippines was ceded to the United States in 1898, after a very brief war, and not without Filipino resistance (Filipinos were, in fact, kept out of Manila by the Americans). Nevertheless, the Philippines declared national independence in 1899. The Americans took over the Philippines to use it as a base for ships engaged in the China trade. As a result of the occupation, the relationship between the Americans and Filipinos deteriorated.

Overall, Spain left a deep and lasting legacy in the Philippines—some aspects beneficial, but many detrimental, especially in terms of social inequality and economic development. Society was divided into "names" depending on where one had been born and race: *peninsulares* (Spaniards born in Spain), *insulares* (Spaniards born in the Philippines), mestizos (mixed-race), and indios (native Filipinos). This structure created persistent inequality in landownership, wealth, and power, many of which remained even after independence. Spain did not industrialize the Philippines or modernize its agriculture in any substantial way. Land was concentrated in the hands of a few (e.g., friar estates), while most Filipinos remained landless peasants. Spain left a highly centralized political system that revolved around Manila and was deeply intertwined with the Catholic Church. Spain neglected infrastructure development, aside from some roads and ports to serve colonial needs. The economy was heavily dependent on the galleon trade. Once that ended, the colony had little industrial or commercial development of its own. On the positive side, Spain introduced formal education, including schools and universities, like the University of Santo Tomas, as early as 1611. It must be noted (and contrary to what is often claimed) that Spain had spread education in the Philippines.[4]

2.3 The American Colonial Period (1898–1946)

The American colonial period was very different from that of Spain. In some ways, it exacerbated the inequalities that had prevailed under Spanish colonization. From the start, American colonial authorities faced strong pleas for independence. To do so, the United States introduced "tutelage colonialism" by giving Filipinos some autonomy. The United States established municipal governments and local elections, public education, and instruction in English; improved public health and hygiene; and built public roads and water supply and irrigation facilities.[5] The intent of the local government laws was to grant as much local autonomy as possible to the Filipino population. Indeed, American domination of the Philippines was intended to be a temporary phenomenon, as the United States did not see itself as an imperial power (although President Theodore Roosevelt was an imperialist). The United States had to sustain the Filipino economy by importing vast quantities of protected agricultural products, such as sugar and coconut oil. The Great Depression had significant effects on the Philippines, as it led to demands for restrictions on the entry of Philippine sugar and immigrants into the United States, as well as the employment of Filipinos on American ships. However, the United States was unable to accept independence immediately on the grounds that it thought the Filipinos were incapable of self-governance (Hall, 1981, chapter 47).

In 1902, the US Congress empowered the Philippine government to classify and dispose of all public lands for the benefit of the people. A mechanism was introduced in 1903 whereby every citizen could acquire up to 24 hectares of public land, while corporations were limited to a maximum of 1,024 hectares. The system, unfortunately, did not work because the procedures were too complicated and because the Bureau of Lands connived at the maneuvers of the land-grabbers. Moreover, in 1904, the American government bought for USD 7 million the lands of the Spanish friars (about 165,000 hectares), which the Filipino leader Aguinaldo had designated for nationalization. However, it was a failure because the United States insisted on a full market price, which tenants could not afford. The consequence was that most land ended up in the hands of businessmen, and no substantive reforms were introduced. The *encomendadores* of Spain's time were replaced by the local oligarchs.

The final blow to the Philippine economy came with the opening of the American market to Filipino sugar. This favored large-scale agricultural production. All these events ended up reducing the majority of owners-cultivators to sharecropping tenants (working under unjust conditions that perpetuated poverty) at the mercy of their landlords. Meanwhile, a powerful group of "sugar barons" emerged. They would eventually control politics (Studwell, 2013, pp. 34–49).[6]

From the start, the relationship between the United States and the Philippines was marked by a series of attempts to negotiate the terms of independence. Eventually, the major problem turned out to be economic: how to protect domestic industries and American business interests. Likewise, there was recognition that the economic base of the Philippine government had to be strengthened. In 1916, the US Congress passed the Jude Law. This provided the Philippines with a constitution and declared the American intention to withdraw sovereignty as soon as a government could be formed. In the meantime, all measures passed by the Philippine legislature had to be reported to the US Congress, which had the power to annul them. Then came the Hares–Hawes–Cutting Act. This was an Independence bill. It became law in 1933. However, Filipino authorities objected to the terms of the Bill and asked for more favorable terms, which were not granted. A new bill, the Tydings–McDuffie Act, was signed in 1934. Under this Act, the Philippines would draw a republican constitution that had to be approved by the president of the United States and the Filipino people. The Act provided for the continuation of trade relations as they existed for five years, but after that, the gradual imposition of tariff duties at 5% a year for the remaining five years of the Commonwealth period (in reality, a semiautonomous

Commonwealth under a Filipino government). The date for independence was scheduled for July 4, 1946.

During the American colonial period, the share of agriculture in GDP hardly declined and stayed at about 38% of total GDP, while that of industry increased from 16.1% to 19.6% between 1913 and 1938/1941 (Booth and Deng, 2017, Tables 2 and 3). Meanwhile, the share of employment in agriculture was 69% in 1939. The production of sugar and tropical fruits developed rapidly, mainly oriented to the American market. Agricultural output, measured in 1938 prices, grew at around 7% per annum between 1902 and 1918 but then declined to about 1% per annum between 1918 and 1938.

The transition to full independence was derailed in 1941, when the Philippines was attacked by Japan. The Japanese installed a puppet government, with Jose Laurel as president. At the same time, resistance was organized in rural areas, mostly peasant movements linked to the Socialist and Communist Parties. The Huk guerrilla movement was organized under the leadership of the Communist Party.[7]

The Philippines finally started sailing as an independent nation in 1946, with a seemingly advanced form of political democracy drawn upon the American system, as established in the Tydings–McDuffie Act. Manuel Roxas was the first elected president of the independent republic, with a term of only two years due to his premature death in 1948. Its economy, however, was in poor shape, not just because it was not well developed (due to the agrarian problem and incipient manufacturing), but also because of the damage caused during World War II.

Spanish and American colonialism introduced changes chaotically and randomly, and they did not really produce a new and coherent form of society; rather, these changes led to rampant dualism. In fact, colonialism brought the Philippines to what Mendels (1972) referred to as *proto-industrialization*, a stage before the full rise of modern industry (with modern factories), the latter associated with the Industrial Revolutions, marked by the rapid growth of traditionally organized but market-oriented rural industry.[8] Under these conditions, a segment of the population lived to a considerable extent from industrial mass production for interregional and international markets. However, the Philippines did not achieve successful modern industrialization because the loss of proto-industrial output and employment was only very insufficiently compensated by the rise of a modern industry.[9]

We note, nevertheless, that De Dios and Williamson (2015) argued that the Philippines was the third Asian country (and the first in Southeast Asia) to enter the so-called "5% industrial growth club"—those countries that had experienced industrial growth rates of at least 5% a year—at the end of the 19th century. This continued until the 1960s, when the Philippines had developed a significant manufacturing sector supported by import protection. Problems came in the 1970s. We return to this point in Chapter 7.

2.4 The Philippines at the End of World War II: Decolonization and Independence

The Philippines, like the rest of Asia, emerged from the war very poor in 1945. Many Asian economies did not see much progress over the next 15–20 years, until the 1960s. The decolonization process differed across countries, and this mattered for future performance. During the years after World War II, some countries were engaged in decolonization wars, and many experienced internal political struggles. These were the cases of Indonesia, the Philippines, Vietnam, Malaysia, South Korea, and Taiwan. Booth and Deng (2017) argued that the different decolonization processes after World War II played an important role in explaining future development. Policymakers in all the new Asian nations were making efforts at learning how to run their countries and tackle the many problems they faced. This situation prevented fast modernization and progress. The United States was the world's market economy leader by this time, and Europe was on its way to fully recover from the physical destruction of World War II.

The 20 years after World War II were a difficult period for many Asian countries. The decolonization process and the Cold War took a toll. At the start of the 1960s, Asia's income per capita was significantly below that of advanced economies (Table 2.1): While those of Western European countries were above USD 1,000, and Canada and the United States above USD 2,000, Japan and Malaya (with Singapore) had the highest per capita income in Asia in 1961, USD 383 and USD 368, respectively. The Philippines was next at USD 188. Other East Asian economies had not reached USD 200, with Taiwan, South Korea, and Thailand just above USD 100, and Indonesia just below this income per capita.[10] Moreover, Asia's average GNP per head in 1961 (excluding Japan and China, the latter with per capita income of USD 83), at USD 84, was the lowest in the world: Africa had USD 100; Latin America, USD 307; Southern Europe, USD 313; the Middle East, USD 187; the Soviet Union, USD 818; and Eastern Europe, USD 550 (Rosenstein-Rodan, 1961, Table I-A, Table 2-C). It is true that the Philippines' per capita income was significantly higher than those of many other Asian countries, including Indonesia, Thailand, South Korea, and Taiwan, but it was a very low level.

The Philippines was in ruins. A vast amount of physical capital in both Manila and the rural areas had been destroyed, work animals had been butchered for food, and inflation was rampant. The American army did much to alleviate the distress, to re-establish order and communications and reopen schools. The United States did a lot to restore transportation facilities, electric power, water supplies, and sanitation.

Although the Philippines was not the central focus of 1974 Nobel Prize winner Gunnar Myrdal's (1968) *Asian Drama*, his analysis encompassed the nation within the broader context of Southeast Asia's economic and political landscape. His observations on the Philippines can be summarized as follows: (1) The

TABLE 2.1 Gross National Product per Capita (USD), 1961

	English-Speaking and European Countries		*Communist Countries*		*Latin America*		*Middle East*		*Asia*		*Africa*	
Over $2,000	United States	2,790										
	Canada	2,048										
$1,000 to $2,000	Sweden	1,557										
	Switzerland	1,555										
	Australia	1,475										
	New Zealand	1,470										
	Belgium	1,348										
	Great Britain	1,345										
	Norway	1,223										
	France	1,203										
	Denmark	1,193										
	West Germany[c]	1,113										
$500 to $1,000	Netherlands	954										
	Finland	893										
	Austria	830	Soviet Union	818								
			East Germany	700								
			Czechoslovakia	650			Israel	733				
	Italy	623			Venezuela	644						
	Ireland	570			Puerto Rico	643						
					Argentina	533						
$250 to $500			Hungary	475								
					Uruguay	449						
			Bulgaria	440								

(Continued)

TABLE 2.1 (Continued)

	English-Speaking and European Countries		*Communist Countries*		*Latin America*		*Middle East*		*Asia*		*Africa*	
	South Africa	427	Poland	440	Cuba	413			Japan	383		
			Romania	440					Malaya[a]	368		
									Singapore	368		
	Greece	383			Jamaica	357						
	Spain	321			Chile	348	Lebanon	319				
			Yugoslavia[b]	306	Mexico	297						
					Colombia	287						
					Panama	283						
					Costa Rica	278						
					Brazil	268						
					Dominican Republic	251						
$100 to $250	Portugal	240	Albania	240								
					Nicaragua	206	Turkey	222				
					El Salvador	191	Algeria	190	Philippines	188		
					Guatemala	184	Syria	173				
					Honduras	180	Saudi Arabia	170	Hong Kong	170	Rhodesia[d] and Nyasaland	161
					Peru	179	Iraq	161				
					Ecuador	159	Tunisia	160				
					Paraguay	129	Egypt	150				
							Morocco	140				
							Jordan	126	Ceylon[a]	123		
							Iran	120	Taiwan	116		

(*Continued*)

TABLE 2.1 (Continued)

	English-Speaking and European Countries		*Communist Countries*		*Latin America*		*Middle East*		*Asia*		*Africa*	
									South Vietnam[a]	111		
									South Korea[a]	106		
									Thailand	101	Rep. of Congo	103
Below					Haiti	99			Indonesia	99		
$100					Bolivia	87					Kenya	94
											Liberia	85
			PRC	83							Nigeria	84
									Cambodia	77	Ethiopia	76
									India	70	Sudan	75
							Libya	62	Pakistan	62	Tanganyika	75
									Burma[a]	61	Uganda	66
									Afghanistan	58	Togoland	55
									Laos[a]	52		
									Nepal	47		
									Bhutan	46		

Notes:

[a] The Table uses the country names in 1961, at the time the source paper was published. Today's names are Malaysia for Malaya, Sri Lanka for Ceylon, Vietnam for South Vietnam, Republic of Korea for South Korea, Myanmar for Burma, and Lao PDR for Laos.

[b] Yugoslavia ceased to exist in 1992. Its territory was split into its constituent republics.

[c] West Germany ceased to exist in 1990, when it unified with East Germany and the country took the official name of West Germany, the Federal Republic of Germany.

[d] Rhodesia ceased to exist in 1980. It became Zimbabwe.

Source: Rosenstein-Rodan (1961, Table 2-C). Figures for the United States, Canada, Japan, Soviet Union, and PRC are from Table I-A. Figures for Sweden, Switzerland, Australia, New Zealand, Belgium, Great Britain, Norway, France, Denmark, West Germany, Netherlands, Finland, Austria, Italy, and Ireland come from Wilcox et al. (1962, Table 1)

Philippines inherited a colonial administrative structure that lacked the robustness needed for effective governance. This legacy contributed to persistent institutional weaknesses post-independence; (2) it suffered from significant disparities in wealth and land ownership, which hindered cohesive national development and perpetuated poverty among large segments of the population; (3) there were deficiencies in the education system, emphasizing that limited access and quality impeded human capital development, which is crucial for economic progress; and (4) political volatility was high, including frequent changes in leadership and policy direction, which disrupted consistent developmental planning and implementation.

The Philippines fits well with Myrdal's notion of "soft state," which he used to describe countries where laws and policies were weakly enforced due to factors like corruption, lack of discipline, and societal indifference. Under these circumstances, politicians who dominate local politics exploit the national resources through patronage politics. The result is that the central government fails to create and implement policies that lead to national economic development.

As noted earlier, the first president of the republic was Manuel Roxas, when the Philippines gained independence in 1946. He won the election on a platform of economic change, promising new economic policies. The first two decades of Philippine independence were characterized by postwar reconstruction and the adoption of a democratic system modeled after the United States'. Yet having attained independence, the Philippines faced a harsh reality. This was that while Spain had ruled through a religious hierarchy and the Americans had set up a government based on the popular will and had brought in the formal institutions of a modern state (local government, a civil service, public works, schools, roads, clean water, health services, and financial institutions), investment into the country and a policy of laissez-faire had combined to perpetuate a colonial economy. Moreover, dependence on the American market led to doubt that ten years would be sufficient to create an economically independent and viable Philippines. The new independent government was not in a position to satisfy the demands that a better-educated population was asking for. The war had also awakened the countryside and aroused expectations that people sought to have fulfilled. Large numbers of people moved to urban areas to escape rural poverty. Increased tenancy, due to the attractions of large-scale production for export, had led to widespread unrest. The American period laid the basis for a modern state, but it also engendered serious problems, including complete economic dependence on the United States.

The key to understanding the future of the Philippines was the feudal agrarian relations and other structural problems, especially in the rural areas, that had been left unaddressed. In the words of Hall (1981, pp. 813–814):

> In effect power was conferred upon the property owners and the intelligentsia, and the men who exercised came almost entirely from the landed gentry; for notwithstanding the most tremendous drive to establish schools, enroll pupils

> and train teachers, education of the masses could never keep pace with political progress. The landed classes, who wielded power, were not at all interested in democratization, but in preserving their own social and economic privileges. And as their co-operation was important to the American authorities, nothing was done to break the big states, save those of the friars, and even then it was not the cultivators who benefited. And one end of the scale there were vast estates and at the other a vast number of holdings of less than a hectare, i.e., just under 2 ½ acres. The number of owner-cultivators too small under the Spanish regime, declined further under the American, and the condition of the peasantry was the worst in the whole of Southeast Asia.

The lack of a land reform and the poor state of agriculture would be a key impediment to Philippine modernization and takeoff. This exacerbated the Huk problem.[11] Filipino landlords extracted excessive rents (over 50% of the crop) from the tenants and lent at very high rates. In 1946, the government passed a law that reduced landlords' share to 30%. It was, however, violated. Moreover, tenants had no working capital. The situation in the countryside was very complex, resulting in the rise of Communism.

The second key theme to understand and evaluate the future of the Philippines, which marked the country during the decades after independence, is the economic arrangements with the United States. They were complex and became key to understanding the country's future development. American assistance started immediately after the war. The US Congress passed two acts in 1946, the Philippine Rehabilitation Act ("Tydings Act") and the Trade Act ("Bell Act" by Congressman Jasper Bell).[12]

The Tydings Act dealt with compensation for war damages. This provided USD 620 million and extensive technical assistance to the Philippines. A military base agreement was also negotiated in 1947. This gave the US armed forces a 99-year lease on Philippine bases.[13] This was subject to the Philippine Congress accepting the Bell Act, which stipulated the following:

- From 1946 to 1954, the Philippines would enjoy duty-free exports into the United States, subject to certain quotas. Between 1954 and 1974, Philippine exports to the United States paid a duty that started at 5% of the American tariff and increased gradually by 5% per annum until it reached the full amount of the American tariff in 1974. The quotas affected the following products: raw sugar, refined sugar, hemp, rice, cigars, tobacco, copra oil, and mother-of-pearl buttons. From 1954, the quota amounts would be reduced by 5% annually.
- The Philippines would not levy export duties.
- The Philippine peso was pegged to the American dollar at the rate of PHP 2 per USD. This rate could not be changed, or convertibility suspended, except by agreement with the president of the United States.

- The Act stipulated no restrictions upon the entry of American products into the Philippines.
- Acceptance of a "parity clause," according to which the exploitation and development of natural resources and lands in the public domain and the operation of public utilities "shall if open to any person, be open to citizens of the United States." In other words, Americans in the Philippines would have equal rights with Filipinos in the exploitation of the natural resources of the country, without reciprocal rights. This last point required an amendment to the Philippine Constitution, which reserved the utilization of the natural resources for Filipino citizens. The Laurel–Langley Agreement of 1955, which extended from 1955 to 1974, replaced the Bell Trade Act. (See later text.)

Filipino sugar interests were, of course, determined to secure the approval of the Bell Act, and this was passed in 1947. The guaranteed export market provided by the quota system encouraged the return to the prewar colonial economy and the return of landed interests in economic and political power. What is important here is the fact that the free entry of American products into the Philippines would have a serious impact on the future development of the country, as it effectively prevented the development of national industries.

The result of the dependence on the United States ensured that landed interests would remain dominant in Filipino politics. US policymakers, for their part, pursued a policy of "attraction," seeking profitable trade and stable government through political alliances with the educated, landholding Filipino elites. The consequence of this was that the United States backed a class deeply dedicated to preserving its own economic and social dominance.

The Philippines depended on the exchange rate earned through exports of agricultural products, and these were grown either on large haciendas (utilizing tenant or unskilled labor) or collected by Chinese middlemen from small independent farmers. This meant that the foreign country's financial resources depended upon groups whose basic political interests were to secure government loans during the planting season, low-cost labor, continuation of the tenancy system, and peace and order in the countryside.

Apart from these powerful landed groups, a new group appeared on the scene. These were the entrepreneurs who grew wealthy during the war as a result of commerce in surplus goods. They invested their surplus capital in commercial enterprises and, as foreign exchange controls were imposed, also in import-substitute industries. They depended on political influence with government agencies and played an increasingly important political role.

President Roxas was followed in 1948 by Elpidio Quirino (1948–1953). Quirino's term was characterized by vigorous economic growth due to reconstruction and a large inflow of foreign assistance. He tried to tackle the country's big problems: social, labor, and agricultural. He also tried to address the Huk problem, and although he was initially successful, negotiations ultimately collapsed. The problem was solved by his secretary of National Defense, Ramon Magsaysay, who, in 1950, captured the top members, while the rest went underground.

The overall economic situation between 1946 and the early 1950s was precarious (Hall, 1981, chapter 51), marked by recurring crises. The prices of exports such as hemp and copra declined, the cost of living went up, and unemployment was high. Despite this, the economy was expanding, and in 1949, production had recovered to 91% of the 1937 level (in 1946, it was only 40%), although the population was about 25% larger. For a number of reasons, the country remained in a state of permanent crisis, however. First, the government refused to levy adequate taxes and failed to collect the existing ones. In 1945–1946, one-third of government revenue came from cigarettes. The Filipino administration was very weak, as shown in its inability to collect taxes. Hall (1981, p. 904) indicated that the government

> assessed some 30,000 individuals and corporations as liable, whereas three months after the date for the receipt of the returns only 1,920 had come in, and of these 1,440 claimed no liability. . . . Government expenditure was only 6.8 percent of the national income, but the tax revenue no more than 4.5 percent.

Another reason that explains this poor state of affairs was the persistent corruption scandals related to the trafficking of import licenses. As a consequence of the precarious fiscal and balance of payments situation, President Truman sent an Economic Survey Mission to the Philippines in 1950, led by Daniel W. Bell, president of the American Security and Trust Company (the Bell Mission). The Mission formulated an economic policy reform for the Philippines and recommended the grant of American aid, USD 250 million, over five years, provided that the Philippines undertook the following reforms and recommendations (Hall, 1981, chapter 52):[14] (1) introduced fiscal measures that increased revenue; (2) revisited the Bell Trade Act; (3) created an Agricultural Credit, Cooperative Financing Administration, and Farmers' Cooperative Marketing Association; (4) established a minimum wage and a Magna Carta of Labor that permitted collective bargaining; and (5) signed a Mutual Security Treaty. These measures (the first two were the most important) did not really have a significant impact, as the level of implementation was low and graft and corruption remained unpunished. Land reform did not advance much, agricultural poverty remained high, and foreign exchange earnings were low.

Quirino was succeeded by Ramon Magsaysay (1953–1957), an anti-Communist and populist president who initiated agrarian reform. He established the National Rehabilitation and Resettlement Administration to encourage internal migration and land settlement, created a Court of Agrarian Relations, and appointed an Agricultural Tenancy Commission. His efforts resulted in an extension of the agricultural cooperative movement and an increase in rural credit. The agrarian reform program, however, stalled, and numerous amendments made by a landlord-dominated Congress rendered it inutile. Nevertheless, he cleaned up the Bureau of Customs and reduced corruption in the allocation of foreign exchange.

Magsaysay did not complete his four-year term, as he died in an accident. He was succeeded by Carlos Garcia (1957–1961), best known for the introduction of the controversial "Filipino First" policy and for his austerity program. He was followed by Diosdado Macapagal (1961–1965), who sought to liberalize the economy (see following text). Both Garcia and Macapagal equally failed to address the country's graft and corruption and its structural problems.

2.4.1 The Great Policy Debates

Economic debate during the three administrations of Presidents Quirino, Magsaysay, and Garcia (13 years in total) was intense, referred to by Takagi (2016, Chapter 4) as the "Great Debate" years over fiscal and monetary policy. While industrialization and the need for the government to lead this process was not put in doubt, policymakers clashed on the details of *how*. The major figures sponsoring different views until the mid-1950s were Finance Secretary (under Presidents Roxas and Quirino), and later central bank governor (1949–1960), Miguel Cuaderno and Secretary of Coordination Salvador Araneta (1950–1952). In essence, Cuaderno argued for a tight fiscal policy and the continuity of a strong peso, the latter a key pillar of the country's import substitution industrialization (ISI) policy (see next section). Depreciation of the peso would increase the price of essential imports of consumer goods as well as of machinery equipment and raw materials. He also argued that exchange controls were needed to constrain imports of luxury products. Araneta, on the other hand, supported a looser fiscal policy; a depreciation of the peso to help exporters, including the sugar industry (a measure openly opposed by Cuaderno); and import substitution. Araneta took ideas from the American New Deal and argued that the government should undertake deficit financing (Keynesian proposals). He was very critical of the tight credit and overvalued exchange rate policies of the central bank. The American-imposed exchange rate of PHP 2 per USD was much higher than the exchange rates of Korea and Japan.

Despite the disagreements, it must be made clear that both were supporters of the industrialization goal. Yet Cuaderno questioned Araneta's views on deficit spending, as the former thought that the Philippines could not implement it successfully because its firms did not have excess capacity to increase the production derived from deficit spending (supply rigidities). Instead, it would increase imports and exacerbate the balance of payments problems and inflation. Cuaderno argued that development could only be achieved with monetary stability.

Cuaderno won the debate and the favor of President Quirino. Araneta resigned in 1952. However, things changed with the arrival of President Magsaysay in 1953, as he was sympathetic of Araneta's economic proposals, though he leaned initially toward Cuaderno's austerity.[15] Yet President Magsaysay changed his view and became convinced that the country needed to use deficit financing (by issuing government bonds) to improve socioeconomic conditions. He reappointed Salvador Araneta as Secretary of Agriculture and Natural Resources (1954–1955). The administration then started examining the feasibility of implementing a New Deal type of package for the Philippines. This would be complemented with devaluation of the peso and the elimination of exchange controls. The Philippines finally used deficit financing for the first time in 1954. Another big win of the Araneta camps was that exporters would be allowed to engage in trade outside the exchange control system (Takagi, 2016, pp. 122–123). This was a first clear departure from the conservative fiscal and monetary policy of the previous administration. Needless to say, Governor Cuaderno continued expressing the need to balance the budget and raised concerns about inflation. Despite the open disagreements between the two officials, the central bank continued supporting industrialization through the allocation of foreign exchange to new industries.[16] Though it is true that prices increased, the president set up a control board rather than abandon deficit financing. Nevertheless, Salvador Araneta resigned in 1955. Again, it seems that Governor Cuaderno won the clash. President Magsaysay died in 1957 and was succeeded by President Carlos Garcia (1957–1961).

President Garcia blamed President Magsaysay for the poor international reserve position that he inherited (declining reserves). He blamed the rapid industrialization program and his liberal credit policy, which, it was claimed by those close to the central bank's position, had led to inflation. The solution was an austerity program. President Garcia seemed to side with Governor Cuaderno, who recommended a stabilization (austerity) program, the pillars of which were restrictive fiscal and monetary policy, together with the gradual lifting of foreign exchange controls. Devaluation was not favored. The government introduced the tariff policy in 1957.

Economic debates during the Garcia administration remained. We highlight three: the exchange rate policy, the austerity program, and the "Filipino First" policy. On the first one, the central bank advocated the gradual (as opposed to a sudden devaluation, advocated by some IMF staff) decontrol of foreign exchange. More precisely, Governor Cuaderno argued that devaluation without fiscal and monetary restraint would not solve the balance of payments crisis. In any case, the IMF did not support his program. This was compounded by opposition by the private sector, which attacked the central bank's strong currency policy. Then, in 1957, Congress asked representative Aldeguer to evaluate the existing control measures. He came up with a proposal to lift exchange controls starting in 1959 and fully eliminate them by the end of 1961. This was interpreted as devaluation, as it was a faster program to lift controls than that advocated by the central bank. President Garcia favored the moderate adjustment of the currency, but along Cuaderno's proposal. We stress again that the industrialization objective remained in this administration's agenda. The Philippine Chamber of Industry, for its part, advocated also a long period for the abolition of controls, about 1968. Finally, the president sided with Governor Cuaderno, and Aldeguer's program was abandoned: The currency would not be devalued, at least for the time being.

The austerity program was also very controversial because the central bank could not really convince the private sector that inflation was an issue. The private sector expected the government to stimulate the economy through expansive fiscal and monetary policies. This was of course Araneta's proposal for deficit financing. This became a tough battle because certain private businesses seemed to have influenced the monetary board. This led to a peculiar situation. This is that while members of the private sector may disagree on their alignment with the central bank on exchange rate controls, they aligned against the austerity program. At one point, the monetary board approved the government's request to issue treasury notes without the governor's knowledge (he was ill). Cuaderno, when he learned about it, stated that it was illegal because it ran against the central bank's charter. President Garcia, while he disagreed with Governor Cuaderno regarding the extent of inflation, agreed with him on the illegality of issuing treasury notes. Independently of this result, "the incident, however, provided only a foretaste of the emerging influence of private business interests over the monetary board and within the Garcia administration" (Takagi, 2016, p. 138).

Finally, as mentioned earlier, the treatment of American and Filipino businesses in the Philippines was unbalanced in favor of the former since the days of the Bell Trade Act. This eventually stoked anticolonial sentiment and resulted in an amendment of the Bell Trade Act under the Laurel–Langley Agreement in 1955, which extended from 1955 to 1974. (See Chapter 7). After the 1960s, exports from the Philippines increased significantly due to the American embargo against Cuba.

This memory left its mark on the 1987 constitution, drafted after the ouster of President Ferdinand Marcos Sr. This constitution included the "Filipino First" clause, articulated by President Garcia in the 1960 State of the Nation Address (the third important economic debate during the Garcia administration, the other two being the exchange rate and austerity). (See Chapter 2.) Takagi (2016, pp. 129–131) notes that the National Economic Council (NEC) had announced the Filipino First policy in 1958. It aimed "to encourage Filipinos to engage in enterprises and industries vital to the economic growth, stability and security of the country" (Takagi, 2016, p. 139). The NEC recognized the importance of the allocation of foreign exchange as the most effective instrument to achieve it. The objective was to favor Filipinos in the allocation of foreign exchange and credit. Its goal was industrialization underpinned by economic nationalism. This policy had indeed a great racial dimension, as it aimed at transforming the colonial economy to benefit the Filipino people. Takagi (2016, Table 5.1) shows the share of imports (a proxy for business) by Filipinos, American, and Chinese between

1948 and 1957. The data shows that the Filipino share increased from 23% to 54%, that of the Chinese declined from 39% to 14%, and that of the Americans slightly declined from 28% to 24% (this last group was protected by the Bell Trade Act, and later by the Laurel–Langley Agreement). As Takagi (2016, pp. 129–131) explains, Filipino First had been effectively implemented since the late 1940s but declined with the end of the Garcia administration in 1961.

Apart from the racial dimension of the policy, there was also the discussion about the achievements of industrialization since independence. While the National Economic Council (NEC) argued that the import substitution industrialization policy had not achieved much to develop a manufacturing sector, the central bank argued that this was incorrect, as the data showed that the share of imports of capital goods had increased from 53% of the total in 1949 to 78% of the total in 1957 (Takagi, 2016, p. 139).

In 1959, the central bank started implementing the Filipino First clause. This was done by reducing the foreign exchange allocation to all aliens except Americans, whose rights, as noted earlier, were protected by the parity clause of the Laurel–Langley Agreement. If the proposal had been completed, the central bank would have decreased to almost zero the allocation of foreign exchange to all foreigners except to the Americans by the end of 1959. Representatives of other nations urged the government to reconsider the policy. At this point, President Garcia had not yet made a clear and open pronouncement about it. Philippine policymakers argued that the policy was necessary to reduce the excessive control of the economy by foreigners. After discussions and hearing all parties (agreements and disagreements), the central bank decided to suspend the allocation of resources, as initially proposed. It decided to maintain the country's foreign exchange allocation at the level of the first quarter of 1959. This was a 50% reduction from the quota set during the last quarter of 1958. The truth seems to be that both NEC and the central bank ultimately found it very difficult to implement the Filipino First policy (Takagi, 2016, p. 145). Governor Cuaderno used Filipino First to carry out his gradual lifting of exchange controls, and with it to avoid an inflationary spike, and to negatively affect infant industries as well as, in general, Filipino businesses. This was a much more moderate program than that of Congressman Aldeguer. While the latter's program was supposed to be completed between 1959 and 1961, Governor Cuaderno designed his program to be completed between 1960 and 1964. When the program was set up, Governor Cuaderno decided to retire from service in 1960. By then, the country had implemented the austerity program that Governor Cuaderno deemed necessary, curtailed deficit financing, and managed to implement a gradual lifting of control measures (allocation of foreign exchange rate, and the peso was devalued).

As stated earlier, President Garcia only acknowledged "Filipino First" as a policy of the administration in the 1960. By 1960–1961, the advocates of the policy had lost momentum. In his 1961 State of the Nation Address, the president pointed out the achievements of his mandate (e.g., favorable balance of payments, increase in reserves) but did not refer to "Filipino First." This was the end of this policy. It was not part of the economic and political agendas of President Macapagal (1961–1965). Likewise, the gradual implementation of the decontrol program signified the end of industrialization (the ISI policy) through foreign exchange controls. As mentioned earlier, the industrialization tools changed with President Macapagal, from foreign exchange controls to tariffs. Efforts to industrialize continued with President Marcos Sr., but they failed (Chapter 7).

2.5 The Evolution of Development Thinking and the American Influence

Underlying the evolution of Philippine economic policy, there is a great deal of American influence, which extended during independence. Nowhere in Asia has been the American influence more obvious and patent than in the Philippines. This influence has shaped Philippine economic policy and thinking, and it remains so until today. It is thus important to contextualize the post–World War II decades. This was the Cold War period, and the Philippines had been an American colony. Because of the fear of a Communist takeover of newly independent yet vulnerable agrarian societies, the United States emphasized economic modernization (economic growth, industrialization, and rising living standards in addition to fundamental social and political changes), but conceived as a means to defeat Communism (Tadem, 2019). Promoting free market liberalism (and avoiding the pitfalls of Socialist- and Communist-leaning economic strategies such as economic planning, as seen in India and China), the World Bank and IMF played a critical role in supporting US-sponsored modernization. This is somewhat ironic, given the American experience (huge mobilization effort by the American government) during the war.[17] The experience of the Philippines was very different from that of the United States.

It is important to note, however, that the earlier description of the American influence as the "promotion of free market liberalism" is a simplification. The reality is that, since the 1930s, a group of Philippine policymakers attempted to create a central bank, something that was not achieved until 1949.[18] The creation of this institution had two purposes: One was to impose foreign exchange controls (the allocation of foreign exchange) to maintain a strong currency policy that encouraged import substitution industrialization (ISI), as discussed earlier. The second purpose of the creation of the central bank was to assert Philippine nationalism, that is, the creation of a central bank was a key pillar of state building. The colonial legacy and the agreements with the United States forced the Philippines to become a producer and exporter of primary products. Thus, the industrialization sustained by the central bank was not only an economic policy but also part of a larger project of state building. The central bank managed to establish its autonomy, which the government used to fend off vestiges of American colonialism and to resist pressure from Philippine agro-export industries. All this means that between the 1930s and the 1960s, the Philippines had a generation of policymakers that tried to create a policy regime that favored industrialization, the same as in other developing nations. Philippine policymakers during these years were determined to achieve the economic decolonization of the country. The role of the central bank was crucial to attain this objective. This endeavor encountered the opposition of American businessmen who attempted to impose neocolonial trade relations.

The implementation of an ISI strategy shows the awareness among economists at that time about the importance of industrialization for development and the role of structural transformation through policymaking. Hirschman (1968) offers a discussion of the problems implementing ISI in Latin America at about the same time. Industrialization has never been a *natural* process (Chang, 2002; Reinert, 2019); rather, it is "a political process whereby policymakers strive to change socioeconomic structures with uncertainty" (Takagi, 2016, p. 13). The role of the state in changing the economic structure is crucial. The first developmental program seeking industrialization drawn up in the Philippines dates back to 1948 (Takagi, 2016, p. 9). We stress that while the ISI policy was seen as an instrument to attain economic development, in the Philippines, the same as in other Southeast Asian nations, it had important racial and ethnic dimensions, insofar as it also aimed at redistributing the gross national product in favor of Filipinos (see Chapter 6 on the "Filipino First" policy of the Garcia administration).

The ISI policy was also recommended by the American administration as part of the 1950 Bell Mission that came to deal with the balance of payments crisis of 1949. In this sense, the Bell Mission represented a shift in American economic policy toward the Philippines. During the next decades, the Philippines had three distinct industrial policy regimes (Takagi, 2016, p. 12). First, as mentioned earlier, ISI worked with foreign exchange controls in the 1950s.[19] Policy during this period focused on strict import substitution with heavy state controls (Teodoro, 1967; Power and Sicat, 1971; Baldwin, 1975a; World Bank Group, 1976). To control imports, the government allocated foreign exchange and issued licenses (quantitative restrictions). The main sectors targeted were (1) consumer goods industries (to replace imports)—textiles and clothing, processed food and beverages, furniture, and footwear and leather products—and (2) light manufacturing and packaging—basic intermediate goods like cement and glass. This allowed the Philippines to develop local industries though focused on the production of consumer rather than export goods. The result nevertheless was the rapid expansion of manufacturing during the 1950s, fueled by high protectionism and import barriers. The manufacturing share of GDP grew from approximately 9.2% in 1949 to 15.3% in 1958 (total industry, 25% of GDP in 1960), while the manufacturing employment share rose from about 6.6% in 1948 to 11.4% in 1958 (total industry, 12%, same year). Meanwhile, the share of agricultural employment in total employment declined from around 72% in 1952 to 58% in 1965, and to 57% by 1967.[20]

We note that while Philippine policymakers before the 1960s could create an efficient and autonomous central bank that could support industrial policy through the exchange rate, they failed to establish cooperative relations with private businesses. These policymakers faced opposition from Philippine entrepreneurs in the export industry, while at the same time they failed to work with domestic industry as a result of the racial dimension of the Philippine economic structure. We take up this point in Chapter 7.

A second ISI regime came with the Macapagal administration (1961–1965). Philippine economic policy changed significantly in the 1960s, as a result of two factors: the arrival of the technocrats and the president's belief in minimal government intervention. This created a new policy regime, including the ISI system. In the 1960s, with the Macapagal administration, the ISI policy continued not through foreign exchange controls (abolished in 1962) but through tariffs (reduced quantitative restrictions in favor of more transparent tariffs). This was combined with the start of an incipient export-orientation industrialization (more so in the 1970s). Foreign exchange controls were lifted, and the currency was devalued, in 1962 (faster than in the plan envisioned by the governor of the central bank), from PHP 2 per USD to PHP 3.90, and protectionist structures started being dismantled. The government created the Program Implementation Agency, the precursor of the National Economic and Development Authority, today's Department of Economy, Planning, and Development. As part of the new policy regime, the Macapagal administration sought to attract foreign investment under a freer trade regime.

The programs of President Ferdinand Marcos Sr. (1965–1986) represented the last major attempt at industrialization undertaken by the Philippines. They failed. We discuss them in Chapter 7.

During the late 1980s, with Corazon Aquino as president (1986–1992), the country entered a third economic regime as it accelerated the pace of liberalization in cooperation with technocrats from the private sector, and it abandoned completely ISI and, more generally, the industrialization objective. This is already clear in the Philippine Development Plan 1987–1992 objectives' language. Apart from a rejection of the previous administration's policies, the second half of the 1980s and the 1990s witnessed a shift in worldwide economic policy (emphasis on liberalization, privatization, deregulation, fiscal discipline, and market-oriented reforms, and IMF–World Bank policy prescriptions for developing countries) that influenced the Philippines. This has prevailed until today.

2.5.1 Technocrats and the New Policy Regime Since the 1960s

As noted earlier, Philippine economic policy changed significantly during the 1960s. This was the result of two factors: One was the American drive to carry out its modernization agenda. To carry out its modernization agenda, the US administrations needed Philippine technocrats who were immersed in US ways of management and free market ideology. These technocrats were Philippine experts who worked with the US government, the World Bank, and the IMF. These gained importance after the 1960s. The second factor was that President Macapagal favored a more liberal management of the country's economic policy.

The American objective through the technocrats was to have a US development worldview. To attain this, the United States started training economists, engineers, and business administrators in the 1950s to organize the development process and prevent new nations from falling prey to communism. President Harry Truman announced the "Point Four Program" on January 20, 1949, defining *poverty* as a strategic threat and linking development to security. For the Truman administration (1945–1953), the biggest fear was that "backward" rural societies, such as those in Asia, would fall prey to Communism (Tadem, 2019, p. 3). To this purpose, disciplines such as business administration and economics were identified as key to providing the technical specialization, knowledge, and managerial training for the experts. For the Philippines, this involved local training and education and graduate study in US colleges. "In the Philippines, it amounted to a program of Americanization with the USA investing in education and training 'experts' who 'spoke the same language' and thought the same way as US mentors" (Tadem, 2019, p. 5). The role of the US-trained technocrats was to lead key economic agencies during the pre–martial law Marcos administration. Some of them became involved in Philippine–US joint business ventures, provided services to the local businesses of the Filipino landed elites who were diversifying into capitalist ventures, and joined the government. In general, these economists advocated economic liberalization and tried to attract foreign investment.[21]

Tadem (2019) noted that, upon independence, education became part of the US Cold War strategy involving the nurturing of an educated elite. This was primarily done in the University of the Philippines (UP), which the United States had established in 1908. UP produced an array of key technocrats who went on to serve in the Marcos regime, both pre-martial law and during the martial law administration (Tadem, 2019, Table 1). The technocrats who studied in the United States took courses that provided them with technical skills and also introduced them to the US worldview of development. UP's College of Business Administration became a regular recipient of US assistance.

The other important factor that influenced the shift in economic policy in the Philippines in the 1960s was the changes introduced by President Macapagal. In January 1962, he eliminated foreign exchange controls (the allocation of foreign exchange), a decision supported by the IMF and the World Bank. He also established the Program Implementation Agency (PIA) the same year, to carry out a socioeconomic development program (with the assistance of the technocrats). To this we add that the "Filipino First" policy of the Garcia administration was not part of Macapagal's agenda. It disappeared. This is important because it represented a significant shift: In the previous policy regime, the central bank was the key institution, with the control of foreign exchange as the policy instrument. The new regime created a new agency to carry out the development program, and the role of the central bank changed. This was a decision made by Philippine policymakers without international pressure.

To understand the rationale behind the change in economic policy, Takagi (2016, Chapter 6) argues that President Macapagal joined with several congressional colleagues in the foundation of the Free Enterprise Society of the Philippines in 1955. This Society advocated minimum interference by the government in private business. It also opposed the central bank's foreign exchange controls. The ideas defended by the Society were very different from those that had, one way or another, been accepted in the Philippines since the 1930s, in particular the role of the state in economic development. During all this time, the idea of free enterprise was associated with the colonial economy.

Apart from decontrolling foreign exchange, the Macapagal administration aimed at scrapping graft and corruption, attaining self-sufficiency in rice and corn, and creating a socioeconomic development program. To complete the decontrol program, the administration had to prepare (together with the IMF and the World Bank) a development program to support the peso in a free foreign exchange market, that is, to have sufficient reserves. The decontrol meant, effectively, a partial devaluation of the peso (the natural concern was, of course, inflation).[22]

Key to all these events was the president's key adviser on economic affairs, Sixto Roxas, who had attended graduate school at Fordham University in New York.[23] Roxas elaborated the plan that was part of the Macapagal economic platform. Under this plan, the government was to set clear directions for monetary, fiscal, and commercial policies, as well as for investment programs. Under this program, the government would implement a series of policies to protect Philippine industry and agriculture from foreign competition during their infant stages. This point is crucial because it meant that, effectively, the Macapagal administration would continue the ISI policy, though not through exchange controls but through tariffs. Finally, the program also encouraged foreign investment into the Philippines.

As noted earlier, President Macapagal created the PIA in 1962 to develop and implement a five-year program. This required a critical mass of technocrats. These economists were very different from those of previous generations. They populated the newly created Philippine Economic Society. Many of them had degrees from American universities. It is also worth noting that this new generation of technocrats would serve later in the Marcos Sr. administration (1965–1986).[24] Interestingly, though the foundation of the Macapagal administration was freedom of enterprise, Takagi (2016, p. 172) notes that the view within the Agency was that "the government should provide market liquidity through expenditure on public works and adopt a more liberal credit policy."

The president also asked Sixto Roxas to address the question of land reform. This showed awareness of the importance of this issue. Moreover, the Philippine administration was aware of Taiwan's great progress in this area. The reality, however, is that land reform did not go far in practice as it was sabotaged in Congress by huge landowners.[25]

Overall, the administration's socioeconomic program aimed at rehabilitating industries affected by the exchange rate liberalization (through tariff protection) while promoting basic and intermediate industries, as well as at expanding and diversifying industrial and agricultural productivity. The main sectors supported were (NEC, 1962, 1963, 1964, 1965; Baldwin, 1975b; Manasan, 1986; Medalla, 1992) (1) intermediate and capital goods industries, which gained attention (e.g., steel, petrochemicals); (2) early moves toward export-oriented industrialization; and (3) the continued presence of light manufacturing, but under growing pressure to modernize. The program also aimed at increasing income in the countryside so as to develop a domestic market for its own industries. We reiterate that the ISI policy to industrialize continued, but through the use of tariff protection.[26] The result was a slight increase in the share of industry in GDP during the 1960s (including the beginning of the Marcos Sr. administration), up to about 32%. Manufacturing output grew between 3% and 8% per annum, and as a share of GDP, it increased to 25%. The share of industrial employment was about 16% in 1965 (11% manufacturing), about the same as in 1980. The share of agricultural employment further declined, but at a slow pace, as it was still 52% in 1980.[27] This means that the decline in the share of agricultural employment between 1965 and 1980 was mirrored by an equal increase in the share of employment in services, from 26% to 33%.

Despite the continuity of some aspects of the economic policy, we conclude that the Macapagal administration signified a deep shift in the Philippine economic regime. This was partly the result of the changing and evolving ideas of a new generation of policymakers. While previous policymakers aimed at economic decolonization in the post-independence years and at decreasing economic dependence on the United States, the Macapagal generation "believed that the effort made by senior policymakers were merely attempts to stick to the status quo and therefore were determined to change the situation even though they had no consensus on the direction of the reform" (Takagi, 2016, p. 179). President Macapagal liberalized the Philippine economy and changed the policy regime. Key to this was a government that played a minimal role in coordinating the economy. Paradoxically, the influence in the government of the technocrats that took over in the 1960s was smaller. The result was that the Philippine government chose to have a small role in the regulation of private business. This state of affairs has lasted until today.

The aforementioned explains, at least in part, why the Philippines skipped the East Asian "developmental state" model and took a more "neoliberal" or market-led route in the ensuing decades. The Philippines decided not to create a well-functioning developmental state, while the neoliberal route has not been successful. As Chang (2002) and Reinert (2019) documented, all relevant cases of development throughout history assigned a significant role to the state, certainly in the take-off years, and certainly in the jump from light manufacturing and agriculture into complex manufactures (e.g., autos, industrial machinery, electronics). The Philippines never engineered a "big push" program, a coordinated investment plan, and a broad strategy of modernization for industry, agriculture, and education (Rosenstein-Rodan, 1943; Nurkse, 1953).[28] We take up this issue in detail in Chapter 7. The dilemma that the Philippines still faces today is whether it can have a government that plays a much more significant role in the economy or whether the state should step back and let the private sector operate without restrictions, thereby (according to members in the private sector) causing minimal damage.

Notes

1 This is an admittedly short account of Philippine history. It intends to highlight major events that have shaped the Philippine economy and which we think are important to understand where the country is today. It skips many details, especially concerning politics.

2 It was in 1521 that they arrived in the Philippines. Miguel Lopez de Legazpi arrived in 1565 and became the first governor-general.

3 Cushner (1971, p.57) indicates that the Spaniard colonist coming to the Philippines was not committed to remaining in the islands for a long time. There was also a revolving population of Mexican merchants who came to profit quickly from the galleon trade (see following text) and then return to New Spain.

4 Contrary to the widespread view that before 1898 the Philippines did not have a well-established system of public education, Manuel Quezon, resident commissioner from the Philippines (in the United States), criticized in a 1914 speech to the American Congress the "lies" by the Philippine Commission about the state of education in the Philippines during Spain's colonization. See details in https://archive.org/details/jonesphilippineb00quez, page 17 onward.

5 Booth and Deng (2017) noted that the United States spread English as a medium of instruction in the Philippines. In 1931, a very high 31% of total budgetary outlays were dedicated to education and health (Booth and Deng, 2017, Table 4). Post-primary education expanded significantly, which probably encouraged many graduates to move into professional and administrative occupations. The American emphasis on education, especially at the secondary and the tertiary levels, reflected the intention to grant self-government to the Philippines. Even so, American educational policy was not a complete success, as many children in rural areas did not enter school or dropped out before completing sixth grade. Moreover, a 1925 inquiry found that the quality of many classes was poor (Booth and Deng, 2017, pp. 33–34).

6 This is much less so today (Coronel et al., 2004, p. 40): "The changes are evident in the sugar industry, as well, portrayed as that sector of the Philippine economy that is the most feudal and least resistant to change. . . . [S]ugarcane planters are losing their power to sugar traders and industrial consumers such as beverage companies and export-oriented food processors. This has also meant a shift in the 'strategies of domination' used by ascendant elites as well as an unprecedented amount of upward mobility and the rapid growth of a middle class."

7 The Huk was a Communist guerrilla movement formed by the peasant farmers of Central Luzon. They were originally formed to fight the Japanese. Communism made its first appearance in the Philippines in 1924, at approximately the same time as in Vietnam and Indonesia. During the next few years, Communism spread and gained adepts in the agricultural provinces of Luzon, where landlordism was worst.

8 The notion of industrialization, as this term is used today, is linked to the capitalist mode of production, where the organization of social production is characterized by private ownership of the means of production and by its separation from labor, hired for a wage.

9 On top of these, there had been little diffusion of technology. The only effective overseas transmission of European technology and science was to the colonies of North America (Maddison, 2001, p. 24). In 1776, the United States had nine universities for 2.5 million people. We shall return to these issues in Chapter 6 in the context of Gerschenkron's (1962) latecomer model of industrialization. The reason is that latecomer countries solved the industrialization problem by using state intervention on a much wider scale than did the United Kingdom, the first industrializer.

10 All qualitative accounts of Singapore seem to indicate that, at that time, it was poor, probably poorer than Hong Kong. Singapore's high per capita income, however, may be due to the fact that it was part of Malaya, shown with the same per capita income.

11 After WWII, the Huk Communist guerrilla movement extended the fight and rebelled against the Philippine government in 1946. Its strength diminished in the 1950s through a series of reforms and military victories by Filipino president Ramon Magsaysay. The movement resurrected during the 1960s, but it never posed a threat to Philippine security.

12 These are, respectively, (1) *Philippine Rehabilitation Act of 1946*, Pub. L. No. 79–370, 60 Stat. 128 (1946), and (2) *Philippine Trade Act of 1946*, Pub. L. No. 79–371, 60 Stat. 141 (1946).

13 The dependence on the United States worsened when the two countries signed the Military Bases Agreement of 1947. This gave the United States a 99-year lease of 23 bases in the Philippines. The initial treaty was for 1947–2046. This was later shortened by amendment in 1966 to 25 years, renewable every 5 years.

14 Hall (1981, Chapter 52, pp. 949–950) noted that between the end of WWII and January 1950, the Philippines received USD 2 billion.

15 The history of austerity in the Philippines is brilliantly documented by Claudio (2025). Austerity was imposed in the Philippines by the Americans.

16 Republic Act 426 (1950) created the Import Control Board. It (1) regulated import quotas, licenses, and allocations; (2) categorized imports into groups—prime, essential, non-essential, luxury—each with different quota reductions, to promote domestic production and conserve foreign exchange; and (3) provided exemptions to, among others, raw materials needed for domestic manufacture. It was repealed by Republic Act 650 (1951), which stipulated that no commodity could be imported without an import license issued under this Act (with a few exceptions). The law empowered the Board to establish quotas, allocate dollar foreign exchange among import commodities, add or delete controlled imports, and reduce or ban non-essential imports. The priorities in foreign exchange and import allocations were as follows: first priority, government agencies for price stabilization, stockpiling, essential goods; next, bona fide producers for capital goods and raw materials not adequately supplied locally; then, other importers based on their average imports in 1949, with some allowance for new Filipino importers. The Act also stipulated that import licenses for non-producer importers had to include the condition that at least 50% of their imports had to be sold to Filipino merchants at the same markup, unless the president granted waiver.

17 The US government created two key agencies that pioneered new methods of economic policymaking. One such agency was the War Production Board (WPB), which focused on the measurement, coordination, and transformation of production. Simon Kuznets, chief economist at the WPB, was the author of the Victory Program, which coordinated economic and military strategies. The other agency was the Office of Scientific Research and Development (OSRD), at the center of science and technology policymaking. It was led by Vannevar Bush, the institutional architect behind the creation of America's organizational capability to design, develop, and produce advanced-technology weapons systems. Together, these two agencies undertook complementary policies that transformed the industrial innovation system, thereby empowering the wartime and postwar growth of the American economy.

18 The central bank was created despite American opposition and neglect by Philippine elites. Takagi (2016) considers the Philippine central bank as an "island of state strength" and a "pocket of efficiency."

19 The foreign exchange policy of the central bank became a contentious issue in the 1950s, when a clash erupted between the institution and the export industry as the latter was not the beneficiary of the former's industrial policy.

20 These statistics are from the four refences mentioned in the text.

21 Tadem (2019, p. 11) noted that the technocrats trained in "market economics" (the belief in small government intervention—hard-core neoclassical macroeconomics) clashed with those in government who advocated nationalist and protectionist development planning. Under the Macapagal administration, protectionism was defended by Hilarion "Larry" Henares Jr., an economist who, while trained at the Massachusetts Institute of Technology, argued for a nationalist economic policy based on import-substitution industrialization.

22 Takagi (2016, pp. 162–168) argues that President Macapagal faced significant opposition from the sugar industry, despite that this important group was supposed to benefit from the foreign exchange control. The intense battle was about the institutionalization of the free enterprise regime.

23 It is interesting to note that Sixto Roxas was not a member of the Free Enterprise Society and that he had questioned the notion of "free enterprise" (Takagi, 2016, p. 162).

24 It is important not to overstretch the argument about the economic and political affiliation of the technocrats, especially during the Marcos Sr. administration. See De Dios et al. (2021, p. 22). While, in general, the technocrats supported economic liberalization (and they were supported by the IMF and the World Bank), it would be erroneous to label them as "neoliberal." This term is more appropriate to describe some policies implemented in the 1990s and the 2000s.

25 A revised Land Reform Act was passed in 1963. See Chapter 6.

26 Disagreements with other members of the Macapagal administration and with the president himself led Sixto Roxas to resign in 1964 (Takagi, 2016, pp. 173–179).

27 The source of these statistics is the World Bank Development Indicators, Hooley (2005), and the Philippine Statistics Authority. The figures provided are slightly different but sufficiently consistent.

28 The idea underlying a big push is that many firms in various sectors of the economy adopt increasing returns technologies (typical of manufacturing) simultaneously to create income that becomes a source of demand for goods in other sectors (i.e., the growth of a sector assists the growth of the rest) and so enlarge their markets and make industrialization profitable; that is, this process creates spillovers. This way, the simultaneous industrialization of many sectors can be self-sustaining even if no sector breaks even industrializing alone. This process of cumulative causation creates a spiral of growth. But if capital formation remains below what this process requires, the result is that only a few segments of the economy experience modernization, we see dualism in the economy, and the full momentum of growth does not develop. This is what seems to have happened to the Philippines.

3

A PRIMER ON GROWTH: FACTS, CONSTRAINTS, AND ENGINES

3.1 Stylized Facts About Growth

Given the importance of growth for a country like the Philippines, this chapter offers a primer. An economy growing at close to 6% per annum could well be the envy of most countries around the globe. In fact, the government often indicates that the Philippines is growing (slightly) faster than its neighbors. This is correct, as shown in Figure 3.1. During the last few years, the Philippine growth rate has been high, only surpassed by Vietnam's.

However, "growing faster than our neighbors" is not an explicit target of the Philippine administration; therefore, it is not a sound way to evaluate the country's growth performance. We noted in Chapter 1, though, that our neighbors overtook us during the past few decades, and this, one way or another, is the result of their faster growth for some time in the past. This is because they had a higher potential growth rate (this concept is elaborated later). This is not the case now: Indonesia's, Malaysia's, and Thailand's actual growth rates are lower as a result of the fact that their potential growth has decreased significantly. This point must be understood. As countries develop and their income per capita increases, growth rates decline. It is possible that a more advanced country like Singapore registers a lower growth rate than the Philippines, and yet the gap between the two increases. This is why catching up is a very steep and difficult escalator.[1]

The proper way to evaluate our growth performance is to compare actual growth with the government's declared target (forecast). The Philippine Development Plan 2023–2028 (NEDA, 2023a) indicates a growth target of 6.5–8% for 2024–2028, which was revised to 6–8% at the end of 2024, then again down in 2025, as things were not going as expected. The question is thus: Why did the government initially choose such a high growth target (up to 8%) and with such a large range? A clear understanding of growth is essential.

DOI: 10.4324/9781003728719-3

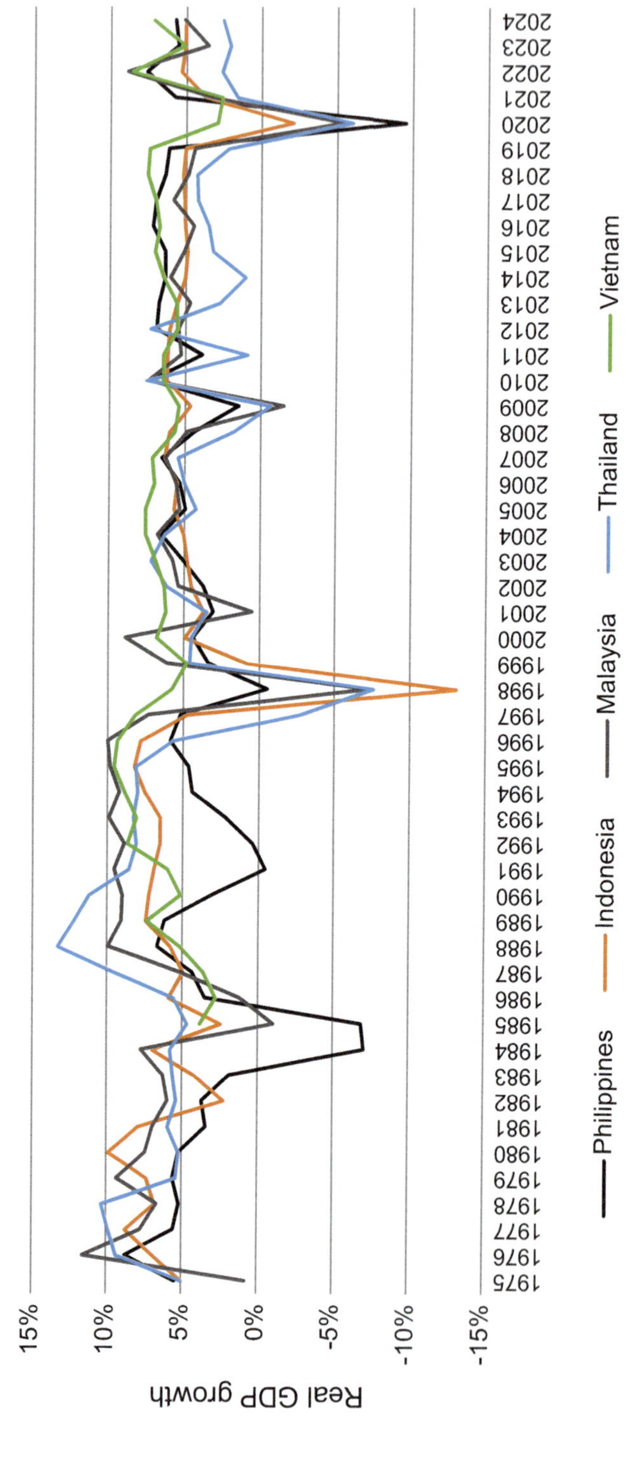

FIGURE 3.1 Real GDP Growth (%), Constant 2015 USD, Selected Southeast Asian Countries, 1975–2024

Source: The World Bank: World Development Indicators (https://data.worldbank.org/indicator/NY.GDP.MKTP.KD.ZG)

In this chapter, we first summarize key stylized facts about growth. Second, we address what we call the two fundamental growth questions: (1) How fast can a country grow, and (2) what drives growth? This chapter is important in our discussion of the Philippines because both the government and the private sector seem not to understand these three issues: what we know about growth, its constraints, and its drivers. The result is that the Philippine Development Plan 2023–2028 (NEDA, 2023a) sets a target growth rate of up to 8%. We elaborate on the feasibility of this target later. The last part of the chapter is an application of the Khan–Pritchett–Sen–Werker political economy framework to the Philippines.

We start the discussion of what we know about growth by summarizing Pritchett and Lewis's (2022) key findings. The title of their paper is telling: "Economic growth *is* enough and only economic growth is enough" (italics in the original). These authors showed that any cross-national measure of human material well-being that is (1) basics (not luxuries), (2) general (uses indicators from multiple domains), and (3) plausible (uses any defensible choices for weights) will have a statistical relationship with the country's GDP per capita with four features:

1. The relationship will be strong, with nearly all cross-national variation in basics associated with variation in GDP per capita.
2. The relationship will be nonlinear, with a stronger elasticity of basics at lower than at higher levels of GDP per capita.
3. GDP per capita is empirically sufficient: While at any given level of GDP per capita, there are countries with higher or lower values, no country has high levels of GDP per capita and low levels of basics.
4. GDP per capita is empirically necessary: No country has high levels of the basics at (very) low levels of GDP per capita.

Their conclusion is clear: The statement "growth is not enough" is demonstrably false for basics.

Pritchett and Summers (2014) and Pritchett et al. (2018) also concluded the following stylized facts about growth:

1. Historically, the distribution of per capita growth has been an average of 2%, with a standard deviation of 2%. A growth rate above 6–8% would be an extraordinary tail event.
2. Today's rich countries experienced steady, moderate, and constant per capita growth of about 2% per annum for a century or more.
3. Poverty (or low-growth) traps. There is a set of countries that are, even today, very near the lowest level of income per capita ever recorded in all of history (a level that could be called "subsistence"). This low level of income today implies that the long-run average rate of their growth must be very low, well

below the long-run rate of the developed economies. This growth differential caused the massive historical divergence in per capita incomes.

4. Accelerations to spectacularly rapid, extended periods of growth are rare. Episodes of super-rapid growth (>6%) tend to be extremely short-lived. Only China, followed by South Korea and Taiwan, has been able to attain super-rapid growth and maintain it for about two decades or longer. Most developing countries tend to see "boom and bust" growth—that is, periods of growth acceleration followed by periods of growth deceleration. Since South Korea was so poor in 1960, its cumulative historical growth rate up to 1960 must have been slow. So a theory of South Korea's growth (or that of other countries that begin episodes of rapid growth from low levels of income) must invoke something that caused an acceleration in growth rates from a previously low level, an acceleration to a very high level which then persisted for decades (as opposed to the long-run persistence of moderate growth of the OECD countries).
5. The principal fact about the growth rates of many countries over the medium run is non-persistent growth with episodes of boom, stagnation, and bust, that is, volatile growth rates—with acceleration and deceleration—and hence a lack of persistence. Circumstances or policies that produce ten years of rapid economic growth appear easily reversed, often leaving countries no better off than they were prior to the expansion.
6. Developing countries spend much more time in negative growth than developed countries. Negative growth increases as per capita income decreases.
7. The end of an episode of super-rapid growth is nearly always a growth deceleration to the world's mean growth rate of about 2% per annum.
8. Present growth is a bad predictor of future growth.[2] This is a very important fact. If it were the case, as many models suggest, that some relatively constant feature of countries—their climate, their culture, their geography, the quality of their institutions, or their openness to the world, as examples—influenced growth importantly, one would expect, because these variables persist, that growth rates would persist. However, in the data, growth rates do not persist. This empirical finding suggests that these constant features affect the level more than the medium-to-long period growth of incomes. It also suggests that even the most favorable conditions will ultimately have diminishing impacts on growth, unless a country can continually improve its policy environment or governance.
9. Although one might have thought that most of the long-horizon growth differences were due to the existence of slow- and fast-growing countries (e.g., the Philippines grew slowly and South Korea grew rapidly), the truth is that nearly all growth variation is due to differences within countries over time.
10. The reason for the low average growth of developing versus developed countries is not the lack of rapid growth—it is the lack of growth *persistence* and the very low growth rates during their periods of negative growth.

Based on these, we extract the following lessons for the Philippines: First, the current Philippine growth of close to 6% per annum is relatively high for historical standards. Second, growth is non-persistent, and the end of an episode of rapid growth is a significant growth deceleration. Third, the Marcos administration may be possibly committing the "Asiaphoria" sin (Pritchett and Summers, 2014) by forecasting or assuming that the Philippine economy can grow by 6–8% per annum for quite some time.

3.2 What Constraints Philippine Growth? The Natural Growth Rate and the Balance of Payments–Constrained Growth Rate

The proper way to understand growth is by answering what we call the "fundamental growth questions": (1) What constrains growth, or how fast can a country grow—what is the maximum rate—and (2) what drives growth? Unless there is a deep economic recession or a war, countries grow, but not at the same rate. To understand these differences, one needs to grasp well the earlier two questions. At the aggregate level, growth can be constrained on the supply or the demand side. In this section, we address the first question.

3.2.1 The Natural Growth Rate

Looking at the economy from the supply side, the maximum growth rate ($\hat{Y}^P$) a country can attain is the sum of labor productivity growth ($\hat{y}^P$) and the growth rate of the labor force ($\widehat{lf}^P$), that is, $\hat{Y}^P = \hat{y}^P + \widehat{lf}^P$. This is what Harrod (1939) called the "natural growth rate" ($\widehat{NGR} = \hat{Y}^P$). This is the maximum sustainable rate of growth that technical conditions make available to the economic system. The natural growth rate sets the ceiling to explosive growth (turning cyclical booms into slumps) and gives a measure of the growth rate around which the economy will gravitate in the long run. At any particular point in time, actual growth ($\hat{Y}$) can (and will) diverge from the natural growth rate, as the functioning of the economy is affected by various restrictions, rigidities, and constraints. Nonetheless, actual growth cannot persistently exceed the rate consistent with the full utilization of productive resources, as this would eventually result in unemployment falling below its natural rate and thus growing inflationary pressures. With wages rising relative to the price of capital, the economy would adopt more capital-intensive techniques, unemployment would rise again to the rate consistent with full employment, and growth would converge to the natural rate. On the other hand, if actual growth were consistently below the natural growth rate, the resulting rising unemployment would trigger an opposite price adjustment process—decreasing wages would, in due course, lead to higher employment through the adoption of more labor-intensive production techniques, until equilibrium in the labor market is achieved and the actual and natural growth rates are brought into line. As a result, in the medium to long term, the economy will tend to gravitate around that particular growth rate consistent with the full utilization of productive resources, stable inflation, and full employment equilibrium in the labor market. This rate is the natural or potential growth rate.

It is the second component, the growth rate of the labor force, that the Philippine government often refers to with optimism—still growing. This is factually correct, but let us not forget that what drives growth in modern economies is the other component, the growth of labor productivity. Moreover, the experience of the developed countries and middle-income countries like China, or Thailand, indicates that the growth rate of the labor force decreases as countries develop and eventually becomes zero, or even negative. The only source of growth will then be labor productivity. The Philippines will reach this point too (Chapter 13).

To estimate the natural growth rate, we follow Thirlwall (1969), Leon-Ledesma and Thirlwall (2002), and Felipe et al. (2022), who used a simple method derived from Okun's (1962) law, the relationship between the change in the unemployment rate (ΔU) and output growth ($\hat{Y}$). Algebraically:[3]

$$\Delta U = \alpha + \beta \hat{Y} \tag{3.1}$$

with $\beta < 0$. If $\hat{Y} > \hat{Y}^P$ ($\widehat{NGR}$), then $\Delta U < 0$; and if $Y < \hat{Y}^P$ ($\widehat{NGR}$), then $\Delta U > 0$. The idea is that actual growth oscillates around potential growth. Therefore, $\widehat{NGR}$ ($=\hat{Y}^P$) is the growth rate that keeps unemployment constant, that is, $\Delta U = 0$. These authors prefer to estimate this relationship in reverse form, that is:

$$\hat{Y} = \gamma + \delta \Delta U \tag{3.2}$$

In this case, $\Delta U = 0$ implies $\hat{Y}^p = \gamma$.

We obtain the natural growth for the Philippines by estimating Okun's regression (Equation 3.2) using annual data from 1971 to 2024.

To test the endogeneity of the potential growth rate (that is, whether potential growth responds to actual growth), Leon-Ledesma and Thirlwall (2002) also estimate:

$$\hat{Y} = \beta_0 + \beta_1 \Delta U + \beta_2 D \tag{3.3}$$

where D is a dummy variable ($D = 1$) for the years where the actual growth rate is higher than the natural growth rate (boom years), resulting from Equation 3.2. Because $(\beta_0 + \beta_2)$ in (3.3) > γ in (3.2), we conclude that the rate of growth to keep unemployment constant in booms must have risen. In other words, the actual rate of growth must have pulled up the natural growth rate.

Using data for the Philippines, the estimated supply-side potential growth of the Philippines during boom periods (years of high growth rate, Equation 3.3) is about 6%, and about 5% in non-boom years (Equation 3.2).

We also used the Hodrick–Prescott (HP) filter to decompose the trend (proxy for potential) and cycle of the GDP series. The growth rate of the trend for the period

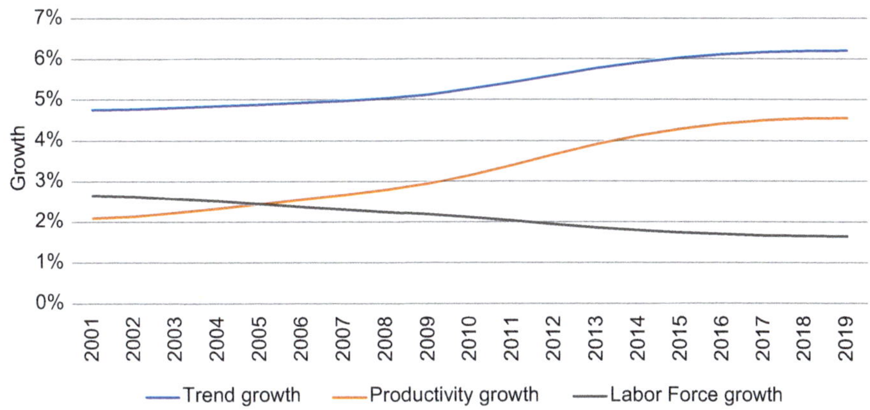

FIGURE 3.2 Potential Growth (Trend) (%) and its Components, Philippines, 2001–2019

Note: Potential growth (trend) is estimated using the Hodrick-Prescott filter to separate trend from cyclical fluctuation.

Source: Authors' calculations based on data from the DLSU ANIMO econometric model database

2000–2019 is shown in Figure 3.2. Then we decompose it into labor productivity growth and labor force growth. The average trend growth rate for 2001–2019 is 5.4%, of which 3.3% is from labor productivity growth and 2.1% is from labor force growth. During the last few years, when trend growth increased to slightly above 6%, most of it (about 4.5%) was due to labor productivity growth, and the rest was due to labor force growth.[4] This means that productivity is the engine of growth in the Philippines, not demographics. Productivity growth is relatively high because the Philippines is far from the technological frontier; therefore, the introduction of the latest technologies embodied in capital leads to productivity growth. The latter is very low or zero in advanced countries because companies there already use modern technologies.[5]

3.2.2 The Balance of Payments-Constrained Growth Rate

Modern neoclassical treatments of growth since Solow (1957) rely on the notion of aggregate production function.[6] These models concentrate on the supply side of the economy (factors of production and technical progress) and apportion the growth of output between the growth rates of capital and labor and a residual called total factor productivity growth. By this approach, growth rate differences are explained in terms of growth differences of factor supplies and productivity. The problem with this approach is that it does not explain why the growth rates of the factors of production and productivity differ across countries. Moreover, it is difficult to argue that labor availability is a constraint on Philippine growth. Capital may be thought to be a constraint, but, as we argue later, not on the supply side.

For these reasons, our preferred explanation of Philippine growth, in the sense of how fast and what constrains it, starts by asking the question of why the growth of factor supplies differs across countries. We believe that the constraint on Philippine growth lies on the demand side of the economy. The question, then, is: Why does demand grow at different rates across countries? We will argue that, in an open economy, the main constraint lies in the balance of payments. Thus, the explanation that we favor to understand Philippine growth (how fast it can grow) is that a country's actual growth rate is consistent with dynamic equilibrium in the current account (Thirlwall, 1979). The rationale is as follows. Most developing countries cannot persistently run current account deficits. Developing countries need to import a myriad of goods that they do not produce, in particular, capital goods. These have to be paid in a currency different from their own (typically US dollars). This currency has to be earned through exports. The problem of many developing countries is that their exports do not cover their imports (the demand constraint). The need to avoid current account deficits sets the maximum growth rate that a country can attain without running into balance of payments problems. In its simplest form, this growth rate, which we call the balance of payments–constrained (BOPC) growth rate ($\hat{Y}^{BP}$), is given by the product of a ratio that measures the degree of non-price competitiveness (that is, product-quality competitiveness) of the country's exports (ε) with respect to the country's imports (π), times the growth rate of the country's trading partners ($\hat{Z}$). Algebraically (McCombie and Thirlwall, 1994, Chapter 3):

$$\hat{Y}^{BP} = \frac{\varepsilon}{\pi}\hat{Z} \tag{3.4}$$

where ε and π are the income elasticities of demand for exports and imports (the percentage by which the country's exports [imports] increase when the income of the trading partners [the country's GDP] increases by one percentage point), respectively. The policy implication of this account of growth, and the message for the Philippines, is that if it wishes to grow faster, it must first raise its balance of payments constraint on demand. If the Philippines wants to attain a faster, sustained growth rate, the economy's BOPC growth rate will have to increase. In our argument that the binding constraint on Philippine growth is on the demand side (the balance of payments), the key is to increase the income elasticity of demand for exports (relative to the income elasticity of demand for imports), that is, to improve the quality of Philippine exports. This entails a great effort, something that will not happen overnight.

Figures 3.3 and 3.4 provide the recursive estimates of these two elasticities (ε and π), obtained through the regressions:[7]

$$\hat{X}_t = \beta_0 + \beta_1\hat{E}_t + \varepsilon\hat{Z}_t \tag{3.5}$$

where X denotes exports, E is the nominal exchange rate, and Z is world's GDP, where all variables are expressed in growth rates, denoted by ^. And:

$$\hat{M}_t = \gamma_0 + \gamma_1\hat{E}_t + \pi\hat{Y}_t \tag{3.6}$$

where M is imports, and Y is the real GDP of the Philippines. Regressions were estimated with annual data for 2000–2023. Both elasticities show a slight increase

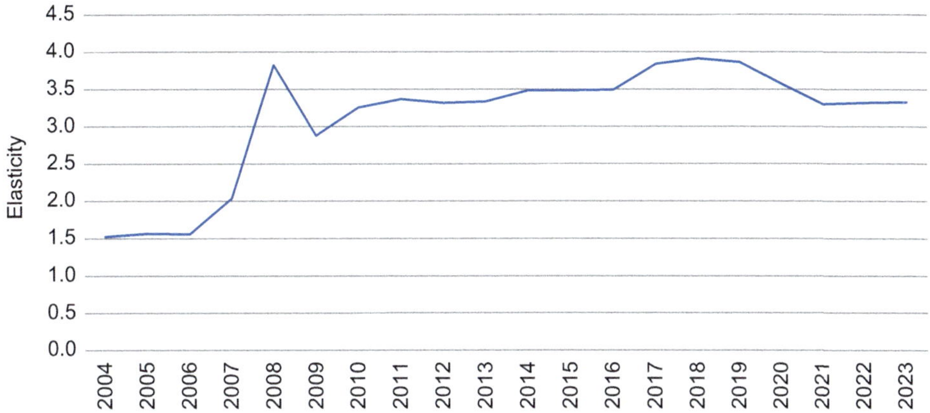

FIGURE 3.3 Income Elasticity of the Demand for Exports, Philippines, 2004–2023

Source: Authors' estimates

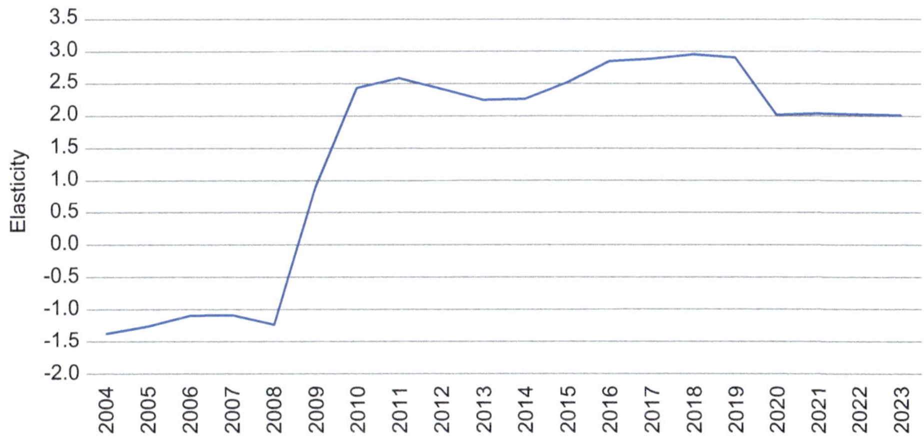

FIGURE 3.4 Income Elasticity of the Demand for Imports, Philippines, 2004–2023

Source: Authors' estimates

after the first few years, with average values of about 3.5 for exports and 2 for imports.[8]

Given these elasticities, we have estimated the BOPC growth rate for the Philippines at about 6%.[9,10] The intuition behind the BOPC growth rate is that, before achieving its (supply-side) potential growth rate, an economy's actual growth performance can be curtailed by macro constraints. For emerging economies, the external constraint associated with the current account balance is particularly significant, given these countries' dependence on the availability of foreign exchange to finance their imports. Current account deficits can be sustainable and, indeed, necessary in the short term, especially when they allow for faster capital accumulation. But countries cannot finance ever-growing current account deficits in the long run, as there is a limit beyond which the deficit becomes unsustainable (or is perceived as such by financial markets), and a balance of payments crisis ensues. Thus, countries with balance of payments problems may be forced to constrain growth while the economy still has surplus capacity and surplus labor—that is, while the actual growth rate is still below the potential growth rate. This growth rate is related to the structure of the economy through the income elasticities of demand for exports and imports (Felipe and Lanzafame, 2020). As noted earlier, this growth rate is about 6%, below the administration's 6.5–8% target. This implies that it will not be possible to attain the administration's target, as pushing actual growth above 6% would lead to current account deficits. The main policy implication is that the economy needs to export products with a higher income elasticity of demand for exports compared to the income elasticity of demand for imports.

The earlier discussion matters because, except during crises, actual growth oscillates around its potential.[11] Market forces are constantly bringing actual growth simultaneously toward and away from its potential. Based on all the approaches we employed, we estimate that the Philippines' potential growth is at about 6%. The average actual growth rate during President Benigno Aquino's III term (2010–2016) was 6.22%. High growth continued under President Duterte: Growth peaked at 7.1% in 2016, but then it came down in the next three successive years: 6.9% in 2017, 6.3% in 2018, and 6.1% in 2019. Yes, growth was above 6% for a couple of years, but it then came down to about potential.

What is the binding constraint (the one that bites first) on the Philippine actual growth rate? The one on the supply side, or the one on the demand side? We believe that the constraint that bites first in Philippine growth is on the demand side, that is, the balance of payments constraint. This was already the case in the 1960s, when growth was constrained by shortages of foreign currency, needed to sustain the demand for imports (De Dios et al., 2021, p. 5).

The BOPC growth rate gives us an estimate of how fast the Philippine economy can grow today, at about 6%. Actual growth in 2023 and 2024 was slightly below. So there is room for actual growth to increase, but not to 7–8%, which is what the government continues to declare as the upper part of the growth target range. This is a very high growth rate, impossible to attain with today's economy. It is just a wish, very unrealistic.[12]

3.3 What Drives Growth? The Roles of Structural Transformation, Exports, and Manufacturing

We now address the related question of what drives growth, implicit in the earlier discussions. Here, economists disagree about the details and about the theoretical model, a discussion that we will skip. In the context of the natural growth rate, the main source of growth is productivity (see previous text). To this we add that, at the current level of development of the Philippine economy, growth is driven by the speed and direction of transformation of the economy, an idea that we will further develop in successive chapters. When looking at the transformation of the economy, we consider three interrelated aspects. First, the shift of workers out of agriculture into other sectors of the economy (more precisely, the decrease in the share of agricultural employment). These sectors are industry and services. Growth is the result of the productivity differential between agriculture and these other sectors, referred to in the literature as the structural bonus. Philippine agriculture still employs over 20% of the labor force. We discuss this in Chapter 4, where we show a decomposition of labor productivity growth into within-sector productivity growth and structural transformation.

The second aspect of the transformation of the economy, linked to the notion of the BOPC growth rate discussed earlier, is that, to progress, countries need to change what they produce and export. There are two important points here: first, about exports in general and, second, about the type of exports.

Exports matter to a country like the Philippines because they are the only true component of autonomous demand in an economy, in the sense that their demand emanates outside the economy. On the other hand, most consumption and investment demand depend on the growth of income itself. Exports are also the only component of demand that can pay for the import requirement of growth. Surely, an economy can experience consumption-led, investment-led, or government expenditure–led growth, but each of these components of demand has an import content. If an economy does not obtain sufficient export earnings to pay for its imports (more precisely, the import content of other components of expenditure), then demand will have to be constrained. For this reason, exports play a very significant role because experience shows that countries, especially developing countries, need to maintain a balance of payments equilibrium in the long run. Otherwise, they run into a crisis. This implies that exports have not only a direct effect on demand but also an indirect effect, allowing all other components of demand to rise faster than they would otherwise. This explains the earlier result, which shows that the long-run rate of growth of an economy becomes attuned to the rate of growth of the dominant component of autonomous demand, which in an open economy is exports. Third, imports may be more productive than domestic resources because certain crucial goods for development (e.g., capital goods) are not produced domestically. This is the supply-side argument for export-led growth. Finally, exports matter because recent work shows that the sophistication of a country's export basket is a good predictor of its future growth.

On the type of exports, a country like the Philippines should aim at exporting products with a higher income elasticity of demand. This is because not all products have the same consequences for development. Some products, mostly those in the manufacturing cluster, offer an upward escalator because the capabilities learnt can be transferred and used to produce other products (see Chapter 8). On the other hand, natural resources, agriculture, and many services do not possess this characteristic. As Figure 3.3 showed, the aggregate income elasticity of demand for Philippine exports increased slightly over the last two decades.

The third important aspect of the transformation of the economy is the role of manufacturing. In practice, aggregate growth is related to the rate of expansion of the sector with the most favorable growth characteristics. This has traditionally been manufacturing. This sector matters because (1) it is the main source of technology-driven productivity growth in modern economies, (2) the capital goods subsector has been the "learning center" of capitalism in technological terms, (3) it has been the source of organizational innovation, (4) it has been the main source of demand for high-productivity activities in other industries (the main customers of high-productivity service activities are manufacturing firms), and (5) as the producer of physical and non-perishable products, it has higher tradability than agriculture and services. For these reasons, we believe that *manufacturing is the engine of growth* (Kaldor, 1967). This means that the faster the growth of manufacturing, the faster the growth of output (GDP).[13] This is not only in a definitional manner but also for fundamental economic reasons connected with induced productivity growth both inside and outside the manufacturing sector. This is a consequence of the large transfer of labor from the low-productivity agricultural sector to the high-productivity industrial sector.

Moreover, the faster the rate of growth of manufacturing output, the faster the rate of growth of labor productivity in manufacturing, owing to the static and dynamic economies of scale (so-called Verdoorn's law). Static economies of scale relate to the size of a production facility, and it is a characteristic largely of manufacturing—for example, when doubling the factors of production, output increases by over two. Dynamic economies refer to increasing returns brought about by induced technical progress and learning by doing. One can think of increasing returns arising from product differentiation, introduction of new processes, creation of new subsidiary industries, and so on.

To elaborate, there is a lot of historical work and empirical evidence to suggest that there is something special about industry, particularly manufacturing. Indeed, there appears to be a close empirical relationship between the level of per capita income today and the share of manufacturing in GDP in the past, as well as between industrial growth and the growth of overall GDP. It is hard to find any cross-sectional relationship between the growth of GDP and the growth of the agricultural sector. The relationship between the growth of GDP and the growth of services is stronger (corroborated for the Philippines), but there is reason to believe that the *direction of causation* may be the other way around, from the growth of GDP to service growth, because the demand for many services is derived from the demand for manufacturing output itself.[14]

There has been much talk about the role of services in the Philippines in recent years. There are two reasons. One is the country's poor industrialization record (Chapter 4) and the belief by many authors that the "window" for manufacturing-led growth may have closed (e.g., De Dios and Williamson, 2015). Overall, we agree with this conclusion if industrialization is understood in the South Korean style. This will not happen today. Yet the Philippines needs to open niches within the manufacturing sector for the arguments explained earlier. The second reason is that, naturally, all activities in all sectors of the economy contribute to growth. Given this, one may ask: If the economy is growing at 5–6%, does it really matter which sectors are leading and which sectors are lagging? We believe it does.

Our view is that the discourse about services in the Philippines is often misguided. For example, the administration regards tourism as a high-productivity sector and a new source of growth. The first statement is not true. The second one could be, but one has to understand what tourism can and cannot do. Tourism, like any other activity that contributes to the nation's GDP, is certainly welcome. But this will not be the "industry" that will make the Philippines a first-world nation. Advanced nations are not high-income economies *because* of this sector, which is a "follower" service of low productivity by its own nature (very labor-intensive). The predictions about the sector are far-fetched and unrealistic: We have read that the government expects the value added of the sector to reach 20% of GDP. This is a very large share. Tourism can be a springboard to develop infrastructure, to bring in foreign income, and to help create decent employment (hotel managers, receptionists, accountants, and chefs). This will help us reach upper middle income. High income requires much more than tourism.[15]

As we shall show in Chapter 4, the problem in the Philippines is that while the share of labor in agriculture declines, the shares that increase are those of low-productivity service activities. This is Fabella's "development progeria," a concept related to Baumol's cost disease (Baumol, 1967).[16] High-productivity (hence high wages) service activities of the type that exists in advanced economies (advanced logistics, engineering, consulting) are a function of manufacturing and are not what Philippine companies do. It is true that, over the last decades, the Philippines has developed a thriving business process outsourcing (IT-BPO) sector, leveraging information and communication technology (ICT) since the early 1990s, when Accenture established the first contact center in the country (although this sector truly gained momentum in the 2000s). This was primarily because of the abundance of English-speaking workers, competitive wages, and various economic policies that encourage the flow of jobs (Palisada, 2010). Yet whether this sector's growth has driven GDP growth or whether causation goes the other way around is a moot point. Even in the possible case that a part of the IT-BPO sector is a growth driver, the sector is not a large employer, and concerns remain about its ability to absorb the large pool of underemployed workers who would have found opportunities in industry, and about the fact that many (most) of these jobs are call centers.[17] Unless the Philippine ICT sector moves into more sophisticated activities, it will not be able to pay higher wages. Surely, the sector provides valuable employment to the Philippines, but these jobs are not the same as those in advanced economies (much lower wages).[18]

Moreover, the country's dependence on external markets for service exports makes it vulnerable to global economic shifts and rising competition from emerging economies. Finally, artificial intelligence (AI) is reshaping labor markets, creating new challenges for workers in sectors like the IT-BPO. We insist: Philippine income per capita over the past 25 years (IT-BPO sector boom) has increased to just above USD 4,400. This means that the services the Philippines got into have not achieved what manufacturing did in South Korea in a similar period.

Serafica (2024) discussed options for the service sector, yet he acknowledged that the Philippine service sector is absorbing an increasing share of the nation's labor force but service worker productivity remains low. Our view is that even if the global economy has outgrown the 20th-century manufacturing-led development model, the Philippines needs a few niches within manufacturing (more on this in Chapter 7).

To emphasize why it will be very difficult to reach high income while skipping manufacturing, Felipe et al. (2019) documented three important historical facts about industrialization. First, to achieve a high income, it is necessary to attain a high manufacturing employment share (at least 20%). This is more important than a high share of manufacturing value added in GDP. Second, most developing countries today have not been able to attain the same share of manufacturing employment that advanced economies attained in the 20th century, with a share of 20% and above. Employment in today's developing countries is shifting out of agriculture into non-tradable services, many of which are of low productivity (Chen et al., 2021). Third, even in the context of low manufacturing employment shares, many developing countries are de-industrializing, a phenomenon known as "premature de-industrialization." Likewise, using a large cross-global database of national manufacturing employment and output levels covering the period 1970–2010, Felipe and Mehta (2016) documented that rapid within-country manufacturing productivity growth was counterbalanced by a shift of manufacturing jobs toward lower-productivity economies, most notably China.

We do recognize that industrialization, similar to that seen in other East Asian economies (manufacturing-driven) in the latter part of the 20th century, is a chimera for the Philippines today (see Chapter 4). The reality of the Philippines, as we will document in this book, is that the share of employment in agriculture is declining, but the sectors that create most of the employment are service activities of low productivity, particularly wholesale and retail trade. However, we will argue that unless the Philippines attains a higher degree of industrialization (especially in employment), it will be very difficult to accelerate and sustain growth. Services of the type one sees in high-income economies (modern logistics like Maersk, Amsterdam's flower market, or engineering consulting) are a function of manufacturing.

We think that the three dimensions of structural transformation mentioned earlier should be at the center of Philippine economic policy. Long-run growth is much less determined by the central bank's monetary policy than by how fast workers move out of agriculture into manufacturing and by how fast the export structure changes. To be fair, the transformation of the economy is mentioned in the Philippine Development Plan 2023–2028 (NEDA, 2023a), but it is hidden among a myriad of other possible determinants of growth; thus, its relevance is buried.

3.4 The Khan–Pritchett–Sen–Werker (KPSW) Political Economy Framework: Political Settlements, Rents, and Deals

The final section of this growth chapter applies the Khan–Pritchett–Sen–Werker (KPSW hereafter) political economy framework (Khan, 2010; Pritchett et al., 2018) to discuss the Philippine growth experience in its relation to the structure of political settlements, rents, and deals. It contributes to our understanding of the determinants of Philippine growth. The KPSW framework provides a unified growth theory capable of explaining the dynamics of growth rates, both the persistence and the transitions. More specifically, why are some countries able to sustain growth episodes over many decades of rapid (or steady) growth while other growth episodes end in reversion to stagnation or collapse? The framework consists of two core variables, the *political settlement* and the *rents space*, and one intermediary variable, the *deals space*. The analysis focuses on the reality of politics and the way political actors interact with economic actors or, indeed, at times morph into one. The authors put forward a framework that offers insights about when the political economy is favorable to growth-enhancing reforms and when it is not.

Political settlement refers to the balance of power among different social groups and classes. Khan (2010) argued that the group that holds power shapes the distribution of rents and uses institutional arrangements to maintain peace and economic stability within society. There are two dimensions of power in the political settlement, as seen in Table 3.1. The first is horizontal power (the power of excluded factions), defined as the concentration of power in one dominant group or in multiple groups vying for power. The other one is vertical power (the power of lower-level factions), defined as the distribution of power between elites and non-elites.

TABLE 3.1 The Distribution of Horizontal and Vertical Power in Dominant and Competitive Settlements

Vertical/Horizontal Distribution of Power		*Horizontal Distribution of Power: The Power of Excluded Factions*	
		Weak	*Strong*
Vertical Distribution of Power: The Power of Lower-Level Factions	*Weak*	Strong dominant party	Vulnerable authoritarian coalition
	Strong	Weak dominant party	Competitive clientelism

Source: Pritchett et al. (2018, Table 1.10).

TABLE 3.2 The Rents Space

	Regulatory Rents	*Market Competition*
Export-oriented	Rentiers	Magicians
Domestic market	Powerbrokers	Workhorses

Source: Pritchett et al. (2018, Table 1.11).

The second core variable is the rents space, which explains how economic opportunities are structured. This framework is divided into two dimensions where firms within an economy are analyzed on the standard of the target market and the source of profitability. The first dimension is whether a firm only sells within the domestic market or exports to the global market. The second dimension refers to whether firms profit through discretionary rents (e.g., licenses for commercial use of a resource or bestowing firm-specific tax advantage) or through rents derived from normal market competition. This leads to four types of firms, as shown in Table 3.2.

This classification does not imply that rentiers and powerbrokers are "bad" because of their monopolistic tendencies, and that magicians and workhorses are "good" because they exhibit innovative characteristics. Indeed, rentiers can sustain growth during growth accelerations because they control a large portion of the export market. Meanwhile, powerbrokers can provide basic services to the public at the lowest prices and in the most convenient ways possible.

Different firms in each sector have varying demands from the government regarding policy implementation (Pritchett et al., 2018). These demands encompass contract enforcement, barriers to entry, infrastructure, subsidies or tax reductions, and clear rule-setting. All firms except powerbrokers prioritize contract enforcement, whereas powerbrokers favor barriers to entry instead of regulated competition due to the advantages they receive from the confusion of bureaucratic procedures and inconsistent enforcement. Magicians and workhorses equally require better infrastructure and clarity in contract regulations. Magicians and rentiers also advocate specialized infrastructure, such as special economic zones and port facilities. Additionally, magicians and rentiers call for subsidies or lower taxes, though for different reasons: Rentiers seek subsidies for increased profits, whereas magicians aim for improved competitiveness and greater market presence overseas. Understanding these demands is essential for analyzing the interest of the elites in promoting growth.

The intermediary variable is the deals space, which refers to the informal and personalized relationships between those who make deals and those to whom deals are made available. These are not based on rules and how the deals are planned but on how these planned deals are carried out. This variable takes into consideration two factors. The first factor is to whom the deals are made available, that is, whether they are only open to a certain group of people (closed deals) or open to everyone (open deals). The second factor is whether these deals are honored (ordered deals) or not (disordered deals). This is shown in Table 3.3.

How does this framework work? It suggests that economic growth is influenced by the openness and enforcement of deals in an economy, which, in turn, is influenced by the core variables of the political settlement and rents spaces. A growth episode creates a feedback loop that impacts the core variables and ultimately affects the openness of deals, influencing future growth episodes. For instance, a growth acceleration can occur when there is a shift in the deals space from disordered to ordered, as investors feel confident that their resources will not be subject to corruption and the ruling elites will enforce contracts.

The evolution of institutions and the shift from closed deals to open and ordered deals are not predetermined. Growth can have a positive or a negative impact on the deals space through the economic and political feedback loops. The economic feedback loop is influenced by the growth process by strengthening powerbrokers and rentiers, or magicians and workhorses. If the power of powerbrokers and rentiers increases, the deals space may become closed as these groups benefit from closed deals. On the other hand, if the power of magicians and workhorses increases, the deals space may become more open due to these groups' dynamic nature and the potential for "creative destruction" to occur in these sectors. The political feedback loop is influenced by the evolution of the political settlement, which is affected by the relative power of different firms in the rents space and the constraints of the settlement. In cases where rentiers and powerbrokers hold more influence, it may negatively impact institutional quality unless there is a dominant party with strong enforcement capabilities that sees magicians and workhorses as important for maintaining growth.

TABLE 3.3 The Deals Space

	Closed (Deals Are Available Only to Specific Individuals/ Organizations)	*Open (Deals Depend on Actions of Agents but Not Identities)*
Ordered (Once Negotiated, Deals Will Be Honored)	Only those with political connections get to make deals, but they can be confident that officials will deliver.	Anyone can make a deal, and they can be certain that officials will deliver.
Disordered (Deals Will Be Honored so Long as They Are in the Short-Term Interests of the Political Elite)	Only those with political connections get to make deals, and even they cannot be certain that officials will deliver.	Anyone can make a deal, but no one is certain that officials will deliver.

Source: Pritchett et al. (2018, Table 1.14).

If positive growth is fueled by closed, ordered deals that do not become open, both economic and political feedback loops will likely turn negative, and the closed-ordered deals may become disordered, ending the growth episode. However, if the deals space becomes more open and the magician and workhorse sectors become more prominent in the growth process, it can lead to sustained growth through positive feedback loops. Political elites may offer different deals to different groups of firms, such as closed, ordered deals to politically connected firms and open, ordered deals to magicians, depending on the political settlement and the relative power of different firms. This can impact growth and structural transformation.

3.4.1 An Application of the KPSW Framework to the Philippines

Given the path dependence inherent in the deals and development framework of a country, it is imperative that we understand how it has evolved since the Philippines attained independence in 1946. We divide the period 1946–2024 into five episodes.[19] Figure 3.5 shows the growth rates through different growth episodes.

Table 3.4 provides a summary of the three variables for the different administrations since 1946, together with the average growth rate of the period. Details are provided by Felipe et al. (2023). The Philippines experienced very high growth for about 25 years, between independence in 1946 and the declaration of martial law in 1972. It is true that this was the period of reconstruction after WWII (investment, industrialization, American assistance).[20] However, it proves that a country can grow fast for some time despite corruption and institutions that could not be better than those of today. It was the declaration of martial law in 1972 that sent the country through a long dark journey.[21] Then, it experienced two and a half decades (the administrations of Presidents C. Aquino, F. Ramos, and J. Estrada) with growth of 3–4%.[22] Growth picked up during the administration of Gloria Macapagal-Arroyo and increased during that of Benigno Aquino III. It went down

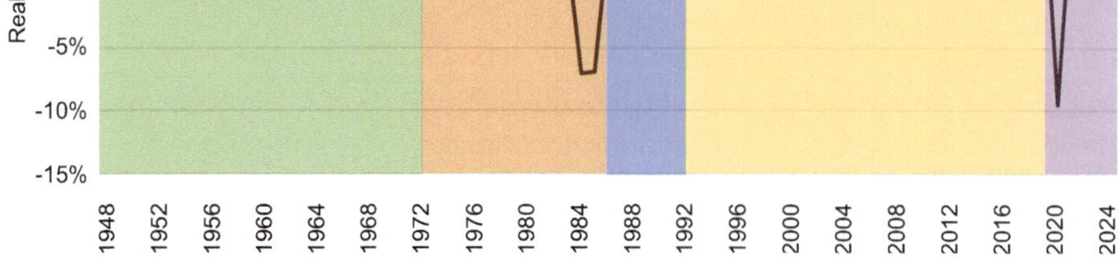

FIGURE 3.5 Real GDP Growth (%), Constant 2018 PHP, Philippines, 1948–2024

Source: Authors' calculations based on data from the Philippines Statistics Authority (https://openstat.psa.gov.ph/Database/Economic-Accounts/National-Accounts-of-the-Philippines/Annual-National-Accounts)

TABLE 3.4 Political Settlement, Rents Space, Deals Space, Philippines, 1946–2022

Presidents	*Period*	*Annual Growth (%)*	*Political Settlement*	*Rents Space*	*Deals Space*
Roxas; Quirino; Magsaysay; Garcia; Macapagal, D.; Marcos Sr.	1946–1972	7.25	Vulnerable authoritarian coalition with two major ruling parties (Nacionalista and Liberal)	Economy dominated by rentiers and powerbrokers	Closed and ordered
Marcos Sr.	1972–1986	3.22	Strong dominant party (Martial Law years)	Rentiers and powerbrokers	Enforced deals for allies, leaving others in chaos
Aquino, C.	1986–1992	3.35	Vulnerable authoritarian coalition amidst a revival of democratic institutions	Rentiers and powerbrokers with an incipient presence of magicians	A reversal toward ordered deals for all
Ramos; Estrada; Macapagal-Arroyo, G.; Aquino, B.; Duterte	1992–2022	3.60 3.59 5.02 6.22 3.67	Multiparty-based vulnerable authoritarian competitive clientelism during 1998–2001 (Estrada)	The rise of workhorses and magicians	Elite dominance persistence in an ordered deal–making setting
Marcos Jr.	2022–2028	5.61 (2022–2024)	Reinforced vulnerable authoritarian	Will conglomerates venture into untapped magician sectors? Maybe . . .	Will deals finally be open to competitive industries? Slowly.

Source: Authors.

again to an average of below 4% during the Duterte administration as a result of COVID–19.

3.4.1.1 The Marcos Jr. Administration

In 2022, Filipinos participated in one of the largest and most significant elections in the country since the Snap Elections orchestrated by Ferdinand Marcos Sr. in 1972. Ferdinand "Bongbong" Marcos Jr., the son of the late president, won by a landslide.

Since the fall of the Marcos Sr. regime in 1986, the Marcoses have gradually restored their reputation and built strong political ties with the ruling elite, paving the way for multiple seats in the legislative and executive branches. The new Marcos administration promised to recover from the pandemic, attain annual growth of 6.5–8% during 2023–2028, and reduce the poverty rate from 18.1% as of 2021 to 9% by 2028. To do this, his administration vowed to continue Duterte's massive infrastructure program and implement a multitude of tax reforms to encourage foreign direct investment. He even emphasized the importance of investing in the agriculture sector and improving value chains within it. However, unless there are plans to structurally transform the country, we argue that such economic goals will be unachievable.

The last row of Table 3.4 shows the characterization of the current administration. We are in the middle of the six-year period, and what we have seen is a return to growth after COVID-19, but it is well below the administration's target. The political settlement during the last years of the Duterte administration and the start of the Marcos Jr. administration remained a vulnerable authoritarian coalition, given only minute differences in terms of horizontal and vertical power. Growth collapsed in 2020 as a result of the COVID-19 pandemic. Horizontal power (the power of excluded factions) remained strong because elections retained the feature of multiple groups aiming for political control. During the Duterte administration, opposition members were given the opportunity to hold government positions. This included individuals from varying groups with differing interests, such as former Vice President Leni Robredo and Senator Risa Hontiveros from the opposition, Senator Lito Lapid and former Senator Tito Sotto from the entertainment industry, and several military officials appointed as department secretaries.

The main reason for this is the continuation of patronage and personality politics present in the previous eras, which makes it hard for one party or one person to dominate. Although it was good that many political parties and party lists vied for political control, the majority of those who eventually won belonged to the political and economic elite. Nonetheless, a weak vertical distribution of power (the power of lower-level factions) remains intact, given that the middle and working classes have been willing to accept institutional arrangements if these help them recover from the ravaged effects of the COVID-19 pandemic.

Philippine conglomerates have wielded significant influence in the business sector and have played a substantial role in the country's economic advancement.[23] These conglomerates predominantly focus on the production of non-tradables and rely on regulatory rents, establishing themselves as key players in the powerbroker sector. The majority of the subsidiaries of the conglomerates operate in sectors such as banking, finance, construction, utility generation or distribution, and real estate. However, it should be noted that some subsidiaries do engage in exporting to the global market, with a particular focus on food, beverages, and agricultural-related products.

This export composition has resulted in cycles of growth (relatively high growth attained for very short periods) as closed deals within the politically connected powerbroker sector have stifled competition and hindered the development of more competitive industries through negative feedback loops. Filipino conglomerates primarily export low-complexity goods.[24] Workhorses and magicians, who often operate small and medium-sized enterprises (SMEs) and retail, constitute 99.51% of businesses in the country and provide the majority of employment and income, particularly for vulnerable workers (Department of Trade and Industry, 2021). The influence of social media and online shopping has helped the SMSE industry to transition into the digital realm, making it easier for newly established entrepreneurs to open a shop (Reyes, 2021). The top industries that they heavily focus on are wholesale and retail trade, repair of motor vehicles and motorcycles, and food service activities, indicating that the country has become a service-led economy.

In line with the political settlement, we have discussed the prevalence of clientelism or interpersonal political relationships that enable firms to gain access to exclusive deals. Even though the democratic reforms of the post–martial law era have maintained the ability of the government to enforce deals, the political system continues to be dominated by dynasties and oligarchs. This blurs the lines between government and business and has led to the emergence of crony capitalism (Mendoza et al., 2022). Business oligarchs, who often come from traditional economic sectors such as trade and agriculture before branching out into banking, manufacturing, retail, and logistics, rely on personal relationships with the elites in the government to maintain their businesses. The stability of these businesses is often linked to the political influence and transactional deals cultivated over time with these government elites. The growth of business oligarchs is paralleled by a similar rise in political dynasties, according to Mendoza et al. (2022).

So far, the Marcos Jr. administration has also adopted a dualistic deals approach by continuing the signature infrastructure programs of past administrations and by partnering up with multinational corporations to set up manufacturing plants in the Philippines. He is currently in talks (we read) with American, European, and Chinese companies to build a manufacturing plant for personal care products, to develop the shipbuilding industry, and to build an electric-vehicle facility. He has also stated that he is keen to boost the country's manufacturing sector, particularly in areas of high-value manufacturing activities, such as battery manufacturing and mineral processing (Atienza, 2023). As we shall discuss in Chapter 7, we believe that the recent initiatives of the Philippine administration will not lead to a significant change in the structure of the economy.

Past administrations have been slowly introducing reforms that benefit the manufacturing and export market, especially with the introduction of the dualistic deals approach. They actively pursued talks with multinational corporations to secure investment pledges and sign laws and investment incentives. There was an attempt to open up deals with the rise of electronics firms, but they remained closed because politically connected families continued to have access to deals where they continued to profit from a rent-seeking behavior. During this time, the majority of conglomerates grew and diversified their subsidiaries into sectors that rely on regulatory rents, such as banking and real estate. They are politically and economically well-established, enough to remain as partners of the government, and will continue to do so. They do not have incentives to move away from regulatory rents and shift into competitive industries and make the deals space more open to everyone. However, it is worth noting that staying in these industries is not an unfavorable outcome in itself. Banking services, for instance, being provided in a cost-effective way by conglomerates, are needed. Even reforms introduced by the government to reduce regulatory rents are good. But is this enough to achieve high and sustainable growth? We do not think so. If the magician sector remains relatively weak, where firms remain stuck in activities such as assembly rather than upgrading and venturing into complex manufacturing, it would still hinder the growth outcome of the country.

3.4.1.2 Settlements, Rents, and Deals for Growth

For the Philippines to sustain a long period of high growth, economic policy needs to focus on transforming the economy by increasing its complexity, that is, by diversifying and making its export basket more unique. Are the conditions to jumpstart a significant process of structural transformation of the economy ready today? Who is going to lead this process? As argued earlier, the Philippines' actual growth is constrained in the long run by the need to avoid current account deficits (the balance of payments constrains the growth rate). This, in turn, depends (to a significant extent) on the non-price characteristics of the goods and services exported. Thus, unless the export basket of the Philippines becomes more complex and is based on products with a higher income elasticity of demand for exports, it will be very difficult to increase actual growth and maintain it for a significant period. Economic transformation is the key to the nation's future. The question is, once again: Who will lead this process?

The history and politics of the Philippines have created a system such that the future of the nation will remain in the hands of the economic-turned-political elites. Over each growth episode, the interaction of a political settlement that was mainly a vulnerable authoritarian coalition with a rents space dominated by powerbrokers and workhorses suggests three key points. First, no matter which group ends up winning the elections, reliance on a group of rich and powerful individuals will remain. Although multiple groups vie for power, the most prominent seats in politics are still occupied by the same elites and their family members, retaining control over Philippine laws and institutions.

Second, the majority of the conglomerates' subsidiaries feed on regulatory rents, meaning that their ability to profit is not so much defined by their ability to compete in foreign markets through clear competitive advantages and brand differentiation but by their ability to secure exclusive deals and certain protections from the government. Because the growth episodes in the Philippines have promoted the rise of powerbrokers and rentiers, the implication for the future of the country's export structure is that the government needs to plan better incentives to induce the jump from non-tradable goods and simple products toward more complex products, most of which should be exported to global markets. Overall, the problem of the Philippines is not that it has too many powerbrokers and rentiers. On average, the same number of powerbrokers and rentiers can still exist in the most developed nations. The problem, ultimately, is the lack of magicians. This has been detrimental to the state of the country and its lack of competitiveness in the world economy.[25]

Lastly, the fact that the nature of deals strongly involves elite families implies a lack of a clear distinction between those who control the government and those who control businesses. Integration of the interests of the political and economic elite led to a lack of export-oriented firms because they thrive on regulatory rents; hence, there is a constant negative feedback loop that benefits powerbrokers and takes away the competitive sectors' opportunities for growth. When extensive business interests are developed among these two players, the interests of both sides must be fulfilled to create solutions that enable the process of structural transformation.

To start a process of much-needed structural transformation of the Philippine economy, it is necessary to implement a comprehensive roadmap that guides the country's major conglomerates toward producing and exporting tradable goods. Only the nation's large companies have the capacity to lead this process. SMEs do not have the required financial and organizational muscle and knowledge to do it by themselves. A country like the Philippines needs to create a clear plan to attract the type of FDI that the country requires, along with a strategy for learning. Even if some SMEs are part of the value chain of multinational enterprises (MNEs), unless there is a clear program not only to link multinationals to domestic suppliers but also to acquire technology and upgrade it, these concerns remain unaddressed. Consequently, the country will remain doing low-value activities, such as assembly. Therefore, it falls upon the conglomerates to take on the task of empowering the magician sector. Although we are not implying that MNEs are incapable of doing so, it is even more challenging to convince them to undertake such endeavors relative to the conglomerates.

The involvement of conglomerates in the transformation of the economy can be achieved through discussions and negotiations with them, followed by an analysis of each organization's current capabilities to identify potential product opportunities. In this process, it will be important to identify any market or contracting failures that may be preventing these companies from diversifying and producing more complex products so that the appropriate public goods can be provided. Deals should be made available to any able conglomerate willing to create a subsidiary that competes in export markets, produces non-tradable products, and continually improves its export quality (Gutierrez and Rodriguez, 2013).

Non-market capabilities also make it easier for conglomerates to get into powerbroker industries because these offer them certain advantages vis-à-vis manufacturing. The decentralized structure of service industries helps equalize the competition for local conglomerates against foreign multinational rivals, as they do not need to make substantial investments in exclusive technologies that can ensure a lasting competitive edge. Furthermore, having non-market capabilities, such as strong political connections and the presence of regulations in many service sectors where Philippine business groups are involved, gives local firms an advantage in navigating interactions with regulatory authorities.

Meanwhile, the government ought to focus on a select number of highly complex sectors with promising returns to maximize the effectiveness of these efforts. It is important to avoid leaving conglomerates to their own devices, as this can result in the monopolization of deals within powerbrokers, depriving magicians and workhorses of the resources they need to succeed, leading to negative feedback loops. By investing in and cultivating these competitive sectors, positive feedback loops are more likely to emerge, leading to openness in the deals spaces. The first positive feedback loop results in the growth of magicians and workhorses as new investments and support from the government allow them to improve their production processes and organizational capabilities. In turn, the economy faces robust and sustainable economic growth.

The second positive feedback loop is that government elites recognize the importance of investing in competitive industries, which is why politically connected powerbrokers slowly lose their economic significance and political lobbying prowess, transforming the deals spaces into a more open and ordered one. Although competitive industries can sometimes be detrimental due to the critique that they can hinder competition and impede innovation, as in the case of the Japanese keiretsu system, this is unlikely to happen in the Philippines. Competition policy can promote an environment that encourages innovation and efficiency rather than creating barriers. Additionally, a clear plan for integrating smaller firms into the value chain of conglomerates, as long as there is also a plan to acquire and upgrade the technology used in manufacturing, can foster healthy competitiveness within the economy.

Our analysis suggests that this is difficult and will first require an understanding of what development is ultimately about—structural transformation. The key constraint is that the country has to relax its balance of payments. Second, it will require the active participation and commitment of the country's main conglomerates to lead the transformation of the economy, that is, the shift from non-tradables to tradables. Deals will have to become open to allow smaller players to participate. This is not to say that improving the service sector is the wrong strategy, but it is difficult to become a high-income economy without a burgeoning manufacturing sector. With almost 25% of the labor force still employed in agriculture, the transfer of labor into higher-value services (e.g., professional services, logistics) is much harder than the transfer of labor into the manufacturing sector. Some conglomerates may be reluctant to do this. The conglomerates that are most likely to oppose any changes are likely those that engage in low-complex manufacturing activities, such as mining and agricultural products, because a shift to more complex exports means losing a lot of the perks they currently benefit from.

Recent economic growth in the Philippines has been attributed to non-competitive sectors, which are dominated by politically connected conglomerates and elites. As the deals space remains closed and ordered, economic growth will likely bring negative feedback loops, where there is no impetus for deals to become open to less politically connected individuals and competitive sectors, because the government is already satisfied with the fact that the economy is growing.

Short of a significant and lasting change in the structure of the economy, the country can still attain 5–6% annual growth rates without forcing macroeconomic imbalances, given that labor force and productivity growth rates are both positive. The Philippines can continue growing, but this growth is based on a still high population growth rate and through the provision of services to the domestic economy. Sooner or later, this growth will end as population growth converges to zero, much like in the case of China. When this happens, the economy will continue to be internationally uncompetitive. Because the differential in growth between the Philippines and advanced economies is very high, there will be some convergence. This convergence, however, will be slow. Moreover, if deals do not open up to competitive sectors, the Philippines will either face boom–bust periods of growth or stagnation, and a significant share of its workers will still be employed in the agricultural sector, or most output will be generated by regulatory rents prone to corruption and monopolization.

Faster growth than the current rate will be feasible if and only if the administration makes fast structural transformation the cornerstone of its economic policy. Much-discussed reforms (from addressing the high cost of electricity to competition policy) will not deliver what is expected from them unless they are embedded in a framework of economic transformation. The deals space must be open to everyone, especially the competitive sectors, as growth should move away from enriching politically connected powerbrokers and rentiers. Succeeding governments must create projects that are dedicated to supporting the private sector and ensure continuity by each administration, or else, development will either stagnate or reverse.

Notes

1 To show this point, let's take an extreme (but true) example, Singapore and the Philippines. Why is Singapore farther and farther away if the Philippines grows faster? Suppose Singapore's income per capita is USD 70,000 while that of the Philippines is USD 4,500. The difference between the two countries is USD 70,000 – USD 4,500 = USD 65,500. Now, suppose Singapore's income per capita grows by 1% while that of the Philippines by an amazing 10%. Next year, Singapore's income per capita will be USD 70,700, while that of the Philippines will be USD 4,950. The income gap has increased: USD 70,700 – USD 4,950 = USD 67,750. This is what is happening in reality.

2 This is true for the Philippines. Indeed, a regression with annual data of actual growth on last year's growth has a statistically insignificant coefficient, not different from zero and a negative point estimate, and a fit of virtually zero.

3 Different specifications of the regressions discussed here, including lags or error corrections, yielded the same conclusions, with relevant coefficient estimates about the same as those discussed here.

4 We applied the Hodrick–Prescott (HP) filter to the time series of real GDP and labor productivity. We used annual data from 2000 until 2019. Then we calculated the growth rate of these two series and obtained the growth rate of the labor force residually as the difference between thew first two. We do not include the pandemic years, because the HP filter is sensitive to large shocks and can misrepresent the trend. The result was very similar to that given by Okun's law, that is, a (trend) growth rate of about 6% in recent years.

5 Felipe and Estrada (2020) estimated a model that takes into account the relationship between financial factors and the output gap. The estimated potential growth for the Philippines was 4.6% during 2000–2007, 4.4% during 2008–2009, and 5.9% during 2010–2018.

6 Solow's (1957) work differs from Harrod's in that the latter relies on the concept of aggregate production function. We note, though, that the neoclassical growth model is consistent with Harrod's natural growth rate. Indeed, the steady-state solution of this model indicates that the growth rate of output equals the sum of the growth rates of total factor productivity and the labor force.

7 Different specifications of the regressions discussed here, including lags or error corrections, yielded the same conclusions, with relevant coefficient estimates about the same as those discussed here.

8 As a result of having just a few data points in the initial years of the recursive estimation, the income elasticity of demand for imports is poorly estimated the first few years.

9 To obtain a point estimate of the income elasticity of demand for exports (ε), we estimate the export function (3.5) $\hat{X}_t = \beta_0 + \beta_1\hat{E}_t + \varepsilon\hat{Z}_t$, where X is exports (in real terms),

E is the nominal exchange rate, and Z is the world's GDP, where all variables are expressed in growth rates, denoted by ^, with annual data for 2000–2023. To obtain the income elasticity of the demand for imports (π), we estimate equation (3.6) $\hat{M}_t = \gamma_0 + \gamma_1\hat{E}_t + \pi\hat{Y}_t$, where M is imports (in real terms), and Y is the real GDP of the Philippines. Regressions are estimated for 2000–2023. The exchange rate elasticities β_1 and γ_1 are very low and statistically insignificant. The estimates that we obtain for the income elasticities are $\varepsilon = 3.3$ and $\pi = 2.01$. These two values are about the average of the recursive estimates in Figures 3.3 and 3.4. The growth rate of the world economy ($\hat{Z}_t$) is 3.45%. This gives a BOPC growth rate of 5.72% (period average).

10 We have also estimated a version of the model that includes the growth remittances as an additional factor determining the BOPC growth grate. Although this is positive, it has to be multiplied by the share of remittances in total payments (about 0.25), and then the share of exports reduced (from 1 on the first model to 0.75 now). This does not change the estimate of the BOPC growth rate.

11 COVID-19 in 2020–2021 delayed efforts to transform the economy by forcing many workers to seek employment in the countryside (Biswas, 2021).

12 Felipe et al. (2012) estimated a cross-country regression using data for 147 countries. Their model combined variables that captured countries' accumulated capabilities and the capacity to undergo structural transformation. Using this model, they forecasted an average growth rate for the Philippines for 2010–2030 between 5.85% and 7.06%.

13 Using annual data for the Philippines from 2000 to 2023, we estimate a simple growth regression where real output growth is dependent on real manufacturing value added, $\hat{Y} = \beta_0 + \beta_1\hat{Y}^M$, Kaldor's first growth law. We find that an increase of 1% in manufacturing growth is associated with a 0.76% increase in output growth. We also find that there is a strong correlation between real output growth and the excess of growth in manufacturing over the growth in non-manufacturing sectors, $\hat{Y} = \beta_0 + \beta_1\left(\hat{Y}^M - \hat{Y}^{NM}\right)$, with a positive and significant coefficient $\beta_1 = 0.65$. Finally, the Verdoorn coefficient of the regression of employment growth on output growth for the manufacturing sector, $\hat{E}^M = \beta_0 + \beta_1\hat{Y}^M$, Kaldor's second growth law, is $\beta_1 = 0.86$, indicative of increasing returns to scale.

14 Again, using annual data for 2000–2023, we find a positive and significant relationship between manufacturing growth and the growth in services, $\hat{Y}^S = \beta_0 + \beta_1\hat{Y}^M$, where $\beta_1 = 0.7$; that is, there is a 0.7% increase in the growth of services for every 1% increase in the growth of manufacturing output.

15 It is important to understand that tourism is a business of the advanced economies: With a few exceptions, virtually all major tourist destinations in the world, by country and by city, are advanced economies. Think of Paris, London, Rome, New York, Madrid, Bangkok, or Istanbul. People do not travel there because of their beaches (which many countries have too) but because of the "package" these places offer: culture (monuments, museums, cultural activities; high-end shopping), parks, restaurants, and public transportation to commute. The Philippines does not have these. We need much better infrastructure, but more importantly, we have to upgrade our tourism package to compete with Thailand or Mexico first . . . then think about competing with the world's largest tourist destinations, France and Spain.

16 Baumol's cost disease refers to the following: To attract workers, sectors of low productivity, like education, health care, the arts, or public services, must raise wages at the same pace as in high-productivity sectors, like manufacturing. The result is that costs in slow-growing productivity sectors rise faster than their productivity, leading to higher relative prices. This explains why health care, education, and public

services get more expensive over time and shows that the rising costs in these sectors are not necessarily due to inefficiency or waste but due to a structural feature of the economy.

17 The IT-BPO sector employs about 1.82 million workers. This is about 3.7% of total employment (almost 49 million workers). This is a significant share, but much smaller than those of agriculture, wholesale and retail trade, or construction (Chapter 4).

18 This is not to say that all jobs in advanced countries in services pay high salaries. What we claim is that the share of high-paying jobs in services is much higher in advanced economies, and this is because these jobs are linked to (or a function of) the industrial sector in general.

19 Obviously, there is subjectivity in choosing these subperiods. Yet we think that they are sufficiently homogeneous (and different among themselves) for the purposes of our analysis.

20 The very high growth rate of 1946–1972 is the result of the growth rates during the first few years: 38.42% in 1946–1947, 15.93% in 1947–1948, 6.66% in 1948–1949, and 10.60% in 1949–1950. Average growth during 1951–1972 was 5.66%.

21 De Dios et al. (2021) stress the fact that average growth was below 4% per annum during the whole Marcos Sr. administration, not just in the martial law years. The best performance of the Marcos Sr. era was during 1972–1980.

22 The two decades from 1972 to 1992 have been the most difficult in recent Philippine history, marked by low growth, political instability (including the martial law years), restoration of democracy, and the collapse of the manufacturing sector.

23 Torio et al. (2021) found that the top 15 conglomerates in the country generated approximately one trillion pesos of value added, equivalent to 6% of the total national output, in 2018. Yet it is not clear to us how they calculated the value added of these companies.

24 We admit that there might be exceptions to this broad statement. However, as documented in Chapter 4, most of what the Philippines does in electronics is assembly. Werker et al. (2014) provided an excellent overview of Ayala Corporation. Ayala's Integrated Micro-Electronics Inc. signed a noteworthy USD 65 million deal with Zero Motorcycles, an American company, to manufacture battery-powered motorcycles for Europe and other Asian markets (Ramos, 2023). This is not a complex product. Although Ayala's collaboration with American companies in manufacturing seemingly highly complex products aligns with the country's structural transformation process, multinational companies still dominate a significant portion of the export market. In particular, multinational electronics firms, rather than local conglomerates, exert control over the semiconductor and electronics industries, which collectively constitute nearly half of the value of the Philippines' exports (Desiderio, 2022). Companies like Texas Instruments, Intel, Philips, and Sanyo outsource low-paying and labor-intensive activities, such as assembly and testing, to the Philippines in order to reduce costs (Castillo, 2005).

25 Another factor that can be considered to understand the lack of competitive exports is poor trainability. It is not so much that consistently high levels of education are needed for the development of comparative advantage. In fact, Felipe et al. (2024) concluded that basic education, as long as it is of high quality, matters more for export diversification than college attainment. The process of training workers is a learning-by-doing process, which, coupled with good organizational capabilities, is crucial for creating high and sustained export-oriented growth, much like South Korea and Singapore in their emerging stages of development.

4

THE STRUCTURE OF THE PHILIPPINE ECONOMY

4.1 Introduction

This chapter provides a detailed account of the structure of the Philippine economy and how it has changed during the last decades. As explained in previous chapters, this is the first main theme in our account of why the Philippine economy got behind those of many of its East Asian peers. The structure of the economy, and more precisely, the speed and direction of its changes, determines a country's growth. We argued in Chapter 3 that aggregate growth is related to the rate of expansion of the sector with the most favorable growth characteristics. This has traditionally been manufacturing. This has been the case since the Middle Ages with the emergence of Europe (Reinert, 2019). Growth and, more generally, development are the results of changes in the structure of the economy (both in output and, more importantly, in employment), particularly the shift from agriculture to manufacturing. This process was common to all advanced economies.

If there is a simple way to explain what the successful Asian economies (first Japan, then Hong Kong, Singapore, South Korea, and Taiwan, and finally China) did to attain fast growth, it can be summarized in the following statement: very fast economic transformation. Felipe, McCombie, et al. (2025) provide an in-depth discussion of the structural transformation literature in relation to East Asia's fast growth. They argue that it is impossible to comprehend East Asia's success without bringing into the discussion the significant structural transformation that these economies underwent between the mid-1960s and the early 1990s, from the point of view of both output and employment. These authors also argue that the shift of workers out of agriculture into industry and services happened because these economies created companies with the capabilities to manufacture products of increasing complexity. These capabilities allowed these economies to upgrade their export structures. Finally, the role of the government in

DOI: 10.4324/9781003728719-4

facilitating and encouraging structural transformation through different tools of industrial policy was also key. Chapter 7 provides a discussion of Korea's industrial policy.

Likewise, what has the Philippines not done? Transform its economy the way successful East Asian economies did. The Philippines is still largely an agrarian economy from an employment point of view, and the sectors that create employment today are service activities of low productivity. Consequently, productivity and the employment structure explain the country's relatively low per capita income.

The rest of the chapter is structured as follows: First, we provide an account of the transformation and upgrading of successful East Asian economies. Then we describe the structure of the Philippine economy: (1) productivity and output growth; (2) employment shares, productivity growth, wages, occupations, and education; and (3) Philippine firms and their participation in global value chains. We emphasize three points: (1) The largest shares of employment are those of agriculture and wholesale and retail trade, both sectors of low productivity; (2) the manufacturing sector is important but lags those of other countries in the region; and (3) Philippine exports remain globally uncompetitive. This analysis provides the departure point (where is the Philippine economy today?) for our forecasts, in Chapter 5, until 2028 and, in Chapters 12 and 13, until 2050.

4.2 Structural Transformation and Upgrading in East Asia

This section provides a synthesis of what East Asian countries did during the decades of high growth. Its purpose is not to argue that the Philippines should imitate Korea or Taiwan in their industrialization efforts (impossible today); what we argue instead is that these countries succeeded because they made efforts to accumulate capabilities and to upgrade. This materialized in a very fast transformation of their economic structures. If the Philippines does not industrialize, then we wonder what service activities will deliver the fast progress that we need.

The economic transformation of successful East Asian economies is best summarized by the transfer of workers out of agriculture (the sector with the lowest productivity) into industry, characterized by manufacturing growth (Kaldor, 1967), and, second, in the diversification and upgrading of their export baskets. As documented by Felipe et al. (2016), the share of agricultural employment in total employment in Korea and Taiwan declined much faster during their period of high growth—at about 1 percentage point per annum—than it did in advanced Western economies in the 19th and 20th centuries (at between 0.22 and 0.5 percentage points per annum between 1870 and 1979).[1] Figure 4.1 shows the fast decline in the agricultural employment share in two East Asian economies. We note that the agricultural employment share was about 23% (today's Philippine share) in Taiwan in the late 1970s and in Korea in the mid-1980s. Today, about four decades later, the agricultural employment shares in these two economies are about 5% (attained around 2015).

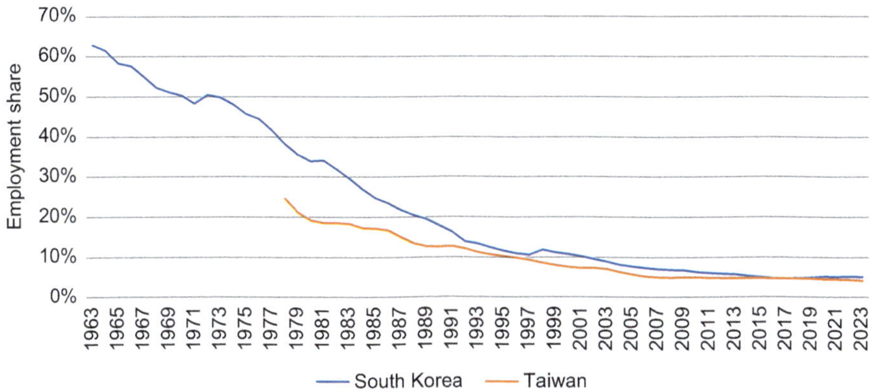

FIGURE 4.1 Share of Agriculture, Forestry, & Fishing in Total Employment (%), South Korea and Taiwan, 1963–2023

Source: Authors' calculations based on data from the International Labour Organization (https://ilostat.ilo.org/data/) and the Directorate-General of Budget, Accounting and Statistics (DGBAS) of Executive Yuan (https://manpower.dgbas.gov.tw/dgbas_community/Common_Inquire/index_eng/)

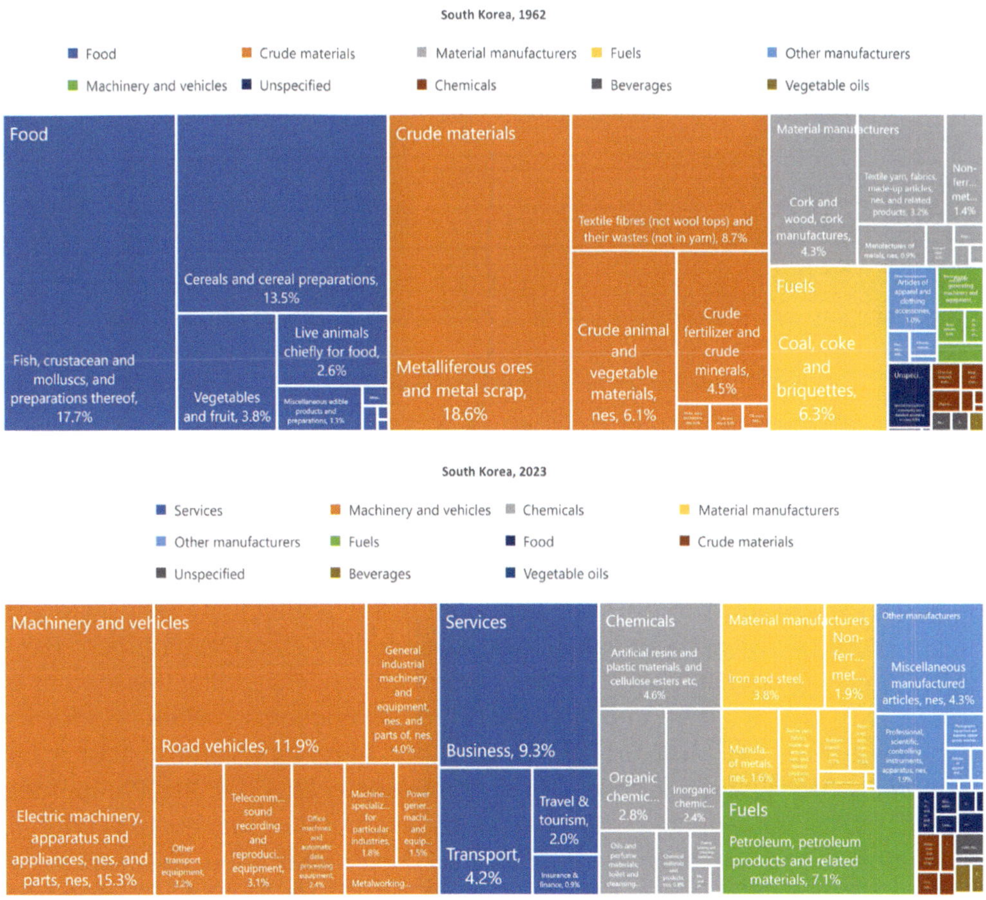

FIGURE 4.2 Export Structures, South Korea and Taiwan, 1962 and 2023

Source: Growth Lab at Harvard University, The Atlas of Economic Complexity (https://atlas.cid.harvard.edu/). Last accessed 5th June, 2025

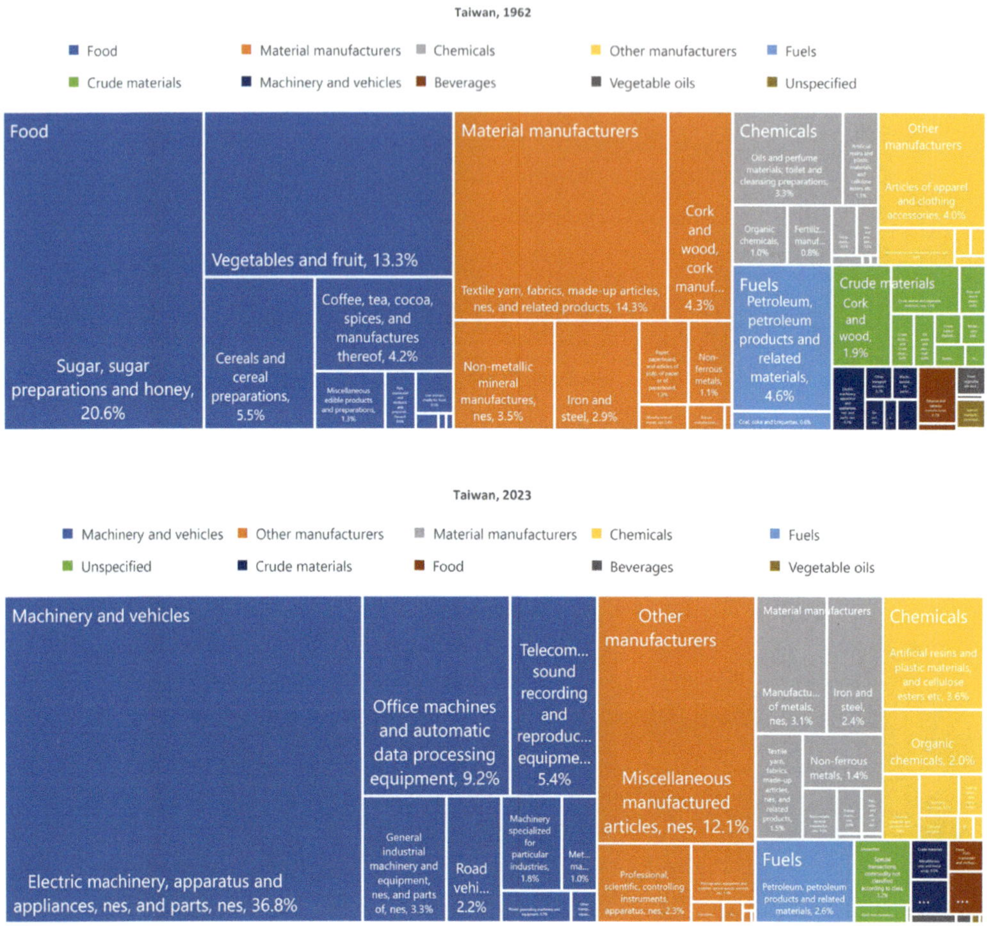

FIGURE 4.2 (Continued)

This is the essence of what development was about during the early periods of transformation: the movement of workers out of low-productivity activities into high-productivity activities, in particular, into manufacturing. The decompositions of productivity growth into the "within sectors" and "structural transformation" (the shift of workers from sectors of lower productivity into sectors of higher productivity) components undertaken by the Asian Development Bank (2013) and Rodrik et al. (2017) are very helpful in understanding the sources of productivity growth. They indicated that both components (within-sector productivity growth and structural transformation) were significant in East Asian economies. We also undertake this decomposition later for the Philippines. Szirmai (2012) documented that all historical examples of success in economic development and catch-up since 1870 have been associated with successful industrialization. The Asian Development Bank (2013) provided a thorough analysis of Asia's economic transformation and highlighted the significant differences across economies. Industrialization played a key role in East Asia's development in the 20th century, but not in most other Asian countries. Szirmai and Verspagen (2015) also highlighted the importance of manufacturing for development (the engine of growth hypothesis) and documented the interaction effects of manufacturing on education and income gaps.

Apart from the fast decline in the employment share documented in Figure 4.1, another key contributing factor to East Asia's growth was the change in the export mix. Figure 4.2 shows how the export mixes of Korea and Taiwan changed between 1962 and 2023 from very simple manufactures and agricultural products into cars, electronics, or chemicals. This change in the composition of the export basket was reflected in an increase in *complexity*. This concept provides a summary of how diversified an economy is and how unique the products it exports are.[2]

The recent literature on the product space of Hidalgo et al. (2007) and the concept of complexity by Hidalgo and Hausmann (2009) make the very important point that not all products have the same consequences for development. This work explains economic development as a process of learning how to produce (and export) more complex products. This literature, in effect, implies that development is slow for countries with productive structures geared toward low-productivity and low-wage activities, producing mostly low-value commodities or agricultural products. Development is fast, on the other hand, for countries with productive structures geared toward high-productivity and high-wage activities.

While East Asian economies' export mixes in the early 1960s were somewhat more diverse and complex than those of other countries in the region (e.g., the Philippines and Indonesia provide a contrasting comparison), their dynamism was far greater. All East Asian economies developed comparative advantages in many more products and more complex products over the next three decades, and they grew rapidly as they did so (Hausmann et al., 2014).

The notion that development takes place in the productive structure of an economy and that firms' capabilities form the foundation of this structure is a powerful way to understand why some countries advance rapidly while others progress more slowly. *Capabilities* refer to (1) the set of human and physical capital, the legal system, and institutions, among others, that are needed to produce a product (hence, they are product-specific, not just a set of amorphous factor inputs); (2) at the firm level, the know-how or working practices held collectively by the group of individuals comprising the firm; and (3) the organizational abilities that provide the capacity to form, manage, and operate activities that involve large numbers of people. Capabilities manifest themselves in quality–productivity combinations. A given capability is embodied in the tacit knowledge of the individuals who comprise the firm's workforce. The quality–productivity combinations are not a continuum from zero; rather, there is a window with a minimum threshold below which the firm would be excluded from the market and not export. Therefore, capabilities are largely non-tradable inputs. Khan (2015) argued that because they reflect mostly tacit knowledge, the way to acquire them is through learning by doing (LBD). Such LBD requires external (to the firm) financing (i.e., it has to be subsidized). Simultaneously, it requires efforts from both the firm and its workers. We return to this point in Chapter 8.

Through this lens, economic development is a process that requires acquiring more complex sets of capabilities to move toward new activities associated with higher levels of productivity. In the case of East Asian economies, the implication is that their success in industrial upgrading ignited a series of processes of capability improvement, including some measure of technology development, human capital accumulation, and institutional development. Chapter 6 discusses, using Gerschenkron's latecomer model, the fundamental role of the state in backward economies.

All this has been lacking in the Philippines, contributing to the current state of the economy. In the following section, we take a deeper look at the structure of the Philippine economy and explore several key features that will help us better understand its underlying reality.

4.3 The Structure of the Philippine Economy

This section provides an in-depth analysis of the structure of the Philippine economy. To do so, we rely on the following datasets:

1. The De La Salle University (DLSU) ANIMO econometric model database. The series are discussed in Aragones et al. (2024), and the model is described in Chapter 5, Appendix 5.[3]
2. A database containing employment, education, and wage data for the Philippines from 2000 to 2023, discussed further in Chapters 10 and 13.
3. A dataset constructed by Felipe, Mathew, et al. (2025a), with data for the largest 1,000 firms of the Philippines covering the years 2018 to 2021 (Section 4.3.3).
4. A dataset (value added, employment, and wages from 2000 to 2023) constructed by Felipe, Mathew, et al. (2025a) with data for the manufacturing sector of the Philippine economy, disaggregated into 13 subsectors (Section 4.3.3).

To gain a clearer understanding of the current state and structure of our economy, we examine several factors which, combined, help explain why we are still catching up with our neighbors.

First, we examine labor productivity, delving into sectoral value-added and output growth. Second, we take a closer look at the labor market, covering employment shares, wages, occupations, and education. Finally, we discuss global value chains and firms in the Philippines, given that firms are the main agents of transformation in an economy.

4.3.1 Productivity and Output Growth

We start by examining productivity in the Philippines across three dimensions: at the aggregate level, by sector, and by city or province. Figure 4.3 and Table 4.1 show aggregate labor productivity in the Philippines and in selected Asian countries. The data indicate that Philippine productivity was one of the lowest during 2000–2023, and it has been the lowest since 2021. In 2023, China's productivity, which was lower than that of the Philippines in 2000, became twice that of the Philippines.

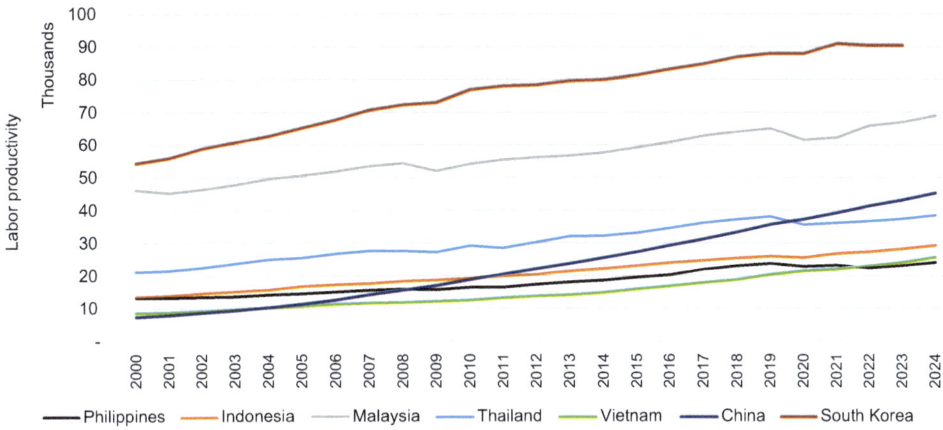

FIGURE 4.3 Labor Productivity (Constant 2021 PPP, international dollars), Selected Countries, 2000–2024

Note: Productivity is measured as GDP per person employed (constant 2021 PPP, international dollars) as per the World Bank.

Source: The World Bank: World Development Indicators (https://data.worldbank.org/indicator/SL.GDP.PCAP.EM.KD)

TABLE 4.1 Labor Productivity (Constant 2021 PPP, International Dollars), Selected Countries, 2023

Country	*Labor Productivity, 2023*
South Korea	90,534
Malaysia	66,895
China	43,341
Thailand	37,582
Indonesia	28,576
Vietnam	24,333
Philippines	23,099

Note: Productivity is measured as GDP per person employed (constant 2021 PPP, international dollars) as per the World Bank.

Source: The World Bank: World Development Indicators (https://data.worldbank.org/indicator/SL.GDP.PCAP.EM.KD).

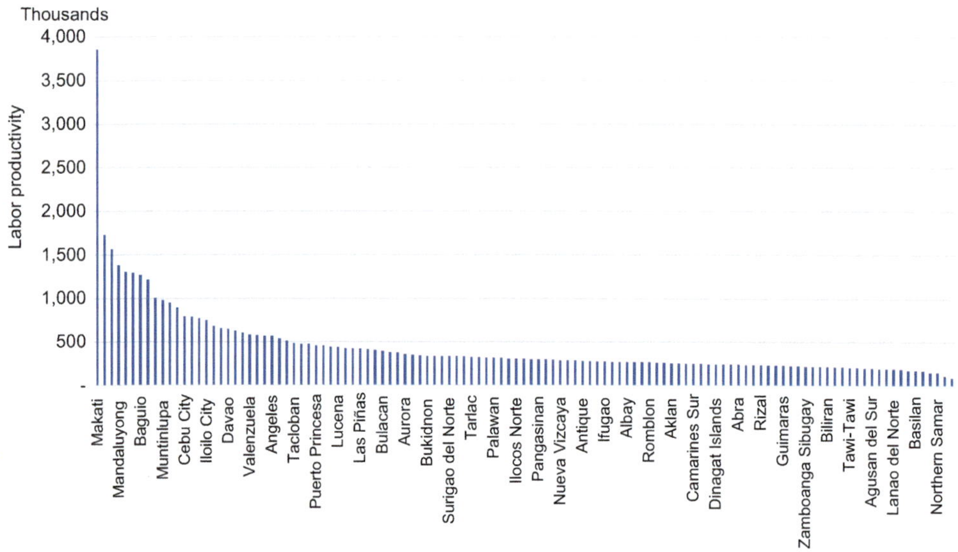

FIGURE 4.4 Labor Productivity by Province and Highly-Urbanized City (Constant 2018 PHP), Philippines, 2023

Notes: Labor Productivity is calculated as the GDP per province and highly-urbanized city (constant 2018 PHP) divided by the number of workers employed in each area.

Source: Authors' calculations based on data from the Philippine Statistics Authority's Provincial Product Accounts (https://openstat.psa.gov.ph/Database/Economic-Accounts/Provincial-Product-Accounts) and the Philippine Statistics Authority's (2023a) Preliminary 2023 Annual Provincial Labor Market Statistics

Figure 4.4 shows that the low level of productivity for the economy is the result of a significant number of cities with low productivity (PHP 100,000 in the poorest). At the other extreme, Makati's productivity at almost PHP 4 million makes it a high-income area. Given that the overall economic environment and institutions are the same across all cities (i.e., national government, laws, and business requirements), the reason for this significant differential must lie somewhere else.

Analyzing productivity by sector, real estate, utilities, and finance and insurance are the highest (Figure 4.5).[4] It must be kept in mind that the seemingly high productivity of these sectors is the result of not having physical measures of output. Instead, we use real value added, which is a very imprecise measure. If we take out the sectors where productivity is not a well-defined concept, the other sectors with high productivity are information and communication and manufacturing. Sectors of low productivity that are important to take note of at this point are wholesale and retail trade, construction, transport and storage, and agriculture.

Figure 4.6 shows the six sectors that make up about 70% of real output. The sectors that contribute the most are manufacturing and wholesale and retail

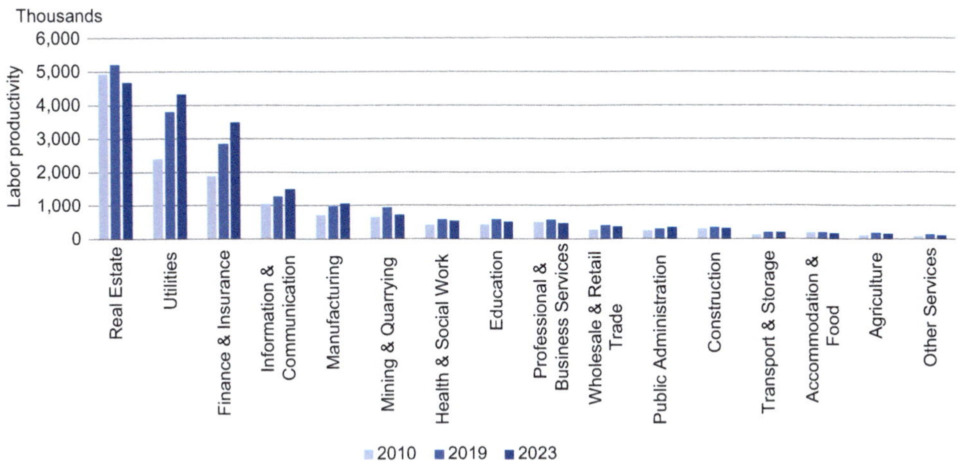

FIGURE 4.5 Labor Productivity by Sector (Constant 2018 PHP), Philippines, 2010, 2019, and 2023

Note: Labor Productivity is calculated as the gross value added per sector (constant 2018 PHP) divided by the number of workers employed in each sector.

Source: Authors' calculations based on sectoral gross value added data from the Philippine Statistics Authority (https://openstat.psa.gov.ph/Database/Economic-Accounts/National-Accounts-of-the-Philippines/Annual-National-Accounts), and sectoral employment from the Philippine Statistics Authority's (2015, 2018, 2023, 2024b) Statistical Yearbooks

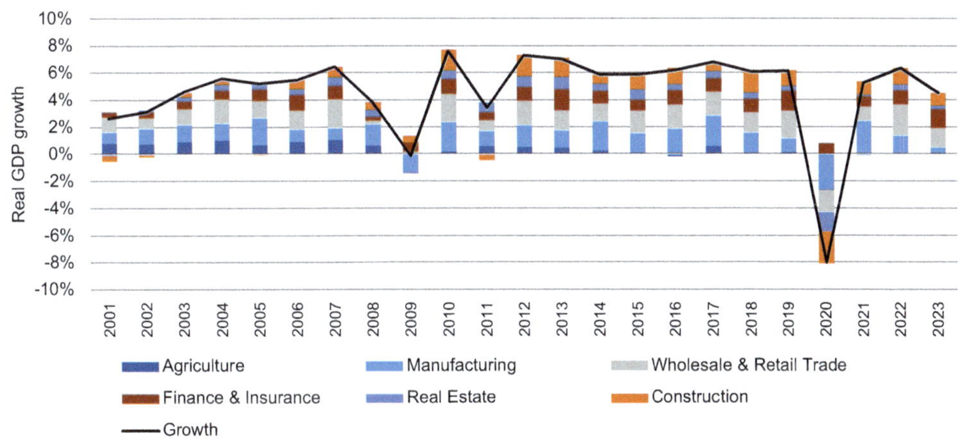

FIGURE 4.6 Decomposition of Real GDP Growth (%), Philippines, 2001–2023

Source: Authors' calculations based on data from the Philippines Statistics Authority (https://openstat.psa.gov.ph/Database/Economic-Accounts/National-Accounts-of-the-Philippines/Annual-National-Accounts)

trade. On average, they contribute about 35% of total output, and they contribute about 50% of output growth. However, note that wholesale and retail trade is a sector of low productivity. Manufacturing, on the other hand, is a sector of high productivity, with both a high output share and a relatively high

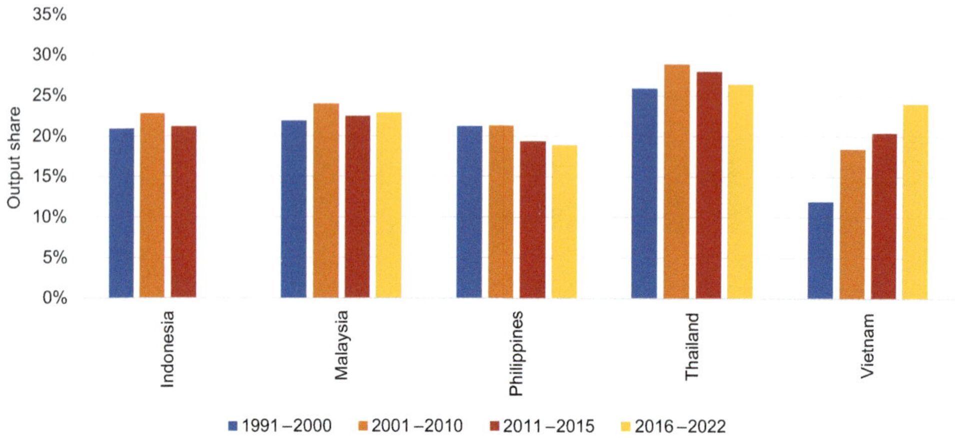

FIGURE 4.7 Share of Manufacturing in GDP (%), Selected Southeast Asian Countries, 1991–2022

Source: Authors' calculations based on data from the United Nations Industrial Development Organization's National Accounts Database (https://stat.unido.org/data/table?dataset=national-accounts#data-browser)

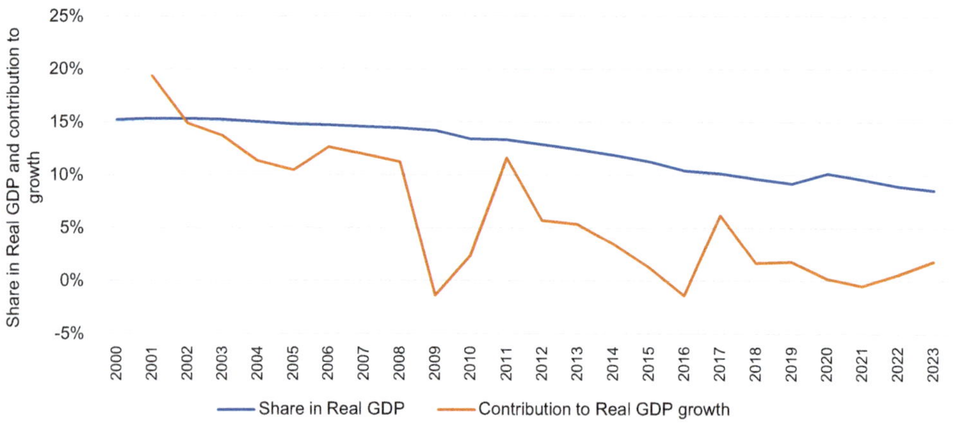

FIGURE 4.8 Share of Agriculture, Forestry & Fishing in Real GDP, and Contribution to Real GDP Growth (%), Philippines, 2000–2023

Source: Authors' calculations based on data from the Philippines Statistics Authority (https://openstat.psa.gov.ph/Database/Economic-Accounts/National-Accounts-of-the-Philippines/Annual-National-Accounts)

contribution to output growth. Compared to its neighbors, however, the share of manufacturing in total output is quite low (Figure 4.7).

In the case of agriculture, aside from being a sector of very low productivity (Figure 4.5), both its share in total output and its contribution to output growth have been declining since 2000 (Figures 4.8).

Understanding productivity across sectors leads us to the next section, where we analyze where Philippine workers are employed, their occupations, wages, and educational attainment.

4.3.2 *Employment Shares, Productivity Growth, Wages, Occupations, and Education*

Analyzing sectoral employment, we find that the employment share of agriculture has decreased since 2000—an indication of development, as previously discussed (Figure 4.9). However, in 2023, agriculture still employed over one-fifth of our workers (23%)—21.6% in 2024. Recall that this was the share in Taiwan in

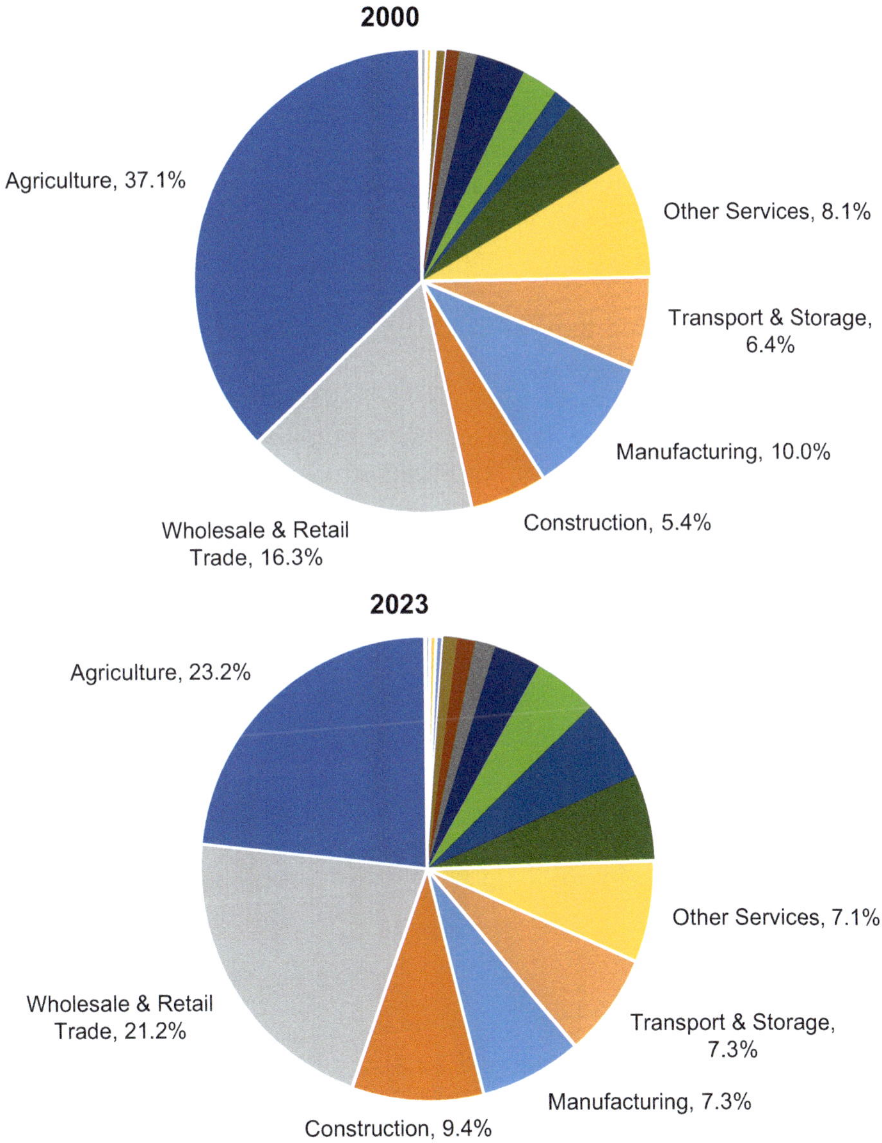

FIGURE 4.9 Employment Share by Sector (%), Philippines, 2000 and 2023

Source: Authors' calculations based on data from the Philippine Statistics Authority (2002, 2024b), and the DLSU ANIMO econometric model database

the late 1970s and in South Korea in the mid-1980s, and it took their economies about three decades for this share to reach the current one of about 5%. If we add wholesale and retail trade and construction to agriculture, slightly over 50% of our workers are employed in low-productivity sectors.[5] Meanwhile, manufacturing employs only about 7% of all workers (3.6 million), a share that has seen a reduction of 3 percentage points since 2000. It is worth noting that in absolute terms, employment in the sector has increased. In 2000, manufacturing employed 2.7 million workers. The problem is that employment in services has increased faster, leading to a decrease in the manufacturing share.

The manufacturing employment share is very low compared to what developed economies had in the past. In high-income East Asian economies and in most advanced countries, this share was about 30% at some point in the 20th century (Felipe et al., 2019). Figure 4.10 shows the share of manufacturing for employment for selected Southeast Asian countries, and that of the Philippines has always been low compared to its neighbors. In Vietnam, the manufacturing employment share is about twice as high.

It is worth emphasizing that, until today, the share of employment in agriculture remains very high (in terms of the number of workers, it has remained quite stable at around 10 to 11 million). Unless the economy can create jobs in other sectors at higher wages (so that employment declines), it will be difficult to mechanize the sector, and agriculture will continue to be a low-productivity sector and contribute very little to our output growth.

We summarize the earlier discussion in Figure 4.11, which shows employment shares and productivity levels by sector for the years 2000 and 2023. This

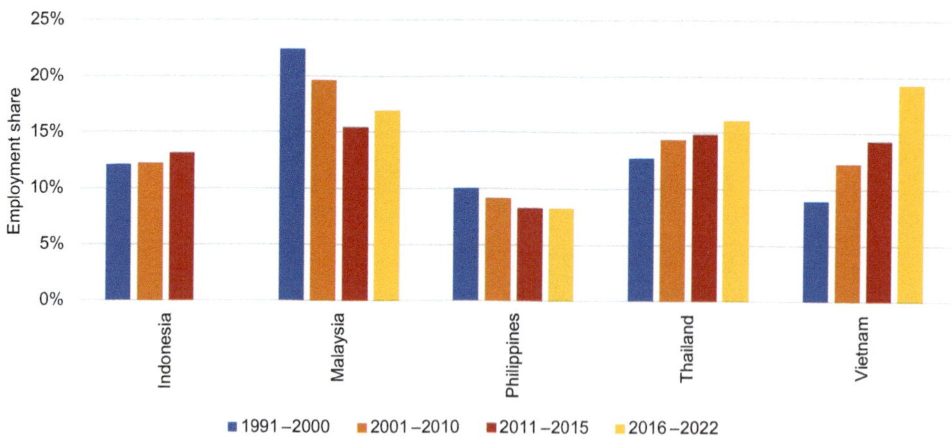

FIGURE 4.10 Share of Manufacturing in Total Employment (%), Selected Southeast Asian Countries, 1991–2022

Source: Authors' calculations based on data from the Groningen Growth and Development Centre's 10-sector database (Timmer et al., 2015), the International Labour Organization (https://ilostat.ilo.org/data/), and the DLSU ANIMO econometric model database

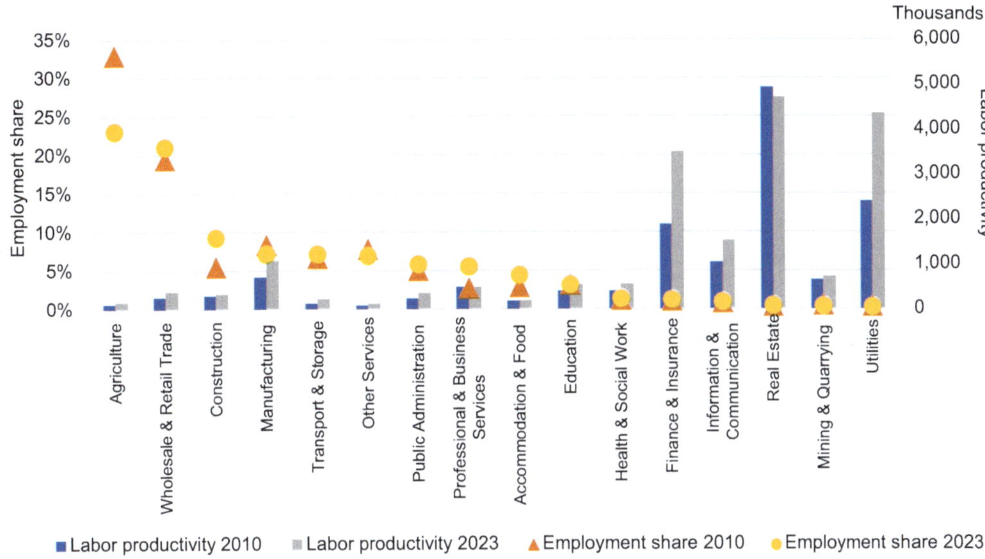

FIGURE 4.11 Employment Share (%) and Labor Productivity (Constant 2018 PHP) by Sector, Philippines, 2010 and 2023

Source: Authors' calculations based on data from the DLSU ANIMO econometric model database

indicates that, over the last two decades, employment has been concentrated in sectors of low productivity. Meanwhile, the sectors with the highest levels of productivity each account for only about 1% of the workforce.

When we decompose productivity growth into the within-sector effect (productivity growth due to the growth of productivity in each sector) and the structural transformation effect (productivity growth due to the sectoral reallocation of employment), we can observe that during 2010–2023, overall productivity growth amounted to 41% (Figure 4.12).[6] Manufacturing had the largest within-sector effect, yet the sector's employment share declined, resulting in the negative contribution of the structural transformation effect. In the case of agriculture, we find that it has a positive within effect and a larger negative structural transformation effect, implying that the contribution of the sector to overall productivity growth is negative. It can be noted that sectors such as construction and accommodation and food do not contribute much to productivity growth in terms of the within effect; instead, their contribution to productivity is largely from the structural transformation effect, which reinforces the fact that workers are moving to sectors that have a low contribution to overall productivity growth.

Since Philippine productivity is low, particularly in the largest employers, wages are low. We find that 75% of the Philippine workforce is employed in six sectors (out of 16, identified in the figure with colors and labels in bold) with some of the lowest wage rates (Figure 4.13).

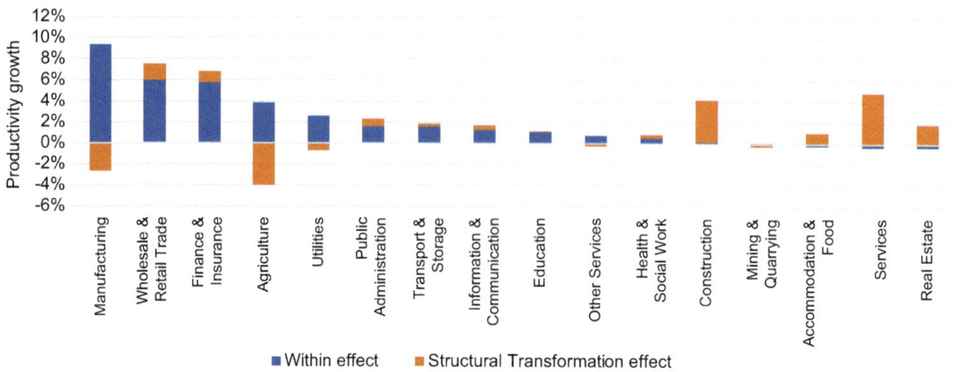

FIGURE 4.12 Decomposition of Productivity Growth by Sector (%), Philippines, 2010–2023

Source: Authors' calculations based on data from the DLSU ANIMO econometric model database

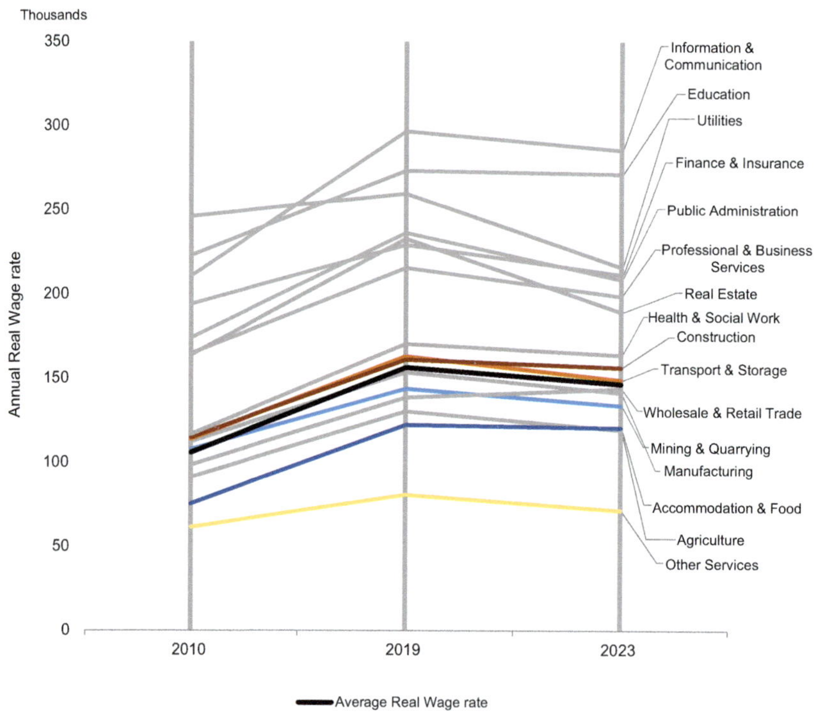

FIGURE 4.13 Annual Real Wage Rate by Sector (Constant 2018 PHP), Philippines, 2010, 2019, and 2023

Source: DLSU ANIMO econometric model database

Figure 4.14 shows the number of workers by occupation in the Philippines. It shows that most workers are laborers, followed by sales workers, and then agriculture workers.[7] These occupations make up about 50% of our workforce.[8]

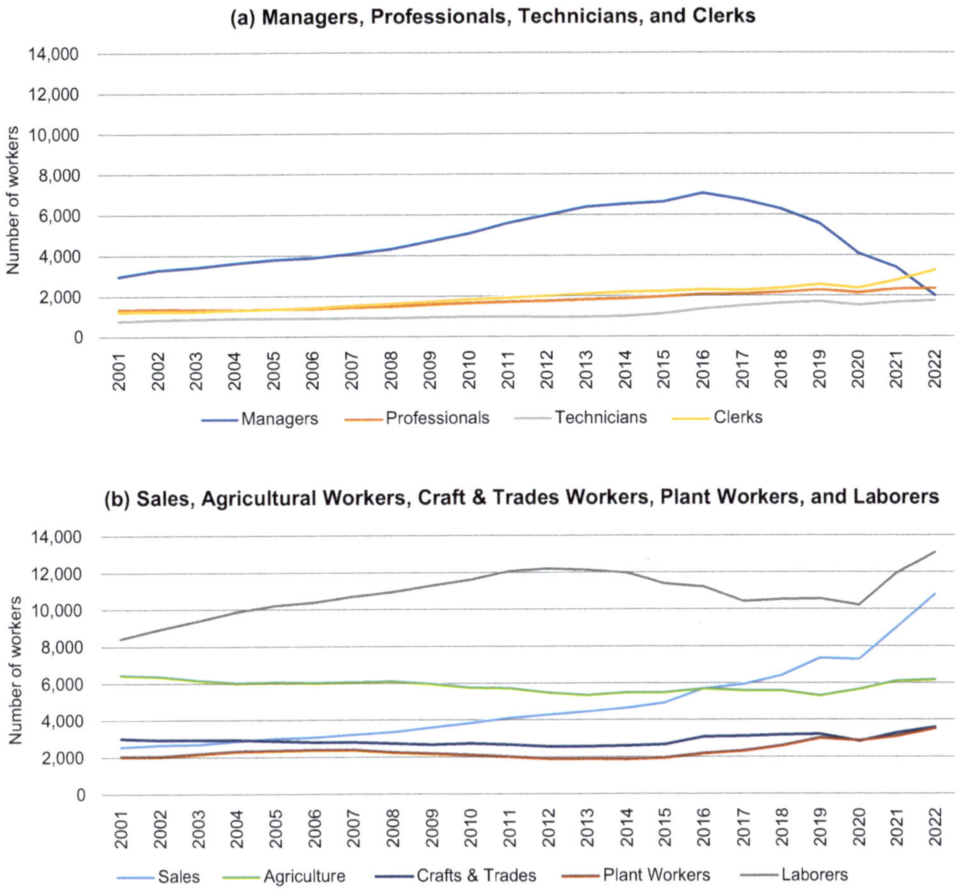

FIGURE 4.14 Number of Workers by Occupation, Philippines, 2001–2022

Note: "Technicians and Associate Professionals" is shortened to "Technicians"; "Clerical and Support" is shortened to "Clerks"; "Sales and Services Workers" is shortened to "Sales"; "Skilled Agriculture, Forestry, and Fishery Workers" is shortened to "Agriculture"; "Crafts and Trades Workers" is shortened to "Crafts and Trades"; "Plant Machinery Operators & Assemblers" is shortened to "Plant Workers"; and "Elementary Occupations" is shortened to "Laborers".

Source: Authors' calculations from the Philippine Statistics Authority's Labor Force Survey (https://psada.psa.gov.ph/catalog/LFS/about)

Panel (A) of Figure 4.14 shows that the number of professionals, technicians, and clerks grew steadily between 2001 and 2022. The number of managers shows the largest increase—it more than doubled between 2001 and 2016, after which the number declined significantly. It is important to note that managers range from chief executives and senior officers (often responsible for highly complex tasks, such as planning, research, and decision-making) to line supervisors and hospitality supervisors (mainly tasked with overseeing frontline employees or operational staff). Managers in the Philippines also have varying levels of education, with 47% having lower than tertiary education. This goes against

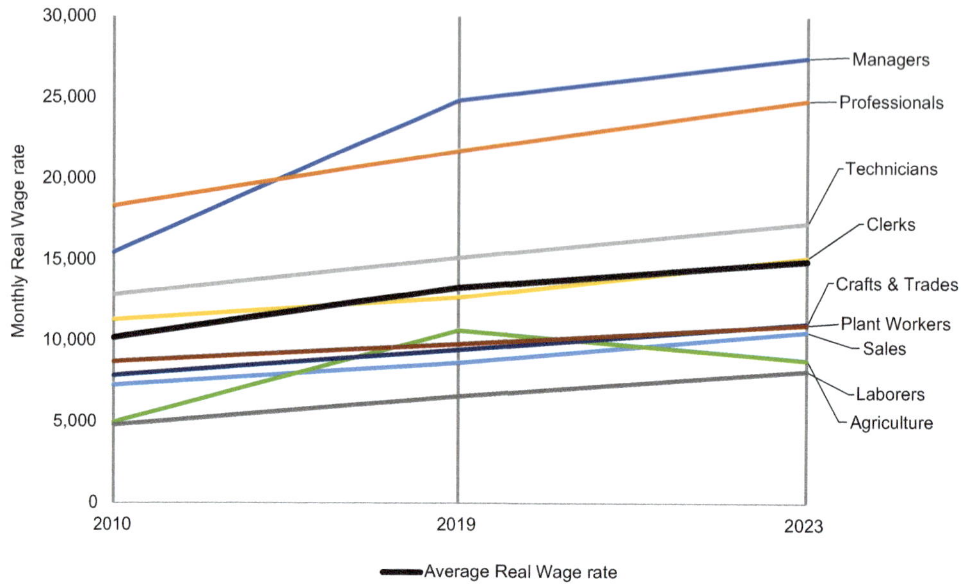

FIGURE 4.15 Monthly Real Wage Rate by Occupation (Constant 2018 PHP), Philippines, 2010, 2019, and 2023

Note: 2010 and 2019 figures are based on the October round of the Labor Force Surveys and 2023 is based on the April round of the Labor Force Survey.

Source: Authors' calculations from the Philippine Statistics Authority's Labor Force Survey (https://psada.psa.gov.ph/catalog/LFS/about)

the International Standard Classification of Occupations' (ISCO) recommended qualifications for managerial roles. This may be due to changes in education, labor market conditions, or definitions of occupations, and it warrants further investigation. Panel (B) shows that the number of workers classified as laborers and sales increased significantly in the last few years.

Average wages for these occupations in 2023 differ systematically (Figure 4.15).[9] Excluding armed forces occupations, the highest-paying occupations are managers and professionals, which comprise 10% of our workforce. These occupations correspond to ISCO level 1 (Table A4.3). The rest of the workforce (90%) are in occupations that match ISCO levels 2–4 in terms of skills, and these occupations earn much lower wages. Managers and professionals earn an average monthly wage of PHP 26,146, while the rest of the occupations earn an average monthly wage of PHP 11,708.

Furthermore, based on the 2023 Labor Force Survey, the largest employment shares by occupation are sales workers, agriculture workers, and laborers—all low-wage jobs (Table 4.2). Sales workers; market-oriented skilled agricultural workers; agricultural, forestry, and fishery laborers; and laborers in mining, constructions, manufacturing, and transport make up close to 50% of all our workers—these are occupations that pay low wages.

TABLE 4.2 Highest Employment Shares (%) by Occupation Based on the 2-Digit Philippine Standard Occupation Classification, Philippines, 2023

Primary Occupation	*Share in Total Employment (%)*
Sales workers	15.81
Market-oriented skilled agricultural workers	11.42
Agricultural, forestry, and fishery laborers	11.38
Laborers in mining, construction, manufacturing, and transport	9.96
Drivers and mobile plant operators	6.49
Cleaners and helpers	4.22
Personal service workers	3.35
Customer service clerks	2.88
Teaching professionals	2.85
Market-oriented skilled forestry, fishery, and hunting workers	2.76

Note: These are the ten occupations with the largest employment shares, identified from 43 categories under the Philippine Standard Occupational Classification used in the Philippine Labor Force Surveys.

Source: Authors' calculations from the Philippine Statistics Authority's Labor Force Survey (https://psada.psa.gov.ph/catalog/LFS/about).

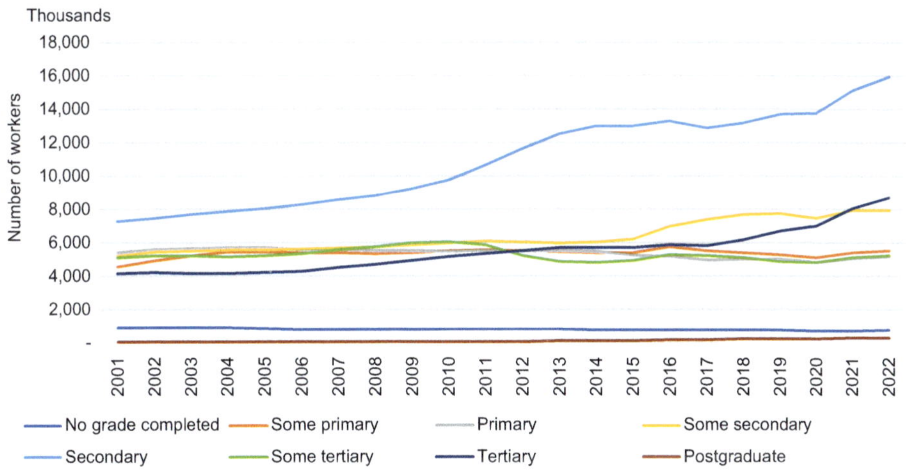

FIGURE 4.16 Number of Workers by Educational Attainment, Philippines, 2001–2022

Source: Authors' calculations from the Philippine Statistics Authority's Labor Force Survey (https://psada.psa.gov.ph/catalog/LFS/about)

Figure 4.16 shows the educational degrees that workers possess. We observe that the growth rates of the supply of workers with no grade completed, unfinished primary, secondary, and tertiary education have slowed since 2015. This implies that more workers complete their education and acquire their high school and college diplomas. A significant proportion of the labor force has completed secondary education, which, in 2022, was around a third of the workforce (about 16 million). This is followed by those with tertiary degrees and by those with graduate

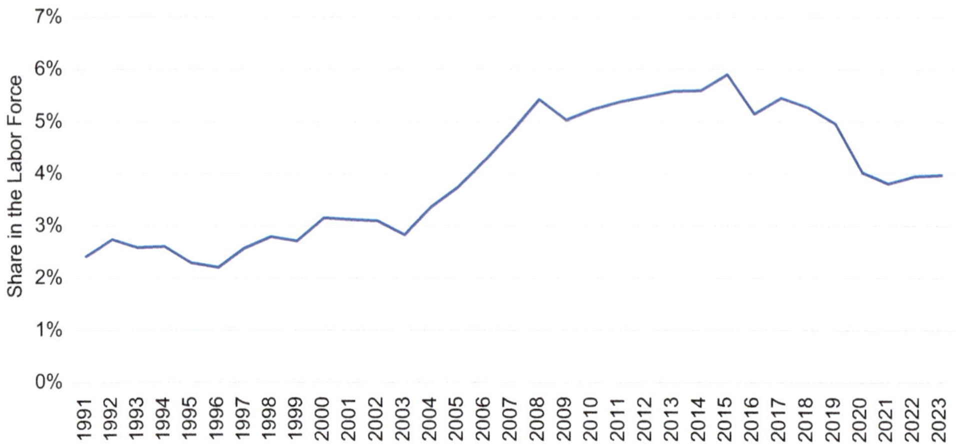

FIGURE 4.17 Overseas Filipino Workers (% of Labor Force), Philippines, 1991–2023

Source: Authors' calculations based on data from the DLSU ANIMO econometric model database

degrees. Those with a master's or PhD have steadily increased over the past two decades. Overall, the Philippine labor force appears to have become "more educated" over time. Although this seems like a positive trend, it marks an underlying issue that the country has yet to address. This concern is discussed in Chapter 10.

As a consequence of the low wage rates, the number of overseas Filipino workers (OFWs) increased in the early 2000s (Figure 4.17). Indeed, the number of OFWs doubled between 2001 and 2011, an indication that our wages are not growing at the same rate as those of the migrant-destination countries. Overall, however, migrant workers represent only about 4% of the labor force.

This quite thorough look at the labor market of the Philippine economy through the lens of structural transformation highlights two important points. First, most of the nation's workers are still concentrated in sectors of low productivity (agriculture and low-productivity services). Second, the vast majority of the country's relatively more educated workforce remains in low-wage occupations (laborers, sales workers, and agricultural workers). Given that most of those employed are in sectors with low productivity that pay low wages, it becomes crucial to understand where productivity happens and where jobs are actually created: firms.

4.3.3 Understanding Philippine Firms and Their Participation in Global Value Chains

To make sense of why overall Philippine productivity is low, it is important to understand the structure of Philippine firms. In most countries, a large majority of firms (about 95%) are micro, small, or medium-sized enterprises. The key difference with the Philippines is that, in advanced industrial countries, there are dozens, if not hundreds, of large firms—each employing thousands of workers and manufacturing complex products for the world market.

In the Philippines, the typical firm is small and unproductive, which keeps wages low. Productivity remains low for two reasons. One is that small firms cannot mechanize. The other reason is that these firms' abilities to carry out tasks using available resources—their organizational capabilities—are rudimentary. On the other hand, large Filipino conglomerates with better organizational capabilities have chosen domestic safety, preferring to expand into non-tradable sectors, such as banking, real estate, education, health care, and so forth, instead of competing internationally.

4.3.3.1 The Largest Firms

Felipe, Mathew, et al. (2025a) built a unique dataset with information on sales, profits, and assets; sector (agriculture, manufacturing, services); status as multinational versus local (domestic) company; and status as exporter versus non-exporter of the largest 1,000 Philippine firms for 2018–2021. The authors found that, in 2021, the top 1,000 Philippine companies earned PHP 17.3 trillion (sales), while the entire economy's gross output was PHP 58.9 trillion.[10] This represents 29%. Firms in this dataset earned an average of PHP 13.4 billion in gross sales in 2021. They had an average profit rate (the ratio of profits to sales) of 12%. Also in 2021, 663 of the largest 1,000 firms were services companies, 309 were manufacturing companies, while the remaining companies were in agriculture and mining. On average, manufacturing firms were larger than those in other sectors in terms of sales but smaller in terms of assets.

Analyzing sales and assets, Felipe, Mathew, et al. (2025a) found that the distributions are highly skewed, with most firms "on the left side." Table 4.3 shows the size distribution of the top 1,000 Philippine companies in 2021. Out of the 1,000 largest firms, 816 earned between PHP 2 billion and PHP 16.75 billion in 2021. Only two firms earned more than PHP 200 billion: Petron, the country's largest petroleum company, and Manila Electric Co. (MERALCO), the largest electricity provider. For assets, 960 out of the 1,000 largest firms had assets between PHP 0.18 billion and PHP 173 billion in 2021. The largest companies in terms of assets are BDO, Landbank, Metrobank, Bank of the Philippine Islands (BPI), and Philippine National Bank (PNB), all financial institutions, with assets up to PHP 3.5 trillion.

In 2021, 663 of the top 1,000 firms were services companies, 184 were exporters, and 372 were multinationals. When the 1,000 firms were divided into subgroups based on the three dimensions, the authors found that almost half of these companies (476) are domestic, service providers, and non-exporters. This is followed by multinational services firms that do not export (150). The two largest subgroups in manufacturing are domestic manufacturing firms that do not export (110) and multinational manufacturing firms that export (107). This information is shown in Table 4.4.

Focusing on manufacturing and services, Table 4.5 shows the five largest firms within each of the eight subgroups. There is a stark contrast between the two most populated manufacturing subgroups—type I and type IV firms. While type I firms are in the fuel, food, basic metals, and other resource-based industries (such as Petron, San Miguel, and Steel Asia), type IV firms are mostly electronics manufacturers (such as Toshiba, TI, and Epson).

TABLE 4.3 Size Distribution of the Top 1,000 Companies, Philippines, 2021

	Sales	
Lower Bound (PHP Billions)	*Upper Bound (PHP Billions)*	*Number of Companies*
2.25	16.75	816
16.75	31.24	91
31.24	45.73	36
45.73	60.22	17
60.22	74.71	7
74.71	89.21	9
89.21	103.70	4
103.70	118.19	6
118.19	132.68	3
132.68	147.17	3
147.17	161.66	1
161.66	176.16	2
176.16	190.65	2
234.12	248.62	1
277.60	292.09	1
	Assets	
Lower Bound (PHP Billions)	*Upper Bound (PHP Billions)*	*Number of Companies*
0.18	173.47	960
173.47	346.76	19
346.76	520.06	8
520.06	693.35	1
693.35	866.64	2
866.64	1039.93	3
1039.93	1213.22	2
1906.38	2079.67	1
2079.67	2252.97	1
2426.26	2599.55	1
3292.71	3466	1

Source: Felipe, Mathew, et al. (2025a, Table 4).

It is also worth noting that the six largest Philippine companies are non-exporters: MERALCO, Petron, Shell, BDO Unibank, Philip Morris International, and Mercury Drug (highlighted in bold in Table 4.5). These companies, together, earned PHP 1.37 trillion in gross sales in 2021, equivalent to 8% of the largest 1,000 firms' total gross sales. The seventh largest firm is an exporter—Toshiba, an electronics manufacturer.

TABLE 4.4 Breakdown of the Top 1,000 Firms by Year, Sector, Exporting, and Multinational Status, Philippines, 2021

	Agriculture (n = 9)		*Mining (n = 18)*	
	Non-Exporter	*Exporter*	*Non-Exporter*	*Exporter*
DOM	2	2	4	12
MNC	1	4	1	1
	Manufacturing (n = 309)		*Services (n = 663)*	
	Non-Exporter (183)	*Exporter (126)*	*Non-Exporter (626)*	*Exporter (37)*
DOM (129; 478)	110	19	476	2
MNC (180; 185)	73	107	150	35

Note: DOM = domestic companies; MNC = multinational corporations.

Source: Felipe, Mathew, et al. (2025a, Table 5).

TABLE 4.5 Largest Firms by Subgroup Based on Gross Sales, Philippines, 2021

	Manufacturing		*Services*	
	Non-Exporter	*Exporter*	*Non-Exporter*	*Exporter*
Local	Type I • **Petron** • San Miguel Brewery • San Miguel Foods • Zenith Foods • Steel Asia Manufacturing	Type II • Universal Robina • SFA Semiconductors • Integrated Micro-electronics • Monde Nissin	Type V • **MERALCO** • **BDO Unibank** • **Mercury Drugs** • Philippine Airlines • Puregold Price Club	Type VI • Acquire Asia Pacific • Seven Seven Global Services
MNC	Type III • **Pilipinas Shell** • **PMFTC** • Nestle • Coca-Cola • JT Intl.	Type IV • Toshiba • TI Phils. • PASAR • Epson • House Technologies Industries Inc.	Type VII • Chevron • SunLife • Philippine Seven Corp. • AXA Life • Pru Life UK	Type VIII • Sitel Phils. • Sykes Asia • RMS Collect • Cognizant Technology Solutions • IBM Business Services

Note: MNC = multinational corporation.

Source: Felipe, Mathew, et al. (2025a, Table 6).

TABLE 4.6 Largest Firms by Subgroup Based on Assets, Philippines, 2021

	Manufacturing		*Services*	
	Non-Exporter	*Exporter*	*Non-Exporter*	*Exporter*
Local	Type I • Petron • San Miguel Brewery • Monde Nissin • JG Summit Olefins • San Miguel Foods	Type II • Universal Robina • Integrated Micro-electronics • Universal Harvester Inc. • Philbest Canning Corp. • SFA Semicon	Type V • **BDO Unibank** • **Landbank** • **Metrobank** • **BPI** • **PNB**	Type VI • Acquire Asia Pacific • Seven Seven Global Services
MNC	Type III • Pilipinas Shell • Coca-Cola • PMFTC • JT Intl. • Nestle Phils.	Type IV • TI Phils. • PASAR • Taganito HPAL Nickel Corp. • Toshiba • Epson	Type VII • SunLife • AIA • Hongkong and Shanghai Banking Corp. • AXA • Pru Life	Type VIII • SPI Technologies • Sitel • Qualfon • Cognizant • TPPH

Note: MNC = multinational corporation.

Source: Felipe, Mathew, et al. (2025a, Table 7).

Table 4.6 provides information on firms classified by assets. The largest are all type V, finance companies.

The dominance of services and non-exporting firms extends to the conglomerates. The authors applied uniform criteria in linking individual firms in the data to conglomerates: (1) They must be reported in a conglomerate's financial statements, annual reports, or conglomerate "maps," and (2) the conglomerate must own more than 30% of the firm directly, or indirectly, through another subsidiary. Table 4.7 shows the share of manufacturing in the total annual sales of the conglomerates that had two or more firms that belonged to the top 1,000 (the remaining share is that of services). The authors identified five conglomerates—San Miguel, GT Capital, Monde Nissin, NutriAsia, and Century Pacific—with a significant percentage of sales coming from manufacturing.

Additionally, the authors found that most of the local conglomerates' subsidiaries are type V firms, as shown in Table 4.6. In particular, 66 of the 83 firms that they were able to link to the local conglomerates belong to this subgroup. This means that most of the conglomerates are into services and barely engage in any exporting activities. Notable type V firms, for example, include local banks, such as BDO Unibank of the Ayala Group; wholesale and retail firms like SM Investments; and real estate companies like Ayala Land and Vista Residences.

TABLE 4.7 Sectoral Structure of Philippine Conglomerates, 2021

Conglomerate	*No. of Firms in Top 1,000*	*Share of Manufacturing in Total Sales (%)*
Century Pacific Food	**2**	**100**
Monde Nissin Corp.	**2**	**100**
San Miguel Group	**22**	**67.44**
NutriAsia Inc.	**2**	**55.69**
GT Capital Inc.	**10**	**53.66**
LT Group	5	46.83
JG Summit	8	40.05
REBISCO	2	37.66
Aboitiz Equity Ventures	15	34.81
Alliance Global Inc.	7	17.9
Jollibee Foods	3	12.76
Lopez Group	10	9.44
Ayala Group	8	4.2
SM Investments	12	1.26
COSCO Capital	2	0
Filinvest Development Corp	7	0
Udenna Corp.	2	0
Villar Group	5	0

Source: Felipe, Mathew, et al. (2025a, Table 8).

Felipe, Mathew, et al. (2025a) tested if sales, assets, and profit rates are statistically different across different groups of firms (manufacturing and services, local and multinational, exporter and non-exporter). Results are shown in Table 4.8. Their results indicate that (1) the largest companies in the Philippines in terms of sales are multinational firms engaged in manufacturing but are non-exporters. The smallest are multinational firms, service-oriented, and exporters. (2) The largest companies in the Philippines in terms of assets are domestic, service-oriented, and non-exporters. And (3) the most profitable companies in the Philippines are domestic, service-oriented, and non-exporters. Multinational companies engaged in manufacturing and are exporters obtain the smallest profit rates.

For reference, firms in the combination "manufacturing-domestic-non-exporter" obtain PHP 12.70 billion in sales, a 4.40% profit rate, and PHP 13.10 billion in assets. The columns in Table 4.8 show the estimated value of sales, profit rate, and assets for each group of company, while Table 4.9 shows the most profitable companies in 2021.

To complement the analysis, Felipe, Mathew, et al. (2025a) further analyzed profit rates by subsector. Real estate is the most profitable subsector, with an average profit rate of 26.22%. This is followed by electricity and water supply, which has an average profit rate of 17.43%. Firms belonging to the real estate and utilities sectors are type V. Wholesale and retail trade firms are less profitable than manufacturing, with average profit rates of 1.68%. The rest of the services subsectors' average profit rates are not statistically different from those of manufacturing, the reference sector, at 4.62%.

TABLE 4.8 Estimation Results: Sales, Profit Rates, and Assets by Type of Company, Philippines, 2021

Manufacturing Domestic Non-Exporter			
	(1)	*(2)*	*(3)*
Subgroup	*Estimated Sales in PHP Billions*	*Estimated Profit Rate (%)*	*Estimated Assets in PHP Billions*
MFG, multinational, non-exporter	19.14***	5.47***	12.26
	(1.48)	(1.41)	(10.4)
MFG, domestic, exporter	10.85***	5.60***	11.23
	(2.93)	(2.76)	(20.64)
MFG, MNC, exporter	13.57***	3.01**	10.58
	(1.22)	(1.15)	(8.61)
SERV, domestic, non-exporter	12.69***	8.46***	64.60***
	(0.56)	(5.54)	(3.96)
SERV, multinational, non-exporter	9.73***	4.01***	21.31***
	(1.09)	(1.06)	(7.72)
SERV, domestic, exporter	3.52	4.34	1.95
	(8.72)	(8.23)	(61.49)
SERV, MNC, exporter	6.77***	8.03***	4.84
	(1.67)	(1.57)	(11.75)
Observations	3,892	3,691	3,892
R-squared	0.010	0.009	0.02

Notes:

(1) MFG = manufacturing; SERV = services; MNC = multinational corporation.

(2) Standard errors in parentheses: *** $p < 0.01$, ** $p < 0.05$, * $p < 0.1$.

(3) Agriculture and mining firms were excluded from these regressions. The reference sector is manufacturing. For the profit rate regressions, firms with profit rates higher than the average profit rate plus two standard deviations were excluded.

Source: Felipe, Mathew, et al. (2025a, Table 9).

TABLE 4.9 Most Profitable Companies, Philippines, 2021

Company	*Sector*	*Profit Rate (%)*
Megaworld Corp.	Real estate	68.99
AREIT Inc.	Financial and insurance activities	68.77
Therma Power Inc.	Financial and insurance activities	66.71
SM Investments Corp.	Financial and insurance activities	65.12
SMC Global Power Holdings Inc.	Financial and insurance activities	64.97
Philip Morris Manufacturing Inc.	Manufacturing	63.52
Double Dragon Corp.	Real estate	62.71
Filinvest Land Inc.	Real estate	61.57
All First Equity Holdings Inc.	Financial and insurance activities	61.36
Aboitiz Power Inc.	Financial and insurance activities	61.15

Note: Profit rates are calculated as profit divided by gross sales. Firms with profit rates higher than the average profit rate plus two standard deviations were excluded.

Source: Felipe, Mathew, et al. (2025a, Table 10).

4.3.3.2 Inside the Manufacturing Sector

Felipe, Mathew, et al. (2025a) also constructed a database for 13 manufacturing subsectors for 2000–2022. The dataset covers subsector output, value added, wages, employment, wage rates, and labor productivity as the main indicators.[11]

The largest manufacturing subsectors in the Philippines are food and electronics. These are observed for gross output, employment, and gross exports (Figures 4.18 to 4.20). Food and electronics make up 60% of all manufacturing output and 50% of total employment in manufacturing. Out of total gross exports

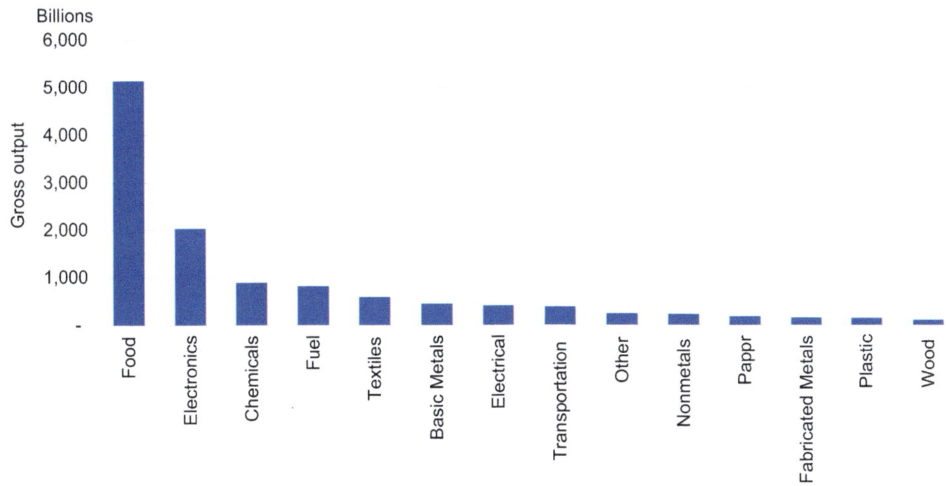

FIGURE 4.18 Gross Output by Manufacturing Subsector (PHP), Philippines, 2019

Source: Felipe, Mathew and Sevilla (2025a, Figure 2)

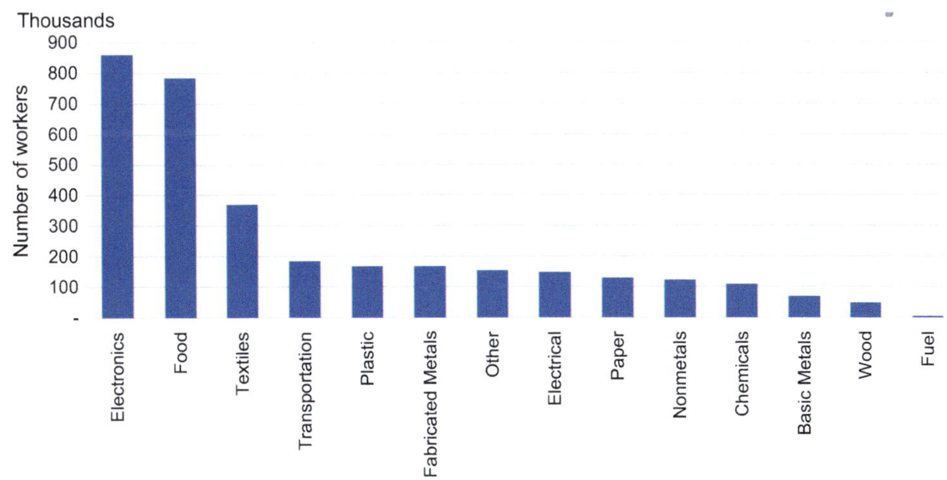

FIGURE 4.19 Employment by Manufacturing Subsector, Philippines, 2021

Source: Felipe, Mathew and Sevilla (2025a, Figure 3)

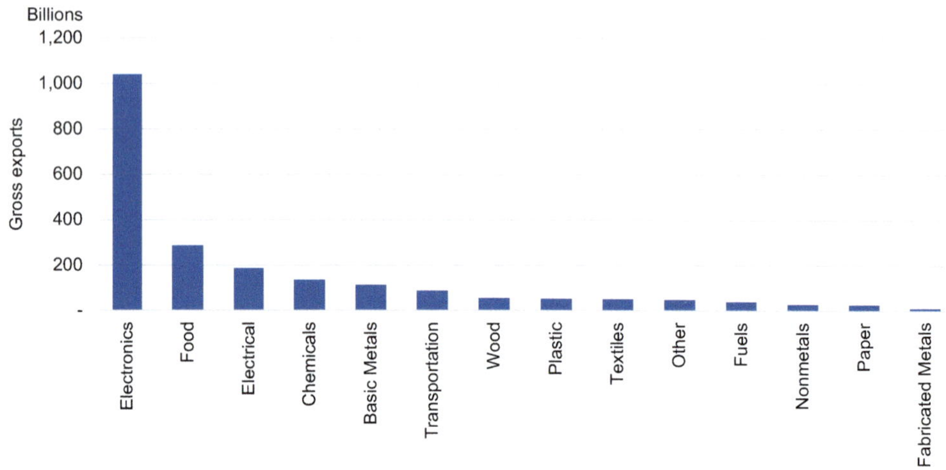

FIGURE 4.20 Gross Exports by Manufacturing Subsector (PHP), Philippines, 2019

Source: Felipe, Mathew and Sevilla (2025a, Figure 4)

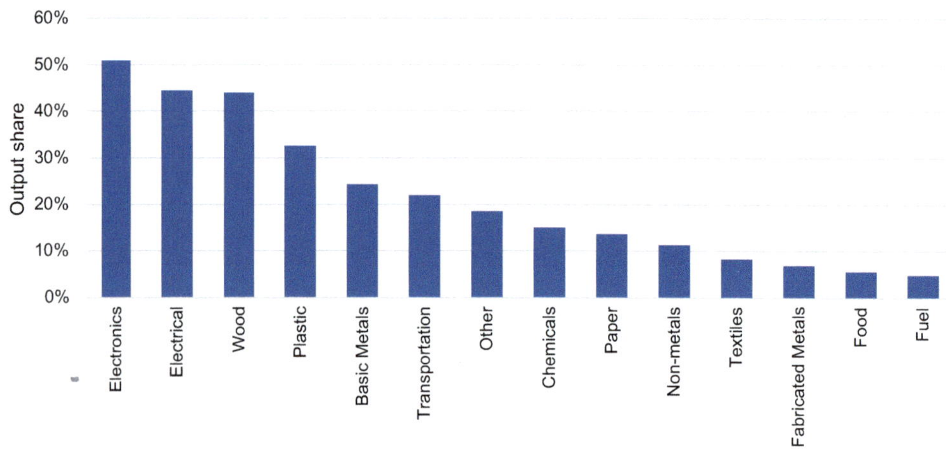

FIGURE 4.21 Share of Gross Exports in Total Output by Manufacturing Subsector (%), 2019

Source: Authors' calculations based on the Organisation for Economic Cooperation and Development Trade-in-Value Added Database (https://data-explorer.oecd.org/?pg=0&bp=true&tm=%22%28TIVA%29%202025%20edition%22&snb=5)

in manufacturing, 48% is from the electronics subsector, and 60% is from electronics and food combined.

Figure 4.21 shows that out of the total output, the share of gross exports is highest in electronics (50%) and is very low in food (6%).

Out of the largest 309 manufacturing firms in the Philippines, the largest proportion is that of food (89 firms, almost 30%), followed by electronics (62 firms; Figure 4.22).

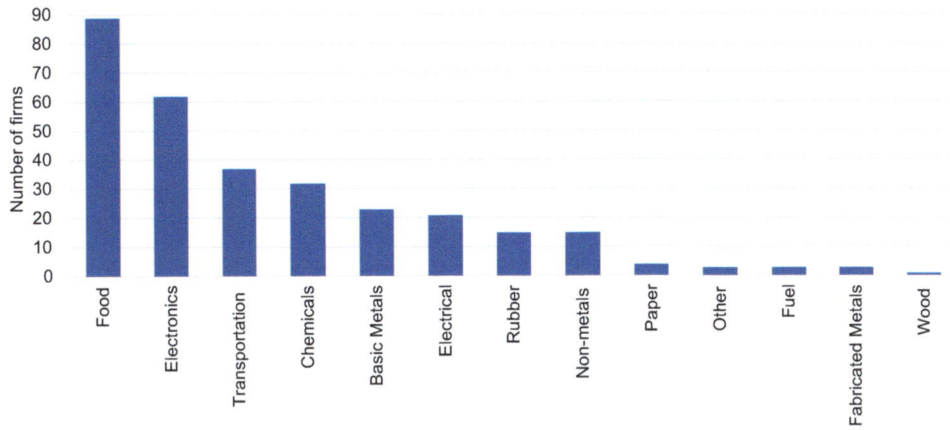

FIGURE 4.22 Number of Firms by Manufacturing Subsector, Top 309 Manufacturing Firms In The Philippines, 2021

Source: Felipe, Mathew and Sevilla (2025a, Figure 5)

TABLE 4.10 Number of Manufacturing Firms by Subgroup, Philippines, 2021

	Manufacturing (n = 309)		
	Non-Exporter (183)	Exporter (126)	Total
Domestic	110	19	129
Multinational	73	107	180
Total	183	126	309

Source: Felipe, Mathew, et al. (2025a, Table 12).

An important consideration is whether Philippine manufacturing firms can compete in global markets. According to Felipe, Mathew, et al. (2025a), only 126 of the 309 top manufacturing firms export. Of the 126, 107 are multinational firms. As shown in Table 4.10, only 19 of the firms that export are domestic. Multinational firms make up 85% of the firms that export. They discuss that most exporters are multinational firms in electronics.

In addition to this, the foreign content of gross exports in electronics is about 40% (Figure 4.23).

These authors also reported that only one product makes up 31.68% of total manufacturing exports, monolithic integrated circuits, and 8 of the 10 firms (PSIC 26200: *Manufacture of computers and peripheral equipment and accessories*) that export this product are multinational companies.[12]

The export basket of the Philippines (Figure 4.24) has also changed significantly since the 1960s, when it was not different from those of Korea and

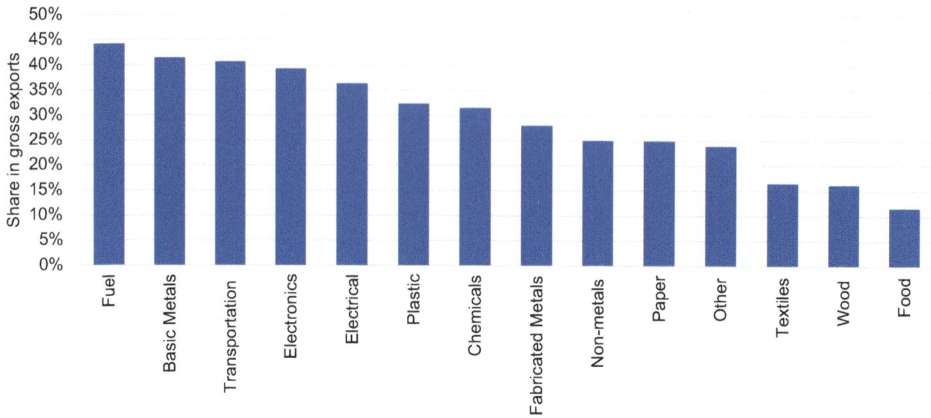

FIGURE 4.23 Share of Foreign Content in Gross Exports by Manufacturing Subsector (%), Philippines, 2019

Source: Felipe, Mathew and Sevilla (2025a, Figure 6)

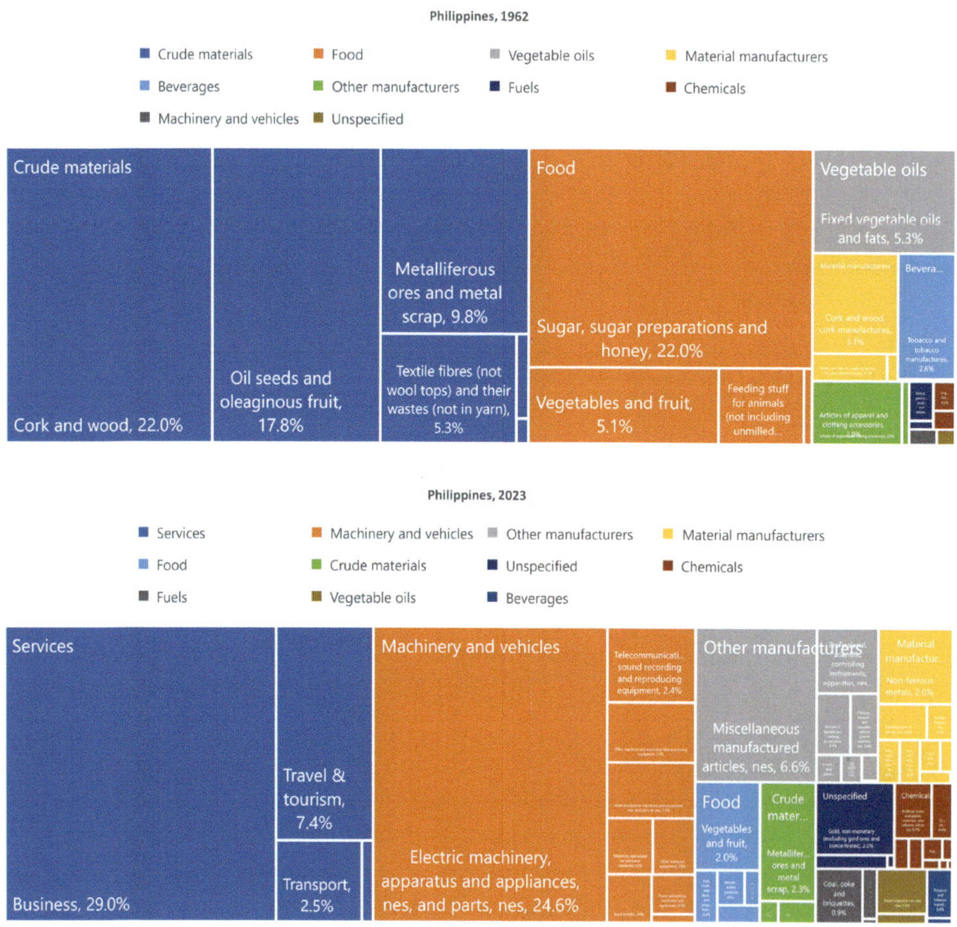

FIGURE 4.24 Export Structure, Philippines, 1962 and 2023

Source: Growth Lab at Harvard University, The Atlas of Economic Complexity (https://atlas.cid.harvard.edu). Last accessed 5th June, 2025

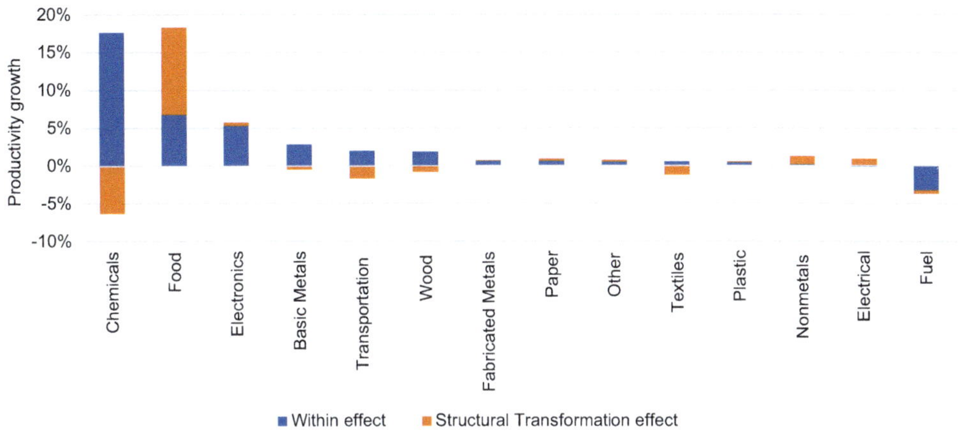

FIGURE 4.25 Decomposition of Manufacturing Productivity Growth by Subsector (%), Philippines, 2010–2023

Source: Authors' calculations based on data from the Philippine Statistics Authority (https://openstat.psa.gov.ph/Database/Economic-Accounts/National-Accounts-of-the-Philippines/Annual-National-Accounts), the United Nations Industrial Development Organization (https://stat.unido.org/data/table?dataset=indstat) and the DLSU ANIMO econometric model database

Taiwan (Figure 4.2). However, during the last six decades, it has not reached the complexity level of South Korea and Taiwan.

Overall productivity growth in the manufacturing sector during 2010–2022 amounted to 36%. Figure 4.25 shows the decomposition into the within and structural transformation effects (parallel to the decomposition of overall productivity growth in Figure 4.12).[13] A significant portion of the sector's overall productivity growth came from only three sectors: chemicals, food, and electronics. The chemical sector registered significant within productivity growth. However, it registered a negative structural transformation effect, indicating that labor shifted away (the sector's employment share declined during this period). In the case of food, the majority of its contribution to manufacturing productivity growth is from the structural transformation effect. Electronics' contribution to productivity growth is almost entirely from the within-sector effect. The contribution of other manufacturing subsectors to manufacturing sector productivity growth is quite limited and close to zero in some cases. In several low-productivity sectors, the structural transformation effect contributed minimally or, in some cases, worsened the net contribution to manufacturing productivity growth.

4.3.3.3 Do Exports Matter?

Felipe, Mathew, et al. (2025b) used a firm-level panel dataset from 2014 to 2020 to examine whether exporting and export diversification contribute to firm-level growth in the Philippine manufacturing sector. Contrary to conventional expectations, they found no significant evidence that exporting, per se, leads to improved firm performance (measured as growth in sales, employment, or labor productivity). Firms that export do not, on average, grow faster than their non-exporting counterparts, suggesting that the benefits of trade may be conditional on the nature and complexity of the export activity. This suggests that many Philippine exporters may not be integrated into sufficiently high-value segments of the global value chain to realize growth benefits. In contrast, they find that export diversification—defined as the introduction of new products into a firm's export basket—has a positive and significant effect on both sales and employment growth, even though these benefits do not extend to labor productivity. These findings highlight the importance of not only participating in trade but also upgrading and diversification as key mechanisms through which trade contributes to firm growth.

4.3.3.4 *Global Value Chains*

Finally, Felipe, Foster-McGregor, et al. (2025) documented that the Philippines is not as well integrated into global value chains (GVCs) as some of its East Asian neighbors. These authors documented the following facts about Philippine integration into GVCs, input complexity, and patenting and Fourth Industrial Revolution (4IR) technologies:

1. An acceptable level of backward integration given its income per capita, but a relatively low level of forward integration.[14]
2. Between 2007 and 2019, backward GVC integration increased, but forward GVC integration declined. This suggests a movement toward more final assembly-type activities.
3. Foreign input complexity in electricals increased between 2007 and 2009. This suggests an improvement in capabilities and the complexity of electrical production, with a movement toward the production of more sophisticated products requiring more sophisticated inputs. The complexity of Philippine domestic inputs has also increased in electricals. And overall, the final output complexity of electricals increased.
4. Textiles experienced an increase in final output complexity alongside a decline in foreign input complexity.
5. Positive revealed technology advantage in 4IR technologies in 2007, maintained in 2019. The Philippines also had a positive revealed technology advantage in imports of 4IR in both years.[15]

Summing up, all these suggest that Philippine firms are not like the firms we find in advanced nations—in terms of size, products, organizational capabilities, and supply chains. The sector that drives productivity in a nation is industry, particularly *manufacturing*. This is also true in the Philippines. Yet overall Philippine productivity is low because the manufacturing sector is small and has gotten smaller in terms of employment share.

4.4 A Recap: What the Philippine Economy Has Missed

This chapter has argued that a fundamental reason that the Philippine economy finds itself in its current state, with a per capita income of USD 4,400 and still lagging behind its neighbors, is its failure to undergo structural transformation, in particular industrialization. We have described the structure of the Philippine economy in depth, analyzed sectoral productivity, employment shares, occupations, wages, the manufacturing subsectors, and firm-level characteristics. This comprehensive analysis points to an economic structure that is significantly different from that of advanced nations. Unlike our East Asian neighbors, which are manufacturing-driven economies, the Philippine economy's largest employers are agriculture and low-productivity services. The economy's current productivity level and its economic structure are simply not allowing it to keep pace with its more advanced neighbors. In Chapter 3, we discussed the three main drivers of growth, and we summarize this chapter by discussing each point, drawing from earlier discussions.

The first one is the shift of workers out of agriculture. As we showed earlier, the share of employment in agriculture has declined from 37% to 23% over the last two decades. Although the intrasectoral productivity growth of the sector has been positive, this has been compensated for by a negative reallocation effect (the latter is normal at this stage of development). The result is that agriculture does not contribute to the overall productivity growth. Although the economy's total workforce grew from 27 to 48 million from 2000 to 2023, the number of workers in agriculture remained quite stable (roughly 10 million workers), and it is still the sector with the largest share. That both the share of agriculture in total output and the contribution of agriculture to output growth have been decreasing renders the shifting of workers out of agriculture even more imperative. Meanwhile, over the last two decades, the largest increases in the number of workers and their employment shares have occurred in these sectors: wholesale and retail trade, construction, and transport and storage. The result is that the majority of Filipino workers are employed in sectors of low productivity. These are sectors that pay the lowest wage rates. Moreover, while the Philippine labor force has, in general, become more educated, with better completion rates in both secondary and higher education, the vast majority of the workers are employed in occupations in sectors that pay very low wages. All this translates into a low per capita income.

The second driver is the manufacturing sector, which, as mentioned earlier, is the main engine of growth. Since the year 2000, the number of workers in manufacturing has increased by roughly 800,000, yet the share of employment in this sector in total employment—which is what matters more—actually decreased from 10% to 7%. In addition, college diploma holders are concentrated in other high-productivity sectors, such as finance and insurance and information and communication, and not in manufacturing. While countries such as South Korea and Taiwan were able to strengthen their manufacturing sectors through strategic industrial policies and clear government support, the

Philippines has struggled to implement similar measures. Despite the products that Philippine firms produce and export and the characteristics of the country's firms, the manufacturing sector continues to play a significant role in the country's total real output and output growth. Our earlier discussion also highlights the importance of understanding the manufacturing sector. The largest manufacturing subsector is food. The foreign content of exports of other key subsectors is also very high, for example, 40% in electronics and 30% in chemicals. Yet efforts by the government to improve manufacturing do not seem well defined. Relying on reforms such as Executive Order No. 18 (2023) on green lanes makes us doubt whether the government really understands (1) that we need to take industrialization seriously if we want to see real and sustainable changes in the economy and (2) that the kind of industrialization needed by the economy requires policies that are more focused and strategic than EO18 or initiatives like *Tatak Pinoy*. Chapters 7 and 8 discuss in detail the current initiatives of the administration and what a modern industrial policy entails.

The third driver of growth concerns what we produce and export. As we discussed earlier, most of the largest manufacturing firms are in the food and beverages and electronics sectors, and a large portion of Philippine electronics exports is sourced globally. This means that we are relying on assembly and packaging, both low-value-added activities. Philippine-made products simply lack global competitiveness; this emphasizes the importance of understanding the balance of payments–constrained growth rate discussed in Chapter 3. Unlike neighboring economies that have built competitive, export-oriented industries, the Philippines has remained dependent on imports rather than developing high-value sectors. Furthermore, findings show, as discussed earlier, that Philippine firms that export do not seem to perform better than non-exporters, highlighting the need to diversify their portfolio of products and to improve their product offerings. In addition, most Philippine firms are small in size and lack the capital needed to increase the competitiveness of their products. Philippine firms also lack organizational capabilities. And it just so happens that the firms that might have the capacity to develop globally competitive goods, the conglomerates, are into non-tradable services.

Without addressing these factors, the aggregate productivity level and the structure of the economy will not improve in such a way that we will see a generalized increase in wages and, consequently, income per capita. Perhaps it is high time for the government to seriously reconsider industrialization and focus on supporting firms in developing their organizational capabilities.

Notes

1 For reference: In the 18th century, agriculture was the largest employer of the economy across the world, although in the Netherlands (the leading country at that time), employment in industry and services already represented 33% and 27%, respectively, of total employment in the year 1700. In the United Kingdom (also in 1700), the share

of employment in services was significantly larger than that in industry, 25% versus 15% (Maddison, 1982). By 1890, the service sector was already the largest employer in the Netherlands and in the United Kingdom, with 36% and 40%, respectively, of total employment. In the United States, this sector employed 34% of total employment, ahead of industry's 27% share. In Japan, however, agriculture employed 72.6% of total employment in 1880. The corresponding percentage in 1870 in the United Kingdom was 22.7%. The Industrial Revolution brought the rise of industry and services. In the United Kingdom, between 1820 and 1890, employment in agriculture declined from 40% of total employment to 16% (a decline of about 3.45 percentage points per decade).

2 For an introduction to the concept of complexity, see Hausmann et al. (2014). Harvard's *The Atlas of Economic Complexity* (https://atlas.hks.harvard.edu/countries/608/export-complexity) provides complexity indices at the country and product levels.

3 We have data for 16 sectors of the economy. The key variables are value added, employment, and wages. We reconciled the data provided by the Philippine Statistics Authority, based on the Labor Force Surveys, and the International Labour Organization, and missing values were interpolated. Details on the construction of the wage series are provided in Aragones et al. (2024). This database is primarily used for the DLSU ANIMO econometric model, described in Appendix 5.

4 A description of the sectors and examples on the activities included in the sectors are in Appendix 4, Table A4.1.

5 When we disaggregate the data further, to the 2-digit Philippine Standard Industrial Classification (PSIC) level, close to 50% are in (1) crop and animal production, hunting, and related service activities; (2) retail trade, except of motor vehicles and motorcycles, and (3) construction of buildings. See Table A4.2 in Appendix 4.

6 To decompose productivity growth between periods $t - n$ and t, we calculate the within and the structural transformation effects as follows: $\hat{y}_t = \sum_i \frac{\left(y_t^i - y_{t-n}^i\right)}{y_{t-n}} q_{t-n}^i + \sum_i \frac{\left(q_t^i - q_{t-n}^i\right)}{y_{t-n}} y_t^i$, where y^i is productivity and q^i is the employment share of each sector i. The first term, $\sum \frac{\left(y_t^i - y_{t-n}^i\right)}{y_{t-n}} q_{t-n}^i$, is the within effect, and the second term, $\sum \frac{\left(q_t^i - q_{t-n}^i\right)}{y_{t-n}} y_t^i$, captures the structural transformation effect. The sum of the bars in Figure 4.12 is not exactly 41% due to rounding.

7 This follows the Philippine Standard Occupational Classifications (PSOC), which the Philippine Statistical Authority uses. This is based on the International Standard Classification of Occupations (ISCO), which provides a classification of skill levels based on educational requirements and tasks. The codes are described in Table A4.3 in Appendix 4.

8 We pool the 2001–2023 rounds of the Labor Force Survey published by the Philippine Statistics Authority into a time series, harmonizing categories of educational attainment, occupation, and sector, and we observe workers by educational attainment and by occupation.

9 We use the October Labor Force Surveys for 2010 to 2022 and the April Labor Force Survey for 2023.

10 *Gross output* (intermediate expenses plus value added) is the aggregate counterpart of gross sales. The authors use the gross output figure for the Philippine economy from the Asian Development Bank's (ADB) Input-Output Database. They could not obtain firms' value added to compare with GDP.

11 See Felipe, Mathew, et al. (2025a) for a description of how the dataset was constructed and the main sources.

12 The manufacturing process of monolithic integrated circuits is more complex than that of assembly.

13 The bars do not add up exactly to 36% due to rounding errors.

14 Backward integration: the share of value added supplied to a sector from foreign sources as an indicator of GVC integration. Higher values of this indicator imply that final demand in a country-sector contains a relatively large share of value added from third economies, suggesting that this country-sector is engaged in activities such as assembly within GVCs, which require inputs from other countries. Forward integration: This indicator captures the extent to which a country-sector is engaged in GVCs as a supplier of intermediate goods, raw materials, and service inputs to third economies, with higher values of this indicator indicating that the country-sector is intensive in activities that serve other economies' final production activities.

15 The Revealed Technology Advantage index shows whether an economy is a more intensive producer of Fourth Industrial Revolution (4IR) patents (relative to total patenting) than the world as a whole. This index does not take into account the absolute number of patents but only involves a comparison of 4IR patenting with overall patenting in the country. An economy may have a high intensity of 4IR patenting despite having a small number of 4IR patents, with these patents accounting for a relatively high share of overall patents.

APPENDIX 4

Sectors and Definitions

In what follows, we further disaggregate the sectors into subsectors and subgroups for a clearer idea of the activities covered by each sector. We include examples of activities to help us understand the sectors better. For brevity, some subsector or activity names may not be complete. Descriptions, activities, and sector names are taken directly from the 2009 Philippine Standard Industrial Classification.

TABLE A4.1 Sectors and Corresponding 2-Digit and 6-Digit Industrial Classifications

Sector and Brief Description	*Subsectors Based on 2-Digit PSIC Codes*	*Examples of Activities Roughly based on 6-digit PSIC*
Agriculture *(Agriculture, forestry, and fishing)* Includes growing crops, breeding animals, harvesting plants and other products from farms or their natural habitats	Crop and animal production Hunting and related service activities Forestry and logging Fishing and aquaculture	Growing of specific fruits and vegetables Plant propagation Operation of irrigation systems Rental of farm machinery Growing of timer forest species Culture of freshwater crustaceans Pearl culture
Construction Includes general and specialized construction activities for buildings and civil engineering works; construction of entire dwellings, office buildings, farm dwellings, or civil engineering works, such as motorways, bridges, industrial facilities, etc.	Construction of buildings Civil engineering Specialized construction activities	Assembly and erection of prefabricated construction on the site Construction of railways and subways Dredging of waterways Demolition and site preparation Electrical installation Building completion and finishing

(Continued)

TABLE A4.1 (Continued)

Sector and Brief Description	*Subsectors Based on 2-Digit PSIC Codes*	*Examples of Activities Roughly based on 6-digit PSIC*
Utilities *(Electricity, gas, steam, and air conditioning supply; water supply; sewerage, waste management, and remediation activities)* Includes the activity of providing electric power, natural gas, steam, hot water, and the like through a permanent infrastructure of lines, mains, and pipes; also includes the operation of electric and gas utilities	Electricity, gas, stem, and air conditioning supply Water collection, treatment, and supply Sewerage Waste collection, treatment, and disposal activities Materials recovery Remediation activities and other waste management activities	Operation of generation facilities Sale of electricity to users Manufacture of gaseous fuels Collection of rainwater Operation of irrigation canals Operation of sewer systems or treatment facilities Cleaning up of oil spills and other pollutions on land
Mining and quarrying Includes the extraction of minerals, liquids, or gases, supplementary activities for preparing crude materials for further processing	Mining of coal and lignite Extraction of crude petroleum and natural gas Mining of metal ores Other mining and quarrying Mining support service activities	Mining of hard coal Process to obtain crude oil Production of natural gas Mining of gold ores, silver ores, copper ores Marble quarrying Limestone quarrying Extraction of salt Directional drilling for oil and gas extraction Exploration services
Manufacturing Includes the physical or chemical transformation of materials or other inputs into new products; raw materials products from agriculture or mining and quarrying, or other manufacturing	Manufacture of food products Manufacture of beverages Manufacture of tobacco products Manufacture of textiles Manufacture of wearing apparel Manufacture of leather and related products Manufacture of wood and products of wood, bamboo, rattan, cane Manufacture of paper and paper products Printing and reproduction of recorded media Manufacture of coke and refined petroleum Manufacture of chemicals and chemical products Manufacture of basic pharmaceutical products	roduction of fresh, chilled, or frozen meat or poultry Production of fermented fish, fish paste, or fish balls Manufacture of crude vegetable oils Coffee roasting or processing Manufacture of chewing and smoking tobacco Preparation and spinning of textile fibers Manufacture of carpets and rugs Manufacture of felt, net fabrics, canvas Manufacture of other clothing accessories Custom tailoring Manufacture of luggage, shoes Sawmilling and planing of wood Manufacture of other builders' carpentry and joinery Manufacture of newsprint

(Continued)

TABLE A4.1 (Continued)

Sector and Brief Description	*Subsectors Based on 2-Digit PSIC Codes*	*Examples of Activities Roughly based on 6-digit PSIC*
	and preparations Manufacture of rubber and plastic products Manufacture of other non-metallic mineral products Manufacture of basic metals Manufacture of fabricated metal products Manufacture of computer, electronic products Manufacture of electrical equipment Manufacture of machinery and equipment Manufacture of motor vehicles and trailers Manufacture of other transport equipment Manufacture of furniture Manufacture of other manufacture Repair and installation of machinery and equipment	PBookbinding and related work Production of motor fuel Manufacture of dyes and pigments Manufacture of plastics and synthetic rubber Preparation of botanical products for pharmaceutical use Manufacture of artificial stone Manufacture of glass and glass products Manufacture of cement, lime, and plaster Operation of blast furnaces and steelmaking furnaces Manufacturing of steam generators Treatment and coating of metals Manufacture of printers, monitors, keyboards Manufacture of aircraft engine instruments Manufacture of electricity distribution and control apparatus Manufacture of electric lighting equipment Manufacture of ovens, furnaces, and furnace burners Manufacture of agricultural and forestry machinery Building of pleasure and sporting boats Manufacture of parts and accessories of bicycles Finishing such as upholstery of chairs and seats Manufacture of jewelry Manufacture of string instruments Manufacture of pens and pencils Installation of industrial machinery and equipment
Accommodation and food *(Accommodation and food service activities)* Includes the provision of short-stay and long-term accommodation; also includes the provision of complete meals and drinks fit for immediate consumption	Accommodation Food and beverage service activities	Hotels and motels, resort hotels, pension houses, camping sites Food and beverage service activities, such as restaurants, cafeterias, mobile food carts, bars, coffee shops Events catering

(Continued)

TABLE A4.1 (Continued)

Sector and Brief Description	*Subsectors Based on 2-Digit PSIC Codes*	*Examples of Activities Roughly based on 6-digit PSIC*
Education Includes education at any level or for any profession, oral or written, as well as by radio and television or other means of communication	Education	Public and private preschool, elementary, high school education Technical and vocational secondary education Public and private higher education Sports instruction Cultural education
Finance and insurance *(Financial and insurance activities)* Includes financial service activities, including insurance, reinsurance, and pension funding and activities to support financial services	Financial service activities Insurance, reinsurance, and pension funding Activities auxiliary to financial services	Central banking Expanded commercial banking, savings and mortgage banking, cooperative rural banking Trusts, funds, and other financial vehicles Pawnshop operations Administration of financial markets Risk and damage evaluation Fund management activities
Health and social work *(Human health and social work activities)* Includes the provision of health and social work activities	Human health activities Residential care activities Social work activities without accommodation	Hospital activities Medical and dental practice activities Ambulance transport of patients Assisted-living facilities Halfway group homes Welfare and guidance counselling Community and neighborhood activities Child day-care activities Welfare and guidance counseling
Information and communication Includes the production and distribution of information and cultural products, as well as data or communications and information technology activities	Publishing activities Motion picture, video, and television production Programming and broadcasting activities Telecommunications Computer programming, consultancy Information service activities	Publishing of books, periodicals, advertising materials, photos Publishing of ready-made software, such as operating systems, business applications, computer games Postproduction activities, such as editing, closed captioning, processing motion picture films

(Continued)

TABLE A4.1 (Continued)

Sector and Brief Description	*Subsectors Based on 2-Digit PSIC Codes*	*Examples of Activities Roughly based on 6-digit PSIC*
		Production of original (sound) master recording Publishing of music Radio broadcasting Provision of internet access by the operator Mobile telecommunication services Computer programming activities Computer consultancy and facilities management activities Specialized activities, such as web hosting, streaming services, data processing
Professional and business services *(Professional, scientific, and technical activities; administrative and support service activities)* Includes specialized professional, scientific, and technical activities	Legal and accounting activities Activities of head offices; management consultancy activities Architecture and engineering activities; technical testing and analysis Scientific research and development Advertising and market research Other professional, scientific, and technical activities Veterinary activities	General counselling and advising, preparation of legal documents Accounting, bookkeeping, and auditing Architectural consulting activities Land surveying services Research and experimental development Creation and realization of advertising campaigns Activities of graphic designers, interior decorators Digital photograph processing Translation and interpretation, weather forecasting, patent brokerage
Public administration *(Public administrative and defense; compulsory social security)* Includes activities of governmental nature	Public administration and defense, compulsory social security	Executive and legislative administration of central, regional, and local bodies Regulation of the activities of providing health care, education, cultural services, and other social services, excluding social security Foreign affairs Administration of defense-related R&D policies and related funds Compulsory social security activities

(Continued)

TABLE A4.1 (Continued)

Sector and Brief Description	*Subsectors Based on 2-Digit PSIC Codes*	*Examples of Activities Roughly based on 6-digit PSIC*
Real estate *(Real estate activities)* Includes acting as lessors, agents, and/or brokers in selling or buying real estate, renting real estate, and providing other related services	Real estate activities	Provision of homes and furnished or unfurnished apartments Development of building projects Renting or leasing services of residential properties
Transport and storage *(Transportation and storage)* Includes the provision of passenger or freight transport by rail, pipeline, road, water, or air and associated activities	Land transport and transport via pipelines Water transport Air transport Warehousing and support activities for transportation Postal and courier activities	Urban and suburban railway transport Transport via buses Operations of jeepneys, tricycles, freight trucks Interisland water passenger transport Operation of storage and warehouse facilities for all kinds of goods Operation of parking lots, toll roads, and bridges Cargo handling Distribution and delivery of mail and parcels Messenger service
Wholesale and retail trade *(Wholesale and retail trade; repair of motor vehicles and motorcycles)* Includes wholesale and retail sale of any type of goods and the rendering of services incidental to the sale of these goods	Wholesale and retail trade and repair of motor vehicles and motorcycles Wholesale trade Retail trade	Sale of off-road motor vehicles Car auctions Wholesale on a fee or contract basis Activities of commission agenda, brokers Retail selling in groceries, supermarkets, sari-sari stores Retail sale via internet Door-to-door retailing
Other services *(Arts, entertainment, and recreation; activities of private households as employers and undifferentiated goods and services and producing activities of households for own use; activities of extraterritorial organizations and bodies; other service activities)*	Rental and leasing activities Employment activities Travel agency, tour operator, reservation services, and related activities Service and investigation activities Services to buildings and landscape activities	Rental and leasing of motor vehicles, household, other personal goods such as furniture, electrical appliances Labor recruitment and provision of personnel Arranging and assembling tours Event tickets, entertainment, and recreational

(Continued)

TABLE A4.1 (Continued)

Sector and Brief Description	*Subsectors Based on 2-Digit PSIC Codes*	*Examples of Activities Roughly based on 6-digit PSIC*
Includes a variety of activities that support general business operations; activities to meet varied cultural, entertainment, and recreational interests of the general public; activities of membership organizations, repair of computers and personal and household goods; and other activities	Office administrative, office support, and other business support activities Creative, arts, and entertainment activities Libraries, archives, museums, and other cultural activities Gambling and betting activities Sports activities and amusement and recreation activities	Provision of support activities, such as general interior cleaning, maintenance, guard and security Photocopying, document preparation Call centers and other related activities Customer relationship management activities Production of live theatrical presentations Concerts and opera or dance production
	Activities of membership organizations Repairs of computers and personal and household goods Other personal service activities Activities of households as employers Activities of extraterritorial organizations and bodies	Botanical and zoological gardens and nature reserve activities Sale of lottery tickets Operation of sports facilities Activities of amusement parks and theme parks Activities of chambers of commerce, guilds, and similar organizations Activities of trade unions Repair and maintenance of computer terminals, like automatic teller machines Repair and servicing of household appliances Personal services for wellness Laundry services Coin-operated machines activities Activities of households as employers of domestic personnel Foreign diplomatic missions Activities of extraterritorial and international organizations

Note: In selecting activities to include, we choose a mix of both expected and unexpected ones to gain a better understanding of what a sector covers. These are by no means a complete representation of the components of each sector.

Source: National Statistical Coordination Board (2009).

TABLE A4.2 Highest Employment Shares (%) by Subsector Based on the 2-Digit Philippine Standard Industrial Classification, Philippines, 2023

Industry Division	*Share in Total Employment (%)*
Crop and animal production, hunting, and related service activities	21.61
Retail trade, except of motor vehicles and motorcycles	17.80
Construction of buildings	7.30
Public administration and defense; compulsory social security	6.82
Land transport and transport via pipelines	5.47
Other personal service activities	5.46
Fishing and aquaculture	3.86
Food and beverage service activities	3.58
Education	3.21
Office administrative, office support, and other business support activities	2.63

Note: These are the ten occupations with the largest employment shares, identified from 85 categories under the Philippine Standard Industrial Classification used in the Philippine Labor Force Surveys.

Source: Authors' calculations from the Philippine Statistics Authority's Labor Force Survey (https://psada.psa.gov.ph/catalog/LFS/about).

TABLE A4.3 1-Digit Philippine Standard Occupational Classifications (PSOC) and Skill Level Requirements Based on the International Standard Classification of Occupations (ISCO)

1-Digit PSOC	*Occupation*	*Task Description*	*Skill Level, Educational Requirement, and Specialization*	*Occupation Sub-Major Groups Based on 2-Digit PSOC Codes*
1	Managers and supervisors	Plan, direct, coordinate, and evaluate activities governments and enterprises or smaller units within. These include the formulation and review of policies and laws. Tasks include: • Planning and direct operations • Formulating and advising on policy, budgets, laws • Establishing objectives and standards • Formulating and evaluating programs • Managing material, human, and financial resources • Selecting and approving staff during hiring • Ensuring compliance with different requirements • Representing institutions, enterprises, and governments in meetings	ISCO skill level 4 (generally applicable for managers and professionals) • Highly complex, specialized tasks • Requires higher academic education • Requires extensive language, numeracy, communication skills, advanced comprehension, and being able to convey complex ideas • Solving complex problems, making decisions based on theoretical and practical knowledge • Research with the aim of increasing knowledge in a specific field, diagnostics and treatment of disease, design of structures, machines, construction projects, and production processes	• Chief executives, senior officials, and legislators • Administrative and commercial managers • Production and specialized services managers • Hospitality, retail, and other services managers
2	Professionals	Increase the stock of knowledge, apply scientific or artistic concepts and theories, and teach in a systematic manner.		• Science and engineering professionals • Health professionals • Teaching professionals

(*Continued*)

TABLE A4.3 (Continued)

1-Digit PSOC	*Occupation*	*Task Description*	*Skill Level, Educational Requirement, and Specialization*	*Occupation Sub-Major Groups Based on 2-Digit PSOC Codes*
		Tasks include: • Conducting analysis and research • Development of concepts, theories, methods, and application of existing knowledge across various fields • Teaching theory and practice at different education levels • Rendering business, legal, and social services • Creating and performing works of art • Supervision of other workers		• Business and administration professionals • Information and communication technology professionals • Legal, social, and cultural professionals
3	Technicians and associate professionals	Perform technical and tasks related to research and the application of scientific or artistic concepts and methods. Tasks include: • Undertaking technical work connected with research and the application of concepts and methods in fields of physical, life, and social sciences • Carrying out technical services related to trade, finance, and administration • Providing technical support for arts and entertainment • Supervision of other workers	ISCO skill level 3 • Complex tasks • Secondary, post-secondary, or higher education required • Excellent language and numeracy skills, well-developed communication skills • Includes operation of highly technical equipment, such as medical equipment, and computers • Requires factual, technical, and procedural area-specific knowledge, such as radiology, architecture, IT support	• Science and engineering associate professionals • Health associate professionals • Business and administration associate professionals • Legal, social, cultural, and related professionals • Information and communication technician

(*Continued*)

TABLE A4.3 (Continued)

1-Digit PSOC	*Occupation*	*Task Description*	*Skill Level, Educational Requirement, and Specialization*	*Occupation Sub-Major Groups Based on 2-Digit PSOC Codes*
4	Clerical and support	Record, organize, store, compute, and retrieve information, perform clerical duties in money-handling operations, travel arrangements, information requests, appointments. Tasks include: • Stenography, typing, operating word processors and office machines • Entering data into computers • Secretarial duties • Recording and computing numerical data • Keeping records on passenger and freight transport • Filing documents • Duties in libraries, mail services • Preparing and checking material for printing • Operating telephone switchboards	ISCO skill level 2 (Generally applicable for clerical and support; sales and service workers; skilled agriculture, forestry, and fishery workers; crafts and trades workers; plan machinery operators and assemblers) • Low to moderate complex tasks • Primary or general secondary education required; post-secondary and technical-vocational education may also be required • Requires language and numeracy skills, communication skills, and manual dexterity skills • Operating machines and devices, driving vehicles, maintenance and repair of electrical and mechanical equipment, processing and organizing and storying of data • Use of hand and hand-powered tools to reduce physical effort and time spent for tasks and improve product quality	• General and keyboard clerks • Customer service clerks • Numerical and material recording clerks • Other clerical support workers
5	Sales and service workers	Provide personal and protective services related to travel, housekeeping, catering, personal care, public safety; demonstrate and sell goods in wholesale or retail establishments, stalls, and markets.		• Personal service workers • Sales workers • Personal care workers • Protective services workers

(Continued)

TABLE A4.3 (Continued)

1-Digit PSOC	*Occupation*	*Task Description*	*Skill Level, Educational Requirement, and Specialization*	*Occupation Sub-Major Groups Based on 2-Digit PSOC Codes*
		Tasks include: • Organizing and providing services related to travel, housekeeping, food and beverage preparation and service, childcare, personal and basic health care • Providing security services and public safety • Posing as models for advertising, artistic creation, and display of goods • Selling of goods at wholesale or retail establishments, stalls, and markets, and demonstrating product usage	• Requires experience with and understanding of machinery used in various fields	
6	Skilled agriculture, forestry, and fishery workers	Grow and harvest field or tree and shrub crops; gather fruits and plants; breed, tend, or hunt animals and produce animal husbandry products; cultivate, conserve, and produce forestry products; breed or catch fish. Tasks include: • Preparing soil • Sowing, planting, spraying, fertilizing, harvesting crops		• Market-oriented skilled agricultural workers • Market-oriented skilled forestry, fishery, and hunting workers • Subsistence farmers, fishers, hunters, and gatherers

(Continued)

TABLE A4.3 (Continued)

1-Digit PSOC	*Occupation*	*Task Description*	*Skill Level, Educational Requirement, and Specialization*	*Occupation Sub-Major Groups Based on 2-Digit PSOC Codes*
		• Growing fruit, tree, and shrub crops • Growing garden vegetables and horticultural products • Gathering fruits and plants • Breeding, raising, tending, and hunting animals to obtain animal products (meat, milk, fur, etc.) • Cultivating, conserving, and logging forests • Breeding or catching fish and cultivating and gathering aquatic life • Storing and carrying out basic processing • Selling products		
7	Crafts and trades workers	Apply specific knowledge and skills for the construction and maintenance of buildings; form metal; erection of metal structures; set machine tools, make fit, maintain and repair machinery, equipment, or tools; carry out printing work; produce or process foodstuffs, textiles, or wooden, metal, and other equipment or tools, and handicrafts; use hand and hand-powered tools to reduce physical effort and time spent for tasks and improve product quality.		• Building and related trades workers, excluding electricians • Metal, machinery, and related trades workers • Handicraft and printing workers • Electrical and electronics trades workers • Food processing, woodworking, garment, and other craft and related trades workers

(Continued)

TABLE A4.3 (Continued)

1-Digit PSOC	*Occupation*	*Task Description*	*Skill Level, Educational Requirement, and Specialization*	*Occupation Sub-Major Groups Based on 2-Digit PSOC Codes*
		Tasks include: • Constructing, maintaining, and repairing buildings and other structures • Casting, welding, shaping metal • Installing, erecting heavy metal structures • Making machinery, tools, equipment, and other metal articles • Setting for operators and operating machine tools • Fitting, maintaining, and repairing industrial machinery, electrical and electronic instruments, engines, vehicles • Making precision instruments, jewelry, precious metal articles, pottery, glass • Printing • Producing and processing foodstuffs, and articles made of wood, textiles, leather, and handicrafts		

(*Continued*)

TABLE A4.3 (Continued)

1-Digit PSOC	*Occupation*	*Task Description*	*Skill Level, Educational Requirement, and Specialization*	*Occupation Sub-Major Groups Based on 2-Digit PSOC Codes*
8	Plant machinery operators and assemblers	Operate and monitor industrial and agricultural machinery and equipment; drive and operate trains, motor vehicles, and mobile machinery and equipment; assemble products. Tasks include: • Operating and monitoring mining and other industrial machinery and equipment for the processing and production of articles made from metals, minerals, glass, ceramics, wood, paper, chemicals, rubber, plastics, fur, leather • Driving and operating trains and motor vehicles • Operating and monitoring mobile, industrial, and agricultural machinery and equipment • Assembling products from component parts according to specifications and procedures		• Stationary plant and machine operators • Assemblers • Drivers and mobile plant operators
9	Elementary occupations	Simple routine tasks that may require the use of handheld tools and considerable physical effort. Tasks include: • Cleaning, sweeping in various locations	ISCO skill level 1 • Physical and manual routine work • Requires elementary or primary education level • Some basic reading and writing • Uses hand tools	• Cleaners and helpers • Agricultural, forestry, and fishery laborers • Laborers in mining, construction, manufacturing, and transport

(Continued)

TABLE A4.3 (Continued)

1-Digit PSOC	*Occupation*	*Task Description*	*Skill Level, Educational Requirement, and Specialization*	*Occupation Sub-Major Groups Based on 2-Digit PSOC Codes*
		• Restocking supplies and performing basic maintenance in apartments, houses, kitchens, hotels, offices, and other buildings • Washing cars, windows • Helping in kitchens and in simpler tasks in food preparation • Delivering messages and goods • Carrying luggage, handling baggage and freight • Collecting and sorting refuse • Performing simple tasks related to farming, fishing, hunting, trapping, mining, construction, manufacturing • Packing and unpacking • Pedaling and hand-guiding vehicles for transport of passengers and goods	• Includes cleaning, shoveling, manual lifting, assembling, operating non-motorized vehicles, picking fruits, helping in the kitchen	• Food preparation assistants • Street and related sales and service workers • Refuse workers and other elementary workers
10	Armed forces	Includes army, navy, air force, conscripts for military training, and auxiliary services. Tasks are similar to civilian occupations, depending on function—medical doctors, radio operators, cooks, secretaries, heavy equipment operators, and drivers.	May vary from ISCO skill level 1 to 4	• Commissioned armed forces officers • Non-commissioned armed forces officers • Armed forces occupations, other ranks

Note: Information on the skill level and educational requirements are from Statistics Netherlands (2023), based on the International Standard Classification of Occupations (ISCO) by the International Labour Organization.

Source: Philippine Statistics Authority (2022), International Labour Organization (n.d.).

5

PHILIPPINE DEVELOPMENT PLANS: DEVELOPMENT MISUNDERSTANDINGS

5.1 Introduction

The Philippine economy is in a difficult spot: It must pursue goals ambitious enough to catch up, yet these goals must be realistic and attainable. In this context, government planning is of particular importance, as development plans not only enumerate targets and discuss strategies but also reveal how policymakers understand long-term growth. The paradox of Philippine development planning is that it combines decades' worth of economic targets set too low to propel the country into high-income status, but also too high to be achieved consistently. Both hint at a sobering reality: Regardless of political affiliation, a long succession of presidential administrations has failed to grasp what it would take for a nation to develop. As a result, the country has bet on the same strategies again and again—strategies that have delivered the undoubted benefits of macroeconomic stability, a few growth spurts, steady poverty reduction, and the approval of global institutions . . . but, ultimately, just over USD 4,400 per capita income, along with a growing list of neighbors that have overtaken it.

Every president since independence has published a Philippine development plan (PDP), or a variant thereof. While government development plans are aspirational by definition, they can reveal much about the strategic thinking of governments as well as their seriousness and ability to deliver, by comparing what they are willing to commit publicly and what they remain silent about.

Ferdinand Romualdez Marcos Jr. won the Philippine presidential election in May 2022, and the PDP 2023–2028 (NEDA, 2023a) was published in early 2023. This 400-page document is a "plan for economic and social transformation." It discusses the priorities and programs of the government in areas such as human development, education, food security, incomes, agriculture, industry, trade, and

DOI: 10.4324/9781003728719-5

competition. It outlines the government's priorities, strategies, and programs for the economic and social transformation of the Philippine economy.

As explained in the preface of this book, the authors started a research program on the "future of the Philippine economy" in 2022. The PDP 2023–2028 document became a useful resource in shaping our discussions, and it guided some of the deliverables in our research program. The program focuses on the long-term prospects of the Philippine economy—in particular, what the next two and a half decades might hold. If the PDP 2023–2028 is intended as a stepping stone toward achieving *Ambisyon Natin 2040,* then it is important to evaluate the targets set for 2028. After all, an economy's short-run performance determines the trajectory of its long-run growth path.

In Chapter 3, we discussed the importance of potential growth, and in Chapter 4, we emphasized the critical role of structural transformation in achieving sustained growth, something the Philippine economy has failed to achieve. In this chapter, we turn first to PDP 2023–2028 (NEDA, 2023a) and the ambitions contained therein. Using the DLSU ANIMO econometric model, we present forecasts up to 2028—the end of President Marcos Jr.'s administration—and assess whether the PDP's 2023–2028 targets will be achieved. Our analysis indicates that most of the targets set under 7 of the 11 indicators will eventually be met, but not by 2028. This suggests that the economy will advance, but at a slower pace than anticipated. We find a similar pattern with respect to growth and poverty incidence targets in previous Philippine development plans (NEDA, 1982, 1988, 1993, 1996, 1999, 2004, 2017). This reflects recurring issues: that the potential growth of the economy is sorely misunderstood and that the necessary foundations for structural transformation have been neglected. Finally, a comparison of government development plans in the Philippines, Malaysia, and Vietnam reveals that the latter two demonstrate a clearer grasp of the drivers of long-term economic growth far more than the Philippine government has so far shown.

5.2 The Philippine Development Plan 2023–2028: Will Its Targets Be Met?

While *Ambisyon Natin 2040* (released in 2015) is a true vision statement (meant to be more of an inspirational declaration of the desired future for the country), the PDP 2023–2028 is filled with an overwhelming number of strategies, targets, and goals. Although it is understandable for government plans to be detailed, the sheer number of targets contained in the plan is questionable. Based on a rough count, the document contains over 350 targets (Table 5.1).

Perhaps it is not simply the number of targets identified but whether or not the administration fully understands what achieving each of the 350-plus targets entails—what mostly *human* resources may be needed to achieve each one, and the level of *coordination* needed across agencies. It is also likely that focusing on some targets may simply mean not meeting others. For example, the government has made fiscal consolidation a priority, yet meeting the deficit-to-GDP ratio

TABLE 5.1 Number of Targets in the Philippine Development Plan

Area	*Number of Targets*
Headline Indicators	11
Promote human and social development	>60
Reduce vulnerabilities and protect purchasing power	>40
Increase income-earning ability	>20
Modernize agriculture and business	>15
Revitalize industry	>20
Reinvigorate services	>10
Advance research and development, technology, and innovation	>10
Promote trade and investment	>7
Promote competition and improve regulatory efficiency	>20
Ensure macroeconomic stability and expand inclusive and innovative finance	>40
Expand and upgrade infrastructure	>25
Ensure peace and security and enhance administration of justice	>30
Practice good governance and improve bureaucratic efficiency	>30
Accelerate climate action and strengthen disaster resilience	>15
Total	**>350**

Note: Targets that did not specify a clear figure were not counted.

Source: Authors, based on the National Economic and Development Authority (2023a).

targets of below 3–4% may mean that, by limiting spending, other targets will not be met.[1] In our view, it would be more beneficial to identify a few targets—and the right ones, that is, targets that will eventually lead to sustained growth and the Philippine economy's development—and focus on them.

It is also not clear how the targets are determined. This applies, for example, to the growth targets. As discussed in Chapter 3, our estimates of the potential growth of the Philippine economy do not go above 6%, and this renders the (fundamental) growth target of up to 8% ineffective and maybe even counterproductive. In setting goals and targets, ambition is necessary, but understanding the reality of our economy is also an important part of the process.

The key outcomes of the plan are accompanied by a table of the annual targets for the 11 headline indicators, shown in Table 5.2. Each of the subsequent chapters then covers a designated area, lists the outcomes and strategies therein, and shows a results matrix. Each results matrix contains a list of indicators and targets per year from 2023 to 2028. In some cases, the targets are numerical and measurable; in other cases, an "increase" or "decrease" is stated. In some, they are left blank, intended to be updated at some point. The indicators listed in each of the results matrices state how the indicator will be tracked and measured and which agency is in charge. Understandably, such a document would be sizable and all-encompassing. Ensuring the transition of the country, with

TABLE 5.2 Philippine Development Plan 2023–2028 Targets for Headline Indicators

Indicator	*Annual Target*					
	2023	*2024*	*2025*	*2026*	*2027*	*2028*
GDP growth (%)	6.0–7.0	6.0–8.0	6.5–8.0	6.5–8.0	6.5–8.0	6.5–8.0
GNI per capita (USD)	4,130–4,203	4,454–4,592	4,814–4,920	5,256–5,563	5,645–6,056	6,044–6,571
Headline inflation rate (%)	2.5–4.5	2.0–4.0	2.0–4.0	2.0–4.0	2.0–4.0	2.0–4.0
Food inflation rate (%)	2.5–4.5	2.0–4.0	2.0–4.0	2.0–4.0	2.0–4.0	2.0–4.0
National government deficit-to-GDP ratio (%)	5	5.1	4.1	3.5	3.2	3.0
Outstanding national government debt stock-to-GDP ratio (in %)	60–62	57–61	56–59	54–58	50–55	48–53
Global Competitiveness Index rank (score and rank %)	Top 43	Top 41	Top 39	Top 37	Top 35	Top 33
	Score: 62.1	Score: 62.7	Score: 62.9	Score: 64.3	Score: 64.9	Score: 65.1
Global Innovation Index rank	57th	54th	52nd	49th	46th	43rd
Ratio of wage and salary workers in private establishments to total employed (%)	50.3–50.7	50.9–51.5	51.4–52.4	51.9–53.3	52.5–54.1	53.0–55.0
Unemployment rate (in %)	5.3–6.4	4.4–4.7	4.8–5.1	4.0–5.0	4.0–5.0	4.0–5.0
Poverty incidence rate (% of population)	16.0–16.4	–	12.9–13.2	–	10.0–10.3	8.8–9.0

Note: GDP = gross domestic product; GNI = gross national income.

Source: National Economic and Development Authority (2023a, Table 1.1).

112 million people, from a lower-middle-income status to a high-income one is not an easy feat. At the outset, the level of detail provided is highly commendable, but we are unsure whether the government truly understands the effort and coordination required to track each indicator and, more importantly, how they all interact together.

The Development Budget Coordination Committee released joint statements on December 2, 2024 (189th joint statement), and on June 26, 2025 (191st joint statement), where several of the targets were revised, including those for real GDP growth, inflation, deficit-to-GDP ratio. In these statements, targets are often referred to as projections or assumptions, prompting questions about the basis for such revisions and the criteria used to determine them in the first place. At this point, growth targets have been revised downward twice, and the deficit-to-GDP ratio has been adjusted twice to accommodate a larger deficit. In September 2025, a midterm update of the PDP 2023–2028 was published with the updated targets for the headline indicators, shown in Table 5.3. On January 23, 2025, a statement on the release of the 2024 Philippine Development Report was circulated by the Department of Economy, Planning, and Development (DEPDev), formerly National Economic Development Authority (NEDA), claimed that we are "on track toward socioeconomic transformation" (NEDA, 2025). In this statement, Secretary Arsenio Balisacan claimed that we have "achieved many of our targets and delivered tangible results." We use our forecasting tools to assess whether this is indeed true.

The 11 headline indicators in PDP 2023–2028 guide the economic policy of the current administration, and here we present our forecasts of seven of these indicators until 2028. These forecasts are derived from both the DLSU ANIMO

TABLE 5.3 Revised Headline Indicators and Targets for 2025–2028

Indicator	*Annual Target*			
	2025	*2026*	*2027*	*2028*
GDP growth (%)	5.5–6.5	6.0–7.0	6.0–7.0	6.0–7.0
GNI per capita (USD)	4,814–4,920	5,124–5,210	5,452–5,589	5,582–6,081
National government deficit-to-GDP ratio (%)	5.5	5.3	4.8	4.3
Outstanding national government debt stock to GDP ratio (%)	56–59	60–63	59–62	58–61
Poverty incidence rate (% of population)	12–13	–	10.0–11.0	8.0–9.0

Notes:

(1) Targets were revised in the Philippine Development Plan 2023–2028, 2025 Midterm Update.

(2) GDP = gross domestic product; GNI = gross national income.

Source: Authors, based on Department of Economy, Planning, and Development (DEPDev, 2025).

TABLE 5.4 DLSU ANIMO Econometric Model Forecasts for the PDP 2023–2028 Headline Indicators, 2025–2028

Indicator	*2025*	*2026*	*2027*	*2028*
GDP growth rate (%)*[b]	5.4	5.6	5.8	5.3
GNI per capita (USD)[b]	4,767	5,039	5,308	5,509
Headline inflation rate (%)	1.9	3.6	3.5	4.0
National government deficit-to-GDP ratio (%)[b]	3.6	3.4	3.4	3.9
Outstanding national government debt stock-to-GDP ratio (in %)[b]	56.5	54.1	52.3	51.8
Unemployment rate (%)	3.2	2.5	2.7	3.2
Poverty incidence rate (% of population)[b]	14.3	13.3[a]	12.12[a]	11.8

Note: Forecasts shown are from both the DLSU ANIMO econometric model (generated in the 4th quarter of 2024) and the DLSU Philippine high-frequency model (generated in September 2025). Those in green indicate that the target will be achieved, and those in red will not be achieved. If a target has been revised, we use the targets in the revised version.

(1) There is no explicit target for poverty incidence for 2026.
(2) We are using revised targets, as shown in Table 5.1.

Source: DLSU ANIMO econometric model and DLSU Philippine high-frequency model.

econometric model, which uses annual data, and the DLSU Philippine high-frequency model, which uses monthly and quarterly data. Appendix 5 describes the main features of the ANIMO econometric model of the Philippine economy. Appendix 5 also provides a description of the high-frequency model.[2] Our forecasts from the annual model are the result of a rigorous academic exercise based on our knowledge of the Philippine economy and a model that captures the interactions and relationships of more than 800 variables. We focus on the narrative that the model reveals and make sense of its projections.

Although it may be true that certain targets are being realized, our forecasts for the key headline indicators show otherwise. The country will continue to grow, but not fast enough to reach all its targets by 2028. Table 5.4 provides a summary of our forecasts for seven headline indicators. The corresponding charts are in Figures 5.1 to 5.7.[3]

Our real GDP growth forecasts (Figure 5.1) indicate that neither the initial targets nor the revised targets for 2025 to 2028 will be met. Although a two percentage point range for a growth target (6–8%, as indicated in the original PDP 2023–2028) appears imprecise, we emphasize that it will be extremely difficult for the country to meet and sustain growth rates above the economy's potential. As discussed in Chapter 3, the potential growth rate for the Philippine economy is around 6%. In 2024, we forecasted that growth for the year would be 5.9% at best. The Philippine Statistics Authority released the 2024 growth rate while we were writing this book. It was 5.7%. We maintain our analysis, that is, that the Philippine economy cannot attain the government's target of

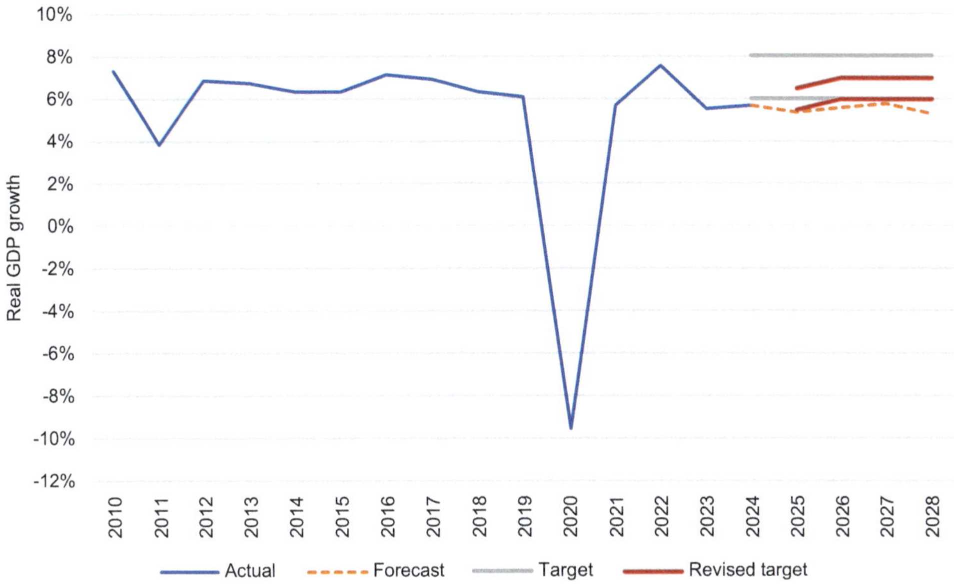

FIGURE 5.1 Real GDP Growth (%), Constant 2018 PHP, Philippines, 2010–2028

Source: Actual values for 2010–2024 are from the Philippine Statistics Authority (https://openstat.psa.gov.ph/Database/Economic-Accounts/National-Accounts-of-the-Philippines/Annual-National-Accounts). Forecasts are from the DLSU ANIMO econometric model.

6–8% (certainly not above 7%). The revised targets, especially for 2025, are more consistent with our estimates of the country's potential growth, although our recent forecasts show that these growth rates will still not be achieved. For 2025 and 2026, we forecast (as of the second half of 2025) growth rates of 5.4% and 5.6%, respectively.[4] We insist that sustained faster growth without hitting macroeconomic imbalances requires increasing the potential.

Additional reasons why it is difficult to grow significantly faster than 6% are, first, that the world economy is growing at about half as fast, at 2.8% in 2025 and 3.0% in 2026 (International Monetary Fund, 2025). It is difficult for a small, open economy like that of the Philippines to attain (and sustain) a growth rate twice as high. Another reason is that, as noted in Chapter 3, there are only a few countries (all in East Asia) that managed to grow by more than 6% for a long time. Sustained economic growth above 6% (the government target) is rare, much more so 8%. Moreover, history shows that fast growth episodes result in a massive deceleration in growth (Chapter 3).

Given our gross domestic product (GDP) growth rate forecasts for the next four years, as well as those of remittances as a percent of GDP, projected to decrease from about 7.7% in 2024 to 6.8% in 2028, we can project gross national income (GNI) per capita. This is shown in Figure 5.2. The projection indicates that the Philippines *should* become an upper-middle-income country in 2025 (based on

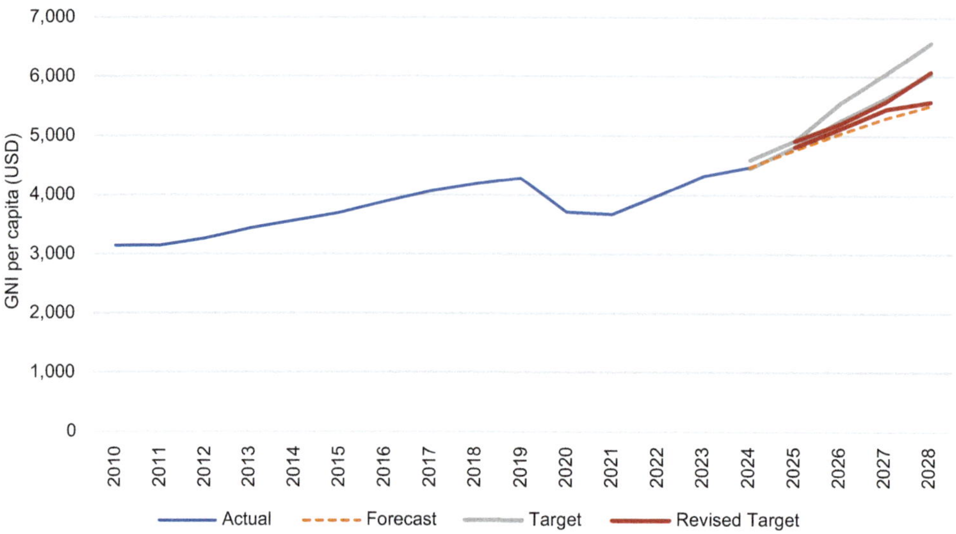

FIGURE 5.2 GNI per Capita (USD), Constant 2023 Prices, Philippines, 2010–2028

Note: Our projections are based on the DLSU ANIMO econometric model's forecasts of Gross National Income (PHP) and the Philippine Statistics Authority's (2024a) forecasts of population. To express future values in present-day terms, we adjust the series using the 2023 consumer price index (CPI) and the 2023 PHP-USD exchange rate.

Source: Actual values for 2010–2024 are authors' calculations based on data from the DLSU ANIMO econometric model database. Forecasts are from the DLSU ANIMO econometric model.

the forecast for 2024 of USD 4,546 and the World Bank's 2024 income threshold of USD 4,515). However, the GNI per capita will surpass the lower bound of the administration's initial 2028 target three years later instead, in 2031 (the initial target range of USD 6,044 to USD 6,571 in 2028 is shown by the continuous lines). However, according to World Bank figures published in mid-2025, the Philippines did not make it into the upper-middle-income category (with the new threshold of USD 4,496) and is a mere USD 26 from the threshold. While the GNI per capita targets were revised downward for the remainder of this administration's term, our forecasts show that they will not be achieved.

The inflation rate will be slightly lower than the 2.0 lower bound in 2025, and the inflation target band of 2.0–4.0% will be achieved in 2026, 2027, and 2028 (Figure 5.3). The overall price level is a weighted average of food and non-food consumption prices.[5]

Meanwhile, the unemployment rate will be quite low until 2028 and will be even lower than the target range for all the years (Figure 5.4). The unemployment rate is calculated from the labor force and employment forecasts. The labor force forecasts are obtained from the forecasts of labor force participation rates per age and sex (eight groups).[6] Employment forecasts are derived from the forecasts for gross value added and productivity per sector.[7] From 2025 to

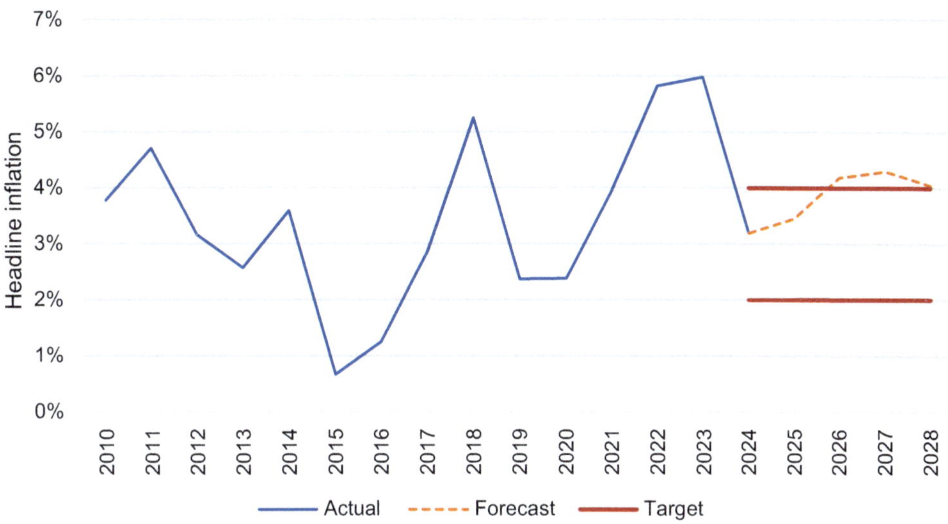

FIGURE 5.3 Headline Inflation (%), Philippines, 2010–2028

Source: Actual values for 2010–2024 are authors' calculations based on data from the Bangko Sentral ng Pilipinas (https://www.bsp.gov.ph/Statistics/Prices/prices2018.xls). Forecasts are from the DLSU ANIMO econometric model.

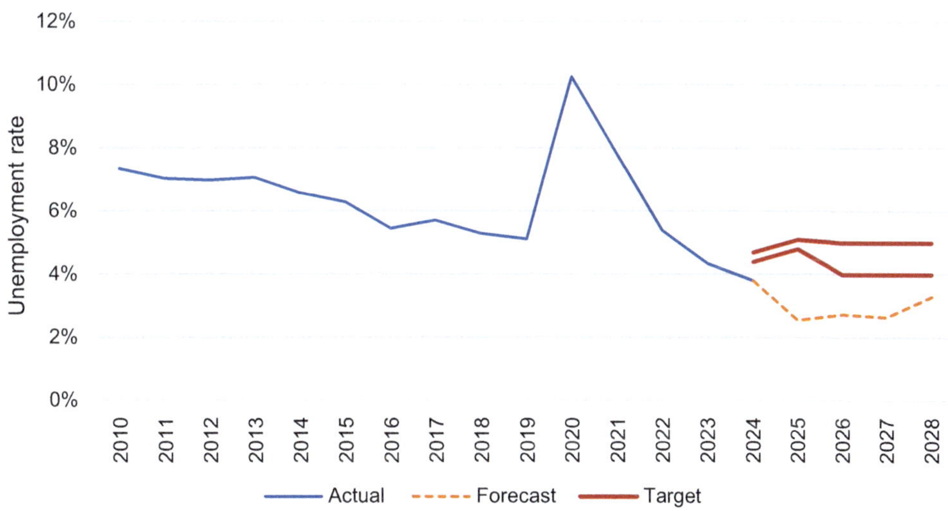

FIGURE 5.4 Unemployment Rate (%), Philippines, 2010–2028

Source: Actual values for 2010–2024 are from the Philippine Statistics Authority (https://openstat.psa.gov.ph/). Forecasts are from the DLSU ANIMO econometric model.

2028, both the labor force and employment will grow at quite similar rates, on average, leading to the unemployment rate staying close to 4%.

Figure 5.5 shows that the debt-to-GDP ratio would have stayed within the initial target range through 2028; however, the revised targets will be missed

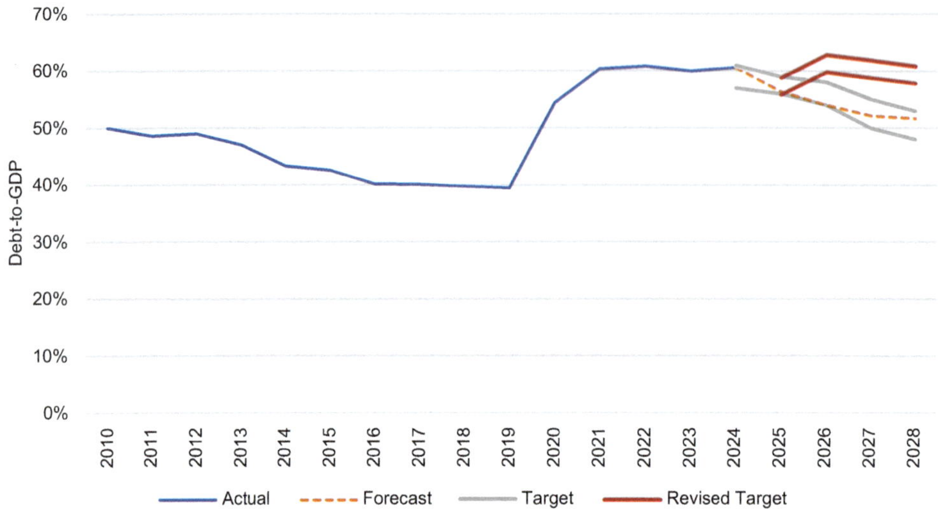

FIGURE 5.5 Debt-to-GDP Ratio (%), Philippines, 2010–2028

Source: Actual values for 2010–2024 are from the Republic of the Philippines, Bureau of the Treasury (https://www.treasury.gov.ph/wp-content/uploads/2025/02/DEBT-STOCK-ANNUAL-1986-2024.xlsx). Forecasts are from the DLSU ANIMO econometric model.

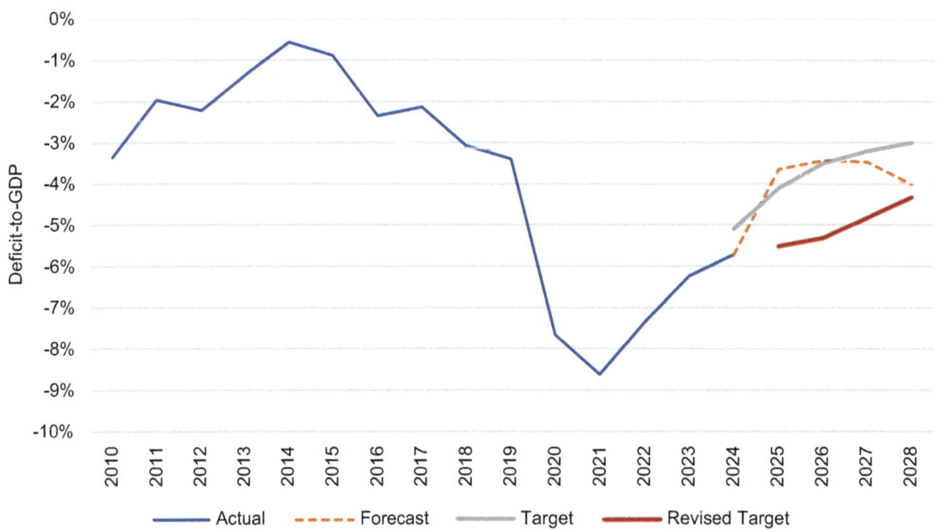

FIGURE 5.6 Deficit-to-GDP Ratio (%), Philippines, 2010–2028

Source: Actual values for 2010–2024 are from the Republic of the Philippines, Bureau of the Treasury (https://www.treasury.gov.ph/wp-content/uploads/2025/09/COR_Summary_Annual_1986-2024.xlsx). Forecasts are from the DLSU ANIMO econometric model.

from 2026 to 2028. Figure 5.6 shows that the initial deficit-to-GDP ratio targets would only have been achieved in 2025 and 2026. Since the targets until 2028 were revised to accommodate a larger deficit-to-GDP ratio, our forecasts show that the new targets will now be met. These forecasts are also based on the behavioral equations for government spending and government revenues.

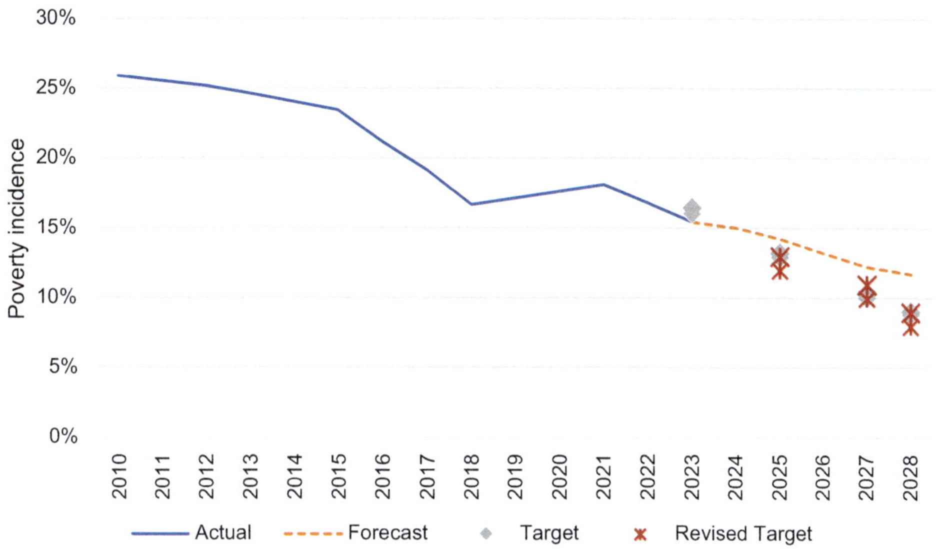

FIGURE 5.7 Poverty Incidence (%), Philippines, 2010–2028

Notes: Poverty Incidence rates are provided only every three years, as it is based on the Family Income and Expenditure Survey. We interpolate the values for the missing years for use in the econometric model.

Source: Actual values for 2010–2023 are authors' calculations based on data from the Philippine Statistics Authority (2016, 2023b, 2024c). Forecasts are from the DLSU ANIMO econometric model.

Finally, the government's goal of reducing poverty incidence to a single digit is projected to be attained in 2034, when it will reach 9% (Figure 5.7).[8] Our forecasts show that poverty incidence will meet neither the initial nor the revised targets.

Based on the earlier figures, most of the headline indicator targets for the remainder of this administration's term will not be met. Instead, they will be met a few years later. Two reasons account for this: (1) The targets do not reflect the current reality of the economy, and (2) the government's programs and policies are not fully aligned with what is needed to achieve the targets. These points emphasize the importance of setting goals and targets grounded in the economy's capacity and potential, as well as in a clear understanding of the relationships among various indicators and what it truly means for the economy to develop. As we reviewed targets set in previous Philippine development plans, similar issues emerged, prompting us to reflect on whether we have been learning from our past or if we are inadvertently repeating similar patterns.

5.3 Philippine Development Plans—a Heritage of Smallness

A close look at past Philippine development plans reinforces the need to clarify misunderstandings about the potential growth of an economy and re-evaluate the targets set and how they are defined. Figure 5.8 compares the GDP growth targets stated in the last seven administrations' development plans, since that of President Corazon Aquino (1986–1992), against actual recorded growth. There

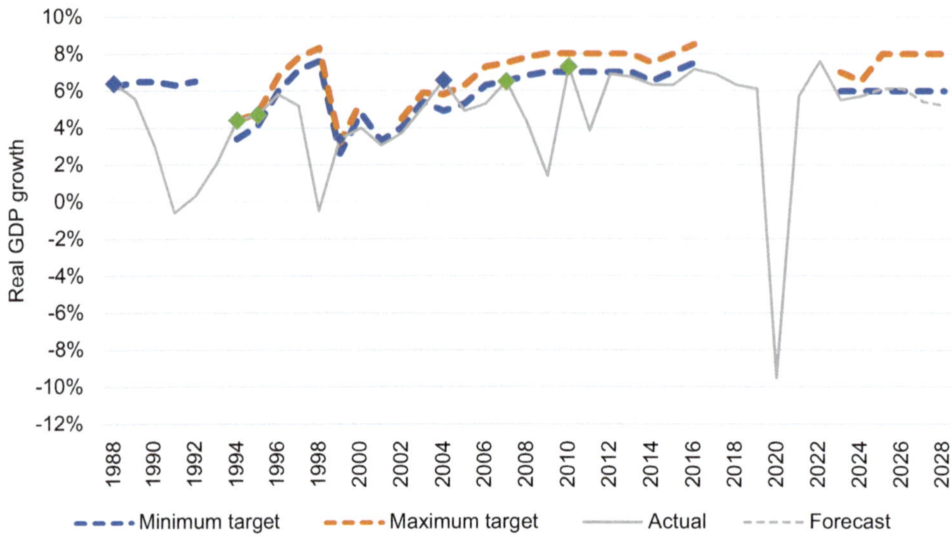

FIGURE 5.8 GDP Growth Targets in the Philippine Development Plan vs Actual (%), 1988–2028

Notes: (i) From 1988 to 1992, a single value was given as the target; in other years, a minimum and maximum are given. (ii) There were no growth targets identified in the Philippine Development Plans for the year 1993 and for the years 2017–2022. (iii) Markers in blue indicate the years when actual growth was higher than the target, while markers in green indicate the years when the targets were met.

Source: Targets are from the National Economic and Development Authority (1988, 1993, 1996, 1999, 2004, 2014, 2017, 2023a) and the Department of Economy, Planning, and Development (2025). Actual values for 1988–2024 are from the Philippine Statistics Authority (https://openstat.psa.gov.ph/Database/Economic-Accounts/National-Accounts-of-the-Philippines/Annual-National-Accounts). Forecasts are from the DLSU ANIMO econometric model.

were no targets provided for the years 2017–2022. Until 2024, actual growth fell within the target range (green markers) for only 4 years out of the 30 with a specified growth target. Growth exceeded the provided target or the target range (blue markers) in three years. This means that if we exclude the three instances when the actual was higher than the target or target range, the Philippines has missed its annual growth target 20 times out of the 30 in which it had a specific target. This recurring gap between actual and desired growth emphasizes the need to have a clearer understanding of the potential growth of our economy, as discussed in Chapter 3. Otherwise, we are likely to continue to fall short of our growth targets.

The same can be said about the poverty incidence ratio. A comparison of poverty incidence targets and actual outcomes across seven administrations is shown in Figure 5.9. Targets were specified for 17 years in the period covered, and of those years, as reported by the Philippine Statistics Authority, the actual poverty incidence ratios were within or below the target range in just three instances (green markers). This implies that the Philippines has missed its annual poverty incidence targets 13 years out of the 17 in which it set targets.

Sustaining high growth and reducing poverty seem to be reasonable indicators for a country like the Philippines. However, under the last seven administrations,

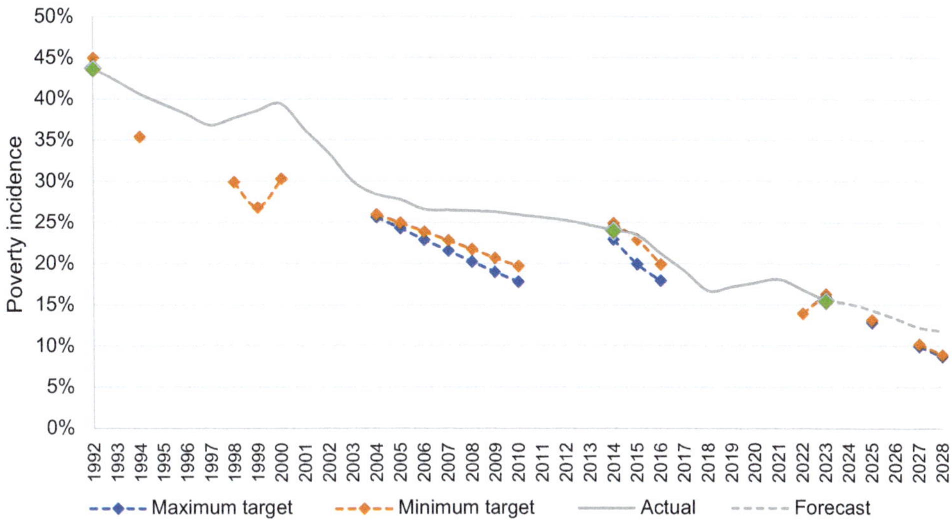

FIGURE 5.9 Poverty Incidence Targets in the Philippine Development Plan vs Actual (%), Philippines, 1992–2028

Notes: (i) Markers in green indicate the years when the targets were met. (ii) Poverty Incidence rates are provided only every three years, as it is based on the Family Income and Expenditure Survey. We interpolate values for the missing years.

Source: Targets are from the National Economic and Development Authority (1988, 1993, 1996, 1999, 2004, 2014, 2017) and the Department of Economy, Planning, and Development (2025). Actual values for 1991–2023 are authors' calculations from the Philippine Statistics Authority (2002, 2010, 2016, 2023b, 2024c). Forecasts are from the DLSU ANIMO econometric model.

it has missed its targets year after year. It is important to acknowledge that our government needs to carefully rethink targets and the way these are established.

The other important aspect about the targets is to recognize that no matter how they are set, we also seem to be missing something. Knowing what we know now about the centrality of structural transformation, productivity and product complexity, the irreplaceability of manufacturing and exports, the crucial requirement of firms with constantly upgrading organizational capabilities, and the decisive role of the state, Philippine development plans make for compelling reading—often not for what is there but for what has been absent all this time.

An assessment of the last seven Philippine development plans provides us with a grim confirmation of why the Philippines has made modest gains but ultimately missed the boat. Our view differs from that of most commentators, who argue that Philippine underperformance is a result of some form of poor implementation. This is true, but there is more. We find that our national leadership's thinking about development, codified in its key visioning and strategy documents, has missed systematically the essential elements of industrialization. Each successive administration since that of President Corazon Aquino in the second half of the 1980s seems to have chosen an alternative development path, despite their real-time ability to observe how our neighbors transformed the structures of their economies. In the decades when Korea, Singapore, and Taiwan were implementing big push industrialization programs, driven by the goal of becoming major exporters of complex goods, successive Philippine administrations balked. Reconstruction, agricultural rehabilitation, and macroeconomic stability often took precedence over industrial development. The result was that, compared to the South Korean development plans of the period (see Chapter 7), Philippine sectoral strategies were much less detailed, lacked clear ideas about the sequencing of products, and had no long-term export orientation. Montes (1994, p. 140) argued that

> Philippine development plans have tended to be cheerleading exercises instead of decisions about which potential priorities have to be sacrificed in the current plan period. This mode of planning permits private interests to justify almost any project as being consistent with the current development plan.

Even with the Marcos Sr. administration lasting nearly two decades, and whose plans for industrialization scored favorably compared to those of other presidents after him, the vision remained limited when set next to the manufacturing ambitions of neighboring countries, such as Taiwan, Malaysia, and even Thailand. Post–Marcos Sr., a common thread has run through successive Philippine development plans: the notion that industrial development can be led by the private sector, with the state playing only a limited, facilitating role, and always in compliance with international trading bodies and credit agencies. Regardless of which political party has been in power, the same underlying ideological posture has persisted: one that regards industrialization as something that can be achieved organically by ensuring a stable macroeconomy within which private enterprise can thrive. It need not be socially engineered, presents too much of a risk if government were to be too heavily involved, and perhaps can be supplanted anyway by a service-based economy.

We end this section with a reference to National Artist for Literature Nick Joaquin. Philippine industrial ambitions seem to corroborate the title of his well-known essay, *A Heritage of Smallness*

> Society for the Filipino is a small rowboat: the barangay. Geography for the Filipino is a small locality: the barrio. History for the Filipino is a small vague saying: *matanda pa kay mahoma; noong* peacetime. Enterprise for the Filipino is a small stall: the *sari-sari*. Industry and production for the Filipino are the small immediate searchings of each day: *isang kahig, isang tuka*. And commerce for the Filipino is the smallest degree of retail: the *tingi*.
>
> *(Joaquin, 1988/2004, p. 351)*

5.4 Learning From Our Neighbors

If a historical analysis of Philippine development plans confirms continuity in the way industrialization has been overlooked in favor of other priorities, such as macroeconomic stabilization, or alternative paths, such as leapfrogging to services, a simple cross-country comparison can establish present-day contrasts. Table 5.5 summarizes key features of the current development plans of

TABLE 5.5 Comparing Current Development Plans: Philippines, Malaysia, Vietnam

	Philippine Development Plan 2023–2028 Briefer	*Twelfth Malaysia Plan 2021–2025 Executive Summary*	*Vietnam Industrial Development Strategy 2025 Vision to 2035 (English Translation)*
Pages of Content	*6*	*12*	*11*
Structure of plan	Goals and targets Key strategies What to expect	Three key themes Four policy enablers Selected targets 14 game changers	Vision/viewpoints Industrial strategy Objectives Solutions Organization
Overall goal, vision	"[T]o reinvigorate job creation and accelerate poverty reduction by steering the Philippine economy back to its high-growth trajectory and effect economic and social transformation for a prosperous, inclusive, and resilient society." (p. 3)	"Prosperous, high-income, inclusive, low-carbon, high-tech and sustainable nation, globally competitive, united, harmonious and dignified." (p. 11)	"By 2025, Viet Nam's . . . industrial sector will be competitive, have modern technologies, and participate in the global value chain in a number of specialized sub-sectors, and can fundamentally meet the requirements of the economy and export; its workforce will be qualified to meet the needs of a modern production system. "By 2035, it will develop with a majority specialized industries having advanced technologies and product quality up to international standards, deeply participating in global value chains." (pp. 2–3)
Key targets	Annual growth 6.5 to 8.0%, 2024–2028 Unemployment 4–5% Percentage of workers in private establishments 55% Food and overall inflation 2.0–4.0% Deficit to GDP 3.0% Debt to GDP 53% Global Competitiveness Index top 33% Poverty incidence 8–9%	GDP growth 4.5–5.5% per annum GNI per capita RM 57,882 Labor productivity growth 3.6% per annum Employee compensation 40% of GDP Average monthly household income RM 10,065 Malaysian Wellbeing Index growth 1.2% per annum	Industry value-added growth 7.0–8.0% Industrial production value growth 11.0–12.5% Industry and construction 40% of GDP Industrial exports 90% of total exports Value of high-tech industrial products 45–50% of GDP Industrial incremental capital-output ratio (ICOR) 3.0–4.0%

(*Continued*)

TABLE 5.5 (Continued)

	Philippine Development Plan 2023–2028 Briefer	*Twelfth Malaysia Plan 2021–2025 Executive Summary*	*Vietnam Industrial Development Strategy 2025 Vision to 2035 (English Translation)*
Key economic/ production strategies	Modernize agriculture and agribusiness to move up value chain, promote diversification and food security Revitalize industry through business matching, innovation, servicification Reinvigorate services, tourism, IT, creative industries, business process management through partnerships with enterprises and local government units	Develop future talent by improving technical and vocational education and training (TVET) Accelerate adoption and application of digital technology; align R&D toward commercialization, wealth generation, and economic growth Improve logistics infrastructure by focusing on last-mile connectivity Transform public service through whole-of-government approach, enhancing budgeting and project management	Priority to processing and manufacturing industries: mechanical engineering and metallurgy, chemicals, agricultural product processing, garments, textiles, leather and footwear, electronics and telecommunications, renewable energy
Key public investments	Strengthen public–private partnerships (PPPs) to upgrade energy, logistics, telecoms, water, etc. Reform Foreign Investment Act, Retail Trade Liberalization Act, Public Service Act, Corporate Recovery and Tax Incentives for Enterprises Law	"Transformational" strategies for high-impact industries: electrical and electronics, global services, aerospace, creative, tourism, halal, smart farming, biomass MSME digitalization and second chance support Sustainable health financing Tax to finance poverty alleviation Kedah, Kelantan, Perlis, Sabah, Sarawak, Terengganu to receive at least 50% of total basic development expenditure JENDELA plan to achieve full 4G coverage	Improve state management mechanisms, reasonably decentralize, supplement technical regulations consistent with international standards Restructure industrial sector, with special attention to increasing proportion of large and medium-sized enterprises nationwide Develop quality standards for training at all levels, focusing on occupational skill standards to reach international levels Concentrate investment on a number of scientific and technological research institutes to acquire and master new technologies Encourage enterprises to expand scale of investment

(Continued)

TABLE 5.5 (Continued)

	Philippine Development Plan 2023–2028 Briefer	*Twelfth Malaysia Plan 2021–2025 Executive Summary*	*Vietnam Industrial Development Strategy 2025 Vision to 2035 (English Translation)*
		Fifty percent of all government research funding to experimental development with high commercialization potential	Promote exploitation of non-traditional markets, such as BRIC group for output, East Asia, Japan, US, EU for inputs
			Publish list of industries eligible for investment promotion, industries subject to restriction, products and components eligible for financial support
		Centralized planning and development of logistics hubs	
		Performance-driven culture in civil service	Strictly control import of technologies through regulations on conditions, criteria, categories
			Develop specific preferential mechanisms and policies for industrial parks and clusters, with priority to those of high scientific and technical content
			Vigorously develop industrial investment consultancy services for planning and adjustment
Key departments cited	Local government units	Commission for Small Business, Federal and District Poverty Units, Digital Nasional Berhad (DNB), Research Management Unit (RMU)	Ministry of Trade and Industry, Ministry of Planning and Investment, Ministry of Finance, Ministry of Education and Training, Ministry of Labor-Invalids and Social Affairs, Ministry of Agriculture and Rural Development, Ministry of Information and Communications, Ministry of Construction, Ministry of Natural Resources and Environment, Ministry of Science and Technology, State Bank of Vietnam, provincial-level peoples' committees

Source: National Economic Development Authority (2023b), Economic Planning Unit of Malaysia's Prime Minister's Department (2021), Socialist Republic of Viet Nam (n.d.).

the Philippines vis-à-vis those of two ASEAN neighbors, Malaysia and Vietnam. By design, we selected the most abridged version of each plan, on the assumption that the limited space (under 20 pages each) would force authorities to declare priorities explicitly and reveal what they consider to be the most important features of the national strategy. We elicit key elements over several rows and reproduce key passages verbatim across the three documents to provide primary evidence of the differences in the way the Philippine (NEDA, 2023b), Malaysian (Economic Planning Unit of Malaysia's Prime Minister's Department, 2021), and Vietnamese (Socialist Republic of Viet Nam, n.d.) governments strategize over their respective futures.

The Philippines has set long-run targets in its *Ambisyon Natin 2040* vision paper, but its 2023–2028 development plan seems a classic case of insular, "more of the same" thinking. The terms *reinvigorate, accelerate,* and *steer the country back* are much more low-key and muted in ambition compared to Malaysia's and Vietnam's plans. Malaysia does not hesitate to include *high income, low-carbon,* and *globally competitive* in its visioning, and Vietnam is equally intent on making its mark internationally, explicitly declaring a desire to *participate in global value chains,* to *export,* and to *develop advanced products that meet international standards.*

The difference in outlook is not trivial. Easterly (2006), in a paper delivered at a conference in the Asian Development Bank (ADB) in Manila 20 years ago, distinguished between two paths to development and poverty alleviation: the path of planners versus that of searchers. The main difference in results (i.e., poverty has never been alleviated by planners, only by searchers) comes from the mechanisms of feedback and accountability. Planners are much less likely to seek feedback about what works and what does not. They often proceed from the assumption that large problems are well-defined, that they know what gaps exist, and that they simply need to fill them by spending. If unelected, they often do not have to bear the consequences of failure. Indeed, they can perversely use failure to justify the expansion of their programs.

Searchers, on the other hand, must engage with customers and markets as they offer products and solutions to smaller-scale problems; this frequent feedback encourages innovation and accountability because failure to deliver and satisfy carries real costs.

At the level of overall vision, Malaysia's and Vietnam's public commitment to tie their development efforts to the global market is not a mere statement of ambition. It orients their economies—their firms and institutions—toward an environment that demands quality results. Whatever resources are committed by their governments toward favored firms and sectors, accountability is maintained by an external and apolitical arbiter: the international customer. The Philippine vision already looks weaker by comparison.

Comparing key targets is instructive as well. The full versions of each plan no doubt contain dozens of more granular figures. But the half-dozen or so that have been considered most critical reveal each government's thinking about what it means to develop and how to get there.

All three countries share an interest in annual growth and employment figures, as well as various versions of social welfare (poverty incidence, well-being). Yet one does not have to be an ideologue to notice how only the Philippines names macroeconomic stability and reform indicators among its key targets: inflation, deficit-to-GDP ratio, debt-to-GDP ratio, and Global Competitiveness Index. We argue in Chapter 11 that these belie a misunderstanding of a country's monetary reality, and have provided decades-long justification for underspending on critical public goods, indeed for absconding from directly providing them, in favor of the private sector. Fiscal conservatism seems baked into the country's economic vision.

Malaysia and Vietnam, on the other hand, provide fewer key targets, nearly all of which are attuned to the country's productive capacity. They explicitly track labor productivity growth and industrial productivity (the Philippines merely tracks employment in the private sector). Malaysia sets targets for household income (twice what would be considered "decent income," not merely non-poor income in the Philippines). Vietnam declares targets for industrial output, industrial productivity (including capital–output ratios), and industrial exports. It is clear from their choice of key targets that the Philippines has bet on fiscal discipline and reforms to encourage economic activity. Malaysia and Vietnam understand that development is ultimately about productivity, industrialization, and exports.

These alternative visions and targets unfold logically into key strategies, notably the industries and sectors each of the respective governments is willing to invest in. The essence of strategy is taking calculated risks on ventures that one believes will yield the best outcomes. In the Philippines, these are placed on essentially the same industries successive administrations have bet on since 1986: agribusiness, tourism, services, IT, creative industries, and business processes. There is simply no reference to heavy industry manufacturing, never mind aggressive exporting of complex goods. For that, one would have to look to Malaysia and especially Vietnam, which do not hesitate to name their favored industries: metallurgy, chemicals, agricultural processing, textiles, garments, leather, footwear (i.e., "the products that make a nation"—see Chapter 8), as well as sunrise industries, such as renewable energy.

The section on key public investments reveals glaring differences in how each government pursues its strategies—literally, how much it is willing to invest, both in resources and direct participation. In the case of the Philippines, it is clear that the government sees its main role as enabler and reformer, relying on public–private partnerships to fund the upgrading of physical and digital infrastructure. It sees its major responsibility as delivering critical legislation, which will presumably ignite rapid growth via the private sector and foreign investment.

Malaysia and Vietnam, on the other hand, have no qualms about state involvement in transforming industries, completing the provision of public goods, and defining preferences and restrictions based on a national agenda. Malaysia is willing to commit a definite figure ("at least 50 percent") of its total basic development expenditure to six underserved provinces. It can declare a plan to ensure 100% 4G coverage and other costly undertakings without any reference to budget deficits. Vietnam, interestingly, understands the role that medium and large enterprises play in advancing industrialization and is prepared to back these efforts with state resources, including resources devoted to making state mechanisms more efficient and performance-driven.

Finally, we can look at state organizational capabilities and accountability, proxied here by explicit mentions within each plan of the responsible government agencies. The premise, as noted by Easterly (2006), is that having too many targets and objectives weakens principal–agent relations. Agents can always use multiple objectives to play their principals against each other and, indeed, are incentivized not to focus on delivering on any one target. For this reason, national plans that directly delegate responsibilities to specific agencies are more likely to enhance accountability than those that set targets but without clear public indications of who will do what by when.

PDP 2023–2028 is weakest in this regard, with not a single mention of any national agency tasked with delivering any of the targets; only "local government units" appear. In Chapter 9, we discuss this as a case of "spatial fragmentation," which has retarded efforts at national development. Malaysia, on the other hand, lists three new agencies tasked with specific mandates, along with an overall declaration of civil service reform. Vietnam, however, devotes the final section of its industrial plan to a section called "Organization." In it, 12 separate national agencies are named and paired with specific responsibilities and actions, including the country's finance authorities and provincial authorities.

Time will tell whether Malaysia's and Vietnam's targets are met, but there is no doubt of their clarity and ambition around the indicators that we believe matter most for countries that are serious about rapid development: productivity, industrial output, and exports. Unlike the Philippines, neither is shy about the indispensable role of the state in directly providing public goods and driving industrial policy.

5.5 From Plans to Prospects

Overall, based on the forecasts generated by both the annual and the high-frequency models, the Philippine economy is not likely to perform in line with the expectations of the current administration. Most of the targets under 7 of the 11 headline indicators set for 2028 will not be achieved. A review of past Philippine development plans reveals the same pattern—persistent underperformance in growth and poverty incidence targets. A comparison with the development plans of Malaysia and Vietnam reveals that the Philippines continues to misunderstand what it truly takes to develop. Instead of prioritizing policies and programs that address the transformation of the structure of the economy (productivity, the competitiveness of exports, a robust manufacturing sector, and shifts in employment shares), the Philippine government continues to reuse and recycle plans that repeat the same narrative and deliver little in terms of sustained economic growth.

A more solid understanding of the type of reforms we implement is crucial at this point. Either we do something different or we accept that the current state is as far as we are going to go. We need to understand the potential growth of the economy, as emphasized in Chapter 3. We need to address the structure of the economy and productivity, as discussed in Chapter 4. In our view, the reforms directed toward these are what will really change the trajectory of our growth path. Otherwise, we may improve efficiencies here and there and reach some targets, but we will most likely see more of the same in the next 25 years.

Notes

1 As we explain in Chapter 11, making fiscal consolidation a top priority is based on a flawed understanding of government finances.

2 The forecasts presented in this book come from the DLSU ANIMO econometric model, generated in the fourth quarter of 2024, and the DLSU Philippine high-frequency model, generated in September 2025.

3 Note that these forecasts were generated in August 2024. Hence, we used available data until 2023. Employment data for 2023 was updated by the International Labour Organization (ILO) at the end of 2024, and we used our 2023 forecasts for these series. As of this writing, our 2023 forecasts for employment are very close to the actual 2023 figures from the ILO.

4 For months during 2024, our growth forecasts for 2025 and 2026 were more optimistic, 6.1%. The significantly lower growth than expected in 2024 and the geopolitical uncertainties at the start of 2025 require caution.

5 All forecasts are derived from the solution of the complete DLSU ANIMO econometric model. For reference, we indicate here that food and non-food consumption prices are a function of what we call "theoretical prices," which we construct as a weighted average of sectoral output and import prices, given by the input–output tables. This is described in the ANIMO econometric model database by Aragones et al. (2024).

6 Labor force participation rates are a function of the average wage rate, the number of overseas Filipino workers, and social benefits.

7 Gross value added per sector (16 sectors) is a function of a variable that we call "theoretical gross value added," which we construct from the input–output tables. Productivity per sector (18 sectors) is estimated using different demand components and gross value added as regressors.

8 In the DLSU ANIMO macroeconometric model, poverty incidence is a function of the share of employment in agriculture, the consumer price index, and remittances. As the share of employment in agriculture is projected to decrease to 17.5% by 2028, this contributes substantially to the reduction in poverty incidence. This is offset by the decrease in remittances (negatively related to poverty) and the increase in the consumer price index (positively related to poverty).

9 A complete and detailed description of the database we have created is in the DLSU AKI working paper on the ANIMO econometric model database, Aragones et al. (2024).

APPENDIX 5

The De La Salle University (DLSU) ANIMO Econometric Model of the Philippine Economy

This Appendix provides a mostly nontechnical brief of the main features of the DLSU ANIMO econometric model. The DLSU ANIMO model is a large-scale macroeconometric model of the Philippine economy. In its current version, the model contains 592 equations and 842 variables. Out of the 592 equations, 136 are behavioral equations. The remaining equations are a mix of definitions, identities, and transformations. Out of the 842 variables, 592 are endogenous, 64 are exogenous, and 186 are additive factors that are used for simulations.

Figure A5.1 shows a diagram of the model. We show the three main blocks of the model: supply (gross value added), demand (gross domestic product), and income (gross disposable income), and others, and the main variables in each block. The diagram does not contain all the details; it contains the main parts and relationships that are important to understand the model's structure.

The key feature of this model is that the structures of employment and output drive productivity, which drives wages and, consequently, income per capita. This process is captured in the supply block of the model. The model has Kaldor–Verdoorn features. In this block, gross value added (GVA) is derived from the sectoral value added. This part of the model is made up of 16 sectors: agriculture, construction, utilities, mining and quarrying, manufacturing, accommodation and food, education, finance and insurance, health and social work, information and communication, professional and business services, public administration, real estate, transport and storage, wholesale and retail trade, and other services. For each sector, the model contains real and nominal GVA, the GVA deflators, productivity, employment, employment shares, and wage rates. We use the input–output tables to arrive at a theoretical real GVA, which is derived from the gross value added of all the sectors and the real gross output of the demand components. We also determine labor force participation rates, which helps us determine the labor force and, consequently, the unemployment rate. From gross value added and productivity, we derive sectoral employment and employment shares. This block contains 74 behavioral equations.

In the demand block, the demand components are also disaggregated. Consumption is disaggregated into food and non-food; investment into construction, equipment, and other investment; exports into agriculture, electronics, chemicals, other goods, travel, and other services; imports into agriculture, chemicals, electronics, industrial machinery, metals, other imports, and services. Then there is government spending. In the demand block, the input–output tables are also used to determine theoretical prices, which, along with a simultaneous price model, leads to the demand deflators. Import prices are determined from the exchange rate and a representation of foreign incomes. The demand block has 41 behavioral equations.

In the incomes block, we track the incomes and expenses of the three main agents: households, corporations, and the government. For households, incomes include gross operating surplus, compensation of employees, social benefits, property income, and transfers. Expenses include taxes, social contributions, property expenses, fees, and transfers. For corporations, incomes include gross operating surplus, property income, and transfers. Expenses include taxes, property expenses, fees, and transfers. For the government, incomes include gross operating surplus, taxes on products, taxes on incomes, social contributions, property incomes, fees, and transfers. Expenses include social benefits, property expenses, subsidies, and transfers. We include other variables and behavioral equations in this block, such as government debt, balance of payments and its components, the exchange rate, interest rates, compensation of employees from the rest of the world, overseas Filipino workers, and remittances. This block has a total of 21 behavioral equations.

We built a database of annual data containing 990 indicators, and 471 of these indicators are used as inputs into the model. We used annual data from 2000 to 2023 taken from the Philippine Statistics Authority, the Bangko Sentral ng Pilipinas, the World Bank, the International Monetary Fund, and the International Labour Organization, among others.[9] We also used these main sources for forecasts of our exogenous variables.

The baseline assumptions for the main exogenous variables are summarized in the following:

TABLE A5.1 Main Exogenous Variables Assumptions, 2025–2050

Variable	*2025*	*2030*	*2035*	*2040*	*2045*	*2050*
Philippine government investment growth (%)	2.5	2.5	2.5	2.5	2.5	2.5
World GDP growth (%)	3.18	3.4	3.4	3.4	3.4	3.4
China's growth (%)	4.5–5.0	3.5–4.5	3.5–4.5	3.5–4.5	3.5–4.5	3.5–4.5
India's growth (%)	6.5–7.0	6.5–7.0	6.5–7.0	6.0–6.5	6.0–6.5	6.0–6.5
GNI per capita growth, Saudi Arabia (%)	4.3	3.8	3.3	2.8	2.3	1.8
US Fed policy rate (%)	3.9	2.6	2.6	2.6	2.6	2.6
Brent oil price (2018 = 100)	110.9	114.3	117.7	121.1	124.4	127.8

Source: Authors, based on International Monetary Fund (2024), Federal Reserve Board (2024), Pricewaterhouse Coopers (PwC, 2017), United States Energy Information Administration (2023).

To estimate the relationships among our variables, we mostly use error-correction type of regressions. Given the autoregressive-distributed lag of order (p,q), we have:

$$y_t = c + \sum_{i=1}^{p} \alpha_i y_{t-i} + \sum_{j=0}^{q} \beta_j x_{t-j} + \epsilon_t$$

This can be expressed in error-correction form to represent the relationship in terms of differences and levels. In the simplest case of an ARDL $(1,1)$ in levels (variables in logarithms):

$$y_t = c + \alpha y_{t-1} + \beta_0 x_t + \beta_1 x_{t-1} + \epsilon_t$$

which can be rewritten as:

$$\Delta y_t = c + \beta_0 \Delta x_t - (1-\alpha)(y_{t-1} - \theta x_{t-1}) + \epsilon_t$$

where β_0 reflects the short-run dynamics between the dependent and independent variables, while $\theta = \frac{\beta_0+\beta_1}{1-\alpha}$ is the long-run elasticity, and $(y_{t-1} - \theta x_{t-1})$ is the error correction term.

After estimating all the behavioral equations, we generated a model solution and evaluated the model solution using in-sample estimates using EViews13. We then entered forecasts of our exogenous variables into the model and solved the model to generate forecasts for all endogenous variables until 2050.

The De La Salle University (DLSU) High-Frequency Model

The DLSU Philippine high-frequency model generates monthly and quarterly forecasts of the quarterly national accounts provided by the Philippine Statistics Authority. The model uses seasonally adjusted quarterly national accounts and over 50 monthly indicators of the Philippine economy. The process involves pooling the indicators into factors used for predicting both the national accounts and the indicators themselves. The predicted values of national accounts undergo disaggregation and benchmarking to obtain the forecasts.

Examples of indicators for the demand side include (1) private consumption, including cash remittances and the consumer price index (CPI); (2) public consumption, including employment volume in education and tax revenues; (3) investment, including outstanding loans and ten-year treasury bond rate; (4) exports, including outgoing international cargo and the PHP/USD exchange rate; and (5) imports, including incoming international cargo and merchandise imports.

Examples of indicators for the supply side include (1) agriculture output, with farmgate prices of palay and loans outstanding for agriculture, forestry, and fisheries; (2) industrial output, with average capacity utilization rate and foreign direct investment in industry; and (3) services output, with tourist arrivals and international aircraft traffic.

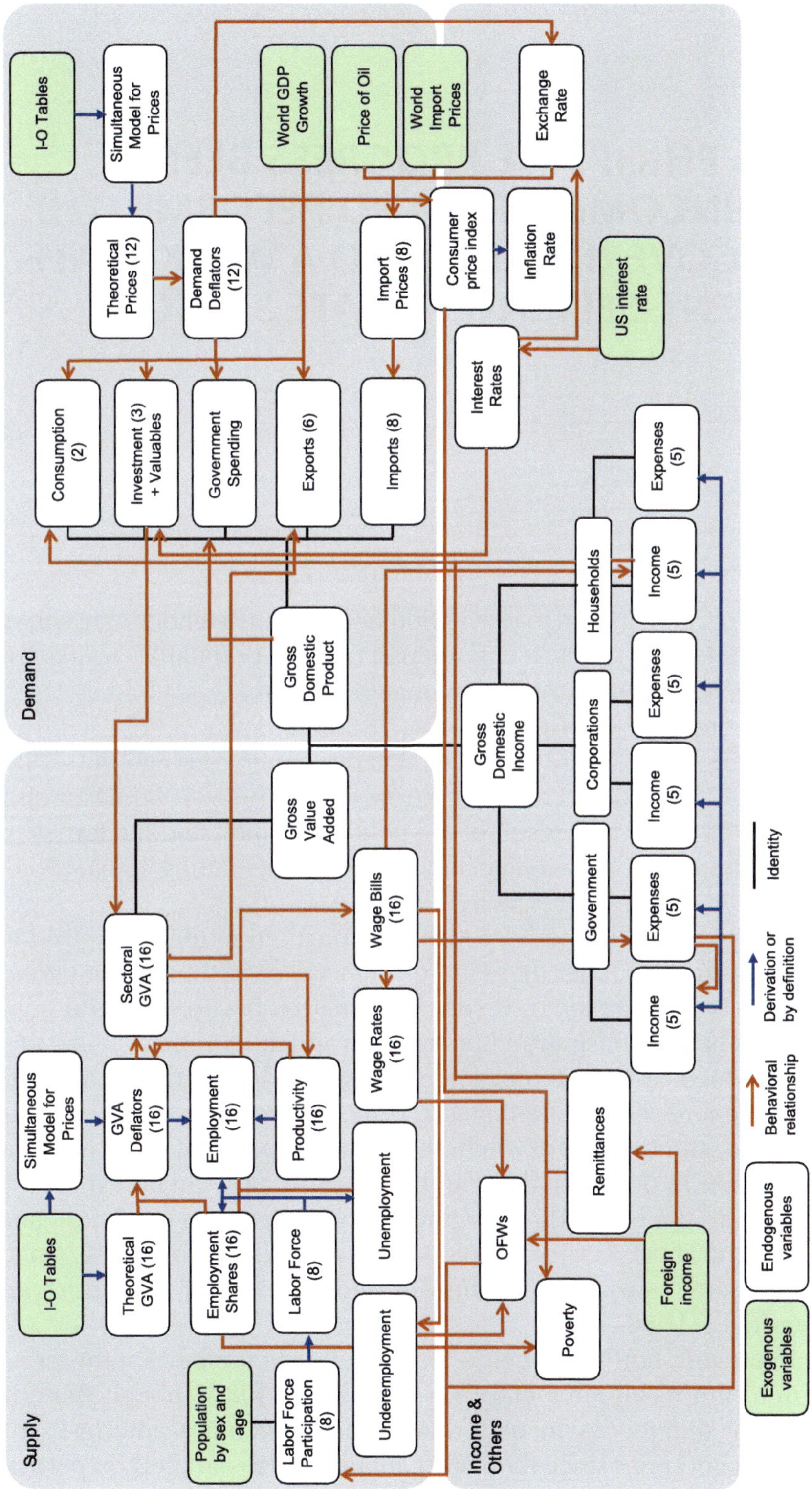

FIGURE A5.1 Diagram of the DLSU ANIMO econometric model. Note: The numbers in parentheses indicate the number of sectors or types that belong to that component.

6

WHY HAS PHILIPPINE PROGRESS BEEN SLOW? I: INCOMPLETE LAND REFORMS, THE ROLE OF GOVERNMENT, AND A WEAK STATE WITH A RENT-SEEKING PRIVATE SECTOR

6.1 Introduction

The Philippines never managed to join its Southeast Asian neighbors' growth spree of the mid-1960s to mid-1990s. It was not part of the World Bank Group's (1993) *The East Asian Miracle*. This is not to say that the country was a basket case. The average annual growth rate of GDP during 1960–1991 was 3.96%, with crises in the middle. Growth increased from 4.94% per annum during 1960–1970 to 5.64% during 1970–1975 and reached 6.07% during 1975–1980. Then disaster came during 1983–1985 as a result of the political turmoil and the foreign debt crisis, with the result that the average annual growth rate during 1980–1985 was –0.98%.

The Philippines had an American-inspired constitution that conferred great power to the president. Under these circumstances, everything went wrong after 1972, when President Marcos Sr. declared martial law to deal with popular discontent with his administration (the agrarian situation in particular), to deal with the Huk armed resistance movement, as well as to overcome the prohibition of a president to serve more than six years. To deal with the latter, Marcos redrafted the Constitution after switching to another political party to secure a nomination again. To deal with the country's chronic agrarian unrest, he promised that he would use his martial law powers to break up the landed oligarchy. He failed, and the EDSA Revolution of 1986 ended with his mandate. Corazon Aquino, the wife of assassinated political opposition leader Benigno Aquino, became president (1986–1992).

Growth improved, but it was below that achieved by other Southeast Asian countries until the Asian Financial Crisis of 1997–1998.[1] Though there have been significant differences in performance and outcomes among East and Southeast Asian countries since the 1960s, there are also parallels, in particular,

DOI: 10.4324/9781003728719-6

fast structural transformation with the rise of manufacturing and the implementation of an export-led growth model (Chapter 3), as well as the significant role of the public sector (industrial policies) supporting firms that were competing in international markets to survive.[2] In the cases of Japan, South Korea, and Taiwan, land reform was key. Ultimately, firms in the private sector played a key role in the East and Southeast Asian story of technological upgrading and structural change. This was where learning and upgrading came from, namely, the latecomer firm model.

These features are not present in the Philippine setting, and this is where the country differs from its neighbors. The first few decades of the post-colonial period of the Philippines were difficult. The country did not undergo any serious land reform, and the Bell Act of 1946, imposed by the United States as a condition to grant independence, did not facilitate the industrialization of the country (Chapter 2).

In what follows, and in the next chapter, we elaborate upon four important issues that help explain why the Philippines did not join East Asia's fast-growth club and which, in different forms, remain as obstacles to our country's progress: (1) failed land reforms and the state of agriculture, (2) the role of government, (3) the nature of the relationship between the state and the private sector, and (4) failed industrialization programs. This last point is taken up in Chapter 7.

6.2 Failed Land Reforms

As noted earlier, land reform was key in Japan, South Korea, and Taiwan. Land reforms allowed the modernization of the sector by redistributing land. This created plots of such a size that mechanization made economic sense. Second, workers left agriculture and found jobs in activities that paid higher wages. It was in this way that these countries reached the Lewis turning point, that is, the transition in a developing economy when surplus labor in the traditional sector (like agriculture) is fully absorbed into the modern, industrial sector. This shift typically leads to a rise in wages for both agricultural and unskilled industrial workers as the supply of cheap labor diminishes. With almost 25% of employment in agriculture, the Philippines has not reached such a point.

Probably no Asian country has produced so many land reform programs as the Philippines. Also, it is likely that no ruling Asian elite has devised so many ways to avoid implementing them. As mentioned in Chapter 2, the first land reform of the Philippines dates back to 1904, shortly after the transfer of colonial powers from Spain to the United States. It was a failure. Rural poverty in the next decades led to agrarian unrest (despite measures such as the introduction of a general minimum wage of one peso/day or an eight-hour day). The Huk rebel movement in Luzon, which fought the Japanese during World War II, increased in scale. Local politicians responded to this with a new tenancy law, which was not enforced; instead, they resettled a few thousand landless farmers. After World War II, many landowners recovered their land from the rebels by raising private armies.

Two reports issued by the United States, in 1950 and 1951, stated clearly that redistributive land reform was the only way to tackle the situation.[3] This never happened, and all successive governments have done since the 1950s is implement cosmetic changes to avoid civil war. Examples are the Philippine Rural Reconstruction Movement that the United States helped set up and fund—it did not promote compulsory land redistribution—or the 1954–1955 legislation to expropriate private tenanted estates over 300 hectares, which in 1963 was lowered to 75 hectares—compulsory purchase only occurred when a specific locality was declared a "land reform area."

President Diosdado Macapagal tried to undertake significant land reform during his tenure (1961–1965). His most notable achievement in this area was the passage of the Agricultural Land Reform Code of 1963, Republic Act No. 3844 (1963). However, as noted in Chapter 2, this was a very revised version by landlords in Congress. The key features of the 1963 Agricultural Land Reform Code were:

1. *Abolition of share tenancy.* The law aimed to replace the exploitative share tenancy system with a leasehold system, granting farmers more control over the land they tilled.
2. *Land-to-the-tiller program.* It set the foundation for land redistribution, allowing tenant farmers to purchase the land they worked on through government assistance.
3. *Creation of the Land Authority.* This agency was tasked with implementing land reform policies and overseeing land distribution.
4. *Emphasis on cooperatives.* The law promoted cooperatives and rural credit to help farmers become more independent and financially stable.

Macapagal's land reform efforts were progressive, but they faced implementation challenges due to resistance from landowning elites and inadequate government resources.

The result of all this was that, in 1969, the Huk movement, together with a reformed Communist Party of the Philippines, created the New People's Army (NPA). In the 1970s, the NPA started cooperating with Christian socialist activists who set up rural-based areas following the Chinese Revolution. The NPA enforced rent and interest reductions and, occasionally, the redistribution of land.

It was in this context that Ferdinand Marcos Sr. declared martial law in 1972. He justified it by arguing that only an authoritarian government could enforce land reform. Despite the promises, there was very little land reform: It affected only corn and rice land, it involved a high 7-hectare retention limit, and most of it targeted the properties of his political enemies (e.g., the Aquino family).

During the almost 14 years that martial law lasted, the NPA increased its presence across the country. As an act of desperation and shortly before fleeing the country, President Marcos Sr. ordered the government to hand out thousands of titles to plots of land, called "emancipation patents," to farmers who had not completed their land reform application process. This came too late, and Marcos Sr. was forced to leave with his family. It is estimated that between 1900 and 1986, land reform in the Philippines led to the redistribution of 315,000 hectares of land, just about 4% of the cultivated areas (Studwell, 2013, p. 37).

Marcos's successor, President Corazon Aquino (1986–1992), did not do much more to advance land reform.[4] She was only pushed to act when, in 1987, a farmers' demonstration in Manila ended up with the police killing 13 people (known as the "Mendiola massacre"). As a result, President Aquino asked Congress to develop a new land reform program, the 1988 Comprehensive Agrarian Reform Law (CARL), Republic Act 6657, which targeted 8.2 million hectares of farmland.[5] It was time-limited for ten years (1988–1998). Unlike Presidential Decree 27 under President Ferdinand Marcos Sr., which was limited to rice and corn lands, the CARL aimed to redistribute land, regardless of crops or fruit produced and irrespective of tenurial arrangements, to farmers and regular farmworkers who were landless. The objective was to lift the economic status of the beneficiaries.

As a result of peasant unrest, in August 2009, Congress extended the program's implementation until June 2014 (Republic Act 9700, Comprehensive Agrarian Reform Program Extension with Reforms, or CARPER). Beyond this, the program has been extended multiple times due to several challenges. The Department of Agrarian Reform continues implementing agrarian reform initiatives, including land distribution and support services to agrarian reform beneficiaries. In July 2023, President Ferdinand Marcos Jr. signed into law the New Agrarian Emancipation Act (Republic Act No. 11953). This legislation waives the unpaid amortizations, interests, and penalties of agrarian reform beneficiaries, effectively freeing over 600,000 farmers from financial burdens associated with land awarded under CARL. The government assumes responsibility for the remaining balance due to landowners under the voluntary land transfer or direct payment scheme. In conclusion, although the original deadlines for land distribution under CARL and CARPER have lapsed, the Philippine government's commitment to agrarian reform persists through ongoing land distribution efforts and supportive legislation like the New Agrarian Emancipation Act.

From the start, the problem with the CARL was that it was unclear whether its purpose was to increase the productivity of land or to dispense social justice. The result is that the CARL has been another insufficient land reform that contains plenty of loopholes: There was no reliable land survey prior to it, deals were negotiated between landlords and farmers without government supervision, it was not overseen by tenant committees but by government bureaucrats, prawn and fish farms were exempted, and the retention rate was very high, at 5 hectares, plus another 3 for every owner's child above the age of 15. Sadly, as it happened with previous attempts, the Filipino elite undermined it.[6] Today, there seems to be a stalemate to leave things where they are (Coronel et al., 2004, p. 41). As of 2025, the CARL is still in effect, and Republic Act 9700 (signed in 2009) amended it to extend the deadline of distributing agricultural lands to farmers by five more years.

During the last two decades, agriculture's share in total gross domestic product (GDP) and its contribution to output growth have declined, as Figure 4.8 in Chapter 4 showed. Given that this sector still employs over 20% of all workers (about 10 million) at low productivity, it is of paramount importance that the number of workers employed in this sector decrease significantly. This important point does not seem to be understood. Keeping low-productivity jobs and fearing imports hurt the sector itself. Indeed, although there is awareness about the need to improve the sector's performance and productivity, this cannot happen without a significant reduction in the number of workers in the sector. This will occur when other activities create employment at higher wages. Only then will it be possible to mechanize the sector and introduce modern technologies to increase productivity. Likewise, the sector needs to industrialize to generate more value added.

To be successful, perhaps the CARL should have followed the *enclosure movement* of European countries during the second agricultural revolution for the crops where this is a sensible strategy.[7] In the Philippines, weaker farmers are not allowed to be taken over by better farmers, resulting in no land consolidation. Moreover, non-tariff barriers and government regulations make it nearly impossible for the private sector to import agricultural products that are much cheaper in other countries.

The consolidation of farms (especially in the coconut sector, fragmented by the CARL, and in other high-value tree or crops, such as cacao, coffee, mangoes, avocado, durian, bamboo, and palm oil) is necessary (perhaps to a minimum of 25 hectares). Only then will Philippine agriculture take off. These commercial plantations are the only means to attain growth in the agricultural sector. There is no alternative to increasingly consolidate some of the small farms to attain the necessary economies of scale to significantly increase the productivity of the agricultural sector. This consolidation can be done through cooperatives.

The Philippine government, nevertheless, claimed that the CARL met its targets (Studwell, 2013, p. 39). Official data indicate that by the end of 2006, 6.8 million hectares of the targeted 8.2 million hectares of farmland had been subject to land reform, benefiting 4.1 million rural households. The truth is that Philippine statistics count all kinds of new land titles that have been issued, not practical and physical changes in ownership. Moreover, much of the land that on paper has been redistributed has been leased back or sold illegally to its original owners or others (Studwell, 2013, p. 39). Finally, only about a third of the targeted 8.2 million hectares under land reform is private; the rest is publicly owned forest where some farming takes place.

Certainly, there is no such thing as a one-size-fits-all. Farm consolidation, perhaps, is not the solution for crops such as rice. The agrarian reform reduced the average rice farms to 1.3 hectares. Yields remain low, slightly over 4 tons per hectare. Yet the experience of other rice producers indicates that productivity can be high in small plots. The average Vietnamese farm size is only 0.5 hectares, and yet the average yield is 6 tons per hectare. In Taiwan, the average yield is also slightly above 6 tons per hectare. The disparity in yields can be attributed to several factors: (1) *Agricultural practices.* Taiwan employs advanced farming techniques, including the use of high-quality seeds, efficient irrigation systems, and modern machinery, which contribute to higher productivity. (2) *Government support.* Taiwan's government provides substantial support to farmers through subsidies, research and development, and infrastructure development, enhancing agricultural productivity. (3) *Climate and soil conditions.* Taiwan's climate and soil are conducive to high rice yields, benefiting from favorable weather patterns and fertile soils. In contrast, the Philippines faces challenges such as limited access to modern farming technologies, inadequate infrastructure, and vulnerability to natural disasters, which lower agricultural productivity.

Given the importance of rice in the Philippines, the government passed the Philippine Rice Tariffication Law (RTL), officially known as Republic Act No. 11203 (2019). This legislation aimed to liberalize the rice sector in the Philippines and reform the way rice is imported into the country. One key goal of the law was to lower rice prices for consumers by increasing supply through more competitive rice imports. The government hoped that this would help address food security issues and inflation, particularly because rice is a staple food in the Philippines. Overall, the RTL represents a significant shift in the Philippines' agricultural policy, aiming to create a more market-oriented rice sector. At the same time, it tries to safeguard the interests of local farmers. The law removed the previously imposed quantitative restrictions (QRs) on rice imports, which limited the amount of rice that could be imported into the Philippines. Under the former system, the National Food Authority (NFA) had a monopoly on rice imports. The RTL ended the monopoly and enabled the private sector to import rice. The NFA was transformed into a mere public warehouse firm for the country's rice buffer stock. The RTL was also approved to comply with the country's legal obligation to impose tariffs on import QRs in agriculture as a member of the World Trade Organization. This was done for other agricultural products in 1996, but the government kept deferring it for rice, on the grounds that rice farmers were not ready for it. But the tariffication could no longer be postponed by 2019, and the finance department had to urge Congress to impose tariffs on the rice QR.

The RTL has made rice import decisions more transparent and reduced the country's vulnerability to import shortages and high rice prices. Instead of QRs, the law has established a system of tariffs on imported rice. This means that imported rice would be subject to import duties rather than to strict quotas. The tariffs were set at 35% for rice imports from countries within the ASEAN (Association of Southeast Asian Nations) and higher rates for imports from non-ASEAN countries. A portion of the tariff revenues collected from rice imports was allocated to the Rice Competitiveness Enhancement Fund (RCEF), which aims to support local rice farmers. The fund is intended to provide assistance in areas such as farm mechanization, seed distribution, credit, and training programs, aiming to enhance competitive farming practices. While the law aimed to make rice more accessible and affordable for consumers, it also included provisions to support local farmers to help them adapt to new competition from imported rice. The idea was to enhance the productivity and competitiveness of local rice farmers.

The RTL does not allow the NFA to engage in rice trading, except for keeping the emergency buffer stocks. The problem with not permitting the NFA to conduct commercial operations is that it deprives the national government of the capacity to effectively countervail rice price manipulation by a few rice traders/importers.

What has been the impact of the RTL? In 2019, the year the Rice Tariffication Law was implemented, the Philippines imported a record 3.0 million metric tons of rice, the first time any country imported that much of the staple (with similarly large imports in 2022, 2023, and 2024). That opened the floodgates for reckless, greed-driven rice imports. The RTL failed to bring down rice prices significantly. When the Philippine government slashed rice import tariffs from 35% to 15% in July 2024, the expectation was simple: Lower tariffs would mean lower retail prices for consumers. Yet months later, while rice prices had fallen, the reality is that the decline was not the result of the tariff cut. Domestic rice prices dropped by 19–23%, but the real driver was global dynamics. International prices of Vietnam's 5% broken rice fell by 35% over the same period, thanks to shifting supply and demand in the world market. In theory, a competitive domestic market should have passed on much of the tariff reduction to consumers. The fact that it did not reveals a deeper structural issue in the Philippine rice market. Why didn't the tariff cut work? The gap suggests that rice importers and traders are not passing on cost savings efficiently. Instead, the benefits of tariff reduction are being absorbed within the supply chain rather than flowing to Filipino households.

Things are not much better in 2025. One possibility is that a *de facto* rice cartel, involving a few large traders and importers, sets rice prices to maximize profits. The government resorted to using suggested retail prices for rice, a measure that is costly to enforce and thus ineffective. The most effective measure that the national government could use is to countervail rice price manipulation. This could be done through a state-controlled importing corporation that could purchase rice alongside private traders. This would inject competition into the market and limit the ability of traders to manipulate prices. However, the government does not have this capacity today, as the RTL disallowed commercial operations of the NFA. No matter how this is done, government participation must be carefully designed.[8] If a state corporation dominates trade, private traders may be crowded out, creating new inefficiencies. The aim should be a level playing field where both government and private importers compete transparently. If the government can import rice at competitive rates, private traders will be compelled to follow suit, ultimately benefiting consumers. The bottom line is that lowering tariffs alone will not fix the Philippines' rice conundrum. Unless domestic market structures are reformed, consumers will remain vulnerable to high prices and asymmetric price transmission. The tariff cut may have been a bold first step, but without addressing the underlying market inefficiencies, its impact will remain muted.

The problem is not importing rice. It is about productivity. In fact, the NFA had several mandates in addition to its monopoly over imports and exports of rice, although the country has not exported rice since the 1970s. It supported farmgate *palay* (unmilled rice) prices, subsidized rice prices for the poor, managed the country's emergency rice stocks, and regulated the domestic rice and corn trade. It also helped increase the productivity of rice farms and reduce post-harvest waste. The RTL is silent on these important functions.

The result of all this is that agriculture in the Philippines has not served the same purpose it did in Japan, South Korea, or Taiwan, that is, to kick-start development. As we have mentioned already, primary agriculture still provides employment to over 20% of Filipino workers (75% of whom are landless), and yields are low in a country where cultivable land accounts for only one-third of the land mass and has a climate and soil quality that are conducive to high yields. One such example is the case of sugar, where big landlords (justifying the need to maintain large plots) claimed that sugar growing can only be competitive on plantations of a minimum scale. However, Philippine yields are significantly lower (around 63 tons per hectare) than in Taiwan or the PRC (around 80–85 tons). The reason is that in Japan, South Korea, and Taiwan, land reforms were accompanied by significant state involvement: Not only did the state redistribute land quickly and fairly, but it also provided irrigation, fertilizers, credit, service extension, and marketing support. This did not happen in the Philippines, where farmers have received very little state infrastructural support. Low yields also extend to crops such as corn, at 3.3 tons per hectare, against Taiwan's 5.3 tons.

Efforts are underway in the Philippines to address these challenges, including the implementation of programs like the *Masagana* Rice Industry Development Program, which aims to boost rice yields to 7.5 metric tons per hectare. Achieving yields comparable to those of Taiwan will require sustained investment in technology, infrastructure, and farmer education. And we insist: Productivity in the sector will not increase unless the number of workers it employs declines.

It is ironic that land reform has failed in the country that pioneered Asia's Green Revolution, a project of the International Rice Research Institute (located in Los Baños) with United States assistance. Apart from deep-seated interests to prevent the full implementation of a genuine land reform, the Green Revolution was biased because instead of helping the most needed farmers, it was implemented in the most favored areas (with the objective of replicating laboratory results), which were already enjoying higher yields than the rest. Moreover, the mechanization of some areas increased inequality and fostered a peasant rebellion. The consequence is that the gap between the rich and the poor regions has widened. Those responsible for the program picked progressive farmers (often the richest) and gave them a package of seeds, credit, and advice. The thought was that there would be a demonstration effect. This effect was only partial because poorer farmers introduced the new technologies later and on a much lower scale than their richer neighbors did.

6.3 Gerschenkron's Latecomer Model and the Role of the State

One important difference between the Philippines and its more successful East Asian neighbors (see the discussion in Chapter 4) is the role that the state played. We do not mean to imply that the Philippine government must follow the same path, yet we ask the following question: Is it possible that the structure of the Philippine economy changes (becomes more sophisticated) quickly without an active government?

The intellectual underpinnings of government intervention in East Asia go back to Gerschenkron's (1962) *latecomer model*, based on the following tenets:[9] (1) Poor countries enjoy the advantages of backwardness, that is, their development is based on learning and mastering products and processes invented by the more advanced countries. (2) The more backward a country is, the more important the role of the state as the facilitator of this process. Without the government pushing to alter the structure of production of the economy toward advanced industries (from light manufacturing and agriculture into ships, steel, autos, industrial machinery, and electronics), growth and development would have happened much more slowly in these poor (latecomer) countries. This means that the ultimate purpose of industrial policy and targeting certain sectors was more than addressing market failures; it was to induce distortions in the short term to realize long-term gains. And (3) the more backward a country, the less likely was its agriculture to play any active role by offering to the growing industries the advantages of an expanding industrial market based, in turn, on the rising productivity of agricultural labor.

Amsden (1989) used this model to explain East Asia's success, and Hobday (1995) to document how East Asian firms climbed the development ladder in the electronics industry. The experience of East Asia's latecomers shows that they focused on industries with dominant technologies. In these industries, competition centers on cost minimization and on building mass production capacities as fast as possible. The experience of East Asia's late industrializers (starting with Japan after World War II) shows that they all had effective developmental states that provided extensive support to their firms, not only by boosting the profits of those firms that were prepared to enter the competitive arena, through subsidies, tax breaks, or low interest rates on loans, but also through mechanisms designed to curb rent-seeking. Some of the most cited cases are those of South Korea and Taiwan, where governments provided support in terms of subsidies or tax breaks in exchange (i.e., reciprocity) for firms achieving certain export targets. Failure to meet these targets would lead to the withdrawal of support. This was very much a results-oriented performance mechanism. It proved to be a powerful means to discipline both government and firms, as well as to control rent-seeking. All this assistance to their firms was complemented by a complex set of catch-up institutions, such as the Singapore Economic Development Board and Taiwan's Industrial Technology Research Institute, whose goal was to capture technologies and raise skill levels. The industrialization problem, namely, whether the development of a modern capitalist industry is possible in a backward country, is equally relevant today.

In the context of successful East Asian economies, exporting played a signaling role for governments. Studwell (2013) argued that the governments of South Korea, Singapore, and Taiwan played a crucial role in development by encouraging manufacturing firms to export goods, thereby subjecting them to foreign competition. This was often achieved by offering incentives to firms that engaged in exporting, such as direct subsidies and subsidized credit, privileges with regard to importing raw materials, as well as additional tax benefits and permission to seek financing from abroad. In more extreme cases, firms were harassed and forced into entering export markets. Studwell further argued that differences in the extent to which the governments of South Korea, Singapore, and Taiwan were able to embed domestic firms in international markets set these countries apart from other countries in Asia that did not enjoy such rapid development.

Exporting provided a mechanism and a signal through which governments could learn whether their efforts and interventions in developing manufacturing sectors were fruitful or not. It allowed them to observe whether domestic firms could compete in the global marketplace. For this reason, exporters were required to report on their exporting activities regularly. One aspect of government policy in Korea, Singapore, and Taiwan, as emphasized by Studwell (2013), was their willingness to cast aside firms that were incapable of competing in world markets, creating a policy of weeding out losers rather than picking winners. This was achieved through bankruptcy, forced mergers, the withdrawal of capital, and the withholding of production licenses. This process was most clear with South Korea's *chaebols*, as many of those that existed in the 1960s disappeared by the mid-1970s, and then again in the 1980s. In a majority of these cases, forced mergers and bankruptcy led to the death of the firm. A similar development also emerged during the Asian Financial Crisis of 1997–1998, with a number of companies, including Daewoo, Hanbo, Halla, and Sambi, also being culled through a process of state negotiation.

Amsden (1995), comparing the old, advanced economies (including Japan) with those of South Korea, Singapore, Taiwan, Indonesia, Malaysia, and Thailand, elaborated upon the latecomer industrialization model and highlighted three important differences. First, on the question of why latecomers needed more government, she claimed that "industrial policy was invented to raise productivity levels" (Amsden, 1995, p. 792), given that the two other options to lower unit labor costs were to lower nominal wages or to miss industrialization at all. The United Kingdom did not need much government support because it was the first one and it was the developer (through trial and error) of the steam engine and the other technologies developed at that time, which increased productivity. Something similar happened in Germany and the United States about 100 years later in the context of the Second Industrial Revolution. They progressed based on the new technologies developed at that time, chemicals and electricity, as well as a whole array of new organizational forms, with professional managers and much more formal R&D. Governments intervened more than in the case of the United Kingdom, mostly protecting infant industries. Then came Japan and, later, South Korea, Singapore, and Taiwan (and a few more countries around the world). These countries "did *not* achieve their growth in productivity by new products and processes . . . [it involved] . . . 'pure' learning" (Amsden, 1995, p. 793; italics original), that is, by borrowing and becoming proficient in existing technologies. This process is very different from those in the United Kingdom, Germany, or the United States. Although the first group focused on R&D, the new industrializers needed to make sure that the borrowed technologies could be adapted and improved to suit the specific needs of their factories. Because these countries did not have the competitive advantage that new products and processes confer, the role of government had to be greater and go beyond protecting infant industries.

Second, Amsden (1995) argued that the actual experience of the degree of government intervention in the economy did not squarely follow Gerschenkron's prediction, namely, the more backward the economy the more intervention. Rather, intervention was greater in countries with smaller *competitive assets* in relation to global competitive needs. A competitive asset is anything that contributes to the international competitiveness of raw labor power and raises labor productivity, for example, being a port or being endowed with natural resources. Why did the British government not intervene heavily in Hong Kong, except for providing mass subsidized housing, which lowered labor costs? Because in the 1950s and the 1960s, the colony was able to access Commonwealth preferences, which provided it with a market shielded from Japanese competition in clothing and textiles. Hong Kong also had a significant influx of experienced textile engineers and technicians who had moved after the Chinese Revolution. Indonesia, Malaysia, and Thailand also had a competitive asset, a natural resource base; hence, government intervention was initially modest. It increased as time passed by, as these countries sought to diversify their economies, because all three lacked a key competitive asset: entrepreneurial skills. Government intervention in Japan, as seen earlier, was notable because it was the first Asian country to develop an industrial base prior to World War II. Which governments intervened most heavily and why? Those of South Korea, Singapore, and Taiwan, because they lacked competitive assets. Yes, Singapore was a port, but at the time of independence in 1965, its economy, with 2 million people and a land area of only 581 km^2, was adrift. The other two were in political disarray in the 1950s.

Third, she argued that the governments of Japan, South Korea, Singapore, and Taiwan did a better job than those of Indonesia, Malaysia, and Thailand because they were much more forceful in applying the reciprocity principle of providing subsidies in exchange for performance standards, often in the form of export targets. This system of reciprocity disciplined both firms and the government itself. Interventions in the first group were of higher quality because their bureaucracies were of higher quality.

The Philippines does not conform to Gerschenkron's predictions like other East and Southeast Asian countries. Only the third proposition about agriculture applies to the Philippines. Though it has competitive assets, including access to the sea, and it is endowed with natural resources, these were never utilized to a significant extent, and hence, this cannot justify the small government intervention. Instead, we believe that the Bell Act of 1946, and decades of American intellectual influence, prevented the development of a strong government that could push the economy like it happened in its neighbors. The situation today demands swift action. Although we believe the private sector (thousands of firms) is not in a position to do what a well-functioning government does (in particular, to provide public goods for an egalitarian society), the reality is that the Philippine government (public sector) is incapable of doing it. The Philippine government believes that it has to tax prior to being able to fund its expenses. This is incorrect, and it has negatively affected the nation's development. Arguing this way amounts to stopping the flow of blood into the economy. As we shall elaborate in Chapter 11, our view is that the government should use its ability to pay in its own currency to fund all the services the country needs (public goods). At the same time, the government should allow the private sector to operate with minimal interference (and enable and help it) in all those areas truly under the realm of the private sector.

6.4 The State and the Private Sector in the Philippines

This section complements the analysis in Chapter 3 with the KPSW framework and the historical account in Chapter 2 about the economic debates within the government in the decades after independence. It looks specifically at the relationship between the state and the private sector.

The economic relationships developed during the American colonization of 1898–1946, and afterward with the agreements post-independence, undermined and crippled Philippine economic development. Indeed, the Bell Act of 1946 both rehabilitated the sugar industry and provided the free entry of American products into the Philippines. These made it difficult to develop national industries, in particular, the manufacturing sector. From here on, it can be said that the Philippines' history after independence is a case of a country that developed "extractive" institutions, in the terminology of Acemoglu and Robinson (2012), and was dominated by a landed oligarchy of great families who fought for economic and political power and took over the House of Representatives, the Senate, and all other important political positions (Chapter 3). They became the country's own colonialists. This has been the case since the first Constitution in 1898. This naturally led to a weak state. Government capture (many powerful landowners are congressmen, much more so in the old days) has prevented change. In the words of Bardhan (2001, p. 277): "The political stumbling blocks to beneficial institutional change in many poor countries may have more to do with distributive conflicts and asymmetries in bargaining power." These distributive conflicts lead to the persistence of dysfunctional institutions. Countries like the Philippines have developed self-reinforcing mechanisms that perpetuate socially suboptimal institutions. Some initial adopters chose these institutions at some point in the past because they suited their interests, but then the whole system became "locked in." One may wonder why these institutions have not changed. The answer would seem to be that powerful vested interests make institutional change politically difficult in terms of distributive conflicts and asymmetries in bargaining power (Aldaba et al., 2005). The tenacity of vested interests, the difficulty of mobilizing collective action to bring about institutional change, and the differential capacity of different social groups for mobilization and coordination are long-lasting barriers to economic progress.

On paper, the Philippines developed early on a sophisticated system of legal codes governing elections, commerce, and corporations. They indeed read like strict regulations. In practice, however, politicians learn to manipulate these regulations to siphon off rents, and they get rich. Education is key to entering this club (Coronel et al., 2004). The wealth of politicians was derived from agricultural land for a long time. While this is still important, its role has declined as landowners moved to commercial, real estate, or industrial enterprises (Coronel et al., 2004, Table 1.24). This led to a shift during the 1990s from a *rentier* mentality among rural agrarian elites to a more urban-based entrepreneurial and competitive mindset. To be fair, today the Philippines is more open to competition and new entrants than agricultural landowners ever were.

To better understand the differences between the private sector and the state of the more successful Asian economies and those of the Philippines, it is important to appreciate the role of rents, that is, returns over and beyond the normal economic opportunity earnings, such as extra earnings obtained from enjoying a favorable location, created out of state intervention operating through social processes of political positioning. Given that successful Asian governments intervened much more than the Philippine government did, it follows that these other economies created more rents as a share of GDP. The difference lies in how rents were used and the type of firms that dominate in each type of economy (Montes, 1994). Although successful Asian countries had profit-seeking firms that operated in a more or less competitive atmosphere and were driven to innovate to lower costs, the Philippines was dominated by a few large firms that lived on capturing rents through political influence and then applying those rents to retain or expand their standing. The state was not powerful enough to either turn their investments to contribute to social interests or to intervene to open the market to other firms. Montes (1994, p. 143) described it as follows:

> These dominant firms are controlled by large family business groupings that have historically arisen out of landholdings, rural credit, state allocations of war reparations finance after World War II, timber logging concessions, and perhaps the original land grants obtained during the Spanish colonial period (though the last is unlikely since in the time scale of decades the membership of this select group has been quite unstable).

Coronel et al. (2004) provided a good account of who these families were. Where did their rents come from? These were often derived from the exploitation of natural resources, resulting from the difference between international prices and low domestic extraction costs, or from government-controlled access to the resource. There were also rents that derived from industrialization policy. These were state tax revenues and international financing. The latter came between independence and the early 1990s from US military bases. The state served "as the source of newly available rent resources packaged from foreign savings" (Montes, 1994, p. 145).

To emphasize this point, certainly, successful Asian economies also engaged in rent-related activities; however, in these cases, the state played an important role in determining the flows of rent-generated resources. In the Philippines, however, powerful groups spent (and still do) a significant amount of time on political struggles and political competition (much more than on economic competition), with the consequence that if an entrepreneur decides not to invest in these activities, they will be able to expand their business only to the point where they will start infringing on the business interests of other groups.

How were these firms incentivized to undertake development investments? The state had to offer them a return that was competitive with land from land rents, natural resource extraction, trading, and other traditional business activities. This means that reforms have a double effect: On the one hand, they dismantle the power of the state to extend these privileges. On the other hand, they undermine the state further, particularly in terms of having the capacity to open opportunities for other firms to prosper. Moreover, liberalization reforms have taken away protection from activities with the greatest potential for generating growth, while maintaining protection for slow-growing industries.

Chapter 2 discussed the "Filipino First" policy of the late 1950s. It seemed to end with President Macapagal (1961–1965). Two decades later, however, Sections 10 and 11 of Article XII of the 1987 Constitution, and the Public Sector Act, limited foreign investors' participation to 40%, implying that foreign investors would have to partner with local firms to participate in key economic sectors, such as power, telecommunications, and water. Likewise, foreigners are prohibited from owning land in the Philippines. Only Filipinos or corporations at least 60% owned by Filipinos are permitted to own land. Foreigners can lease, though.[10] This again gave Filipinos preferential treatment in the national economy over foreigners. The unintended consequence was to limit the sectors available to foreign investors and the local capture of business ventures by a few uncompetitive oligarchs. Likewise, after 1987, there was significant privatization of government assets. Because of the foreign participation limitation, the conglomerates did not encounter foreign competition in their bid to take over government assets. Competition was among a handful of powerful groups.

These constitutional provisions have been subject to discussions, with proposed amendments aimed at liberalizing foreign investment in the Philippines, in recent years. For instance, in March 2024, the Philippine House Committee on Constitutional Amendments approved "Resolution of Both Houses No. 7," proposing to amend economic provisions of the 1987 Constitution, including removing the 40% foreign ownership limit for public utilities, education, and advertising firms. The Philippines has undertaken several legislative initiatives to relax foreign ownership restrictions and attract more foreign investment. Notable efforts include (1) *The Public Service Act (PSA) Amendatory Law.* Signed into law on March 2, 2022, the PSA Amendatory Law redefined the term "public utility" to exclude certain sectors, thereby removing the 40% foreign ownership cap in these areas. This change allows foreign investors to own 100% of businesses in sectors such as telecommunications, transportation, and power generation. (2) *The Foreign Investments Act (FIA) Amendatory Law.* Enacted on July 11, 2022, the FIA Amendatory Law eased restrictions on foreign ownership in micro- and small enterprises. This amendment facilitates foreign investment in small and medium-sized businesses, including those in financial technology and precision agriculture. And (3) *the Corporate Recovery and Tax Incentives for Enterprises (CREATE) Act.* Signed on May 28, 2021, the CREATE law reduced the corporate income tax rate from 30% to 25% and introduced additional fiscal incentives—updated in 2024 as the CREATE MORE Act, discussed in Chapter 7. These measures, and others mentioned in Chapter 7, aim to enhance the Philippines' competitiveness and appeal to foreign investors. As we discuss there, we doubt they will lead to the changes in the structure of the economy that we argue the Philippines needs.

Notes

1 The Asian Financial Crisis of 1997–1998 affected the Philippines, but the impact was much smaller than in Indonesia, Malaysia, and Thailand.

2 While the manufacturing sector was, like in many other countries, an engine of growth, Montes (1994) indicates that the structure of the Philippine economy changed very little between 1960 and 1990. The share of agriculture in GDP declined from 30% to 22.5%, while that of manufacturing increased from 24.85% to 25.45%. The manufacturing employment share even declined slightly during this 30-year period. This is in stark contrast with the structural changes of East Asian economies.

3 Studwell (2013, p. 36) noted that "while radical land reform was supported by the US Embassy in Manila, it did not win support in Washington."
4 President Aquino belonged to the Cojuangco family, a landed family.
5 It originally targeted 10.3 million hectares and with considerably more private land, but for unclear reasons, this was reduced to 8.2 million.
6 For example, the large Hacienda Luisita received permission to avoid breakup by exploiting one of the many loopholes of the CARL, the stock distribution option (SDO), which allowed the family to give its tenants equity in a new farming business rather than family plots. However, by overvaluing non-land inputs and management expenses and undervaluing land, the shareholders work for very little return. The result is that Hacienda Luisita has been hardly affected by the reform. Variants of the SDO have also been used by other Philippine landlords, for example, form a joint venture with the tenants that involved the nominal transfer of land to them but with the landlord retaining management control.
7 "Enclosure" was the removal of common rights to establish exclusive private ownership of land. In the 16th and 17th centuries, civil authority mandated the enclosures of these fragmented lands through acts of parliament. The most productive enclosed farms meant that fewer farmers were needed to work in the same area, leaving many villagers without land and grazing rights. Many of them moved to the cities in search of work in the emerging factories.
8 We do not suggest that this has to be done through the NFA, which was responsible for not making the market price more competitive.
9 In more detail, the model was conceived to characterize the industrialization of countries like Germany, Italy, and Russia. Additional propositions of the model are thus: (1) The more backward a country's economy, the more likely its industrialization to start discontinuously as a sudden great spurt proceeding at a relatively high rate of manufacturing output. (2) The more backward a country's economy, the more pronounced the stress in its industrialization on bigness of both plant and enterprise. (3) The more backward a country's economy, the greater the stress upon producers' goods as against consumers' goods. (4) The more backward a country's economy, the heavier the pressure upon the levels of consumption of the population. And (e) the more backward a country's economy, the greater the part played by special institutional factors designed to increase the supply of capital to the nascent industries and, in addition, to provide them with less decentralized and better-informed entrepreneurial guidance; the more backward the country, the more pronounced the coerciveness and comprehensiveness of those factors.
10 Since 2025, foreign investors can now lease land for up to 99 years, in some special cases.

7

WHY HAS PHILIPPINE PROGRESS BEEN SLOW? II: FAILED INDUSTRIALIZATION PROGRAMS

7.1 Failed Industrialization Programs

This chapter addresses the fourth reason that explains the slow progress of the Philippines for decades: its failed industrialization programs.

As noted in Chapters 2 and 6, the Bell Act of 1946, imposed by the United States as a condition to grant independence, did not facilitate the industrialization of the Philippines. However, De Dios and Williamson (2015) argued that the Philippines was the third Asian country (and the first in Southeast Asia) to enter the so-called "5% industrial growth club"—those countries that had experienced industrial growth rates of at least 5% a year, in the early 20th century. This indicates that the Philippines managed to start developing a manufacturing sector before independence in 1946. Likewise, the discussions in Chapters 2 and 6 indicates that Philippine policymakers understood the importance of industrialization for a new nation like the Philippines.

Bénétrix et al. (2015) provided information on how early countries achieved a 10-year average industrial growth rate of 5% or above. A summary for Asia is shown in Table 7.1. These countries posted a cumulative 10-year growth of at least 5% per annum. This means that growth was fast during the 10 years preceding the year shown in the Table. Table 7.1 indicates that several Asian countries joined the group of fast growers during 1896–1913. High growth rates in Asian industrial production started in Japan and China. The Philippines was the next one. Among the countries in the top part of the Table, all but South Korea had joined the modern industrial growth club by World War I. The region took advantage of the war, and growth picked up during 1913–1920. Growth slowed down during the de-globalization period after World War I, but it remained respectable in most countries. World War II delivered a significant blow to Asia, and manufacturing growth turned negative. This recovered after 1950, reaching its highest

DOI: 10.4324/9781003728719-7

TABLE 7.1 Year Asian Economies Entered 5% or Higher Annual Industrial Growth, and Annual Growth Rates (%)

Country	*Year Entered*	*1870–1896*	*1896–1913*	*1913–1920*	*1920–1938*	*1938–1950*	*1950–1973*	*1973–1990*	*1990–2007*
Japan	1899	3.3	5.9	6.5	6.7	−3.7	12.4	4.1	1.0
China	1900	7.8	7.8	9.4	5.3	−2.2	9.2	8.3	9.8
Philippines	1913		6.3	10.1	3.4	9.4	7.0	1.8	3.3
Taiwan	1914		5.1	9.8	4.4	−10.4	11.6	8.7	4.9
South Korea	1921		8.0	9.3	7.1	−4.0	13.6	11.7	7.4
Other Asian Economies That Did Not Register Fast Manufacturing Growth Prior to WWII									
Country	*Year Entered*	*1870–1896*	*1896–1913*	*1913–1920*	*1920–1938*	*1938–1950*	*1950–1973*	*1973–1990*	*1990–2007*
India	1929	0.9	2.6	−4.3	3.4	1.4	6.9	5.1	6.5
Indonesia	1941	1.3	1.3	1.0	2.7	−6.6	3.4	12.8	5.1
Myanmar	1982		0.3	3.5	2.6		3.2	3.0	12.0
Thailand	1971	0.9	2.3	1.6	2.3	2.4	11.2	8.1	5.9

Note: Other economies for which the "year entered" 5% growth is provided: Pakistan (1961), Sri Lanka (1968), Bangladesh (1971), Vietnam (1973), Mongolia (1975), Singapore (1977), Malaysia (1979), Fiji (1981), Nepal (1986), Tonga (1986), Bhutan (1992), Hong Kong (1993), Kiribati (1994), Lao PDR (1995), Papua New Guinea (1999), Cambodia (2004), Kyrgyz Republic (2004), Armenia (2005), Tajikistan (2005), Georgia (2007).

Source: Bénétrix et al. (2015, Table 3, Table 7, Table 12).

rate of growth. During World War I, Asian countries' manufacturing sectors responded to the stimulus provided by the reduction in the supply of manufactured goods to the region. After World War II, many Asian countries employed various forms of so-called import-substitution industrialization (ISI) policies, including the Philippines (Chapters 2 and 6).[1]

Bénétrix et al. (2015, Table 4) showed that the Philippines was one of Asia's top 10 industrial performers in terms of growth during 1896–1913, 1913–1920, 1920–1938, 1938–1950, and 1950–1973. It then disappeared from the list of top performers. Philippine industrialization stagnated from the 1970s onward (during the second part of the Marcos Sr. administration) (Table 7.1), thereby missing the East Asian Miracle, which brought the dramatic ascent of newly industrialized economies across Asia from the 1970s to the mi-1990s. Why did this happen? It is complicated to provide a single answer, and a review of the literature suggests that different causes were likely at play.

As noted in Chapter 2, between independence and the early 1960s, Philippine administrations tried import substitution industrialization (ISI) policies. Philippine policymakers tried to steer the direction of the economy by implementing industrialization policies. Following Balance of Payments problems in 1949, the Philippines imposed import and foreign exchange controls. The major purpose of these was to ration foreign exchange. However, in the late 1950s and 1960s, the policy was also used, like in other countries, as a means of building an industrial base through an import-substitution strategy. This strategy was based on a system of protection that relied on an overvalued exchange rate defended by tariffs and quantitative restrictions. Toward the end of the 1950s, the tariff structure changed such that duties on raw materials, intermediate goods, and essential goods that were not domestically available, were reduced. In contrast, duties on non-essential finished goods and items that could be produced domestically, increased. Over time, this had the effect of encouraging the use of artificially cheap imported inputs while penalizing exports, and encouraging the import of cheap capital, which led to domestic industries that were highly capital-intensive. The import substitution policy was indeed quite successful in shifting imports away from consumer goods and toward capital goods, with the share of consumer goods in imports falling from 37% in 1949 to 14% by the end of the 1950s. Over the same period, the share of capital goods increased from 10% to nearly 20%. This, however, would prove to be problematic later. The reason is that the purpose of limiting imports of finished consumer goods was to encourage the development of the local industries. This policy worked during the 1950s, but it ran out of steam (see following).

In addition to the highly protectionist trade regime, policies aimed at promoting domestic industries were also implemented. These policies included the granting of fiscal incentives, such as tax exemptions on imported capital and equipment and tax credits on domestic capital equipment, exemptions from most revenue taxes, and targeted lending. Controls on entry into crowded industries were also implemented. During the 1940s and 1950s, the state became directly involved in manufacturing as well as in other activities. By the early 1950s, the national government was operating railroads, hotels, electric power, gas and water works, as well as directly producing coal, cement, steel, pulp and paper, and textiles and yarns. It was also operating a shipyard for both repairs and construction, as well as engineering shops. As an example, Executive Order No. 356 (1950) created the National Shipyards and Steel Corporation (NASSCO), tasked with operating shipyards and fabrication facilities—corroborating government participation in shipbuilding and heavy industrial activity. The company's steel mill turned scrap metal into ingots, bars, steel shapes, and rods—mostly for ships. The logic behind combining the steel and shipbuilding businesses under one roof had been that the Philippines—a nation of islands—needs lots of ships. The objective was to build those ships at home and gain experience in them for future export. In 1955, the government granted NASSCO 50 million pesos to set up pig iron plants. When completed, it would make it an integrated steel mill. NASSCO would be Asia's second such facility. Only the Japanese would attempt such a thing sooner than the Filipinos. Jon (2022) provides an instructive summary of the history of NASSCO, from its inception in 1950 to its demise in 1999 as a result of a series of unfortunate economic and political events. The company managed to do very well in the 1970s. However, the decline started in the 1980s: South Korean and Taiwanese imports as a result of much lower tariffs, flooded the market; the company hadn't yet become a truly vertically integrated steelmaker—it lacked iron and steel making capabilities; privatization under President Ramos (poor Malaysian management); and the *coup de grâce* with the Asian Financial Crisis in 1997.[2]

The industrialization efforts continued during the administration of President Macapagal (1961–1965). The result was that, as concluded by Power and Sicat (1971), by the late 1960s (with Marcos Sr. already as President), the Philippines had developed a significant manufacturing sector supported by import protection, which means that the measures taken yielded some success. However, this is qualified by De Dios et al. (2021, pp. 4–5) as follows:

> Imported consumer goods were indeed replaced by manufactured local substitutes, but the composition of the country's imports and the state of its dependence merely shifted to imports of capital goods and intermediate imports. Even as the country stopped importing refrigerators and air conditioners, for example, it began to import sheet steel, compressors and other machinery. It stopped imported canned milk but began importing tin plate and powdered milk to produce substitutes. By the late 1950s, almost all of the country's imports (around 90%) already consisted of producer goods and no further easy possibilities existed for import substitution. The domestic market proved too small to reap economies of scale and reduce costs, while protection removed the pressure for the "infant industries" to become efficient.

On top of the aforementioned, the country's export basket remained confined to raw materials and semi-processed products, the demand for which was sluggish and inelastic (the BOPC growth rate; see Chapter 3). As a result, the pre-martial law economy ran trade deficits. Moreover, exporters were penalized as they had to surrender their foreign exchange earnings at an unfavorable (overvalued) exchange rate (see Hirschman (1968) on the same problem for Latin America). And in a context of foreign exchange allocation, corruption (foreign exchange to friends in exchange for kickbacks), was the norm. De Dios et al. (2021, p. 4) concluded that the Philippine economy started slowing down in the 1960s (during pre-martial law) as a result of the "prolonged failure of the government's program of industrial protection." However, in our view, the failure was not due to the use of industrial protection *per se*, but to the poor implementation of the import substitution strategy, together with the fact that it was not accompanied by mechanisms to promote (force) exports and to induce manufacturing upgrading. This assessment is not different from Hirschman's (1968) about the success and then failure of ISI in Latin America (i.e., exaggerated criticism). There are significant parallels with the Philippines.

The Philippines pushed forward the export-oriented regime in the mid-1970s under President Marcos Sr. (this had started during the Macapagal years when the country shifted from foreign exchange allocation to a tariff system), although high import tariffs on finished products remained (higher than on intermediate inputs and capital goods) in place until the late 1980s. The peso was devalued from PHP 3.90 per USD to PHP 6.40 in 1970. The central bank abandoned the fixed exchange rate system and adopted a floating rate. This was complemented by a system of import controls that created a highly protective and restrictive trade structure. This meant that industries continued to be geared toward the small domestic market, and the high tariffs continued facilitating fraud and corruption (smuggling). Moreover, the economy continued relying on traditional exports. Current account deficits continued. The reforms of the 1970s and 1980s were undertaken in collaboration with and with support from the World Bank and the IMF, involving tariff reductions and more flexible exchange rates. Foreign trade and capital markets were also liberalized to introduce competition into the domestic economy and to dismantle cartels and monopolies.

To further understand the administration of President Marcos Sr., we highlight two additional issues. The first one was concern with the end of the Laurel–Langley Agreement in 1974. The end of the Agreement signified (1) the completion of the elimination of mutual tariff preferences (the process had started in 1955); (2) the right of the Philippine government to decide on monetary and exchange rate policies (the agreement ended the authority of the United States to control the exchange rate of the Philippine peso); (3) the end of the automatic parity rights of US investors in the Philippines, restoring constitutional restrictions that reserved natural resources and public utilities for Filipinos (or corporations at least 60% Filipino-owned); and (4) the end of the free American market for sugar produced in the Philippines, which had been, before the agreement, exported to the United States duty-free.

The chief concern was that Philippine exports would immediately face the full US tariff rates, removing a key competitive advantage.[3] Also, the removal of the fixed exchange rate implied that the Philippines had the authority to control the exchange rate of the Philippine Peso.

President Marcos argued in the 1966 State of the Nation Address (Marcos, 1966/2022) that this situation should be counterbalanced by the exploitation of new markets in Europe and the Asian neighbors, the diversification of the export basket, and a switch in export emphasis from unprocessed and semi-processed raw material to intermediate manufactures and finished goods.

The second issue was the fact that, although President Marcos thought about industrialization, he did not have a clear understanding of what it entailed. There was an "industrial policy" embodied in the Investment Incentives Act (1967). He also established the export processing zones (EPZ) through RA No. 5490 (1969) and Presidential Decree 66 (1972). The Export Incentives Act of 1970 (1970) provided export incentives, and Presidential Decree No. 34 (1972) updates the Tariff and Customs Code. The Bataan EPZ started operating in in 1970, Mactan-Cebu in 1979, and in Cavite and Baguio in 1980. Yet, the extent of the success of these measures is mixed. The 1967 Investment Incentives Act was "weak" because it amounted to a package of tax incentives and exemptions (the carrot) but without imposing strict targets (the stick). Examples of the incentives provided are: accelerated depreciation of assets, Net Operating Loss Carry-over, Tax Exemption on Imported Capital Equipment, Tax Credit on Domestic Capital Equipment, or Deduction for Expansion Reinvestment. This applied to registered enterprises with at least 60% Filipino ownership in capital and board. It was required for ventures exploiting natural resources and operating public utilities. This rule was applied to non-pioneer industries, while 100% foreign ownership was allowed only for pioneer projects introducing new products or technologies. The government's role was passive. It amounted to offering a favorable tax environment. This, by itself, does not ensure the transformation of the economy.

It is true though that the composition of exports started changing and that the share of labor-intensive manufactured exports increased (e.g., semiconductors and other electronics, garments, footwear). Yet, the new exports involved mostly assembly and testing of imported components that involved low value added. Moreover, the non-traditional export sector did not progress much because it was located in export processing zones and was mostly foreign owned. Yet these were the companies benefitting from, for example, tariff and tax-free imported inputs. The benefits did not apply to the companies outside the zones. This explains the low manufacturing share that the Philippines attained. Multinational companies in export processing zones created employment but this was not a high share of total employment, and it did not have links with domestic companies out the zones.[4]

The result is that while the share of manufacturing value added in GDP increased up to 28% during the 1970s (it was already about 25% in the mid-1960s, compared to 17% in South Korea and 10% in Malaysia), and that of industry reached 40% in the early 1980s (Hooley, 2005, Table 3), the manufacturing employment share peaked in the 1970s at only slightly above 11% (and the employment share of total industry peaked at 40%) (Aldaba, 2014, Table 5). Since then, these two shares have been declining, until today. This shows that while the Philippines was industrializing in output during the 1970s–1980s (the shares reported are similar to those in other countries), the manufacturing employment share did not progress. While in the mid-1960s the Philippine manufacturing employment share (at 11%) was significantly higher than those of South Korea or Malaysia, 9% and 6%, respectively, by 1986 (the end of the Marcos Sr. regime), the shares of these countries were higher than that of the Philippines (11%), 25% for Korea and 15% for Malaysia. Likewise, the output share increased to 30% in the case of South Korea and to 20% in the case of Malaysia (below that of the Philippines in the latter case). These figures matter because, as documented by Felipe et al. (2019), the Philippine manufacturing employment share is very low for international standards (with respect to that attained by the countries that have attained high income, at least 20%—the manufacturing employment share is a much better predictor of attaining high income than the share in GDP. Notice that both Philippine premature deindustrialization in output, and the low manufacturing employment share, happened well before China entered the picture and became the global manufacturing power, so it is not that China crowded out the Philippines in the 1970s and 1980s.[5]

We conclude that the cause behind the Philippine low manufacturing employment share was the fact that the sector was developed in export processing zones by multinational companies. These did not create much employment (as a share of total employment) and were delinked from the rest of the economy. Later on, austerity measures since the second half of the 1980s contributed to deindustrialization by causing a contraction in public and private investment and by limiting the government's ability to support struggling industries.

Another issue that added to the difficulties to industrialize, was the lack of coordination between tariff, import restrictions, and exchange rate. This is essential for a successful implementation of an import substitution strategy (to start manufacturing products domestically) combined with an export-oriented strategy (to be able to compete abroad). This requires reliance on tariffs rather than on discretionary import restrictions; tariffs at about the same rate for all types of products; and an exchange rate at a level that encourages exports and discourages imports. Moreover, a serious policy mistake was to reduce tariffs while at the same time increase non-tariff barriers, as the Philippines was doing in the 1970s.

Finally, corruption in the form of monopoly rents through import privileges, a myriad of government-franchised or contracted activities, the creation of state monopolies, or giving the control of key exports such as sugar and coconut to R.

Benedicto and E. Cojuangco, respectively, created a political system that allowed a small group of people in the private sector to amass an immense economic power (crony capitalism). De Dios et al. (2021, pp. 22–28) offer an excellent summary of crony capitalism.

We stress that the Philippine government was passive (simply offered incentives), certainly compared to that of Korea, reviewed later. Historically, countries have not progressed as a result of standard Ricardian comparative advantage, beyond what is obvious, and by announcing a package of tax incentives. Moving up decisively in the development ladder has always required active governments that directed the economy. This included a central bank that set an exchange rate that favored exports (a type of industrial policy).

The 1980s marked a shift in Philippine public investment strategy toward a greater emphasis on industrial development. One aspect of this policy was continued investment in, and expansion of, the country's export processing zones. A second aspect was that the Philippine government created the Major Industrial Projects (MIPS) program. The MIPS was a large industrialization strategy that aimed at import substitution through heavy industrialization. The goals were to deepen Philippine industrial structure, reduce the heavy dependence of domestic industry on imported materials, and establish growth poles away from Manila. The Philippine government was influenced by the heavy industrialization policy initiatives of many East Asian countries during this period. South Korea and Taiwan had adopted extensive efforts to encourage heavy industry, but neighboring countries in Southeast Asia–Malaysia, Thailand, and Singapore, were also supporting investments in petrochemicals, aluminum smelting, pulp and paper, and other heavy industries.

The MIPS was a series of 11 major industrial programs. These programs were (1) copper smelter, a joint venture with Marubeni (Japan), with operational target ~1983; (2) phosphatic fertilizer, which used sulfuric acid by-products from the smelter, with international support from the United States, Japan, Germany, the UK, Belgium, and Spain and a target start ~1983; (3) aluminum smelter, a 50/50 venture with US Reynolds Metals, launch anticipated ~1984; (4) integrated steel mill, joint effort with Austria, estimated operation by ~1985; (5) alcogas program, a nationwide production of 20% alcohol and 80% gasoline blend for vehicles using sugar as a raw material; (6) heavy engineering industries, with Germany, aimed at producing machine tools and parts for major industrial plants; (7) integrated pulp and paper, which is pulp and paper expansion, including newsprint—the only such plant in Southeast Asia; (8) petrochemical complex, located near the Bataan Nuclear Power Plant, with assistance from the United States and Taiwan and a start ~1983; (9) cement industry expansion, converting existing plants from oil- to coal-based systems, with a target ~1984; (10) coconut industry rationalization (fatty alcohol), involving the production of commercial alcohol (for detergents) from coconuts, with a start ~1982; and (11) diesel engine manufacturing, JV with Japanese and German firms and a production start ~1982.

The plan was for these industrial infrastructures to spur the growth of supporting manufacturing activities. Their locations across the country were also strategically chosen to disperse economic activities and generate rural employment. Financing was to come from external loans, foreign equity, and suppliers' credits.[6] IMF and the World Bank, as well as the country's technocrats and voices representing the business community, expressed concerns about the rationale of the projects, especially financing them with (private) external resources (dollars). The estimated cost was estimated between USD 3.8 billion and USD 4.7 billion (of the early 1980s).[7]

The MIPS program did not contribute to the country's industrialization. In the early 1980s, the economy started deteriorating due to mounting foreign debt. This was the result of the increases in interest rates in the United States (the US Federal Funds rate rose from 9% in 1980 to 19% in 1981) with Paul Volcker as chair of the Federal Reserve. This affected interest rates on emerging countries' foreign debt as they carried floating interest rates. This caused a major debt crisis in these countries. De Dios et al. (2021, pp.12–14) provide details of the impact on the Philippines. The result was that many projects stalled, were privatized, or never fully realized. While a bold developmental strategy, most projects floundered due to financial, political, and external pressures. Out of the eleven projects, only five were completed: copper; smelter; diesel engine manufacturing; cement industry coal conversion; phosphatic fertilizer; and coconut-based chemicals. Heavy engineering and the integrated steel plant projects were started but deferred in 1983 as a result of the debt moratorium, and the remaining four were deferred at an earlier stage, before contracting took place. The expenditure on the seven projects that went forward amounted to USD 2.8 billion, almost entirely financed through foreign loans (Dohner and Intal 1989, p. 410).

The result was that, unlike other Asian countries that managed to catapult their economies into the league of industrial nations, the Philippines could not free itself from the constraints of narrow export specialization, import dependence, and a shallow knowledge base. Indeed, before any of these big-ticket projects could take off, the country plunged into another economic and political crisis, triggered by the assassination of leading opposition leader Benigno Aquino Jr. in 1983. The industrialization programs had to take a backseat to stabilize the economy and reduce the deficits in the balance of payments and government budget.

Between the 1980s and the early 2000s, manufacturing growth was very slow, about 0.9% per annum. During 2001–2010, growth averaged 3.5% per annum, and during 2011–2019, 5.6%, still below growth in other Asian countries. These growth rates were not enough to increase the share of manufacturing output during the period. The share of employment even dropped from about 11% in the 1970s to 9% in the 2000s, and to 7% currently.

The reality is that although the government developed plans and industrial policy programs, these were never implemented as effectively as those in other East Asian countries, South Korea being the reference (see Section 7.2). Many have traditionally seen government failure and state-created inefficiency as the main culprits behind the Philippine development failure. Government policies have been harmful to the country's development prospects, hence the need for market-oriented reforms. Although this is a well-rehearsed argument, Montes (1994, p. 136) contended that a significant problem for the Philippines after independence was the nature of state and business relations, as well as the nature of the Philippine private sector (see Chapter 6). The Philippines never developed institutions that accelerated the transformation of its economic structure. It never had a powerful state that forced change, like in the other East and Southeast Asian economies. Moreover, as we argued in the earlier chapters, the private sector is dominated by a group of elite families whose objective is to attain political dominance in society. This latter fact may partly explain the lack of competitive Small and Medium Enterprises (SMEs) in the Philippines, particularly when compared with other more successful Asian economies. To this, one should add the discord in trade, investments, domestic regulation, human resources, and science and technology policies that were supposed to complement the industrial programs during the 1960s and until the 1980s. Overall, the manifest lack of coherence between the industrial blueprints and supporting policies, the policy flip-flops, and the institutional deficiencies undermined the implementation of seemingly well-crafted programs.

This lack of coherence is most obvious in the failed automotive, shipbuilding, and steel industry programs. For example, while the country was trying to develop its shipbuilding industry in the 1970s, it allowed liberal entry of cheap imported secondhand vessels from Japan, offered financing schemes for the acquisition of imported vessels, but none for locally constructed vessels, and neglected the ancillary sectors (metal casting, forging, and machining). The automotive program failed because of the neglect of small and medium-sized parts manufacturers, whereas assemblers were subjected to weak regulations on local content and limits on the number of brands and models. As a result, the expectation that the cost penalty of localization would compel foreign assemblers to develop local parts production did not materialize, and the program failed to generate externalities for the rest of the economy. Some of these same problems remain today.

Under these circumstances, it was very difficult for the Philippines to complete its structural transformation and become an advanced economy. As discussed in Chapters 2 and 6, and in this one, the economic policies of the government and central bank since independence (e.g., the aversion to deficit spending (with some exceptions) and the strong currency for a long time), the relationship between public and private sectors, and the political problems after martial law was imposed in 1972, ended up crippling an incipient manufacturing sector. The decline in the manufacturing share started during the administration of President Corazon Aquino in the second part of the 1980s and has continued until today (18% of GDP in 2024). As argued in Chapter 2, efforts to industrialize were abandoned because with the collapse of the economy in the mid-1980s, there was a significant shift in policy afterward. This was the key turning point. We should also add that Philippine industrialization efforts were never at the Korean level. After all, President Ferdinand Marcos Sr. was not President Park Chung Hee (see next section).

Today, most Philippine manufacturing companies are small, whereas large conglomerates are mostly involved in non-tradable activities such as real estate or banking. With a much weaker state than its neighbors, the export-led industrialization growth model eluded the Philippines. This situation remained during the successive administrations of Corazon Aquino (1986–1992), Fidel Ramos (1992–1998), Joseph Estrada (1998–2000), Gloria Macapagal-Arroyo (2000–2010), Benigno Aquino (2010–2016), Rodrigo Duterte (2016–2022), and Ferdinand Marcos Jr. (2022–2028). The "industrialization question" has always been mentioned, but the reality is that it has never been addressed decisively.

De Dios and Williamson (2015) concluded the well-trodden route to industrialization "has been missed forever" and that the Philippines needs a different path. Perhaps they are right. Ten years after the publication of their work things have not improved. Over four decades after the manufacturing debacle, perhaps it will be difficult to reopen that route unless there is a conscious effort. Unit labor costs are high and the only way to reduce them to gain competitiveness is to increase productivity and capabilities (See Chapter 8).

With the relative decline of manufacturing in the Philippines came the rise of services in the 1990s and 2000s. Workers from rural and agricultural areas seeking better living standards often found themselves in low-skill, traditional service-oriented jobs, or as contract workers overseas. Having skipped industrialization, the Philippine development model had to rely on the service sector, and economic policy tried to address seemingly important issues, such as lack of physical and human capital, liberalization/deregulation/reforms/less government, attraction of FDI, infrastructure improvement, tax breaks, improvement in the ranking in the World Competitiveness Report, and macro stability. Typical interventions (structural reforms) took the form of increasing tax collection, spending more on infrastructure, reducing the budget deficit, and reforming the economy (eliminating burdensome regulations). We refer to these as Reforms Type I. As argued in Chapter 1, all this in a context of freedom of enterprise, trade, and investment. Together with these came the mantra of adjectives qualifying growth since the 1990s and 2000s, such as "inclusive," "pro-poor," "sustainable," "equitable," "broad-based," "resilient," etc., and the Millennium and Sustainable Development Goals, which the latest administrations bought into. None of these have delivered what the Philippines needs: plain growth.

We do agree that addressing some of these issues is necessary. The fact is, however, that this development model has delivered only about USD 4,400 per capita income. It has not been enough because it has missed what is crucial for growth and development, namely, a focus on changing the structure of the economy with industrialization at its center. Unless a new set of reforms, which we refer to as Type II, is implemented, fast progress will not occur. What are these reforms? All those that facilitate the transformation of the economy. These reforms must aim at upgrading the manufacturing sector and at exporting, and not at doing more of the same (perhaps a bit better). Although some of these reforms are general, such as building roads and ports, or providing electricity and water efficiently, many others should be area specific. This is because producing and exporting mangoes, for example, requires specific private and public goods and knowledge, such as property rights, refrigeration systems, phytosanitary regulations, health and safety standards, agricultural R&D, specific packaging, air shipping, and market-access agreements. Moreover, they are sold through supermarkets, distributors, and direct retailers. These private and public goods are very different from those needed to manufacture and export, for example, furniture: Usually transported via sea freight; it requires quality and safety standards (e.g., fire resistance); it has a steady market with trends affecting demand (e.g., modern designs); it is sold via wholesalers, online marketplaces, or showrooms; and it requires specific packaging. However, the most significant problem here, as we shall discuss in Chapter 8, is the lack of firms with high organizational capabilities.

7.2 The South Korean Industrialization Miracle

This section provides, for comparison, a brief account of South Korea's drive to industrialization between the 1960s and the 1980s, precisely when Philippine industrialization lost momentum.

In 1961, the Korean army took control of power through a coup led by General Park Chung Hee, who was formally elected President in 1963, following the return to civilian rule. He was in power until 1979. Park not only normalized relations with Japan but also engineered the Korean economic miracle. At the time, Korea's income per capita was lower than that of the Philippines, and in 1962, still 69% of Korean workers were employed in agriculture (Felipe et al., 2016). Perhaps one of the most positive assets of the country at the time (different from the Philippines) was that it had already undertaken a land reform in the 1940s under the Rhee government. Beyond this, Park transformed the country into a developmental state that followed the steps of the latecomer industrializers. He quickly reversed previous economic policies (e.g., import substitution) and transformed the country into an export-led industrial power following the Japanese model, which involved channeling funds to the industrial sector.

Between the 1960s and the 1980s, Korea's industrial policy followed Japan's steps, but in a much more intense way, for two reasons. First, Korea was far behind Japan technologically. Catching up fast required significant government intervention. Second, Korea had a short history of capitalism. Except perhaps during 1953–1960, under the Syngman Rhee regime, Korea had never experienced an extensive free-market economy, certainly not during the agrarian Korean society that prevailed until the 19th century, nor during the Japanese colonial government's years of heavy interventionist policy.

Korea's industrial policy before 1961 was simply a strategy of import substitution, mostly for consumer goods. The priority industries were sugar, fertilizer, spun yarn, cement, and glass. However, the country soon reached a saturation point as a result of the small size of the domestic market and growth constraints due to a current account deficit. Moreover, while substantial US aid during the 1950s and early 1960s facilitated accumulation and industrialization, this declined during the 1960s, with the consequence that Korea was forced to export. Moreover, Korea could not rely on exports of primary products to finance its imports. It became obvious that it needed a different model. During the developmental decades after 1961, the government again turned to heavy interventionism and created a particular business-state relationship that made the country neither a free-market economy nor a centrally planned economy. Jung (1994) referred to it as a *regulated market economy*.

Korea's state intervention had the objective of building an independent economy and achieving industrial upgrading by transferring labor from low-productivity sectors to high-productivity sectors. This was clearly institutionalized in the 1970s with the heavy and chemical industries program of 1973 (see following); and in the 1980s (e.g., Industrial Development Law of 1986) to nurture sunrise industries, to restructure sunset industries, or to provide assistance to critical industries. The institutionalization of growth as a prime objective gave reformist technocrats tremendous political space and power. This did not happen in the Philippines.

When the new regime came to power in 1961, it lacked a coherent economic plan but had a series of sectoral targets. South Korea switched to an export-oriented development strategy in 1962. This was prompted by the realization that it had a relatively small domestic market and a large pool of low-wage labor. The first phase of the export program ran until 1972. The initial focus was on the development of the light industry. During the 1960s, firms had concentrated mainly on basic assembly, beginning with the manufacture of standard, simple goods, often supplying foreign MNCs from Japan and the United States through Original Equipment Manufacturing (OEM).

Starting in 1973, South Korea moved into the second phase of its export-oriented program. It made conscious and concerted efforts to move into higher value-added areas through complementary investments in human capital and infrastructure. Korean policymakers felt that the country should develop the Heavy and Chemical Industries (HCI), which required more skill and capital-intensive manufacturing (e.g., ships, machinery, steel, automobiles, computer electronics), like Japan. Unlike the latter, however, the key reason behind this drive was to manufacture weapons and defend itself. However, instead of building military factories, Korean policymakers decided to build dual-use industrial complexes with a target production ratio of 70% civilian and 30% military. The machinery sector was regarded as a critical industry not only for its high value-added and extensive linkages with other industries, but also for its contribution to defense. This is what sets apart the industrial policy of the Philippines from that of South Korea.

South Korea launched the HCI program in 1973, partly to address the problems generated by the increase in oil prices, and partly to make sure that Korea became a self-reliant economy and to achieve USD 10 billion in exports by 1981 (which Japan had reached in 1967). This would help the country pay for its imported oil. The program also aimed to achieve a USD 1,000 per capita income by 1981, up from about USD 300 at the start of the program. Another important objective was that the HCI sector should account for at least 50% of manufacturing value added and contribute 60.5% to manufacturing exports, also by 1981. At the time, international organizations thought that the program was beyond Korea's reach and not in accordance with its comparative advantage. Hence, they discouraged the government from pursuing it.

Korean planners believed that, given the country's comparative advantage in light manufacturing (e.g., apparel, footwear, electronic appliances) at that time, plus a benchmark against Japan, Korea could make it into the HCI. Moreover, some companies in the light manufacturing sectors had already started demanding products that the HCI would produce. Policymakers looked into industries deemed critical for their high value added, extensive linkages with other industries, and contribution to defense. The specific industries "picked" were (with specific subsectors within each) (1) iron and steel, (2) non-ferrous metals, (3) shipbuilding, (4) machinery, (5) electronics, and (6) chemicals. Sectors that had already developed considerably were excluded, as were activities within the realm of the private sector, as well as sectors deemed impossible to develop at that time.

Planners consciously chose to develop these sectors not just for the domestic market, but also aimed to achieve a global market size, thereby enabling export. This was to be done by relying on a group of state-owned enterprises together with private companies such as Hyundai, Samsung, and LG (there was relatively little foreign investment in Korea because the large *chaebols* provided the necessary entrepreneurship). The program relied on four key pillars:

1. *Finance*. The nine-year program amounted to USD 9.6 billion (equivalent to Korea's GDP at that time), with foreign funds accounting for 60% of the total requirements. The government established the National Investment Fund (NIF) to finance long-term investment through direct credit. The NIF interest rate was 9%, while the prevailing three-year interest rate on bank loans was 15.5%. Likewise, government-controlled banks supported the program by providing policy-oriented loans on favorable terms. Other instruments used were tax credits on income earned from exports, tariff reductions on necessary imported inputs, selective protection, entry restrictions, land, and in some cases, direct government involvement in industrial decision-making. In terms of this latter aspect, the government tended to select large family-owned firms (the *chaebols*) to enter specific industries. Over the period 1973–1979, almost 60% of total bank loans and more than 75% of total manufacturing investment were allocated to the selected sectors, and therefore largely to the *chaebols*,

reducing the available funds for light manufacturing industries and small and medium enterprises (SMEs). See Tan (1999, pp. 100–104, 108–110) and Edwards (1999, pp. 254–256).

2. *Land and infrastructure*. The program followed a "cluster approach" where related industries were concentrated in a single location, such as the machinery complex in Changwon, the petrochemical complex in Yeocheon, and the electronics complex in Gumi. This required the development of not only infrastructure, such as roads, ports, water, and electricity, but also schools, research institutes, public administration offices, banks, hospitals, and housing facilities.
3. *Human resources*. The HCI drive needed the development of a technological base. Under the presidential declaration "the scientification of all people," Korea changed its educational curricula to make them very applied. To achieve this, it reinforced its vocational schools, technical education, and engineering, based on the German model. Ninety-five technical high schools were divided into four types—mechanical (19), model (11), specialized (10), and general (55)—to train a wide variety of technicians and skilled workers. The result is that between 1977 and 1991, Korean students placed first in the International Vocational Olympics. As part of this process, private companies also contributed significantly as suppliers of education services for their own interests in securing needed workers.[8]
4. *R&D*. The government set up several research institutes to develop science and technology, as well as industry-specific institutes and science parks. To develop its defense industry, and given that the United States was reluctant to share defense technologies, Korea had to resort to reverse engineering.

Macroeconomic imbalances as well as political problems forced the Korean Government to call off the HCI drive in 1979. Likewise, the promotion of strategic industries, which dominated policy during the 1970s, came to an end at the start of the 1980s, when a process of trade liberalization, including an opening up of domestic markets and a reduction in export subsidies, was adopted. Many of the earlier policies were thus phased out, with the number of strategic industries gradually decreasing and the extent of preferential treatment regarding taxes and credit also reduced.

The eventual maturity of the industry's part of the HCI program provided Korea with an undeniable boost to its economy. Despite all the problems, the HCI program helped lay the foundation for many of Korea's leading industries, including steel, shipbuilding, machinery, electronics, petrochemicals, and later on, semiconductors and the automotive industry. The policies adopted also helped materialize a dramatic change in industrial structure throughout the 1970s. Although the HCI industries contributed around 12% to GDP in 1970, the figure increased to more than 25% by 1980, and to more than 30% by 1988. The success of this program can be further seen in the shift in the composition of exports, with HCI increasing its share of total exports from around 13% in 1970 to more than 50% by 1988 (Kim et al., 1995). By 1978, Japanese manufacturers operating in South Korea thought that Korean companies would catch up with Japan within 5 years, or were already at a comparable level, in many manufacturing sectors (Hayashi, 1990, Table 2, pp. 30–31). Recently, Lane (2025) has evaluated the effects of South Korea's industrial policy by examining differential changes in outcomes between targeted (treated) and non-targeted (untreated) manufacturing industries before and after the policy's implementation. His analysis yields three principal findings. First, the policy package generated substantial positive effects on industrial performance in the treated sectors. Relative to pre-intervention levels, output in targeted HCI industries increased by more than 100% compared with non-treated manufacturing, while labor productivity rose by over 15%. Positive impacts were also observed for employment growth, export performance, and output prices, indicating that the HCI program produced durable, long-run benefits for supported industries. Second, the policy coincided with a reorientation of dynamic comparative advantage toward the targeted export sectors. Post-1979 indicators such as employment and output shares remained significantly higher in treated industries than in their non-treated counterparts. In addition, after 1973, treated sectors were 10 percentage points more likely to achieve comparative advantage in international markets, with revealed comparative advantage in HCI products increasing 13% more than that of other manufacturing exports. These effects, however, emerged only gradually, underscoring the limitations of short-term evaluations in capturing the full dynamic consequences of industrial policy. Third, HCI-oriented measures were associated with the expansion of downstream industries, as sectors with strong linkages to those targeted experienced significant growth during the policy period.

Finally, the HCI also set the stage for Korea's transition years later into an innovation-driven economy, strengthening backward and forward linkages among these industries, as well as among related industries. During the 1980s, there was also increased pressure to upgrade and restructure the industry to shift from labor- and capital-intensive production to more technology-intensive production.

During the rapid industrialization of the 1960s and 1970s, Korea developed a monitoring and evaluation system that, while simple, was highly effective. In the 1960s, the president held monthly export promotion meetings, which were chaired by himself and attended by ministers, the central bank governor, and experts from the private sector, including business leaders, and prominent engineers and scientists. The president effectively chose and groomed specific chaebols to lead in strategic sectors like automobiles (Hyundai), electronics (Samsung, LG), and shipbuilding. The government provided the blueprints, and the chaebols executed them. In exchange, these companies received preferential treatment and support in the form of low interest rate credits, tax incentives, and a protected domestic market.[9] These meetings primarily focused on monitoring export progress against the annual targets set by the Ministry of Commerce and Industry.[10]

The business community had the opportunity to voice complaints and offer suggestions. Based on their input, the president would set new goals and pressure ministers to address grievances and resolve issues within a specified time frame.

This was a top-down system. The government didn't just advise; it dictated industrial policy, picked "winners," and heavily subsidized or punished chaebols based on their adherence to national goals, particularly export targets. Chaebols received immense government support (cheap credit, tax breaks, protected markets) but also faced severe consequences if they failed to perform or deviated from the state's industrial plans. Park even arrested businessmen early in his rule to assert state supremacy. The Korean economy indeed transformed rapidly under this very authoritarian mechanism.

Under President Marcos Jr., the Philippines created the Philippine Private Sector Advisory Council (PSAC) in 2022. However, its *modus operandi* is very different from that of Korea's meetings with President Park, top-down and directed toward industrialization and exports. The PSAC is explicitly an *advisory* body. It is comprised of prominent business leaders who provide recommendations and insights to the President on various economic sectors (e.g., agriculture, infrastructure, digital infrastructure, education, health care, tourism). The stated goal is to foster stronger collaboration between the public and private sectors to achieve the country's economic objectives. It's a more democratic and participatory model of engagement. The PSAC operates through sectoral groups, addressing specific issues like digital transformation, job creation, healthcare reforms, and infrastructure development. They identify problems and propose solutions. The PSAC has been an active and influential body that has successfully channeled private sector insights and recommendations to the President. Its direct access and the President's apparent receptiveness to its proposals suggest a degree of effectiveness in shaping policy discussions and driving specific initiatives. However, like any such council, its ultimate long-term effectiveness will be measured by the concrete improvements it brings to the Philippine economy and the well-being of its citizens, and its ability to balance the interests of various stakeholders.

7.3 Does the Philippines Have an Industrial Policy Today?

As we argued in Chapters 2 and 6, as well as in the preceding text, the Philippine administrations undertook different forms of industrial policy to industrialize the country until the 1980s, even though during the Macapagal administration (1961–1965) the economic regime had started changing. Even in the 1980s, with President Marcos Sr., the Philippines tried to pursue state-led industrialization.

Since the mid-late 1980s with President Corazon Aquino (1986–1992), however, the role of the state guiding the economy has declined and industrial policies, understood as the targeting (favoring) of particular sectors by the government, disappeared. This view remains very much alive today, and it manifests in the decades-long quasi-aversion to undertaking industrial policy. This coincided with a decline in the use of industrial policy across the world. In the words of Montes (2024, p. 1), "In the Philippine context, the consideration of industrial policy is a contravention of the state project since the 1980s to rely on an open trade regime as a key pillar of a development strategy." We know the result.

However, since the early 2000s, the economics profession at large has reconsidered industrial policy. Many governments (in both developed and developing countries) have realized that it is very difficult to get into complex activities (associated to high wages) without government assistance. There seems to be agreement by now that the discussion should not be about *whether* industrial policy is needed or not, but about *how* to implement it properly (Felipe, 2015).

The Philippines has not been immune to this new trend, and numerous legislative initiatives have sprung during the last decade aimed at supporting industrialization Yet, these initiatives could hardly be considered as a coherent industrial policy. Some of these programs (not all) have poorly stated rationales (why are they needed, that is, what problem do they want to solve that the private sector cannot on its own?), objectives, instruments, sunset clauses (for how long is the assistance provided?), and conditions (assistance is provided only if certain targets, for example, exports, are attained). With this setting, it is very difficult to move in the direction of industrialization. Also, we wonder why legislators have not passed a single comprehensive policy, instead of several piecemeal ones. As we argue in Chapter 8, Philippine industrial policy needs to focus more on increasing firms' capabilities, a simple design of the initiatives, and a simple implementation program.

Today, the most important Philippine policy initiatives that one way or another aim at supporting industrialization are: the Inclusive Innovation Industrial Strategy (i3S), the CREATE MORE Act (Republic Act 12066, 2024), the *Tatak Pinoy* Act (Republic Act 11981, 2024), and the CARS program (Executive Order 182, 2015).[11] We review their main features later. It would be unfair to say that these programs (and others in place) are a failure. Yet, the reality is that they will not be the game changer that their proponents claim. These programs tend to focus on rewarding the production of complex products. While this has merit, we wonder why these initiatives do not include, explicitly, the manufacture of high-quality products such as furniture, cutlery, or glasses (potentially high-quality "expensive" products), for example, many of them imported by the Philippines, often from developed countries (which means their manufacture requires high skills). The Philippines needs an industrial policy that focuses on firms and on the manufacturing of a wide range of products that "make a nation," with emphasis on high quality. We stress that this industrial policy should include agriculture and services.

In what follows, we review these four initiatives:

7.3.1 The Inclusive Innovation Industrial Strategy (i3S)

Introduced in 2017, this is a grand vision that only highlights major ideas. It aims to (1) upgrade and modernize industries, (2) promote innovation and R&D, (3) foster entrepreneurship and startups, (4) encourage investments in priority sectors, (5) integrate micro- and small enterprises into global value chains, and (6) support regional industry development and clustering. It integrates innovation, investment, and industrial upgrading across various sectors, hence its name, i3, or "i-cube."

The i3S is anchored on high-potential sectors identified in the Department of Trade and Industry's industry roadmaps: (1) electronics and semiconductors, (2) automotive and auto parts, (3) aerospace, (4) agro-industrial processing, (5) chemicals and petrochemicals, (6) IT-BPM and creative industries, (7) green and sustainable industries, and (8) tourism and transport.

The i3S itself does not directly grant fiscal incentives, but it is strategically linked to incentive-granting mechanisms, particularly through the CREATE Act (already updated; see following) and the Strategic Investment Priority Plan (SIPP).

7.3.2 The Corporate Recovery and Tax Incentives for Enterprises to Maximize Opportunities for Reinvigorating the Economy, or CREATE MORE (RA 12066)

It was signed into law by President Marcos Jr. and took effect on November 28, 2024. It aims to generate jobs, spur economic growth, and enhance the investment landscape by providing tax reforms and financial incentives to a preferred set of industries listed in the Bureau of Investment's Strategic Investment Priorities Plan (SIPP). CREATE MORE is the updated version of the Corporate Recovery and Tax Incentives for Enterprises Act (CREATE Act of 2021, R.A. 11534), which aimed at simplifying procedures, eliminating overlapping tax incentives, and clarifying the mechanics of fiscal incentives.

The CREATE MORE Act provides essentially a series of tax benefits that reduce operational costs. It may be said nevertheless that it has features of an industrial policy. Its key features are as follows:[12] (1) It amends the National Internal Revenue Code. (2) Registered business enterprises availing of enhanced deductions are subject to a 20% corporate income tax rate, regardless of net taxable income and total assets. (3) It clarifies VAT treatment on the sale, transfer, or disposal of previously VAT-exempt imported capital equipment, raw materials, spare parts, and accessories and specifies conditions under which VAT exemption and zero rating apply, particularly for registered export enterprises with export sales comprising at least 70% of total annual production. (4) It introduces additional deductions for registered business enterprises, such as a 100% additional deduction on power expenses and deductions for reinvested profits in manufacturing and tourism sectors and extends the period during which income tax–based incentives can be availed of, with options approved by investment promotion agencies and the Fiscal Incentives Review Board. (5) Registered business enterprises engaged in activities under the Strategic Investment Priority Plan of 2022 may be entitled to an income tax holiday of four to seven years, followed by a special corporate income tax or enhanced deductions for up to 20 years, And (6) it mandates the Fiscal Incentives Review Board to decide on applications for tax incentives within

20 working days from receipt of all requirements and empowers the president to craft appropriate fiscal and non-fiscal support packages for highly desirable projects or specific industrial activities.

The CREATE MORE Act classifies registered businesses into three categories: (1) registered export enterprises, (2) domestic market enterprises, and (3) high-value domestic market enterprises. Registered business enterprises may avail of six primary types of tax incentives:

1. *Income tax holiday.* ITH grants full exemption from income tax on projects or activities of the firms for four to seven years. This is offered to all the types of businesses mentioned earlier.
2. *Special corporate income tax (SCIT).* Instead of paying the standard corporate income tax of 25% and other local government taxes, as well as other fees, registered export enterprises have the incentive to use a flat tax of 5% on their gross income earned.
3. *Enhanced deductions regime (EDR).* It offers nine types of financial deductions to export and domestic enterprises.[13]
4. *Duty exemption.* All registered businesses may be fully exempt from fees and import duties on equipment, materials, parts, or accessories, including those for administrative purposes.
5. *Value-added tax exemption.* VAT exemption applies to registered businesses' imports, and zero-rated VAT applies to local purchases.
6. *Registered business enterprise local tax.* This provision mandates local government units to impose a tax rate of no more than 2% of the gross income of a registered business enterprise.

The CREATE MORE Act has elements of an industrial policy, as it focuses on strategic industries under the Strategic Investment Priorities Plan (SIPP) of 2022.[14] Industries under the SIPP are classified into three tiers: tier I, essential activities; tier II, support industries; and tier III, advanced and emerging technologies.[15]

To qualify for the incentives, the businesses must (1) be registered with an investment promotion agency (IPA) or the Fiscal Incentives Review Board (FIRB); (2) fall under the government-prioritized industries listed in SIPP; and (3) identify whether the business would classify as a registered export enterprise, a domestic market enterprise, or a high-value domestic market enterprise.

Moreover, a minimum capital investment threshold of PHP 15 billion, specific for high-value domestic market enterprises, is required. Additionally, to receive the incentives, the projects of the registered businesses must be inside the export processing zones, economic zones, and freeports.

The conditions to qualify for the benefits of the CREATE MORE Act are as follows:

- Export performance for registered export enterprises. They must export at least 70% of their products/services.

- Export level for high-value domestic market enterprises. At least USD 100 million in export sales the following year.
- A minimum investment capital of PHP 50 billion or a minimum direct local employment of 10,000 workers within three years upon issuance of a certificate for incentives.
- The business and its project must have a comprehensive, sustainable development plan with clear, inclusive business approaches and a high level of sophistication and innovation.
- A periodic review by the FIRB will be conducted every three years to assess the performance of the registered businesses.

If these conditions are not met, the FIRB will recommend to the president the cancellation of the incentives. Registered business enterprises that do not comply with filing and reportorial requirements may be fined PHP 100,000 to PHP 500,000, or their registration will be cancelled. Moreover, government officials or employees who fail to furnish and provide the required tax incentives report will be penalized. A fine equivalent to the government employee's basic pay of one to six months will be imposed, or a suspension from government services of not more than one year and a criminal and administrative penalty will be imposed.

In April 2025, the government decided to extend incentives under the CREATE MORE Act to export-oriented enterprises (EOE). DTI's Export Marketing Bureau started accepting applications for the EOE certification under Republic Act 12066.[16]

7.3.3 The Tatak Pinoy (TP) Act (Republic Act 11981)

It was enacted on February 26, 2024, to mandate the formulation, funding, implementation, monitoring, and evaluation of a comprehensive and multiyear *Tatak Pinoy* (Proudly Filipino) strategy to oversee the initiatives and appropriate funds. The TP Act is a policy that directs the government to support and promote the production of Philippine products and services with increased diversity, sophistication, and quality to make domestic enterprises globally competitive (https://lawphil.net/statutes/repacts/ra2024/ra_11981_2024.html). It was approved by President Marcos Jr. in October 2025 (Memorandum Circular No. 104).

Section 2 of Republic Act No. 11981 states that the state's objective is to "encourage, support, and promote the production and offering of the Philippine products and services of increasing diversity, sophistication, and quality by domestic enterprises that are globally competitive." The statement aligns with Article XII, Section 1 of the Constitution, emphasizing the promotion of industrialization and full employment through industries that make full and efficient use of human and natural resources and are competitive in both domestic and foreign markets. The TP Act aims to strengthen local enterprises, boost exports, attract investments, and elevate the country's position in the global value chain. Its main objective is to diversify the Philippine industrial base by manufacturing a broad range of value-added goods for both domestic and international markets. The TP Act is keen on pushing domestic production to provide opportunities for Filipino businesses to gain market access and an international presence through exports.

Following Republic Act 11981, Section 8, *Tatak Pinoy* Strategy (TPS) intends to achieve its objectives by implementing plans and programs organized into the following key pillars: human resources, infrastructure, technology, innovation, investments, and sound financial management.

The TP Act also provides green lanes for investments and exports. According to Section 15 of Republic Act No. 11981, green lanes are mandated in government and public offices to streamline the processes and requirements for issuing permits, licenses, or certifications under the TPS. Green lanes ensure market access for *Tatak Pinoy* products and services, making them eligible to reach both domestic and global markets. Thus, an export green lane facility shall be established for qualified exporters for advanced processing and clearances for export requirements. *Tatak Pinoy* domestic enterprises are encouraged to participate in these programs and initiatives to enhance their product and service offerings. This follows Executive Order No. 18 (EO18) of 2023. This is a government-wide response to enhance the ease of doing business (see following) by mandating the creation of government offices (green lanes) that will expedite, streamline, and automate government processes for so-called "strategic investments." What are these investments? The list includes, among others, clean energy sources, defense-related projects, aerospace, electric vehicles, and specialty hospitals.

In late 2024, we contacted the Bureau of Investments (the agency coordinating the program) and inquired about the state of the program. We received information that indicates that of the about 170 projects approved by then, 80% corresponded to "clean energy sources," many of them floating solar projects.

Section 12 of the TP Act ensures that, for a period of ten years, Philippine-made products and services will be prioritized in government purchases. Government agencies will prioritize sectors covered by the TPS and apply this to all procurement levels, including raw materials, components, and final goods. The businesses must comply with SIPP requirements to qualify.

The preference for these can be waived if local production of the product is insufficient or not available for commercial quantities. Another reason would be that the desired quality or specifications cannot be met domestically. Finally, the preference will be waived if it violates international trade agreements of WTO commitments. After the ten-year period, the preference becomes subject to a "margin of preference"; the minimum margin is 15%.

As of March 2025, the *Tatak Pinoy* Market Access Initiative had supported 38 projects, mobilizing PHP 51.82 million in funding and benefiting 232 micro- and small enterprises, generating actual and booked sales of PHP 6.08 billion, projected revenues of PHP 4.85 million, and investments of about PHP 5.24 billion. Through international trade fairs, trade and investment missions, and business-to-business matching, *Tatak Pinoy* strives to allow Philippine products and services to compete globally, with continuous efforts to support micro- and small enterprises.

Overall, the *Tatak Pinoy* Act has commendable intentions to support the diversification, sophistication, and quality of locally produced goods to become globally competitive. The TP Act has been able to establish a *Tatak Pinoy* Council and a TPS to coordinate various government agencies and key private representatives to meet and develop strategies or policy recommendations. However, despite prioritizing key pillars such as human resources, infrastructure, technology, innovation, and investment, the TP Act does not get to the specifics. Moreover, as noted earlier, it ensures that, for ten years, Philippine-made products and services will be prioritized in government purchases of common-use items, such as supplies, construction materials, government uniforms with tropical fabrics, and defense materials. This is potentially problematic and runs counter to the overall objective of increasing international competitiveness.

Currently, the TP Act can best be thought of as an organizing framework that wants to set the tone, gather key actors, and get them all to agree toward a shared vision, moving up higher in global value chains and international competitiveness.

7.3.4 The CARS Program (EO 182, 2015)

It aims to attract new investments, stimulate demand, and effectively implement industry regulation to revitalize the Philippine automobile industry and develop the country as a regional automotive manufacturing hub. The program aims to provide time-bound and performance-based fiscal support to attract strategic investments into the manufacturing of motor vehicles and parts, with other non-fiscal measures already provided by existing laws, rules, and regulations (https://lawphil.net/executive/execord/eo2015/eo_182_2015.html).

The specific objectives of the CARS program are as follows: (1) boost manufacturing capability, enhancing the overall industrial sector by improving the automotive industry's manufacturing capacity; (2) stimulate SME growth, encouraging the development of small and medium enterprises linked to the automotive supply chain; (3) create jobs, generate employment opportunities through increased industrial activity; and (4) integrate regionally, positioning the Philippines as a competitive player in the ASEAN automotive market and deepening participation in regional supply chains.

The CARS program requires participating car manufacturers to be international brands with proven track records, while local parts manufacturers are required to be endorsed by participating car manufacturers. Moreover, local parts manufacturers are further required to have already been supplying parts for these models with original equipment manufacturing (OEM) standards and be a member in good standing of the Philippine Parts Maker Association. This program supports car manufacturers, parts makers, and the construction of shared testing facilities through fixed investment support, which is based on capital expenditures for tooling and equipment to manufacture parts, including training costs. Additionally, it offers a production volume incentive (PVI) based on the number of cars produced. Specifically, over a period of six years, and with three available model spots, each model was eligible for fiscal support of up to PHP 9 billion, with 40% coming from fiscal investment support (FIS) and 60% coming from the PVI. Particularly, its quota and tax incentives would be given through a tax payment certificate. The CARS program will end in 2025.

The program specified a goal of 200,000 units to be produced for each model within a six-year period, although only 100,000 units are needed to avail the incentive. Two manufacturers were selected through a competitive evaluation based on their investment proposals, production capacity, and ability to comply with the localization, employment, and technology-transfer goals of the CARS program. These were Toyota Motor Philippines Corporation and Mitsubishi Motors Philippines Corporation, which enrolled their Vios and Mirage models, respectively. Moreover, there is a local content requirement that requires car manufacturers to manufacture 50% of the assembly weight in the case of the body shell assembly in order to avail the PVI. Specifically, the *body shell* refers to the full metal weight of a car before it has been painted. There is also a requirement to manufacture major components of the assemblies locally, in the case of large plastic parts such as dashboards and bumpers. To avail the FIS, registered participants are required to either invest in the manufacturing of parts or the establishment of a shared testing facility. Other provisions include timely delivery of parts to the program participant's compliance monitoring (PCM), consistent meeting of the criteria for the PCM, and introduction of the enrolled models in the Philippine market using the parts manufactured under the CARS program. In addition, the fiscal support for the program would be computed based on the segment weighted average price, standard production support, and logistics efficiency index, as defined in this executive order, during the manufacture of the enrolled models. The program uses the segment weighted average price (net manufacturer's price minus an estimated 5% profit) and a standard production support (60% of the budget divided by production over 100,000 units within six years), targeting strategic parts that are not locally produced and not in OEM standards.

The program is coordinated and implemented mainly by the Board of Investments (BOI) and is required to submit annual performance reports. An interagency committee composed of various government agencies that administer the program, together with the BOI serving as the secretariat, functions as the body that evaluates applications for the models, monitors compliance, and recommends actions to the BOI, as well as the availability of fiscal support.

Overall, the CARS program has stimulated investment, created jobs, and revived local car assembly. Indeed, Toyota and Mitsubishi invested billions of pesos in modernizing their local assembly lines. The Vios and Mirage models have been manufactured locally on a large scale, supporting domestic production. The program helped create thousands of jobs directly and indirectly (through suppliers, logistics, etc.) and boosted local parts manufacturing, especially for body shells, bumpers, and plastic parts. It has been estimated that the program has provided 110,000 direct and ancillary jobs and saved the country USD 1.01 billion in forex. Likewise, CARS facilitated the transfer of advanced automotive manufacturing technologies, helping local firms meet international standards and become more competitive. CARS improved the localization of parts, which is now above 40% for both enrolled units (previously 22% and 32%, respectively).

On the other side of the scale, the CARS program fell short of becoming the transformative game changer it aimed to be, as it only engaged two manufacturers (the government allowed up to three participants, but only the two mentioned enrolled) that produced just over 200,000 units of Mitsubishi Mirage and Toyota Vios, though this is already a good output, as the manufacturers started in 2017 and 2018, respectively, in addition to the economic downturn caused by the pandemic. The reality is that the program did not significantly lift the entire local auto industry or turn the Philippines into a major regional hub.

The program lacked export incentives despite its objective to attain regional competitiveness. A second fundamental problem is that the local content requirements only affect the assembly of car parts, not the use of locally manufactured machines. This is what would make the industry truly competitive. As it stands now, further manufacturing after the program requires the involvement of international brands rather than local manufacturers having the capability to manufacture cars themselves.

The program is a good way to temporarily solve the country's reliance on imported cars and has created jobs in high-value sectors, which stimulates economic growth. Yet it has not lived up to its objectives—it even failed to attract a third model. This could be seen as a problem of the incentives or the procedures involved in applying for the program. Moreover, its implemented instruments, such as the requirements and the standards for the PCM and local parts manufacturers to achieve technology transfer, could only serve as a foundation for local parts manufacturers but would not make the country regionally competitive, nor would it allow the parts manufacturers to take off and create their own cars.

The government has decided to extend the CARS program to support the industry, having achieved some of the original goals, such as reviving the automotive manufacturing industry. Furthermore, the Revitalizing the Automotive Industry for Competitiveness Enhancement (RACE) program has not yet been outlined but is scheduled to replace the CARS program in 2025, with Mitsubishi pledging to introduce a new model and invest PHP 7 billion in the next five years, noting that the Philippines is their number one market in the ASEAN. Electric and hybrid vehicles were not included—a gap that the upcoming RACE program aims to address. The RACE program is designed to build on the gains of the CARS program while shifting the focus toward future-ready vehicles, especially electric, hybrid, and energy-efficient models. Possibly, the following vehicle types would be eligible for this new program: battery electric vehicles (BEVs), hybrid electric vehicles (HEVs), plug-in hybrid electric vehicles (PHEVs), and energy-efficient conventional vehicles (EECVs). The expected incentives would be tax breaks, duty exemptions, non-fiscal support in the form of streamlined importation and regulatory easing, and encouragement of local parts manufacturing.

* * *

To the aforementioned four key initiatives we add two more as examples that illustrate how the Philippine government thinks of growth, industrialization, and development in general today. The first one is the Maharlika Investment Corporation (MIC). This initiative confuses what it does with development. It was established in July 2023 to manage the Maharlika Investment Fund (MIF), the Philippines' first sovereign wealth fund (seed capital of PHP 500 billion, about USD 8.7 billion).[17] Its "core mandate is to generate optimal long-term returns on investments while fostering the socioeconomic development of the Philippines . . . and drive positive impact for future generations" (https://www.mic.gov.ph/about). Some of its initial actions have been a memorandum of agreement to upgrade Mindoro's and Palawan's power infrastructures, a strategic partnership with the Bases Conversion and Development Authority (BCDA) "to explore opportunities in transport, logistics, affordable housing, and agro-industrial urbanization," and a memorandum of understanding with Clark International Airport Corporation for further infrastructure and development projects in Central Luzon. Again, it would be churlish to dismiss these efforts to spark regional growth. Yet the reality is that there is nothing in the MIF to promote economic and social development that is not presently undertaken by existing public institutions in collaboration with the private sector. The Maharlika Investment Fund cannot contribute to the nation's *development* because *development* is, as discussed throughout this book, something different. Absent a clear national plan to rapidly industrialize and enable our firms to export complex products, how can we expect anything other than a "more of the same" (MOTS) outcome?

The other one is a significant tax reform, approved in May 2025: the Capital Market Efficiency Promotion Act (CMEPA), Republic Act No. 12214.[18] The CMEPA is designed to simplify the complex taxation of passive income in the Philippines. It also seeks to align and promote the Philippine capital market within the context of financial globalization, increased international mobility, and financial inclusion.[19] These may be needed measures that we applaud. Yet again, they will not deliver 8% growth, much less encourage ordinary Filipinos to invest in the Philippine capital markets and promote inclusive growth (as its proponents argue). It will not promote long-term economic growth and prosperity for all Filipinos because long-term growth is the result of very different initiatives.

7.4 Is the Philippines' Lack of Industrialization the Result of a Poor Business Environment?

This is a much-used argument by the business community. The business community at large claims that the Philippines scores relatively low (especially vis-à-vis some of its regional neighbors) in the Ease of Doing Business (EDB) indicators of the World Bank. The implicit claim is that if the private sector faced a more appropriate business environment (see later how this is measured), the country would do much better.

To better understand this claim, we collected the World Bank data on the EDB. The EDB score is a measure of regulatory performance across 10 Doing Business areas, averaged to get the main EDB score. The World Bank's EDB database provides information for 190 countries. An economy's EDB score is reflected on a scale from 0 (minimum) to 100 (maximum possible), where 0 represents the lowest and 100 represents the best possible performance. The 10 business areas covered are as follows: Starting a Business; Dealing with Construction Permits; Access to Electricity; Property Registration; Access to Credit; Protection of Minority Investors; Tax Payment; Trading Across Borders; Contract Enforcement; and Insolvency Resolution.

Figure 7.1 shows the distribution of the EDB overall score in 2020. The overall score of the Philippines is 63.06, right on the average (mean = 62.98), and note that the maximum value is 86.4.

Table 7.2 provides a summary of the scores for the ten indicators, as well as the overall score for the Philippines, including the mean value, standard deviation, and maximum value. These figures corroborate that the Philippines is about

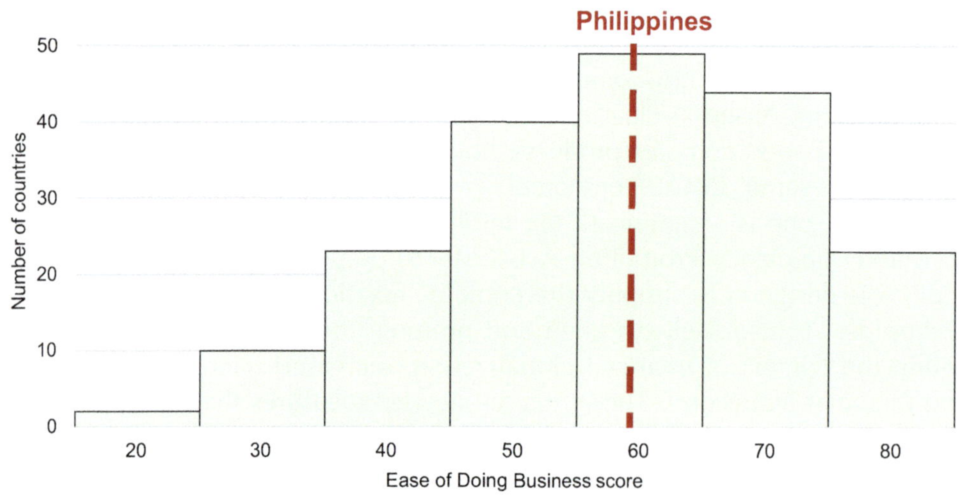

FIGURE 7.1 Distribution of the Overall Ease of Doing Business Scores, All Countries, 2020

Source: Authors' calculations based on data from The World Bank (2021)

TABLE 7.2 Indicators of the Ease of Doing Business, Philippines, 2020

Indicator	*Philippine Score*	*Average Score of the Indicator*	*Standard Deviation of the Indicator*	*Maximum Score of the Indicator*
Starting a business	71.28	84.02	11.36	99.62
Dealing with construction permits	71.63	65.47	15.84	93.47
Access to electricity	87.44	69.73	20.23	100
Property registration	57.57	62.10	18.16	95.41
Access to credit	40.00	54.24	23.94	100
Protection of minority Investors	60.00	51.80	20.04	92.00
Tax payment	73.17	69.80	16.86	100
Trading across borders	68.45	71.08	22.57	100
Contract enforcement	45.96	56.29	13.41	84.15
Insolvency resolution	55.08	45.28	24.20	92.69
Overall EDB score	63.06	62.98	13.87	86.40

Note: The average score, standard deviation, and maximum score of each indicator are based on the ease of doing business scores across 191 countries reported in the World Bank (2021).

Source: Authors' calculations based on data from the World Bank (2021).

average, and even earlier in some indicators, or within one standard deviation from the mean in others (note that the maximum score in some cases is below 100). The Philippines obtains the lowest score in the indicator of starting a business, 71.28, which is slightly below the average minus one standard deviation. The indicator starting a business under the EDB looks into four aspects for a small- to medium-sized limited liability company to start up and formally operate in each economy's largest business city: (1) number of procedures to legally start and formally operate a company, (2) time required to complete each procedure, (3) cost required to complete each procedure (% of income per capita), and (4) paid-in minimum capital (% of income per capita). The Philippines requires 13 procedures that take 33 days under EDB 2020. Time and costs to accomplish them are measured accordingly. For comparison, Vietnam requires a total of eight procedures that take 16 days, Thailand requires five procedures that take 6 days, South Korea requires three procedures that take 8 days, China requires 4.5 procedures that take 9 days, and Malaysia requires eight procedures that take 17 days.[20] With these values, it is perhaps legitimate to argue that there is room to do better, but it would be incorrect to conclude that, overall, the Philippine business environment is a binding constraint on industrialization or growth.

It is also important to note that if the sample is restricted to emerging and developing countries, the Philippines performs even better, as the mean of this group of countries is 59.15.

To analyze the impact of the EDB on industrialization, we ran a series of regressions of several proxy variables for industrialization on the EDB score. These variables are the share of industry's value added in GDP, the share of manufacturing value added in GDP, the share of industry's employment in total employment, the share of manufacturing employment in total employment, and the share of investment in GDP.[21] We control GDP per capita and GDP per capita squared and add country and time (decade) fixed effects.[22] Results are shown in Table 7.3. The dataset covers 190 countries for the period 2010–2020. The expectation is that these proxies for industrialization and the EDB will be positively correlated. A summary of the most significant results is as follows:

1. *Columns 1 and 2.* We first ran regressions of the share of industry in GDP as a function of the EDB. Without controlling for income (column 1), we obtain an elasticity of 0.128, that is, a 1% increase in the overall ease of doing business score corresponds to a 0.13% increase in the share of industry in GDP. However, after controlling for income (*gdp*) and income squared (*gdpsq*) (column 2), the coefficient becomes statistically insignificant. The predicted values for the estimation years by the regression in column 2 are about the same as the actual values.
2. *Columns 3 and 4.* We replicate (1) but use the share of manufacturing employment in total employment as our indicator of industrialization and find similar results: While the regression with no controls yields a positive and significant coefficient estimate for the EDB score, controlling for income and its squared term yields a statistically insignificant coefficient estimate. Again, the predicted values of the EDB for the Philippines closely approximate the actual scores. We use this regression to simulate an improvement in the Philippines' EDB, such that its score equals that of South Korea, 84 in 2020. We find that an increase in the Philippines' EDB score from 63 to 84, while holding income constant, increases the share of manufacturing employment from 8.75% to 8.91%.
3. *Columns 5 and 6.* Finally, we replicate (1) and (2) and use the investment share as the dependent variable, with largely the same results as in columns (1) and (2): a positive and significant coefficient estimate for the EDB without control variables, and an insignificant coefficient estimate upon controlling for income. Predicted values are also close to the actual values.

One of the major concerns of the Filipino private sector is the cost of electricity (access to electricity is not a problem, as Table 7.2 shows), thought to be very high and a binding constraint. Ravago (2022) offered a detailed analysis of the causes of high electricity prices. Filipino businessmen often mention as examples Indonesia, Malaysia, or Thailand, where electricity is cheaper (Rimando and Mercado, 2012; Remo, 2014). A high cost of power may act as a deterrent to investment in power-intensive industries, thereby biasing growth toward more labor-intensive sectors. However, not all countries with lower electricity rates are world manufacturing powerhouses, and not all countries with higher electricity rates than the Philippines are industrial underperformers. Hence, it is important to explore the extent to which the price of electricity impedes industrialization.

TABLE 7.3 Estimation Results: Ease of Doing Business and Industrialization Indicators

	(1)	(2)	(3)	(4)	(5)	(6)
	s_{IND}^{VA}	s_{IND}^{VA}	s_{MFG}^{EMP}	s_{MFG}^{EMP}	s^{GCF}	s^{GCF}
EDB	0.128***	−0.075	0.244***	0.065	0.145*	−0.182
	(0.054)	(0.051)	(0.058)	(0.056)	(0.080)	(0.138)
gdp		1.549***		2.843***		1.926
		(0.325)		(0.374)		(1.487)
gdpsq		−0.081***		−0.150***		−0.085
		(0.018)		(0.021)		(0.081)
constant	1.619***	−4.180***	1.199***	−11.34***	1.943***	−5.539
	(0.200)	(1.289)	(0.241)	(1.699)	(0.299)	(5.766)
Country fixed effects	YES	YES	YES	YES	YES	YES
Decade fixed effects	YES	YES	YES	YES	YES	YES
Observations	1,512	1,481	874	861	1,418	1,413
R-squared	0.970	0.972	0.967	0.970	0.704	0.722
ACTUAL: Average value observed for the Philippines (2010–2020) (%)	24.10	24.10	8.38	8.38	22.25	22.25
PREDICTED: Average value estimated for the Philippines (2010–2020)	24.102	24.113	8.384	8.400	22.058	22.110

Notes:
(1) Robust standard errors in parentheses: *** $p < 0.01$, ** $p < 0.05$, * $p < 0.1$.
(2) s_{IND}^{VA} is the share of industry value added in GDP; s_{MFG}^{EMP} is the share of employment in manufacturing in total employment; s^{GCF} is the investment rate, or the share of gross capital formation in GDP.
(3) All variables are in natural logarithms (coefficient estimates are elasticities).

Source: Authors' estimations based on the ease of doing business data from World Bank (2021), data from the World Bank: World Development Indicators (https://data.worldbank.org), the United Nations Industrial Development Organization's National Accounts Database (https://stat.unido.org/data/table?dataset=national-accounts#data-browser), the Groningen Growth and Development Centre's ten-sector database (Timmer et al., 2015), and the International Labour Organization's ILOSTAT database (https://ilostat.ilo.org/data/).

Ravago et al. (2019) studied whether power prices play a significant role in hampering industrialization, specifically whether higher electricity prices explain the industrial share. Specifically, these authors studied the impact of electricity prices on the share of industry's value added in GDP (total industry, not just manufacturing), using annual data for 33 OECD and Southeast Asian countries from 1980 to 2014. We note that while the Philippine industrial share in GDP is lower than that of its Asian neighbors, it is not low for international standards.

Ravago et al.'s (2019, Table 4, column 4) estimates indicate that the impact of the price of electricity on industry's share in GDP is negative. Yet, this impact is not excessively large: For a power price of USD 0.19 kWh (at the 80th percentile, the Philippine residential price), the predicted peak industrial share is 31.7% of GDP. By contrast, for a power price of USD 0.10 kWh (at the 20th percentile), the predicted peak industrial share is only marginally higher at 33.3%. These values are averages, not specific on the Philippines.

To focus on the Philippines, we obtained a large sample of electricity rates (USD/kWh) from two databases, Liddle (2022) and the World Bank (2020). Both provide very different data. Figure 7.2 shows the distribution of these prices in 2014, the common year for which both provide information. According to the Liddle data-set, the Philippine price is among the highest in the world. On the other hand, the World Bank database gives a much lower price, and the distribution indicates that the Philippine price is about average. The reason is that the prices provided are very different. Liddle's (2022) electricity prices are in 2015 US cents per kilowatt hour. The price is a weighted combination of residential and industrial prices. Meanwhile, the distribution from the World Bank refers to electricity prices in US cents per kilowatt hour. This is a component of the information used to calculate the ease-of-doing-business index. As seen in Figure 7.2, based on data measured and collected through Liddle's methodology, the Philippines had an electricity price of 40 US cents per kilowatt hour in 2014, which is 2.6 standard deviations

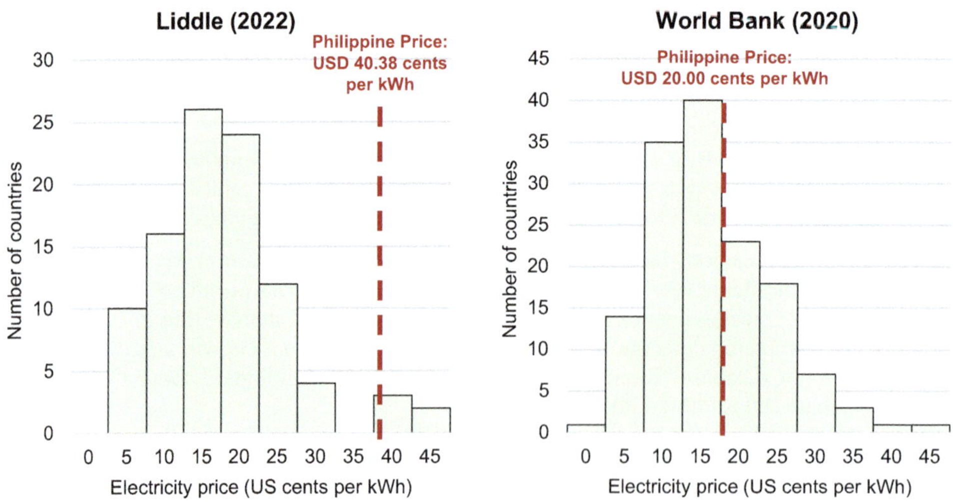

FIGURE 7.2 Distribution of Electricity Prices, 2014

Notes: (i) Liddle (2022) has price data for 97 countries in 2014 (left), while The World Bank (2021) has data for 112 countries in 2014 (right). (ii) We removed Venezuela from The World Bank's data set as the price provided is USD 955 cents per kWh in 2014.

Source: Liddle (2022) and The World Bank (2020).

higher than the average price for electricity across the world in the same period. Meanwhile, using the World Bank's methodology to measure electricity prices, the Philippines has a price of 20 US cents per kilowatt hour, and it is much closer (albeit still higher) than the average world price.[23]

Figure 7.3 presents data for the Philippines, Indonesia, Malaysia, Thailand, and Vietnam, as provided by both Liddle (2022) and the World Bank (2020). Across both datasets, the Philippines has a higher electricity price than its neighbors, with a more pronounced price differential in Liddle's (2022) dataset.

Meanwhile, as discussed in Chapter 4, while the share of manufacturing employment in total employment is lower in the Philippines than in its neighbors, the Philippine share of manufacturing in GDP was quite similar to those of Indonesia and Malaysia, and even Vietnam before 2016.

To further investigate the potentially negative role that electricity prices play on Philippine industrialization, and with the caveat about the reliability of the electricity prices that we gathered, we regressed the industrialization proxies used in the EDB analysis against electricity prices, and GDP per capita and its square. The regressions include country and decade fixed effects. We used the Liddle (2022) series because this is where the Philippines appears with a very high price. Note also that 2014 is the latest year for which data on the Philippines is available. Does this high price explain the country's low industrialization? Liddle provided an unbalanced panel of electricity prices in real terms (in 2015 US cents per kilowatt hour) that combines residential and industrial prices, available for 107 countries from 1960 to 2019.

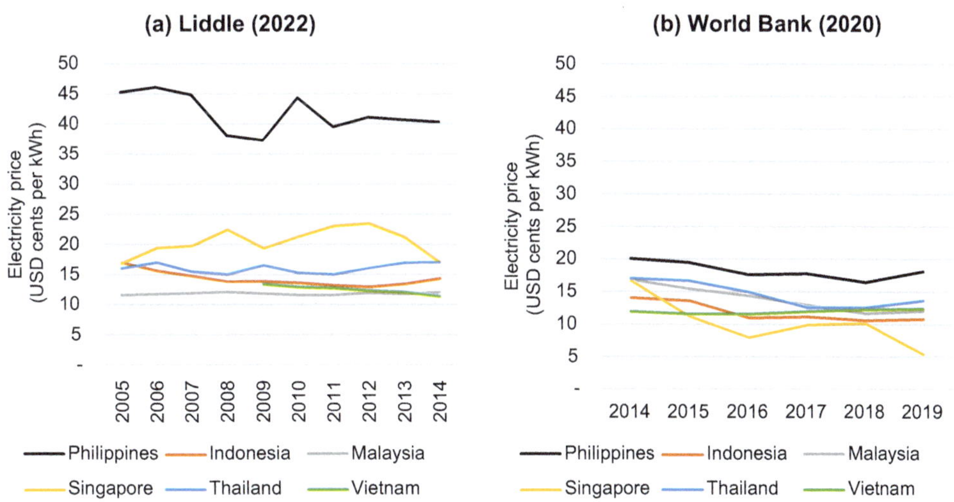

FIGURE 7.3 Electricity Prices (USD cents per kWh), Selected Southeast Asian Countries, 2005–2014 (Panel a) and 2014–2019 (Panel b)

Source: Liddle (2022) and The World Bank (2020).

TABLE 7.4 Estimation Results: Electricity Prices and Industrialization Indicators

	(1)	(2)	(3)	(4)
	s_{IND}^{VA}	s_{IND}^{VA}	s_{MFG}^{EMP}	s^{GCF}
eprice	−0.031***	−0.038***	−0.0325***	−0.133***
	(0.010)	(0.011)	(0.010)	(0.026)
gdp		0.521***	2.949***	1.275***
		(0.105)	(0.104)	(0.155)
gdpsq		−0.026***	−0.158***	−0.059***
		(0.006)	(0.006)	(0.008)
constant	3.072***	0.478***	−11.16***	−3.673***
	(0.020)	(0.447)	(0.498)	(0.700)
Country fixed effects	YES	YES	YES	YES
Decade fixed effects	YES	YES	YES	YES
Observations	2,366	2,313	2,381	2,921
R-squared	0.923	0.926	0.926	0.514
ACTUAL: Average value observed for the Philippines (2010–2020) (%)	25.28	25.28	8.64	18.94
PREDICTED: Average value estimated for the Philippines (2010–2020)	25.28	25.28	8.64	18.86

Notes:
(1) Robust standard errors in parentheses: *** $p < 0.01$, ** $p < 0.05$, * $p < 0.1$.
(2) s_{IND}^{VA} is the share of industry value added in GDP; s_{MFG}^{EMP} is the share of employment in manufacturing in total employment; s^{GCF} is the investment rate, or the share of gross capital formation in GDP.
(3) All variables are in natural logarithms (coefficient estimates are elasticities).

Source: Authors' estimations based on electricity price data from Liddle (2022), data from the World Bank: World Development Indicators (https://data.worldbank.org), the United Nations Industrial Development Organization's National Accounts database (https://stat.unido.org/data/table?dataset=national-accounts#data-browser), the Groningen Growth and Development Centre's ten-sector database (Timmer et al., 2015), and the International Labour Organization's ILOSTAT database (https://ilostat.ilo.org/data/).

Results are summarized in Table 7.4. The key finding for our purposes is that the price of electricity (denoted *eprice* in Table 7.4) is consistently negative across all specifications; that is, a higher price of electricity affects industrialization negatively. In what follows, we comment on the different specifications in Table 7.4 and, in particular, on the impact of the electricity price on the Philippine industrialization:

1. *Column 1.* Not adding any control variable, the actual share of industry in GDP (average of 25.27% for 2005–2014) is about the same as that predicted by the regression (average of 25.28% for the same period).

2. *Column 2*. Controlling for income (denoted *gdp*) per capita and income per capita squared (denoted *gdpsq*), the negative sign of the electricity price remains, and again, the actual and predicted values of industry's share in GDP are about the same (average of 25.27% actual share for 2005–2014, vis-à-vis 25.28% average predicted share for 2005–2014). We used this regression to estimate the effect of a 50% reduction in the Philippine price of electricity, evaluated in 2014. We find that the industry's share in GDP increases, but by less than one percentage point, from 24.59% to 25.25%.
3. *Column 3*. When we repeat the same exercise as in (1) and (2) with the manufacturing employment share, conclusions remain generally consistent; that is, the electricity prices carry a negative sign, and the employment share predicted by the regression is identical to the actual one (average of 8.64%). A reduction in the Philippine price of electricity by 50% leads again to a marginal increase in the share of employment in manufacturing, from 8.63% to 8.82%.
4. *Column 4*. The exercise with the investment share as the dependent variable does not lead to a radically different assessment—the price of electricity has a negative sign. The actual investment shares are slightly lower than those predicted by the regression (18.87% period average predicted value vis-à-vis 18.94% period average actual value). A decrease in the price of electricity by 50% leads to only an increase in the investment share by 1 percentage point, from 19.91% to 21.84%.[24]

Overall, we conclude that the business environment, including the price of electricity, probably plays some role in explaining the country's industrial underperformance. Yet we do not think it is the binding constraint on Philippine industrialization. If the Starting a Business indicator improved significantly, or if the price of electricity decreased to the levels of Vietnam or Indonesia (less than a half of the Philippine price, according to our data), we would not be able to create a much larger (especially in employment) and advanced manufacturing sector that would compete in the world economy. Most of today's developed nations attained high income in the decades after WWII. The data do not exist, but we doubt they had a much better business environment than the Philippines today.

The country's industrialization problems are longstanding and are attributed to a myriad of reasons. They go back to the three decades after independence in 1946. During these three decades, the Philippines, like all new independent nations, made efforts to industrialize. It failed when it should have succeeded. As discussed earlier, the real problem with Philippine industrialization emerged in the 1970s and 1980s, when the country faced a "perfect de-industrialization storm": political instability, the debt crisis, foreign-capital dependency, missed FDI opportunities, and poor coordination of the exchange rate and trade regimes. Yet, upgrading the manufacturing sector is imperative to create links with other sectors, to undertake R&D, to pull agriculture and services, and to employ our engineers. Certainly, it will not be possible for the Philippines to industrialize in today's world like South Korea did in the 1970s and 1980s (think of China), but the country needs to strive and develop a few niches in manufacturing.

Not having a manufacturing sector, many of the service activities that have flourished in the Philippines are of low productivity. Many of them are non-tradable, such as wholesale and retail trade (e.g., department stores and malls). These sectors certainly exist everywhere. Our point is that the Philippines has not been able to create a sizeable tradable sector, that is, manufactured goods that can be exported and compete in the world economy. This matters because the wages in many non-tradable activities depend on the wages of the tradable sector.[25] Unless this point is understood, wages in the Philippines will continue to be low.

Notes

1 These authors do not provide details about the manufacturing sector, for example, subsectoral composition, employment and output shares, etc.

2 Also, in the 1950s, there were government-run projects such as the Mariveles shipyards and the Iligan steel mills, along with operations like the Manila Gas Corporation and the Cebu Portland Cement Company. An example in the hotel sector is the Manila Hotel, which was acquired by the Philippine government after World War II. The state also invested in tourism-related facilities as part of nation-building and international projection in the 1950s.

3 When President Marcos took over in 1965, the tariff rate was 40% of the US full rate. The tariff would increase until reaching 100% in December 1973.

4 Broad (1988, p. 124) indicates that the World Bank had projected the creation of 360,000 new jobs between 1980 and 1985 under a successful export-oriented industrial promotion strategy. The reality was that employment in the three operating export processing zones did not even reach 25,000.

5 China officially entered the World Trade Organization (WTO) on December 11, 2001. The agreement for accession was the culmination of 15 years of negotiations, involving a US–China bilateral agreement reached in November 1999. After China joined the WTO, it experienced massive economic growth, becoming the world's largest exporter in 2009. China's imports increased substantially, and the country attracted significant foreign direct investment (FDI).

6 The Marcos Sr. administration had started financing growth using recycled petrodollars in the 1970s. These loans carried floating interest rates. The result is that foreign debt mounted (De Dios et al., 2021).

7 The two figures correspond to those provided in the Five-Year Philippine Development Plan 1983–1987 (NEDA, 1982, Table 5.1) and by the World Bank Group (1984, Table 4.1).

8 Edwards (1999, pp. 254–255) indicated that there are questions about the quality of Korea's education, that it focused on repetition and put a heavy emphasis on moral education and discipline. He quoted Alice Amsden, who claimed that it is easy to exaggerate the role of formal education in Korea's development. Nevertheless, this is not to dismiss the role of education, and he pointed out that the state played a large role in, for example, de-packing technology, promoting overseas training, or in coordinating the acquisition and application of existing technologies.

9 (a) State-controlled banks provided preferential loans at very low interest rates to chaebols that aligned with the government's development goals. The government often guaranteed repayment of foreign loans, making it easier for chaebols to secure international financing. (b) Chaebols received significant tax breaks and other financial incentives. (c) The government insulated domestic industries from foreign competition through import restrictions and high tariffs, giving chaebols a protected market to grow and consolidate. (d) The government facilitated chaebols' access to crucial foreign technology and expertise.

10 Chaebols were given strict performance quotas, especially related to export targets. Meeting these targets meant continued government support and privileges; failure could lead to serious consequences, including the withdrawal of support or even the threat of asset confiscation.

11 RepublicAct12066isanactamendingSections 27, 28, 32, 34, 57, 106, 108, 109, 112, 135, 237, 237-A, 269, 292, 293, 294, 295, 296, 297, 300, 301, 308, 309, 310, and 311 and adding new ones, Sections 135-A, 295-A, 296-A, and 297-A, of the National Internal Revenue Code of 1997, as amended, and for other purposes, enacted November 8, 2024, *Official Gazette* (Phil.), published Nov. 13, 2024.

- Republic Act 11981: *Tatak Pinoy* (Proudly Filipino) Act, Republic Act No. 11981 (Phil. Feb. 26, 2024).
- Executive Order No. 182: Comprehensive Automotive Resurgence Strategy (CARS) Program, Exec. Order No. 182, s. 2015 (Philippines May 29, 2015).

12 https://lawphil.net/statutes/repacts/ra2024/pdf/ra_12066_2024.pdf

13 The Enhanced Net Operating Loss Carry Over (NOLCO); 50% additional deduction on four types of expenses—labor, domestic input, trade exhibitions or trade fairs, and electricity; 100% additional deduction on two types of expenses—R&D and training expenses; reinvestment allowance for manufacturing and tourism industries. A deduction of up to 50% of the amount reinvested in manufacturing or tourism-related projects, deductible within five years from the time of reinvestment; depreciation of qualified capital expenditures. An additional deduction of 10% for buildings and 20% for machinery and equipment used directly in registered projects or activities.

14 https://firb.gov.ph/download/2022-strategic-investment-priority-plan-sipp/

15 Tier I, essential activities: infrastructure and logistics; health and medical products; disaster risk reduction and climate change adaptation; defense-related activities; mass housing, renewable energy projects; agriculture, forestry, and fishery; export activities; and activities supporting the *Balik Probinsya* Program.

Tier II, support industries: manufacture of parts and components; processing of agricultural and fishery products; digital infrastructure; research and development activities; skills development and technical education.

Tier III, advanced and emerging technologies: artificial intelligence, robotics and automation, biotechnology, nanotechnology, advanced digital production technologies, space technology, advanced materials, electric vehicles, and green manufacturing. Although the SIPP includes horizontal elements, its tiered structure reflects a more targeted approach—channeling incentives toward priority sectors. In this way, tax instruments are used not just for general investment promotion but as a means to influence the performance of strategic industries. Specifically, Tier III contains the following activities for innovation: (a) research and development (R&D) and activities adopting advanced digital production technologies of the Fourth Industrial Revolution, such as, but not limited to, robotics, artificial intelligence (AI), additive manufacturing, data analytics, digital transformative technologies (e.g., cloud computing services, hyperscalers, data centers, and digital infrastructure), nanotechnology (includes nanoelectronics), biotechnology, production and/or adoption of new hybrid seeds, and other Industry 4.0 technologies; (b) highly technical manufacturing and production of innovative products and services, such as, but not limited to, manufacture of equipment, parts, and services; commercialization of intellectual property and R&D products/services, aerospace, medical devices (except personal protective equipment); Internet of Things (Iot) devices and systems (includes wireless sensors and devices); full-scale wafer fabrication; and advanced materials; (c) establishment of innovation support facilities, such as, but not limited to, R&D hubs; centers of excellence; science and technology parks; innovation incubation center; tech startups; startup enablers: incubators and accelerators; and space-related infrastructures.

16 The Department of Trade and Industry (DTI) announced in June 2025 that it had certified the first four companies as export-oriented enterprises (EOEs) under the CREATE MORE law: (a) Dole Philippines Inc. (est. 1963). A global leader in tropical fruit exports, Dole cultivates vast plantations across Mindanao and Luzon, supplying fresh and processed pineapples and juices to markets in the Americas, Europe, and Asia. The company is also expanding into sustainable agriculture and biofuel production. (b) Philsaga Mining Corporation (PMC) (est. 2001). PMC operates the Coo Gold Mine in Agusan del Sur, extracting over 900,000 metric tons of ore annually. (c) Krystle Exports Philippines Inc. (est. 1987). Krystle Exports is a distributor of premium Filipino food and non-food products. It also partners with local manufacturers to deliver high-quality goods to the United States, Hong Kong, and the Middle East. (d) Bosch Service Solutions Inc. (est. 2010). Based in Taguig City, Bosch provides business process outsourcing and customer experience services to global clients, including the Bosch Group.

17 Maharlika Investment Fund Act of 2023, Republic Act No. 11954 (Philippines July 18, 2023).

18 Capital Markets Efficiency Promotion Act, Republic Act No. 12214 (Philippines May 29, 2025).

19 For details, see: https://www.grantthornton.com.ph/insights/articles-and-updates1/lets-talk-tax/whats-next-a-new-tax-reform-for-the-capital-market/

20 Methodology of the World Bank's Doing Business: https://archive.doingbusiness.org/en/methodology. The specific methodology for the indicator "starting a business" is: https://archive.doingbusiness.org/en/methodology/starting-a-business.

21 Data on the share of industry value added and manufacturing value added in GDP is taken from the United Nations Industrial Development Organization (2025) National Accounts' database. Industry value added comprises ISIC Rev. 4 sections B–E, or mining and quarrying, manufacturing, and utilities. The share of employment in industry and in manufacturing to total employment is derived from the International Labour Organization's (2025) ILOSTAT database. Employment share in industry includes mining and quarrying, manufacturing, utilities, and construction.

22 Income per capita is measured as the GDP per capita of each country, in constant 2015 USD. Data is obtained from the World Bank's (2024) World Development Indicators (WDI).

23 While the World Bank figures are in current prices, we also checked whether the Philippines' place in the distribution holds after deflating the price using each country's electricity price deflator (2015 = 100) (see Parker, 2024). There is minimal change in the Philippines price (20 cents in current prices, 18.6 cents in 2015 prices), and the Philippine price remains within one standard deviation to the right of the mean.

24 The investment share is measured as gross capital formation as a share of GDP (%). Data are taken from the World Bank (2024) WDI.

25 This is the case of, for example, taxi drivers or barbers, who earn much more in Switzerland or in France than in the Philippines.

8

INNOVATION, FIRMS, CAPABILITIES, AND MODERN INDUSTRIAL POLICY

8.1 Introduction

This chapter discusses four intimately related themes: innovation, firms, capabilities, and industrial policy, with a particular focus on the type of industrial policy that the Philippines needs, which we call "modern industrial policy." Consistent with the first theme of this book (i.e., the transformation of the economy), modern industrial policy refers to the restructuring policies (both horizontal—generic, and vertical—for specific sectors) that facilitate the transfer of resources to the more dynamic activities of the economy, whether in agriculture, industry, or services. Thus, industrial policy clearly aims at facilitating (forcing?) changes in the structure of the economy. Industrial policy is *necessary* in a developing country context because the market alone will not lead to the economic transformation (upgrading, diversification) that is associated with development. Economic transformation (beyond small changes) is not a natural process. In market economies, firms are the agents of transformation, but their actions need to be inserted in a framework of public action. This is especially important in developing countries because their firms face significant market failures and lack organizational capabilities. Firms in developing countries also face another problem: network failures, especially those that aim at producing complex products. If a country wants to enter advanced industrial fields, progress is not achieved as a result of competitive transactions, but rather through mutual learning processes fostered by well-managed collaboration between specialists in different fields. This is, for example, the case of the creation and development of high-cost, complex products and systems (Hobday, 1998).

DOI: 10.4324/9781003728719-8

8.2 Industrial Policy Levers for a Weak State: Is an Effective Industrial Policy for the Philippines Possible?

We concluded Chapter 7 by arguing that the Philippines needs a true industrial policy, different from the initiatives currently being implemented. Apart from the deficit in national vision discussed in previous chapters, the Philippine state has often lacked the capability to carry out long-term, strategic, industry-shaping policies. Unlike its more successful neighbors, it has not been able to consolidate state power to direct or even discipline the private sector. It has also suffered from a self-inhibiting view of government finance that has weakened its ability to provide long-needed public goods. Individual presidents may have adopted the postures of strongmen, but the Philippine state itself is widely viewed as weak.

Could an effective industrial policy be introduced under such conditions? We argued it can be done. Analyzing the possibilities of African countries implementing an industrial policy, South Korean economist Chang (2013) disagreed with all the standard arguments adduced against it, including climate, geography, history, culture, natural resource abundance, political economy, bureaucratic capabilities, and the changes in global economic rules. All these are highly biased and partial arguments. The implementation of a sound industrial policy requires a mix of vision, realism, institutional reform, and investments.

The Philippines is a somewhat similar story: It needs a vigorous executive sponsorship of a sweeping industrial strategy, together with well-defined pilots whose success would build credibility and could then be replicated or scaled up. The key would be for planners to identify sectors with productive firms willing to improve (and without entrenched interests), involve individuals with a strong reputation for generating results, and most of all, standardize the use of clear time-bound goals and key performance indicators.

Any "development deals" (Chapter 3) must be open, as political capture thrives on discretion. One safeguard is to propagate rules-based incentives with automated criteria, for example, all subsidies are matched 1:1 with private R&D spending and are automatically reviewed after three years. They may not eliminate capture entirely, but will raise the transaction cost of rent-seeking. Openness in development deals also means maximizing competitive processes and third-party evaluation, as opposed to opaque selection. Academic institutions or even international partners may be brought in to conduct performance-based ranking, publish dashboards, and solicit public feedback, not because they are immune in themselves, but because they are often less embedded in domestic patronage networks. Indeed, some state agencies, such as PEZA (Philippine Export Zone Authority) and DOST (Department of Science and Technology, have built reputations even within the business community for relative professionalism. Along with other "islands of competence," they can reinforce layers of insulation and credibility.

Legislation like *Tatak Pinoy* probably embodies the current extent of Philippine industrial policy. It is undeniably modest compared to comparable legislation from Taiwan, Malaysia, and even Vietnam. But the tools described there can still, with some enhancement, serve as force multipliers for the upgrading of Philippine firms. Public procurement, for instance, can be used to extract better performance. The Philippine government remains a significant buyer, especially in infrastructure, health, education, and defense goods. If procurement policies are designed to favor local high-performing firms (e.g., by requiring local content levels or elevated quality standards by local SMEs), they can encourage capability building in targeted sectors. It may even be possible to pilot a new procurement track: Instead of awarding government contracts purely to the lowest bidder, bidders who meet ISO standards or who complete a pre-bid quality audit may be preferred—with the proviso that winning bidders are required to then join a free "supplier development" track, say covering workshops on inventory systems, packaging, quality enhancement, and so forth.

The current set of Special Economic Zones could be improved by clustering firms around particular supply chains, then providing support for workforce training, R&D, and supplier development. The government might designate one to two industrial zones near Clark or Calabarzon to move from electronics assembly to more advanced electronics manufacturing ("small to medium jump") and offer significant tax breaks and matching grants to firms that locate there and meet transparent criteria. For example, achieving at least 50% exports within three years, R&D partnerships with local universities, and workforce training programs. For firms able to branch into, say, EV components, the Department of Transport may commit to procuring locally produced basic EV buses (evaluated by a panel of DOST, academe, and PEZA representatives) over five years, creating an anticipated and predictable pipeline of demand.

Incentives are already offered by the Fiscal Incentives Review Board (FIRB), but these must be more closely tied to clear performance metrics to discipline firms and guide industrial upgrading. The government will need to invest in better monitoring capacity, but as a lever, one might consider identifying 10–15 large anchor firms (conglomerate retailers, exporters, construction companies, food processors, etc.) willing to open their supply chains to local SMEs. Participating suppliers then go through benchmarking assessments, focusing on process, cost, delivery time, defect rates, and the government co-finances ISO certification, coaching, lean manufacturing workshops, and even digital adoption plans, on a 1:1 matching basis with the conglomerates.

Throughout the book, we argue that industrial policy is essential. The notion that Philippine peculiarities make it impossible to undertake it at the same scale as Japan, South Korea, Malaysia, and Vietnam is not a reason for benign neglect or a vain hope in "leapfrogging." Manufacturing matters because, as an activity, it is the most reliable way to absorb large swaths of the labor force, organize them productively within firms, and develop capabilities that allow them to produce more complex goods for the world market, ultimately raising wages and incomes. Historically, a strong state has always been needed for such an undertaking. But a strategy based on (1) starting with whoever is already producing and wants to improve; (2) tying significant financial support to demonstrated effort and market validation; (3) investing in capabilities building—diagnostics, coaching, standards enforcement, and peer learning; and (4) using city-level or sectoral approaches to distribute political risks can build exemplars or "islands of competence" and generate momentum for more ambitious moves.

8.3 A Question of Ideology?

As discussed in Chapter 2, after World War II, the Philippines remained under American influence and thinking when it came to economic policy. Yet, as we also discussed in that chapter, Philippine policymakers had their own views and, in fact, the country ran an import substitution industrialization policy for quite some time. What is true, is that the American-trained technocrats pursued economic modernization by promoting free market liberalism and by ensuring that the country would not fall prey to socialist-communist ideology. This influenced how business and economics programs were set up, especially at the University of the Philippines, which soon became the most prestigious.

When President Marcos Sr. declared Martial Law in 1972, he retained the technocrats, who then intensified development assistance from the World Bank and the IMF as part of the United States' Cold War strategy. The economic policies pursued by the technocrats were in consonance with the United States-IMF-World Bank global economic policies and were part and parcel of the tenets of the Bretton Woods system, meant to boost the post-World War II economy. Although these policies had a political objective (e.g., avoid the communist insurgency in the countryside), they also aimed to transform the agricultural and industrial sectors and shift from import-substitution manufacturing to export-oriented industrialization. Although Marcos Sr. also prioritized industrialization and the expansion of heavy industries (see Chapter 7), the technocrats of the Marcos administration believed in economic liberalization and encouraged trade and foreign investments. They tried to abandon the import-substitution strategy, which they viewed as hampering development and limiting foreign exchange, and promoted Export-Oriented Industrialization, following the footsteps of Taiwan and South Korea.

However, the overall United States' Cold War development strategy failed. One key cause was the dominance of political dynasties that did not fully support the technocrats' policies, in particular, economic liberalization and free trade (e.g., the coconut and sugar landlords).[1] The power of these politico-economic elites derived from the rents discussed in Chapter 7 and the concomitant decrease of central government control over the provinces. This led, for example, to the privatization of public goods, with deleterious consequences for the nation to this day. This situation allowed these political dynasties to utilize patronage politics to perpetuate their wealth and power. There were elites who opposed the technocrats' liberalization of the economy as they believed foreign investment would compete with their own protected industries. This required compromises. For example, the Bureau of Investments (BOI) instituted pioneer and non-pioneer investments. Under this policy, the BOI identified industries where foreign investors could freely venture (pioneer industries) and those reserved solely for Filipinos (non-pioneer industries). Pioneer industries were those that had not been in operation in the Philippines and could be 100% foreign-owned. Those industries where Filipinos were already operating (e.g., cement) were classified as non-pioneer. In these industries, the voting stocks of the corporation had to be at least 60% Filipino-controlled (Tadem, 2019, p. 13).[2]

The technocrats' failure to implement the modernization ideology was clear in the late 1960s and early 1970s, when social contradictions reemerged with student demonstrations, peasant marches, and workers' strikes. The economic and political crises were a struggle between two groups: those who favored nationalist programs and technocrats who wanted more openness. In the 1970s, the emphasis of the export industrialization strategy on a few export crops under a free-trade arrangement paved the way for a dependent and predominantly agricultural economy, benefiting a small sector of landowners. Both industry and agriculture stagnated (Tadem, 2019, p. 13).

Some technocrats supported Marcos' martial law. They thought that it gave them the opportunity to clear the legislative backlog and introduce essential reforms to develop faster. The reforms further liberalized the economy to allow more foreign investment and facilitated the country's entry into the General Agreement on Tariffs and Trade (GATT). The IMF and the World Bank also supported martial law as it allowed them to fully restructure the Philippine economy along the lines desired by the liberalization strategy. Also, crony capitalism was initially tolerated by technocrats, the IMF, and the World Bank, as the global economy was doing well and there was no problem in extending financial assistance to the country. However, these conditions soon changed when crony capitalism continued unabated. At one point, there were three groups in the country with different interests and objectives: technocrats, cronies, and multilateral institutions.

The technocrats had access to foreign development funds from the World Bank, the IMF, and other international creditors. This was facilitated during the martial law period with the formation of the Consultative Group for the Philippines, chaired by the World Bank (Tadem, 2019, p. 15).

Moreover, these development strategies failed to halt the growth of the communist insurgency due to the failure of economic policies (e.g., the failures of IMF/World Bank structural adjustment policies) to address poverty and underdevelopment, as well as uncontrolled crony capitalism. As discussed in Chapters 6 and 7, the lack of land reform, the rentier relationship between the government and the private sector, and the clear failures in implementing industrial policy, have made development very difficult.

This situation has remained until today. The initiatives discussed in Chapter 7 do not amount to a coherent system of industrial policy. In the following sections, we argue that the Philippines needs an industrial policy, although one adapted to the current circumstances.

8.4 Innovation in Developing Countries to Accelerate the Behind-the-Frontier Catch-Up

Lack of innovation is one of the most important market failures that developing countries face. Innovation refers to the creation of a new idea, method, device, product, service, or process, or the introduction or use of such novelties in economic and social spheres. Innovation matters because it leads to productivity gains. These can be passed on to workers in the form of higher wages, and to consumers in the form of lower prices and products of higher quality. The term innovation is used in the literature to refer to both original inventions and the creative use of existing products or processes. Economists argue that the former is what advanced economies do, that is, invent. This is so because their governments and companies have developed national innovation systems and invest in research and development. This is what allows them to make high-cost, complex (unique) products and systems such as airplanes, robotics equipment, satellite systems, intelligent buildings, submarines, dams, luxurious yachts and cruise liners, or nuclear power plants (Hobday, 1998). These are not just products but entire "systems" that require knowledge and coordination that most developing countries do not have. Historical experience tells us that this type of innovation is passed on to workers in the form of higher wages.

As discussed in Chapter 3, a country's potential (maximum) growth is given by the sum of the growth rates of the labor force and labor productivity. Both are low in advanced economies, resulting in low growth. In many of them, labor force growth is zero or even negative. Labor productivity growth is also relatively low because these countries are on the technological frontier, which means that firms are already highly mechanized and have high organizational capabilities (these refer to how to organize the flow of work in both a manufacturing shop floor and in an office). Therefore, labor productivity is high in developed countries, but at the same time, the growth rate is low. If they want to grow, they need to create new products and invent. Innovation and R&D became buzzwords in the 1980s and 1990s in the growth literature, which was created to explain growth in developed countries (so-called endogenous growth models), but not in developing nations. Yet, many scholars started trying to explain growth in developing countries by appealing to the innovation paradigm.

Although advanced nations primarily depend on innovation to fuel economic growth, much of the growth in developing countries stems from adopting and adapting existing technologies. Although innovation is certainly present in many developing nations, their growth is largely driven by the use and modification of established technologies. For example, East Asia experienced rapid growth during the 1960s and 1970s through swift technology transfer and imitation, mainly of Japanese and American innovations. With the introduction of trade-related aspects of intellectual property rights under the World Trade Organization and other intellectual property protection agreements, the approach to catching up had to evolve because the use of many of the classic tools of industrial policy was either banned or significantly circumscribed.[3] In light of the global framework safeguarding technology rents, it is now believed that developing countries must convincingly enforce intellectual property rights to attract foreign technology providers, as international firms tend to favor locations where the risk of unauthorized imitation is low. Yet, we must note that while the World Trade Organization (WTO) has certainly made industrial policy more difficult to implement, the constraints imposed by it should not be exaggerated.[4] Although it is true that the range of industrial policy measures that developing countries can use has become considerably smaller compared to the 1960s and the 1970s, in reality, there is still room to maneuver for countries that are creative and determined enough.

As a result, strong intellectual property rights protection is frequently advised for middle-income developing countries seeking to attract high-tech foreign direct investment. However, this also raises significant governance challenges. Simply ensuring effective intellectual property protection is not sufficient. These countries must also identify the most beneficial technologies and establish suitable incentives to draw them in. Governments require specialized negotiation skills and a solid understanding of World Trade Organization regulations to structure incentives and agreements with multinational corporations, ensuring that the technologies with the greatest potential for spillover into domestic industries are transferred.

It is worth noting that the high degree of protection has arguably made it harder for developing countries to imitate technologies, engage in reverse engineering, or establish their own component supply industries without relying on the location choices of global multinational corporations. Today, developing countries have significantly less flexibility to enhance their position within global value chains through independent efforts to catch up, as they are increasingly constrained by the strategic decisions of multinational firms.

Given that current international agreements are likely to remain in place for the foreseeable future, using intellectual property rights protection to attract high-technology foreign investment presents both opportunities and challenges for developing countries. Upon joining the World Trade Organization, these countries lose the ability to simply replicate advanced technologies or impose domestic content requirements that compel foreign technology holders to share their knowledge with local firms. Nevertheless, facilitating technology transfer to domestic companies remains crucial for achieving broad-based and sustained national development. To attract the right technologies and promote effective transfer to local firms, a more sophisticated set of incentives and strategic approaches is now necessary. Policy failure in this area could hinder growth, especially for middle-income nations. Over the long term, there may also be a need to reassess the global trade and intellectual property framework to create a more balanced system that better reflects the interests of all countries.

The Philippine administration has argued that the future of the nation is innovation, as this is the catalyst for sustaining growth. Chapter 8 of the Philippine Development Plan 2023–2028: Advance Research and Development, Technology, and Innovation (NEDA, 2023a), lays out strategies, programs, and legislative priorities to be pursued to promote innovation among industries and identifies metrics to measure the country's progress in harnessing research and development, technology, and innovation. In this vein, Aldaba and Aldaba (2024) postulated that the lack of domestic innovation in the Philippines has resulted in low productivity levels and that this is a crucial barrier to industrial transformation.

However, as argued earlier, developing countries like the Philippines do not create new products. At best, they do process innovation and adaptation (small changes in products created by developed countries). These types of innovations are most often not transferred to workers in the form of higher wages but instead lead to lower prices. In these countries, potential growth can be high, as labor force growth remains positive (certainly it is in the Philippines), and labor productivity growth is significant because developing countries are adopting technologies created in advanced economies. This type of progress is called behind-the-frontier catch-up. This is what the East Asian countries did during the period of high growth in the 1970s and 1980s. South Korea is the best example. China's labor force growth has already reached developed-nation rates: zero and even negative. Hence, output growth is about labor productivity. China is still adopting technologies from the advanced nations and, at the same time, developing its own (innovating and inventing) and competing with the advanced economies in the most advanced sectors. No other developing nation can do this.

The Philippines is clearly far from the technological frontier (De Dios, 2024). Moreover, it lacks the capabilities to invent and compete through research at the frontier, particularly in the areas of the Fourth Industrial Revolution. The optimal strategy is to accelerate behind-the-frontier catch-up. In order to accelerate this process, the Philippines has to think along two axes, discussed in the next section.

8.5 Modern Industrial Policy to Acquire Organizational Capabilities

The first axis concerns products: *What* types of products could the Philippines successfully produce and export, and where are the possibilities to innovate? The answer seems to be obvious: everything it imports that is not high-tech and highly complex, including footwear, furniture, textiles of all sorts, glasses, cutlery, and agriculture/food (packaging, food quality, variety, reliability, speed of delivery, and distribution network). We would add all the imported construction materials. We are not picking winners but stating the obvious. The key is to produce high-quality (*pulido*) as opposed to low-quality (*puwede na*) products. It is not just about manufacturing but about producing high-quality products to compete in the world economy (export). These are the products that "make a nation." Surely there are companies in the country that manufacture these products. All it takes is to identify them and help them move up to make high-quality products that can be exported and compete in the world economy.

We recognize that Republic Act No. 11981 (Tatak Pinoy Act, 2024) contains elements similar to those proposed here. We need to see its implementation and what it delivers. Focusing on the production of electric cars, for example, may not be the right choice given the Philippines' current stage of development. The Philippines also needs to manufacture some of the machines that make these goods, that is, develop a machinery cluster that employs productively engineers. In other words, processing coconuts into juice, oil, or soap, will not take the Philippines very far if it has to import the machines that transform coconuts into these products. This is the fundamental difference with the advanced economies when these were industrializing: Unlike the very late industrializers like the Philippines, they were producing their own capital goods (Hirschman, 1968).

These examples do not imply disregarding services and agriculture. Our point is that we believe that *manufacturing is the engine of growth* (Chapter 3), and most innovations take place within the manufacturing sector. Creating a strong manufacturing sector will contribute significantly to the development of more advanced services in finance or logistics, for example, and to reducing the number of workers in agriculture.

The second axis, which, in our view, is more important, concerns *who* is going to manufacture those products. This requires thinking about firms and the capabilities that they have, including entrepreneurship (Hirschman, 1968).

We have argued that productivity is the fundamental long-run driver of income per capita. Productivity is a firm-level concept, and ultimately, it must be understood at this level: A nation's productivity is low because its firms' productivity is low. In a seminal paper, Nobel Prize winner Michael Kremer (1993) asked, "Why are wage and productivity differentials between the industrialized nations and developing countries so large?" He used the "O-ring" analogy (the collapse of the space shuttle *Challenger* in 1986) to explain this along the following lines: Production is often the result of a series of tasks, such as one found on an assembly line. These tasks can be performed at different levels of "skills," where the latter refers to the probability of completing the task successfully. For the final product or service to be successfully made or delivered, every single task must be completed correctly. Kremer showed that the value of each worker's efforts depends on the quality of all other workers' efforts. In this setting, the problem of developing countries is that, as a result of O-ring failures (poor organization that leads to failures), they end up having low productivity and manufacture poor-quality products that cannot compete in international markets.

Kremer's model has a series of important implications that help understand development and the large discrepancies in income per capita among countries: (1) Workers of similar skills have strong incentives to match together, that is, highly skilled workers will attempt to work with other highly skilled workers, and likewise for low-skilled workers. The consequence is that highly skilled workers complement each other, giving rise to increasing returns to skills, with the result that productivity will be even higher, and unskilled workers, when they match together, lower each other's productivity even more. (2) Rich countries specialize in the production of complicated products, firms are larger in industrial countries, and firm size and wages are positively correlated. (3) Differences in product quality are associated with differences in workers' skills. A small difference in workers' skills leads to a proportionally larger difference in wages and output, so wages and productivity differentials between countries with different skill levels are enormous. And (4) rich and skilled nations will produce "advanced" and "high-value" goods (or the final stages of a process in a global value chain), while poor nations will produce raw materials (primary production in general) and "low-value" goods.

All the aforementioned is the result of the fact that a significant number of firms in most developing countries are poorly organized, with the consequence that their labor productivity is low. The question is, what can they do? The argument we develop here is that industrial policy in the Philippines needs to focus more on firms than on products. Ultimately, we believe that industrial policy is less about the efficacy of government intervention and the allocation of funds or subsidies than about public–private collaboration in the design of mechanisms of transparency and accountability, sunset clauses, and time-bound assistance.

To acquire capabilities requires learning, adopting, and improving fast what others have done (Khan, 2015). This is a productivity-enhancing process and a form of innovation that does not require huge investments in capital. Without firms, the nation will not be able to move forward. In fact, we believe that the most important constraint to the development of modern sectors in the Philippines is the absence of a broad base of firms with the technological and organizational capabilities to adopt, adapt, and use available technologies. The skills of workers and managers refer to their capacity to operate specific machines and technologies. These skills are developed in part through formal education and training. However, gaining essential tacit knowledge through hands-on experience and experimentation is often even more crucial. This is particularly important for operating various machines and production processes, including advanced equipment that can be managed by workers with limited formal education.

The technological capabilities of individuals within a firm are important, but the firm's overall competitiveness relies even more on its ability to function as a cohesive team (Kremer, 1993; Khan, 2015). A key characteristic of an effective team is that individual productivity is not solely determined by personal skills or effort but is instead shaped by the collective organization of the team. An individual's productivity is influenced by the type of team he/she belongs to. On a production line, a worker's efficiency depends on how well the firm is organized, which, in turn, is the result of tacit production capabilities accumulated over time and embedded in the firm's routines. These routines go beyond defining specific processes; they also dictate how the firm adapts to challenges and modifies existing practices.

A firm's organization encompasses its internal management systems, incentive structures, and mechanisms for monitoring work, ensuring quality control, minimizing input wastage, and managing inventory efficiently. These systems are crucial in determining both the firm's overall competitiveness and the productivity of its individual workers. However, achieving competitiveness is not as simple as replicating the organizational structures of successful firms in more advanced economies. Each country has unique initial conditions that shape the most effective organizational structures, which must develop through experimentation and the gradual acquisition of tacit knowledge via intensive learning-by-doing.

The key point is that a worker's productivity depends not only on her own technological capabilities, both formal and tacit, but also on the organization of the firm she works for, which can be described as its tacit productive capability. Even a highly skilled worker will have low productivity if poor inventory management or operational bottlenecks lead to prolonged idle time. Likewise, input productivity is affected by material wastage and product rejection rates, both of which can stem from ineffective organizational design. Similarly, capital productivity is influenced by factors such as capacity utilization and downtime, which are directly tied to the firm's overall organizational efficiency.

As a result, all the key productivity measures that determine competitiveness are shaped by a firm's tacit productive capabilities, which are embedded in its production routines. In developing countries, new firms typically have weak organizational capabilities, making them less competitive even when they acquire the right machinery and employ workers and managers with the formal knowledge required to operate the technology. This challenge applies not only to advanced manufacturing but also to lower-technology industries like garment production. The ability to develop tacit productive capabilities is one of the most widespread obstacles to technology acquisition for developing countries and is often hindered by significant contracting failures. Without addressing these issues, both individual firms and entire countries may struggle to establish competitive enterprises, ultimately undermining their technology acquisition efforts.

Countries with few firms possessing the necessary tacit productive capabilities will struggle to benefit from industrial policy strategies that address other challenges. For instance, initiatives to increase the supply of skilled workers or to support first-mover investments assume the existence of firms capable of leveraging these strategies. However, in reality, many firms lack these capabilities and must acquire tacit knowledge about routines and processes. As tacit knowledge cannot be learned through formal education, it must be developed through hands-on experience and experimentation. Consequently, progress in this area cannot be easily assessed using traditional methods such as examinations.

Despite these challenges, the process of building capabilities must still be financed, even though its outcomes are difficult to monitor, evaluate, and control. The issue is that simply funding "doing" (what some of the initiatives discussed in Chapter 7) without significant effort is unlikely to result in meaningful "learning." Effort is especially crucial for developing organizational capabilities, as this process requires continuous adjustments in firm structure, entails adjustment costs, and often encounters internal resistance. Managers and other stakeholders must take on risks and costs throughout this transformation, making them hesitant to proceed unless they are strongly compelled to enhance competitiveness. Given the substantial internal costs associated with continuous organizational improvements, effective learning demands external pressure or incentives that push managers and workers to achieve competitiveness swiftly.

This brings us to the challenges these investments encounter. Investors from developing-country firms who start as uncompetitive must take considerable risks to finance this process independently. The difficulty in monitoring effort exposes external financiers to significant uncertainty. Because the learning effort cannot be directly observed, assessing it based on intermediate outcomes can sometimes lead to incorrect conclusions. At the same time, if the effort is insufficient, the entire investment in infrastructure, machinery, and learning may become unprofitable.

The policy solution to this challenge is for the government to share some of the risks and costs associated with financing. Measures such as protecting domestic markets, providing export subsidies, and offering other explicit or implicit subsidies can support infant industries in developing their productive capabilities. However, public financing is likely to be ineffective if it does not address the core issue of ensuring a high level of effort. Without conditions that incentivize strong effort, competitiveness will not improve quickly enough, and industrial policy will not deliver the expected results. When infant industries remain uncompetitive despite decades of support, it is almost always due to a failure to enforce the necessary effort to achieve competitiveness.

This is the most fundamental challenge in technology adoption. A firm without tacit productive capabilities will remain uncompetitive, even if other constraints on its competitiveness are addressed. Therefore, strategies for building organizational and technological capabilities are a crucial part of effective industrial policies. The challenge for policymakers is that successful learning support strategies have varied widely across countries, as states differ significantly in their ability to monitor and enforce policies. Consequently, financing approaches that proved effective in one country have often failed in others.

Historical experience indicates that successfully supporting capability development through top-down industrial policy, as seen in South Korea, requires government agencies to have strong monitoring and enforcement capabilities. However, in most developing countries, the political and institutional foundations necessary for such enforcement are often lacking. Without these capabilities, top-down industrial policies risk allocating resources to firms without ensuring high effort, making it unlikely that competitive enterprises will emerge. Nevertheless, the experiences of other developing countries—such as India, Bangladesh, and Thailand, in specific cases—demonstrate that productive capabilities can still be developed. This can be achieved by designing industrial policy instruments differently and ensuring that conditions promoting high effort are enforceable within the existing institutional and political constraints of the state.

The earlier considerations do not imply that a nation like the Philippines cannot innovate at the frontier in some sectors (complex products). We reiterate that innovation certainly matters for the future of the nation, but we must be clear about what type of innovation makes sense and is feasible in the Philippines. This will be the result of fast assimilation and adaptation of advanced technologies, rather than of grand research and development (except in well-targeted areas); and of the improvement of firms' organizational capabilities to increase productivity.

Besides China, take the case of Vietnam. It has developed its own electric automobile, the VinFast. What is impressive is that it has done it in less than a decade. It is already making inroads in Europe and in the United States, some of the world's most sophisticated markets. Vietnam is clearly determined to nurture its new national champions with a package of proactive trade and industrial policies. This requires a very clear and well-focused industrial policy that targets a few key products, led by the government and a group of companies willing to invest, develop a competitive product, and sell it to the whole world, not just the domestic market. Vietnam will certainly move forward. It is already slightly ahead of the Philippines in GDP per capita, and it will continue opening the gap in the coming decades.

Finally, we emphasize that the Philippine government needs to develop a coherent industrial policy to support the development of firms. Some basic principles are as follows (Felipe, 2015): (1) Set up mechanisms of transparency. (2) Set clear benchmarks for success and failure. (3) Build in a sunset clause. (4) Public support must target activities, not sectors. (5) Subsidize activities with clear potential for spillovers and demonstration effects. And (6) monitor by a principal stakeholder who has political authority at the highest level (see Esguerra et al., 2024). This is what successful East Asian countries did in different forms. There are also important lessons from developed countries, which, as Cimoli et al. (2009, p. 545) indicated, "undertook indeed relatively high degrees of intervention to support the accumulation of technological capabilities and the transformation of their organization of production, especially in the early period of industrialization." Some of these lessons are thus: (1) Emulate and even leapfrog. (2) Nurture infant industries. This can be done even in the context of the World Trade Organization (Felipe, 2021)—circumvent the loopholes, safeguard clauses, and exceptional provisions to deal with trade-related aspects of intellectual property, and do not believe that intellectual property rights are "good" for development. (3) Manage the distribution of rents to favor learning and industrialization. (4) Avoid the natural resource curse. While the Philippines can and should add value to the extraction of minerals, natural resources are not the staircase to development. And (5) macroeconomic and industrial policies must be consistent.

Notes

1 This also included First Lady Imelda Marcos, who embarked on personal projects financed by government agencies but which were not accounted for in the budget (Tadem, 2019, p. 15).

2 Additional obstacles for the technocrats to implement their agenda were (Tadem, 2019) (a) the oil price hikes in 1980 and the debt default in October 1983 and (b) the growing anti-dictatorship movement, fueled by massive corruption, gross human rights violations, and the assassination of ex-senator Benigno S. Aquino Jr. In this highly politicized context, the technocrats could not find support for their development agenda from the business community, which had abandoned the regime and the technocrats.

3 The most important change brought about by the World Trade Organization was the prohibition of quantitative restrictions (e.g., quotas). Likewise, tariffs were reduced and bound. Export subsidies are also banned. Most other subsidies (except those frequently used by rich countries, such as those for agriculture, R&D, and regional equalization) have become open to countervailing duties and other retaliatory measures. New issues, like regulations on FDI (foreign direct investment) and IPRs (intellectual property rights), have been brought under the jurisdiction of the WTO, making it difficult for countries to "borrow" foreign technologies for free by violating IPRs or put performance requirements (regarding things like local contents) on the TNCs (transnational corporations) that make FDI.

4 Chang (2013, pp. 14–16): (a) WTO by no means obliges countries to abolish all tariffs—only to bind them. (b) The use of emergency tariff increases ("import surcharges") is allowed under some circumstances. (c) Not all subsidies are illegal for everyone. (4) The trade-related investment measures agreement banned certain policy measures, such as local contents requirements or trade balancing requirements, but allows other measures. These include conditions regarding the hiring of local labor, technology transfer, and the conduct of R&D in the host country. Countries can also provide targeted subsidies, directed credits, and tailor-made infrastructure (measures that Singapore and Ireland have used to attract FDI into targeted industries, insofar as these do not violate the most-favored nation provision.

9

WHY IS THE PHILIPPINE STATE WEAK?: SPATIAL AND TEMPORAL FRAGMENTATION OBSTRUCTING STRUCTURAL TRANSFORMATION

9.1 Introduction

As discussed in earlier chapters, Philippine development has been slow compared to forecasts and the performance of neighboring countries. In this chapter, we take a closer look at the political factors (national, local, and political parties) that have hindered the structural transformation of the economy, in particular, a faster reduction in agricultural employment and the creation of a manufacturing sector that absorbs employment, as well as some advanced services that complement manufacturing.

A strong government facilitates economic transformation by providing public goods such as infrastructure, health, and education. This has been largely absent in the Philippines. We explore the political factors that contribute to the specific type of incapacity of the Philippine government. We propose a conceptualization that combines multiple factors and argue that government weakness occurs as a result of *spatial* and *temporal fragmentation*. At one level, *spatial fragmentation* refers to the devolution of national powers to subnational units called local government units (LGUs). At a second level, *temporal fragmentation* refers to the lack of strong institutionalized political parties that can provide continuity for long-term planning in a democratic political system like the Philippines, characterized by term limits at the executive and legislative levels. The proposed concept is particularly useful as previous literature on the political economy of the Philippines has focused on isolated factors such as patronage, vote-buying, and the effects of fragmentation. However, little literature has looked at the combination of necessary and sufficient factors that make up government weakness. Moreover, spatial or temporal fragmentation, when present in isolation, does not necessarily contribute to the stunted economic performance we see in the Philippines.

DOI: 10.4324/9781003728719-9

We start with a discussion of spatial fragmentation, that is, the emergence of LGUs, and provide a brief history of their establishment, their functions, and their impact on the economy. Next, we discuss temporal fragmentation arising from the lack of strong, institutionalized political parties in the Philippines. More specifically, we look at what political parties are in the Philippine context, how they function, and the economic outcomes of these functions. This is followed by a comparative analysis of the Philippines with other neighboring countries, namely China and Thailand. The basis of this comparison is the presence of one of the dimensions of government weakness but not the other. In the case of China, the similarity with the Philippines lies in the presence of subnational units and the use of patronage in lieu of democratic representation. In the case of Thailand, the effectiveness of political parties is restricted by a more powerful military institution. Research on the role of institutions suggests that extractive institutions in both countries would result in lower levels of development (Acemoglu and Robinson, 2012). Empirical work, however, shows unexpected results, as the economic performance of both countries differs drastically from that of the Philippines. Thus, we further investigate the ways in which these countries are different and whether there are lessons to be learned for the Philippines. Finally, we conclude by arguing that all is not lost. The Philippines does not have to be locked in a vicious cycle of weak institutions. Political reforms could help alleviate some of the weaknesses.

9.2 Spatial Fragmentation: National vs. Local Government

The first element that makes up government weakness is *spatial fragmentation*, that is, the devolution of national power to LGUs. This type of weakness can be particularly obstructive to the delivery of consistent, high-quality public services across different regions and within sub-regions. It also makes it more challenging for the national government to implement and oversee national plans that would encourage the shift of labor from low-wage, low-productivity sectors, such as agriculture, to manufacturing. This national-subnational relationship was institutionalized in the Philippines with the introduction of the Local Government Code (LGC) in 1991 (League of Provinces of the Philippines, n.d.). The LGC mandated the devolution of powers from the national government, including taxing, borrowing, and spending, to subnational units of different sizes and jurisdictions, such as provinces, municipalities, cities, and barangays (the smallest government unit). The institutionalization of the LGC has strongly impacted the national government's ability to create a nationally cohesive development plan that would result in the transformation of the economy. Although not a federal system, the Philippine political structure of national and subnational units of varying sizes and responsibilities results in the spatial fragmentation of authority among LGUs across regions and within LGU subcategories in the same region. At the vertical level, political power is decentralized and shared between the national government and local government units. On the horizontal level, LGUs' jurisdiction is demarcated by territorial lines, but authority can at times overlap among different types of LGUs with responsibility for the same area. This is because a territory can, for example, fall under the jurisdiction of a barangay, municipality, and province. Moreover, competing interests between local politicians and business elites can further hinder the ability of LGUs to function effectively. To elaborate on spatial fragmentation, the following sections review the history and rationale of the LGC and its economic impact.

9.2.1 Brief History and Description of the Local Government Code

This section traces the justification for the LGC to its historical and political roots. The political system in the Philippines is one of the most decentralized systems in Southeast Asia. Although the passing of the LGC in 1991 formalized the national-local relations, the roots of decentralization can be traced back to earlier times. The LGC delegates its fiscal, administrative, and political authority to sub-national entities. The objective is to encourage the design and implementation of policies and projects at the local level to better reflect their specific needs. It is noteworthy that this system of local governance existed long before the introduction of the LGC in 1991. It dates back to the pre-colonial period and included functions such as tax collection and the provision of services such as infrastructure. During the American colonial period, the national government was encouraged to enhance regional autonomy via the creation of local government units (Hutchcroft, 2014). Some of the reasons why the United States encouraged local autonomy include ideological convictions resulting in forging a polity in the image of the American federal political system. Additionally, the participation of local elites in the political process was seen as a way to discourage them from joining guerrilla independence movements. These efforts resulted in the promotion of political participation and representation at the expense of enhancing bureaucratic capacity and encouraging the creation of nascent political parties, which were back then little more than patronage instruments. This remains true until today.

This system of governance continued after the Philippines became independent in 1946, with elected officials representing local interests at the national level (League of Provinces of the Philippines, n.d.). The earliest attempts to establish LGUs can be traced back to these early days following independence. The Local Autonomy Bill was passed in 1957 after reforms were proposed by city and municipal representatives (League of Provinces of the Philippines, n.d.), paving the way for the Local Autonomy Act of 1959 (Tapales, 1992). This Act allowed for the election of representatives of smaller local government units. These bodies took part in the allocation of the internal revenue allotment (IRA) (League of Provinces of the Philippines, n.d.). Local representation initiatives, however, came to a halt between 1972 and 1986, during the administration of Ferdinand Marcos Sr. Soon after taking office, he moved to consolidate his executive power by replacing agreements with local units with policies that expanded his own authority at the expense of other players. In 1973, he issued Presidential Decree No. 144 stating that local government representatives would cease to participate in the IRA, giving way for the Ministry of Budget to take over these decisions (League of Provinces of the Philippines, n.d.). A number of other decrees, orders, and directives further limited the powers of local government units, including limiting their ability to run for local elections and setting term limits.

This later changed with Corazon Aquino (1986–1992). The Executive Order No. 262, introduced in 1987, established the League of Provinces, which paved the way to the creation of separate leagues, including the League of Municipalities of the Philippines, League of Cities of the Philippines, and eventually the Liga ng mga Barangay (League of Provinces of the Philippines, n.d.). On October 10, 1991, the LGC was enacted into law. Politically speaking, the LGC stipulated that national political powers would be devolved to LGUs. Fiscally, the LGUs were to receive 40% of national taxes to fund their programs. Revenue would be shared based on each unit's Internal Revenue Allotment (IRA), which is computed based on a formula that takes into account each unit's national proportion of population and land. The LGC institutionalized the League of Provinces of the Philippines (LPP) as a unit that would represent the provinces (total of 82 members) in terms of issues and proposed solutions. Following several Supreme Court rulings, the LPP has continued to lobby for the expansion of its allotment of the IRA. However, a number of hurdles and delays continue to impact the ability of the LPP to receive and utilize these allotments in a timely and effective manner (League of Provinces of the Philippines, n.d.).

9.2.2 Economic Functions of LGUs and Political Impact

In theory, LGUs enjoy enough authority to enable them to provide a number of economic functions. This broad mandate was established by the national government, giving LGUs responsibility for issues ranging from culture and education to welfare issues. Specific examples include authority over agricultural research, environmental and pollution management, primary health and hospitals, social welfare, maintenance of infrastructure, water supply and irrigation, and planning of land use (Republic Act No. 7160, sect. 17, 1991) (Supreme Court E-Library, 2019). These were added to the existing functions of tax collection, regulation of business activities, and sanitary services, among others. Additionally, LGUs enjoy the authority to raise necessary funds and the ability to spend them on the provision of public services (Diokno-Sicat, 2019), such as funding infrastructure projects (Capulong et al., 2024). They are also able to provide other basic services such as health and education, tax generation and collection (Alvina, 2019), and manage local resources (Gumba, 2023). As a result, LGU policies directly impact productivity and employment within their jurisdictions (Gumba, 2023).

To enable LGUs to execute their functions, taxes controlled by the national government (including income tax, estate and inheritance tax, customs tax, VAT, and vehicle tax) are shared with LGUs. Out of all taxes collected by the Bureau of Internal Revenue (BIR), 40% is allocated to various LGU offices (Department of Finance, 2025). This share is apportioned as follows: Provinces receive 23%; another 23% goes to cities; 34% is for municipalities; and barangays receive the remaining 20%. In addition to the shared national tax, LGUs are also able to collect taxes locally. Cities are the most effective unit in generating taxes locally (compared to other units) and are, thus, the least dependent on revenue allocated through national tax distribution.

In terms of expenditure, a large share of the LGU budget goes toward infrastructure projects with local development funds as the primary source (Maddawin et al., 2020). Among the budget sources, the Department of Public Works and Highways' Local Infrastructure Program and the Department of Agriculture's Farm to Market Road Programs are utilized almost fully. However, poorer LGUs experience lower utilization of local development funds. The LGC, however, has had a limited impact on the provision of public services and economic growth, largely due to "low technical and absorptive capacity" of LGUs (Ibañez, 2021). In addition to financial constraints, political challenges exist as local families and clans have found the perforated system beneficial, allowing them to exercise patronage politics by dispensing funds and public positions as private goods to family members and allies. The actors that stand to benefit from reform of the current system are bureaucratic departments. In response to doubts about LGUs providing services adequately, there have been calls to push back the date for a full devolution from 2024 to 2027 following the Mandanas-Garcia ruling that allowed LGUs to receive higher budget allocation (Ill-prepared for full devolution, 2022). While the LGC ensured the automatic allocation of tax revenue to government units, it inadvertently expanded the number of veto players in the political system from just national-level legislators at Congress to local politicians as well.

This political reality has often hindered the delivery of LGU functions at an optimum level, resulting instead in informal institutions and practices that divert public funds into private pockets, leading to waste and inefficiency. The weak supervisory capacity of LGUs and the strong patronage connections have, in some cases, turned LGUs into channels for the delivery of votes to national politicians (Hutchcroft, 2014). Although LGU officials are limited to three consecutive terms, each running for three years, they are not barred from running for other positions, local or national, once they have exhausted their term limits. This has created an incentive to maintain patronage linkages, even though the specific contours of the constituents may change depending on the office. Additional patronage incentives exist at the national level. The president has the capacity through discretionary funds to distribute payments to legislators and local officials (De Dios, 2007). Thus, the guaranteed funds from the LGC have not in any way dampened the incentives of local politicians to supplement their budgets through direct patronage relationships with the national government, especially the president in office. Some of these transfers take the form of non-productive infrastructure, such as basketball courts or sponsorship of personal events like weddings and funerals (Hutchcroft, 2014).

Shair-Rosenfield (2016) attributed the ineffectiveness in delivering these objectives to the slow process of implementing LGC processes, the hesitance of the national government to share resources (especially prior to the Mandanas-Garcia ruling), and the widespread corruption and cronyism that shield local and national elites from accountability when dispersing funds. Conflict of interest between local and national political elites has meant that any reform to the system remains at a standstill. Moreover, national officials fear that attempts at centralizing power might alienate their local supporters. At the electorate level, there seems to be little popular support for a stronger national government, as it is often seen as incompetent and reminiscent of the Marcos Sr. administration. Thus, the delivery of services has been hindered by a lack of adequate administrative expertise, weak supervisory capacity that would ensure the quality of services delivered, and, last but not least, conflicting interests between political and business elites, creating incentives to buy votes rather than invest in long-term projects.

Some literature on the number of interest groups and veto players has suggested that decision-making, when not dominated by the interests of a single entity, might reflect the interests of a wider public and potentially result in the provision of more public goods (Kurdli, 2023). On the one hand, this does make the political system more porous, allowing for increased chances of rent-seeking opportunities. On the other hand, the higher number of veto players means that politicians have a higher incentive to provide more goods that benefit a wider segment of the population (De Mesquita et al., 2004). Hutchcroft's (2014) typology differentiates between goods targeting a small group (e.g., individuals and households) and have a specific benefit accrued to that specific target, and goods that are delivered to a wider segment (i.e., programmatic or meso-particularistic goods), which benefit a wider segment of the population. For ease of reference, we refer to these different types of patronage as public versus private goods. This typology and the implications for the Philippines are discussed further in section 10.3.2.

9.3 Temporal Fragmentation: Weak and Uninstitutionalized Political Parties

The second dimension of Philippine government weakness that has contributed to lower industrialization is the lack of continuity in planning. Autocratic political systems can ensure this continuity under leaders with long-term horizons (Olson, 1993). Leaders in democratic systems are able to provide this as well, not due to personal long-term horizons, as democratic systems ensure term limits, but due to continuity under their ideological platforms and affiliations, that is, political parties. The Philippines has a political system where neither type of continuity exists. It is neither a personalistic autocracy nor a democracy that enjoys robust, ideologically coherent political parties. The result is that elections place in power leaders with short-term horizons who are more concerned with buying votes and ensuring immediate returns rather than investing in long-term projects that yield long-term returns on investment, such as industrial development.

Although political parties are defined as organized groups that share the same ideological and political objectives, the de facto setting in the Philippines is built around personalities rather than programs or ideologies, as the parties are practically identical to one another in terms of their proclamations and broad policy statements (Quimpo, 2007). Membership is also weak as politicians routinely shift from one party to another. This is termed as *turncoatism*. The parties use vote-buying vehicles during elections. Quimpo (2007) termed these institutions as clientelistic parties that have evolved into patrimonialistic parties, which function as mediums for the political consolidation of elites through patronage and clientelism networks, coercion, and, at times, outright violence. The following section provides a brief background that explains why this is the case, outlines the causal mechanism that enables short-termism, and discusses its economic impact.

9.3.1 A Brief History of Political Parties in the Philippines

Following independence, a two-party system similar to that of the United States emerged in the Philippines, namely, the Nacionalistas and the Liberals. These two major parties gained the majority of votes in presidential, congressional, and gubernatorial elections. Although minor parties were present, they posed no real competition in terms of votes and longevity when compared to the two major parties. Quite interestingly, the two parties were essentially identical in terms of ideology and program (Lande, 1967). In other words, neither had a distinct regional association, championed causes, an ideological orientation or a strong electoral membership. It is, therefore, no wonder that party loyalty is almost absent in the Philippines, both among politicians and the electorate. Politicians are motivated to switch to the party of the winning presidential candidate, and the electorate is motivated to vote for parties that provide them with the most immediate benefits, that is, private goods provided through vote-buying.

The political scene of the 1960s and 1970s was characterized by rampant vote-buying as well as outright, violent, coercive tactics against the opposition. This changed during the rule of Marcos Sr., who in 1972 imposed Martial Law to allegedly curb Communist and Muslim opposition. Marcos Sr. worked to expand his powers at the expense of local politicians. In 1978, he established his own ruling party, the Kilusang Bagong Lipunan (KBL or New Society Movement). Responding to a combination of incentives and punishments in the form of dispensability, the KBL drew broad participation from national and local-level politicians. However, these new dynamics did not mean a complete change in the nature of state-society relations. It simply meant that the decentralization of power meant that patronage relationships were tightly controlled and decided by the President as opposed to the more fragmented nature during the pre- and post-Marcos Sr. eras, as evident by the creation of his own political party, the KBL. Perhaps the only ideologically coherent party in the Philippines is the Communist Party of the Philippines (CPP). However, instead of working within the existing political system, the CPP has opted to engage in armed opposition, oftentimes boycotting elections.

The emerging political parties failed to develop coherent programs and ideologies. Instead, they quickly turned into instruments for private goods disbursement rather than ideological platforms, as their programs and objectives were practically indistinguishable. Moreover, the weak institutionalization meant that politicians often switched alliances in search of higher benefits. Quimpo (2007, p. 277) described parties as "convenient vehicles of patronage that can be set up, merged with others, split, resurrected, regurgitated, reconstituted, renamed, repackaged, recycled, or flushed down the toilet anytime." Hutchcroft (2014) argued that the emphasis on political representation before the creation of strong bureaucracies highlighted opportunities for patronage politics to emerge at the expense of providing broader public services. He added that the emergence of patronage politics can be attributed to four key policies during the administration of American President William Howard Taft. These factors are emphasis on local autonomy, high support for local politicians, prioritization of electoral and legislative institutions rather than bureaucratic capacity, and encouragement of the establishment of political parties while discouraging ideological diversity (particularly socialist or communist currents). This has had direct implications on accountability and performance legitimacy. Running candidates do not necessarily need to prove their track record to get reelected. They often resort to buying votes directly through the provision or promise of provision of private goods. Thus, vote-buying can substitute service delivery. As local elites can be immune from electoral repercussions due to poor performance, there is little incentive for them to reform, and little incentive for national governments to do so as well.

9.3.2 Economic Functions of Political Parties and Political Impact

Political parties are essential for the provision of public goods. Strong institutionalized parties enable the delivery of welfare, address coordination challenges, resist capture by interest groups, and connect with a broad segment of the population (Rasmussen and Knutsen, 2021). Huntington (2006) differentiated between weak and strong political parties, as well as institutionalized and uninstitutionalized. Parties are considered strong if broad support has been institutionalized, organizational capacity is effective, and membership is loyal.

In the case of the Philippines, political parties are best described as weak and un-institutionalized. Mergers are quite common, and candidates can easily either switch parties or even be affiliated with more than one party at a time. They are also not ideologically centered and thus, their policy is quite vague. This suggests that party lines have little influence on decision-making and are not a factor when voting. Moreover, allocation of discretionary funds in the House of Representatives is facilitated by the President and the Speaker of the House. This phenomenon encourages legislators to switch political parties to the president's party. This then provides the president with less resistance in the lower house (Hutchcroft, 2014).

Literature on the politics of the Philippines differentiates between patronage, clientelism, vote-buying, rent-seeking, and corruption as different mechanisms for gaining the support of voters and allies in order to get to and stay in office. To avoid confusion, and in alignment with the terminology in the political economy literature, this chapter primarily uses the term "provision of private goods", that is, goods and benefits that are exclusionary and rivalrous using public and private resources, versus public goods. Borrowing from the typology by Hutchcroft (2014), three types of goods may be differentiated. The first is programmatic macro type of goods that benefit the majority of the electorate (public goods). On the opposite end of the spectrum are micro-particularistic types of goods that benefit one person or a very small group of people (private goods). In the middle are meso-particularistic types of goods that benefit a slightly larger portion of the population (broader types of private goods). Table 9.1 differentiates between them.

Building on the earlier typology in addition to works on veto players that suggest they are associated with higher levels of rent-seeking, and the selectorate theory developed by De Mesquita et al. (2004), which suggests that leaders faced with larger winning coalitions are likely to provide more public goods, we agree that the high number of veto players in the national and local political scene results in rampant rent-seeking. Although this is no surprise, it is important to distinguish the different types of rent sought and their overall impact on the economy. The selectorate theory suggests that a larger winning coalition provides leaders with an incentive to provide more public goods over private goods in order to maintain office. Here, we deviate from Hutchcroft's (2014) analysis in which he argued that leaders in the Philippines are more likely to provide micro-particularistic types of goods, that is, narrow private goods. Instead, we suggest that meso-particularistic goods are more likely to be provided (broader private goods). This is because the higher number of rent-seekers is associated with the type of patronage that benefits a wider segment of the population rather than the micro-particularistic. This partially explains our argument in this book that while the Philippine economy has performed well, it has not performed at an optimal capacity.

TABLE 9.1 Continuum of Programmatic and Particularistic Politics

	Programmatic	*Meso-Particularistic*	*Micro-Particularistic*
Target	Universalistic categories	Specific intermediate-level targets, as in sectors/districts/cities shading into villages and neighborhoods	Individuals and households
Character	Impersonal policies	Impersonal patronage	Personalistic/clientelistic patronage
Examples	National health-care system, revenue sharing based on uniform models, environmental protection, etc.	Targeted infrastructure/skewed apportionment of district/agricultural subsidies/US-style pork barrel (via legislation) shading into Philippine-style pork barrel (via grants to legislators)	Spoils system, personal networks of candidates, buying of individual votes, etc.
Key actors and relationships	Bureaucrats, parties, politicians, interest groups, citizens	Bureaucracies, parties, politicians, interest groups, citizens	Revolves around various patron–client (or boss–retinue) ties: oligarchs and officials, oligarchs and politicians, politicians and officials, politicians of higher and lower levels, politicians and constituents, etc.
Source of benefits	General public revenue	Mostly general revenue	A combination of general public revenue as well as private and quasi-public sources, including legislator-controlled pork barrel, causal employee payroll, personal wealth of the politician and his/her supporters, kickbacks on public infrastructure projects, profits from illicit or semi-illicit activities

Source: Hutchcroft (2014, Table 8.2).

9.4 Comparative Analysis: The Philippines vis-à-vis China and Thailand

In this section, we seek to contextualize our conceptual framework by comparing the Philippines to other cases in the region. The case of China is particularly interesting as the country is ruled by a single strong and institutionalized party, the Communist Party of China (CPC), but is spatially fragmented due to the devolution of some political powers to local administrative divisions composed of provincial, prefecture, county, township, and village, much similar to the Philippines. Another interesting case for comparison is Thailand, which, similarly to the Philippines, has weak political parties but is not administratively run by smaller government units. In other words, Thailand has temporal fragmentation but not spatial fragmentation. We argue that in the case of the Philippines, the combination of devolved political power into subnational units (spatial fragmentation) and weak political parties (temporal fragmentation) has resulted in slower structural transformation. The following sections illustrate these points by providing a comparison with the cases of China and Thailand.

9.4.1 *Spatial Fragmentation in China*

China's political system is characterized by a hierarchical system with the Communist Party of China at its center and apex. Although its ideology has evolved since the early days of the Revolution, it remains quite coherent with regards to its objectives, which are focused on maintaining high levels of growth and political stability. In this highly centralized political system, local governments play a key role in implementing the broad objectives of the central government, with mandates that enable them to own enterprises and attract foreign investment (Cheng, 2016). The electorate does not play a direct role in assessing the performance of local governments due to a lack of popular participation. However, local government officials are directly accountable to higher-level and national government officials (Cheng, 2016). Economic growth also acts as a direct measure of performance. This provides a direct incentive for local politicians to prioritize long-term growth as opposed to short-term rent-seeking.

Local governments operate to implement the CPC policies and are accountable to higher levels of office, particularly the State Council (Cheng, 2016). Local governments are responsible for providing public services, overseeing economic development, and executing the broad national objectives set by the central government (Yu, 2019). Representatives and officials of the local government are appointed directly by higher-level officers and are not elected by voters (Cheng, 2016). Because local government representatives do not get to office through elections, they are less preoccupied with developing patronage networks. The top-down approach of decision-making in China, however, does not mean that local governments simply implement top-down decisions without any input. In reality, they have the ability to adapt central policies and implement them according to local needs (Li, 2006), giving them flexibility and the ability to engage with local actors such as the private sector (Ahlers et al., 2019).

The decentralized political system in China has supported growth through the presence of three factors: high administrative capacity, the ability to obtain private benefits, and high levels of competition among local governments. To illustrate, local governments in China have enormous administrative capacity, enabling them to support private firms, which then benefits the local officials by generating more profits that directly benefit these local politicians. At the national level, the intense competition between local government units diminishes the predatory ability of any one local unit that would otherwise harm businesses (Bai et al., 2019). This has not translated to the Philippines, which has a similar politically decentralized system, because the primary incentives for politicians are different. The absence of electoral democracy and representation in China has meant that economic performance becomes the legitimizing factor for rulers, both local and national. In the case of the Philippines, broad economic legitimacy is replaced with direct vote-buying (the provision of meso and micro types of private goods as discussed earlier). Moreover, unlike China, the weak administrative capacity at the LGU level means that local officials are not able to fully capitalize on the growth that could be accrued by working with private firms. Another difference is that the plethora of political parties may give the illusion of variation and representation. However, as discussed earlier, parties differ little in terms of their functions, that is, ensuring votes for candidates. While spatial fragmentation of political power explains part of the puzzle of Philippine government weakness, it does not tell the whole story. Thus, we move to the second part of the story, which is the role of political parties.

9.4.2 Temporal Fragmentation in Thailand

In the case of Thailand, the political system is characterized by weak political parties. This is evident by the ability of the military to overthrow a seated government through military coups (19 successful and unsuccessful coups since the government's transition into a constitutional monarchy in 1932) at times of clashing interests with the elected branches of government. Decision-making in parties tends to be centralized within the executive committee, with other members of the party providing minimal input. Recruitment is often implemented through patronage networks (Laiprakobsup, 2022; Croissant and Chambers, 2010). Although political parties play an important role in aggregating and communicating the populace's interests (Chambers, 2005), especially in rural areas, the power of the military and monarchy severely limit the role of political parties, particularly when interests clash (Naruemon, 2016). Their ability is also often negatively impacted by the less-than democratic dynamics mentioned (Laiprakobsup, 2022), internal conflict, and fragmentation within parties (Chambers, 2005). Like in the Philippines, Thai parties also suffer from low levels of institutionalization and a weak ideological platform, resulting in constant formation and dissolution of parties (Kuhonta, 2014).

Similar to the Philippines, Thai political parties are often personalistic and lack longevity or coherent ideological platforms. However, Thailand is different from the Philippines in that its cohesive bureaucracy and strong national government are able to implement policies effectively in both urban and rural areas, with promotion being a main motivator for performance (Hutchcroft, 2014). Provincial officials are not elected but appointed directly by the Ministry of Interior. Although this does not mean at all that vote-buying does not exist, it does mean that local politicians are tasked with implementing a cohesive national vision. It also means that the system is less porous than the Philippines. Thus, the strong capacity of the Thai national government compensates for the lack of strong political parties, allowing it to oversee local units. Additionally, the national government enjoys high supervisory capacity, and local-national connections are based on the provision of public goods rather than the provision of private goods.

Table 9.2 summarizes the different types of fragmentation among the three case studies: the Philippines, China, and Thailand. The Philippines is unique in that it has both types of fragmentation, spatial and temporal; whereas China and Thailand exhibit only one type of fragmentation. This enables them to provide basic public services and transform their economies in a way that the Philippines cannot.

TABLE 9.2 Different Types of Fragmentation in the Philippines, China, and Thailand

	The Philippines	*China*	*Thailand*
Spatial fragmentation	Fragmented political system; LGUs having high autonomy in raising taxes, spending nationally allocated budget, providing public services, and electing officials	Fragmented political system through decentralized subnational administrative units, but officials appointed by the national government	Strong bureaucracy, centralized system of service delivery overseen by national government
Temporal fragmentation	Weak political parties, inconsistent platforms, and agendas highly dependent on personality of political leaders	Strong political party (CPC), long-term plan to transform structure of economy, consistent vision of industrial policy	Weak political parties, high threat of dissolution and military coups

Source: Authors.

9.5 Solutions Within the Context of Spatial and Temporal Fragmentation

This chapter provided a diagnosis of the political factors that hinder Philippine economic development. More specifically, it answered the question: What are the political obstacles to facilitating structural transformation? To answer this question, this chapter has argued that government weakness can be observed on two levels. The first is spatial fragmentation in the form of devolved national political powers into subnational local government units. The aim of this process is to increase local autonomy and responsiveness. However, the delivery of public services has been complicated by a number of political factors, including local elite competition and conflicting interests between local and national officials, a lack of administrative capacity, and rampant corruption, particularly vote-buying, which often substitutes for effective public service delivery. In addition to the political challenges, LGU expenses often exceed their allocated budgets, hindering their ability to deliver services. At the second level, temporal fragmentation refers to the lack of institutions with long-term horizons that are able to implement and oversee developmental policies. In democracies, continuity is provided through strong political parties. However, these institutions in the Philippines often serve less the purpose of organizing groups under shared interests but more as vehicles for the distribution of private goods.

It is the presence of these two dimensions simultaneously that has left the Philippines behind other countries in the region, where only one of these dimensions is observed, for example, China and Thailand. While weak administrative capacity has prevented the Philippines from addressing developmental challenges, we argue that the solution is not the consolidation of power or transition to less democratic forms of governance. We do not advocate for a repeat of the Martial Law era. Instead, the Philippines would benefit from strengthening the administrative capacity of LGUs, such as their supervisory capacity, and from reforming regulations around political parties to prevent issues such as turncoatism.

Given the status quo where incumbent interest groups maximize their benefits, there is little incentive for reforming the current arrangement. To address these issues, reform should aim to improve the capacity of bureaucratic agencies for service delivery and reporting. Similarly, reform should improve accountability and governance. We argue that enhancing the administrative capacity of local governments by incentivizing reporting and compliance is also an important piece of the puzzle. Shair-Rosenfield (2016) called for the reward of observable outcomes rather than vague criteria such as good governance. Moreover, the generation of tax at the local level must be encouraged to achieve fiscal autonomy. LGUs can also be encouraged to facilitate the creation of new businesses by streamlining processes and applications at the national level.

10

EMPLOYMENT AND EDUCATION IN THE PHILIPPINES: MISCONCEPTIONS AND REALITIES

10.1 Introduction

Chapter 3 provided a primer on growth, highlighting the role that structural transformation plays in determining the balance of payments–constrained growth rate through the income elasticities of demand for exports and imports. Chapter 4 looked into the structure of the Philippine economy and found that a significant share of the workforce is employed in low-productivity sectors and low-paying jobs. And yet, we found that the Philippine labor force has become more educated over time, as the proportion of unfinished degrees has decreased, and the shares of secondary and tertiary graduates have increased. This begs the question: Is education (or a lack thereof) a constraint on growth?

In this chapter, we argue that education is not the primary constraint to Philippine growth. This is not to say that the educational system of the country does not have problems. What we argue is that there are fundamental misunderstandings about the role that education plays in the economy and the type of education that the Philippines needs to pay attention to. Education is not the constraint to growth in the sense that more (even better) education will lead to higher growth. We take as reference the growth diagnostics framework of Hausmann et al. (2005), where low human capital is a possible constraint to growth.[1] As we will argue in the chapter, addressing low human capital will not necessarily address the problem of low social returns to economic activity, and will not guarantee improvements in private investment.

Education is *not* an engine of growth like manufacturing. Yet, certainly education matters. For this reason, it is important to understand what education does and does not do. Basic education is responsible for producing competent citizens capable of contributing to nation-building. This cannot be emphasized enough, considering the ongoing learning crisis at the time of writing this book. Moreover,

DOI: 10.4324/9781003728719-10

while it has become widely accepted that education promotes economic growth, the mechanisms through which this occurs require further clarification. In the context of industrial policy and structural transformation, education can facilitate the diffusion of knowledge and learning-by-doing. Education, particularly post-graduate education, is needed to generate knowledge capital—R&D—which is essential in producing new products and techniques to spur innovation (Viotti, 2002). However, the role that education plays largely depends on the product, or industry diversification strategy of the country. Education, particularly good quality basic education, facilitates a country's "jump" toward new, existing products, or products that are unrelated to the existing comparative advantage but not necessarily toward more complex or education-intensive products (Felipe et al., 2024). Education explains very little about a country's industrialization, which is determined more by governments deliberately developing stepping-stone industries to reach further products.

However, a country like the Philippines does not need to reinvent the wheel. The country does not need to invent new or even more complex products. There is much to gain by focusing on its behind-the-frontier catch-up, or by producing the existing products that "make a nation," as discussed in Chapter 8. Education, particularly basic education, can support this. What about higher education? Or even postgraduate education, which was said to be important to spur innovation? In the Philippines, the number of tertiary education graduates has significantly increased in the past few decades, and yet, when we look at the jobs they undertake, we can hardly say that their degrees are fully utilized. This is called "overeducation," which is one of the issues we tackle in this chapter. It is true that firms require well-trained workers to carry out the tasks needed to support their activities—workers who can do their tasks well, communicate properly, read manuals, and learn quickly on the job. However, for most of the jobs that firms create, basic education should be sufficient. Without companies engaging in productivity-enhancing activities, workers are stuck working jobs that offer low pay. This limits the returns to education, especially of the ever-growing number of workers with tertiary degrees. It hampers social mobility and casts doubt on the widespread belief that "higher education is a necessary condition for a better life."

Government labor market initiatives globally and in the Philippines have been largely supply-side interventions, including training, education, and up-skilling. However, they do not necessarily lead to higher pay. This is a misconception about how the labor market operates. A more educated workforce does not guarantee higher wages across the board. The Philippines is following the global trend of increasing enrollments in higher education. However, in a country with a low domestic absorptive capacity of workers, this leads to overeducation—workers with higher-level degrees working in jobs that require a lower level of education. The irony is that despite this, it has recently been reported that almost 25 million Filipinos are functionally illiterate—people who can read, write, and apply basic numeracy, but struggle with comprehension (Philippine

Statistics Authority, 2025a). The quantity of education is not a constraint on growth, but the education system itself is constrained by the issues we mention in this chapter, which negatively impact the quality of education, contributing to the current learning crisis. There is a need to refocus on the right type of education.

We start this chapter with a brief review of labor market policies and provide a different view of the labor market. We then clarify two misconceptions about employment and education that have long misled Philippine policies.

10.2 Labor Market Policies: An Overview

It is true that, over time, the country has made strides to provide employment and improve the income-earning ability of Filipinos. The labor market objectives outlined in the Philippine Development Plan 2023–2028 (NEDA, 2023a) include creating better and resilient jobs, reducing unemployment, and increasing paid work. It has also sought to increase the income-earning ability of the workforce in three ways. First, by increasing employability through upskilling and retooling (via strengthening technical and vocational education and training) and to develop a system of recognizing prior learning (via the implementation of the Philippine Qualifications Framework and the Philippine Skills Framework). Second, by expanding employment opportunities through career development support (via Public Employment Service Offices), by providing greater labor market information (through improvements in the labor market portal, PhilJobNet), and by encouraging greater labor force participation among women and youth (through a variety of employment programs). Lastly, by improving labor market governance by promoting tripartite dialogue and collaboration among government, industry, and employees.

During the May 2024 economic briefing conducted by the country's economic managers, it was reported that the employment rate has reached historic highs, with a significant portion made up by wage workers. The December 2024 press release of the Labor Force Survey by the Philippine Statistics Authority (2025b) indicated that the employment rate reached 96.9%, with 50.19 million people (3.1% unemployment rate, 1.63 million). Paid workers accounted for 63.1% of employment, whereas 28.5% were self-employed workers and 6.8% were unpaid family workers. Underemployment rates decreased to 10.9% from 11.9% in December 2023. Transportation and storage, as well as construction workers, experienced the largest increases in employment, whereas agriculture and manufacturing decreased.

Government policies addressing labor market challenges have been mostly labor-supply focused, that is, emphasis on the development of workers. Apart from the objectives of the PDP 2023–2028, this is also embodied in the *Trabaho Para sa Bayan* Act (TPB) (Republic Act No. 119621, 2023). The TPB Inter-Agency Council unveiled the 10-year TPB Master Plan in June 2024 to address the law's objective of poverty reduction by promoting decent work, sustainable enterprises, and economic transformation (Presidential Communications Office, 2024). Although there is a provision for identifying key sectors and industries, encouraging investments, and targeting subsidies to enhance the value-added of supply chains, most of the law's objectives mainly target developing skills, providing training, protecting worker rights, and supporting MSMEs.

However, we cannot help but notice how the discussion on decent jobs—whether in the PDP or the TPB—is done without a plan for raising wages, which we could argue is what would mostly constitute a decent job. The reality is that despite improvements in earnings over the past two decades, nearly 88% of workers earn no more than PHP 20,000 (USD 350) monthly (Figure 10.1). Earning more than PHP 50,000 (less than USD 1,000 at today's exchange rate) would already put a worker at the top 1% of wage earners.

Most of the employment in the country is concentrated in jobs and industries that do not provide decent work (Figure 10.2). For purposes of our work, the term decent work is not meant to prescribe what makes work *decent*—which arguably could be based on things like work environment, career advancement, and work relationships—things that are unobservable in the typical labor force survey conducted by national statistical authorities. Rather, our definition of decent work here is more descriptive, based on the distribution of key indicators across sectors and occupations. Thus, we define decent work using an aggregate normalized index based on wages, work hours, and tenure—indicators that are available in the Philippine Statistics Authority's Labor Force Survey. These are weighted using

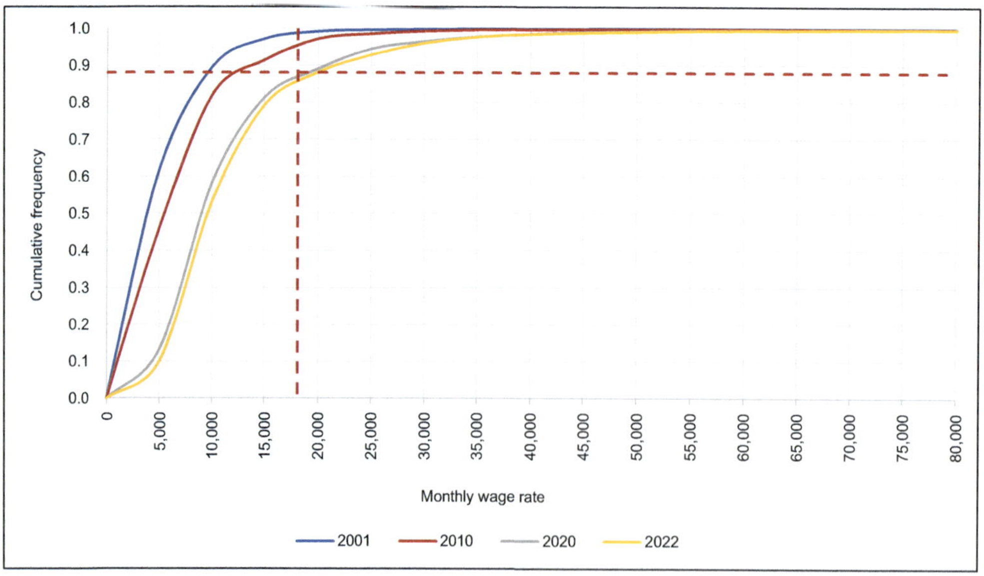

FIGURE 10.1 Cumulative Distribution of the Monthly Wage Rate (PHP), Working-Age Employees (15–64), 2001, 2010, 2020, and 2022

Note: Cumulative frequency is the % of workers earning up to a given monthly wage rate.

Source: Authors' calculations from the Philippine Statistics Authority's Labor Force Survey (https://psada.psa.gov.ph/catalog/LFS/about)

the first component from a Principal Components Analysis. The analysis shows that decent work happens in sectors and occupations that come with high wages, high prevalence of permanent workers, and low work hours.

According to this definition, the largest employers of the country (agriculture, wholesale and retail trade, and construction) are creating jobs with the lowest pay and job **security** (see Appendix 4 in Chapter 4 for the full list of sectors and their activities). Transport and storage may have a positive decent work score, but there is a wide disparity in wages between those working in water and air transport subsectors (where ship captains and engineers and pilots work, respectively), and the land transport subsector (comprised mainly of tricycle, jeepney, and bus operators). Land transport has the lion's share of employment, but workers also have the lowest earnings.

Unpaid workers *still* number 3.4 million, mostly in agriculture and wholesale and retail trade. Although self-employed workers make up a third of total employment (around 14.3 million, mostly in agriculture, wholesale and retail trade, and transport and storage), these are not startups that are scaled up by investors; rather, these are "sari-sari store" owners, smallholder farmers, private tricycle operators, and gig economy workers (drivers for ridesharing and transport network companies and delivery riders). To be clear, there is nothing wrong with these jobs; they provide honest work. However, these are low-paying jobs. Although the largest proportion

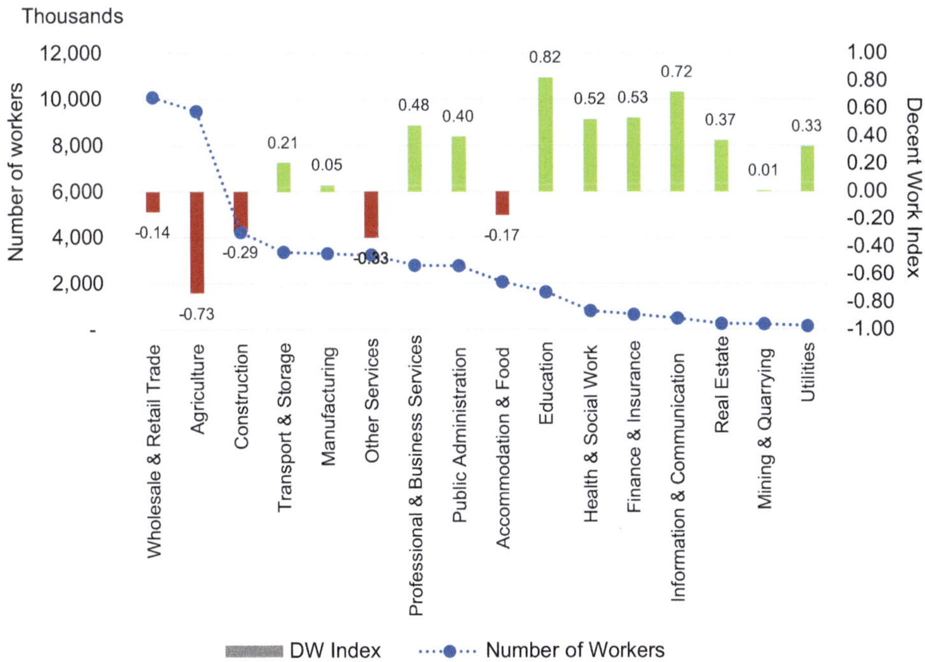

FIGURE 10.2 Employment and Decent Work Scores by Sector, Philippines, 2023

Source: Authors' calculations based on data from the Philippine Statistics Authority's Labor Force Survey (https://psada.psa.gov.ph/catalog/LFS/about)

of employment is paid work, the reality is that most of these jobs pay low wages. We estimate that, in 2023, about a third of workers in paid-work jobs received below minimum wage. Why do the PDP or TPB not address these issues directly?

Labor market regulations and executive plans to raise wages have been limited to minimum wage setting. The national minimum wage setting in the 1950s was described as a bilateral monopoly bargaining process, which disproportionately penalized low-wage and low-skilled workers, further pushing them into marginal occupations or unemployment (Paqueo et al., 2014; Sicat, 1986). Republic Act 6727, or the Wage Rationalization Act (Republic Act No. 6727, 1989) created Regional Tripartite Wages and Productivity Boards to prescribe minimum wages at the regional level to account for local preferences and labor market conditions. Although these seek to protect workers and are meant to help them form more firm-specific skills, these policies may also lead to unemployment, especially among the poor, the less educated, the young, and women (Paqueo et al., 2014)—demographics that are often part of the informal sector which is "exempt" from minimum wage laws (because they are paid lower than the minimum wage).

Reiterating that the government's plan in both the Philippine Development Plan 2023–2028 (NEDA, 2023a) and the TPB is to further enhance skills accumulation and improve labor market information dissemination and governance, will these supply-side improvements translate into wage increases? This may not necessarily be the case.

We posit that this response is driven by two *misconceptions*:

1. A better-educated workforce leads to overall higher employment and wages.
2. The workforce is not educated enough and education is a key constraint to the growth of the Philippine economy.

We hypothesize that the first is the result of confusing micro and macro evidence of the link between education and employment. While there is *some* truth to the second, it confuses the quality and quantity of education. Moreover, it results from a misunderstanding of the type of education (whether early childhood, basic, or tertiary) that is more directly relevant to the sector that drives economic growth. Both potentially explain the obsession with supply-side interventions without batting an eye toward demand-side, industry-driven factors that are more likely to create employment and raise wages. In reality, these are the types of interventions that have led the country to where it is today, where we celebrate higher employment rates and increases in the proportion of salaried workers, yet we do not reflect on the fact that many of the jobs created do not meet the standards of "decent" that the government promised to deliver.

10.3 Misconception 1: A Better-Educated Workforce Implies Higher Wages

When surveying the literature on the impact of education, training, or other human capital-enhancing activities on employment and wages, studies often converge on a positive association between both, whether causal or just correlation. Policy discussions would then be steered toward thinking that more education is necessary to attain higher wages, and hence, that everybody should (and be presented with the opportunity to) pursue as much education as possible. However, not all those who have acquired more years of education are paid higher salaries. The Philippines has also experienced brain drain, or the exodus of professionals to other countries in pursuit of better economic opportunities due to a lack of them domestically. People ask why aren't there better and higher-paying jobs for our educated workers? The important point to keep in mind is that this is not a (labor) supply problem; rather, it is a question of (labor) demand.

10.3.1 Education Leads to Higher Employment for an Individual, but Not Necessarily for Everyone

The misunderstanding that because a workforce is better educated on average then employment rates and wages will be higher confuses what education does for the person versus what it does for the country—a confusion of the micro and macro impacts of education. It is true that highly educated workers enjoy greater employability (i.e., they are more likely to be employed) and higher wages (Huang et al., 2022; Brunello et al., 2009), but this does not guarantee that *everyone*, not even *most* workers, or even the *average worker*, will enjoy the same benefits. This does not guarantee that more workers will be employed or that higher wages will be paid across occupations, across industries, or across the country. Just because a worker is more educated does not necessarily mean that he/she will earn a higher salary than a worker with a lower level of education in the same occupation. A person will only be paid a higher wage for the skills he/she has accumulated (whether these are firm-specific skills acquired via training, certifications, internships, and on-the-job training, or general skills acquired from formal education) if the firm she works for values these skills and is willing to pay a wage premium. In fact, there are inequalities in the impacts of education on employment and wages that favor high-skill sectors (those with a larger demand for non-routine tasks, such as IT and finance) over low-skill sectors (e.g., clerical and basic production), thereby widening the wage gap between high-skilled and low-skilled workers (Autor, Katz, et al., 2006). This can be seen in Table 10.1, where we present the returns to tertiary education relative to graduates of secondary education, categorized by sector.[2] Workers with tertiary education get higher wages than graduates of secondary education, but only for high-skill service sectors, such as information and communication (31% higher compared to secondary graduates in other services), finance and insurance (19% higher returns), professional business services (8%), public administration (30%), education (60%), and health and social works (26%). This is driven by what we mention in the next sections, "occupational sorting." There is room for tertiary education graduates, particularly engineers, in the mining and quarrying (21%) and utilities (35%) sectors. In sectors like agriculture,

TABLE 10.1 Estimation Results: Differential Returns to Tertiary Education Relative to Graduates of Secondary Education by Sector, Philippines, 2023

Sector	*Returns*	*Sector*	*Returns*
Agriculture	−0.03 (0.07)	Information and communication	0.31*** (0.07)
Mining and quarrying	0.21** (0.09)	Finance and insurance	0.19*** (0.06)
Manufacturing	0.03 (0.04)	Real estate	0.17 (0.11)
Utilities	0.35*** (0.10)	Professional and business services	0.08* (0.04)
Construction	0.05 (0.05)	Public administration	0.30*** (0.05)
Wholesale and retail trade	−0.03 (0.04)	Education	0.60*** (0.07)
Transport and storage	−0.01 (0.05)	Health and social work	0.26*** (0.05)
Accommodation and food	−0.01 (0.04)		

Notes:
(1) Robust standard errors in parenthesis: *** $p < 0.01$, ** $p < 0.05$, * $p < 0.1$.
(2) Base category is secondary graduates in other services.

Source: Authors' calculations based on data from the Philippine Statistics Authority's Labor Force Survey (https://psada.psa.gov.ph/catalog/LFS/about).

construction, wholesale and retail trade, transport and storage, and accommodation and food, college graduates are paid no higher than high school graduates. Keep in mind that the bulk of our workforce is employed in these latter sectors.

It is worth noting that the difference in returns between secondary and tertiary graduates is not statistically significant for Manufacturing. The sub-sectors within Manufacturing are very diverse, and this is indicative of the sector's failure to expand in terms of activities that require tertiary education. It has been shown that the polarizing effect that skill-biased technical change [SBTC] (the shift toward non-routinary tasks augmented by computerization) has on the wage distribution is not driven by rising educational attainment or higher participation of women, and is more driven by shifts in the demand for job tasks spurred by technological advancement and structural transformation (Autor, Katz, et al., 2006; Autor, Levy, et al., 2003). Philippine manufacturing has not made major strides in either one.

How does education increase employability and earnings for a worker? The channels through which more education potentially lead to higher employability and earnings occur through (1) a larger wage premia paid by sectors with greater use for higher cognitive or analytical abilities (usually engineering, IT, finance), which is the SBTC hypothesis that gives rise to industry-specific variation in wages;

(2) signaling, where accomplishing a certain level of education or type of degree signals to employers that a person has attained a certain level of skill or possesses a particular skillset; or (3) occupational sorting (selection) and mobility, where a person chooses a specific course in higher education that allows them to move up the occupational ladder, usually to occupations that get paid higher wages (e.g., non-routinary, cognitive-intensive jobs such as professionals). The difficulty, particularly for the third channel, is that without an expansion of the sectors that would receive highly skilled workers, even well-educated workers will not be able to access high-paying jobs. This is a labor mismatch issue, a supply and demand problem. The increase in the supply of skilled labor without a corresponding increase in demand for skilled labor would lead to overeducation. Not only does this increase competition for workers with higher levels of education, but it also erodes the wage premium paid to higher levels of education (Chen and Chen, 2021).

10.3.2 Average Wages Increase If Firms' Productivity Increases

What can potentially increase wages across the board? Firms' productivity. When productivity (defined as output per worker) increases, it results in a combination of higher output and revenue, and lower costs. This puts companies in a better position to pay higher wages without harming profits. This allows them to attract better and more productive workers. This is where structural transformation and industrialization play key roles, as productivity varies by sector. Depending on the type of activity, some sectors that have a greater demand for higher skills would also be more likely to pay higher wages, thus providing greater returns to higher levels of education (Autor et al., 2003, 2006). Table 10.2 shows regressions of sectoral wage growth on growth of productivity and employment with tertiary education.[3] The growth of employment with tertiary education consistently shows no significant relation with wage growth. Whereas productivity growth shows a consistent and statistically significant positive, albeit modest association: 0.07–0.10 percentage point faster wage growth for every 1 percentage point increase in productivity growth.

This provides strong evidence that productivity, and not more workers with tertiary education, drives wage growth. This also explains the finding in Table 10.1 that service sectors like IT and finance provide higher returns on tertiary education, as opposed to sectors with low productivity like agriculture, retail, or construction.

Countries often aim at expanding manufacturing as a means to drive economic growth. What is particularly crucial to attaining high income is the share of manufacturing employment in total employment rather than the share of manufacturing value added in GDP (Felipe et al., 2019). Shifting labor from the "traditional" agricultural sector to the "modern" manufacturing sector increases labor productivity in terms of value added per worker (Lewis, 1954). Manufacturing also enables unconditional convergence. This means that developing countries can "converge" or catch up with richer countries in terms of labor productivity, independently of

TABLE 10.2 Estimation Results: Sectoral Wage Growth, Productivity Growth, and Growth of Employment With Tertiary Degrees, Philippines, 2005–2022

	Dependent Variable: Annual Sectoral Wage Growth							
	(1)	*(2)*	*(3)*	*(4)*	*(5)*	*(6)*	*(7)*	*(8)*
	OLS	*WG FE*	*ARDL*	*OLS*	*WG FE*	*ARDL*	*OLS*	*ARDL*
Productivity growth	0.08*	0.07*	0.10**				0.08*	0.09*
	(0.04)	(0.04)	(0.04)				(0.05)	(0.05)
Growth of employment with tertiary education				−0.02	−0.01	−0.03	−0.02	−0.02
				(0.02)	(0.02)	(0.02)	(0.02)	(0.03)
Constant	0.04***	0.02***	0.04***	0.04***	0.02***	0.05***	0.04***	0.04***
	(0.007)	(0.003)	(0.01)	(0.01)	(0.01)	(0.01)	(0.01)	(0.01)
ARDL(1, 1) term	No	No	Yes	No	No	Yes	No	Yes
Observations	288	288	272	288	288	272	288	272
R-squared	0.08		0.09	0.06		0.07	0.08	0.10

Notes:
(1) Robust standard errors are reported in parentheses: *** $p < 0.01$, ** $p < 0.05$, * $p < 0.1$.
(2) OLS and ARDL specifications include sector fixed effects.

Source: Authors' calculations based on data from the Philippine Statistics Authority's Labor Force Survey (https://psada.psa.gov.ph/catalog/LFS/about) and the DLSU ANIMO econometric model.

country-specific policies, institutions, or even geography (Rodrik, 2013). This is because the sector produces tradable goods, rapidly integrates into global production networks, and benefits from and facilitates further technological progress, transfer, and adoption. As a result, the manufacturing sector is also able to pay higher wages for low-skilled labor and higher wage premiums for higher skills and education (Pandian, 2024).

The expansion of employment in the sector also reduces income inequality more in developing countries because it absorbs low-skilled labor from agriculture and informal work. As a result, the expansion of manufacturing often leads to broad-based wage growth and to a reduction in inequality (Pandian, 2024) because it raises wages for low- and middle-skilled workers (which typically only have completed basic education). On the other hand, the expansion of services that are biased toward high-value services (finance, healthcare), increase wage dispersion due to high skill premiums and high entry barriers (due to higher skill requirements). The expansion of manufacturing has even been found to reduce poverty, whereas the expansion of services tends to increase it (Fabella et al., 2023). Low-productivity jobs in retail, hospitality, or gig work also pay low salaries and do not provide job security.

We must not confuse how education influences the earnings of a worker with the role it plays in economic growth. Education is not an engine of growth; a better-educated workforce will not guarantee that all workers will be paid higher wages. Productivity, firms, and manufacturing job creation are more likely to be the engines of growth and the road to high per capita income. Education must provide the railway . . . but which type of education?

10.4 Misconception 2: Education Is a Key Constraint to the Growth of the Philippine Economy—the Workforce Is Not Educated Enough

We have argued so far that increasing the number of highly educated workers may not necessarily increase earnings or the number of people with jobs, because these are likely to be demand-driven. This does not imply that we argue that education does not matter. On the contrary, much work is needed to reform the education system. The broad consensus that education is positively associated with earnings and growth has given policy circles enough munition to discuss how education is the nation's key bottleneck, and, consequently, how we must increase everybody's education, without reflecting on the *type*, *amount*, and *quality*.

Education matters, but there are significant misunderstandings in this area, particularly the difference between education in the traditional sense (i.e., the "cultural experience") and *trainability*. Education refers to the transmission of knowledge to develop an understanding and appreciation of more complex processes in the world. This allows a person to appreciate things like classical music, good literature, good movies, and be aware of history. *Trainability*, on the other hand, is what matters for employability, growth, and productivity. This distinction is not the same as that about the roles of different levels of education: basic vs. technical/vocational vs. higher vs. postgraduate education.[4] Many people do not realize that these different levels contribute to trainability heterogeneously—some more than others.

Education, understood as the process of receiving systematic instruction, matters for political reasons, as it helps societies acquire political philosophies based on individual rights. These rights are necessary for political and social developments that overcome the privileges of special interests and satisfy individual and consumer desires better. Education is necessary to understand complex political systems that facilitate advanced economic performance. It is possible that poor countries (like the Philippines) today will not escape poverty traps without political changes, and these political changes may only be possible with broader education. Although this is an important issue, it differs from the emphasis on education in the public debate, very focused on tertiary education, especially with the passing of Republic Act 10931 or the Universal Access to Quality Tertiary Education Act in 2017—the "Free Tuition Law." The law provides free tuition, covers miscellaneous fees, offers affirmative action for minorities, offers subsidies and loan programs. Prior to the law's passage, the expansion of tertiary education had already started in the 1990s as a response to the increasing number of secondary education graduates who wanted to pursue higher education (De Jesus, 2011). Several state universities and colleges (SUCs) were established to meet the demand. Students and parents alike started viewing higher education as necessary to attain social mobility (Chan and Zhang, 2021). This belief has been firmly placed in *Philippine culture*.

10.4.1 Overeducation Among Tertiary Graduates

Does the Philippines need more tertiary graduates? Is this a constraint? No, in fact, the Philippines suffers from severe overeducation—especially tertiary graduates. Firms offer graduates who have completed tertiary education jobs that typically require only primary or secondary education. The Philippine government recognizes this and tracks the proportion of tertiary degree holders working in elementary occupations (Classification 9) as laborers, cleaners, and helpers (Philippine Statistics Authority, 2025b). However, this underestimates the problem of overeducation because jobs and tasks in occupational classifications 4–8 also require no more than a high school diploma.[5] Figure 10.3 reports the distribution of tertiary graduates who work in various occupations. In 2022, the number of tertiary education graduates working as sales and service personnel, agricultural workers, crafts and tradesmen, plant machinery operators and assemblers, and laborers was approximately 3.1 million—around 35% of all tertiary degree holders.

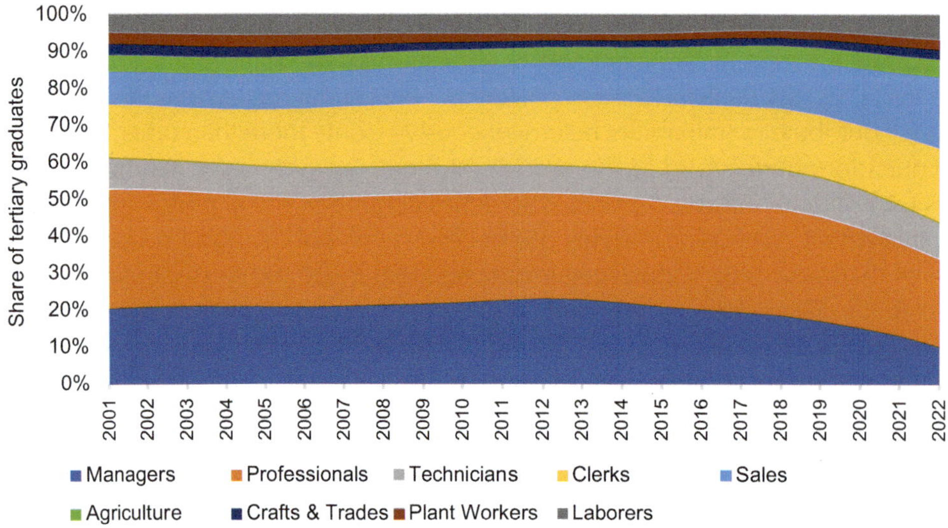

FIGURE 10.3 Share of Tertiary Graduates by Occupation (%), Philippines, 2001–2022

Source: Authors' calculations based on data from the Philippine Statistics Authority's Labor Force Survey (https://psada.psa.gov.ph/catalog/LFS/about)

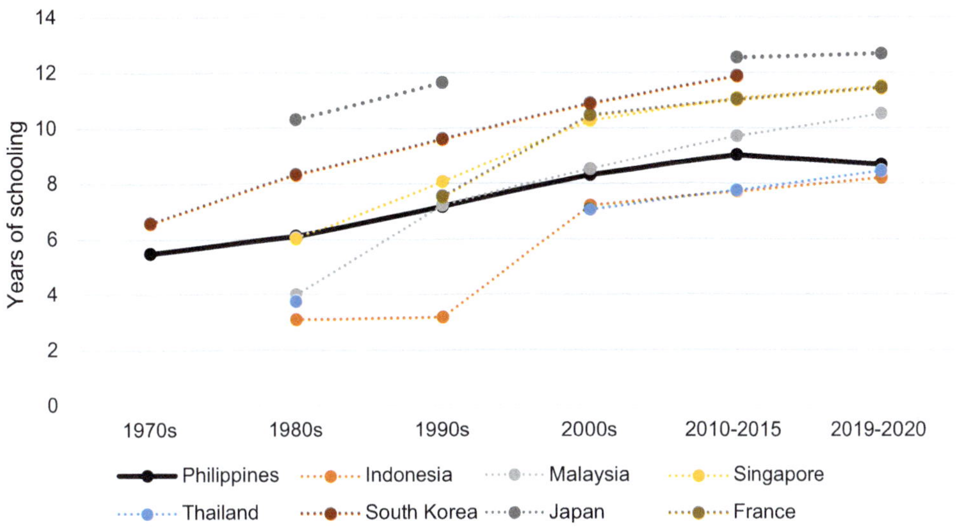

FIGURE 10.4 Mean Years of Schooling, Selected Countries, 1970–2020

Source: Authors' calculations based on data from the UNESCO Institute of Statistics (https://databrowser.uis.unesco.org/browser/EDUCATION/UIS-EducationOPRI/mys)

The public debate has been misled for decades by the "upgrading thesis." This is the idea that the changing conditions of work require a better-trained, better-educated, and, therefore, upgraded working population. This is a myth resulting from three observed trends. One is the increasing average level of skills (in terms of average years of education) (Figure 10.4). This is the global trend of increasing mean years of schooling and the growing pursuit of tertiary degrees. Everybody is now more learned. However, it is misleading to argue that, with the development of technology, *all* labor processes now require greater scientific knowledge and skills compared to the past. This only affects some jobs, not all, and certainly not most. Indeed, as mentioned previously, today's technological world has magnified the returns of those with strong math and science skills and used them in fields such as finance, software development, or genetics. However, this also increases inequality in both developed and developing countries.

Many of the jobs modern societies create do not require high skills. In the Philippines, workers who benefit from higher returns to math and science skills represent a small percentage of the labor force, given that the country is not a leading nation in the development of advanced technologies.

A second trend is the shift of workers from some major occupational groups into others through structural transformation. Figure 10.5 reports the occupational distribution of the Philippine workforce. The shares of agricultural workers, laborers, and even managers have slowly declined over the last two decades. Meanwhile, the share of sales and service personnel has increased significantly,

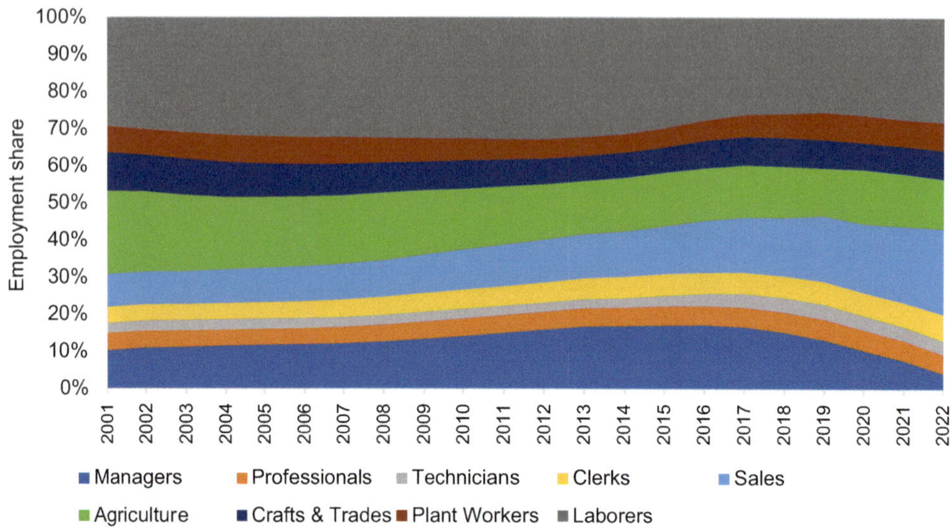

FIGURE 10.5 Employment Share by Occupation (%), Philippines, 2001–2022

Source: Authors' calculations based on data from the Philippine Statistics Authority's Labor Force Survey (https://psada.psa.gov.ph/catalog/LFS/about)

whereas the shares of crafts workers, plant workers, clerks, professionals, and technicians remain stable.

Workers classified by the statistics in the secondary sector (e.g., crafts and tradespeople, assembly line workers) are believed to need and have more skills than those classified in the primary sector (e.g., laborers, farmers). Those working in services (typically professional and clerical work) are believed to need and to have even higher skills. Indeed, managers, professionals, and technicians are expected to have tertiary education; clerks, sales, agriculture, crafts and trades, and plant workers are expected to have secondary education; and laborers are expected to at least have primary education. This is what is dictated in the International Standard Classification of Occupations set by the International Labour Organization (ILO), which is also adopted by the Philippine Statistics Authority in the Philippine Standard Occupational Classifications, and other statistical agencies across the world. While this view is standard and widely accepted, it raises questions about why an assembly line worker is presumed to have greater skills than a fisherman or an oysterman. Even pick-and-shovel work takes more learning before it can be done to the required standards than many assembly or machine-feeding jobs.

The third observed trend is the prolongation of the period of education, as seen in the trend of mean years of schooling presented earlier (Figure 10.4), and the upward trend in gross tertiary enrollment rates across the world, particularly in Asia (Figure 10.6). This indicates how people have increasingly perceived tertiary education as necessary for upward social mobility. This has been ingrained in

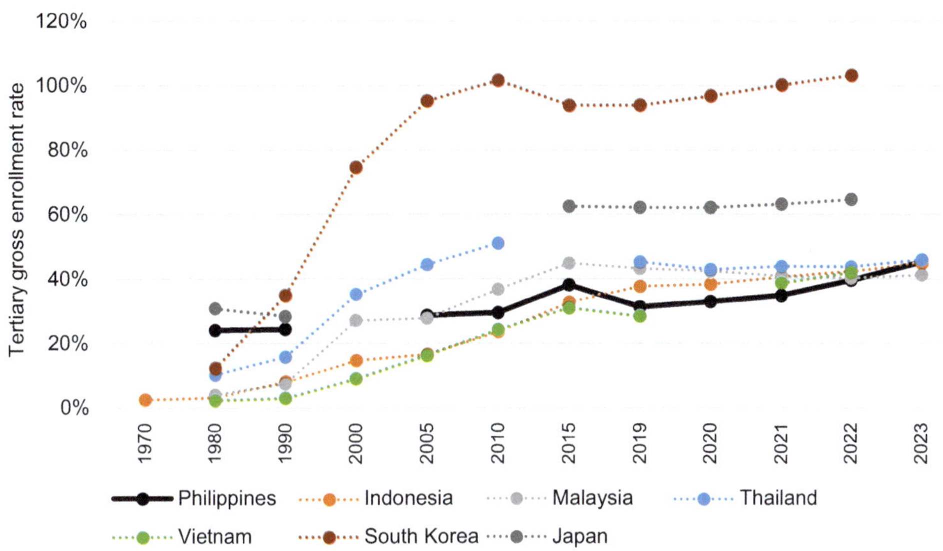

FIGURE 10.6 Tertiary Gross Enrollment Rates (%), Selected Asian Countries, 1980–2023

Source: The World Bank: World Data Indicators (https://data.worldbank.org/indicator/SE.TER.ENRR)

Philippine culture—kids being told that a college education is a must for a better life. However, the difference with countries like Korea and Japan is that they have "superstar firms" that lead the development of new technologies. When kids from these countries graduate from college, there *will* be jobs that make proper use of their skills.

The reality is that we do not spend so many years at school today because the jobs that the marketplace creates require at least 12 years of formal schooling. Laborers perform very simple tasks, and it is internationally recognized that these require only primary education. The lengthening of the school period started in advanced nations in the 20th century. This had more to do with the need to reduce unemployment and the fact that laws recognized that 12-year-old children should not be sent to the labor market. In time, developing countries followed suit. Yet, the reality is that many of the jobs created today in most developing countries in the services sector (e.g., delivery, sales) do not require more than basic literacy (i.e., reading, writing, and arithmetic). These qualifications are demanded by the urban environment in which many people now live, so that they learn how to conform to the rules of society and obey the law. Beyond this need for basic literacy, schools play a key role in the socialization process of children and teenagers, as a venue to learn about and adapt to modern life.

These reflections are not to undermine the Philippine K-12 program's objectives. Rather, they reaffirm it. As discussed previously, basic education is necessary to produce "good citizens." This, by itself, is an outcome that society must work toward.

Graduates of K-12 can begin working, as the majority of jobs require around secondary education. The K-12 program provides a "natural stop" for graduates-a clear transition into either the labor market, or post-secondary or tertiary education. In principle, K-12 graduates should be able to start working. This assumes that companies will be ready to hire *mostly* K-12 graduates and will hire graduates with tertiary education degrees specifically for high value-added activities. However, the program fails to achieve this because companies choose college graduates over secondary graduates, as the former are ready to pounce on the same low-paying jobs—that do not require tertiary education. How can K-12 graduates compete? To begin with, there are few jobs that do really require tertiary education. What company would not hire a worker with a higher education level, for the same salary?

Many secondary graduates still desire to get into college, considering how the Free Tuition Law grants admission to SUCs and LUCs. However, in attempting to accommodate more students, the expansion of SUCs and LUCs has led to issues of both access and quality (Bayudan-Dacuycuy et al., 2024). This includes a lack of classrooms, facilities, and equipment, low faculty wages (leading to low retention rates), and the inability of SUCs to fulfill its core function of producing research. This requires a greater allocation of government resources toward the public higher education system. Note that the benefits of tertiary education accrue more to the individual and his/her household rather than to society. Couple this with the reality of overeducation, it becomes a misguided solution, as the jobs that await college graduates do not use their specialized skills. Nor would they pay decent wages that justify the investment made by parents and the government. Do the benefits still outweigh the costs? Or is it time to rethink this strategy?

One can hardly argue that, for the Philippines, the key constraint on development is education. There might be specific sectors that lack qualified professionals, but this is not true at the national level. This is a country where helpers, guards, and drivers have college degrees. Claiming that education is the binding constraint is barking up the wrong tree. When France reached high-income status, approximately in the early 1970s, its workers had an average of 6.05 years of total education, split into 4.05 years of primary education, 1.75 years of secondary education, and 0.25 years of tertiary education. The same four figures for the Philippines at the time were 5.56 (total), 3.65 (primary), 1.52 (secondary), and 0.38 (yes, more tertiary). These were not so different to justify how France had fifteen times higher income per capita than the Philippines at the time. In the 1990s, average years of schooling in France and the Philippines were 7.55 and 7.18, respectively. While this gap has widened in the two succeeding decades (11.46 and 8.68 in 2020 for France and the Philippines, respectively), the per capita income ratio of 10 cannot be attributed to it. No, it is not the quantity of education. For these reasons, the public policy debate should shift toward a different paradigm: trainability.

10.4.2 Missing the Critical Window in Early Childhood and Basic Education

Trainability is the ability to learn quickly on-the-job, pick-up new skills, make informed decisions, and master different tasks. Well-trained workers perform well, regardless of whether they are in an office, or in an assembly line. They can read and understand a manual, write correctly, and know how to convey a message, and can be easily redeployed to perform new tasks. Filipino workers can be trained to achieve much higher productivity levels. A key aspect of trainability is cognitive aptitude. This is the capacity to think critically, solve problems, and digest and apply new information. Do students need to wait until they reach tertiary education to develop cognitive aptitudes? *No*. The acquisition and development of cognitive aptitudes begins in the first few years of life.

This is where *the real (and more severe) bottleneck is—basic education and early childhood education* (ECE). Currently, the Philippines suffers from a learning crisis, particularly learning poverty, where about 91% of late primary age children cannot comprehend age-appropriate texts (World Bank Group, 2022). Moreover, 25 million Filipinos 10 to 64 years old, regardless of highest educational attainment, are said to be functionally illiterate, that is, they lack comprehension skills. In the 2022 PISA, the Philippines had an average score of 355 in mathematics, 347 in reading, and 356 in science, making it the sixth lowest in the world for mathematics and reading, and third lowest in science (Organisation for Economic Co-operation and Development, 2023).[6] This is driven by problems in both access and quality, and combinations of supply-side and demand-side factors (Ulep et al., 2024).

Supply-side factors are primarily personnel-related problems: high student-teacher ratios, teacher mismatches (e.g., PE teachers teaching economics), and a lack of childcare or daycare workers. There are also shortages in terms of physical resources: textbook shortages; infrastructure deficiencies such as deteriorating buildings; overcrowded classrooms; a lack of access to electricity, water, and sanitation; and a shortage of childcare facilities. The Department of Education was also threatened with budget cuts of about PHP 12 billion (Chi, 2024), given the already low government spending on basic and early childhood education. The K-12 curriculum has also been criticized for "overworking students by design"—that is, students in the Philippines spend about 3–9 hours more per week in school compared to students in Vietnam, Malaysia, and Thailand (Largoza, 2024). Although weather disruptions have decreased the number of class days, and because of classroom and teacher shortages, many schools operate with double and triple shifts, reducing potential contact time for students by half.

Is the newly implemented *Matatag* Curriculum, which promises to loosen student workloads, the solution? Could rolling back the two additional years from the K-12 program be the solution? In principle, the plan to revise the curriculum sounds like a much-needed breath of fresh air for our overworked students. However, similar to the initial rollout of the K-12, the implementation left a lot to be desired. Professionals in the public education sector were—and are still—underprepared, with no channels of feedback, and no clear systems of monitoring and evaluation, leading to a messy rollout and culminating in an overall underwhelming attempt to address the supply-side issues of education quality.

On the demand side, while primary and secondary net enrollment rates have increased over time, participation rates in pre-kindergarten programs remain low, with about 20% in 2022 (Ulep et al., 2024). The most pressing problem preventing Filipino children from learning is *malnutrition*. In 2021, 26.7% of Filipino children under five were stunted (low height for their age), surpassing the global average of 22.3%, one of the highest in the world, and 16.8% experienced wasting (i.e., low weight for their height; Second Congressional Commission on Education [EDCOM2], 2024). Stunting and wasting are not only indications of poor physical development, but also of poorer mental development. This high prevalence of stunting and wasting is linked to inadequate nutrition during the first 1,000 days of life, with only 25% of children meeting the recommended energy intake (Ulep et al., 2024). However, supplemental feeding and nutrition interventions have been inadequate. Some may think that school lunch (and breakfast) programs are just "Band Aid solutions." Yet, this is a misconception. The truth is that these are great and proven low-cost interventions. The logic is simple: How can children focus and pay attention to their lessons when they go to school hungry? And so, for many Filipino children, this critical window has been missed, impacting their learning and cognitive development in the long term. Good nutrition is linked to better school attendance, lower dropout rates, improved learning ability, enhanced concentration during class, and better information retention and reading comprehension, which translate to better cognitive ability test results and boost earnings later in life (Ulep et al., 2023). Furthermore, poverty, cultural norms, and the lack of awareness by parents, further limits participation in ECE (Ulep et al., 2024).

The benefits of good nutrition and early childhood education are severely underestimated. By age 5, a child's brain reaches around 90% development, and the foundations for success in school and later in life are already in place (Zubairi and Rose, 2017). Hence, there is a need to expand ECE programs to increase access and awareness, public spending, increase childcare centers and their workers, and revisit the implementation of the feeding programs to address gaps (Ulep et al., 2024). However, we cannot stop at simply increasing the quantity of ECE. There is a need for strong ECE programs that focus on enhancing life, language, motor, and socio-emotional skills such as communication, task orientation, independence, and prosocial behavior. These interventions are what give the most "bang for the buck" in the long term, as claimed by none other than the 2000 Nobel laureate in the Economic Sciences, James J. Heckman himself (Garcia et al., 2020).

Our children do not develop "critical thinking" or even "trainability" in tertiary education. This is done in the first five years of their lives, followed through and reinforced in the next 11 to 13 years (regardless of K-10, *Matatag*, or K-12). With a strong start and addressing the gaps in basic education, every child will have the right fundamentals to succeed later in life—to eventually enter the job market, quickly absorb training and develop firm-specific skills in a company, and become productive workers. For this reason, the government's efforts must go into ensuring that children from all backgrounds receive high-quality early childhood and basic education that propel their cognitive ability.

In conclusion, what the Philippines needs is a well-trained labor force, and we would want our workers to have good jobs—decent pay, job security, and reasonable work hours. These jobs exist, and while it is true that higher education helps a worker increase his/her earnings, this occurs only through occupational and sectoral sorting or selection. But this does not move the needle for every person. Ultimately, wages are paid by firms, and we have argued that only when firms engage in activities that drive up their productivity can then wage rates increase. Supply-side interventions, such as upskilling or retooling, do not guarantee wage increases for every person. This does not mean we should forget about these. The workforce will eventually need to be prepared of changing labor market conditions, particularly the rise of AI and automation, which threatens to render some jobs and roles obsolete.

While we forego an in-depth discussion of AI, we recognize that AI and automation clearly play a role in both job creation (or displacement) and redefining the tasks of some occupations. We forego the discussion on the impacts of AI and automation in the Philippines for two reasons. First, studies estimating the threat of job displacement or vulnerability typically base these indicators on the tasks that each job does, whether physical or cognitive, and whether they are routine or non-routine (Frey and Osborne, 2017). These are not conservative estimates as they do not factor in the likelihood or the rate at which firms will adopt these technologies, which is a function of the firm's activities and the costs of these technologies. Acemoglu (2025) also cautioned us how the positive gains of AI are modest at best. Second, it is important to understand that the adoption of AI and automation in the workplace is inevitable, but what will determine the rate of job displacement or replacement is the type of activities that firms are engaged in, as well as the cost of integrating AI into their production processes. The structure of occupations and industries in the Philippines typically favors physical, routine work (work that is typically in danger of replacement by AI and automation in developed countries), and Philippine manufacturing does not develop new products. Complemented by low labor costs relative to the costs of developing AI technologies, what would be the likelihood that Philippine firms automate or adopt AI? Not very high. Will salespersons, hotel and restaurant staff (all services) be replaced by robots? The country is ironically saved by this structure. The country's laggard manufacturing sector, which is supposed to benefit the most from technological progress, has a very low rate of mechanization and automation. However, this may not be the case of sectors such IT-BPO, particularly voice operations in contact centers. This sector is the stopgap to absorb the excess supply of tertiary graduates but it is not a large employer at the national level. The reality is that this type of work does not require a tertiary degree. We add that this sector is only a second-best destination for workers who are unable to get jobs in their first industry of choice—nurses, for example. Hence, while we should understand what AI and automation are, this cannot be considered the number one problem of the country, even when considering education. As argued earlier, we should focus on pressing matters such as providing decent jobs, addressing overeducation, and the learning crisis.

Decent jobs exist in the Philippines, but these are a minority. The reality is that not everybody can be a professional in the IT or finance sectors. The bulk of the jobs the economy needs are plumbers, electricians, carpenters, bricklayers, mechanics, welders, and so forth. This is why the discussion on education, training, or upskilling should be refocused toward trainability, to produce workers who can build a road properly, mid-level technicians, and workers with skills to make quality products (shoes, furniture, bricks, cement, plastic, glass) that meet international standards and can compete in world markets (i.e., be exported). The skills of most of these workers do not require college degrees. This is why there is a need to refocus the discussion on education toward ECE and basic education. Our children should not have to wait until college to develop their analytical and creative thinking, problem-solving skills, and good communication skills—the skills that are more important for trainability and, by extension, productivity and growth. We have to start instilling these within the first five years of life, and reinforcing them further in the next 10 to 13. In a country like Australia (from early childhood up until year 6), children only appear to be playing around, have no real homework, and do not even have tests, and yet, not only do they rank high in international test scores (Australia scored 487, 498, and 507 in math, reading, and science, respectively, putting it well within the top 15 countries in the world in the 2022 PISA), but children there are also instilled with constructive self-perceptions such as "we are researchers" and "we are self-managers," things that one will not find anywhere in the Philippine curriculum. By looking exclusively through one window (tertiary), we have missed the critical window in early childhood and basic education. The fact that the country is making a fuss of the 25 million functionally illiterate Filipinos only now is indicative that the country is already decades late in addressing these issues and implementing much-needed reforms in education.

Certainly, we need good college and postgraduate students, but the reality is that many of them end up in jobs that in other countries are undertaken by workers with lower educational attainments. Why? Because the country generates very few jobs that require a tertiary education, much less a master's or PhD. This means that, paradoxically, a significant share of the Filipino labor force suffers from overeducation. But this is not a supply problem; rather, it is a demand problem. What type of jobs are firms producing? What levels of education do they require?

There is also a need to start cracking down on unreasonable job ads, such as food cart personnel needing good looks and a pleasant personality, on top of a college degree. Ultimately, the jobs that firms produce are a function of the activities that they are engaged in. Are they engaged in activities like the development of new products or R&D? Do they actively improve their organizational capability? It may be argued that these are activities at the frontier. We cannot dismiss the role of imitation and adaptation in contributing to behind-the-frontier catch-up, which better matches the current stage of the country. While industrialization and structural transformation are not new concepts, the reality is that if we wish to move away from more of the same (MOTS), it is time to change our perspective—and our stance—on employment and education to ensure decent work for every Filipino.

Notes

1 This framework is useful in identifying ways to "ignite" growth, but the question for a growing economy such as the Philippines is more of how to "sustain" growth (Felipe et al., 2011).

2 This is estimated using a conventional Mincerian log-wage equation on a binary tertiary education variable (= 1 if the person finished a tertiary degree, = 0 if they finished a secondary degree), sector fixed effects, and interaction terms of tertiary graduates and the 16 different sectors. The sample is restricted only to workers aged 15 to 64 who are either secondary or tertiary graduates. Secondary Graduates in other services serve as the base category.

3 We estimate a panel regression of wage growth for 16 sectors over the period 2005–2022. Wages, productivity, and employment with tertiary education are expressed as year-on-year growth rates. Ordinary least squares (OLS) provides the baseline estimate. An autoregressive distributed lag (ARDL) of order 1 specification is adopted to check robustness and test for any dynamic relationship. The within-group fixed effects (WGFE) estimator is used to eliminate time-invariant, sector-specific variation in wage growth. The same is done by adding sector fixed effects in the OLS and ARDL specifications.

4 Basic education (primary, lower, and upper secondary) teaches basic literacy, numeracy, and values, which are important factors in producing good, law-abiding, and socially contributive citizens. Technical and vocational education is what produces firm-specific, "blue-collar" skills (e.g., commercial cooking, plumbing, welding, manufacturing skills) that support more routinary and physically demanding tasks. Formal higher education or tertiary education also produces firm-specific skills up to some extent (e.g., accounting, engineering, etc.), but these tasks require greater cognitive ability (e.g., analytical and creative thinking, decision-making, communication, etc.). Postgraduate education is geared toward the production of research and innovation. Of these levels of education, basic education is the level where social returns outweigh private returns. Hence, with these great positive externalities, basic education can be perceived as a public good, and this motivates the mandate for it to be universal and is shouldered by the public sector. The returns to technical and vocational education and higher education accrue more to the person and their household (via the increase in earnings through occupational sorting) rather than society, so typically, tuition at these levels is not free. This is an issue by itself, and we comment on this elsewhere in this chapter. The research and innovation produced by postgraduate education also lead to positive externalities and greater social returns through the expansion of a country's

knowledge frontier. This should be strongly suggestive that governments should also be thinking of investing in growing their country's knowledge capital.

5 While we provide a quick reference here, please see Appendix 4 in Chapter 4 for more details on the Philippines Standard Occupational Classifications. The PSOC is roughly based on the International Standard Classification of Occupations (ISCO), which also provides a classification of skill levels based on educational requirements and skill requirements of tasks. These range from physically laborious to cognitive work, and from routinary tasks to decision-making and problem-solving, which require analytical and creative thinking. 1-digit PSOC classifications include 0 for armed forces, 1 for managers, 2 for professionals, 3 for technicians, 4 for clerks, 5 for sales and service workers, 6 for agricultural workers, 7 for crafts and trades, 8 for plant workers, and 9 for laborers (or elementary occupations). Going up from laborers to managers, primary education is required for laborers, secondary education (and post-secondary or vocational education wherever necessary) is required for plant workers to clerks (although some clerks are more specialized and require tertiary education), post-secondary to tertiary education required for technicians, and tertiary to postgraduate education for professionals up to managers.

6 Indonesia scored 366, 359, and 383, for math, reading, and science, respectively; Thailand scored 394, 379, and 409; and Vietnam scored 469, 462, and 472.

11

THE FISCAL DEFICIT, THE NATIONAL DEBT, AND MONETARY REALITY: OLD HABITS DIE HARD

> Scott Pelley (anchor): Is that tax money that the Fed is spending?
> Chairman Bernanke: It's not tax money. The banks have accounts with the Fed, much the same way you have an account in a commercial bank. So, to lend to a bank, we simply use the computer to mark up the size of the account they have with the Fed.
>
> Interview with the Federal Reserve Bank Chairman Ben Bernanke (2009)[1]

> Recognizing the herculean task at mobilizing resources to fund the projects and programs on the 2025 General Appropriations Act, Secretary Recto reassured the public that the DOF [Department of Finance] has enough funds to meet the needs and that every centavo will be spent efficiently on programs and projects that will greatly benefit the people.
>
> Department of Finance (2024)

11.1 The Government's Finances

The US Federal Reserve Bank chairman acknowledged in 2009 that the Fed did not use taxes to provide liquidity, that all it did was to mark up bank accounts with a computer. Yet the Department of Finance (DOF) of the Philippines claims that it needs to tax in order to spend. Further to the earlier quote, the finance chief explained that of the PHP 6.3 trillion national budget for 2025, only PHP 4.6 trillion is supportable by revenues. This translates to daily government expenditure of PHP 17.3 billion, with the Department of Finance bearing the responsibility of generating PHP 12.7 billion in daily revenue. He further argued that the DOF would strive to not just meet but exceed its revenue targets to generate more resources. These two different statements by Bernanke and Recto raise two points. The first one is that, unless the fiscal/monetary procedures of both countries are different, one of the two statements is "incorrect." The second point refers to the statement by the US Fed: Where did the money that Chairman Bernanke referred to actually come from?

DOI: 10.4324/9781003728719-11

This chapter helps us complete our analysis and understanding of why the Philippines has underperformed. Here we develop the second main theme of the book. The standard view today among most academics, policymakers, and industrialists is that freedom of enterprise, trade, and investment (and the belief in efficacy of the marketplace allocating resources) is the most advantageous path to economic development, accompanied by the belief that budget deficits are "bad" (a necessary evil at times) for the economy because they cause inflation and crowd out the private sector. If they cannot be eliminated, at least they have to be minimized. Because tax collection is low and debt is viewed with suspicion, the result is a level of spending below what the country needs. The fear of larger fiscal deficits in the Philippines brings back memories of the debt crisis of the 1980s.

The fiscal deficit and public debt, the government's finances, as well as central bank operations in general, are arguably the most misunderstood areas in economics, even ahead of the role of education. The framework we provide in this chapter is factual, based on how most treasuries and central banks around the world operate today. We invite the Philippine government to understand what we call the realities of its monetary operations and use them wisely to contribute to the development of the country by at least providing all the public goods it needs, including infrastructure, education, health, and eliminating malnutrition.[2] It can be done. The administration aims at reducing the fiscal deficit to 3% of GDP by 2028, as stated in the Philippine Development Plan 2023–2028 (NEDA, 2023a). We will argue that this is a wrong target. The problem of the 1980s, apart from living in a monetarist policy regime, was the significant borrowing in US dollars.[3] The situation today is very different on both counts.[4] We doubt that what De Dios et al. (2021, pp. 25–28) describe, that is, the financial mismanagement during the years of crony capitalism during the Marcos Sr. years can happen today.[5]

Many of our ideas derive from Abba Lerner's (1943) notion *functional finance*, the idea that fiscal policy should be evaluated by what it does for the economy instead of by whether the budget is balanced or in deficit. Unfortunately, the fiscal and monetary history of the Philippines is plagued by mainstream ideas, and with the obsession to balance the budget, which have led to orthodox austerity.[6]

The key misunderstanding among most people is the belief that the government must raise taxes or borrow in order to spend. It arises from the following two misconceptions. The first one is thinking that the finances of a government are like those of a family or a company. Policymakers, and even the Philippine government officials in key departments, believe so. The reality cannot be further from the truth. Second, terms such as "deficit" (fiscal deficit) and "debt" (national debt) are misleading because they only represent one side of the double-entry accounting inherent in all payments. The deficit/debt is someone else's surplus/wealth.

To correctly understand the government's finances, we have to make two fundamental points. The first one is that discussions cannot start under the premise that "resources are scarce" when the term "resources" refers to money (a very misused term). This premise is factually incorrect. The Philippine (central) government is not financially constrained to the extent that it uses its own currency, pesos (fiat money—which has no intrinsic value), to make payments. This is not a resource and is not scarce.[7]

The second point is that (and much to the surprise of some) the Philippine government (like all governments today) makes payments by simply crediting bank accounts through electronic transfers. There is no physical money involved; it is just somebody authorizing a payment on a computer. This is done by the Federal Reserve in the United States, and by the Department of Budget and Management and the Bureau of Treasury in the Philippines. This is also factually correct, and it is how all modern economies operate. There is no financial constraint to this operation (electronic transfers).[8] Would anybody reject a transfer or a check from the Treasury?

These two points *ought to be* incontestable. Not acknowledging them has led to misunderstandings and questionable economic policies and statements.[9] To make it very clear: The Philippine government does not face a financial constraint like a household, and the term resource in economics refers to labor and capital (which naturally can be scarce), not to pesos (never scarce). Arguing otherwise is wrong, bad economics, and hurts the country. We also emphasize that our arguments in this chapter refer to the use of the domestic currency, the peso, in the Philippines. Incurring debt in a foreign currency is a different matter, as the foreign currency has to be earned to be repaid.

One important implication of the earlier points is that the Philippine government has given in and is happy to allow the private sector to take over some of its functions. This has led to a culture of public–private partnerships (the Philippines is not the only country where this has happened). Instead of building a strong and modern public sector that provides the services the country needs, it believes the private sector can do it and, in fact, it talks about private-sector-led development.

In what follows, we first summarize a series of widely spread fallacies about fiscal deficits and national debt. Then, we explain the monetary reality of the Philippines, what the Departments of Finance, and Budget and Management, as well as Treasury and BSP, actually do, and how they operate. We stress that there is also an administrative and legal reality, as well as self-imposed fiscal rules. The administrative processes that result constrain the government in many ways.

We complement this analysis with an empirical overview of the sectoral balances of the Philippines in Appendix 11. This shows that the fiscal position (mostly deficits) has a mirror image in the private sector (mostly surpluses). One cannot be true without the other. Appendix 11 provides a summary and explanation of the operations of the BSP and the Bureau of Treasury in 2020 in the context of the COVID-19 pandemic, a PHP 300 billion repurchase agreement. The T-accounts of the operation show that this was a very normal transaction between the two institutions. In fact, most Filipinos are completely unaware of the mechanics but have benefited from it.

11.2 Fallacies and Realities About the Fiscal Deficit and National Debt

The two points made in the previous section imply that the Philippine government can certainly fund all social programs and infrastructure the country needs because they require mostly pesos (some foreign currency to import capital goods). There is no financial constraint to do this (i.e., fund in pesos). We need to stress that this does not imply that the government can (or should) spend as if there is no tomorrow (more on this later), or that there might not be resource constraints. We are also very well aware that the Philippines is subject to the vagaries of the international capital flows, sometimes called "sudden stops." This situation may reduce the monetary and fiscal policy space for full employment. Moreover, as we argued in Chapter 3, the Philippines' growth rate is balance of payments constrained because of the need to obtain foreign income (dollars) to pay for its imports (see Vernengo and Pérez Caldentey, 2020). If markets do not trust the Philippines, the exchange rate will depreciate. This means that the Philippines does not have the same degree of monetary power (autonomy, sovereignty) that, for example, the United States or Japan enjoy. Our argument is that the Philippines has gone to the extreme of confusing its own currency with a "resource" (something scarce), of not understanding that its accounting does not follow the same rules and procedures as those of a family, of thinking it needs to collect taxes before it can spend, and, consequently, of not providing at an acceptable level essential public goods like infrastructure, education, or health, or eradicating children malnutrition.

Because of the two fundamental facts summarized earlier, we dismiss as incorrect a number of widely spread fallacies (or variants of them) that constrain governments:

- The government faces the same budget constraint as a household.
- Fiscal deficits (surpluses) are bad (good).
- Fiscal surpluses contribute to national saving.
- The fiscal outcome should be balanced over the economic cycle.
- Fiscal deficits drive up interest rates and crowd out private investment because they compete for scarce private saving.
- Fiscal deficits mean higher taxes in the future (see clarification later).
- Government spending is, by nature, inflationary.
- The government will run out of fiscal space (or money) if it overspends.
- Fiscal deficits lead to big government.

Instead, and following Lerner's (1943) principles of "functional finance," we argue the following factually correct statements:

- Government spending increases the nongovernment's income, peso for peso. Figure 11.1 shows the debits and credits of the four accounts affected when

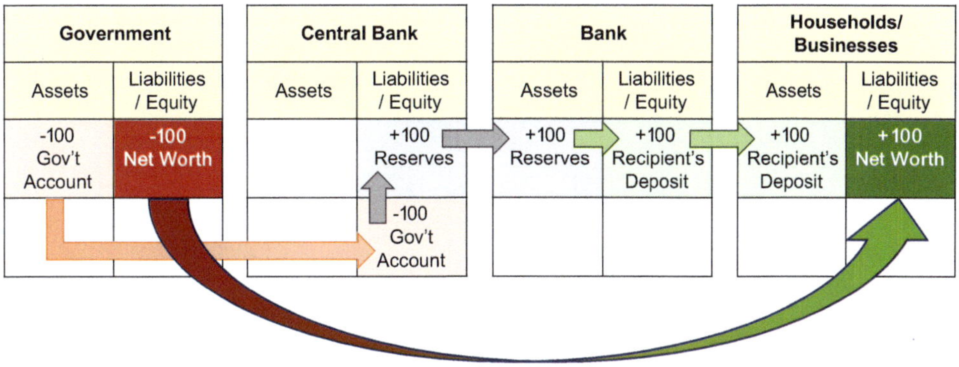

FIGURE 11.1 Bookkeeping: Government Deficit Directly Creates a Private Sector Surplus

Source: Authors

a government makes a payment to someone in the private sector: its own account, that of the central bank (the government's banker), a commercial bank, and the household or business recipient of the funds. It is worth noting that a government deficit increases banks' reserves held in accounts at the central bank (shown in the middle part of Figure 11.1).

- Government deficits raise private saving. Government deficits equal, peso for peso, nongovernment surpluses. A fiscal deficit is part of the private sector's aggregate profits, as reflected in the national accounts.[10] If the government did not spend at all, the net financial wealth of the non-government sector would be much smaller, and consequently, the economy would be much smaller. Many vital services would not exist. This is not a very appealing prospect.
- Government surpluses equal nongovernmental deficits. Government surpluses reduce nongovernment financial saving.
- The government cannot run out of its own money (pesos). The true constraint is our nation's resources, labor, and capital. Thus, there is no financial constraint, although there could be a resource constraint.
- The government's debt is the private sector's asset. The government issues debt to provide the nongovernment sector with a store of value (government debt provides a risk-free financial asset to strengthen nongovernment portfolios) and to manage interest rates instead. Philippine peso–denominated debt poses no solvency risk. The government cannot go broke, and its checks do not bounce.
- The government's banker is the Banko Sentral ng Pilipinas, which creates money (see later on this), *ex nihilo*.[11]
- Economies need money to function. Money can only be *created* (a better and more accurate term than *printed*) by either the banks granting a loan (the vast majority of money in circulation; loans create deposits) or by government spending (effectively, the central bank). (The Philippine sovereign government creates money only indirectly through mechanisms such as central bank

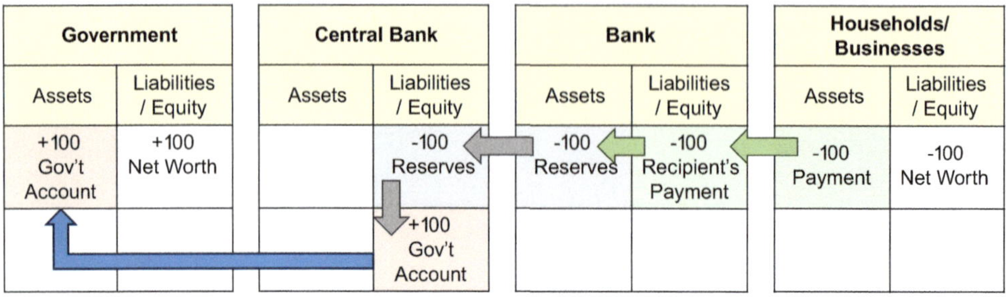

FIGURE 11.2 Bookkeeping: Households Pay Taxes

Source: Authors

actions to fund its services and programs.) This means that the government creates new money when it spends by drawing down its account at the BSP. This process leads to an increase in the *net* financial wealth of the private sector.

- To better understand the previous point, we need to understand money creation in a modern economy. We reiterate that this can only happen in one of two ways: when banks lend and when governments spend. When banks lend, however, they simultaneously create a matching asset and liability that, in effect, cancel each other out. There is no increase in the net financial wealth of the private sector when banks lend. In contrast, when governments spend, they create an asset for the private sector without a corresponding liability. The offset in accounting terms is an increase in the negative equity of the government. The result is an increase in the net financial wealth of the private sector, indeed, the only way this can happen (ignoring the rest of the world). Not only can the government create wealth for the private sector, but it also does so whenever it runs a deficit. It also provides a vehicle for us to store that wealth rather conveniently.
- The central bank cannot control the quantity of money. The latter is determined by borrower demand for bank credit. The central bank can control the cost of borrowing money overnight and can influence the quantity of money through monetary policy.[12]
- The Bangko Sentral ng Pilipinas (BSP) issues its own debt instrument to conduct open market operations. Government bonds are just a portfolio choice that we have to store some wealth as a risk-free asset. Bond sales drain central bank reserve balances, resulting in the BSP using its own debt instrument operations as an offset to achieve its interest rate target. This has nothing to do with saving (S) and investment (I) of the private sector.
- A responsible fiscal policy balances the economy, not the budget. The required balancing act is one that offsets the choice of the Philippine private sector to net save and/or net import—the real reason that the Philippine government ends up running sustained deficits over time (more on this later). Algebraically: $(G-T) \equiv (S-I) - CAB$, where G denotes government expenditures, T denotes taxes (so $(G-T)$ is the fiscal deficit if G is greater than T, and it is the fiscal surplus otherwise), S denotes saving, I denotes investment, and CAB is the current

account balance (in terms of credits minus debits). The symbol ≡ indicates that the relationship is an identity.

- The fiscal balance is largely determined by the economy's performance. The fiscal balance outcome is *not* discretionary. Consequently, trying to achieve a target (e.g., 3% of GDP) is not meaningful from an economic standpoint.
- Fiscal deficits push interest rates downward to zero, not upward. The reason that most people think that fiscal deficits raise interest rates is that they use the loanable funds framework, which only considers the bond sale, not the spending part of the complete operation. In reality, both spending and the bond sale affect the supply of reserve balances. This becomes clear later in Figures 11.2 and 11.3: Spending shifts the supply curve to the right, while the bond sale brings it back.
- *Good* fiscal deficits today create a stronger economy in the future. This will create more tax revenue, to the extent that deficits bring the economy closer to full employment (a good thing for the economy).
- To make payments, governments credit bank accounts using fiat money. Taxes are not, in practice, used for the government to make payments; that is, taxes do not "finance" government spending. The purpose of taxes is to destroy money previously created.[13] The process is shown in Figure 11.2, the reverse of that in Figure 11.1. Taxes, in reality, have other uses: (1) To create demand for the government's currency. Since people are required to pay taxes in the government's currency, they must earn and use it, ensuring its circulation and value. (2) To create non-inflationary fiscal space for the public sector to spend (i.e., take away spending capacity from the private sector). An unconstrained sovereign government can always utilize the available space to ensure aggregate demand is sufficient to maintain full employment and price stability. (3) To penalize "bads" like smoking or driving (pollution and congestion, respectively). and (4) to reduce inequalities.

As stated earlier, many people believe that the finances of the government are like those of a family. Consequently, they are not aware, for example, that many governments "make payments in advance" and that the government's payments create wealth in the private sector, peso for peso.[14] The reality is that before taxes can be collected or bonds be sold, governments must first spend money into the economy, or the central bank must provide reserves.[15] For example, government debt purchased by the private sector is paid with funds *previously provided* by the government or lent by the central bank. This should be obvious if one understands that a government deficit of, let's say, PHP 30 is the result of government spending PHP 100 and taxing the private sector PHP 70. The so-called government *deficit* of PHP 30 is, naturally, the *surplus* of the private sector, we insist, peso for peso. Next, the BSP (or treasury) issues bonds (which add to the national debt) for PHP 30. This leads us to the following points:

- How does the private sector pay for the bonds (PHP 30)? Operationally, the primary dealers finance their purchases of bonds at auctions in the repo market, mostly by using government bonds as collateral, while the newly issued bonds will likely serve as collateral for further credit creation in financial markets. All the private sector does is exchange these liquid funds for a promissory note (government bond). Naturally, these bonds constitute the private sector's wealth. Therefore, the government first transfers funds to the private sector in the form of a fiscal deficit and then offers it a risk-free asset (the bond) in exchange for the funds. This process and sequence do not induce inflation.[16]

- The government does not compete with the private sector for funds. The supply of funds is infinite: The central bank always stands ready to supply currency and reserves on demand to the commercial banking system at its announced target rate.
- Interest on bonds is paid the same way the government makes any other payments: by crediting accounts electronically. These interest payments constitute the disposable income of the private sector.
- Bonds are issued not to fund government expenditures but to prevent the BSP policy rate from going down to zero (and maintaining it within the corridor system—see later), because a budget deficit represents excess reserve balances in the banking system (where all payments of government and private sector are made). A government deficit, consequently, puts downward pressure (not upward, as is often argued) on interest rates.[17] The excess reserve balances (PHP 30 in the example) have to be mopped up. This is the role of bond issuance.[18] More precisely, sovereign bonds are not issued to finance spending but to destroy reserves created via fiscal operations that increase interbank market liquidity and thus lower interest rates beyond the level desired by the central bank.
- Since it is primary bond dealers who compete with each other and not with the government during bond auctions, and since spending pushes interest rates downward and shifts the reserve supply curve to the right, the "crowding out" argument (that the public sector displaces the private sector) is another fallacy.[19] Mainstream economists see government debt as "crowding out" the private sector by competing with private borrowers for the "available stock of loanable funds" (which don't exist) and thus driving up the interest rate. So in their view, excessive government spending adds to the demand for loanable funds and drive up interest rates.[20] By not understanding the accounting and operations involved in government spending/deficits, mainstream economists have wrongly classified them as an increase in the demand for loanable funds when, in fact, they increase the supply of reserves. Deficits crowd in private spending and investment by increasing private income.
- It should be clear that it is not the market that "controls" interest rates. As far back as 1947, Marriner S. Eccles, Chairman of the US Federal Reserve from 1934 to 1948, affirmed the following in a testimony before the Congress in 1947:

> If the Treasury has to finance a heavy deficit, the Reserve System creates the condition in the money market to enable the borrowing to be done, so

> that, in effect, the Reserve System indirectly finances the Treasury through the money market, and that is how the interest rates were stabilized as they were during the war, and as they will have to continue to be in the future. So, it is an illusion to think that to eliminate or to restrict the direct borrowing privilege reduces the amount of deficit financing. Or that the market controls the interest rate. Neither is true.
>
> *(Eccles, 1947)*

- The widespread belief that each Filipino "owes" about PHP 130,000 (the stock of debt was about PHP 16 trillion at the end of 2024) is fiction. To whom is this owed? If anything, it is the other way around: On average, each Filipino "owns" about PHP 130,000 in government securities. Government debt is simply the cumulative number of pesos issued by the BSP due to the government's fiscal operations, which domestic and foreign entities have saved over time as a financial asset.
- Deficits add to national saving (of the nongovernment sector): (1) Government sells, for example, PHP 100 treasuries (this becomes wealth of the private sector), and (2) government spends the PHP 100 it received from the sale of treasuries.

11.3 How Does the Bangko Sentral ng Pilipinas (BSP) Operate?

To understand why bonds are issued to prevent the BSP's policy rate from going down to zero, we provide the basics of how the corridor system of many central banks, including the BSP (since 2016), operates. We note that the BSP is prohibited by law (RA 7653 of 1993, amended by RA 11211 in 2019) from directly financing government deficits. According to the law, it cannot routinely buy government securities in the primary market (no direct lending), and that it cannot create money to cover fiscal shortfalls. As a consequence, the government must fund spending via taxes, *borrowing* from markets (through Treasury bills/bonds), or through foreign *borrowing*—we have already argued earlier that the government does not borrow. The mandate of the BSP is, exclusively, price stability. It does not have a development function.[21]

Most central banks today set interest rate targets or target ranges, necessarily, because of the flexibility in the quantity of central bank reserve balances (RBs), which are central bank liabilities that banks use to settle payments and, where applicable, meet regulatory requirements for liquid balances against their own liabilities. These are required on a daily basis to ensure functioning of the payments system and stability in wholesale funding markets. The BSP carries out daily operations using a corridor system to achieve its interest rate target. This policy rate target is the overnight reverse repurchase (RRP) facility rate. See Figure 11.3.[22]

In the corridor system, the central bank's "penalty rate" for borrowing from its standing facility (BSP calls it overnight lending facility rate) and the rate paid on

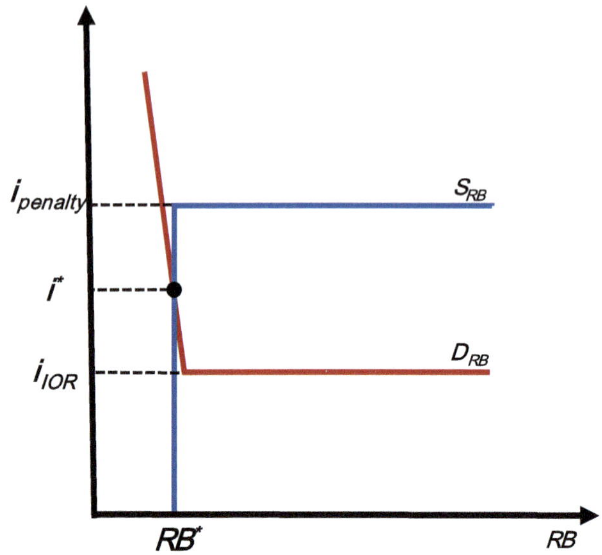

FIGURE 11.3 Corridor System for Central Bank Interest Rate Targeting

Note: RB is Reserve Balance; D_{RB} is the demand for RBs; S_{RB} is the supply of RBs; i^* is the interest rate target; $i_{penalty}$ is the penalty rate; i_{IOR} is the interest on reserves.

Source: Authors

reserves (RBs) (IOR—for "interest on reserves"—or zero for a central bank that does not pay IOR. BSP calls it overnight deposit facility rate) together set a corridor for the market interest rate to fluctuate within. The central bank then adds or drains RBs via open market operations, loans, and so on, to shift the vertical portion of the supply of RBs (S_{RB}) as it accommodates shifts in banks' demand for RBs (D_{RB}) at the CB's interest rate target (i*), or to offset changes to its own balance sheet that would otherwise alter the quantity of RBs and move the market rate away from i*. The quantity of RBs in the corridor system graph is an equilibrium (hence the "*" in RB*), while any quantity of RBs along the horizontal portion of D_{RB} achieves the target rate in the floor system.

It is also important to note that government spending, tax revenues, and bond sales in the domestic currency all occur on the central bank's balance sheet because the government's account is a liability of the central bank. From simple double-entry accounting, the financial flows into and out of the government's account will have the opposite effect on the quantity of RBs circulating. Table 11.1 shows the T-account entries for a government deficit and a government bond sale, respectively. Considering Table 11.1 and Figure 11.2 together, the deficit raises RBs, placing downward pressure on the market rate in the corridor system. The bond sale drains RBs and offsets the deficit's effect on the quantity of RBs; in the corridor system, the pressure on the market rate to fall is reversed.

TABLE 11.1 T-Accounts for Government Deficit and Bond Sale

	Government		*Central Bank*		*Banks*		*Dealers*		*Households*	
	A	*L/E*	*A*	*L/E*	*A*	*L/E*	*A*	*L/E*	*A*	*L/E*
(1) Government deficit	Acct @ CB (-)	Net Worth (-)		RBs (+) Govt Acct (-)	RBs (+)	HH Dep (+)			Dep (+)	Net Worth (+)
(2) Government bond sale	Acct @ CB (+)	Bonds (+)		RBs (-) Govt Acct (+)	RBs (-)	Dealer (Dep) (-)	Dep (-) Bonds (+)			

Note: A = assets; Acct @ CB = government account at the central bank on the government's assets; Dep = deposits; Gov Acct = government account at the central bank on the central bank's liabilities; HH = household; L/E = liabilities and equity; Net Worth = Assets − Liabilities; RB = reserve balance.

Source: Authors.

Even in normal times, the flows to and from the government due to spending, revenues, and bond sales are not perfectly timed. The corollary here is that when CBs finance the government, whether directly (primary market or direct loans) or indirectly (secondary market), they cannot do so without sterilizing these operations. Figure 11.4 shows these operations in the corridor system graph. Both direct and indirect central bank finance shift the SRB to the right. A central bank in a corridor system will need to respond by draining RBs to achieve the target rate, either issuing its own liabilities at a rate similar to its target rate or some combination of reducing its assets via sales or allowing its claims on the private sector to mature and not roll over.[23] There is no "printing money" or "monetization" because it is not operationally possible. See Appendix 11.

A final point relates to interest rates on domestic currency government debt being the yield curve for the risk-free rate, which is a benchmark from which markets price other financial assets. This means that interest rates on government debt are an integral part of the transmission of monetary policy. This is well known in principle, but the implications are usually not. A competitive, highly liquid market for government debt will price the yield curve mostly based on the central bank's current target rate and the market's expected path for the central bank's target rate. This is because sufficient funding liquidity (that is, ability to finance

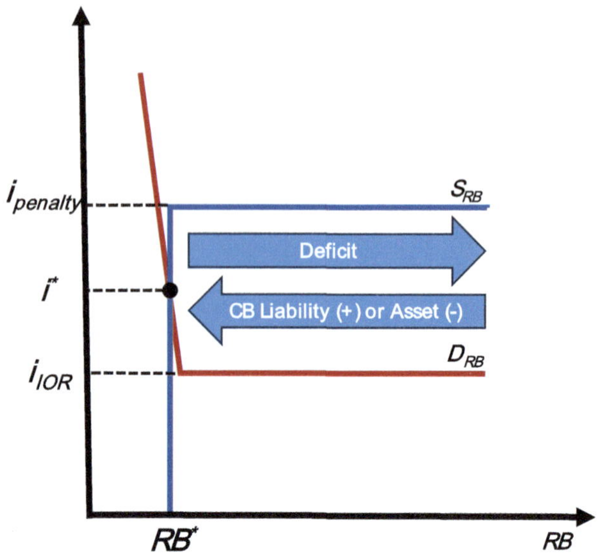

FIGURE 11.4 Sterilizing Central Bank Support of Government in the Corridor System

Note: *RB* is Reserve Balance; D_{RB} is the demand for RBs; S_{RB} is the supply of RBs; i^* is the interest rate target; $i_{penalty}$ is the penalty rate; i_{IOR} is the interest on reserves.

Source: Authors

and refinance asset positions) and market liquidity (ability to buy or sell quickly, in large quantities, and at low cost) in a competitive market bring the returns from holding the government bonds into line (again, mostly) with the borrowing costs of acquiring the funds to purchase them—namely, the current central bank target rate and its expected path. Where government debt markets are highly liquid, central banks enable this via at least an implicit support for markets and funding liquidity for achieving their interest rate targets (or target ranges), especially (or necessarily) where central banks' operations occur with a network of government bond dealers. Appendix 11 summarizes how the BSP authorized a PHP 300 billion repurchase agreement with the Bureau of Treasury in the context of the COVID-19 pandemic.

Given this discussion, it is important to reflect upon the fact that the United States, Japan, or Singapore have much higher debt-to-GDP ratios than the Philippines, and yet, interest rates do not skyrocket, and those economies do not seem to collapse. The reason? Officials in the corresponding departments of these nations understand their *monetary reality* and use it to achieve public purpose.

The earlier arguments are not to say that the Philippine Department of Finance and the BSP are making mistakes. Rather, they mean that officials from key departments (DOF, Budget, BSP, Treasury) ought to

- understand and acknowledge what they actually do, that is, the *monetary reality* that we have summarized;

- reconsider how they approach the budget and discard arguments that boil down to "we do not have money" (and stop considering money as a resource), which is wrong economics; and
- use the government finances wisely to propel the nation's full development.

Our arguments do not imply that the budget should be twice as large, or that the government can spend freely. We reiterate that we do not claim that the government can spend as if there is no tomorrow, and of course, we agree that spending has to be sensible. The capacity of the public sector matters. Rather, we argue thus:

- The Philippine government is in a position to spend "whatever is necessary" to bring the economy as close as possible to full employment and to provide the necessary public goods that the economy needs. By this we mean that the government does not have a financial constraint. Perhaps the budget approved for 2025 (PHP 6.3 trillion) meets this criterion. The limit to spending is the capacity of the government to spend and the achievement of full employment. Fiscal policy can generate inflation only if the economy is running at full productive capacity (and in the presence of a substantial increase in real wages). The private sector will benefit from an economy close to full employment, growth will accelerate, and the debt-to-GDP ratio will decline. Beyond this point, inflation will show up. The solution to cool the economy is to tax.[24]
- It is true that from an "accounting point of view" (the unfortunate conventional thinking), a fiscal deficit occurs when the government spends more into the economy (money created) than it receives in taxation (money destroyed). The economic intuition is that this happens whenever the private sector seeks to net save or net import (or some combination). This means that a fiscal deficit arises ultimately from choices made within the nongovernment sector, rather than from (profligate) government spending. As we saw earlier: $(G-T)\equiv(S-I)-CAB$. The real problem of an economy (what leads to crises) is when the private sector balance goes into deficit. The simplest way to understand the implication of this identity is to assume that $CAB=0$: The only way for the private sector to run a surplus is if the government runs a fiscal deficit. Budget surpluses imply that households have to sell securities so that they can pay for their taxes. Their net financial assets and saving go down by the amount of the surplus. The relationship between the three sectors (government, domestic private, and external) is elaborated upon in Appendix 11.
- The earlier sectoral financial balances accounting identity also implies that statements like "we need to live within our means" is an accounting impossibility for the Philippines, given that the private sector is both a net saver and a net importer at the same time.
- Thinking that taxes at PHP 4.6 trillion cover or support just 73% of total government spending (PHP 6.3 trillion) and that, therefore, the government will have to "generate more resources" to cover the difference up to PHP 6.3 trillion is

incorrect. The government does not need "private sector money" in order to spend, and the Department of Finance should not think in terms of matching taxes and government expenditure. The correct way to state the situation is to say that the PHP 6.3 trillion will be financed out of (1) taxes (PHP 4.6 trillion), plus (2) new bonds, plus (3) the change in the monetary base. We are certain that the difference of PHP 1.7 trillion (fiscal deficit) will be, ex post, identical to the sum of the change in the stock of public debt plus the change in the monetary base (the government's net position with respect to the banking sector).[25] Algebraically: $(G-T) \equiv \Delta B + \Delta M$, where G denotes government expenditures, T is taxes, ΔB is the increase in treasuries (bonds), and ΔM is the increase in base money.[26] The symbol Δ indicates a change in the corresponding variable between two periods, and the symbol $\equiv$ indicates that the relationship is an identity. As we said earlier, currency and reserves are supplied on demand by the central bank demand at an announced rate in a corridor system. Therefore, while the expression is definitionally correct, the relative sizes of ΔB and ΔM are decided by the private sector. Again, monetization is always sterilized. This expression is clearly an accounting identity and not a budget constraint, as it is sometimes misrepresented by writing it as $(G-T) - \Delta M \equiv \Delta B$ to argue that in order to sustain G, the government must issue securities. Note that this expression, apart from being an ex post accounting identity, can be written as $(G-T) - \Delta M \equiv \Delta B + \Delta M^U$, where ΔM^U denotes the unwarranted cash balances that appear as excess reserves in the banking system, clearly showing the possibility that there might be excess reserve balances in the banking system. Of course, these two components are the nongovernment sector surplus (more precisely, the net increase in holdings of financial assets [saving] of the nongovernment sector). Algebraically: $(G-T) \equiv (S-I) - CAB \equiv \Delta B + \Delta M$. The interpretation of these accounting identities is that, given private sector decisions (spending, saving, trade flows), the government can allow its balance to adjust to whatever magnitude is required to maintain full employment and price stability. For example, if $CAB < 0$ and $(S-I) > 0$, the drain on aggregate demand would require the government to run a deficit $(G-T) > 0$ of sufficient size to ensure that total spending is sufficient to absorb the real productive capacity available in the economy. Of course, if the nongovernment sector does not want to net save, it will then increase spending, tax revenue will increase, and there will be no budget deficit.[27]

The real constraint the Philippines faces is of a very different nature: It is the widespread lack of understanding of the nation's monetary reality. A proper understanding would provide the necessary link with the real economy, the drivers of growth and development, that is, the need to transform the economy. The government needs to spend on the key areas that the country urgently needs to transform the economy, as discussed earlier. Government finances can play a decisive role in the development of the nation (a budget deficit is an injection into the economy; a surplus is a leakage) if its mechanics are properly understood.

To reiterate, we argue that the Philippine government is not financially constrained. We can address malnutrition, poor infrastructure and housing, health, and basic education without any financial problems. There could be a resource constraint, though. Providing all these public goods is the role of a good government. The provision of these public goods should not be under the sphere of the private sector. These goods contribute to making an egalitarian society: Children of all classes must receive outstanding public education and health. This is what the governments of today's advanced nations did very early on in their development journey. Certainly, we do not oppose private education and privately provided healthcare for those who can afford it. What we stress is that the government can financially afford to provide these two essential public services to all Filipinos. We learned in 2025 that the Philippine Department of Education had estimated that the country has a shortage of 165,000 classrooms and claimed that the cost of building classrooms increases as population increases. The truth is that when the government announces in its budget that it will spend PHP 100 million, for example, on a new project, that figure does not reflect a cost. The real cost of any program is the extra real resources that the program requires for its implementation. For example, if the government were to build news classrooms, the real costs of the program would be the new materials needed and the extra capital equipment that the companies and workers contracted would use. In other words, government programs have to be appraised by how they use real resources, rather than in terms of the nominal money values involved.

A final point is that FDI (an objective of the government) comes to countries with good infrastructure and human capital. FDI inflows are not driven by lower fiscal deficits.

11.4 Public–Private Partnerships?

We close this chapter by making a reference to the increasing appeal to public–private partnerships (PPPs). PPPS have become popular in developing countries in recent times for the provision of essential public goods. People have been led to believe that their governments cannot undertake certain infrastructure projects because they do not have the capabilities (poor management and delivery) or because they lack the financial resources. In our view, PPPs are poor development advice because they often have a clear political motivation: the privatization of public services. The advice comes from the perennial mantra that PPPs address the limited funding resources for local infrastructure or development projects of the public sector. However, sovereign governments like that of the Philippines do not have limited funding resources because these are set in peso, the national currency. They may have other constraints, such as a lack of know-how, but this is a problem for both the public and the private sectors in most developing countries.

If lack of government know-how is the problem in a middle-income country like the Philippines (is it really?), the solution should be to expedite learning by the government to acquire the necessary capabilities to design and manage these projects, especially in areas such as education and health, which are the cornerstones of society's equality. There might be a reasonable rationale for the government to invite the private sector to contribute to the provision of public goods, for example, an urgent need to build classrooms or housing. Even in this case, it will not be a question of lack of funding, and one would have to pay attention to the conditions stipulated in the PPP contract.

What is the evidence about PPPs? We ask the government to read a report by the European Public Service Union and the European Network on Debt and Development that summarizes well the pitfalls of PPPs (https://www.epsu.org/sites/default/files/article/files/PPPs_EN.pdf). As the report indicates, (1) PPPs do not bring new money—they create hidden debt. (2) Private finance costs more than government borrowing. (3) Public authorities still bear the ultimate risk of project failure. (4) PPPs don't guarantee better value for money. (5) Efficiency gains and design innovation can result in corner-cutting. (6) PPPs do not guarantee projects being on time or on budget. (vii) PPP deals are opaque and can contribute to corruption. And (7) PPPs distort public policy priorities and force publicly run services to cut costs.

Notes

1 The interview was aired in the CBS program *60 minutes* on March 15, 2009. Video: https://www.youtube.com/watch?v=odPfHY4ekHA. Watch 7′57″ to 8′15″.

2 These ideas were presented and discussed at the workshop "Pathways to Progress: Transforming the Philippine Economy" held at the Philippine House of Representatives (organized by the Congressional Policy Budget Research Department) on January 21–22, 2025. Officials from departments such as finance or budget present at the workshop agreed that what this chapter describes (the monetary reality of the Philippines) is correct. They expressed concerns, however, about what they labeled "perceptions" (e.g., a larger budget might be associated with a corrupt government; asked if the private sector is more efficient delivering public goods), as well as about the "influence of the rating agencies" (e.g., credit downgrading resulting from running fiscal deficits), but not about the content (veracity) of our arguments. Despite explaining to them that the arguments behind their fears are largely incorrect, they seemed to prefer the *status quo* and continue doing what they have done for years.

3 We call the reader's attention to the analysis of Punongbayan and De Dios (2025), where they conclude that the debt crisis of the 1980s had a significant long-run impact on the country's growth trajectory. It is important to stress that borrowings were in US dollars. Surely, there was mismanagement and corruption, but the key point is that debt was in a foreign currency.

4 This sentiment was still in vogue in the early 2000s. Gochoco-Bautista and Canlas (2003), for example, argued that inflation in the Philippines up to 1990 was linked to external shocks and excessive peso printing in order to finance government budget deficits. This, in turn, caused the peso to depreciate, even in a fixed currency-exchange rate system. For most of the 1990s, inflation was successfully controlled,

and the authors hinted that central bank independence from national government enabled it to respond more effectively to external shocks and excessive government spending. Likewise, Sicat and Abdula (2003) saw the need for more effective fiscal management to correct perennial budget deficits. They saw these deficits as a major cause of previous bouts of double-digit inflation and peso depreciation. Additionally, they called for more effective revenue-generating programs through stronger tax administration and privatization.

5 The unfortunate case of corruption that surfaced in late 2025 is of very different nature.

6 There are exceptions to this thinking. In 1950, President Quirino (1948–1953) appointed Salvador Araneta as Secretary of Economic Coordination. Araneta defended import substitution, industrial policy, and bold deficit financing in order to eradicate unemployment (see Chapter 2). Araneta criticized those who thought that a large budget deficit would cause inflation and the need to balance the budget (Takagi, 2016, Chapter 4). It is worth quoting him: "There is no choice in the matter. Either we keep our present timid policy of economic development which will increase in intensity our unemployment problem and our peace and order problem, or we courageously decide for a policy or full employment and maximum and rapid development of our land and natural resources which can only be achieved with a huge program of financing" (Takagi, 2016, p. 111). And further: "[W]e will not be able to stimulate private initiative and the government will not be in a position to attend to the building of roads, irrigation systems, hydroelectric projects and basic industries at the rate commensurate with our ever increasing needs" (Takagi, 2016, p. 116). We have not found any policymaker in recent times who has argued in these terms. Unfortunately, Araneta lost the initial intellectual battle over deficit spending to central bank governor Cuaderno and resigned in 1952. As we mentioned in Chapter 2, he was reappointed in 1954 by President Magsaysay and then implemented his deficit spending policy.

7 Under the gold standard, banknotes were effectively debt securities because the central bank was obligated to convert those securities into gold at the request of the banknote holders. Under the gold standard, money was debt, and it was right to classify it as such. This is not the case today with fiat money. What sense does it make to talk about debt? Central banks have no obligation to convert the money they issue into other forms of value (gold). Money does not represent an obligation to anyone, and therefore, according to accounting rules, it is a liability but not a debt. All debt is a liability, but not all liabilities are debt. Currency is an asset to the households and firms that hold it because they can exchange their currency for valuable goods and services. But currency is a liability to the central bank that issues it, a promise to stand behind the currency's value in the future.

8 It is true, though, that countries have self-imposed laws according to which, for example, the government cannot run an overdraft. As we shall see later, this does not affect our arguments. The point remains that the government will make electronic transfers (or issue checks) to make payments, and that these transfers will occur *even without* taxes being collected.

9 An article in the prestigious British newspaper *The Guardian* ("Bad economics at the BBC enabled Tory austerity and its aftermath—and it knows as much," James Meadway, *The Guardian*) in 2023 claimed that bad economics by the British Broadcasting Company (BBC), the reputed British television company, enabled Tory austerity and its aftermath. A BBC internal review noted that too many journalists do not get "basic economics," with a negative effect on UK politics. The review referred to taxation, public spending, government borrowing, and debt output. Poor information is particularly serious when it comes to reporting on the central political issue of government debt, with some journalists apparently instinctively believing that all debt

is inherently bad. The result is that journalists very often frame policy choices, such as making cuts to spending, as if they were decisions of necessity. The reality of so-called national debt is very different from how it is reported and assessed on TV and newspapers, and even by some economists and government officials. The review of the BBC's reporting on government spending and debt is welcome because it serves as an example to countries like ours.

10 It is not difficult to show that aggregate corporate profits = entrepreneurs' consumption + entrepreneurs' investment – workers' savings + trade balance + fiscal balance. Workers' savings are minimal in the Philippines. The last two terms, trade balance and fiscal balance, are "positive" with a surplus and a deficit, respectively. While this equation is true by definition, it is totally missed by the government and the private sector. The equation indicates that total profits that owners of capital collectively receive are equal to the right-hand side of the equation. The relationship highlights the importance of the trade surplus and the government deficit: They enable capitalists to earn profits in excess of their own expenditures and private investment. In the case of a trade surplus, extra profits come from the excess of national income over domestic expenditure due to a surplus of export earnings over import spending. This implies that there is a rational basis for countries' efforts to achieve and maintain trade surpluses, as these tend to boost the profits of domestic firms (holding other factors constant). A fiscal deficit is expansionary because it is equivalent to a private sector surplus with the government. Therefore, deficits provide an increased capacity for entrepreneurs to realize their production plans and sell output as they expand the total aggregate demand in the economy. A fiscal surplus, on the other hand, leads to reduced profits. With a fiscal surplus, aggregate spending falls, which reduces the revenue that firms receive. Moreover, if the surplus is achieved with increased business tax rates, then the firms have lower after-tax profits.

11 The analogy to this is the points that appear in a stadium scoreboard when a team scores. Does anybody know where the stadium got the points from? Of course not. The stadium (or its managers) does not have a box with points. They are simply added, and they show up in the electronic board. This is what central banks do.

12 Mainstream analyses take the view that central banks have it in their power to initiate exogenous changes in the nominal supply of money. This view maintains that monetary change originates in changes in the high-powered base, which allegedly are under the control of the central bank. Following the post-Keynesian endogenous money theory (Moore, 1988), we contend that the supply of credit money is endogenous and responds to changes in the demand for bank credit. Central bank open-market operations affect how required reserves are supplied between borrowed and nonborrowed reserves, rather than the total volume of reserves that is endogenously determined. This view holds that central banks have the ability to set exogenously the supply price of the money market, but not the quantity of credit money.

Key points from McLeay et al. (2014) on this: (a) Whenever a bank makes a loan, it simultaneously creates a matching deposit in the borrower's bank account, thereby creating new money. (b) When a commercial bank issues a loan, it does not hand out existing money—it creates a deposit in the borrower's account. That deposit is new money. This is called endogenous money creation. (c) The central bank creates central bank money (also known as base money), which includes physical cash and reserves held by commercial banks at the central bank. (d) The central bank influences the amount of money created by banks through interest rates and regulations, but it does not directly control the money supply. And (e) Many textbooks (and people) mistakenly believe banks lend out deposits or act purely as intermediaries. The Bank of England explicitly stated that this is incorrect: "[T]he reality of how money is created today differs from the description found in some economics textbooks."

13 The processes of government spending and taxation are totally separate in practice. It is very important to understand that spending creates the money up front that is later destroyed via taxation. Technically, future taxation flows are the collateral that supports the government's ability to draw down on its sovereign line of credit at the BSP when it spends.

14 A point of clarification since we argued that governments cannot run an overdraft or these are cleared very quickly. This, technically, would mean that it is possible to always spend first and receive bond sales proceeds or tax revenues later in the day to clear the overdraft. If the government receives an overdraft, the central bank will pay interest on reserves, and this situation will reduce remittances in kind to the government (since the central bank's profits are lower due to the payment of interest on reserves), so the government still effectively pays interest. The interest rate here is a policy variable. If instead the government issues T-bills, the interest on these will arbitrage with the central target rate. So regardless of the case, the government will pay the interest, and the rate will be a policy variable. There is no loanable funds market. There is no market setting the rates. That is what matters. In the real world, whether spending comes first or not, the government can always run deficits, there will always be interest whether bonds are sold or not (unless there is a zero-interest-rate policy), and the interest rate will always be a policy variable.

15 In the real world, if the government has limited itself from drawing its account at the central bank below zero, then it will need to sell bonds or receive tax revenue before it spends. The exception would be if it were sitting on some huge balance in its reserve account. Then it could draw down without tax revenues or bond sales. But even in this case, how did it acquire this huge balance? Likely through previous surplus or bond sales. In other words, operationally, if the government allowed itself to stop issuing bonds and get an overdraft in its accounts at the central bank, the latter would have to sell its own liabilities, sell assets, or pay interest on reserves to achieve the interest rate target. This tells us that the operational purpose of bond sales is to support the interest rate target of a central bank and a government that issue its own currency since it doesn't need the proceeds from the bond sales in an operational sense. However, the government might need the proceeds in the legal sense, given the self-imposed limit to no overdraft from the central bank.

16 Despite this, many people still link inflation to the growth of the money supply as in the old monetarist system (the link between money demand, price level, and real output), where it was also thought that the central bank could control the money supply. A central tenet of this doctrine is that demand for money is stable: Any increase in the money supply will inevitably be spent on goods rather than stored as savings. Another is that there are predictable "lags" between monetary expansion, the resulting boost in output, and the eventual increase in prices. All this was abandoned decades ago. Central banks learned the lesson in the 1980s, when, in line with monetarist doctrine, they tried to control the aggregate money supply. Measuring—let alone managing—the total quantity of money proved impossible, partly because private banks create money "endogenously" whenever they offer loans. Thus, in reality, the money supply may follow demand, not government-decreed supply. Recognizing this, central banks abandoned the use of monetary aggregates and instead relied on adjusting short-term interest rates as an indirect way of controlling prices. Unfortunately, many people still believe that the root cause of inflation is always a government-induced increase in the money supply.

17 Downward pressure on interest rates occurs on any day when spending is greater than the combination of revenues and receipts from bond sales. Technically, though, whether there is downward pressure would depend on the net of this plus what else

is happening in the central bank balance sheet, and also whether there is a shift in the demand for reserve balances for whatever reason on the same day.

18 In reality, terms such as "monetization" or "printing money" are far from reality. See Appendix 11 and Felipe and Fullwiler (2021).

19 In the Philippines, a Government Securities Eligible Dealer (GSED) is an SEC-licensed securities dealer belonging to a service industry supervised/regulated by the government (Securities and Exchange Commission, Bangko Sentral ng Pilipinas, or Insurance Commission) which has met the (a) PHP 100 million unimpaired capital and surplus account, (b) has the statutory ratios prescribed for the industry, and (c) has the infrastructure for an electronic interface with the Automated Debt Auction Processing System (ADAPS) and the official Registry of Scripless Securities (RoSS) both of the Bureau of the Treasury (BTr) using Bridge Information Systems (BIS) and acknowledged by the BTr as eligible to participate in the primary auction of government securities. Being a dealer is a privilege. To keep the privilege, the institution needs to bid their portion of an auction. The privilege is that it (being a primary dealer) guarantees a profitable business model because now its cost of funds will always be, at most, the central bank target rate.

As of November 2024, these ware the primary dealers in the Philippines: (a) *Government securities:* Australia and New Zealand Banking Group Limited; Asia United Bank; BDO Capital and Investment Corporation; Banco De Oro Unibank Inc.; BDO Private Bank Inc.; Bank of the Philippine Islands; BPI-Capital Corporation; JPMorgan Chase Bank; China Banking Corporation; Citibank N. A.; Philippine Bank of Communications; CTBC Bank (Philippines) Corporation; Development Bank of the Philippines; Deutsche Bank AG; East West Banking Corporation; The Hongkong and Shanghai Banking Corporation Ltd.; ING Banking; Malayan Bank Savings and Mortgage; Maybank Philippines Inc.; Metropolitan Bank and Trust Company; Bank of Commerce; Philippine Veterans Bank; Philippine National Bank; Philippine Business Bank; Rizal Commercial Banking Corporation; Standard Chartered Bank; Security Bank and Trust Company; Sterling Bank of Asia Inc.; Land Bank of the Philippines; Union Bank of the Philippines; BONDS.PH; China Bank Savings Corporation; Bank of China Limited, Manila Branch. (b) *Market makers:* Banco de Oro Universal Bank; Bank of the Philippine Islands; China Banking Corporation; Citibank N. A.; Development Bank of the Philippines; Land Bank of the Philippines; Philippine National Bank; Metropolitan Bank and Trust Company; Security Bank and Trust Company; Standard Chartered Bank.

20 As an example, current interest rates are lower than they were 25 years ago, but in the meantime, US public debt (much larger than that of the Philippines) has increased from USD 6 trillion to a "staggering" USD 36 trillion! If the fairy tales we are told by mainstream economists were true, interest rates should have exploded in the last two or three decades.

21 This is not different from many other central banks. In recent decades, the new conventional policy wisdom has been that independent central banks should set monetary policy. During the last decades, many governments have changed laws under the influence of international finance to legislate central bank independence from governments of the day, especially the executive and legislative branches. Meanwhile, most central banks have come to equate financial stability with price stability as "inflation targeting." With interest rate management as their primary policy tool, central banks may raise interest rates in anticipation of inflation, despite its often-adverse consequences for growth, income, and employment. Such contractionary effects have reduced wages and jobs worldwide. Only a few, mainly large developed economies, have other priorities, such as growth or employment.

22 This also means that the BSP (like all central banks) cannot control the quantity of money. It can control the cost of money and can "influence" the quantity of money through monetary policy.

23 One important clarification: The commercial banking system can experience excess reserve balances not just as a result of a fiscal deficit. This can be the result of any addition to central bank assets or any reduction in central bank liabilities. Or the demand for reserves can shift leftward with no change in the central bank balance sheet, which would again be excess reserve balance.

24 Naturally, inflation may appear before reaching full employment as a result of supply-side bottlenecks. We caution the reader against simplistic explanations of inflation that quickly blame monetary expansion. A good example is Zimbabwe's hyperinflation case in the early 2000s. Hyperinflation in the African country was primarily driven by a severe contraction in the country's productive capacity, rather than by fiscal deficits or monetary expansion. The government's land reform program in the early 2000s that aimed to redistribute land from White commercial farmers to Black Zimbabweans led to a significant decline in agricultural output. The new landowners often lacked the experience and resources to maintain previous production levels, resulting in a sharp drop in food production. This agricultural collapse, in turn, affected other sectors, leading to a broader economic downturn. It is true that Zimbabwe's central bank increased the money supply during this period. However, this action was a response to the economic crisis, not its root cause. Hyperinflation was a consequence of the supply-side shock, and the monetary expansion was an attempt to address the resulting economic challenges. Therefore, attributing the hyperinflation solely to money printing overlooks the underlying structural issues that precipitated the crisis.

25 We say *ex post* because many people think of the relationship between government spending, taxes, the change in the stock of debt and the change in the monetary base as an *ex ante* financial constraint on government. This is incorrect. It is just an accounting identity that tells us *ex post* what the changes in the financial aggregates are as a result of discretionary go0vernment policy choices and the state of the economy.

26 We have tried to get estimates of both ΔB and ΔM to match $(G-T)$, but it has not been possible. Our intuition is that ΔM is a very small component.

27 We are aware that some economists write the identity as $I \equiv S+(T-G)-CAB$. Their causal interpretation is that private saving, government saving, and international saving "finance" investment (e.g., De Dios et al., 2021, pp. 38–39). This view argues that a government deficit is financed by private saving, leaving less financing available for firms' investment spending. In our view, this interpretation is questionable. The reason is that while *saving* (S) is a residual of income that involves changes in net financial assets (and by the way, *what* and *where* is this saving?), *financing* is a gross flow that does not involves changes in net financial assets. The sector financial balances view that we favor argues that a government deficit is about net financial assets of the of the nongovernment sector, not about financing. In the accounting of a government deficit (a decrease in its net worth), households receive a payment (income, an increase in net worth). This represents a change in net financial assets. For the household, the transfer from the government is an increase in income, and keeping consumption and taxes constant, this translates into an increase in (household) saving. Summing up, in the sector financial balances view, $(S-I)\uparrow +(T-G)\downarrow -CAB \equiv 0$, that is, government deficit created a private sector surplus; while under the saving finances investment view, as $I \equiv S\uparrow +(T-G)\downarrow -CAB$, that is, government ran a deficit, private saving increased. Paradoxically, this view shows two things: (a) that investment remains the same and (b) that the government deficit does not reduce private saving. We insist that this view is questionable.

APPENDIX 11

Understanding Sector Financial Balances

We made references to the sector financial balances (SFBs) and their interpretation in the main text. Here we elaborate and show them with numerical values.

From basic accounting principles, one person's spending is another person's income. Applying this to an economy, financial flows comprise a closed system. It is not possible, for instance, for every country to have a current account surplus; if one country has a current account surplus, then at least one other country has a current account deficit. Equivalently, if one sector of an economy has a surplus, at least one other sector must be in deficit.

The following simple identities define the SFBs and their flow-of-funds-based relationships to one another:[1]

Domestic private balance ≡ household sector balance + firm sector balance + financial sector balance (1)

Government balance ≡ tax revenues (T) – government spending, including debt service (G) (2)

Capital account balance ≡ –current account balance (CAB) (3)

Domestic private balance ($S - I$) + government sector balance ($T - G$) – current account balance (CAB) (= –capital account balance) ≡ 0 (4)

Table A11.1 provides the data corresponding to the three sectoral balances of the Philippine economy, from the first quarter of 2108 (2018 Q1) to the third quarter of 2024 (2024 Q3).

Figure A11.1 shows SFBs for the Philippines using Equation (4) and the data in Table A11.1. As Equation (4) shows, the sum of the sector financial balances is 0 (financial flows are a closed system); thus, the three SFBs generate mirror images above and below 0 in every quarter in the figure. In most quarters during the period covered, the Philippines has run fiscal and current account deficits. The mirror

TABLE A11.1 The Three Sectoral Balances (% of GDP), Q1 2018–Q3 2024

Period	*Domestic Private Savings*	*Fiscal Balance*	*Current Account Balance*
2018-Q1	2.71	−3.61	−0.90
2018-Q2	−2.98	−0.87	−3.84
2018-Q3	1.70	−4.21	−2.51
2018-Q4	0.83	−3.65	−2.82
2019-Q1	−0.02	−2.02	−2.04
2019-Q2	−1.79	0.95	−0.84
2019-Q3	5.27	−5.48	−0.21
2019-Q4	6.55	−6.87	−0.32
2020-Q1	2.01	−1.94	0.07
2020-Q2	17.84	−12.45	6.39
2020-Q3	12.31	−7.71	3.60
2020-Q4	13.18	−10.20	2.98
2021-Q1	7.50	−7.53	−0.03
2021-Q2	7.25	−8.50	−1.25
2021-Q3	8.47	−9.56	−1.09
2021-Q4	6.93	−10.20	−3.27
2022-Q1	2.59	−6.87	−4.28
2022-Q2	−0.50	−7.16	−7.66
2022-Q3	0.38	−7.10	−6.72
2022-Q4	10.74	−10.78	−0.04
2023-Q1	1.12	−5.52	−4.40
2023-Q2	1.51	−5.39	−3.88
2023-Q3	6.38	−8.54	−2.16
2023-Q4	8.20	−8.98	−0.78
2024-Q1	3.41	−5.25	−1.85
2024-Q2	1.49	−6.16	−4.67
2024-Q3	1.51	−6.70	−5.19

Note: The domestic private sector balance (S-I) is calculated residually as the sum of the other components, that is, (S − I) = (G − T) + CAB.

Source: Authors' calculations based on fiscal balances data from the Republic of the Philippines, Bureau of the Treasury (https://www.treasury.gov.ph/wp-content/uploads/2025/09/COR_Summary_Annual_1986-2024.xlsx), balance of payments data from the Bangko Sentral ng Pilipinas (https://www.bsp.gov.ph/SitePages/Statistics/External.aspx?TabId=1), GDP data from the Philippine Statistics Authority (https://openstat.psa.gov.ph/Database/Economic-Accounts/National-Accounts-of-the-Philippines/Annual-National-Accounts).

image tends to be domestic private sector surpluses. This is why the Philippine economy is stable, thanks to the fiscal deficits. What else does this mean? It means that the private sector is both a net saver and a net importer. That is "our" (private sector) choice and a feature of the Philippine economy, at least over the period covered. In such a scenario, the government will always run a deficit. It has to; otherwise, neither the accounts nor the economy will be in balance. Thus, if we want to minimize the net borrowing of the government, one of two things has to change: The private sector has to save less/spend more or consume less/produce more.

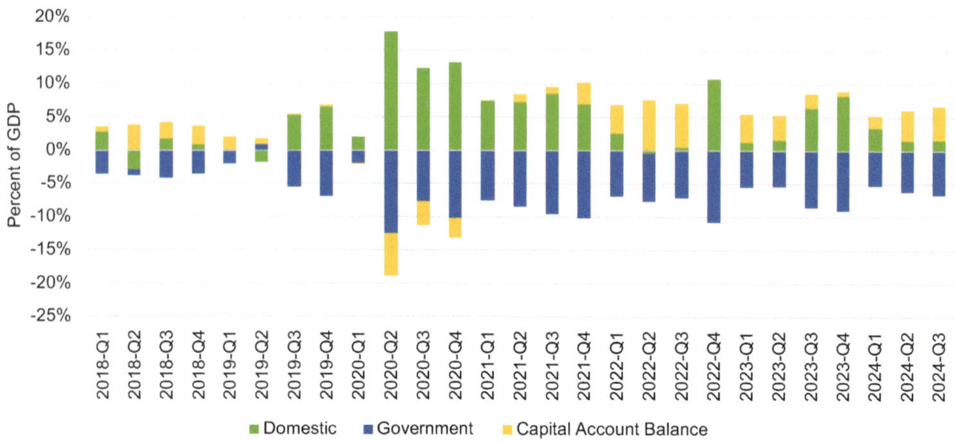

FIGURE A11.1 Sectoral Financial Balances, Philippines, Q1 2018–Q3 2024

Source: Authors' calculations based on fiscal balances data from the Republic of the Philippines, Bureau of the Treasury (https://www.treasury.gov.ph/wp-content/uploads/2025/09/COR_Summary_Annual_1986-2024.xlsx), balance of payments data from the Bangko Sentral ng Pilipinas (https://www.bsp.gov.ph/SitePages/Statistics/External.aspx?TabId=1), GDP data from the Philippines Statistics Authority (https://openstat.psa.gov.ph/Database/Economic-Accounts/National-Accounts-of-the-Philippines/Annual-National-Accounts)

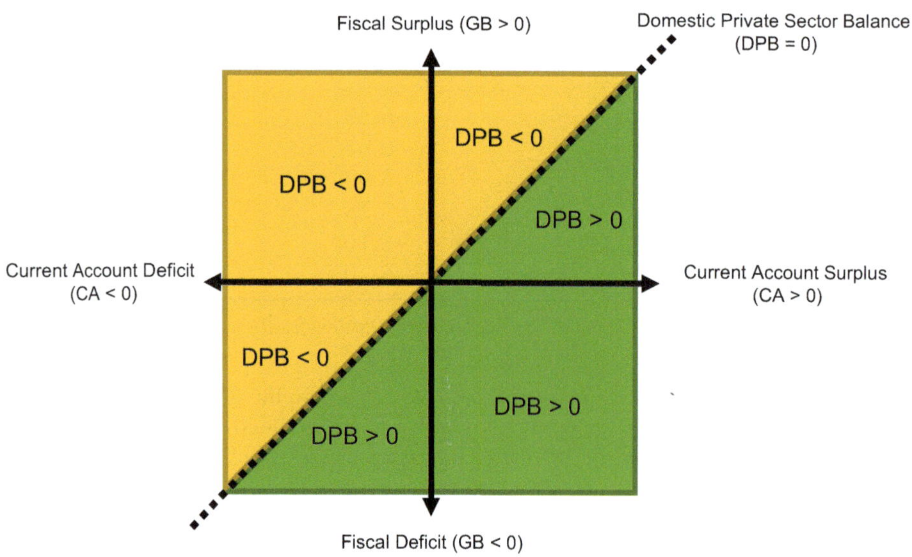

FIGURE A11.2 Sector Financial Balances Map

Notes: CA = current account balance, DPB = domestic private balance, GB = government balance

Source: Authors

An additional useful way to visualize the inherent interactions of the SFBs is shown in Figure A11.2, which presents two axes and a bisecting line that together generate the sector financial balances map (SFBM). The horizontal axis is the current account balance (CAB), and the vertical axis is the government balance (GB). The diagonal dotted line bisects the graph through the origin—the domestic private balance (DPB)—which is 0 at every point along this line. For the SFBM, it is useful to substitute the negative of the current account balance from Equation (3) into Equation (4) and then rearrange as follows:

$$\textbf{Domestic private balance } (S - I) \equiv \textbf{current account balance} - \textbf{government sector balance } (T - G) \tag{5}$$

Using the abbreviations in the figure, Equation (5) becomes:

$$\textbf{DPB} \equiv \textbf{CA} - \textbf{GB} \tag{6}$$

Figure A11.2 visually represents the logic of Equations (5) and (6): The area to the northwest of the DPB = 0 line is where DPB < 0, since CA < GB, while the area to the southeast of DPB = 0 is where DPB > 0, since CA > GB.

Figure A11.3 plots the quarterly SFBs of the Philippines for the period 2020 Q1–2024 Q3 in the SFBM. The figure shows that, for most periods, the Philippines

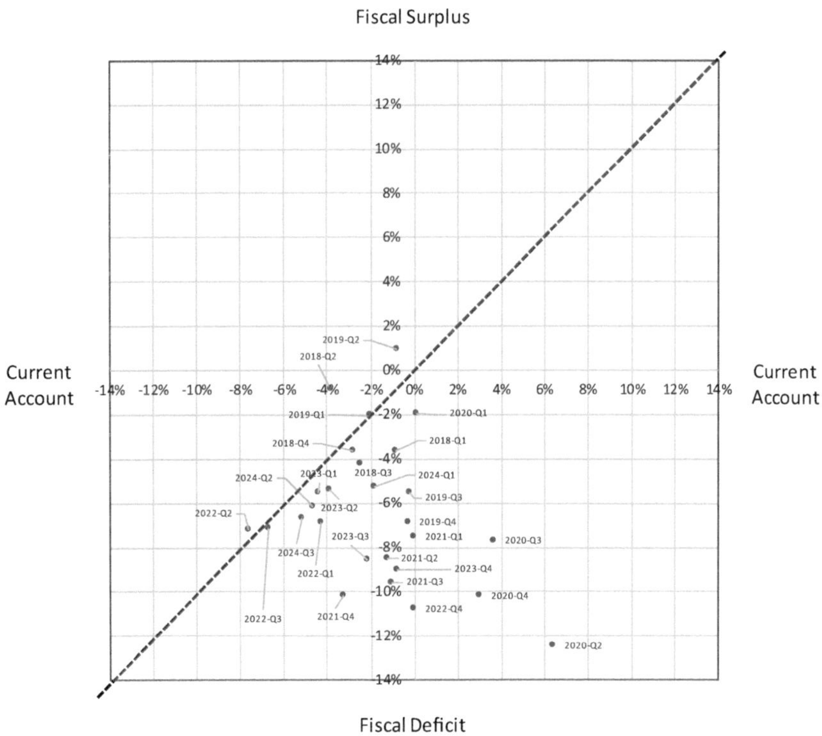

FIGURE A11.3 Sectoral Financial Balances Map, Philippines, Q1 2018–Q3 2024

Source: Authors' calculations based on fiscal balances data from the Republic of the Philippines, Bureau of the Treasury (https://www.treasury.gov.ph/wp-content/uploads/2025/09/COR_Summary_Annual_1986-2024.xlsx), balance of payments data from the Bangko Sentral ng Pilipinas (https://www.bsp.gov.ph/SitePages/Statistics/External.aspx?TabId=1), GDP data from the Philippines Statistics Authority (https://openstat.psa.gov.ph/Database/Economic-Accounts/National-Accounts-of-the-Philippines/Annual-National-Accounts)

was below the horizontal axis (fiscal deficit—often larger than 3%), to the left of the vertical line (indicating current account deficits—only four periods with current account surpluses), and to the right of the 45-degree line (domestic private surplus).[2]

We can return now to the government's objective to reduce the fiscal deficit to 3%. Suppose we draw a horizontal line at –3%, indicating the maximum deficit the economy can achieve. At the same time, recall the private sector's desire to net save, which implies that it would be to the right of the 45-degree line. Under this situation, the sustainable space for the Philippine government is substantially reduced (deficits larger than 3% are not allowed): Either the current account moves toward surplus or the private sector would not be allowed to net save, that is, it would have to run a deficit.

How the Bangko Sentral ng Pilipinas and the Bureau of Treasury Coordinated in March 2020 (COVID-19)[3]

This Appendix describes the PHP 300 billion operation between the Bangko Sentral ng Pilipinas (BSP) and the Bureau of Treasury (BTr) in 2020 to deal with the COVID-19 pandemic. This is an important example to understand monetary operations. As noted earlier, the BSP is prohibited by law from directly financing government deficits. The mandate of the BSP is, exclusively, price stability. It does not have a development function.

However, in 2020, in the context of the COVID-19 pandemic, the BSP directly financed the government through a repurchase agreement.[4] It did not create havoc in the economy. This Appendix provides details of this operation. We follow the arguments in Felipe and Fullwiler (2021). In essence, these authors argued that while central banks do not always overtly "print money" or openly finance government deficits in a simplistic way, the operations they engage in (especially during crises) can amount to de facto monetization—and that some of the constraints (like legal or institutional "no-deficit" rules) may be more smoke screens or partial constraints than fully binding in practice. The use of an interest rate corridor (with facilities for borrowing/lending or deposit/loans) to manage liquidity influences how monetization or "financing" shows up in central bank operations. Even when central banks aren't formally financing government deficits, their coordination with the treasury (or government) plus operation of liquidity facilities mean that debt financing and central bank balance sheet expansion can blur lines.

A background to the BSP and the Bureau of Treasury operation is as follows. The Philippine government bond market encountered several liquidity issues in March and April 2020. In particular, the Bureau of the Treasury (BTr) experienced failed auctions throughout the second half of March (this does not mean there were no buyers; in fact, most of the auctions were almost fully subscribed, though it is not uncommon for the BTr to reject bids it deems too high). The Philippines' BSP responded with the following series of actions:

1. March 17: Cancelled term deposit facility (TDF) auctions that drain RBs to achieve the target rate, so that these would not compete with the BTr's auctions.
2. March 23: Authorized a PHP 300 billion repurchase agreement with the BTr with a maturity of three months, which the BSP could extend for three more months at the due date.
3. March 24: Increased interventions in the secondary government bond market with a new daily one-hour facility to buy select BTr securities.
4. March 26: Remitted PHP 20 billion in advance dividends to the BTr.
5. April 8: Increased interventions again in the secondary government bond market by making all BTr securities eligible for purchase during the new facility's hour of operation.

The action on March 17, 2020, involved the BSP's corridor system for achieving its interest rate target, as the BSP regularly issues its own term liabilities at roughly its own interest rate target to achieve its target rate in normal times.[5] The March 24 and April 8, 2020, actions show the BSP acting as a backstop to the government bond market, attempting to generate greater market liquidity. The March 23 and March 26, 2020, actions are the BSP's direct financing of the government.

The March 23, 2020, repurchase agreement was essentially a six-month direct loan (assuming renewal after the first three months) from the BSP to the BTr. Table A11.2 walks through the operations involved in this PHP 300 billion loan and their effects on the interest rate corridor targeting system for this loan and its eventual repayment. The first transaction is simply the BSP crediting the BTr's account. In transaction 2, the BTr incurs a deficit, and RBs rise. To achieve its target interest rate, the BSP would have to return to TDF auctions to drain any RBs that would otherwise push the market rate below its target rate (transaction 3), and it would have to pay interest on however much is ultimately auctioned (transaction 4). As the loan from the BSP matures, the BSP will reduce outstanding TDF liabilities so sufficient RBs are circulating (or otherwise increase RBs as needed, such as by lending in repurchase agreement markets) in transaction 5. Then, in transaction 6, the BTr issues its own securities to fund the repayment. In transaction 7, the BTr repays the loan.

Note that for the BTr, the BSP, and private financial markets, the primary change is that interest on BTr liabilities has been explicitly set by the BSP. Because the TDF liabilities auctioned by the BSP in transaction 3 are interest-bearing, the BSP reduces its remittances in kind in transaction 8. (The BSP's loan to BTr is a zero-interest loan.) For the BTr, it is as if it issued its own liabilities to financial markets at the rate set by the BSP. From the financial system's perspective, the result is to effectively swap BTr liabilities normally linked to the anticipated path of the BSP's

TABLE A11.2 Operations Involved in the PHP 300 Billion Loan to the Government by the Bangko Sentral ng Pilipinas in 2020

Action	*Effect on Interest Rate Corridor System (Left Side in Figures 11.3 and 11.4)*	*Effect on Bangko Sentral ng Pilipinas' Balance Sheet*	
		A	*L/E*
(1) BSP credits BTr's account		Loan to BTr (+300)	BTr Acct (+300)
(2) BTr incurs a deficit	Shift SRB to the right		RBs (+300) BTr Acct (–300)
(3) BSP's TDF auctions drain excess RBs	Shift SRB to the left		RBs (–300) TDF (+300)
(4) BSP pays interest on new TDF balances			TDF (+int) Equity (–int)
(5) BSP reduces TDFs auctioned	Shift SRB to the right		RBs (+300) TDF (–300)
(6) BTr auctions settles	Shift SRB to the left		RBs (–300) BTr Acct (+300)
(7) BTr repays loan principal to BSP		Loan to BTr (–300)	BTr Acct (–300)
(8) BSP remittances to BTr are lower by the interest paid on TDFs[a]			BTr Acct (–300 –int) Equity int (+300 +int)

Notes:

(1) A = assets; BSP = Bangko Sentral ng Pilipinas; BTr = Bureau of the Treasury of the government's Department of Finance; BTr Acct = BTr's account at BSP; int = size of the interest payment; L/E = liabilities and equity; RB = reserve balance; SRB = supply of RBs; TDF = term deposit facility.

(2) The BSP does not actually debit the BTr's account in transaction 8, but rather, the remittance transfer is less than it would have been in the absence of transaction 1.

Source: Authors.

target rate for TDFs at the BSP that earn roughly the BSP's target rate. Overall, the BSP's explicit backstop of the government securities market and its loan to the BTr show its own interest in ensuring the link remains between the BSP's target rate and interest rates on government liabilities.

As for its March 26, 2020, advance dividend payment to the government, BSP explained:

> To further support the government in its fight against Coronavirus disease 2019 (COVID-19), the BSP will remit [PHP] 20 billion as advance dividend to the National Government (NG). The advance dividends constitute 87% of the

estimated total dividends based on the BSP's unaudited financial statements for the year 2020. . . . BSP will remit the [PHP]20 billion advance dividends today, March 26, 2020, through direct credit to the Treasurer of the Philippines-Treasurer Single Account, which is maintained with the BSP.

(BSP, 2020)

The BSP's advanced dividend payment to the BTr is effectively directly financing the government, and repayment occurs as a reduction in kind of future remittances. The transactions involved in this PHP 20 billion advance payment to the government are in Table A11.3, where transactions 2 through 4 are identical to those in Table A11.1. As with the March 23, 2020, repurchase agreement, once the national government incurs a deficit, the BSP will drain RBs to achieve its interest rate target within the corridor by auctioning interest-bearing TDF liabilities. When the BSP pays interest on TDF liabilities, this reduces its profits. Later on, the BSP will reduce its remittances by the combined amount of the advance and the interest paid on the new TDF liabilities. The advance dividend payment ultimately functions as if the BTr issued its own debt to the private sector at the TDF auction rate.

TABLE A11.3 Operations Involved in the PHP 20 Billion Advance Dividend Payment to the Government by the Bangko Sentral Ng Pilipinas

Action	*Effect on Interest Rate Corridor System (Left Side in Figures 11.3 and 11.4)*	*Effect on Bangko Sentral ng Pilipinas' Balance Sheet*		
		A	*L/E*	
(1) BSP makes advanced remittance to BTr			BTr Acct	(+20)
			Equity	(−20)
(2) BTr incurs a deficit	Shift SRB to the right		RBs	(+20)
			BTr Acct	(−20)
(3) BSP's TDF auctions drain excess RBs	Shift SRB to the left		RBs	(−20)
			TDF	(+20)
(4) BSP pays interest on new TDF balances			TDF	(+int)
			Equity	(−int)
(5) Later, BSP reduces remittances to BTr by combined advance and interest on new TDF balances[a]			BTr Acct	(−20 −int)
			Equity	(+20 +int)

Notes:

(1) A = assets; BSP = Bangko Sentral ng Pilipinas; BTr = Bureau of the Treasury of the government's Department of Finance; BTr Acct = BTr's account at BSP; int = size of the interest payment; L/E = liabilities and equity; RB = reserve balance; SRB = supply of RBs; TDF = term deposit facility.

(2) The BSP does not actually debit the BTr's account in transaction 5, but rather, the remittance transfer is less than it would have been in the absence of transaction 1.

Source: Authors.

The BTr cannot avoid paying interest on new debt created by deficits, even when the BSP finances them directly. Because the BSP must issue its own interest-bearing liabilities in the meantime, it reduces remittances in kind, and the BTr effectively pays roughly the BSP's interest rate target on new increases in the national debt. Overall, the reality of central banks' financing of government is not like printing money, as discussed in textbooks and the financial press, or even by most economists. Instead, the result is an increase in interest-bearing liabilities of the central bank, which the government ultimately services, much like if the government had issued the debt in the first place. The BSP's actions in the first months of the COVID-19 crisis illustrate the point that the primary rationale of central bank support of the government is to keep interest rates on new debt lower or to intervene to reduce liquidity problems, not to add more impact to the existing deficit.

This discussion also implies that "monetization" does not occur in the way most people learn it, including economists. "Direct printing of money," as commonly understood, is not operationally possible. In a corridor interest rate targeting system like that of the Philippines, BSP's purchases of government debt are sterilized by an offsetting reduction in the former's (central bank) assets or an increase in its own interest-bearing liabilities. There is nothing to fear about this.

Beyond the discussion about the Philippines in this chapter, the experiences of the European Central Bank, the Federal Reserve, and Japan in the 2000s and 2010s demonstrate that "printing money" to create inflation is not as easy as some economics textbooks claim. Yet old theories die hard, even when they are inapplicable.

The aforementioned notwithstanding, perceptions and understandings are evolving, if slowly. In September 2020, as the Philippines legislated a temporary increase in BSP lending to BTr (and as Indonesia rewrote laws to both allow Bank Indonesia to directly purchase government debt in the primary market and then also to increase the influence of the Finance Ministry in monetary policy strategy), Standard & Poors' response was:

> We have not seen signs that increased government bond purchases have damaged central bank credibility in India, Indonesia, and the Philippines. Inflation and interest rates have not picked up in these economies, and exchange rate changes have been modest so far.
>
> *(Noble, 2020)*

There are obvious continuing concerns for nations that are not able to withstand or otherwise avoid negative macroeconomic impacts of significant exchange rate depreciations, but it is well past time for recognizing that exchange rates are much more complex than anyone's theory of them.

Our recommendation to the Philippine government is to increase the role of fiscal policy. At some point, this should bring a rethink of the standard approach to "fiscal rules" that international institutions like the International Monetary Fund promote, to instead embed an inherently necessary, active fiscal policy in a macroeconomic and development policy framework that is also consistent with inflation targeting.

Notes

1 We use the old terminology of "capital account." In the modern balance of payments terminology (IMF BPM6), it is called "financial account," and the "capital account" registers *capital transfers* and *transactions in non-produced, non-financial assets* (like debt forgiveness, sale of patents, land, or rights) as a separate account. Therefore, what we call the capital account in the old terminology is the sum of the capital account plus the financial account in the new terminology.

2 The four quarters with current account surpluses are those of 2020 (COVID). These were the result of severe import contractions. During these four periods (especially the last three), the government ran very large deficits. These turned the domestic private sector balance into positive (large).

3 Based on Felipe and Fullwiler (2021).

4 The BSP may grant provisional advances (short-term loans) to the government, but these are capped (up to 20% of government revenues of the previous year) and must be repaid within three months, extendable by another three.

5 As the BSP's own literature on its operations states: "The Term Deposit Facility is a key liquidity absorption facility, commonly used by Central Banks for liquidity management. The TDF is used to withdraw a large part of the structural liquidity from the financial system to bring market rates closer to the BSP policy rate" (Bangko Sentral ng Pilipinas, 2016, p. 5).

12

THE PHILIPPINE ECONOMY TOWARD 2050: ASPIRATIONS AND REALITY

12.1 Can We Do Better . . . or Are We Destined to Experience More of the Same?

Although at a much slower pace than many of its neighbors, there is no doubt that the Philippine economy has progressed in recent decades. Certainly, the economy has moved forward, with clear signs of development in several areas. As the Philippines approaches its 100th year as an independent nation, the country finds itself at an important juncture. Today, we have an economy that has achieved high growth for several years (especially since the 2010s), accompanied by a gradual decline in the share of employment in agriculture and a reduction in poverty incidence.

However, alongside these improvements, there remain unresolved challenges that we must confront. The hard truth is that the Philippines remains a lower-middle-income nation–exactly where it has been since the 1980s. By contrast, Thailand moved into the upper-middle income category (measured in purchasing power parity) in 2004, and Indonesia followed suit in 2009 (Felipe et al., 2017). As of July, 2025, the income categories released by the World Bank shows that Vietnam is now in the same boat as the Philippines–both are at the cusp of becoming an upper-middle-income nation. Yet, it is important to note that Vietnam reached this point after spending only 16 years in the lower-middle-income group. The difference between the two countries' growth trajectories is striking and, as they should be for every Filipino citizen, a true wake-up call.

As we have discussed throughout this book, the country's economic performance in certain areas points to the broader challenges faced by the economy, particularly in key metrics tied to the kind of economic development necessary for the nation's progress in the long run. In Chapter 3, we examined the economy's potential growth, highlighting the important role of labor productivity and

DOI: 10.4324/9781003728719-12

the capacity to export more complex products. In Chapter 4, we emphasized how these are deeply rooted in the structure of the economy, particularly in sectoral employment shares, the labor market, and the role of firms in development. Other chapters have explored the country's weak governance, the shortcomings of education policy, the misguided views and limited understanding of a nation's monetary reality, and the absence of a clear and focused industrialization program. Given everything that has been discussed, we ask: What is the future of the Philippine economy and can we do better?

The government has echoed statements about what the future holds for the country, based on reports from other institutions. It claims that the Philippines will attain a real GDP per capita of USD 6,500 by 2030, that it will be a trillion-dollar economy (real GDP) by 2033, or that it will be 6.6-trillion-dollar economy by 2075. While every Filipino would welcome these outcomes, simple extrapolations show us that becoming a USD 6.6 trillion economy by 2075 means that the economy would have to grow by at least 5.5% every year for the next 50 years. We will show later in this chapter why this will not be the case. A sense of realism is essential to really identify the reforms needed to move toward goals that are ambitious yet truly attainable. Otherwise, we are banking on false hopes to carry us through. Given the points we have outlined in this book thus far, our view is different from the government's: We maintain that the economy will do well, but it will not go as far as it claims. The Philippine economy will continue to grow and experience increases in its standard of living, but it will not be an advanced nation, not even reach the level that many rich nations enjoy today. Future generations will live in a better Philippines. The true question is: Can we do better, or will things be more of the same?

We have already presented our forecasts for the current administration in Chapter 5 (until 2028). In that chapter, we discussed how the targets in the Philippine Development Plan 2023–2028 (NEDA, 2023a) are unlikely to be achieved. In this chapter, we use the DLSU ANIMO econometric model to describe how the Philippine economy will do between now and 2050 (see Chapter 5 for a description of the model). We will focus on key macroeconomic indicators as well as on the areas and variables that have so far mattered to us in this book, including productivity, employment shares, and wages.

To forecast with our DLSU ANIMO econometric model, we need to feed it with values of the variables that are exogenous until 2050. These are variables such as world GDP growth, oil price, or US interest rates, which we take from different sources.[1] It is worth pointing out that our baseline scenario reflects a relatively optimistic view of the world economy. For world GDP growth, we follow the IMF's forecast of 3.0–3.2% annually until 2029, followed by 3.4% per annum from 2030 to 2050. This way, we construct a baseline scenario of the Philippine economy until 2050. Undertaking this exercise with a model avoids the simple extrapolation of a few variables (typically income per capita or real GDP). These extrapolations are most often wrong because they are overly optimistic. Our forecasts up to 2050 are not meant to be correct in the literal sense of the term, that is, the precise numbers we show. As we pointed out in Chapter 5, they are the result of a rigorous exercise with a model that provides a coherent solution. Forecasting the next 25 years is about making sensible statements on how the economy, represented by almost 900 variables, will evolve. We think our model does a good job.[2]

What will happen in the next two and a half decades? How far can we realistically advance? Looking beyond 2028, unless the government takes decisive action to increase the potential of our economy, we will continue to experience progress, but it will mostly be a continuation of the status quo. As discussed in earlier chapters, this stems from fundamental issues related to productivity and the structure of our economy, where half of our workforce continues to be employed in sectors of low productivity.

In this chapter, we will uncover what will happen to the Philippine economy until 2040 and 2050. While *Ambisyon Natin 2040* is more of a national long-term vision with no specific measures, we will comment on the future of our economy as we near 2040. And we will present our forecasts until 2050 to provide a picture of the Philippine economy for the next two and a half decades.

12.2 The Philippine Economy Until 2040

Ambisyon Natin 2040 painted quite a rosy picture of the country when it was released in 2015. It is important to comprehend that the government's plans for each 6-year term are meant to lead to this vision, as was the intention of *Ambisyon Natin 2040*. While we understand this was meant to provide hope to the Filipino people, we also think we should be cautious in making statements such as "no one will be poor" or "we will all enjoy a stable and comfortable lifestyle."[3]

It is understandably very difficult to set measurable targets for 2040, especially when this vision was established back in 2015. However, our forecasts show that the economy's growth rate between now and 2040 will not reach 6–8%. In 2040, it will be about 5.1%. This translates into a per capita income of USD 9,000 in today's money. By 2040, poverty incidence will be 7.9%, which suggests that the Philippine economy will not be free of poverty.

While this may seem disappointing, it is not entirely surprising—no country has completely eliminated poverty. Some nations may have managed to reduce their poverty rates to very low levels, but none has achieved zero poverty. By the year 2040, there will be close to 130 million Filipinos, which means that, at a 7.9% poverty incidence, about 10 million would still be living below the poverty threshold. We discuss poverty in the Philippines in more detail in Chapter 14.

Does an income per capita of USD 9,000, in today's money, imply that Filipinos will be living comfortably? Possibly some, but not all. It is also important to note that, in today's terms, our per capita income will only double—a pace that will fall short of the country's long-term aspirations. The reasons behind this will become clearer as we discuss our projections until 2050.

12.3 The Philippine Economy Until 2050: Improvements, but Possibly More of the Same

We now discuss several aspects of the future of the Philippine economy later, covering actual and potential growth, productivity, output shares and contributions to output growth, agriculture, employment shares, wage rates, GNI per capita, poverty, Overseas Filipino Workers (OFWs), and demographics. Several of the figures we present later extend what was presented in Chapters 4 and 5. Hopefully, by examining these areas, the broader narrative will be more apparent: that the future will largely mirror what we are already observing today. Will the Philippine economy steadily improve? Yes. Will we become a high-income nation by 2050? Unfortunately, not yet.

12.3.1 Actual and Potential Growth

Our forecasts indicate that actual growth will be below 6% and that a large proportion of the workforce will remain concentrated in low-productivity sectors. As a result, while the economy will continue to expand, it will not be at the speed we would like. This must be understood: As discussed in Chapter 3, a growth rate of close to 6% is already high by historical standards. Only a few countries in East Asia have attained such growth rates and maintained them for two decades.

It is also worth noting that the faster an economy grows, the more difficult it becomes to sustain a high growth rate. Our long-run growth forecasts show that the economy will grow at rates below 6% until 2050, as shown in Figure 12.1. In fact, growth will slow to 4% by 2050. By 2040, our actual growth rate will decrease to 5.1% and, by 2050, to 3.6%. Our growth rate projections fall well below the growth rates needed to reach the goals of becoming a trillion-dollar economy by 2033 or a USD 6.6 trillion economy by 2075.

These growth forecasts are not surprising; they are consistent with our estimates of the economy's current potential growth of about 6%, which was covered in Chapter 3.

We also estimate potential growth until 2050 on both the supply and demand sides. On the supply side, using the forecast period 2024–2050, our estimate of the natural growth rate, based on Okun's law (see section 3.2.1), is about 5.7% during the boom years, and 4.5% during non-boom years.

As we did in Chapter 3, we use the Hodrick-Prescott filter to estimate trend growth and decompose it into labor productivity growth and labor force growth. This is shown in Figure 12.2. The first part of this figure reproduces Figure 3.1. Average trend growth for 2024–2050 is 4.8%, and most of the economy's growth will come from labor productivity growth.

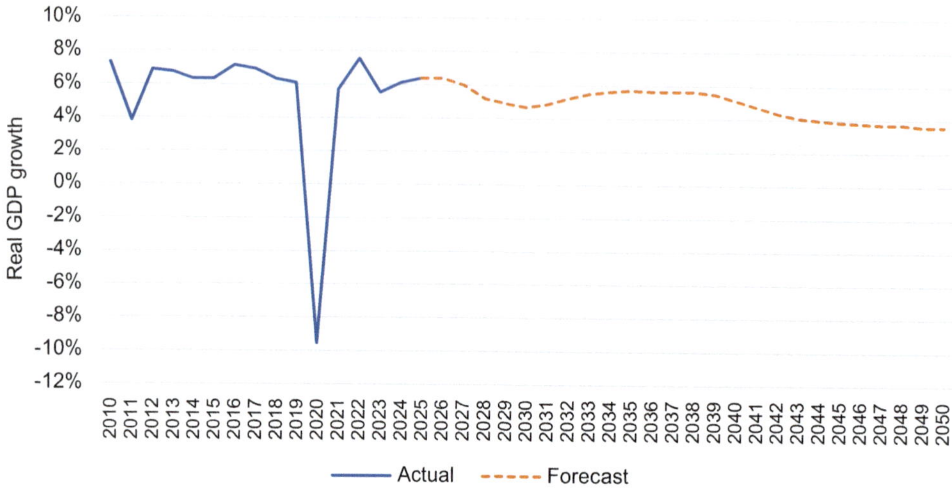

FIGURE 12.1 Real GDP Growth (%), Constant 2018 PHP, Philippines, 2010–2050

Source: Actual values for 2010–2024 are from the Philippine Statistics Authority (https://openstat.psa.gov.ph/Database/Economic-Accounts/National-Accounts-of-the-Philippines/Annual-National-Accounts). Forecasts are from the DLSU ANIMO econometric model.

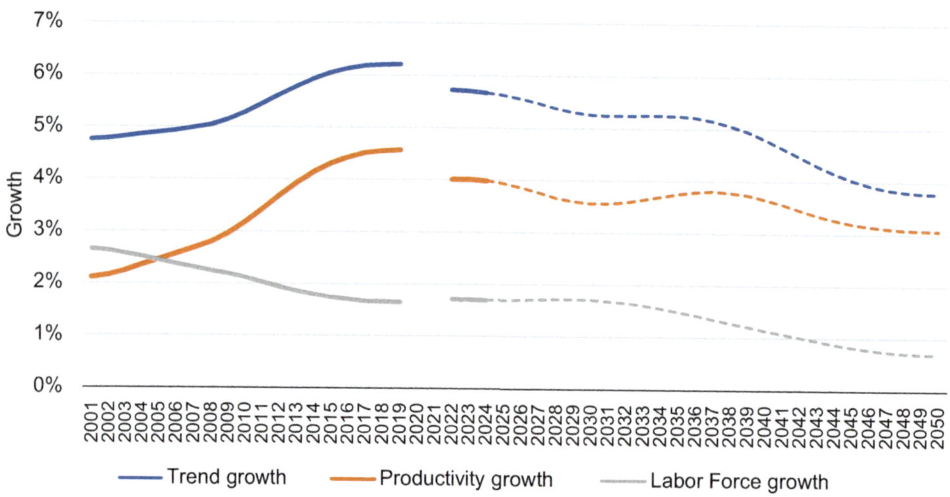

FIGURE 12.2 Potential Growth (Trend) (%) and its Components, Philippines, 2001–2050

Note: Potential growth (trend) is estimated using the Hodrick-Prescott filter to separate trend from cyclical fluctuation. The years 2019–2021 were not included in the exercise.

Source: Actual values for 2001–2023 are authors' calculations based on data from the DLSU ANIMO econometric model database. Forecasts are from the DLSU ANIMO econometric model.

On the demand side, we estimate the income elasticities of the demand for exports and imports to derive the balance of payments–constrained (BOPC) growth rate (see section 4.2.2). For the period 2024–2050, the income elasticity of the demand for exports is 2.5, while the income elasticity of the demand for imports is 2. Given that we assume a world economy average growth rate for the period at 3.4%, the estimated BOPC growth rate is 4%.

We can derive two key implications from these estimates. First, regardless of the method chosen, we are certain that the Philippine economy would not be able to grow by more than 6% in the next two decades. Second, all the forecast-period estimates point to a potential growth of less than 6%, and this suggests that the economy's potential growth will likely decrease until 2050. We argued in Chapter 3 that the binding constraint is on the demand side. It is worth noting that our projected income elasticity of the demand for exports will decrease from 3.5 (Chapter 3) to 2.5, while the income elasticity of the demand for imports will remain steady at about 2. We are also assuming an average world GDP growth rate of 3.4% for the next 25 years, which is quite an optimistic outlook for the world economy. Hence, the policy narrative that has been covered so far in previous chapters becomes even more apparent and urgent: The Philippine economy must develop its manufacturing sector and enable firms to produce more sophisticated and complex goods. Through this, its exports can become more globally competitive, increasing the income elasticity of the demand for exports. This would allow for the economy to increase its potential growth.

The discussions in the next sections will support this perspective as we highlight the role of productivity and the structure of the Philippine economy.

12.3.2 Labor Productivity

Productivity (real value added per worker) is notably highest in real estate, utilities, and finance and insurance (Figure 12.3). However, we stress, as in Chapter 4, that in these sectors, the notion of productivity is somewhat ambiguous. The reason is that, by definition, *productivity* is the ratio of a measure of physical output to labor. While it makes sense in the manufacturing or construction sectors, where the concept is more tangible, it is very difficult to conceptualize output in physical terms in sectors such as real estate or finance and insurance. Other high-productivity sectors include information and communication and manufacturing. In contrast, low-productivity sectors include wholesale and retail trade, transport and storage (with the same caveat for these two), construction, and agriculture.[4] In Figure 12.3, we maintain the ranking according to the sectoral productivity levels in 2023. By 2040, and until 2050, the main difference is that real estate will be the sector with the third highest level of productivity. Education and construction will improve, but not much with respect to what we have for 2023.

We note here that we have not taken into account the possible impact of the new technologies of the Fourth Industrial Revolution (4IR). The reason is that, as shown by Felipe et al. (2025), the Philippines is far from the leaders in the generation of 4IR technologies. Certainly, these technologies will be introduced (adopted) in some sectors, and the impact will be felt (increase in productivity). Yet this will not be something generalized so as to induce a large increase in

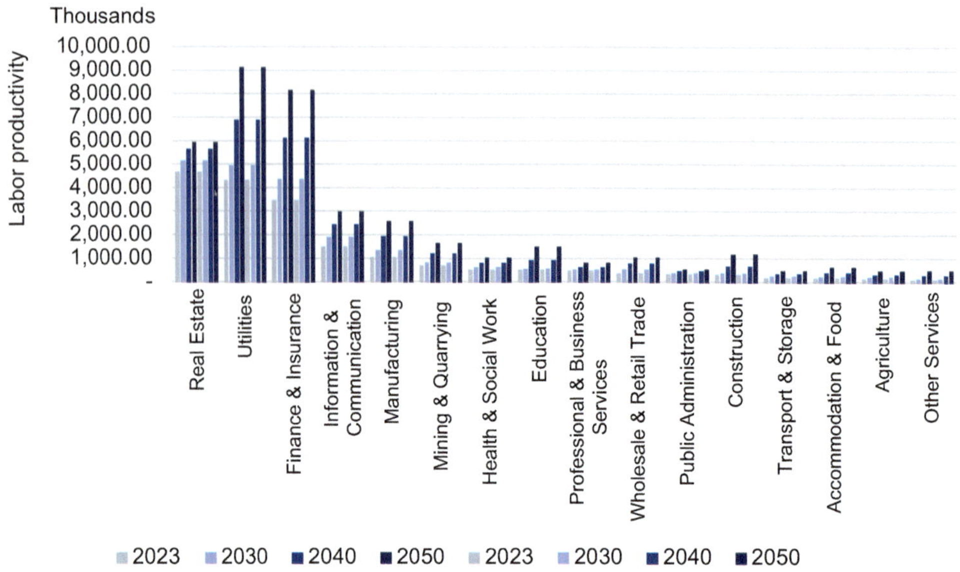

FIGURE 12.3 Labor Productivity by Sector (Constant 2018 PHP), Philippines, 2023, 2030, 2040, and 2050

Source: Actual values for 2023 are authors' calculations based on gross value added data from the Philippine Statistics Authority (https://openstat.psa.gov.ph/Database/Economic-Accounts/National-Accounts-of-the-Philippines/Annual-National-Accounts), and sectoral employment data from Philippine Statistics Authority (2024b), the International Labour Organization (https://ilostat.ilo.org/data/), and the DLSU ANIMO econometric model database. Forecasts for 2030, 2040, and 2050 are from the DLSU ANIMO econometric model.

average productivity. Moreover, as argued in Chapter 10, many Philippine firms have low organizational capabilities, a necessary condition to successfully adopt and adapt foreign (more advanced) technologies.

12.3.3 Output Shares and Contribution to Output Growth

Manufacturing and wholesale and retail trade will continue to be the two sectors with the highest output shares in 2050, collectively accounting for close to 40% of GDP—this is not very different from how things are today (Figure 12.4). In the long run, our forecasts indicate that the output share of wholesale and retail trade will continue to rise, while that of manufacturing will continue to decrease. We also observe that sectoral shares in output, from 2023 to 2050, will not change significantly. The sectors where the difference in output share between 2010 and 2050 is more noticeable are agriculture (decrease from 10% to 4%) and finance and insurance (increase from 4% to 11%).

Figure 12.5 shows the average contribution of each sector to real GDP growth for the indicated time periods. Wholesale and retail trade and manufacturing will continue to make the largest contributions to output growth. Along with finance

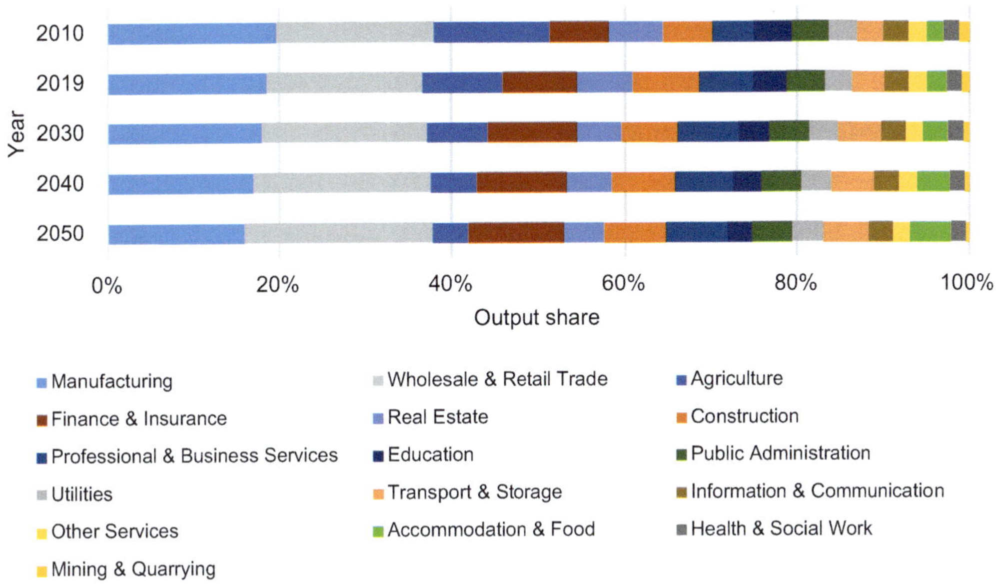

FIGURE 12.4 Output Share by Sector (%), Philippines, 2010, 2019, 2030, 2040, and 2050

Source: Actual values for 2010 and 2019 are authors' calculations based on data from the Philippine Statistics Authority (https://openstat.psa.gov.ph/Database/Economic-Accounts/National-Accounts-of-the-Philippines/Annual-National-Accounts). Forecasts for 2030, 2040, and 2050 are from the DLSU ANIMO econometric model.

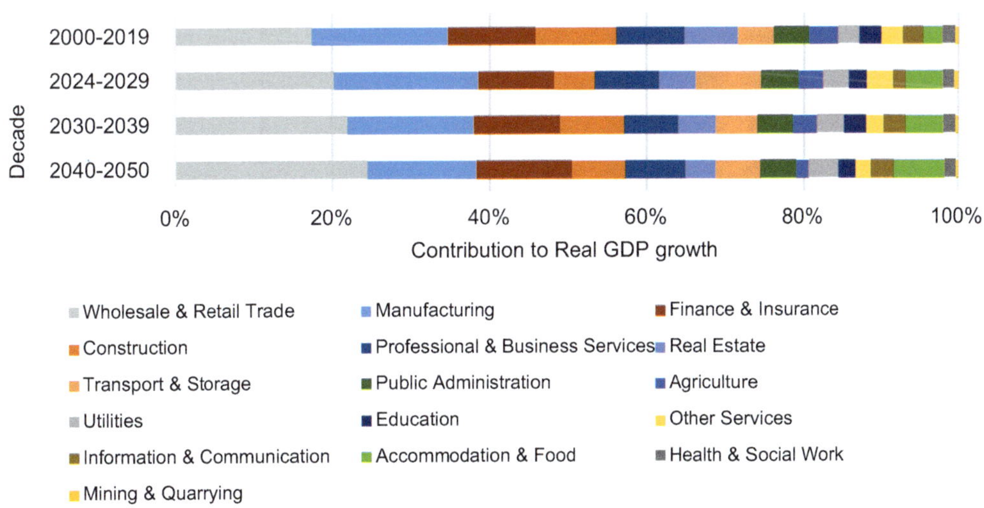

FIGURE 12.5 Average Contribution to Real GDP Growth by Sector (%), Philippines, 2000–2050

Source: Actual values for 2000–2019 are authors' calculations based on data from the Philippine Statistics Authority (https://openstat.psa.gov.ph/Database/Economic-Accounts/National-Accounts-of-the-Philippines/Annual-National-Accounts). Forecasts are from the DLSU ANIMO econometric model.

and insurance, these three sectors account for nearly half of the growth in real value added—a trend predicted to remain largely unchanged until 2040–2050. It can also be observed that the average contribution of agriculture to output growth is projected to decline significantly, from 3.8% to 1.5%.

12.3.4 Agriculture and Employment Shares

As discussed in Chapter 6, agriculture is still a sector of concern for the Philippines. The government currently continues to seek solutions to address the challenges faced by this sector. The key idea is that the productivity of the sector should improve, first, by shifting workers out of agriculture (as mentioned in Chapters 3 and 4) and, second, by modernizing practices, methods, equipment, and systems to make the sector more competitive. Based on our forecasts, agriculture is projected to remain a sector with very low productivity. Additionally, its output share and contribution to real output growth are expected to continue declining. By 2050, agriculture will make up for only 4% of total GDP (Figure 12.6), similar to the contribution in advanced economies.

Agriculture's contribution to output growth will increase sharply in the next few years, and it will gradually decline from 2030 to 2050 (Figure 12.7). In 2040, it will be slightly above 2% and, in 2050, slightly below 2%.

The number of workers in agriculture will decline quite significantly, with a reduction of around 4 million workers and a 14 percentage point decrease in the employment share. As anticipated in Chapter 6, it will become more apparent in the next 25 years that agriculture needs a solution. The decreasing trend in the

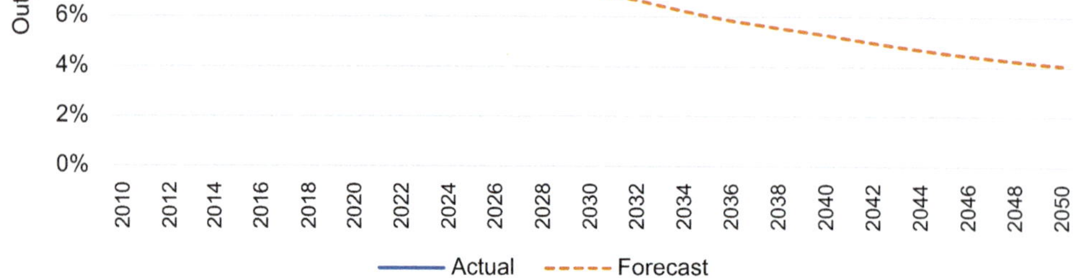

FIGURE 12.6 Share of Agriculture, Forestry & Fishing in Real GDP (%), Philippines, 2010–2050

Source: Actual values for 2010–2024 are from the Philippine Statistics Authority (https://openstat.psa.gov.ph/Database/Economic-Accounts/National-Accounts-of-the-Philippines/Annual-National-Accounts). Forecasts are from the DLSU ANIMO econometric model.

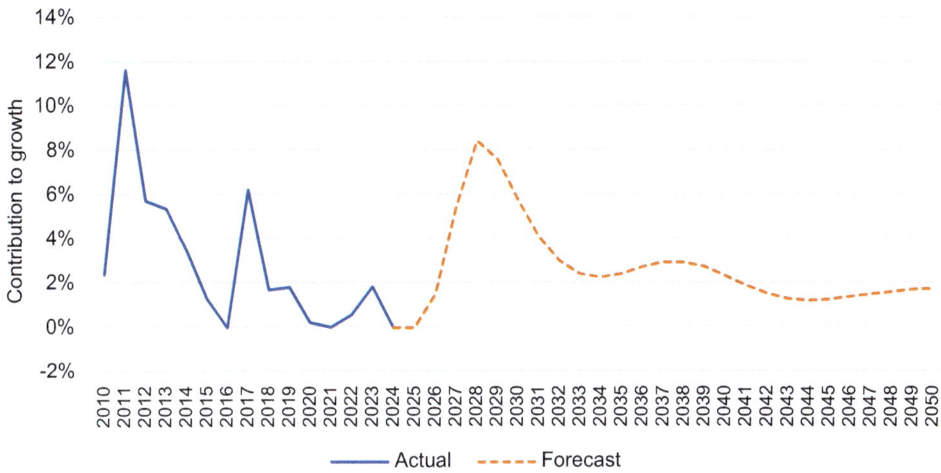

FIGURE 12.7 Contribution of Agriculture, Forestry & Fishing to Real GDP Growth (%), Philippines, 2010–2050

Source: Actual values for 2010–2024 are from the Philippine Statistics Authority's data on the National Accounts (https://openstat.psa.gov.ph/Database/Economic-Accounts/National-Accounts-of-the-Philippines/Annual-National-Accounts). Forecasts are from the DLSU ANIMO econometric model.

employment share of agriculture—a sign of development—will continue until 2050 (see Figure 12.8). For decades, a number of regulations and policy mistakes have stifled the growth of this sector. First, the implementation of the agrarian reform program resulted in minuscule farm sizes. It prevented the attainment of economies of scale in production. Second, the decentralization law mandated local government units to lead in the development of the agriculture sector, a function most of them never took seriously. Third, the protracted protection of the sector through high tariffs on agricultural imports or the imposition of non-tariff barriers to prevent the entry of imported agricultural products. This had the effect of discouraging local producers from enhancing their productivity, innovating, and becoming competitive because they were assured of high prices.

What Philippine agriculture needs today is an integrated development plan (as opposed to piecemeal interventions) that considers the needs for farm-to-market roads, warehouses, logistics, cold chains, irrigation, and so forth. Malaysia and Vietnam have a five-year planning process for their agricultural sector, and once agreed and approved, they devote a block budget for five years to support the development plan. The scheme also prevents unnecessary political interventions by politicians because projects must follow the technically sound and approved five-year plan. Second, we need to consider whether or not the provision of input subsidies leads to increases in productivity and competitiveness. Third, it is of paramount importance to reconsider the rice-centric budget as well as the regional share. Fourth, the private sector must be encouraged to actively participate in agricultural development and the industrialization of the countryside.

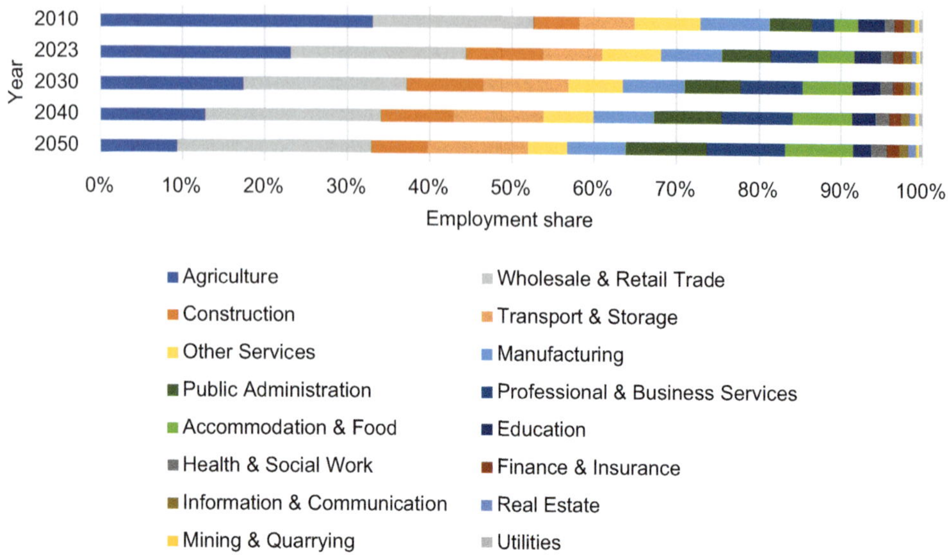

FIGURE 12.8 Employment Share by Sector (%), Philippines, 2010, 2023, 2030, 2040, and 2050

Source: Actual values for 2010 and 2023 are authors' calculations based on data from the Philippine Statistics Authority (2015, 2024b). Forecasts for 2030, 2040, and 2050 are from the DLSU ANIMO econometric model.

Unfortunately, though the employment composition will change slightly, our employment projections show that 75% of the workforce will continue to be in sectors of low productivity. The employment share of construction will also decrease. In contrast, the employment shares of wholesale and retail trade, transport and storage, and accommodation and food will increase, indicating that many of the country's workers will still be employed in low-productivity sectors. Meanwhile, manufacturing's employment share is projected to remain at around 7% (Figure 12.8).

This implies that while both the number of workers in agriculture and the sector's share in total employment will decline (a feature of development), the sectors whose employment shares will increase are sectors of low productivity. Meanwhile, the employment share of Manufacturing, a high-productivity sector that consistently and significantly contributes to output and output growth and is the key sector that will drive growth in the economy, remains at about 7%. A more in-depth look into the labor markets, including occupations and supply and demand mismatches, is covered in Chapter 14.

12.3.5 Wages and Income per Capita

The average real wage is expected to more than double over the next 25 years. However, approximately 75% of the workforce will remain employed in sectors that pay low real wages. Figure 12.9 shows real wage rates by sector from 2010 to 2050.

With three-quarters of the workforce earning low real wages, the implication on income per capita is obvious—the Philippine economy will still be an upper-middle

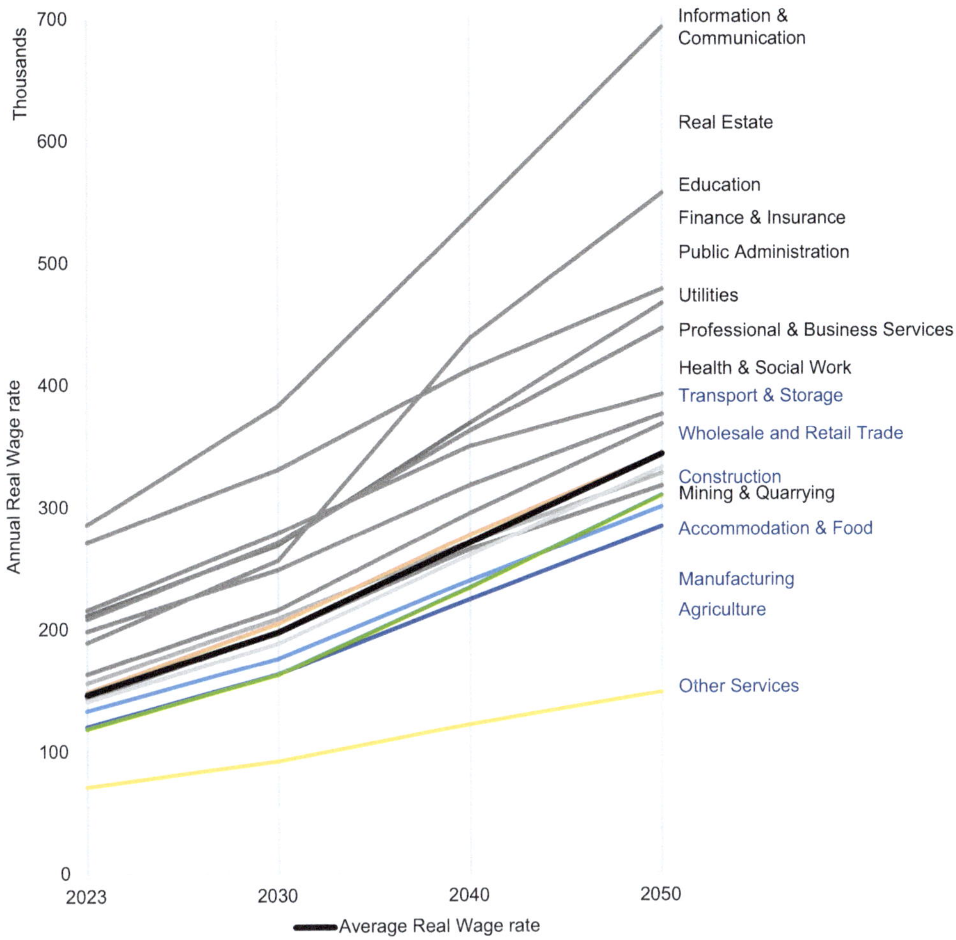

FIGURE 12.9 Annual Real Wage Rate by Sector (Constant 2018 PHP), Philippines, 2023, 2030, 2040, and 2050

Source: Actual value for 2023 is from the DLSU ANIMO econometric model database. Forecasts for 2030, 2040, and 2050 are from the DLSU ANIMO econometric model.

income country by 2050. In Figure 12.10, we show our projection for GNI per capita, using 2023 prices and US dollar to Philippine peso exchange rate.

We argued in Chapter 3 why tourism will not catapult the Philippines to high income—though it can be help achieve middle-income status. Neither will sari-sari stores. We read with concern in June 2025 that the government (the Department of Trade and Industry), together with local industry groups, aim to boost sales of *sari-sari* stores in the country to PHP 2.4 trillion by 2030, as part of a strategy to develop the country's wholesale and retail sector (Desiderio, 2025). This cannot be a development strategy. First, because this is incompatible with the objective of becoming an advanced economy. These stores (low productivity and low wages) will have to disappear from our streets, the same as jeepney drivers, and the still large number of domestic helpers and security guards, amongst other professions that still exist in

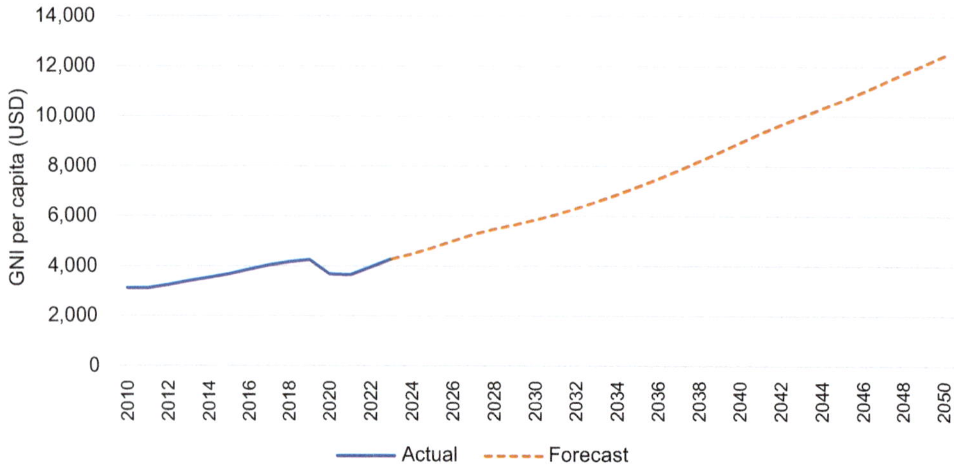

FIGURE 12.10 GNI per Capita (USD), Constant 2023 Prices, Philippines, 2010–2050

Note: Our projections are based on the DLSU ANIMO econometric model's forecasts of Gross National Income (PHP) and the Philippine Statistics Authority's (2024a) forecasts of population. To express future values in present-day terms, we adjust the series using the 2023 consumer price index (CPI) and the 2023 PHP-USD exchange rate.

Source: Actual values are authors' calculations based on data from the DLSU ANIMO econometric model database. Forecasts are from the DLSU ANIMO econometric model.

the Philippines. Why? Sari-sari stores are inefficient places to shop, the graphic sign of the nation's poverty. People in developed countries shop in well-organized, very large, and cheap, supermarkets. And to become an advanced nation, wages will have to increase dramatically, *for everyone*. Who will hire a helper or a guard when their salaries reach PHP 70,000/month (of course, these will have to be formal jobs, and with a contract that includes benefits, paid holidays, etc.). There is a second reason why this objective does not make any sense: PHP 2.4 trillion in 2030 would represent, depending on whether this figure refers to nominal or real pesos, between 5% and 8% of our GDP in 5 years, a ridiculously large percentage.

The government also thinks that artificial intelligence (AI) will be a growth driver. AI matters but it will not be either the game changer of the Philippine economy at large because we are very far from the technological frontier, because 10 million workers are still employed in backward agriculture, and because 25 million Filipinos are functionally illiterate. AI may even exacerbate this problem by increasing inequalities. Certainly, many of our companies (surely the large ones) will use it and see *some* benefits. Indeed, using AI in chatbots, to detect fraud in banks, as voice assistants, to generate text and images, or to manipulate big data, is a step forward and important in order not to be left behind. At this level, AI is already being used everywhere. AI can also help companies in manufacturing. Yet we doubt this will revolutionize the Philippine economy, as long as we do not have the capabilities to generate the advanced technologies of the so-called Fourth Industrial Revolution, including robotics.

Moreover, for a particular technology to have a significant impact on society, including an improvement in productivity, is has to become a *general-purpose technology* (GPT), that is, it has to be used across a wide range of industries and activities, it evolves over time, it leads to complementary innovations, and it alters how people live, work, and interact. Electricity, indoor plumbing (the best invention ever), penicillin, and airplanes are examples of GPTs of the 20th century that changed our lives. Time will tell us if AI becomes a GPT and contributes to productivity growth in the Philippines. Recall what economist Nobel Prize winner Robert Solow said in 1987: "You can see the computer age everywhere but in the productivity statistics."

Summing up, by 2050, we will still fall short of reaching today's high-income classification threshold. Over the next two and a half decades, the Philippine economy will remain largely unchanged. With the vast majority of the workforce expected to remain employed in low-productivity sectors and earning low real wages, we can hardly expect the economy to experience changes significant enough to become a high-income nation in the long run. The structure of the economy will essentially stay the same, and the prospects of becoming a high-income nation in the long run will remain distant.

12.3.6 Poverty and Overseas Filipino Workers

Notwithstanding the earlier forecasts, progress will still be evident: Poverty will decline (discussed in Chapter 14) because this is concentrated in rural areas and the number of workers in agriculture will decline (from 10 million to 6 million workers). Likewise, the number of overseas Filipino workers (OFWs) will decrease as domestic real wages gradually increase (Figure 12.11). The incentive to leave the country will decrease.

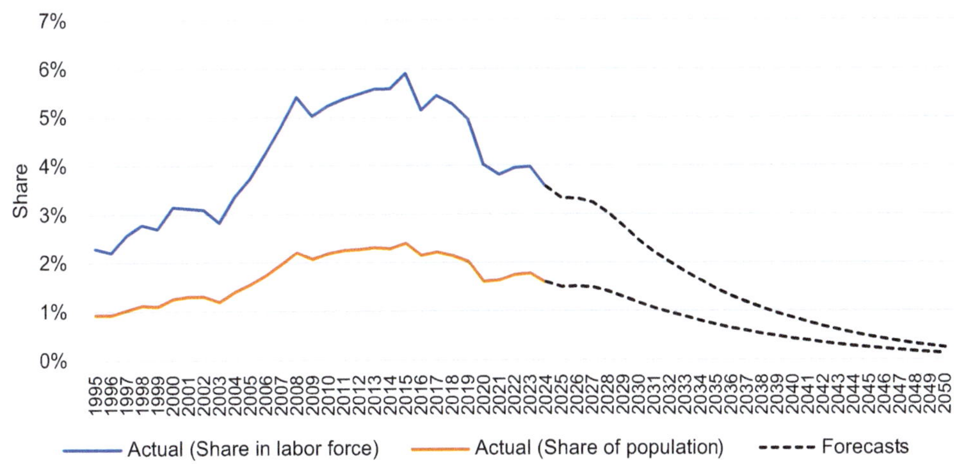

FIGURE 12.11 Overseas Filipino Workers (% of Labor Force, Population), Philippines, 1995–2050

Source: Actual values are authors' calculations based on data from the DLSU ANIMO econometric model database. Forecasts are from the DLSU ANIMO econometric model.

12.3.7 Demographics

As the economy continues to develop, one critical factor to consider is the demographic transition. Based on population projections and our labor force forecasts, our working-age population will grow from 80 million in 2025 to 105 million in 2050 (from 70% to 78% of the total population). The overall labor force participation rate will increase to 66%, translating to a potential workforce of about 70 million. From 2025 to 2050, the labor force coming from the 25 to 54 age group—the prime working-age population—will increase by almost 30% (Figure 12.12).

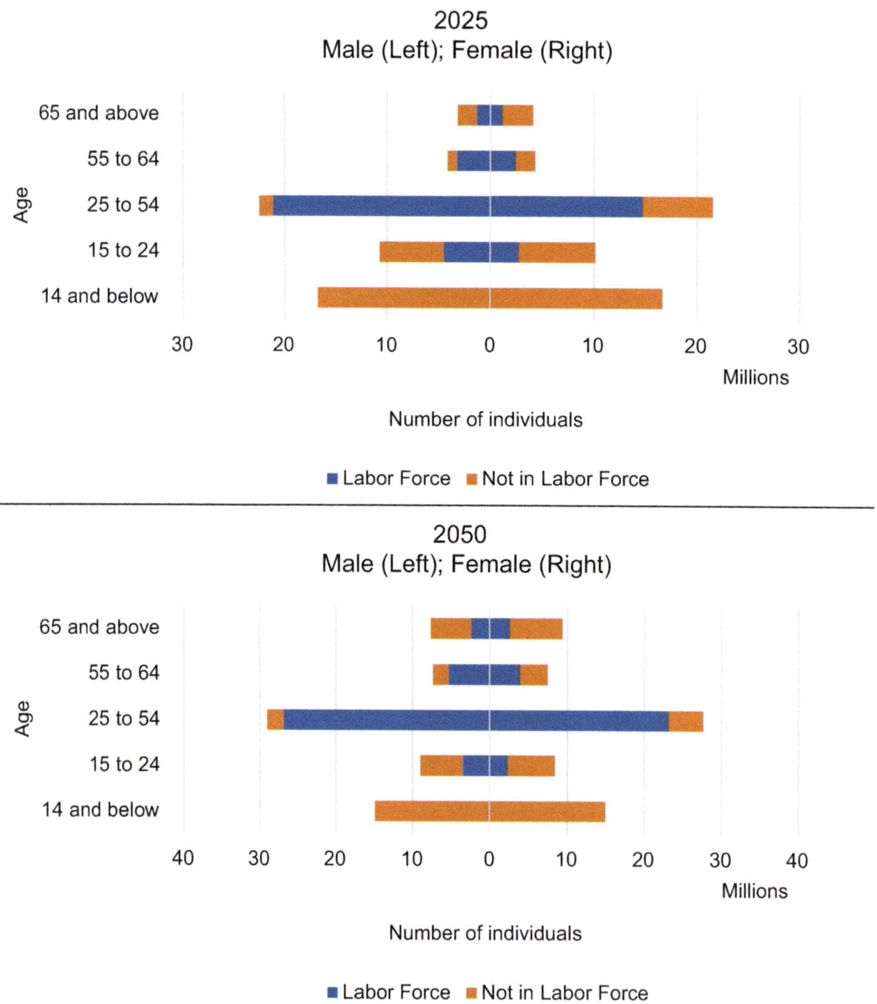

FIGURE 12.12 Population Divided into Individuals in the Labor Force and Not in the Labor Force by Sex and Age, Philippines, 2025 and 2050

Source: Population forecasts for 2025 and 2050 are from the Philippine Statistics Authority (2024a). Labor force projections are from the DLSU ANIMO econometric model, which generates forecasts of labor force participation rates disaggregated by sex and age.

Labor force participation rates by sex and age will largely remain unchanged, except for females aged 25 to 54, whose participation rate is expected to rise from 68% to 83% over the next 25 years. These trends suggest that the economy's labor force participation rates will converge to those observed in more developed countries (Figure 12.13).

This implies that if the country aims at achieving meaningful progress, it has quite a critical opportunity in the next two decades to capitalize on its workforce before the old-age dependency ratio begins to increase, which is projected to occur in 2035.

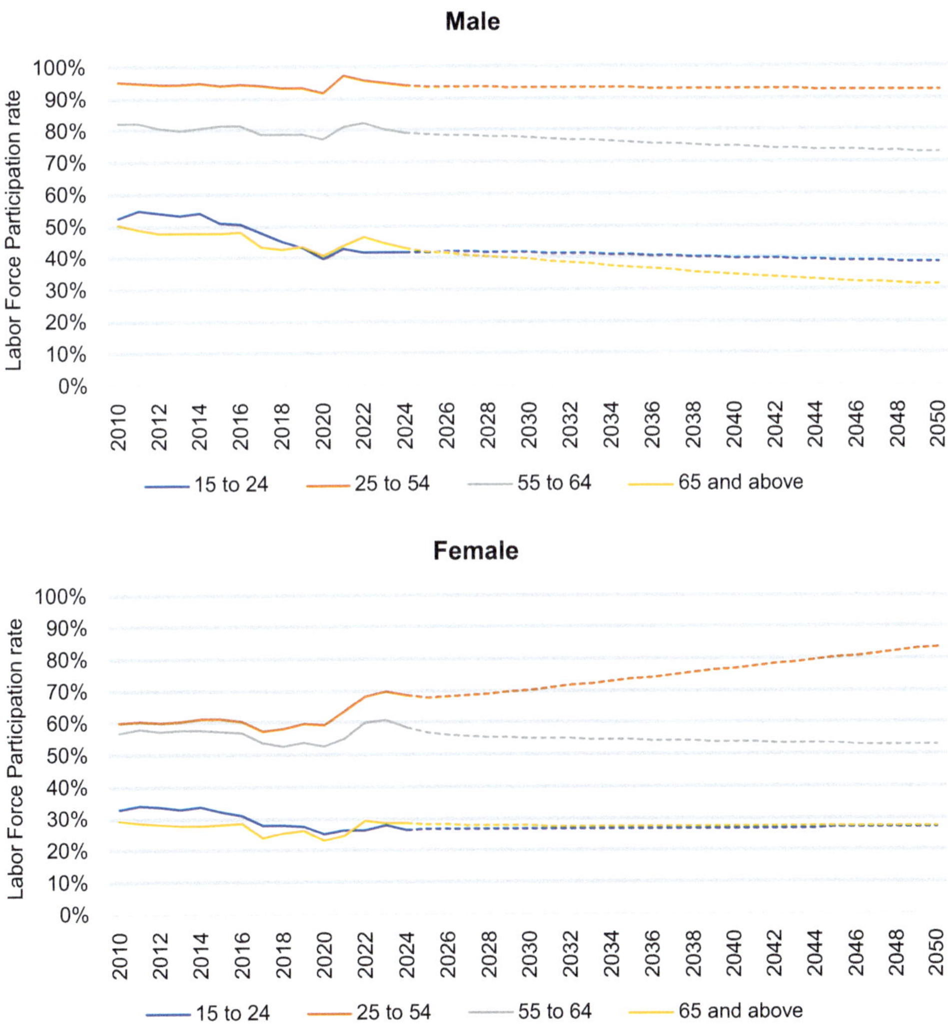

FIGURE 12.13 Labor Force Participation Rates by Sex and Age (%), Philippines, 2010–2050

Source: Actual values are authors' calculations based on data from the DLSU ANIMO econometric model database. Forecasts are from the DLSU ANIMO econometric model.

Our overall assessment is that the economy will continue to do better. Real wages will increase, poverty will decrease, and we will continue being an upper-middle-income country. This is what our economy can achieve given our potential and the current structure of the economy. To do better, the country needs to engineer a massive economic restructuring, like that of South Korea in the 1970s. The likelihood that this happens is minimal.

12.4 Possible Scenarios

Building on the baseline scenario, we now use the model to test two alternative scenarios. The first scenario explores the possibility that our model's forecasts are on the optimistic side. Here we ask: What would happen if the country were to face a crisis? The second scenario revolves around the often-unexamined notion of consistently achieving a 6% growth without first understanding a country's potential growth. We ask: What would it take for the Philippine economy to achieve and sustain such growth for the next two and a half decades?

12.4.1 What If a Crisis Occurs?

As noted, our baseline scenario is based on a quite optimistic view of the economy. In particular, this baseline also assumes no crisis over the next 25 years. Given the frequency of crises historically, we then account for the possibility of at least one crisis occurring between now and 2050. We conduct a simulation exercise in which a global economic crisis occurs in 2036, with the Philippines' real GDP growth decreasing by about 5 percentage points that year (about 0% growth) and returning to its growth path in 2038. The simulation exercise suggests that such a crisis could reduce the GNI per capita in 2050 by around USD1,400.

Figures 12.14 and 12.15 illustrate the baseline forecasts and the alternative scenarios for real GDP growth and GNI per capita, respectively. These results show the significant long-term implications of even just a single crisis. Such an event could easily set back economic progress by roughly three years.

It is important to understand that this scenario is quite likely, given the frequency of crises in the past. It is also possible that recovery will be slower than what we present here. This means that real wages will grow by less, poverty incidence will decrease at a slower rate, and it will take the economy more time to become a high-income nation. This moves the Philippine economy further away from the *Ambisyon Natin 2040* vision.

12.4.2 What Would It Take to Sustain a Growth Rate of 6% for Two and a Half Decades?

Given the government's insistence on sustaining faster growth over the long term, we explored what changes would be necessary for the Philippine economy

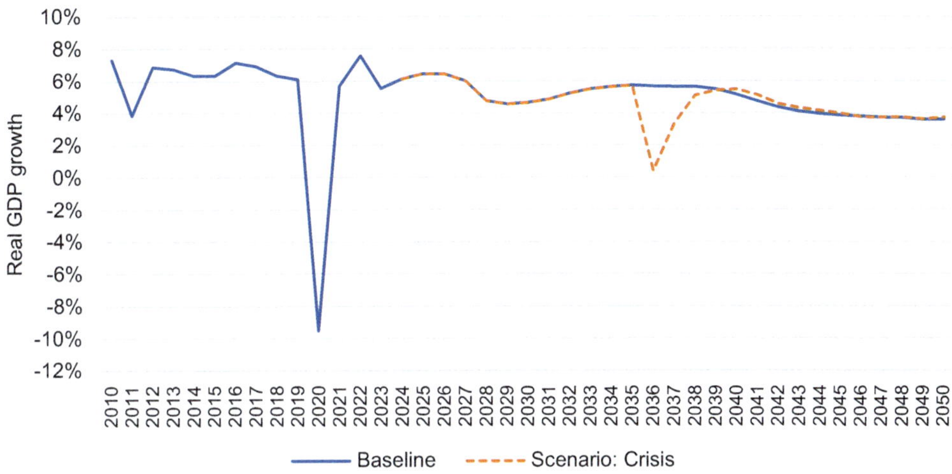

FIGURE 12.14 Simulated Real GDP Growth (%) with a Crisis Occurring in 2036, Philippines, 2024–2050

Source: Values for 2010–2024 are from the Philippine Statistics Authority (https://openstat.psa.gov.ph/Database/Economic-Accounts/National-Accounts-of-the-Philippines/Annual-National-Accounts). Forecasts and simulation are from the DLSU ANIMO econometric model.

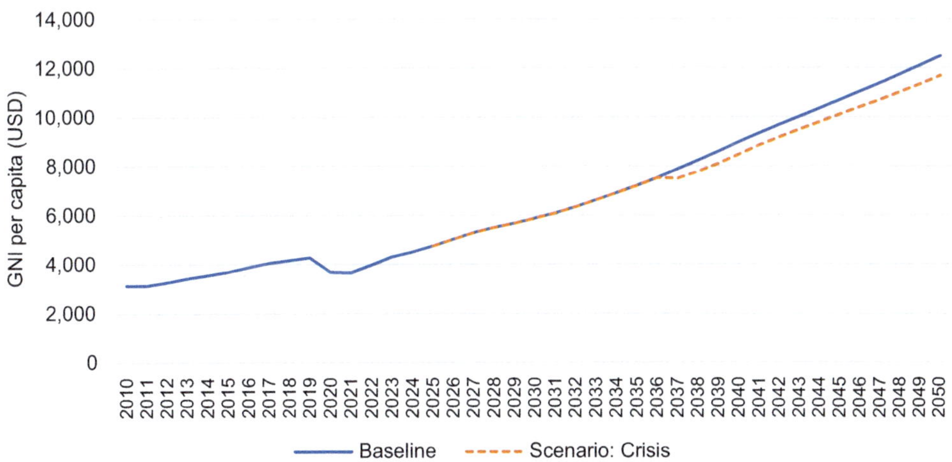

FIGURE 12.15 Simulated GNI per Capita (USD), Constant 2023 Prices, with a Crisis Occurring in 2036, Philippines, 2025–2050

Note: Our projections are based on the DLSU ANIMO econometric model's forecasts of Gross National Income (PHP) and the Philippine Statistics Authority's (2024a) forecasts of population. To express future values in present-day terms, we adjust the series using the 2023 consumer price index (CPI) and the 2023 PHP-USD exchange rate.

Source: Values for 2010–2023 are authors' calculations based on data from the DLSU ANIMO econometric model database. Forecasts and simulation are from the DLSU ANIMO econometric model.

to achieve a sustained growth rate of 6% per annum over the next 25 years. What would it take to maintain such a high growth trajectory? Using the DLSU ANIMO model, the only way the country could grow at 6% for the next two and a half decades is if the investment-to-GDP ratio is forced to grow by 1 additional percentage point per year, reaching 50% by 2050 (Figure 12.16). To put this into perspective, this is similar to China's economy during its phase of aggressive investment. Replicating this in the Philippine context is highly improbable given the structure of the economy. Nevertheless, our model indicates that sustaining this growth rate would propel the economy to high-income status by 2046 (Figure 12.17).

These simulations tell us two important things. First, while the Philippines may continue to do well during the coming decades, things will not be like what the government claims. The Philippine economy will do fine and progress steadily, but this is as far as it can go. Achieving a 7% growth rate and sustaining it is unlikely. Add a crisis into the mix, and the transition into a high-income nation will take longer. Second, the push to achieve even just a 6% growth rate consistently for the next 25 years is simply impossible. As discussed in this chapter and in Chapter 3, the current potential of the economy is no more than about 6%. In the next 25 years, labor force growth will decrease, but so will productivity growth.

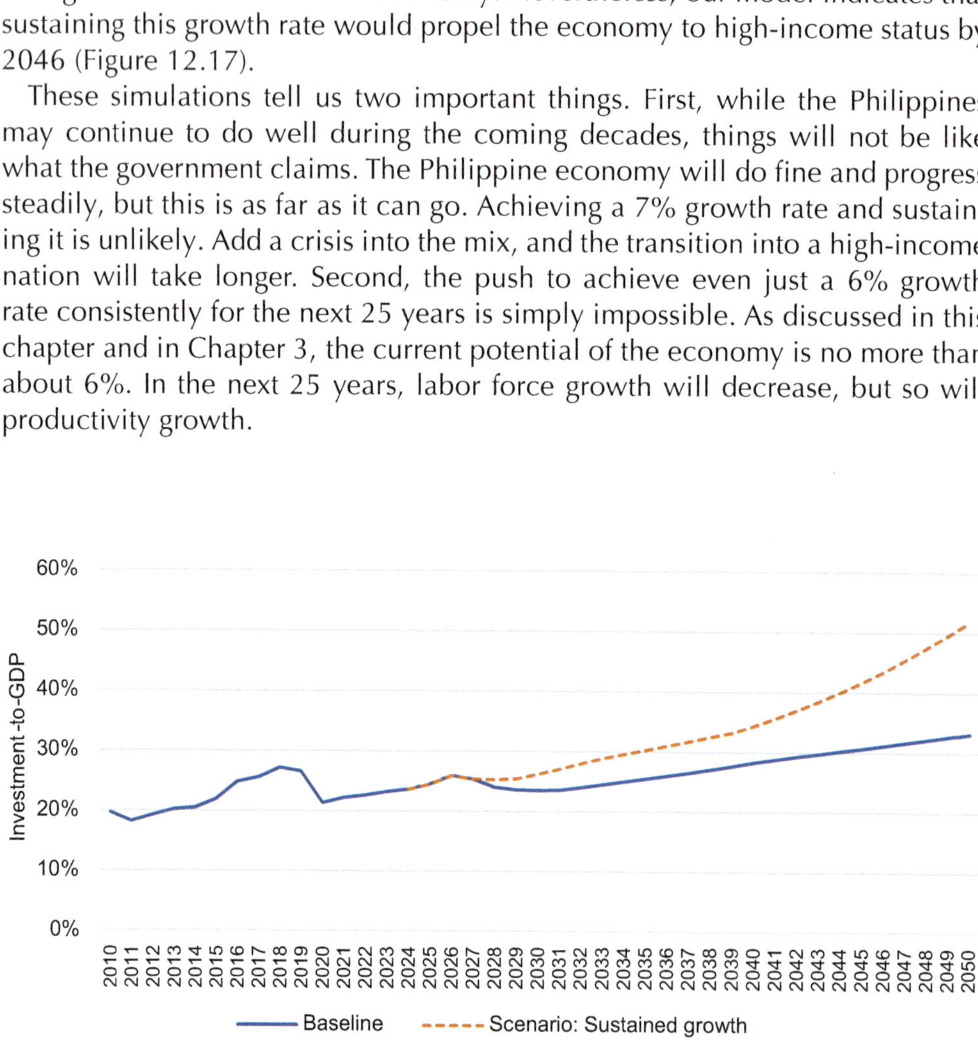

FIGURE 12.16 Simulated Investment-to-GDP (%) required to Maintain Real GDP Growth of 6%, Philippines, 2024–2050

Source: Values for 2010–2023 are authors' calculations based on data from the Philippine Statistics Authority (https://openstat.psa.gov.ph/Database/Economic-Accounts/National-Accounts-of-the-Philippines/Annual-National-Accounts). Forecasts and simulation are from the DLSU ANIMO econometric model.

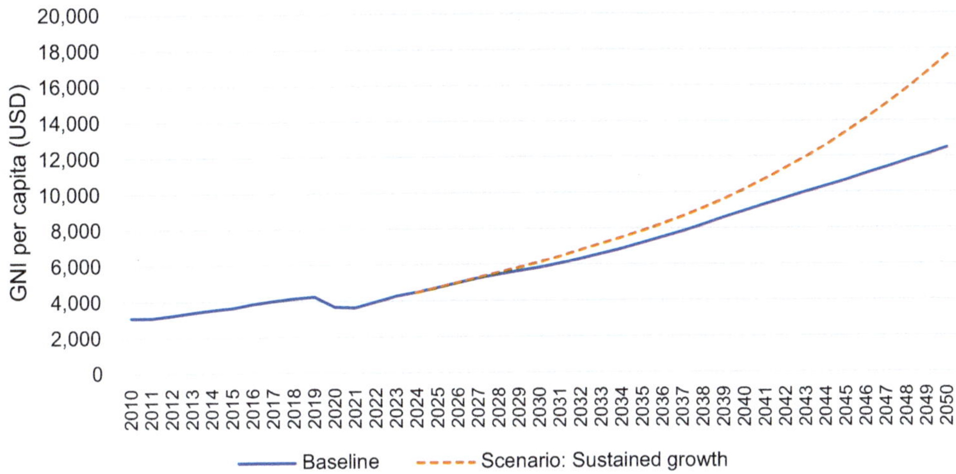

FIGURE 12.17 Simulated GNI per Capita (USD), Constant 2023 Prices, under a Sustained Growth of 6%, Philippines, 2025–2050

Note: Our projections are based on the DLSU ANIMO econometric model's forecasts of Gross National Income (PHP) and the Philippine Statistics Authority's (2024a) forecasts of population. To express future values in present-day terms, we adjust the series using the 2023 consumer price index (CPI) and the 2023 PHP-USD exchange rate.

Source: Values for 2010–2023 are authors' calculations based on data from the DLSU ANIMO econometric model database. Forecasts and simulation are from the DLSU ANIMO econometric model

12.5 The Road Ahead

The results of our exercise with the DLSU ANIMO model indicate that although we will experience progress, things will largely remain the same, and this has one clear implication: If we want to see a much better Philippines, the government must do something different. The economy will continue to progress, and we will reach upper middle income very soon, but it is unlikely that we will attain high-income in the next two and a half decades; and the growth rate will slow to 4%. Given the expected demographic shift beginning in 2035, it is of utmost importance to consider how we can soon make the manufacturing sector thrive (productivity), with firms producing globally competitive products (exporting).

In the end, will the government's aspirations for rapid growth and prosperity become a reality? In the Economic Briefing of May 2024 (Recto, 2024), the government indicated, as we mentioned at the beginning of this chapter, that its target is to reach a real GDP per capita of USD 6,500 in 2030 and to surpass 1-trillion-dollar GDP in 2033. Our model forecasts indicate that the economy will reach these targets in the years 2032 and 2037, respectively. The growth rates assumed for those values are higher than what our model predicts.

We stress that the Philippines will experience progress, income per capita will continue to increase, and poverty will decline, though the pace and scale of change will likely fall short of the ambitious (and unrealistic) goals set by the government. Hence, this presents a good opportunity for the current government. As the government is in the midpoint of its administration, it can choose to make the next 25 years count by shifting gears: to lay the foundations for sustained, long-term growth, and to set up the next administration for success. This requires more than just short-term targets: It demands a well-crafted and coherent industrialization program focused on increasing productivity and on transforming the structure of the economy, and by empowering firms as the main agents of economic transformation and development. If the government seizes this opportunity, it can set the country on a path toward lasting development—one that has eluded the Philippines for decades.

Notes

1 Appendix 5, Table A5.1 in Chapter 5 shows our assumptions about some key exogenous variables.
2 The forecasts presented in this chapter were generated in the latter part of 2024, using actual data up to 2023.
3 As described on the website of the Department of Economy, Planning, and Development (DEPDev), formerly National Economic and Development Authority (NEDA).
4 For a description of the sectors as well as examples of activities that fall under each of the sectors, see Appendix 4.

13

FORECASTING EMPLOYMENT AND EDUCATIONAL NEEDS

13.1 Introduction

Chapter 12 presented and discussed our forecasts of major variables of the Philippine economy until 2050. We argued that despite signs of progress and declining poverty, the Philippines will remain an upper-middle-income country, with most of the workforce still employed in low-productivity, relatively low-wage, sectors. In Chapter 10, we discussed the problem of overeducation and issues in basic education.

In this chapter, we provide forecasts of the Philippine labor market as well as of educational requirements up to 2050. We first study how occupational structures and educational requirements will change by economic sector: (1) What type of jobs will the Philippine economy produce? (2) Will it produce the decent jobs that the Philippine Development Plan (PDP) 2023–2028 (NEDA, 2023a) has promised? Or will it be MOTS (more of the same)? Second, we look at the occupational transition that Filipino graduates are likely to have when they enter the workforce: (1) What type of jobs are they likely to find, given their level of education? (2) What levels of education will be needed to support Philippine industries? (3) Will the country overcome the problem of overeducation? Lastly, by forecasting the supply and demand of occupations and education, we will see what imbalances may occur: (1) Is the country overproducing certain skills? (2) Are there jobs (professions) being unfilled?

To answer these questions, we extract the educational structure of the labor force and the occupational structure of the productive sectors from a pooled annual time series constructed from the 2001 to 2022 October rounds of the Labor Force Survey (LFS) microdata series published by the Philippine Statistics Authority in their microdata catalog (https://psada.psa.gov.ph/catalog/LFS/about).[1] We then combine this with the forecasts of employment by sector and population

DOI: 10.4324/9781003728719-13

by demographics (sex and age group) from the DLSU ANIMO model to see what jobs the economic sectors will be requiring, what level of skills the labor force will be producing, and whether there are mismatches. A more detailed discussion of the methodology is available in Appendix 13.

Where the analysis goes down to sector-specific details, we focus on six sectors in the succeeding discussion: agriculture, wholesale and retail, construction, and transport and storage (the largest employers of the country), manufacturing (a high productivity sector), and information and communication to represent high-value services (the others being finance and insurance, real estate, professional and business services, public administration, education, and health and social work). The forecasts for the other 10 sectors are provided in Figures A13.1 and A13.2 in Appendix 13. We compare the occupational structure of the Philippines with that of Spain (an advanced economy) for 2014–2022 (Figure A13.3 in Appendix 13) and use it as a benchmark.

13.2 Sectors' Occupational Structures and the Levels of Education Needed to Support Them

We start by forecasting the occupational structures of our selected six sectors. The first set of forecasts is a necessary component of the final output of the model. Examining the forecasts of the occupational structures (distribution of workers across occupations) of each sector, is useful in itself to understand the skill composition (of each sector). Figure 13.1 provides forecasts of the distribution across nine occupations (managers, professionals, technicians, clerks, sales, commercial agriculture workers, crafts and trades, plant workers, and laborers) for 2023–2050 (2001–2022 is the actual, historical data from the LFS) for the six sectors.

Agriculture (panel A) has always been a homogeneous sector, requiring only commercial agriculture workers and laborers, who are typically low-skilled, low-pay workers. This trend will persist until 2050 (given how 56% and 43% of the sector's employment in 2050 are made up of those two occupations, respectively). This may be expected. In a developed country like Spain, the structure of Agriculture is similar (Figure A13.3 in Appendix 13). The key difference is that in Spain, professionals, technicians, and plant workers account for a larger share, indicating that the sector requires professionals with higher skills who contribute to its modernization. These occupations are nearly non-existent in Philippine agriculture.

Wholesale and retail trade (panel B) goes to the extreme. With the predicted expansion of the sector in Chapter 12, sales workers will be the dominant occupation, around 94% in 2050. In 2022, salespersons made up nearly 70% of the sector's labor force. The shares of managers and laborers have declined to around 6% and 17%, respectively, in 2022. The declines of these shares will continue until 2050. Clerks, crafts and trades, and technicians represent a very small share in the Philippines, about 7% currently. In Spain, sales workers also represent the

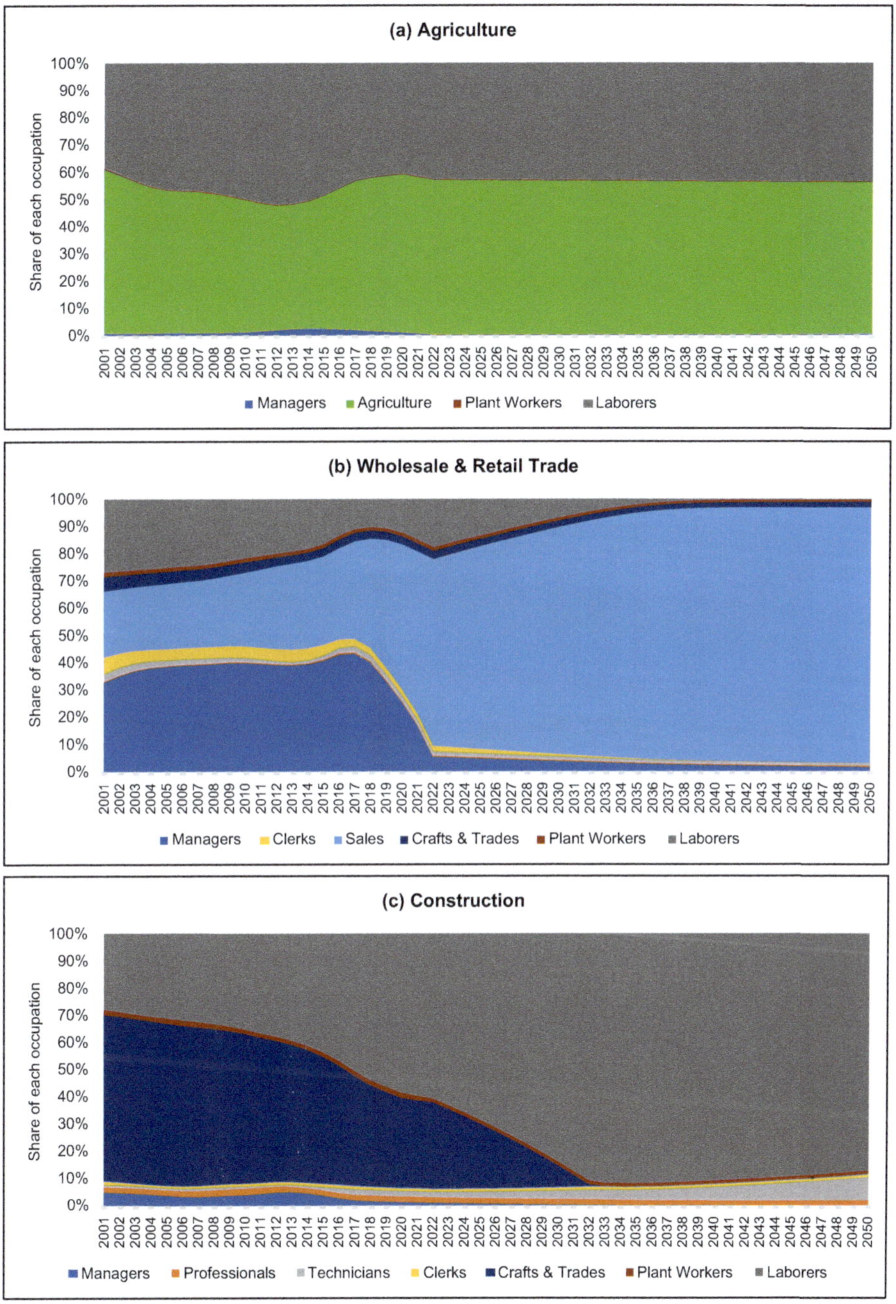

FIGURE 13.1 Occupational Structures for Selected Sectors, Philippines, 2001–2050

Note: Legends for occupations with very small values are suppressed to facilitate better presentation of graphs.

Source: Actual values for 2001–2022 are authors' calculations based on data from the Philippine Statistics Authority's Labor Force Survey (https://psada.psa.gov.ph/catalog/LFS/about). Forecasts are from 2023–2050.

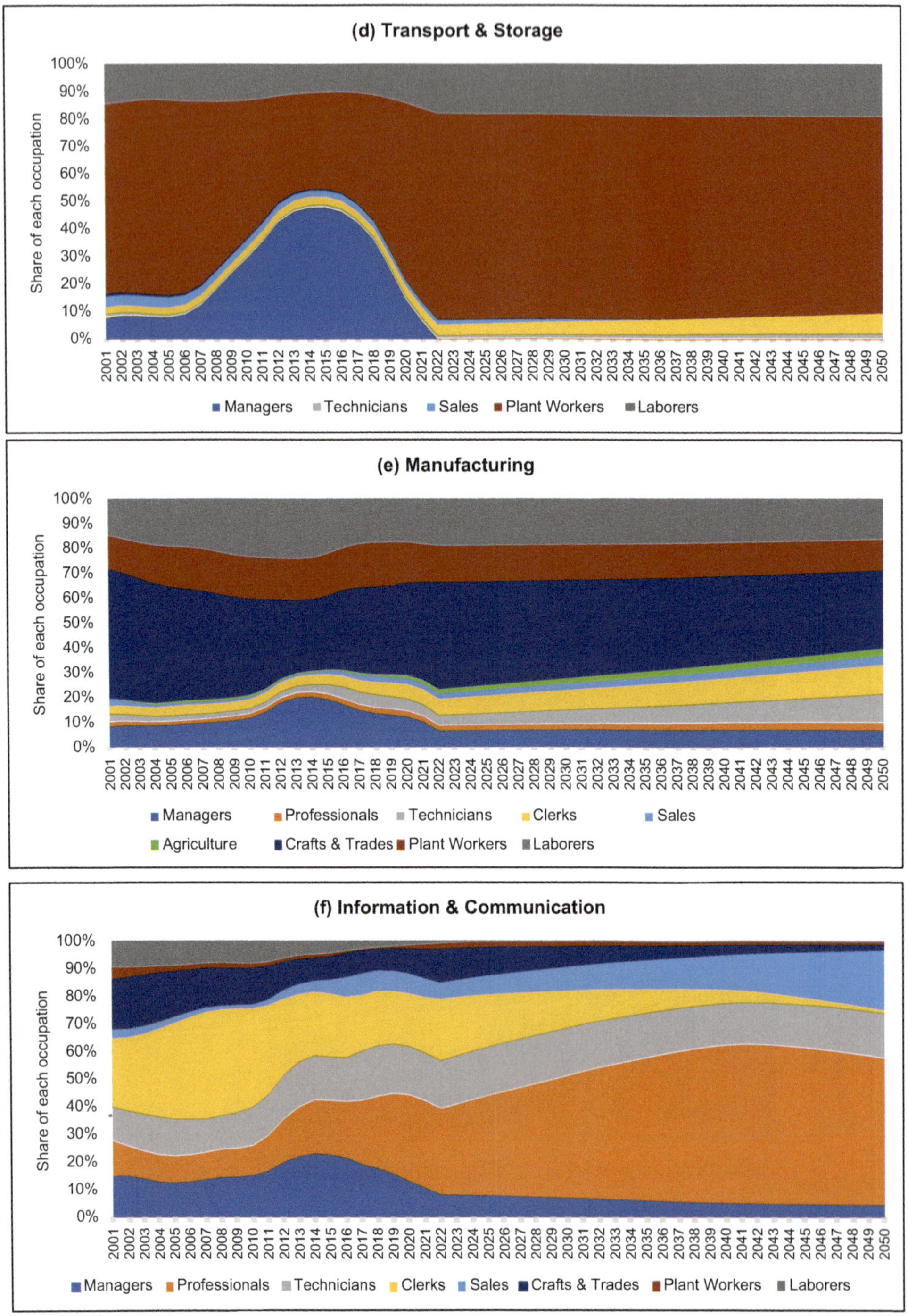

FIGURE 13.1 (Continued)

largest occupation (46%), but a good number of clerks, crafts and trades, and technicians (almost 30%) balances out the sector to provide administrative and technical support.

Construction (panel C) is another sector that goes to the extreme. Between 2001 and 2022, the share of crafts and trades workers decreased steadily, from 61% to 32% of total employment in the sector. During this same period, the reliance on laborers increased from 28% to 61%. This distinctive shift leads the model to predict that laborers will be the main workhorse occupation of the sector in the future. This is puzzling because this runs counter to how the construction sector evolves in developed countries. In Spain, crafts and trades workers are the mainstay of the construction sector—hard hats, steel-toed boots, utility belts, and sophisticated tools and techniques. There are also technicians and professionals (e.g., engineers). Laborers have the lowest education and skill requirements but also receive the lowest salaries. Given that construction is presently the third largest employer, there is a need to investigate this deskilling as this may adversely affect the quality of the country's physical infrastructure.

Transport and Storage (panel D) will mostly be made up of plant workers (around 72% in 2050), particularly drivers and vehicle operators. This is followed by laborers (19%) and clerks (8%). A key difference with Spain's transport and storage sector is that in Spain the share of clerks undertaking coordination and administration activities, is higher than in the Philippines. This is also the case of technicians, who provide the necessary support for maintenance and operations.

Manufacturing (panel E) is a diverse sector that requires a variety of occupations. The largest portion will be made up of crafts and trades workers and plant workers, with a slightly decreasing share of laborers. There is also a growing proportion of clerks and technicians. This may indicate that even a mild expansion of the sector is able to facilitate a shift toward higher skills, productivity, and wages. It is worth mentioning that the distribution of occupations in the Philippines' manufacturing sector, closely mirrors that of Spain, although there are fewer crafts and trades workers and more laborers in the Philippines.

Lastly, information and communication (panel F) is a good example of a highly professional sector. The sector is primarily home to professionals and technicians (software engineers, coders, programmers, etc.) who will be the sector's driving force, representing about 54% and 16% of total employment, respectively, by 2050. The share of clerks is still large, but it has declined from 38% in 2007 to 22% in 2022. This decline will remain until 2050, when clerks will represent only 1%. The composition of the sector is quite similar to that of Spain, that is, mostly professionals, technicians, clerks, sales workers, and managers—although the share of technicians is smaller in the Philippines but that of professionals is larger.

What percentage of workers in each sector will require a given educational level? Figure 13.2 presents forecasts of these educational requirements by sector. As discussed in Chapter 10, wages are ultimately determined by sectoral

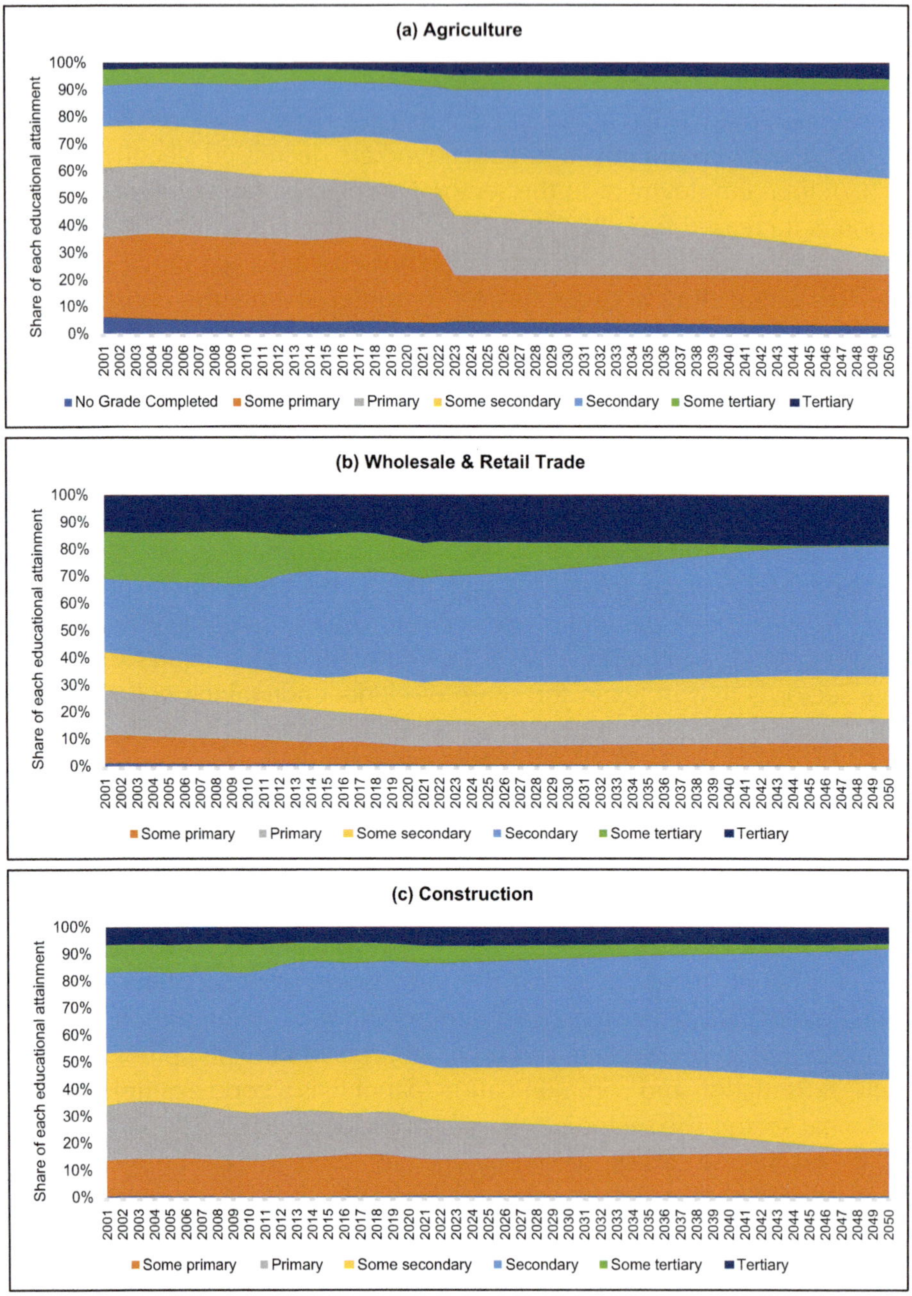

FIGURE 13.2 Educational Requirements for Selected Sectors, Philippines, 2001–2050

Note: Legends for occupations with very small values are suppressed to facilitate better presentation of graphs.

Source: Actual values for 2001–2022 are authors' calculations based on data from the Philippine Statistics Authority's Labor Force Survey (https://psada.psa.gov.ph/catalog/LFS/about). Forecasts are from 2023–2050.

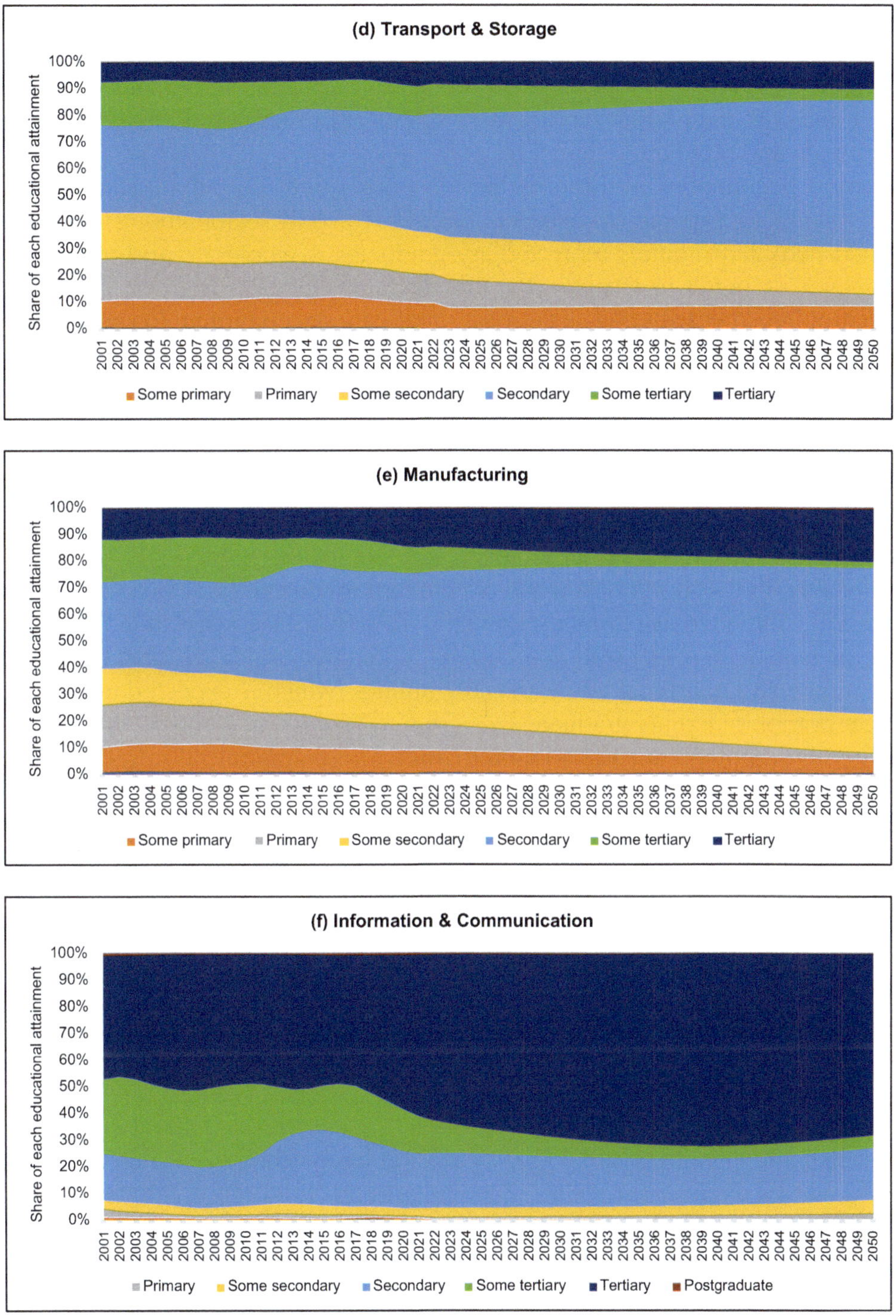

FIGURE 13.2 (Continued)

productivity and skill requirements, and these two will determine the level of education that will be needed to support a sector. The forecasts for educational requirements can be summarized in three findings. First, in sectors of low productivity and with the highest employment shares at present—agriculture (panel A), wholesale and retail trade (panel B), construction (panel C), and transport (panel D), most occupations in these sectors do not require more than a high school diploma. This is expected to persist until 2050. The only sector among those mentioned here that requires more tertiary graduates is wholesale and retail trade. However, as noted in Chapter 10, the Philippines suffers from an overeducation problem, and with the single most significant occupation in the sector being salespersons, college degrees are not needed.

The second finding concerns manufacturing (panel E). Given the potential of manufacturing for high productivity, the sector will not only require greater diversity of occupations and skills, but also more workers with higher education, compared to the sectors in the previous group. Consequently, the sector also provides higher wages and returns to tertiary education. Amidst a mild expansion of the sector, the bulk of workers will still need no more than a high school diploma. But noticeably, the proportion of workers with tertiary degrees will steadily increase and will likely increase further, especially if more firms engage in R&D, exporting, or enhancing organizational capability. Similar trends are also observable for mining and quarrying and especially utilities (which is expected to require a larger portion of tertiary graduates).

The third finding concerns the information and communication sector, which may be extended to the other high-value service sectors like professional business services. These high-productivity sectors require higher skills and higher education than workers in the previous two groups. The lion's share of these workers will require tertiary education. A couple of minor deviations may be noted. For one, real estate, professional business services, and public administration have more room for high school graduates, presumably for the most routine clerical tasks that these sectors require. Second, education and health and social work are likely the sectors that absorb most of the postgraduates of the country, given how academics need master's and PhDs, and, expectedly, medical doctors who study beyond tertiary education. See Appendix 13 for the forecasts for these sectors.

Is the Philippine economy going to create the decent work that the Philippine Development Plan 2023–2028 (NEDA, 2023a) has promised? We noted in Chapter 12 that the employment shares of agriculture and construction will decrease. On the other hand, the employment shares of accommodation and food services, as well as those of wholesale and retail trade and transport and storage, will increase. Unfortunately, these are still sectors of low productivity, and as discussed in Chapter 10, low productivity growth entails low wage growth. The Philippine economy will keep producing a significant share of low-skill, low-pay jobs such as laborers, sales personnel, and drivers who require no more than a high school diploma.

The expansion of manufacturing is stifled. It is a high-productivity sector, yet our forecasts show that the output share of this sector will decline and its share in employment will stagnate. Although the sector will require more better-paid professionals and technicians than other sectors, because they require tertiary, post-secondary, and even postgraduate education in the future, this will only happen more quickly if Philippine manufacturing engages in the development of complex products, exporting, or enhancing organizational capability. Sectors like IT, finance, education, and others with a significant share of professional workers, already approximate the structure of a developed country like Spain. These sectors are the destination of tertiary degree holders. However, as seen in Chapters 4 and 12, the output and employment shares of these sectors will not grow much.

13.3 Job Prospects for the Philippine Labor Force

We now look at the occupations that high school and college graduates are likely to have (Figure 13.3). Secondary graduates (panel a) are most likely to work in sales and as laborers (with shares growing to 43% and 24% by 2050, respectively), which is consistent with the types of jobs the economy is predicted to generate. There may be some who are able to work as managers (typically line managers or supervisors in retail or production), technicians (typically non-specialized medical assistants or recordkeepers), or even as clerks, but the chance that they work as professionals (since this typically requires highly specialized skills) is minimal.

College graduates (panel b) are likely to become clerks, professionals, technicians, and managers, with proportions reaching 28%, 23%, 13%, and 7% in 2050, respectively. However, college graduates may end up in occupations that do not require a college degree. This problem is known as overeducation.

We predict that the country will not be able to meet the Philippine Development Plan 2023–2028 (NEDA, 2023a) target of reducing the proportion of employed college graduates working in elementary occupations to 1.5%–1.7%, given that the proportion will still be about 7% in 2028, which is predicted to persist until 2050. However, restricting the PDP's target to only laborers is a severe underestimation of overeducation because most sales, agriculture, crafts and trades, and plant workers do not require college degrees either. The proportion of college graduates in all these occupations (21%) already surpasses the proportion of college graduates working as laborers. When taken together, workers in these occupations are predicted to account for 28% of the workforce with tertiary education by 2050.

Overeducation will persist. Given where we predict the economy is headed, most of the jobs that will be produced will not require more than a high school diploma. Amidst the aggressive expansion of the public higher education sector, the ambitions that parents have for their children to finish college, and perhaps

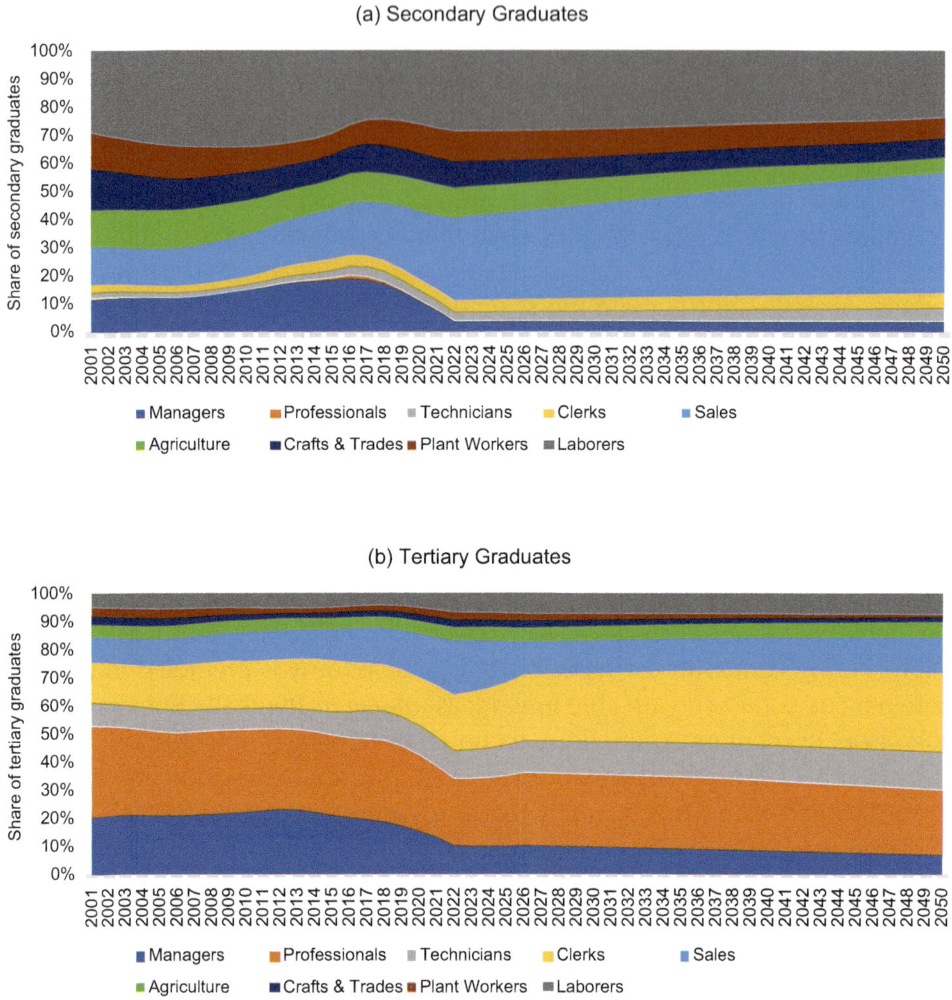

FIGURE 13.3 Share of Graduates by Occupation (%), Philippines, 2001–2050

Note: Legends for occupations with very small values are suppressed to facilitate better presentation of graphs.

Source: Actual values for 2001–2022 are authors' calculations based on data from the Philippine Statistics Authority's Labor Force Survey (https://psada.psa.gov.ph/catalog/LFS/about). Forecasts are from 2023–2050.

the unrealistic job requirements that companies demand of new hires, secondary graduates will increasingly take tertiary education. Certainly, there is nothing wrong with people aspiring to obtain a college degree or to experience college life. However, from society's point of view, this is potentially a misallocation of their time and resources, not to mention the frustration caused by not being able to find a high-paying job. Second, from a moral point of view, college should not be the implicit "minimum" level of education to lead a decent life.

13.4 Supply and Demand Mismatches

Where do imbalances in the demand for and supply of occupations and education lie? Figure 13.4 shows the predicted magnitude of excess supply of occupations up to 2050, while Figure 13.5 shows the ratio of the predicted number of those employed in an occupation (can be considered "employment" or "demand") to the predicted number of those who can work (or are looking for work) in an occupation (can be considered "labor force" or "supply").[2,3] It is apparent that

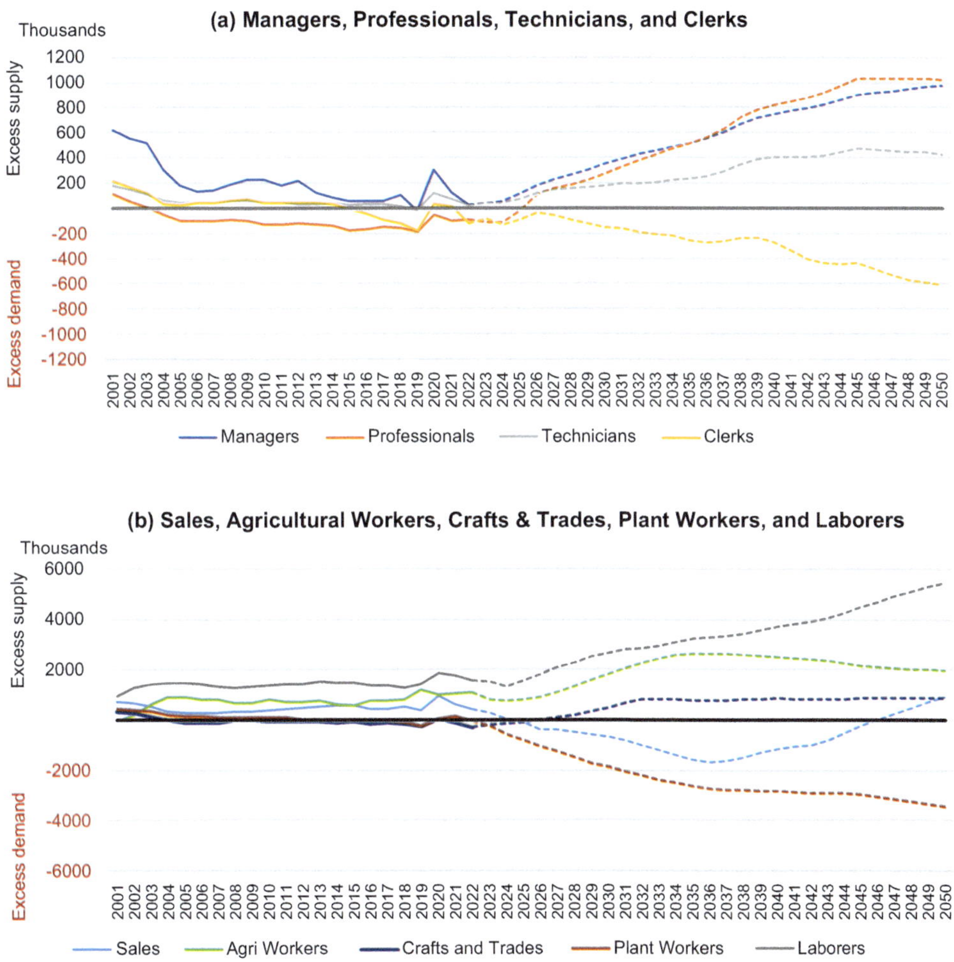

FIGURE 13.4 Supply and Demand Imbalances by Occupation, Philippines, 2001–2050

Note: Positive values indicate excess supply (supply of occupations is greater than demand), whereas negative values indicate excess demand (supply is less than demand).

Source: Actual values for 2001–2022 are authors' calculations based on data from the Philippine Statistics Authority's Labor Force Survey (https://psada.psa.gov.ph/catalog/LFS/about). Forecasts are from 2023–2050.

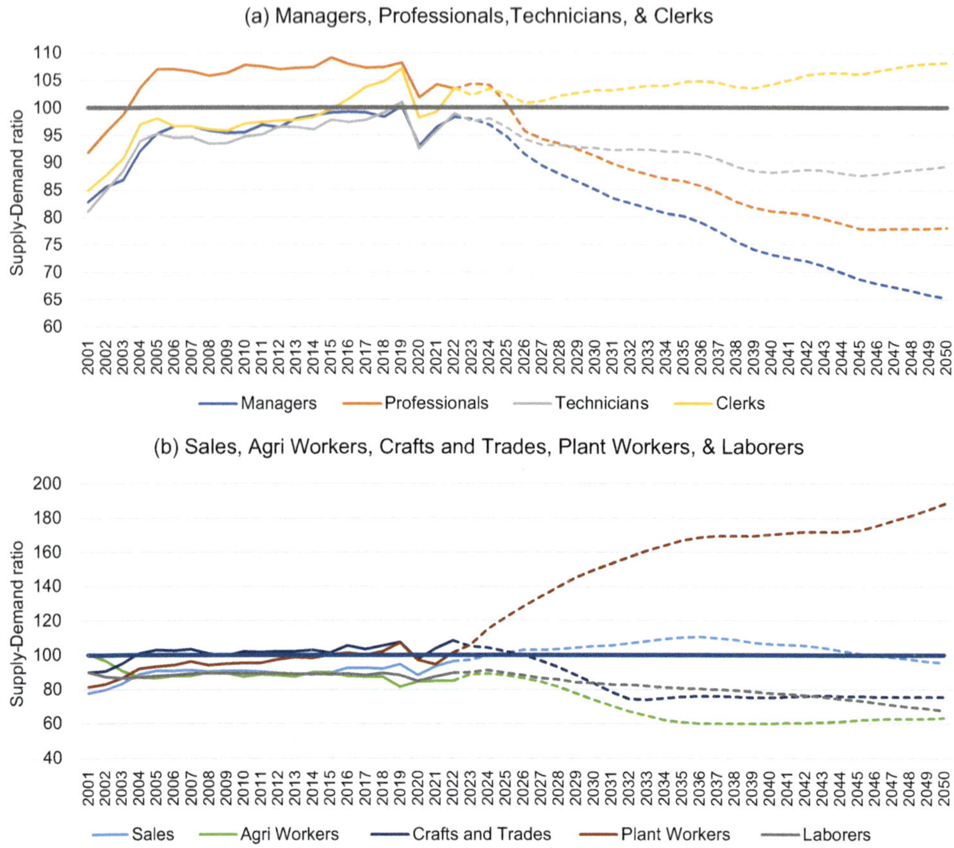

FIGURE 13.5 Supply-Demand Ratios by Occupation, Philippines, 2001–2050

Note: Values greater than 100 indicate unfilled demand of an occupation (demand is greater than supply). Values lower than 100 indicate that not all supply of an occupation is able to find employment (demand is less than supply).

Source: Actual values for 2001–2022 are authors' calculations based on data from the Philippine Statistics Authority's Labor Force Survey (https://psada.psa.gov.ph/catalog/LFS/about). Forecasts are from 2023–2050.

the economy will keep massively overproducing low-skill workers (Figure 13.4, Panel b), such as laborers and agricultural workers, albeit the surplus in the latter will decrease following the decline in this sector's employment share. It should be noted that the demand for laborers is expected to decline. However, this is outpaced by the growing supply—a reflection of the large share of workers transitioning primarily into laborers regardless of educational attainment. In fact, we expect that by 2050, only 67 out of 100 people who can work as laborers, can be employed as such. For agricultural workers, this is estimated to be 63 out of 100. This is a clear sign that the economy will keep producing "bad" jobs, in the sense that these types of jobs receive low wages and do not provide job security. These are workers primarily employed in agriculture, construction, and accommodation and food services, which are also the lowest-paying sectors in the economy.

Meanwhile, occupations such as managers, professionals, and technicians will face surpluses (Figure 13.4, Panel A). Does this mean that the country has a large supply of highly professional workers? While this is true, the correct interpretation is that the economy cannot absorb the types of skills that these workers have. In 2050, only 65 out of 100 people in the labor force who can work as managers will be employed as such. For professionals, this is 78 out of 100, and for technicians, 89 out of 100. These trends and imbalances in occupations will also be reflected in the educational requirements of our productive sectors. The low-skill, low-pay jobs that the economy is producing implies that while we have a more educated workforce overall, as evidenced by the excess supply of secondary graduates, tertiary graduates, and postgraduates (Figure 13.6, Panel A), our sectors are unable to absorb them.[4] In fact, only 84 out of 100 secondary graduates will be able to find employment that requires that level of education, and only 87 out of 100 for tertiary graduates (Panel B). We expect strong demand for workers with postgraduate education between 2022 and 2037, where there is an excess demand of about ten postgraduates on average. However, in terms of absolute magnitudes, these numbers are very low, and the excess demand will become an excess supply from 2038 onward.

This can be related to the perennial question of overseas labor migration: Why do Philippine engineers and other highly skilled individuals leave the country? The lack of domestic demand can be answered in two ways. First, sectors that require workers with these skills are too small in terms of employment share and growth. These include manufacturing, information and communication, real estate, and the financial sectors. Second, as mentioned previously, local companies simply do not engage in activities that require highly skilled workers. Many of them do not develop new products and do not manufacture machinery and equipment to support their own production, let alone export. This is why qualified professionals go abroad to practice their profession.

On the other hand, there are jobs that remain unfilled—those that report an excess demand (negative excess supply in Figure 13.4, or ratios greater than 100 in Figure 13.5). The economy will need more clerks—staple jobs needed to support different business functions. We predict that between 2025 and 2050, there will be an excess of five clerk openings for every 100 workers who can work as such. The demand for sales workers will accelerate following the expected expansion of the wholesale and retail trade sector. We also predict that between 2026 and 2050, there will be an excess of six sales worker openings for every 100 workers who can work as such. However, the labor force is quick to take up these occupations, so the imbalance is predicted to eventually be corrected, and the occupation is once again "overproduced" by 2046. The largest gap to fill will be plant workers, particularly drivers and vehicle operators. Between 2026 and

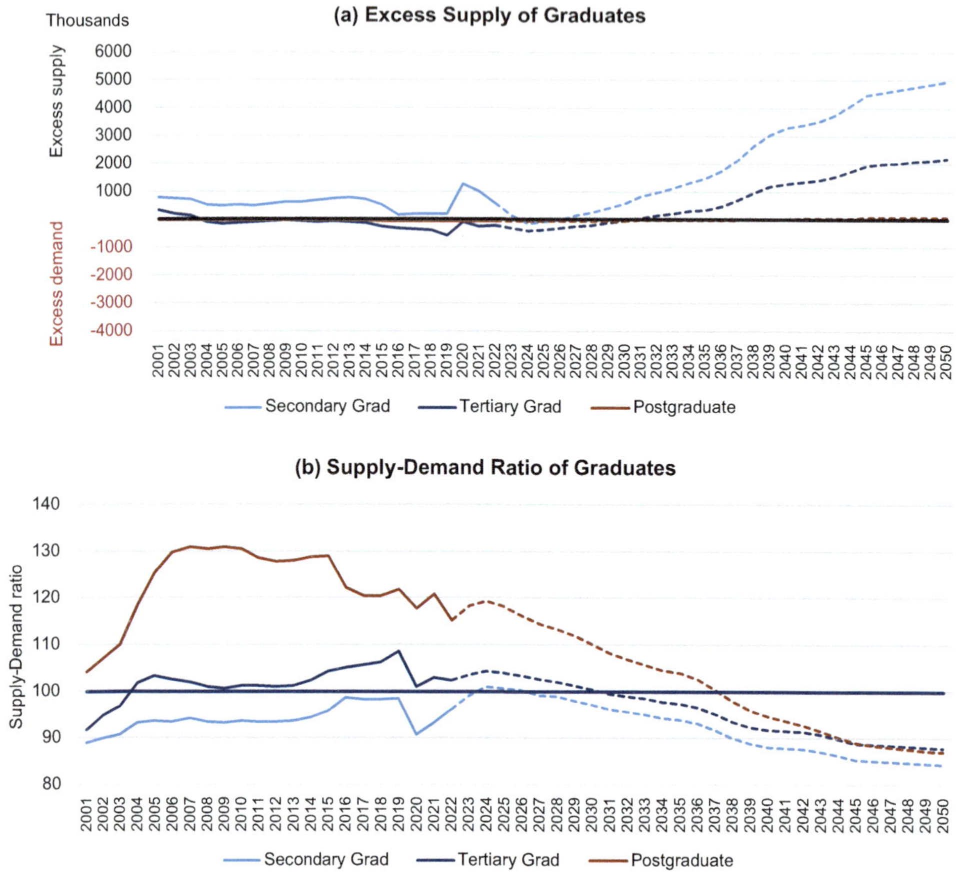

FIGURE 13.6 Supply and Demand Imbalances of Graduates, Philippines, 2001–2050

Notes: (i) Panel (a): Positive values indicate excess supply (supply of occupations is greater than demand), whereas negative values indicate excess demand (supply is less than demand). (ii) Panel (b): Values greater than 100 indicate unfilled demand of an occupation (demand is greater than supply). Values lower than 100 indicate that not all supply of an occupation is able to find employment (demand is less than supply).

Source: Actual values for 2001–2022 are authors' calculations based on data from the Philippine Statistics Authority's Labor Force Survey (https://psada.psa.gov.ph/catalog/LFS/about). Forecasts are from 2023–2050.

2050, we predict that for every 100 workers who can work as plant workers, there will be an annual excess of 65 openings on average, reaching an excess of 88 for every 100 in 2050. This is likely due to the expected expansion of the transport and storage sector.

Given the overproduction of laborers who work in agriculture and construction, there is an opportunity to correct the overall occupational imbalances in the economy by upskilling these workers to allow them to transition into the relatively higher-paying transport sector. However, a stern reminder of the problem of overeducation is necessary: These transport jobs require no more than secondary education. As mentioned in Chapter 10, education matters, but we need to pay attention to the *type* of education. Tertiary and postgraduate education are only relevant if companies engage in R&D to produce new products or improve organizational capability. But for behind-the-frontier catch-up, which is more appropriate for the Philippines, good-quality basic education is key. Hence, there is an urgent need to address the issues plaguing basic and early childhood education mentioned in Chapter 10 (malnutrition, overworked students, and insufficient staffing, backlogs in the building of classrooms), which have led to the learning crisis and the recently uncovered 25 million people functionally illiterate (Philippine Statistics Authority, 2025a). To be fair, the Department of Education has acknowledged the need to address the learning crisis as a "matter of survival." It has set forth to work with different institutions (such as the UNICEF) to enact tutorial and remedial programs, improve early childhood care and development (ECCD), and prevent learning losses due to disasters.

There has also been a recent move to roll back the two years of the K–12 program, allowing grade 10 students to proceed to college if they pass a test, making the two years of senior high school optional. This is potentially another costly move, especially because the K–12 program has taken major criticism but has not undergone proper evaluations, all the while being muddled with implementation issues. There has also been a move to decongest the curriculum in both basic and higher education, where several general education subjects (e.g., arts, ethics, etc.) will be removed from higher education and offered in senior high. This was met with resistance by faculty groups at higher educational institutions. Although these may offer improvements in the long run, the other threats to quality basic education and ECCD must be addressed alongside. These developments can be met with optimism if implemented properly, but only time will tell if they deliver what they promise.

Basic education of higher quality is what is needed for the types of jobs the economy will produce. More specialized knowledge for these occupations can be given through post-secondary and vocational courses. We certainly need to stop producing college graduates who end up working as sales personnel, drivers, or domestic helpers.

13.5 Conclusions

We close this chapter by reiterating our claim: While the country will progress, the Philippines will still be a low-productivity economy, with Filipinos working the same low-paying jobs they are likely working now. These jobs will not require tertiary education, but university graduates will continue being overproduced. Overeducation will persist. With the aggressive expansion of the public higher education sector and the overly demanding job requirements posted by companies operating in low-productivity activities, we will have more workers with college degrees. However, not all of them will be fortunate enough to benefit from higher wages in high-productivity sectors—jobs in these sectors are far too few in number. Because sectors with high potential, like manufacturing, are not producing the goods that "make a country," let alone exporting, opportunities for higher wages in these sectors will remain scarce.

What happened to the resources that the nation and Filipino families have invested into the tertiary education system? The country is getting more and more people through college, promising that a college degree is key to upward social mobility. However, the harsh reality is that we have highly educated security guards, helpers, and sales personnel. We have graduates of bachelor of science in tourism who work as waiters and waitresses. The benefits no longer outweigh the costs.

We call these jobs "bad" not because the work is dishonest or abhorrent but because these are often low-productivity jobs that do not require a college degree. To many people, these jobs still give pride and social mobility up to some extent. However, the persistence of these low-productivity services reveals how much society has become reliant on these jobs—how the system depends on these low-pay jobs that are born out of wide inequality. If workers had a choice, would they really choose to work in these jobs? However, the reality is that *they do not have a choice*; these are the *only* jobs available.

Eventually, as a nation develops, some of these jobs may disappear. In countries like Spain or Australia, household helpers are paid approximately PHP 70,000 monthly, with benefits, on a nine-to-five basis, five days a week. As a result, it is extremely rare to see ordinary households with full-time help. Very far from what household helpers are paid or are entitled to as *mandated by law* in the Philippines (PHP 5,000 monthly—PHP 7,000 in the NCR, with benefits, but often without paid leave). This is the role that structural transformation (and an industrial policy) can play—to eventually phase out "bad jobs" such as elevator attendants, helpers, or laborers in agriculture. This does not mean that the people working these jobs will be left behind; rather, these jobs will disappear because people will have other, better-paying opportunities as an outcome of growth. Hence, the need for strong basic education. Even if these jobs disappear overnight, provided there are new, better jobs available, it would be easy to recalibrate and redirect workers toward these new jobs with a technical or vocational course or two because their foundational skills (trainability, comprehension, and competencies) are strong. However, as mentioned in previous chapters, these jobs can only come from firms. The Philippines needs firms.

Without any strong commitment or vision by the government to transform the structure of the economy, to engage larger firms with the call to shared prosperity, or to at least begin prodding them to engage in higher-value-adding activity or improve organizational capabilities, or to address the challenges in basic education and overeducation, or to produce decent work, not much will change for the Filipino worker.

Notes

1 *Education structure* refers to the distribution (percentage) of people across different levels of education. *Occupational structure* refers the distribution (percentage) of people across 1-digit PSOC occupations.
2 Excess supply is calculated as supply of occupations less demand for occupations. While it is discussed in detail in Appendix 13, to clarify shortly here, the supply of occupations is based on the number of occupations that is produced from the different levels of education attained by the labor force (based on the education-to-occupation transition presented earlier). The demand for occupations is based directly on the structure of occupations (percentage distribution) within each sector multiplied by the total number of employed in the sector, as predicted by the DLSU ANIMO macroeconometric model.
3 The ratio of employed to labor force (demand to supply) is multiplied by 100 for better interpretability. Ratios below 100 indicate that not all workers in the labor force capable of working as an occupation end up employed in that occupation. Ratios above 100 indicate that there will potentially be more openings in that occupation than what can be filled by those able to work in that occupation.
4 Excess supply is calculated as supply of education less demand for education. Supply of education is taken from the forecasted structure of education of the labor force applied to population dynamics from the DLSU ANIMO econometric model. On the other hand, demand for a particular level of education is based on the forecasted proportion of an occupation that have a particular level of education, which is from the occupation-to-education transition, similar to what was presented earlier in Section 13.3. More details are available in Appendix 13.

APPENDIX 13

The Employment–Education Forecasting Model

This Appendix provides a discussion of the model used to forecast employment and education, and presents the figures of forecasts of sectors not presented in the chapter.

The goal of the model is to forecast the supply and demand of education and occupations (in numbers of people) and determine whether imbalances exist. However, the components generated in each step of the process can also provide meaningful insights in our discussion. The process begins with the gathering and treatment of data, which entails getting employment and population forecasts from the DLSU ANIMO model, and the extraction of occupational structures of the economic sectors (e.g., agriculture, manufacturing, etc.) and educational structures of the labor force (by gender and age group) from Labor Force Survey (LFS) microdata. The second step produces the demand for occupations and supply of education. When multiplying the structure (percent distribution) of occupations within a sector to the forecasted total employment of the sector (number of people), this will give the number of people that will be in each occupation. Calculating the levels of education is done similarly. The third step produces two groups of transition matrices: (1) education–occupation matrices capturing what occupations the various levels of education (including undergraduates and graduates) may transition into, and (2) occupation–education matrices, which reveal how each occupation is comprised of people with various levels of education. These are in percentages (e.g., what percent of secondary graduates work as salespersons, etc.). Each occupation–education and education–occupation combination is then collected as a time series and forecasted. In the fourth step, the forecasted demand for occupations is multiplied to the forecasted occupation–education matrix to get the demand for education. The forecasted supply of education is then multiplied to the education–occupation matrix to get the supply of occupations. After this step, the demand and supply of occupations and education can now be compared to see imbalances, whether there is excess supply or excess demand in any occupation or education level.

Step 1: Data Sources

The model uses two data sources:

1. *Macro forecast data.* The following *macro forecast* data up to 2050 are taken from the DLSU ANIMO model and the Philippine Statistics Authority:

   Input 1.1: Labor force forecasts by age group and sex, $LF_{a,s,t}$, in number of people.

   Input 1.2: Employment forecasts by economic sector, $Emp_{n,t}$, in number of people.

2. *Microdata* from the *Philippine Statistics Authority's Labor Force Survey* was compiled, harmonized (since educational, industrial, and occupational classifications change over time), and aggregated into a macro time series. Only the October rounds from 2021 to 2022 were used. The following are extracted:

   a. *Input 2.1*: Structure of educational attainment by age group and sex, $e^{j}_{a,s}$, in percentages—the proportion of a population of age a, and sex s, with a particular level of education, j. There are eight categories of education: no grade completed, primary undergraduate, primary graduate, secondary undergraduate, secondary graduate, tertiary undergraduate, tertiary graduate, and postgraduate. Age categories include below 15, 15 to 24, 25 to 64, and 65 and up—same as in the DLSU ANIMO model.
   b. *Input 2.2*: Structure of occupations by sector, o^{k}_{n}, in percentages—the proportion of workers in sector n working as a particular occupation, k. Sectors are the same 16 sectors specified in the DLSU ANIMO model. Occupations include the ten major groups under the one-digit Philippine Standard Occupational Classifications: managers and supervisors (shortened to *managers*), professionals, technicians and associate professionals (*technicians*), clerical and support services (*clerks*), sales and services (*sales*), skilled agriculture, forestry and fishery (*commercial agricultural workers*), crafts and trades workers, plant machinery operators and assemblers (*plant workers*), and elementary occupations (shortened as *laborers*, given how this typology helps illustrate the majority of this occupation group).
   c. *Input 2.3*: Education-to-occupation transition matrices by age group–sex, in percentages. Each element $y^{j,k}_{a,s}$ represents what proportion of a population

with age a and sex s with a level of education j will end up in a particular occupation k. These may be interpreted somewhat as "transition probabilities."

d. *Input 2.4*: Occupation-to-education transition matrices by sector, in percentages. Each element $z_n^{k,j}$ represents what proportion of a particular occupation k in sector n has different levels of education j. These may be interpreted somewhat as "educational requirements."

The earlier data are extracted for every round of the LFS from 2001 to 2022, and then time series are formed for all values of $e_{a,s}^{j}$ and o_n^k, and every element of the two sets of transition matrices $y_{a,s}^{j,k}$ and $z_n^{k,j}$. In order of the aforementioned, we denote the time series as $E_{a,s,t}^{j}$, $O_{n,t}^{k}$, $Y_{a,s,t}^{j,k}$, and $Z_{n,t}^{k,j}$, respectively, which are all in percentages.

Step 2: Forecasting Structures and Transition Matrix Probabilities

The time series built from *Inputs 2.1 to 2.4* of the microdata in the previous step are forecasted using trend analysis.

For each structure time series $\%X_t$ in $\left\{E_{a,s,t}^{j}, O_{n,t}^{k}, Y_{a,s,t}^{j,k}, Z_{n,t}^{k,j}\right\}$, we do the following:

1. Apply a Hodrick–Prescott filter to separate the trend and cyclical component.
2. Select the best possible trend adjustment among the following specifications and select the one with the lowest forecast mean squared error.

   a. Constant: $\%X_t = \alpha$
   b. Linear trend: $\%X_t = \alpha + \beta * t$
   c. Exponential trend: $\ln \%X_t = \alpha + \beta * t$
   d. Potential: $\ln \%X_t = \alpha + \beta * \ln t$
   e. Stochastic: $\%X_t = \alpha + \beta * \%X_{t-1}$

3. Forecast up to the preferred time horizon using the best trend identified in the previous analysis.
4. Apply a homogenization $\hat{X}\ \%\hat{X}_t = \frac{\%X_{i,t}}{\sum_i \%X_{i,t}}$ such that the summation over i is done across subcategories (i.e., occupations in the sector, educational attainment) to ensure the structures always add up to one; for example, the proportions of different occupations in a sector should always sum to 100% of employment in the sector, $\hat{O}_{n,t}^{k} = \frac{O_{n,t}^{k}}{\sum_k O_{n,t}^{k}}$, for all years.

This produces the following forecasted and homogenized time series:

Output 2.1: $\hat{E}_{a,s,t}^{j}$ is the proportion of population with age a and sex s with educational attainment j.

Output 2.2: $\hat{O}_{n,t}^{k}$ is the proportion of employed persons in sector n with occupation k.

Output 2.3: $\hat{Y}^{j,k}_{a,s,t}$ is the proportion of population with age a and sex s with educational attainment j that gets into occupation k.

Output 2.4: $\hat{Z}^{k,j}_{n,t}$ is the proportion of employed persons in sector n with occupation k that has educational attainment j.

Output 2.2 is organized by sector and gives us the basis for the occupational structures of each sector in Figure 13.1 presented in Section 13.2 of this chapter.

Step 3: Forecasting Sectoral Occupational Demand and Demographic Education Supply

Outputs 2.1 and 2.2 are then combined with the macrodata forecasts from the DLSU ANIMO model to get the quantities of education supply and occupation demand. The following are produced:

Output 3.1: Total education supply of each education level for a particular age group–sex demographic, in numbers of people. This is computed by multiplying Output 2.1 by Input 1.1, $\hat{E}\,S^{E=j}_{a,s,t} = LF_{a,s,t} \times \hat{E}^{j}_{a,s,t}$ for all $a \times s, j$. That is, based on the forecast of how many people there will be in a specific age–sex demographic, what percentage of this demographic will end up with a particular level of education.

Output 3.1.1: When summed up across all age–sex demographics, $S^{E=j}_{t} = \sum_{a \times s} S^{E=j}_{a,s,t}$, this will give us total education supply of education level j.

Output 3.2: Total employment demand by occupation levels per sector, in numbers of people. This is computed by multiplying Output 2.2 by Input 1.2, $\hat{O}\,D^{O=k}_{n,t} = Emp_{n,t} \times \hat{O}^{k}_{n,t}$ for all n, k. That is, based on how many are forecasted to work in a sector per the DLSU ANIMO model, what number will be in occupation k based on the forecasted percentage of this occupation in this sector.

Output 3.2.1: When summed up across all sectors, $D^{O=k}_{t} = \sum_{n} D^{O=k}_{n,t}$, this will give us the total occupation demand for occupation k.

Step 4: Going Through Transition Matrices to Get Sectoral Education Demand and Demographic Occupation Supply

The education–occupation transition time series from Output 2.3 and occupation–education transition from Output 2.4 are then applied to Outputs *3.1* and *3.2* to get occupation supply (Output 4.1) and education demand (Output 4.2).

Output 4.1: Supply of occupations by age–sex demographic, in numbers. Each level of education supply by age and sex $S^{E=j}_{a,s,t}$ (*Output 3.1*) is multiplied by the corresponding cells $\hat{Y}_{a,s,t}^{j,k}$ in the education–occupation matrix (*Output 2.3*) to calculate how many people in a particular demographic a,s and educational attainment j will work in occupation k. This becomes the supply of occupation k from those with educational attainment j in demographic $a \times s$, $S_{a,s,t}^{O=k} = S_{a,s,t}^{E=j} \times \hat{Y}_{a,s,t}^{j,k}$ for all $a \times s, k$.

Output 4.1.1: When summed up across all age–sex demographics, this gives us the total supply of occupation k, $S_t^{O=k} = \sum_{a \times s} S_{a,s,t}^{O=k}$.

Output 4.2: Demand for each level of education by sector, in numbers of people. Each occupation demand by sector $D_{n,t}^{O=k}$ (Output 3.2) is multiplied by the corresponding cells $\hat{Z}_{n,t}^{k,j}$ in the occupation–education matrix (Output 2.4) to calculate how many people in sector n and occupation k have educational attainment j. This becomes the demand for education level j based on occupation k in sector n, $\hat{Z}D_{n,t}^{E=j} = D_{n,t}^{O=k} \times \hat{Z}_{n,t}^{k,j}$ for all n, j.

Output 4.2.1: When summed up across all sectors, this gives us the total demand for education j, $D_t^{E=j} = \sum_{n} D_{n,t}^{E=j}$.

This step produces two by-products that give meaningful insights in this chapter. Output 4.2 is organized by sector, and that gives us the basis for educational requirements by sector in Figure 13.2 of Section 13.2. Output 4.1 is organized by level of education, and that gives us the basis for the occupation–education transitions and the persistence of overeducation highlighted in Figure 13.3 in Section 13.3.

Step 5: Computing Demand and Supply Imbalances

Output 5.1: Occupational imbalances. Total demand for occupations (Output 3.2.1) is then compared with total supply of occupations (Output 4.1.1). Computing for excess supply (or demand) gives the occupational imbalance for occupation k, $XS_t^{O=k} = S_t^{O=k} - D_t^{O=k}$.

Output 5.2: Educational imbalances. Total demand for education (Output 4.2.1) is then compared with the total supply of education (Output 3.1.1). Computing for excess supply (or demand) gives the educational imbalance for education j, $XS^{E=j} = S_t^{E=j} - D_t^{E=j}$.

These represent the final output of the model presented in Section 13.4.

Forecasts of other sectors.

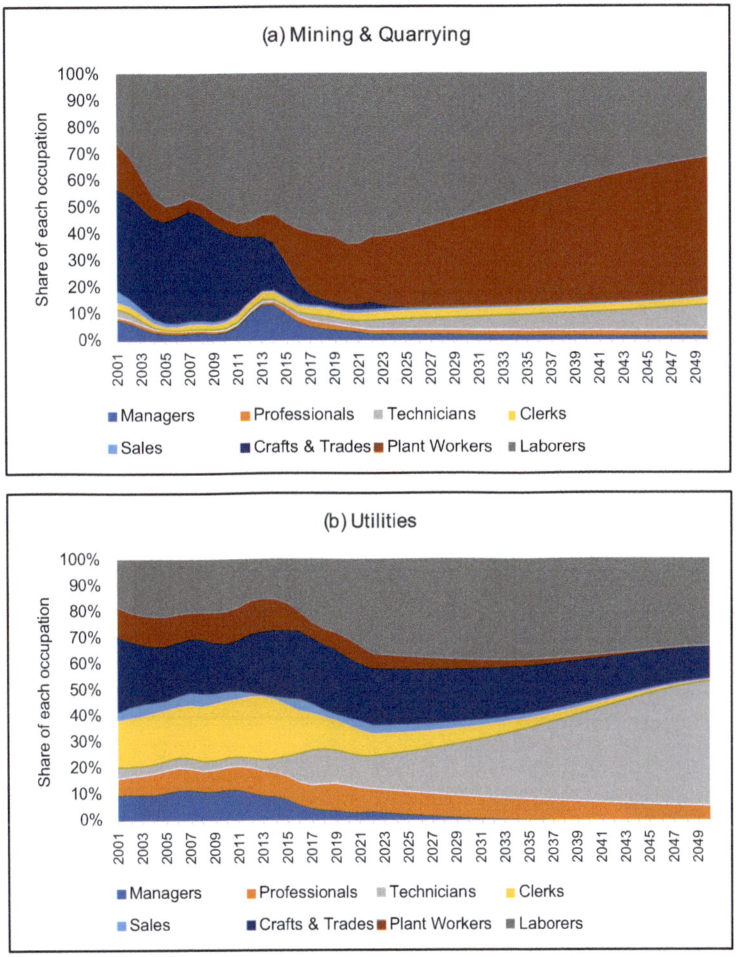

FIGURE A13.1 Occupational Structures for Selected Sectors, Philippines, 2001–2050

Note: Legends for occupations with very small values are suppressed to facilitate better presentation of graphs.

Source: Actual values for 2001–2022 are authors' calculations based on data from the Philippine Statistics Authority's Labor Force Survey (https://psada.psa.gov.ph/catalog/LFS/about). Forecasts are from 2023–2050.

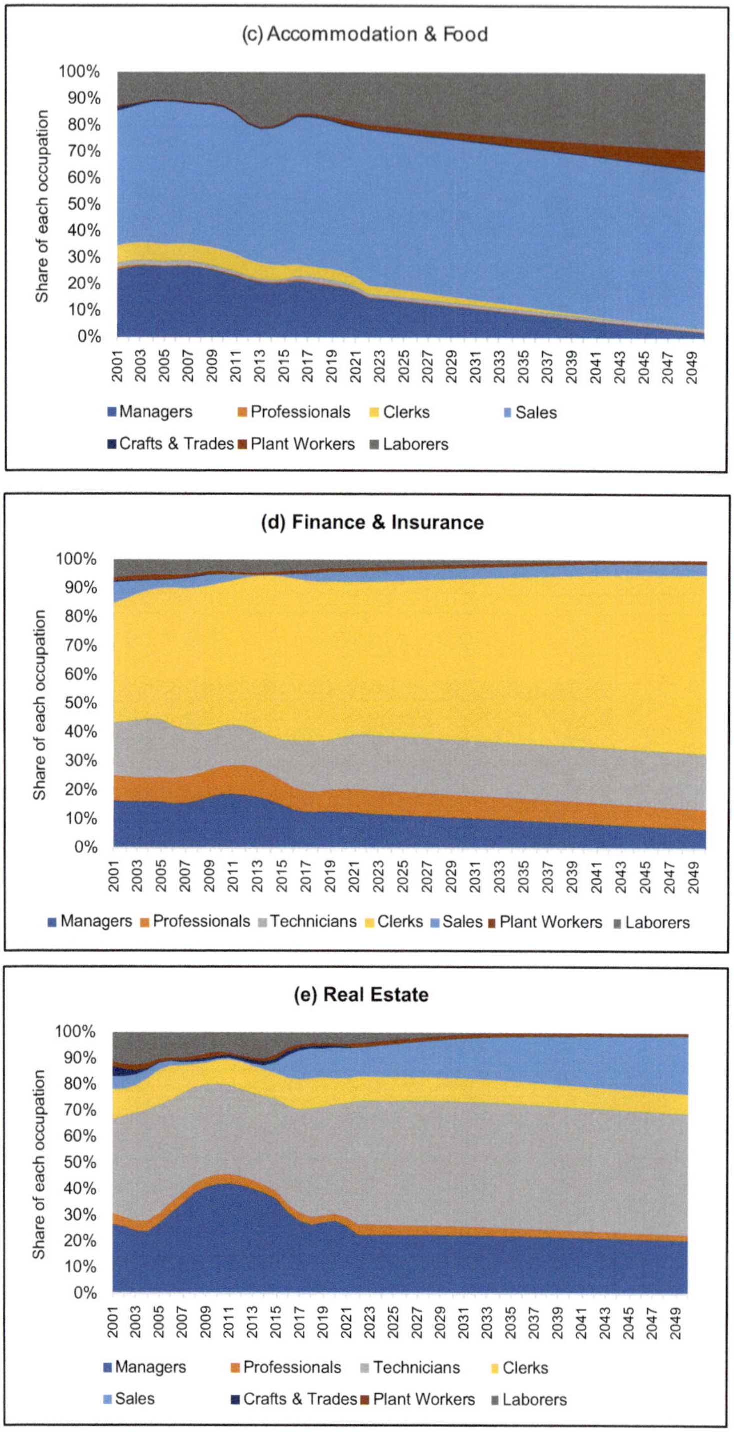

FIGURE A13.1 (Continued)

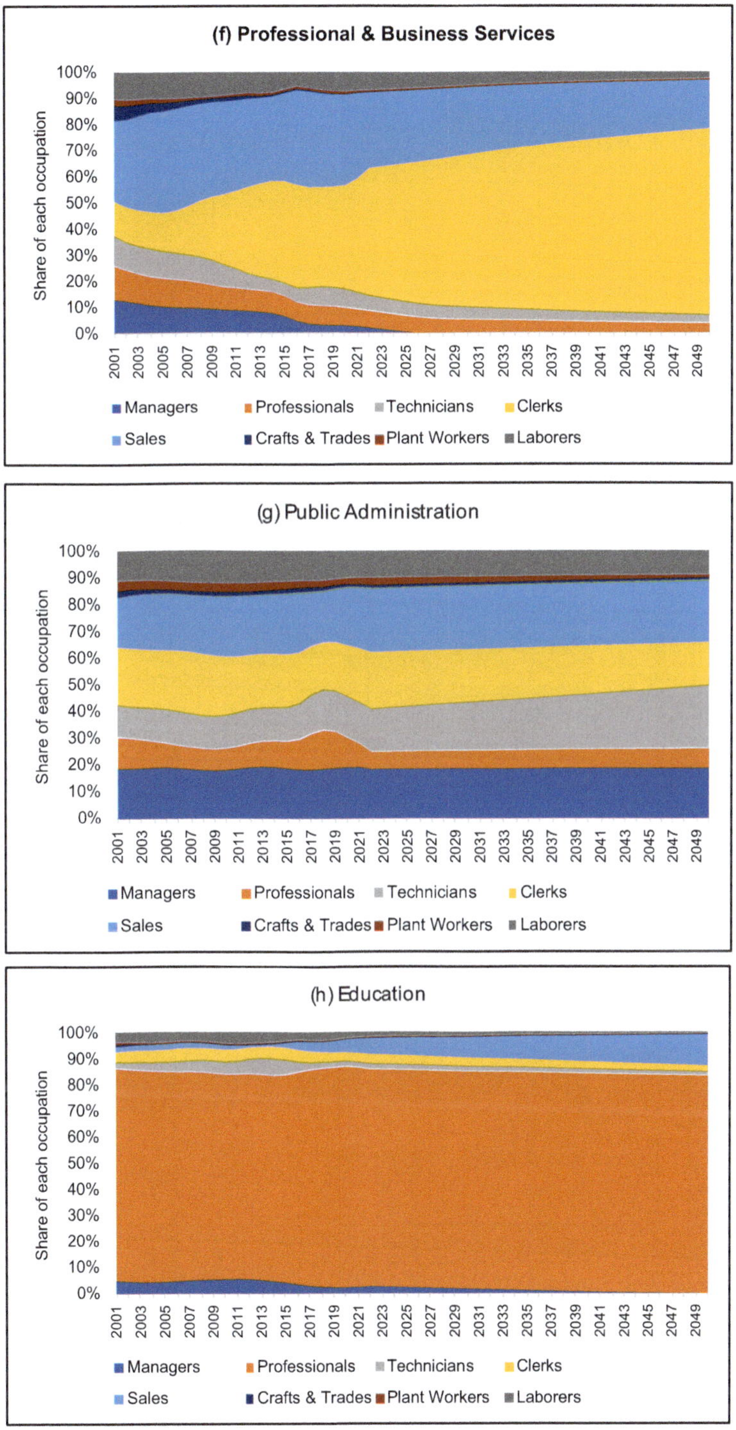

FIGURE A13.1 (Continued)

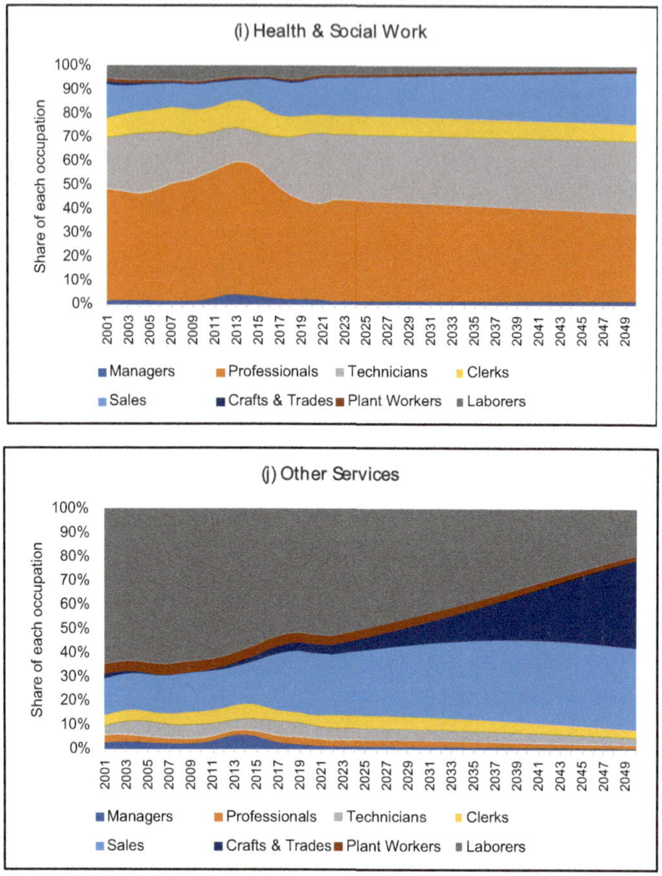

FIGURE A13.1 (Continued)

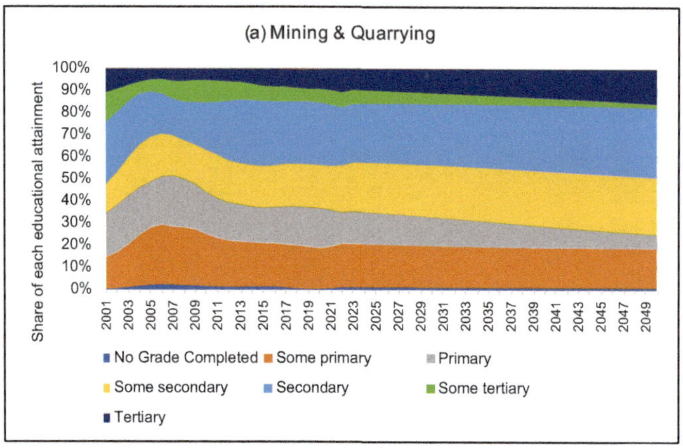

FIGURE A13.2 Educational Requirements for Selected Sectors, Philippines, 2001–2050

Note: Legends for occupations with very small values are suppressed to facilitate better presentation of graphs.

Source: Actual values for 2001–2022 are authors' calculations based on data from the Philippine Statistics Authority's Labor Force Survey (https://psada.psa.gov.ph/catalog/LFS/about). Forecasts are from 2023–2050.

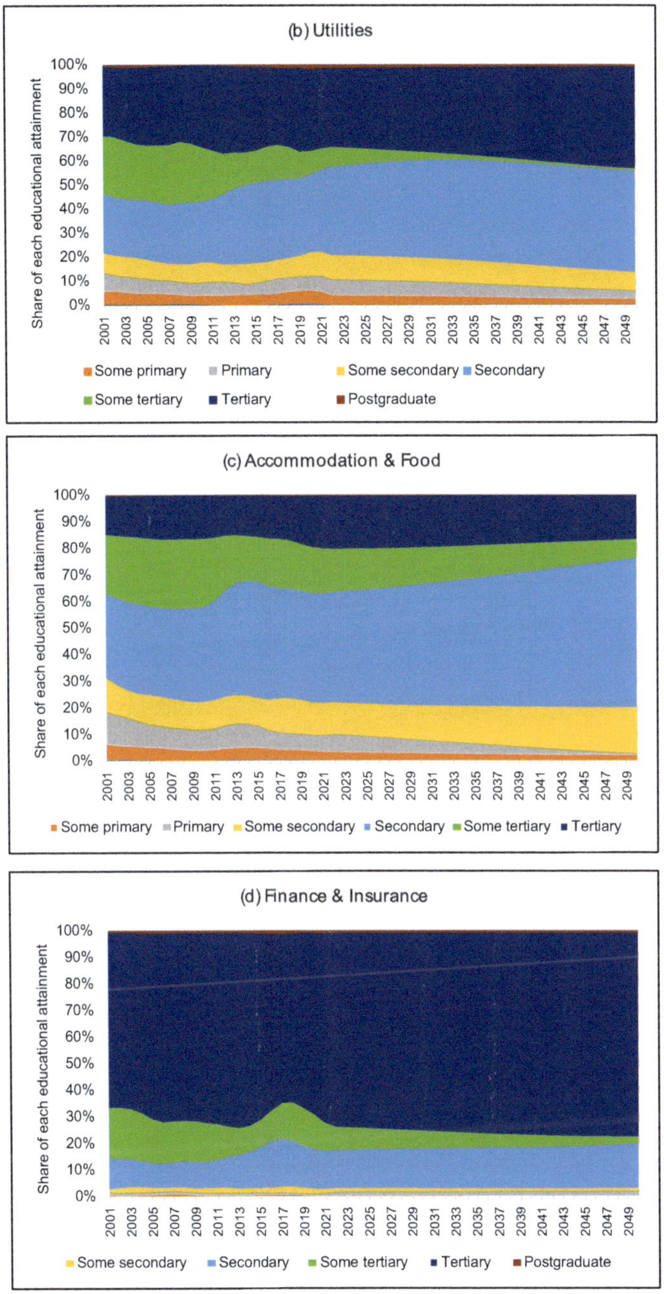

FIGURE A13.2 (Continued)

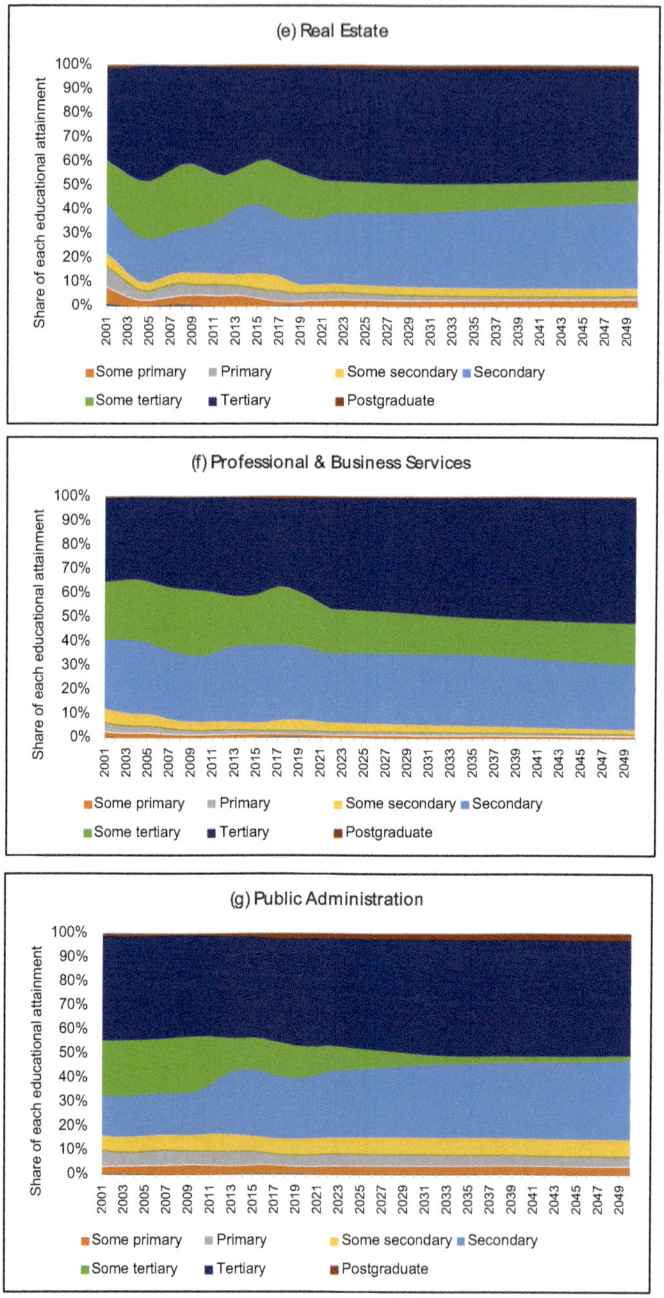

FIGURE A13.2 (Continued)

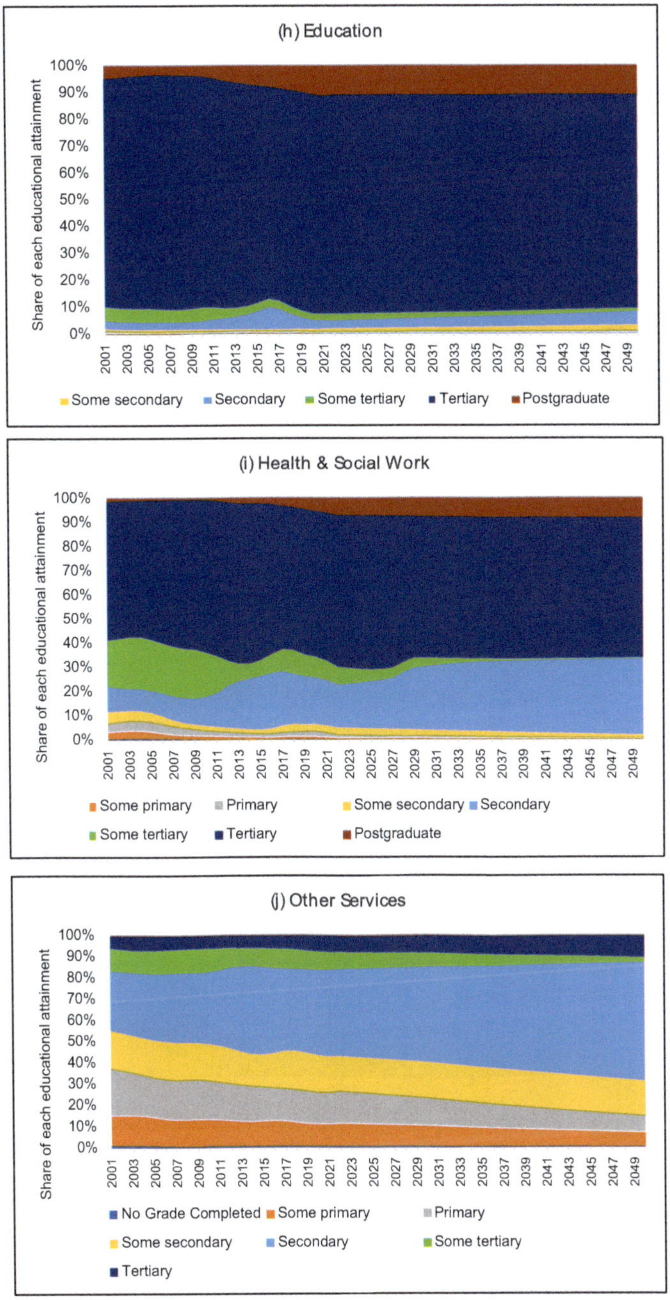

FIGURE A13.2 (Continued)

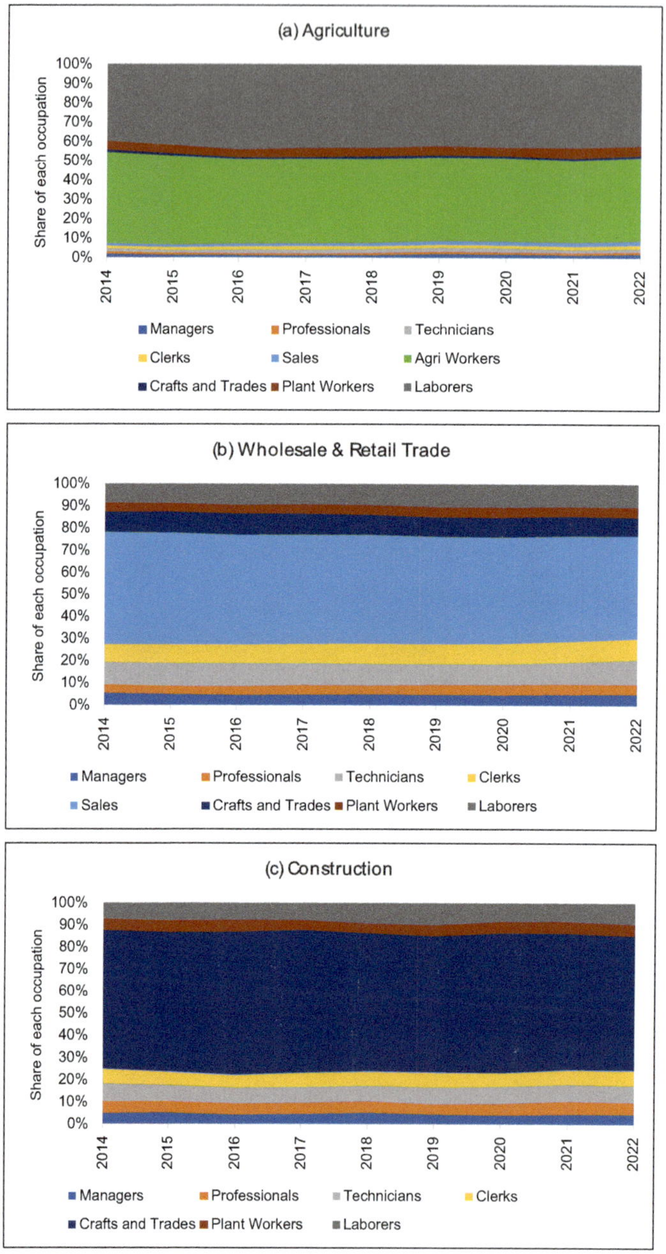

FIGURE A13.3 Occupational Structures for Selected Sectors, Spain, 2014–2022

Note: Legends for occupations with very small values are suppressed to facilitate better presentation of graphs.

Source: Authors' calculations based on data from the Instituto Nacional de Estadistica's Economically Active Population Survey (https://www.ine.es/dyngs/INEbase/en/operacion.htm?c=Estadistica_C&cid=1254736176918&menu=ultiDatos&idp=1254735976595)

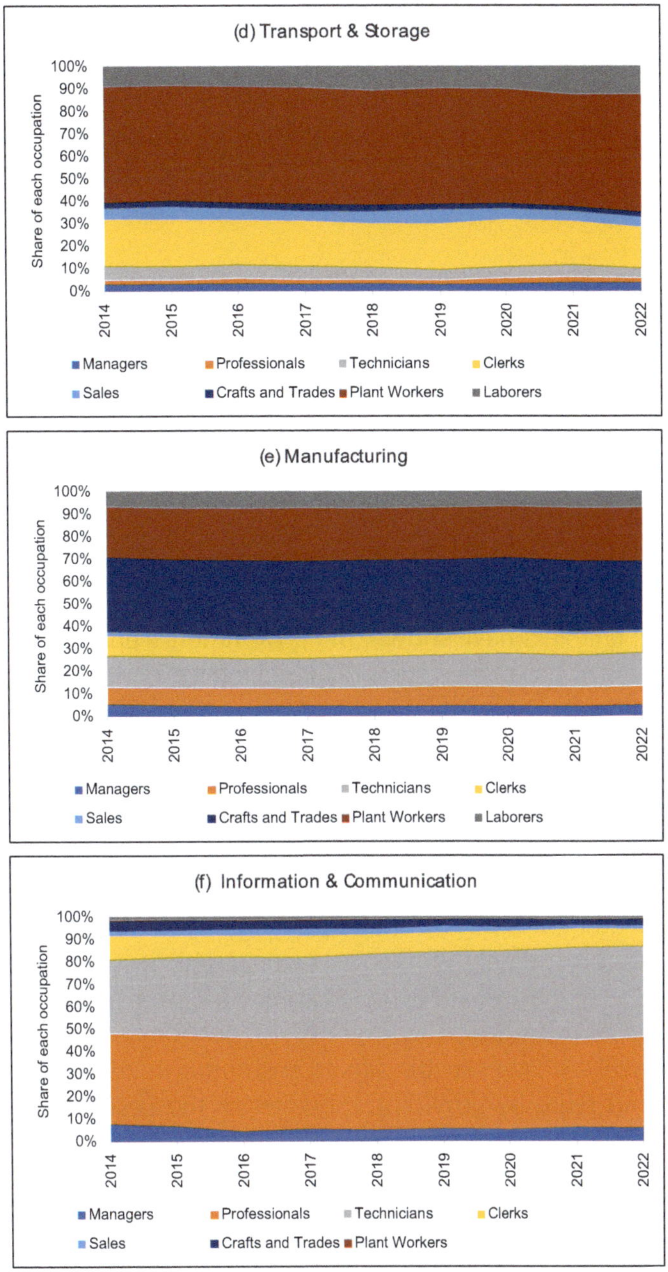

FIGURE A13.3 (Continued)

14

POVERTY AND THE COST OF A DECENT BASKET: WHO CAN AFFORD IT?

14.1 Introduction

As the previous chapters have shown, the government's efforts over the past several decades seem to have fallen short of achieving the progress and development we aspire to. The policies and reforms that the government implemented in previous years have resulted in a per capita income of only about USD 4,400, which is low by international standards. As of 2025, this is below the threshold of the upper-middle-income category. Moreover, poverty remains one of the pressing challenges in the Philippines. In line with this, it is important to closely examine the recent trends in economic growth and poverty incidence while determining whether the government's poverty reduction target is on track. Given the aspirations under the government's *Ambisyon Natin* 2040, it is equally important to determine whether Filipinos will be able to enjoy a "strongly rooted, comfortable, and secure life." We discussed in Chapter 13 our forecasts until 2040, which show that we will be far from the ideals enshrined in *Ambisyon*. This chapter elaborates on this issue by providing estimates of the cost of a "decent" basket and identifying who can afford it in the Philippines.

14.2 Recent Trends in Poverty and Some Forecasts

We focus on a unidimensional definition of *poverty* based on income: A person is poor if their per capita income falls below the official poverty threshold.[1] In other words, the poor are those whose per capita income is not sufficient to meet their basic food and non-food needs. Figure 14.1 shows that poverty in the Philippines displayed a declining trend between 2001 and the COVID-19 pandemic, which disrupted this progress. After the pandemic, poverty incidence resumed its downward trend until 2024. While poverty is generally decreasing over time, one

DOI: 10.4324/9781003728719-14

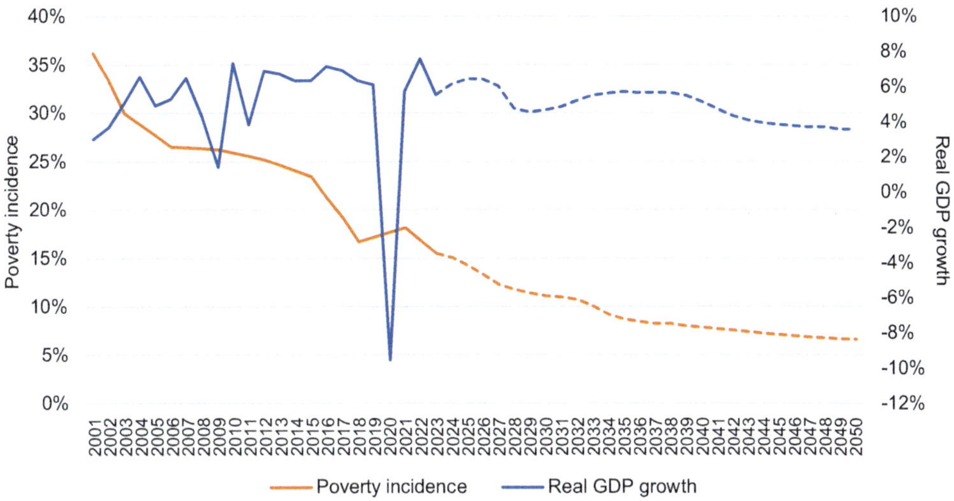

FIGURE 14.1 Poverty Incidence (%) and Real GDP Growth (%), Philippines, 2001–2050

Source: Actual values for 2000–2023 are from the Philippine Statistics Authority's data on the National Accounts (https://openstat.psa.gov.ph/Database/Economic-Accounts/National-Accounts-of-the-Philippines/Annual-National-Accounts) and the poverty incidence estimates reported in Philippine Statistics Authority (2002, 2010, 2016, 2023b, 2024c). Forecasts are from the DLSU ANIMO econometric model.

key question remains: *Is the rate of reduction in poverty fast enough to achieve single-digit incidence by 2028?* Official estimates indicate that poverty rates are declining, but at a slow pace, suggesting that the government needs to adopt different strategies to achieve significant poverty reduction and, hence, allow it to achieve its targets.

The steady decline in poverty from 36.3% in 2001 to 15.7% in 2018 coincided with a relatively robust economic growth, averaging about 5.5% annually. However, the economic growth during the period shows volatility with notable peaks and troughs. For instance, the country recorded only 1.4% growth in 2009, when the world experienced the global financial crisis, and began gaining momentum around 2010. Based on growth, the Philippines was one of the best-performing economies in East Asia before the COVID-19 pandemic of 2020–2021. The pandemic marked a dramatic disruption, with GDP growth plummeting to –9.5% in 2020 and poverty incidence increasing slightly to 17.7%. The post-pandemic period demonstrated a sharp recovery whereby growth bounced back to 7.6% in 2022, 5.5% in 2023, and 5.7% in 2024. In the same manner, poverty incidence gradually declined during the period 2022–2024, reaching 15.1% in 2024. Based on the projections using the DLSU ANIMO econometric model discussed in Chapter 12, the country is expected to record relatively stable growth until 2039 at an average of 5.0%. Between 2040 and 2050, GDP is expected to grow at a slower rate, at an average of 4.1%, while poverty incidence will continue to decline, reaching 6.6% in 2050. Our forecasts suggest that the country will continue to experience a slow decline in poverty incidence until 2050, indicating that if the government maintains its current programs and policies, the reduction in poverty will remain limited.

Looking ahead to 2028, economic growth will gradually slow (we forecast 4.8% in 2028). Although the poverty rate will continue to decline, the rate of reduction will also slow as 2028 approaches. In fact, poverty incidence is expected to reach 11.8% by 2028, which is above the single-digit target for poverty incidence stated in the Philippine Development Plan 2023–2028 (NEDA, 2023a) (see Chapter 5). The most recent official estimates of poverty incidence in 2023 remained at 15.5%. Meanwhile, forecasts based on the DLSU ANIMO econometric model suggest that the country will only reach a single-digit poverty rate by 2034 (at about 9.2%) and not by 2028. In line with the previous discussion, this means that, unless there are significant changes or improvements in the country's current policies and programs, the poverty reduction target will not be attained. In addition, if economic growth is below the government's forecast of 6–8% (and we already predict this will be the case), achieving these poverty reduction targets will become even more challenging.

Although no country in the world has a zero poverty rate, we tried to estimate the time it would take for all poor Filipinos to exit poverty using the 2018 FIES data following the methodology of Morduch (1998).[2] Assuming all incomes of poor families grow by 6–8% annually, it will take between 71 and 95 years for all poor Filipinos to exit poverty using the national poverty line as the threshold. This suggests that the Philippines will fail to achieve zero poverty by 2040, which is one of the key aspirations under *Ambisyon Natin* 2040. Specifically, our projections based on this simple estimation indicate that zero poverty may be realized (if a zero-poverty rate makes sense) between 2092 and 2116. This means that poverty will remain a challenge for the country in the coming decades. If the country's economic growth rate falls below the 6–8% range, as suggested by the DLSU ANIMO econometric model forecasts, approaching zero poverty would take even longer. Moreover, even if we can sustain robust economic growth in the next few years, we need to make sure that the gains are distributed evenly. Investing in human capital and creating better opportunities are crucial in helping the poor secure decent jobs and escape poverty. This may be supported by policies promoting the transition of workers from low-productivity to higher-productivity sectors to boost their incomes and drive more effective poverty reduction.

14.3 Estimating the Cost of a Decent Basket

Although the earlier discussion focused on poverty incidence, most Filipino families aspire not just to meet their basic needs but to achieve a decent standard of living. Given the method used to measure food threshold and poverty incidence, many believe that these metrics do not accurately reflect the true cost of a decent life in the Philippines. In fact, the food threshold in 2023 translates to PHP 64 per day per capita, which is not sufficient for families to afford a nutritious and decent meal at that time.

From this point forward, we shift our focus from the traditional poverty threshold used by PSA to the concept of "living income." According to the Committee on Sustainability Assessment and KIT Royal Tropical Institute (2020), "living income" is the income level that would enable a family to afford a decent standard of living. Similarly, Anker and Anker (2013) defined "living income" as the cost of a basic but decent life for a reference-size family. In other words, we estimate the cost of a decent basket. To apply the aforementioned definitions in the context of the Philippines, we refer to the aspirations outlined in the *Ambisyon Natin* 2040 program. This program represents the collective long-term vision and aspirations of the Filipino people for themselves and for the country by 2040. It envisions Filipinos "enjoying a strongly rooted, comfortable, and secure life" by 2040 (National Economic Development Authority, 2015). More broadly, it states:

> Filipinos enjoy a strongly rooted, comfortable, and secure life. In 2040, we will all enjoy a stable and comfortable lifestyle, secure in the knowledge that we have enough for our daily needs and unexpected expenses, that we can plan and prepare for our own and our children's future. Our family lives together in a place of our own, and we have the freedom to go where we desire, protected and enabled by a clean, efficient, and fair government.
>
> *Department of Economy, Planning, and Development (n.d., par. 1), through: https://2040.depdev.gov.ph/*

In line with this vision, we established a set of criteria to define a "decent standard of living" for a reference family size of five, the typical family size used in the Philippines in research. Given that the Philippine government also aspires to have a prosperous middle-class society by 2040, it is crucial to monitor not only the poverty rates (based on the poverty threshold) but also the proportion of those who are not able to earn a living income (based on the cost of a decent basket).

The Anker methodology is widely regarded as the gold standard for estimating living income. In this chapter, we partially adopt this approach by estimating living income based on expenses on different goods and services that constitute the decent consumption basket. However, unlike the Anker methodology, which uses localized data, our estimates are conducted at the national level. As a result, both the definition of a decent standard of living and the pricing of consumption items are based on national averages rather than local variations.

Let us first briefly discuss how the living income of a Filipino family (having five members) is estimated to understand how it differs from the estimation of the official poverty threshold. The estimation process can be summarized in five key steps. First, we identify the major consumption items that will form the basis of the estimation. In this study, our decent basket consists of ten major consumption categories: (1) food; (2) health care; (3) education; (4) housing, water, and electricity; (5) clothing and footwear; (6) transportation; (7) communication; (8) insurance; (9) recreation; and (10) unforeseen expenses. Where possible, the definition of *decent consumption* for each major category is aligned with the vision of *Ambisyon Natin* 2040 mentioned earlier. Specifically, the decent basket ensures that a Filipino family (1) does not experience poverty or hunger, (2) lives in a comfortable home with essential amenities, (3) can send their children to school, (4) enjoys time with family on weekends (e.g., dining out), (5) can afford domestic or international travel for vacations, and (6) has financial resources to cover unforeseen expenses, among others. By incorporating these elements, the living income approach provides a more comprehensive measure of what it takes for a Filipino family to achieve a truly decent standard of living.

Second, we establish the model diet, which shall be the basis for estimating the amount needed to afford decent food. This approach begins with a model diet used by PSA (and as recommended by the Food and Nutrition Research Institute [FNRI]). Although the model diet meets the minimum daily nutritional requirements of an individual, we modified it to increase the variety of items in the diet while, at the same time, aligning it with what we consider a decent meal. To estimate the cost of a decent meal for the entire day, we used the prices of food commodities from the Department of Agriculture (DA) or the Department of Trade and Industry (DTI), considering both the lowest and highest prices (whenever possible) reported during the study's reference period, which is 2018. In addition, we factored in the assumption that a family eats out for lunch once a week, incorporating this into the annual food expenditures estimates for a family of five. Based on these calculations, Table 14.1 shows that a family of five needs between

TABLE 14.1 Estimated Food Expenditures (PHP) for a Family of Five, Philippines, 2018

	Low	*High*
Breakfast (per capita per day)	19.93	30.31
Lunch (per capita per day)	31.12	65.88
Dinner (per capita per day)	80.27	131.43
Snacks (per capita per day)	8.60	10.30
Food expenditure per capita per day (313 days in one year)	139.91	237.93
Total food expenditure per day per capita if the family eats out for lunch once a week (52 days in one year)	247.47	326.13
Annual per capita food expenditure	56,662	91,430
Annual food expenditure	283,308	457,148
Monthly food expenditure	23,609	38,096

Source: Authors' calculations based on the Philippine Statistics Authority's 2018 Family Income and Expenditure Survey (https://psada.psa.gov.ph/catalog/FIES/about).

PHP 140 and PHP 238 per capita per day to afford decent food for the entire day, covering breakfast, lunch, snacks, and dinner. As expected, these estimates are higher than PSA's most recent estimate per capita food threshold of PHP 64 using their standard model diet (i.e., for the year 2023, in nominal terms). The estimates are even larger on days when the family eats out for lunch (once a week). In fact, to afford a decent meal on those occasions, they need between PHP 248 and PHP 326 per capita per day. Overall, the family of five needs between PHP 56,662 and PHP 91,430 annually to afford decent meals every day, based on 2018 prices. These figures highlight the higher cost of achieving decent meals compared to the official food poverty-based estimates.

The third step extends beyond food to estimate the non-food expenses based on a decent standard of living. The non-food expenses of a family of five include major categories, such as health care, education, housing, water and electricity, clothing and footwear, transportation, communication, insurance, recreation, and unforeseen expenses. To estimate the costs for each major non-food item, we used the average expenditures of a family of five from the 2018 Family Income and Expenditures Survey (FIES). Instead of estimating a single value for the living income, we estimated an interval, with a lower limit and an upper limit. Specifically, we used the estimates for the rural areas as the lower limit and those for the urban areas as the upper limit for most consumption items. For education expenses, we assumed three school-aged children (one in primary and two in secondary school). For health care, we used the costs of accessing public medical facilities as the lower limit, with the costs of accessing private medical facilities as the upper limit. One of the key assumptions in the estimation is that each family has the freedom to move from one place to another (e.g., from urban to rural). At the same time, we assumed that each family can freely choose from among the various goods and services based on prices, preferences, availability, and other factors. This flexibility allows for a more realistic assessment of the range of income needed to achieve a decent standard of living.

Step 4 involves calculating the *total annual expenses* for a family of five using the 2018 FIES, which is based on a one-year reference period. We also determine the *annual per capita expenses* by dividing the *total annual expenses* by the number of family members. This standardization allows for more meaningful comparisons across different family structures, which will be used in the analysis later. The *annual per capita expenses* are then translated to the *annual per capita "living income,"* that is, the per capita income necessary to afford a decent standard of living. For further analysis, this may also be converted to a *monthly "living income"* for a family of five to provide a more practical and accessible benchmark.

Following steps 3 and 4, Table 14.2 presents the estimated costs for each major consumption category, which allows us to calculate both the *total annual expenditures* for a family of five and the corresponding *annual per capita expenditure*. In particular, we estimate that a family of five would need an annual income per capita of between PHP 115,362 (PHP 576,810 annually for the entire family) and PHP 188,282

TABLE 14.2 Estimated Annual Expenditures (PHP) for All Major Consumption Items in the "Decent" Basket for a Family of Five, Philippines, 2018

Consumption Category	*Annual Expenditures*		*Remarks*
	Lower Limit	*Upper Limit*	
1. Food	283,308	457,148	Based on national food bundle reflecting the low and high prices of commodities in 2018 sourced from DA or DTI, with some modification in the food bundle.
2. Health care	19,538	61,498	Upper limit for dental and medical in-patient services refers to private clinic/hospital; lower limit for dental and medical in-patient services refers to public clinic/hospital.
3. Education	33,347	78,814	Assuming three school-aged children: one in primary, two in secondary; includes expense on tuition, allowance, and other educational expenses.
4. Housing, water, electricity, and gas	66,747	116,004	Assuming the family is renting a two-bedroom unit. The toilet is either "flush to pipe sewer system" or "flush to septic tank." Source of water is "community water system piped in dwelling." Roof, wall, and floor made of strong materials. Lower limit is for those living outside NCR; upper limit is those living in NCR.
5. Clothing and footwear	9,331	12,736	Clothes, garments, and footwear.
6. Transportation	39,218	54,590	Transportation services (road, air, sea); operation of own personal transport.
7. Commun-ication	22,407	28,950	Telephone, fax, and services: internet, subscription and prepaid.
8. Insurance	15,622	15,513	Health, life, and dwelling insurance.
9. Recreation	34,855	30,572	Travel (holiday package; individual traveler).
10. Unforeseen expenses; miscellaneous	52,437	85,583	Equivalent to 10% total family expenditures earlier.
Total annual expenditures	**576,810**	**941,408**	
Annual per capita expenditure	**115,362**	**188,282**	

Notes:

(1) The lower limit is for rural areas, while the upper limit is for urban areas, unless otherwise stated. The family size used in the estimation is five.

(2) It is assumed that the family has the freedom to move from one place to another (e.g., urban to rural) and that the family can freely choose from among the various goods and services based on prices, preference, and other factors.

Source: Authors' calculations based on data from the Philippine Statistics Authority's 2018 Family Income and Expenditure Survey (https://psada.psa.gov.ph/catalog/FIES/about), the Department of Agriculture (2018), the Department of Trade and Industry (2018).

(PHP 941,408 annually for the entire family) in 2018 to afford a decent standard of living.[3] However, when we compare this with the actual income levels of families in 2018, a significant gap emerges. The average annual per capita income of Filipino families during the period was only PHP 82,078, which falls well below the minimum required for a decent life (at PHP 115,362). While we would generally expect that incomes in the National Capital Region (NCR) tend to be higher, the average annual per capita income of families in this region in 2018 is only about PHP 124,069, which is only a few thousand pesos above the lower limit for living income. The region, however, clearly performed better when compared to the rest of the regions in the country. In fact, the average annual per capita income of regions other than NCR was approximately PHP 75,575, about 40% lower than NCR's. This also highlights the presence of disparities between NCR and the rest of the regions in the country.

Finally, the fifth step compares the actual *annual per capita income* of each family with the estimated *annual per capita "living income"* to determine whether their current earnings are sufficient to afford a decent standard of living. This comparison is crucial for evaluating income adequacy and identifying potential gaps in earnings among Filipino families. At the same time, this approach provides a comprehensive framework for determining whether the actual income levels in the Philippines are sufficient to sustain a decent quality of life. This can have useful policy implications, particularly in shaping minimum wage policies and in refining poverty reduction strategies to bridge income gaps effectively.

Following the method outlined earlier, we estimated the monthly expenditures for each major consumption category for a family of five in 2018 prices and 2024 prices (Table 14.3) to provide a more practical benchmark. This allows us

TABLE 14.3 Estimated Annual Expenditures (PHP) for a Family of Five, 2018 and 2024

Consumption Category	*Monthly Expenditures (2018)*		*Monthly Expenditures (2024)*	
	Lower Limit	*Upper Limit*	*Lower Limit*	*Upper Limit*
Food	23,609	38,096	30,235	50,401
Health	1,628	5,125	2,022	6,365
Education	2,779	6,568	3,337	7,888
Housing, water, electricity, gas	5,562	9,667	6,741	11,716
Clothing and footwear	778	1,061	928	1,267
Transportation	3,268	4,549	4,249	5,914
Communication	1,867	2,413	1,927	2,490
Insurance	1,302	1,293	1,854	1,841
Recreation	2,905	2,548	3,398	2,981
Unforeseen expenses; miscellaneous	4,370	7,132	5,580	9,107

(Continued)

TABLE 14.3 (Continued)

Consumption Category	*Monthly Expenditures (2018)*		*Monthly Expenditures (2024)*	
	Lower Limit	*Upper Limit*	*Lower Limit*	*Upper Limit*
Monthly living income for a family of 5	**48,067**	**78,451**	**61,272**	**99,970**
Annual living income for a family of 5	**576,810**	**941,408**	**735,266**	**1,199,640**
Annual per capita living income	**115,362**	**188,282**	**147,053**	**239,928**

Notes:
(1) Unforeseen expenses and miscellaneous expenses are calculated residually as the difference between living income and the sum of the other nine categories listed in the table.
(2) The values for 2024 are based on 2018 estimates, adjusted for inflation.

Source: Authors' calculations based on the Philippine Statistics Authority's 2018 Family Income and Expenditure Survey (https://psada.psa.gov.ph/catalog/FIES/about).

to determine the required *monthly living income* of families during these periods. Among all consumption categories, food makes up the largest share, accounting for about 49% of the total family expenditures, followed by housing, water, electricity, and gas, which together represent 11–12% of the total expenditures. Our estimates show that a family of five needed a monthly income between PHP 48,087 and PHP 78,451 in 2018 to afford a decent basket. Adjusted to 2024 prices, this range has increased to PHP 61,272 to PHP 99,970 per month. On an annual basis, this means that a family of five requires an income between PHP 735,000 and PHP 1,200,000 to sustain a decent quality of life.

14.4 Comparing Poverty Threshold and Living Income

Figure 14.2 illustrates the distribution of families' per capita income in the Philippines based on 2018 FIES data, highlighting the difference between the official annual per capita *poverty threshold* and the estimated minimum annual living income per capita. At the same time, it shows that a significantly large share of families was not able to meet the minimum income to afford a decent standard of living in 2018. The annual per capita threshold (marked by the red dashed line), which represents the minimum amount a person needs to afford basic food and non-food needs based on the PSA definition, is PHP 25,813 in 2018. However, the estimated minimum annual living income per capita (marked by the green dashed line) in this study is PHP 115,362, which is more than four times higher than the official *poverty threshold*.

Furthermore, the same figure shows that the peak of the income distribution curve is closer to the poverty threshold rather than the minimum living income, suggesting that a sizable portion of Filipino families earn just above the poverty

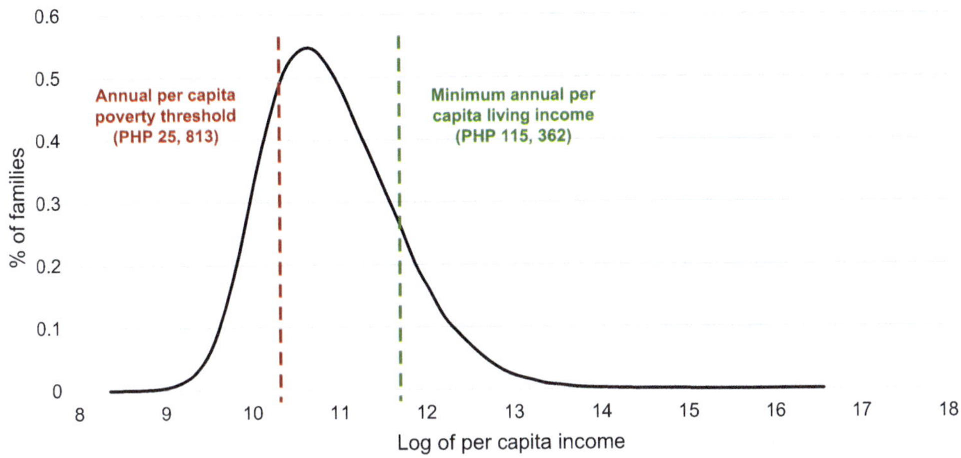

FIGURE 14.2 Distribution of Families' per Capita Income

Note: Kernel = epanechnikov; Bandiwdth = 0.0627

Source: Authors' calculations based on the Philippine Statistics Authority's 2018 Family Income and Expenditure Survey (https://psada.psa.gov.ph/catalog/FIES/about)

line. Relatively few families have incomes that reach or exceed the minimum living income, underscoring the reality that most Filipino families struggle to achieve a decent standard of living. Given that a substantial proportion of families earn below the minimum living income, it is deemed that many families face financial strain, making it difficult to afford decent education, health care, and other essential services. This gap highlights the need for policymakers to implement measures that can provide more opportunities for families to earn higher income, such as "decent job" creation and other livelihood support. The stark contrast between the poverty threshold and the required minimum living income also emphasizes the need for economic policies that go beyond alleviating poverty but also help families achieve a sustainable and decent standard of living.

14.5 Who Can Afford a Decent Life in the Philippines?

Figure 14.3 reveals a stark economic reality where most families find themselves struggling financially to afford a decent basket. A striking 81.7% of families fall below the living income threshold, painting a picture of widespread economic vulnerability. This overwhelming majority suggests that most people are battling to meet a decent standard of living and are likely experiencing significant financial stress and limited opportunities for economic advancement. Notably, while the official poverty incidence among families in 2018 was only 12.1%, our estimates show that about eight in every ten families in the country during the same period failed to meet the minimum income that would allow them to afford the decent basket that we defined earlier in this book.

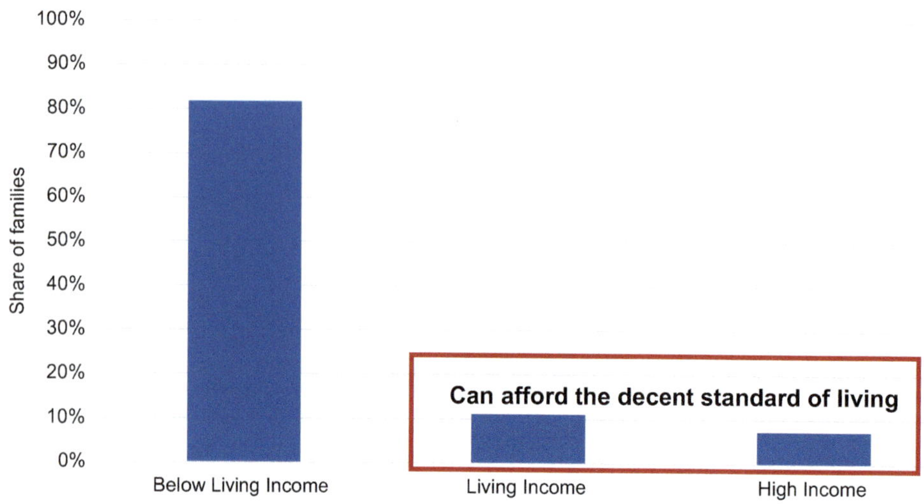

FIGURE 14.3 Share of Families by Income Group (%), Philippines, 2018

Note: The proportion of poor families is 12.1% and the proportion of poor population is 16.7% in 2018.

Source: Authors' calculations based on the Philippine Statistics Authority's 2018 Family Income and Expenditure Survey (https://psada.psa.gov.ph/catalog/FIES/about)

Our estimates also show that only 11.1% of the families meet what is considered a living income, while a mere 7.2% are classified as high-income earners. This small minority represents those who have managed to achieve a decent standard of living, standing in sharp contrast to the vast majority struggling to meet a decent quality of life. This distribution again highlights deep economic inequality, suggesting that most families may be trapped in a cycle of economic hardship, with limited opportunities for upward mobility.

Table 14.4 provides a snapshot of economic stratification, with 20.2 million families—a staggering majority—classified under the "below living income" category in 2018. These families survive on less than PHP 115,362 annually, which translates to just PHP 48,067 monthly for a family of five. The middle category, "living income," encompasses 2.7 million families earning between PHP 115,362 and PHP 188,282 annually. These families exist in a delicate balance, just managing to afford a decent living standard. In contrast, only 1.8 million families are classified under the "high income" category, earning above PHP 188,282 annually or PHP 78,451 monthly for a family of five. This small segment represents a privileged minority with significantly more economic resources and opportunities. When combined, the living income and high income categories account for only 4.5 million families that can afford a decent living standard. Overall, the distribution is deeply unequal, with over 80% of families struggling to meet decent living standards, which again suggests significant systemic challenges in economic opportunity, income distribution, and social mobility.

TABLE 14.4 Annual per Capita Income and Monthly Income (PHP) for a Family of Five and Number of Families by Income Group, 2018

Income Group	*Annual per Capita Income*	*Monthly Income for a Family of 5*	*No. of Families (in Million)*
Below living income	Below PHP 115,362	Below PHP 48,067	20.2
Can afford a "decent" living standard	**PHP 115,362 and above**	**PHP 48,067 and above**	**4.5**
Living income	PHP 115,362 to PHP 188,282	PHP 48,067 to PHP 78,451	2.7
High income	Above PHP 188,282	Above PHP 78,451	1.8
Total families			**24.7**

Source: Authors' calculations based on the Philippine Statistics Authority's 2018 Family Income and Expenditure Survey (https://psada.psa.gov.ph/catalog/FIES/about).

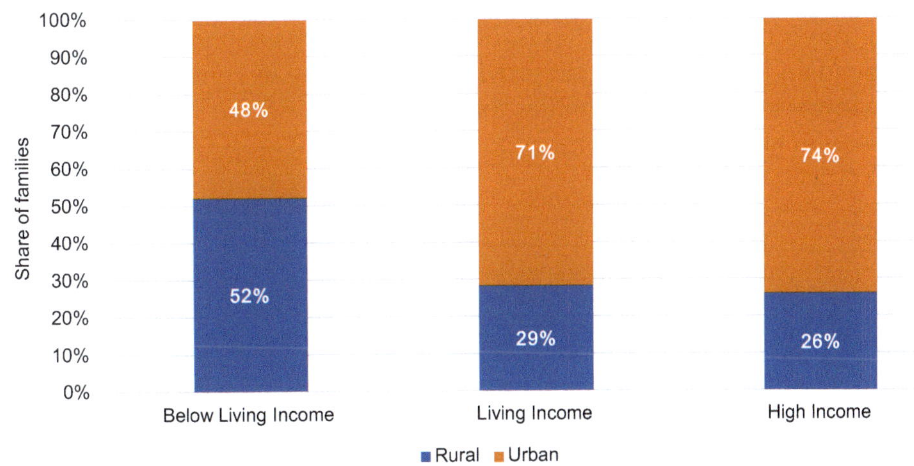

FIGURE 14.4 Share of Families by Income Group and by Location (%), Philippines, 2018

Source: Authors' calculations based on the Philippine Statistics Authority's 2018 Family Income and Expenditure Survey (https://psada.psa.gov.ph/catalog/FIES/about)

Further analysis of the rural–urban distribution reveals that the majority of families below the living income threshold reside in rural areas, accounting for 52.3% (Figure 14.4). However, the substantial proportion recorded in urban areas suggests that many urban families also struggle to afford a decent basket. In contrast, a significant shift toward urban areas is evident among those families living in poverty, with 71.5% of them living in urban settings. This pattern becomes even more pronounced among high-income families (i.e., those who can earn beyond the estimated living income), 73.7% of whom live in urban areas. These findings imply that as income level increases, the proportion of families living in urban areas increases substantially. This urban–rural disparity across income categories can again be linked to the potential inequalities in economic opportunities. For instance, urban areas typically offer greater economic opportunities, higher-paying jobs, and better access to essential services compared to rural areas.

Figure 14.5 illustrates the distribution of income groups across different regions in the Philippines in 2018. It presents the picture of income inequality across Philippine regions, with people "below living income" comprising between 65.6% and 98.9% of the population in each region. The National Capital Region (NCR) recorded the highest proportion of families earning an income of at least equal to the living income at 34.4%. This includes the living income group (20.1%) and the high income group (14.3%), with the latter group exceeding our estimated living income. Although this shows that NCR has one of the more balanced distributions, it is still evidently skewed toward lower incomes. In contrast, the Autonomous Region of Muslim Mindanao (ARMM) recorded the lowest proportion of families that can afford a decent basket at only 1.1%, highlighting its status as one of the most economically disadvantaged regions in the country. When viewed by main island groups, the provinces in Mindanao generally recorded a relatively lower proportion of families that can afford a decent standard of living compared with Luzon and Visayas.

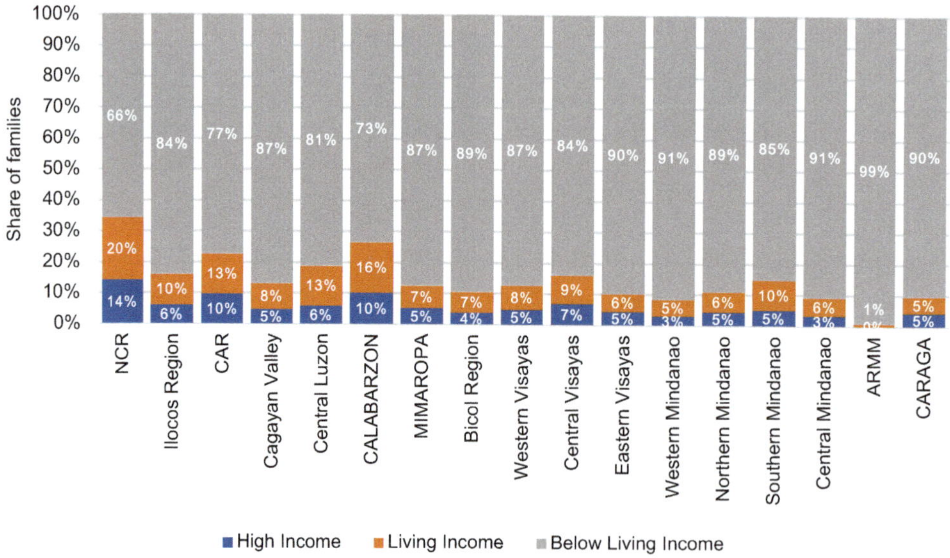

FIGURE 14.5 Share of Families by Income Group and by Region (%), Philippines, 2018

Source: Authors' calculations based on the Philippine Statistics Authority's 2018 Family Income and Expenditure Survey (https://psada.psa.gov.ph/catalog/FIES/about)

Given the patterns discussed earlier, we also estimated the gap between each family's actual income and the living income in 2018, focusing only on families that fall short of affording a decent standard of living (Figure 14.6). This allows us to quantify the average income shortfall and assess how far these families are from meeting the living income threshold. Our estimates indicate that, on average, families below the living income earn only 44.9% of what they need to live a decent life. This translates into a shortfall of 55.1%, which is equivalent to PHP 26,475 monthly income for a family of five (at 2018 prices).

When comparing urban and rural areas, it appears that urban families needed only an additional PHP 23,275 monthly income (2018 prices), on average, as their income shortfall is only about 48.5% of the living income. These estimates are better when compared with rural families, who require a higher additional monthly income amounting to PHP 29,345, representing a gap of 61.1%. These results highlight the more severe income shortfall that occurs in rural areas as compared to urban areas. Across all regions, NCR once again demonstrated a better performance relative to others, similar to our earlier discussions. In particular, NCR families were able to earn 60.6% of the income they needed for a decent living and, hence, face a smaller gap at 39.4% or PHP 18,935 monthly income. Although this suggests that NCR has better economic conditions, many families still fall significantly short of the living income requirements. On the other hand, areas outside NCR (AONCR) faced a larger gap of 57.0%, requiring an additional PHP 27,385 monthly income. All these estimates reveal that families whose incomes are below the living income threshold face substantial gaps

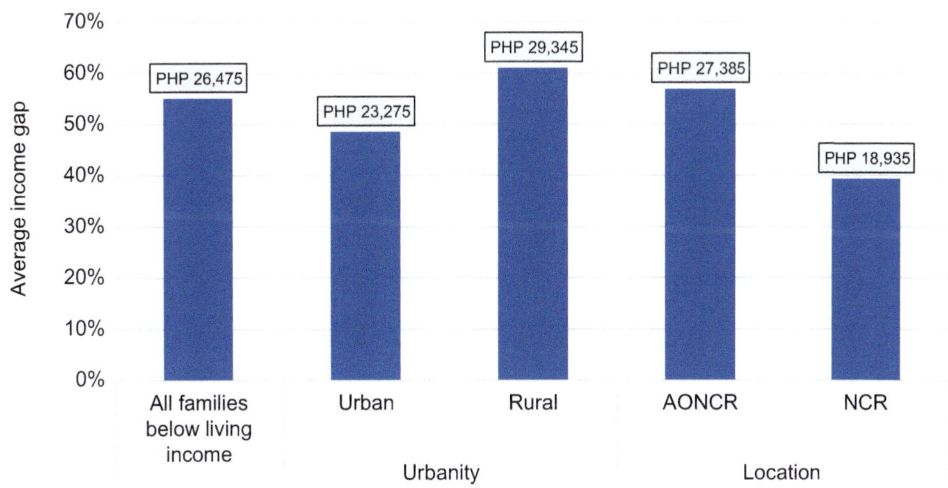

FIGURE 14.6 Average Income Gap (% of Living Income) Among Families Below Living Income by Location, Philippines, 2018

Source: Authors' calculations based on the Philippine Statistics Authority's 2018 Family Income and Expenditure Survey (https://psada.psa.gov.ph/catalog/FIES/about)

between their actual income and our estimated living income. This also points to a question: Do Filipino workers receive wage/salary that will allow them to provide a decent life for their families?

Over the past 26 years, the economic landscape has remained remarkably consistent, yet subtle trends have emerged (Figure 14.7). One of the most striking patterns is the persistent dominance of families unable to afford a decent standard of living (i.e., below living income category), which has hovered around 81–87% throughout the entire period. This suggests a deeply entrenched economic challenge, with the vast majority of the population continuing to struggle financially. Meanwhile, the living income category has shown a gradual but noticeable improvement. Starting at 7.5% in 1997, it has risen incrementally to 11.7% in 2023. This modest increase represents a slow expansion of economic stability for a small segment of the population. Similarly, the high-income category has experienced a slight upward trajectory, rising from 5.4% in 1997 to 6.8% in 2023. This indicates a very modest growth in the number of families achieving a high-income status. The pattern observed during the period suggests a relative economic improvement, though progress remains slow. Again, this implies that the government needs to rethink its existing policies to help ensure a more comprehensive approach in addressing development concerns, which could substantially improve the standard of living of Filipinos.

Meanwhile, the overarching narrative remains one of economic stagnation. Despite small improvements, over 80% of the population continues to fall below a living income standard. The pace of economic mobility is very minimal, suggesting deep-rooted structural challenges in economic opportunity and income

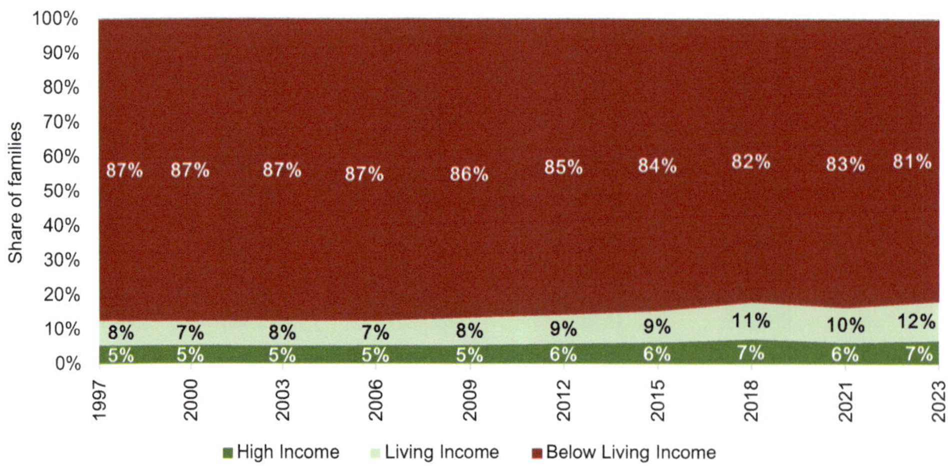

FIGURE 14.7 Share of Families by Income Group (%), Philippines, 1997–2023

Source: Authors' calculations based on the Philippine Statistics Authority's 2018 Family Income and Expenditure Survey (https://psada.psa.gov.ph/catalog/FIES/about)

distribution. In addition, it shows a story of persistent economic inequality, where meaningful change occurs incrementally, and the majority of the families remain trapped living below the minimum decent standard of living, which is a testament to the slow and challenging nature of economic transformation.

14.6 Final Remarks

We have provided an estimate of the minimum annual income required by a family of five to afford a decent standard of living in the Philippines. Based on our definition of *living income*, the cost of a decent basket in 2024 ranges from PHP 735,000 to PHP 1,200,000 per year, depending on location, for a family of five. Although the official poverty rates among families remained below 14% in recent years, the proportion of families with income below our estimated living income is above 80%. The difference in these estimates is expected because, unlike the poverty threshold, which is indirectly measured by using the ratio of food expenditures to total basic expenditures, the living income is estimated directly by accounting for the cost of each major consumption item, given our definition of a decent basket. When examining the distribution of families by location, the majority of families below the living income are located in rural areas. Across all regions, NCR appears to perform better, although it is still evident that the distribution is skewed toward a lower income.

On average, family incomes remain below the minimum income necessary to meet a decent standard of living, highlighting significant income gaps. This finding also has important implications for wages. For instance, if there is only one employed member in a family of five, that individual needs to earn at least PHP 2,168 per day in 2024, assuming 313 workdays in a year. If two adults share financial responsibilities equally, each would need to earn at least PHP 1,084 per day in 2024. Furthermore, for an employed individual who is living alone (assuming no expenses on education), our estimates indicate that the individual needs to earn PHP 822 per day in 2024. All these estimates point to the conclusion that the current minimum daily wages[4] in the country will not allow families to afford a decent basket of goods and services. In other words, the current minimum wage of workers in the country cannot be considered a living wage. This is one of the arguments of lobby groups advocating minimum wage increases in the country, with some arguing that even at current minimum wage levels, many families remain below the poverty threshold.

Notes

1 The poverty threshold is traditionally estimated by the Philippine Statistics Authority as the ratio of food threshold (FT) and the average ratio of food expenditures (FE) and total basic expenditures (TBE), that is, $Poverty\,threshold = \frac{FT}{Average\,\frac{FE}{TBE}}$, using the least cost method. The average nationally determined FE/TBE ratio from 2003, 2006, and 2009

Family Income and Expenditures Survey (FIES) is equivalent to 0.6983, and this ratio is used in estimating the poverty thresholds in the recent rounds of FIES.

2 A household's expected exit time is defined as the time it will take it to reach a given poverty line via income growth. If the income of household i grows at a constant positive rate g per year, the relationship of the poverty line to current income can be written as $z = y_i\,(1+g)^{t_g^i}$. Taking the logarithm and solving for t_g^i yields $t_g^i \approx \frac{\ln(z)-\ln(y_i)}{g}$ for households below the poverty line. The estimation of the time to exit poverty used the data from the 2018 Family Income Expenditures Survey (FIES) administered by the Philippine Statistics Authority (PSA).

3 Albert et al.'s (2020) estimates of the monthly income for a family of five to belong to the middle-income category (defined as having per capita income of twice the poverty threshold up to 12 times the poverty threshold) are between PHP 21,914 to PHP 131,484 in 2018 prices.

4 Each region in the Philippines has its own minimum wage. The highest minimum wage is implemented in the National Capital Region at PHP 645 per day, which took effect in July 2024.

15

FINAL THOUGHTS

We started this book by arguing that we are cautiously optimistic about the future of the Philippines. There is light. The country registers significant growth, the share of employment in agriculture is declining, and so is poverty. Other indicators, such as inflation, suggest a stable macroeconomic environment. We maintain this assessment. However, we have argued that to assess how far the Philippines can realistically advance during the next 25 years, it is important to understand the real constraints that our nation faces. We have focused on two. First, the transformation of the economy toward low-productivity services. Second, a government that, for decades, has underinvested in public goods because it misunderstands the monetary reality of sovereign states. We hope our account in the previous chapters reflects this balance of optimism and realism.

Consistent with these two constraints, we argued in the introduction that the Philippines needs to answer two questions if it is to see faster progress in the next 25 years. One concerns the source of growth: Can services do for the Philippines what manufacturing did for other nations in the 20th century? The second question concerns the role of government: Can it actively coordinate the economy and engineer a big push, or should it stay out of the way and let the private sector lead? Our answers are clear. On the first, the country *must* strive to find niches in manufacturing (what we call the products that make a nation, and some advanced products), as well as create modern firms that export (i.e., compete in the world economy). On the second, the government *must* be willing to drive this change and fund it. This requires a proper understanding of its finances. This includes the central bank (BSP) adding a developmental mandate to price stability.

Both are necessary conditions to progress. The problem is that we have a weak state, a weak political will, and a government and private sectors that share a common misunderstanding of what development is about.

DOI: 10.4324/9781003728719-15

The relative stagnation of the Philippines during the last decades has been the result of bad policies and a development model that has not been conducive to rapid and sustained growth. Neither puzzle nor bad luck. De Dios et al. (2021, pp. 15–18, 19–22) debated if the Philippine debacle during the Marcos Sr. years was the result of bad luck (unfortunate circumstances), bad policy (misguided policy), or bad faith (deliberate malfeasance and corruption). They argued that it was a combination of all three. Surely, political factors (instability), the 1970s oil shocks, foreign borrowing, or corruption, are part of the story.[1] However, other countries also endured their share of the same problems and did better than the Philippines. Moreover, Indonesia, Thailand, China, and Vietnam overtook the Philippines after the Macros Sr. regime ended. We are more convinced by their arguments about the inefficiency of investment (the projects chosen) and the chaos in the trade and investment regimes, that is, bad policy. In this book, we have focused on two complementary arguments about bad policy. What is truly puzzling about the Philippines is the insistence on not understanding how countries progress.

While the governments of many East Asian nations pushed industrialization to change the structure of the economy (with emphasis on manufacturing and with the objective to quickly reduce the share of employment in agriculture), the Philippines skipped it after the administration of President Marcos Sr. The share of manufacturing employment never went beyond a low 11–12%. After President Marcos Sr., successive administrations have focused on implementing a *halo-halo* of reforms (type I), such as increasing tax collection, spending more on infrastructure recently (with no clear results yet), reducing the budget deficit, and eliminating burdensome regulations. The Philippines also tried to attract FDI, to provide tax breaks, and to move up in the rankings in the World Competitiveness Report and Ease of Doing Business. Administration after administration has focused on variants of these programs and actions. Some of these (not all) are fine, as they address some important problems, but we repeat: Evidence indicates that income per capita remains just above USD 4,400. As we completed this manuscript in the second half of 2025, we learned that the World Bank still classifies the Philippines as a lower-middle-income country.[2] Certainly, the Philippines missed something, the real jackpot: changing the structure of the economy in the direction of industrialization (reforms type II). This is what development is about, and the Philippines missed the boat. In the 1960s, the income differential with Singapore was not large. Today, Singapore's GNI per capita is over USD 70,000.

We are under the impression that the current administration is still thinking in the same old way. The initiatives mentioned and discussed in Chapter 7 (e.g., Executive Order No. 18 on green lanes in 2023 and tax reforms like the Ease of Paying Taxes Act 2024, the Real Property Valuation Act 2024, VAT on Digital Services Law 2024, the CREATE MORE Act 2024, or the Capital Market Efficiency Promotion Act 2025) may be necessary, but we do not think they will deliver

8% growth year after year. Let us not confuse actions that, at best, would smooth the workings of some parts of the system with the true *engines of growth* of an economy: productivity, manufacturing, exports, and firms. The same applies to the Maharlika Investment Corporation (MIC), which confuses investment banking–type operations with development.

We have also argued that the government needs to be much more aware of its own monetary reality. This would free the country from old *clichés* about the perceived negative effects of fiscal deficits and debt and would allow the government to provide, without reservations, the public goods that are badly needed to construct an egalitarian society, including the elimination of malnutrition and dire poverty, infrastructure, health, housing, and education. This is the very minimum the government should do, because these services are the rights of all Filipinos. History has also shown that these are preconditions to a productive society. We believe that the Philippine government should do more and take a very active role in guiding the economy.

We are aware of how certain actors in the country think and the difficulties in changing their mentality. It is true that the East Asian type of industrialization and large-scale industrial policy will not happen today. Our proposal is to focus on a few sensible sectors/activities in manufacturing that can take the economy to the next level. We already have a manufacturing sector. It needs to expand to satisfy the domestic economy and to compete in international markets. This does not mean neglecting services, much less agriculture. Both these two sectors can benefit a great deal from a manufacturing sector that pulls them.

Some segments in the country fear that if the government increases spending, we will end up with another crisis like in the 1980s. However, it is very difficult for this to happen with the current monetary system and its current checks and balances. If these deeply entrenched beliefs do not change, all we can do is remain intellectually consistent and stop asking why we do not do better. Some say what we need is much more social pressure for change, triggered by an economic crisis. However, current growth at 5–6% prevents it. So here we are with more of the same: not doing great, just good enough to maintain social peace. If those are the limits to the imagination of all our past, present, and future governments, then so be it.

Our forecasts until 2050, based on the DLSU ANIMO econometric model, could of course be incorrect. Time will tell. Yet they are based on a solid framework, not on extrapolations of GDP *assuming* a growth rate. Quite the opposite, knowing that there is high mean reversion in growth rates, we believe that even the most favorable conditions will ultimately have diminishing impacts on growth, unless the Philippines can continually improve its policy environment or governance. Our model has data for several hundred variables that explain how the Philippine economy works. We also took into account the state of the world economy. This may change in the coming years, but as of today, growth at barely 3% does not help the Philippine case. Arguing that the Philippines is a "consumption-driven" economy does not take the analysis far. Consumption is driven by wages; wages are driven by productivity, and this depends on the type of activities workers are engaged in (the structure of the economy). We understand that the country's economic managers need to set ambitious targets. However, these targets need to be realistic so as not to mislead people with promises or visions of the future that will never materialize in their lifetime. Our analysis shows that the structure of employment will change in the next 25 years, but most Filipino workers will remain employed in services of low productivity (though out of agriculture). We hope this message wakes up policymakers, helps them understand what development is about, and forces them to change course.

Finally, we return to the key question we posed at the beginning of the book: Can the Philippines do better? *"Oo, kaya natin to!"* But we need to understand what this will take, especially to attain and sustain a growth rate above 6% (if this remains the target of successive governments). To grow faster on a sustained basis, the Philippines must increase the balance of payments–constrained growth rate. This will require working on the structure of the economy. If we are proven *wrong* in 2050, in the sense that the economy did significantly better than we forecast here, it can *only* be because policymakers along this journey changed course in the direction we have suggested—the current development model will not do it.

Although political and economic elites have traditionally made decisions affecting the country for their own benefit, this does not have to be incompatible with development. Even in this context, there is room for change. Filipino conglomerates ought to drive the country's progress by getting into the manufacturing of tradable goods that are competitive globally. We also suggest that deals must be more open to all participants. Agreements regarding development and investment should be open to all investors rather than limited to just the elites or their close associates. Though risks are involved in trying to produce and export tradables, there is a lot to be gained in the development process. The current administration's lower growth targets could be achieved (perhaps reach a 6–6.5% growth rate) even without major changes to the nation's political dynamics. We repeat that this requires a slight increase in our balance of payments–constrained growth rate by improving our export basket and productivity. This would benefit the government, conglomerates, and the population at large.

The alternative is to project the same business-as-usual scenario, MOTS (more of the same). In this case, firms catering to the domestic market and benefiting from regulatory rents will continue growing while competitive industries will struggle. Firms in manufacturing will continue to lack organizational capabilities and produce simple products that are not competitive in international markets. This does not mean that the Philippines will not be able to grow. Indeed, it still has a relatively high labor force growth, and attaining productivity growth is possible (given that it is far from the technological frontier). Although the country's potential growth is still relatively high, at about 6%, this will decrease, and the economy will remain vulnerable to global risks. Hence, a more resilient economy is crucial to avoid booms, stagnation, and bust episodes. As Hausmann et al. (2008) have noted, countries with more diversified economies are better equipped to survive export shocks. In essence, episodic growth will persist unless the structure of the economy changes. For this, magicians (exporters) must come in and deals must be open. Even if positive growth episodes occur, growth will not be stable and sustainable in the long run.

We reiterate: The economy will be "okay" . . . if by "okay" we mean 6% growth during very good years, poverty rates in single digits but declining very slowly, more than 80% of Filipino families living above the poverty line yet unable to afford life's "decent basket." All because the economy simply does not produce products that are good enough to compete globally and pay higher wages. Maybe "okay" means we always have a handful of excuses ready to explain our underdevelopment: over 400 years of colonization, venal and shameless politicians, unfair trade relations, weak institutions, rapid population growth, all manner of cultural traits. Never mind that within our own lifetimes we have seen one neighbor after another race past us, burdened with similar, if not worse, initial conditions.

Thirty-five years ago, Paul Krugman (1994) described a peculiar period of American complacency he termed the Age of Diminished Expectations. American society and government, he argued, knew what was needed to return to a high-productivity, high-growth path. But the strategies were just too politically risky, and voters seemed satisfied with mild but steady economic gains. So instead, America settled, downgraded its hopes, and diminished its expectations.

In the case of the Philippines, we argue, it is highly likely that both our government and our people do not really understand what it will take to transform the economy and allow our country to achieve high-income status. We wrote this book to insist—using history, political economy, growth theory, country studies, textual analysis of development plans, novel measures of well-being, and forecasts from what are the most sophisticated models of the Philippine economy currently in use—that we simply cannot have *more of the same* reforms, *more of the same* phobias about debts and deficits.

There is a path up from lower-middle-income to high-income status. We only need to look at the remarkable consistency in the experiences of South Korea, Singapore, Taiwan, Malaysia, Thailand, and Indonesia, which shared our problems in smaller and larger degrees but did not waver in pursuing industrialization. If we remain unconvinced, there is the real-time unfolding of the Vietnamese story.

Throughout the three years we worked on this book, pressed upon by the weight of its arguments, we often came away from meetings with unbearable regret. *The best time to get started would have been 50 years ago.*

But perhaps we can convince you that the next best time is now.

Notes

1 The huge corruption scandal in public works (flood control), as well as the United States' retaliatory tariffs surfaced at the time we were completing the manuscript. It has been impossible to discuss and clarify the finance aspects here.
2 https://blogs.worldbank.org/en/opendata/understanding-country-income--world-bank-group-income-classifica

REFERENCES

Acemoglu, D. (2024, December 8). *Institutions, technology and prosperity* [PDF]. NobelPrize.org. https://www.nobelprize.org/uploads/2025/01/acemoglu-lecture.pdf

Acemoglu, D. (2025). The simple macroeconomics of AI. *Economic Policy, 40*(121), 13–58.

Acemoglu, D., & Robinson, J. A. (2012). *Why nations fail: The origins of power, prosperity, and poverty*. Crown Publishers.

Acemoglu, D., & Robinson, J. A. (2019). *The narrow corridor: States, societies, and the fate of liberty*. Penguin Press.

An Act Amending Sections 27, 28, 32, 34, 57, 106, 108, 109, 112, 135, 237, 237-A, 269, 292, 293, 294, 295, 296, 297, 300, 301, 308, 309, 310, and 311, and Adding New Sections 135-A, 295-A, 296-A, and 297-A of the National Internal Revenue Code of 1997, as Amended, and for Other Purposes, Republic Act No. 12066. (2024, November 8). (Phil.). https://www.officialgazette.gov.ph/2024/11/08/republic-act-no-12066/

An Act Liberalizing the Importation, Exportation and Trading of Rice, Lifting for the Purpose the Quantitative Import Restriction on Rice, and for Other Purposes, Republic Act No. 11203. (2019, February 14). (Phil.). https://www.officialgazette.gov.ph/2019/02/14/republic-act-no-11203/

An Act Making Mariveles, Province of Bataan, a Port of Entry by Amending Section Seven Hundred One of the Tariff and Customs Code of the Philippines, as Amended, Providing for the Establishment, Operation and Maintenance of a Foreign Trade Zone Therein; Creating a Foreign Trade Zone Authority; and Authorizing the Appropriation of the Necessary Funds Therefor, Republic Act No. 5490. (1969, June 21). (Phil.). https://elibrary.judiciary.gov.ph/thebookshelf/showdocs/2/7136

An Act Providing for the Local Government Code of 1991, Republic Act No. 7160. (1991, October 10). (Phil.). https://www.officialgazette.gov.ph/1991/10/10/republic-act-no-7160/

Ahlers, A. L., Heberer, T., & Schubert, G. (2019). The critical role of local governance in China's political system. In J. Yu & S. Guo (Eds.), *The Palgrave handbook of local governance in contemporary China* (pp. 73–93). Palgrave Macmillan.

Albert, J. R. G., Abrigo, M. R. M., Quimba, F. M. A., & Vizmanos, J. F. V. (2020). *Poverty, the middle class, and income distribution amid COVID-19* (Discussion Paper Series No. 2020-22). Philippine Institute for Development Studies. https://pidswebs.pids.gov.ph/CDN/PUBLICATIONS/pidsdps2022.pdf

Aldaba, F., et al. (30 members of the Economics and Political Science Department). (2005). Beneath the Fiscal Crisis: Uneven Development Weakens the Republic. Research Report, Ateneo de Manila University.

Aldaba, R. M. (2014). *The Philippine manufacturing industry roadmap: Agenda for new industrial policy, high productivity jobs, and inclusive growth* (Discussion Paper Series No. 2014-32). Philippine Institute of Development Studies. https://pidswebs.pids.gov.ph/CDN/PUBLICATIONS/pidsdps1432.pdf

Aldaba, R. M., & Aldaba, F. (2024). Industrial policy for innovation: Why does it matter? *Philippine Review of Economics: Special Issue on Industrial Policy, 61*(2), 85–109.

Alvina, N. R. B. (2019). *Credit financing for local development: The subnational debt in the Philippines* (Working Paper No. 966). Asian Development Bank Institute.

Amending the Tariff and Customs Code of the Philippines, Presidential Decree No. 34. (1972, October 27). (Phil.). https://elibrary.judiciary.gov.ph/thebookshelf/showdocs/26/25716

Amsden, A. H. (1989). *Asia's next giant: South Korea and late industrialization*. Oxford University Press.

Amsden, A. H. (1995). Like the rest: South-East Asia's 'late' industrialization. *Journal of International Development, 7*(5), 791–199. https://doi.org/10.1002/jid.3380070508

Anderson, B. (1991). *Imagined communities: Reflections on the origin and spread of nationalism* (Revised ed.). Verso (Original work published in 1983).

Anker, R., & Anker, M. (2013). *The Anker methodology: Estimating living wages and incomes around the world*. Anker Research Institute. https://www.ankerresearchinstitute.org/anker-methodology

Aragones, E. M., Felipe, J., Perez, J., & Sauler, M. M. (2024). *The ANIMO econometric model database of De La Salle University: Variables and technical notes* (Working Paper Series 2024-10-098). De La Salle University-Angelo King Institute for Economic and Business Studies.

Asian Development Bank. (2013). Asia economic transformation: Where to, how, and how fast? In *ADB key indicators for Asia and the Pacific 2013* (pp. 1–90). Asian Development Bank.

Atienza, K. (2023, February 19). Marcos sees manufacturing as key to export growth. *Business World*. https://www.bworldonline.com/economy/2023/02/19/505634/marcos-sees-manufacturing-as-key-to-export-growth/

Autor, D., Katz, L., & Kearney, M. (2006). The polarization of the U.S. labor market. *American Economic Review, 96*(2), 189–194. https://doi.org/10.1257/000282806777212620

Autor, D., Levy, F., & Murnane, R. (2003). The skill content of recent technological change: An empirical exploration. *The Quarterly Journal of Economics, 118*(4), 1279–1333. https://www.jstor.org/stable/25053940

Bai, C.-E., Hsieh, C.-T., & Song, Z. M. (2019). *Special deals with Chinese characteristics* (Working Paper No. 25839). National Bureau of Economic Research. http://www.nber.org/papers/w25839

Baldwin, R. E. (1975a). *Foreign trade regimes and economic development: The lessons of experience*. Columbia University Press for the National Bureau of Economic Research.

Baldwin, R. E. (1975b). *Foreign trade regimes and economic development: The Philippines*. National Bureau of Economic Research.

Balisacan, A., & Hill, H. (Eds.). (2003). *The Philippine economy: Development, policies, and challenges*. Oxford University Press.

Bangko Sentral ng Pilipinas. (2016). *Revised framework for monetary operations under the BSP corridor (IRC) system*. https://www.bsp.gov.ph/Price%20Stability/IRC.pdf

Bangko Sentral ng Pilipinas. (2020, March 26). *BSP to remit P20 billion dividends to fight COVID-19* [Media Release]. https://www.bsp.gov.ph/SitePages/MediaAndResearch/

MediaDisp.aspx?ItemId=5227#:~:text=BSP%20will%20remit%20the%20P20, We%20are%20one%20Filipino%20nation
Bardhan, P. (2001). Distributive conflicts, collective action, and institutional economics. In G. M. Meier & J. E. Stiglitz (Eds.), *Frontiers of development economics: The future in perspective* (pp. 269–290). Oxford University Press and The World Bank.
Baumol, W. J. (1967). Macroeconomics of unbalanced growth: The anatomy of urban crisis. *The American Economic Review, 57*(3), 415–426. http://www.jstor.org/stable/1812111?origin=JSTOR-pdf
Bayudan-Dacuycuy, C., Cabuay, C., & Luzon, P. (2024). *Expansions, quality, and affirmative action in public higher education institutions* (Discussion Paper Series No. 2024-16). Philippine Institute for Development Studies. https://doi.org/10.62986/dp2024.16
Bénétrix, A. S., O'Rourke, K. H., & Williamson, J. G. (2015). The spread of manufacturing to the poor periphery 1870–2007. *Open Economies Review, 26*(1), 1–37.
Biswas, R. (2021). *Philippine economy hit by rising COVID-19 wave*. S&P Global Market Intelligence. https://www.spglobal.com/marketintelligence/en/mi/research-analysis/philippines-economy-hit-by-rising-covid19-wave-apr21.html
Booth, A., & Deng, K. (2017). Japanese colonialism in comparative perspective. *Journal of World History, 28*(1), 61–98.
Broad, R. (1988). *Unequal alliance: The World Bank, the international monetary fund, and the Philippines*. University of California Press.
Brunello, G., Fort, M., & Weber, G. (2009). Changes in compulsory schooling, education and the distribution of wages in Europe. *The Economic Journal, 119*(536), 516–539. https://www.jstor.org/stable/20485330
Burnside, C., & Dollar, D. (2000). Aid, policies, and growth. *American Economic Review, 90*(4), 847–868.
Canlas, D. B., & Fujisaki, S. (Eds.). (2001). *The Philippine economy: Alternatives for the 21st century*. University of the Philippines Press.
Capital Markets Efficiency Promotion Act, Republic Act No. 12214. (2025, May 9). (Phil.). https://www.officialgazette.gov.ph/2025/05/29/republic-act-no-12214/
Capulong, C. M., Abing, M. J. J., Teves, M. R. Y., & Babanto, G. A. C. (2024). Determinants of economic dynamism among the 22 municipalities in the Philippines. *Journal of Economics Research and Social Sciences, 8*(2), 184–196.
Castillo, P. (2005). *Regional production networks and implications on trade and investment policies, and regional cooperation: The case of the Philippines*. De La Salle University-Angelo King Institute for Economic and Business Studies.
CBS. (2009, March 16). *The chairman part 1* [Video]. YouTube. https://www.youtube.com/watch?v=odPfHY4ekHA
Chambers, P. (2005). Evolving toward what? Parties, factions, and coalition behavior in Thailand today. *Journal of East Asian Studies, 5*(3), 495–520.
Chan, W., & Zhang, J. (2021). Can university qualification promote social mobility? A review of higher education expansion and graduate employment in China. International *Journal of Educational Development, 84*, 102423. https://doi.org/10.1016/j.ijedudev.2021.102423
Chang, H.-J. (2002). *Kicking away the development ladder: Development strategy in historical perspective*. Anthem Press.
Chang, H.-J. (2013). *Is industrial policy necessary and feasible in Africa? Theoretical considerations and historical lessons*. Working Paper Prepared for JICA/IPD Africa Task Force Meeting Yokohama, Japan, June 2–3. https://www.jica.go.jp/Resource/jica-ri/publication/booksandreports/jrft3q00000029ds-att/Is_industrial_policy_necessary_and_feasible_in_Africa,Chang-JICA_IPD_Working_Papers.pdf

Chen, C., & Chen, L. (2021). The impact of higher education expansion on the educational wage premium in Taiwan: 1985 to 2015. *International Journal of Financial Studies, 9*(38), 1–12. https://doi.org/10.3390/ijfs9030038
Chen, L., Felipe, J., & Mehta, A. (2021). Is employment globalizing? *Structural Change and Economic Dynamics, 56*, 74–92.
Cheng, J. Y. (2016). Local governments in China. In U. Sadioglu & K. Dede (Eds.), *Comparative studies and regionally-focused cases examining local governments* (pp. 207–227). IGI Global Scientific Publishing.
Chi, C. (2024, December 16). What we know so far: DepEd's P12 billion 'budget cut'. *Philstar Global.* https://www.philstar.com/headlines/2024/12/16/2407813/what-we-know-so-far-depeds-p12-billion-budget-cut
Cimoli, M., Dosi, G., & Stiglitz, J. E. (Eds.). (2009). *Industrial policy and development: The political economy of capabilities accumulation*. Oxford University Press.
Clarete, R. L., Esguerra, E. F., & Hill, H. (Eds.). (2018). *The Philippine economy: No longer the East Asian exception?* ISEAS-Yusof Ishak Institute.
Claudio, L. E. (2025). *The profligate colonial: How the US exported austerity to the Philippines*. Cornell University Press.
Clemente, T. S. (2012). Chines trade in pre-Spanish Philippines: Credit, hostage and raid regimes. *Journal of Southeast Asian Studies, 17*, 191–206.
Committee on Sustainability Assessment, & KIT Royal Tropical Institute. (2020). *Guidance manual on calculating and visualizing the income gap to a Living Income Benchmark*. Living Income Community of Practice.
Coronel, S., Chua, Y. T., Rimban, L., & Cruz, B. B. (2004). *The rulemakers: How the wealthy and well-born dominate Congress*. Philippine Center for Investigative Journalism.
Creating the Export Processing Zone Authority and Revising Republic Act No. 5490, Presidential Decree No. 66. (1972, November 20). (Phil.). https://www.officialgazette.gov.ph/1972/11/20/presidential-decree-no-66-s-1972/
Croissant, A., & Chambers, P. (2010). Unravelling intra-party democracy in Thailand. *Asian Journal of Political Science, 18*(2), 195–223.
Cushner, N. P. (1971). *Spain in the Philippines: From conquest to revolution*. Ateneo de Manila University.
De Dios, E. S. (2007). Local politics and local economy. In A. M. Balisacan & H. Hill (Eds.), *The dynamics of regional development* (pp. 157–203). Edward Elgar Publishing.
De Dios, E. S. (2024). Comment on "Industrial policy for innovation: Why does it matter?" *Philippine Review of Economics: Special Issue on Industrial Policy, 61*(2), 110–113.
De Dios, E. S., Gochoco-Bautista, M. S., & Punongbayan, J. C. (2021). *Martial law and the Philippine economy* (UPSE Discussion Paper No. 2021-07). University of the Philippines School of Economics. https://hdl.handle.net/10419/266061
De Dios, E. S., & Williamson, J. (2015). Deviant behavior: A century of Philippine industrialization. In A. Balisacan, U. Chakravorty, & M. Ravago (Eds.), *Sustainable economic development: Resources, environment, and institutions* (pp. 371–400). Elsevier Academic Press.
De Jesus, E. (2011). Access, equity and capacity: Managing tradeoffs in the Philippines. In D. Neubauer & Y. Tanaka (Eds.), *Access, equity, and capacity in Asia-Pacific higher education* (pp. 155–170). Palgrave MacMillan.
De Mesquita, B. B., Morrow, J. D., Siverson, R. M., & Smith, A. (2004). Testing novel implications from the selectorate theory of war. *World Politics, 56*(3), 363–388.
Department of Agriculture. (2018, December 28). *Daily price monitoring report: Selected wet markets in Metro Manila*. https://www.da.gov.ph/wp-content/uploads/2019/02/Price-Watch-December-28-2018.pdf

Department of Economy, Planning, and Development. (n.d.). *The Life of all Filipinos by 2040 Matatag, Maginhawa at Panatag na Buhay*. Retrieved September 2025, from https://2040.depdev.gov.ph/

Department of Economy, Planning, and Development. (2025). *Philippine development plan 2023–2028: 2025 midterm update*. https://depdev.gov.ph/wp-content/uploads/2025/09/PDP-2023-208-Midterm-Update-September-24-2025-compressed.pdf

Department of Finance. (2024, December 30). *Recto: PHP 6.326 trillion national budget for 2025 most powerful tool to deliver the biggest economic benefits to Filipinos, reaffirms DOF's commitment to work hard in funding it*. https://www.dof.gov.ph/recto-php-6-326-trillion-national-budget-for-2025-most-powerful-tool-to-deliver-the-biggest-economic-benefits-to-filipinos-reaffirms-dofs-commitment-to-work-hard-in-funding-it/

Department of Finance. (2025). *DOF clarifies determination of the national tax allotment shares for LGUs, ensures transparency and strict compliance with Mandanas-Garcia ruling*. https://www.dof.gov.ph/dof-clarifies-determination-of-the-national-tax-allotment-shares-for-lgus-ensures-transparency-and-strict-compliance-with-mandanas-garcia-ruling/#:~:text=The%202019%20Mandanas%2DGarcia%20ruling,of%20Internal%20Revenue%20(BIR)

Department of Trade and Industry. (2018, December 5). *Suggested retail prices of basic necessities and prime commodities as of 05 December 2018*. https://drive.google.com/drive/folders/0B9g4z7P_-NePVUhpX2NuS0VJS28?resourcekey=0-0P2WXuFc4yLXDp8Jmxa55A

Department of Trade and Industry. (2021). *Basta e-commerce madali: Ecommerce Philippines 2022 roadmap*. https://ecommerce.dti.gov.ph/wp-content/uploads/2022/02/Madali_01042022_FINAL-web.pdf

Desiderio, L. (2022, January 28). Electronics exports may expand 10% this year. *Philstar Global*. https://www.philstar.com/business/2022/01/28/2156805/electronics-exports-may-expand-10-year

Desiderio, L. (2025, June 18). Sari-sari store sales to hit P2.4 trillion by 2030. *Philstar Global*. https://www.philstar.com/business/2025/06/18/2451288/sari-sari-store-sales-hit-p24-trillion-2030

Diokno-Sicat, J. (2019). *Philippine (Metro Manila) case study on municipal financing* (MPFD Working Paper No. WP/19/02). United Nations Economic and Social Commission for Asia and the Pacific (ESCAP). https://repository.unescap.org/server/api/core/bitstreams/e31643d6-f833-41b0-a2cb-792c2bbdb916/content

Dohner, R., & Intal, P., Jr. (1989). Government expenditures and revenues. In J. D. Sachs & S. M. Collins (Eds.), *Developing country debt and economic performance, volume 3: Country studies—Indonesia, Korea, Philippines, Turkey* (pp. 401–433). The University of Chicago Press.

Domar, E. D. (1946). Capital expansion, rate of growth, and employment. *Econometrica, 14*(2), 137–147.

Ease of Paying Taxes Act, Republic Act No. 11976. (2024, January 5). (Phil.). https://www.officialgazette.gov.ph/downloads/2024/01jan/20240105-RA-11976-FRM.pdf

Easterly, W. (2006). Planners versus searchers in foreign aid. *Asian Development Review, 23*(2), 1–35.

Eccles, M. S. (1947). Statement of Marriner S. Eccles on behalf of the Board of Governors of the Federal Reserve System before the Committee on Banking and Currency, U.S. House of Representatives, 80th Congress, Tuesday, December 2. U.S. Government Printing Office

Economic Planning Unit of Malaysia's Prime Minister's Department. (2021). *Twelfth Malaysia plan 2021–2025*. https://faolex.fao.org/docs/pdf/mal210617.pdf

Edwards, S. (1999). *Crises and reform in Latin America: From despair to hope*. Oxford University Press.

Esguerra, E. F., Dacuycuy, L. B., Dakila, F. G., Jr., Estudillo, J. P., Floro, M. S., Llanto, G. M., Peña-Reyes, S. P. K., & Rufo, H. R. R. (Eds.). (2024). Special issue on industrial policy. *The Philippine Review of Economics, 61*(2). https://pre.econ.upd.edu.ph/index.php/pre/issue/viewIssue/131/11

Export Incentives Act of 1970, Republic Act No. 6135. (1970, August 31). (Phil.). https://elibrary.judiciary.gov.ph/thebookshelf/showdocs/2/6494

Fabella, R. (2011). Development thinking and the rise of human agency. In R. Fabella, J. Faustino, M. G. Mirandilla-Santos, P. Catiang, & R. Paras (Eds.), *Built on dreams, grounded in reality: Economic policy reform in the Philippines* (pp. 225–252). The Asia Foundation.

Fabella, R., Daway-Ducanes, S., & Ducanes, G. (2023). Quality of growth and poverty in low-income countries: The role of manufacturing. *DLSU Business & Economics Review, 33*(1), 1–10.

Federal Reserve Board. (2024, March 20). *Summary of economic projections*. https://www.federalreserve.gov/monetarypolicy/files/fomcprojtabl20240320.pdf

Felipe, J. (Ed.). (2015). *Development and modern industrial policy in practice: Issues and country experiences*. Asian Development Bank; Edward Elgar. https://doi.org/10.4337/9781784715540

Felipe, J. (2021). Structural transformation, old and new industrial policies, and implications for development. In N. Foster-McGregor, L. Alcorta, A. Szirmai, & B. Verspagen (Eds.), *New perspectives on structural change: Causes and consequences of structural change in the global economy* (pp. 648–675). Oxford University Press.

Felipe, J., Bayudan-Dacuycuy, C., & Lanzafame, M. (2016). The declining share of agricultural employment in China: How fast? *Structural Change and Economic Dynamics, 37*, 127–137.

Felipe, J., & Estrada, G. (2020). What happened to the world's potential growth after the 2008–2009 global financial crisis? *Journal of The Japanese and International Economies, 56*, 1–13.

Felipe, J., Estrada, G., & Lanzafame, M. (2022). The turnaround in Philippine growth: From disappointment to promising success. *Structural Change and Economic Dynamics, 62*, 327–342. https://doi.org/10.1016/j.strueco.2022.03.016

Felipe, J., Foster-McGregor, N., Nomaler, Ö., & Verspagen, B. (2025). *Innovation and structural transformation in Asia*. Routledge (Taylor & Francis Group).

Felipe, J., & Fullwiler, S. (2021). How 'monetization' really works: Examples from three Asian nations' responses to Covid–19. *Review of Political Economy, 34*(3), 397–419. https://doi.org/10.1080/09538259.2021.1908777

Felipe, J., Jin, H., & Mehta, A. (2024). Education and the evolution of comparative advantage. *Structural Change and Economic Dynamics, 70*, 530–543. https://doi.org/10.1016/j.strueco.2024.05.011

Felipe, J., Kumar, U., & Abdon, A. (2012). Using capabilities to project growth, 2010–2030. *Journal of the Japanese and International Economies, 26*, 153–166.

Felipe, J., Kumar, U., & Galope, F. R. (2017). Middle-income transitions: Trap or myth? *Journal of the Asia Pacific Economy, 22*(3), 429–453.

Felipe, J., & Lanzafame, M. (2020). The PRC's long-run growth through the lens of the export-led growth model. *Journal of Comparative Economics, 48*(1), 163–181. https://doi.org/10.1016/j.jce.2019.08.004

Felipe, J., Mathew, N., & Sevilla, J. (2025a). *A profile of the Philippines' largest 1,000 firms and the manufacturing sector* (Working Paper No. 2025-05-099). De La Salle University-Angelo King Institute for Economic and Business Studies.

Felipe, J., Mathew, N., & Sevilla, J. (2025b). *No change, no gain: Exporting, diversification, and firm growth in the Philippines* (Working Paper No. 2025-05-099). De La Salle University-Angelo King Institute for Economic and Business Studies.
Felipe, J., McCombie, J. S. L., & Mehta, A. (2025). Is anything left of the debate about the sources of growth in East Asia 30 years later? A critical survey. *Journal of Evolutionary Economics, 35*, 247–280. https://doi.org/10.1007/s00191-025-00894-w
Felipe, J., & Mehta, A. (2016). Deindustrialization? A global perspective. *Economics Letters, 149*, 148–151. https://doi.org/10.1016/j.econlet.2016.10.038
Felipe, J., Mehta, A., & Rhee, C. (2019). Manufacturing matters . . . but it's the jobs that count. *Cambridge Journal of Economics, 43*(1), 139–168. https://doi.org/10.1093/cje/bex086
Felipe, J., Miranda, B. E., & Empeño, E. D. (2023). *Economic transformation and growth in the Philippines: An analysis of political settlements, rents, and deals* (Working Paper No. 2023-07-087). De La Salle University-Angelo King Institute for Economic and Business Studies.
Felipe, J., Usui, N., & Abdon, A. (2011). Rethinking the growth diagnostics approach: Questions from the practitioners. *Journal of International Commerce, Economics and Policy, 2*(2), 251–276.
Frey, C., & Osborne, M. (2017). The future of employment: How susceptible are jobs to computerization? *Technological Forecasting and Social Change, 114*, 254–280. https://doi.org/10.1016/j.techfore.2016.08.019
Fukuyama, F. (2014). *Political order and political decay: From the industrial revolution to the globalization of democracy*. Farrar, Straus and Giroux.
Garcia, J., Heckman, J., Leaf, D., & Prados, M. (2020). Quantifying the life-cycle benefits of an influential early-childhood program. *Journal of Political Economy, 128*(7), 2502–2541. https://doi.org/10.1086/705718
Gerschenkron, A. (1962). *Economic backwardness in historical perspective*. Belknap Press.
Gochoco-Bautista, M. S., & Canlas, D. (2003). Monetary and exchange rate policy. In A. Balisacan & H. Hill (Eds.), *The Philippine economy: Development policies, and challenges* (pp. 77–105). Oxford University Press.
Gumba, B. (2023). Efficiency analysis of the community health programs of the Partido District in the Philippines. *Asian Journal of Multidisciplinary Studies, 6*(1), 68–76.
Gutierrez, B., & Rodriguez, R. (2013). Diversification strategies of large business groups in the Philippines. *Philippine Management Review, 20*, 65–82. https://journals.upd.edu.ph/index.php/pmr/article/view/3597
Hall, D. G. E. (1981). *A history of Southeast Asia* (4th ed.). Malaysia: Macmillan.
Harrod, R. (1939). An essay in dynamic theory. *The Economic Journal, 49*(33), 14–33.
Hausmann, R., Hidalgo, C. A., Bustos, S., Coscia, M., Simoes, A., & Yildirim, M. A. (2014). *The atlas of economic complexity: Mapping paths to prosperity*. MIT Press.
Hausmann, R., Rodriguez, F., & Wagner, R. (2008). Growth collapses. In C. M. Reinhart & C. A. Vegh (Eds.), *Money, crises, and transition: Essays in honor of Guillermo A. Calvo* (pp. 377–428). MIT Press.
Hausmann, R., Rodrik, D., & Velasco, A. (2005). *Growth diagnostics* (Working Paper). Harvard University Kennedy School of Government.
Hayashi, T. (1990). *The Japanese experience in technology: From transfer to self-reliance*. The United Nations University Press.
Hidalgo, C., & Hausmann, R. (2009). The building blocks of economic complexity. *The Proceedings of the National Academy of Sciences, 106*(26), 10570–10575. https://doi.org/10.1073/pnas.0900943106
Hidalgo, C., Klinger, B., Barabasi, A. L., & Hausmann, R. (2007). The product space conditions the development of nations. *Science, 317*(5837), 482–487.

Hill, H., Ravago, M.-L. V., & Roumasset, J. A. (Eds.). (2022). *Pro-poor development policies: Lessons from the Philippines and East Asia*. ISEAS-Yusof Ishak Institute.
Hirschman, A. O. (1968). The political economy of import-substituting industrialization in Latin America. *The Quarterly Journal of Economics, 82*(1), 1–32. https://doi.org/10.2307/1882243
Hobday, M. (1995). *Innovation in East Asia: The challenge to Japan*. Edward Elgar.
Hobday, M. (1998). Product complexity, innovation and industrial organization. *Research Policy, 26*, 689–710.
Hooley, R. (2005). American economic policy in the Philippines, 1902–1940: Exploring a dark age in colonial statistics. *Journal of Asian Economics, 16*(3), 464–488.
Huang, B., Tani, M., Wei, Y., & Zhu, Y. (2022). Returns to education in China: Evidence from the great higher education expansion. *China Economic Review, 74*, Article 101804. https://doi.org/10.1016/j.chieco.2022.101804
Huntington, S. P. (2006). *Political order in changing societies*. Yale University Press.
Hutchcroft, P. D. (2014). Linking capital and countryside: Patronage and clientelism in Japan, Thailand, and the Philippines. In D. A. Brun & L. Diamond (Eds.), *Clientelism, social policy, and the quality of democracy* (pp. 174–203). John Hopkins University Press.
Ibañez, J. (2021, December 29). *LGU spending inefficiency won't drag growth—analyst*. Business World. https://www.bworldonline.com/top-stories/2021/12/29/420500/lgu-spending-inefficiency-wont-drag-growth-analyst/
Ill-prepared for full devolution. (2022, December 15). *Philippine daily inquirer*. https://opinion.inquirer.net/159525/ill-prepared-for-full-devolution
International Labour Organization. (2025). *Employment by sex and economic activity (thousands)—annual* [Database]. https://rshiny.ilo.org/dataexplorer52/
International Labour Organization. (n.d.). *International standard classification of occupations* (ISCO). https://ilostat.ilo.org/methods/concepts-and-definitions/classification-occupation/
International Monetary Fund. (2024). *World economic outlook, April 2024* [Data Set]. Retrieved May 15, 2024, from https://www.imf.org/-/media/Files/Publications/WEO/WEO-Database/2024/April/WEOApr2024all.ashx
International Monetary Fund. (2025). *World economic outlook, April 2025* [Data Set]. Retrieved July 9, 2025, from https://www.imf.org/-/media/files/publications/weo/weo-database/2025/april/weoapr2025alla.xls
Investment Incentives Act, Republic Act No. 5186. (1967, September 16). (Phil.). https://www.officialgazette.gov.ph/1967/09/16/republic-act-no-5186/
Joaquin, N. (2004). *Culture and history: Occasional notes on the process of Philippine becoming*. Anvil Publishing Inc. (Original work published 1988).
Jon, Y. (2022, November 3). The sad fall of a Philippine steel giant. *The Asianometry Newsletter*. https://www.asianometry.com/p/the-sad-fall-of-a-philippine-steel
Jung, K.-H. (1994). Changing business government relations in Korea. In R. Fitzgerald (Ed.), *The state and economic development* (pp. 98–112). Toppan Company (S) Pte. Ltd.
Kaldor, N. (1967). *Strategic factors in economic development*. New York State School of Industrial and Labor Relations, Cornell University.
Khan, M. H. (2010). *Political settlements and the governance of growth-enhancing institutions* (Working Paper). School of Oriental and African Studies, University of London. https://soas-repository.worktribe.com/output/389203/political-settlements-and-the-governance-of-growth-enhancing-institutions
Khan, M. H. (2015). Industrial policy design and implementation challenges. In J. Felipe (Ed.), *Development and modern industrial policy in practice: Issues and country experiences* (pp. 94–126). Edward Elgar Publishing. https://doi.org/10.4337/9781784715540
Kim, K. S., Leipziger, D., & McDonald, J. (1995). *The Korean Miracle (1962–1980): Policies, growth, and lessons*. Washington, DC: World Bank.

Kremer, M. (1993). The O-ring theory of economic development. *The Quarterly Journal of Economics, 108*(3), 551–575.
Krugman, P. R. (1994). *The age of diminished expectations: U.S. economic policy in the 1990s* (3rd ed.). MIT Press.
Kuhonta, E. M. (2014). Thailand's feckless parties and party system: A path-dependent analysis. In A. Hicken, A. Arbor, & E.M. Kuhonta (Eds.), *Party system institutionalization in Asia: Democracies, autocracies, and the shadows of the past* (pp. 280–306). Cambridge University Press.
Kurdli, S. N. (2023). *How interest groups shape industrial policy: The case of MENA countries* [Doctoral dissertation, Nanyang Technological University]. Digital Repository of NTU. https://hdl.handle.net/10356/170473
Laiprakobsup, T. (2022). The analytical framework for the policymaking process of Thai political parties under the CESE model. *Asian Journal of Comparative Politics, 7*(4), 1247–1267.
Lande, C. H. (1967). The Philippine political party system. *Journal of Southeast Asian History, 8*(5), 19–39.
Landingin, R., & Medalla, F. (Eds.). (2019). *Momentum: Economic reforms for sustaining growth*. Foundation for Economic Freedom.
Lane, N. (2025). Manufacturing revolutions: Industrial policy and industrialization in South Korea. *The Quarterly Journal of Economics, 40*(3), 1683–1741. https://doi.org/10.1093/qje/qjaf025
Largoza, G. (2024, October 4). Are K-12 students overworked—by design? *Philippine Daily Inquirer*. https://opinion.inquirer.net/177289/are-k-12-students-overworked-by-design
League of Provinces of the Philippines. (n.d.). *History*. https://lpp.gov.ph/history/
Leibenstein, H. (1957). *Economic backwardness and economic growth: Studies in the theory of economic development*. John Wiley & Sons.
Leon-Ledesma, M. A., & Thirlwall, A. P. (2002). The endogeneity of the natural rate of growth. *Cambridge Journal of Economics, 26*(4), 441–459.
Lerner, A. (1943). Functional finance and the federal debt. *Social Research, 10*, 38–51.
Lewis, A. (1954). Economic development with unlimited supplies of labor. *The Manchester School, 22*, 139–191.
Li, L. C. (2006). Differentiated actors: Central–local politics in China's rural tax reforms. *Modern Asian Studies, 40*(1), 151–174.
Liddle, B. (2022). Introducing a large panel dataset of economy-wide real electricity prices and estimating long-run GDP and price elasticities of electricity demand for high-and middle-income panels. *Journal of Energy History, 7*(2), 1e–9e.
Machiavelli, N. (1984). *The prince* (D. Donno, Trans.). Bantam Classics. (Original work published 1532).
Maddawin, R. B., Diokno-Sicat, C. J., & Castillo, A. F. G. (2020). *Philippine local government public expenditure review: A survey of national government local government support programs* (Discussion Paper Series No. 2020-48). Philippine Institute for Development Studies. https://pidswebs.pids.gov.ph/CDN/PUBLICATIONS/pidsdps2048.pdf
Maddison, A. (1982). *Phases of capitalist development*. Oxford University Press.
Maddison, A. (2001). *The world economy: A millennial perspective*. Development Centre of the Organisation for Economic Co-Operation and Development.
Manasan, R. G. (1986). *Public finance in the Philippines: A review of the literature* (Working Paper No. 81-03). Philippine Institute for Development Studies. https://www.pids.gov.ph/publication/working-papers/public-finance-in-the-philippines-a-review-of-the-literature
Marcos, F. E., Sr. (1971). *Today's revolution: Democracy*. Office of Media Affairs.

Marcos, F. E., Sr. (2022). *First state of the nation address*. https://www.spot.ph/newsfeatures/policy/101775/first-sona-ferdinand-marcos-sr-full-text-a4671-20220717-lfrm5 (Original work published 1966).

McCombie, J. S. L., & Thirlwall, A. P. (1994). *Economic growth and the balance-of-payments constraint*. Palgrave Macmillan.

McLeay, M., Radia, A., & Thomas, R. (2014). Money creation in the modern economy. *Quarterly Bulletin, Q1*, 14–27. Bank of England. https://www.bankofengland.co.uk/-/media/boe/files/quarterly-bulletin/2014/money-creation-in-the-modern-economy

Medalla, E. M. (1992). *Trade and industrial policy beyond 2000: An assessment of the Philippine economy* (Discussion Paper Series No. 98-05). Philippine Institute for Development Studies. https://pidswebs.pids.gov.ph/CDN/PUBLICATIONS/ris-old-backups/pdf/pidsdps9805.pdf

Mendels, F. (1972). Protoindustrialization: The first phase of the industrialization process. *Journal of Economic History, 32*(1), 241–261.

Mendoza, R., Bulaong, O., Jr., & Mendoza, G. (2022). *Cronyism, oligarchy and governance in the Philippines: 1970s vs 2020s*. http://dx.doi.org/10.2139/ssrn.4032259

Montes, M. F. (1994). The private sector as the engine of Philippine growth: Can heaven wait? In R. Fitzgerald (Ed.), *The state and economic development: Lessons from the Far East* (pp. 132–147). Toppan Co. (S) PTE Ltd.

Montes, M. F. (2024). Philippine industrial policy: Why not? *Philippine Review of Economics: Special Issue on Industrial Policy, 61*(2), 1–21.

Moore, B. (1988). *Horizontalists and verticalists: The macroeconomics of credit money*. Cambridge University Press.

Morduch, J. (1998). Poverty, economic growth, and average exit time. *Economics Letters, 59*(3), 385–390. https://doi.org/10.1016/S0165-1765(98)00070-6

Myrdal, G. (1968). *Asian drama: An inquiry into the poverty of nations*. Pantheon Books.

Naruemon, T. (2016). Contending political networks: A study of the "Yellow Shirts" and "Red Shirts" in Thailand's politics. *Southeast Asian Studies, 5*(1), 93–113.

National Economic and Development Authority. (1982). *Five-year Philippine development plan 2023–2028*. Author.

National Economic and Development Authority. (1988). *Updates on the medium-term Philippine development plan 1988–1992*. https://drive.google.com/drive/folders/1n3DSI1dnkcThg1XCIt-HsgAsDAjnRAT

National Economic and Development Authority. (1993). *Medium-term Philippine development plan 1993–1998*. https://drive.google.com/drive/folders/13XYQg10cdVBPOx3BGfleAHPaYMD47bBI

National Economic and Development Authority. (1996). *Updated medium-term Philippine development plan 1996–1998*. https://drive.google.com/drive/folders/13XYQg10cdVBPOx3BGfleAHPaYMD47bBI

National Economic and Development Authority. (1999). *Medium-term Philippine development plan 1999–2004*. https://drive.google.com/drive/folders/0B4nUTV4owtcY3RYVGhEdlk1V3M?resourcekey=0-EZtHW6WNsFgnQiujQIiBYQ

National Economic and Development Authority. (2004). *Medium-term Philippine development plan 2004–2010*. https://drive.google.com/drive/folders/1S7ZTSRs8_I6s6UNYtY3EBB-zCjZHTooq

National Economic and Development Authority. (2014). *Philippine development plan 2011–2016 midterm update*. https://drive.google.com/file/d/1LGA1oXVmkkRzXo9LVSMD8-mJqZpt5awE/view

National Economic and Development Authority. (2015). *Ambisyon Natin 2040: A long-term vision for the Philippines*. Author.

National Economic and Development Authority. (2017). *Philippine development plan 2017–2022*. http://pdp.neda.gov.ph/wp-content/uploads/2017/01/PDP-2017-2022-10-03-2017.pdf

National Economic and Development Authority. (2023a). *Philippine development plan 2023–2028*. https://pdp.depdev.gov.ph/wp-content/uploads/2023/09/Philippine-Development-Plan-2023-2028.pdf

National Economic and Development Authority. (2023b). *Philippine development plan 2023–2028 briefer*. https://pdp.depdev.gov.ph/wp-content/uploads/2023/01/PDP-2023-2028-Briefer.pdf

National Economic and Development Authority. (2025, January 23). *2024 PH dev't report: On track toward socioeconomic transformation, but no room for complacency*. https://depdev.gov.ph/24thnedaboard/

National Economic Council. (1962). *Annual economic report to the President of the Philippines, 1962*. National Economic Council.

National Economic Council. (1963). *Annual economic report to the President of the Philippines, 1963*. National Economic Council.

National Economic Council. (1964). *Annual economic report to the President of the Philippines, 1964*. National Economic Council.

National Economic Council. (1965). *Annual economic report to the President of the Philippines, 1965*. National Economic Council.

National Statistical Coordination Board. (2009). *2009 Philippine standard industrial classification*. https://client.emb.gov.ph/crs/uploads/PSA_PSIC_2009-CODES.pdf

Noble, L. W. T. (2020, September 15). BSP can lend more to government under Bayanihan II. *Business World*. https://www.bworldonline.com/editors-picks/2020/09/15/316714/bsp-can-lend-more-to-govt-under-bayanihan-ii/

North, D. C. (1990). *Institutions, institutional change and economic performance*. Cambridge University Press.

Nurkse, R. (1953). *Problems of capital formation in underdeveloped countries*. Basil Blackwell.

Office of the President, Constituting Green Lanes for Strategic Investments, Exec. Ord. No. 18. (2023, February 23). (Phil.). https://www.officialgazette.gov.ph/2023/02/23/executive-order-no-18-s-2023/

Office of the President, Creating the National Shipyards and Steel Corporation and Dissolving the National Shipyard and Heavy Industries Department, the Engineer Island Shops, the Steel Mill Project and the Reparation Tools Department of the National Development Company, Exec. Ord. No. 356. (2023, February 23). (Phil.). https://www.officialgazette.gov.ph/1950/10/23/executive-order-no-356-s-1950/

Okun, A. (1962). Potential G.N.P.: Its measurement and significance. In *Proceedings of the business and economics statistics section of the American statistical association* (pp. 98–104). American Statistical Association.

Olson, M. (1993). Dictatorship, democracy, and development. *American Political Science Review*, *87*(3), 567–576.

Organisation for Economic Co-operation and Development. (2023). *PISA 2022 results (Volume I): The state of learning and equity in education*. PISA, OECD Publishing. https://doi.org/10.1787/53f23881-en

Palisada, S. (2010, February 11). The light and shade of the Cyber Corridor. *ABS-CBN News*. https://news.abs-cbn.com/views-and-analysis/02/10/10/light-and-shade-cyber-corridor-stanley-palisada

Pandian, R. (2024). Globalization of production, manufacturing employment, and income inequality in developing nations. *Social Science Research*, *118*, Article 102975. https://doi.org/10.1016/j.ssresearch.2023.102975

Paqueo, V., Orbeta, A. C., Jr., Lanzona, L. A., Jr., & Dulay, D. G. C. (2014). *Labor policy analysis for jobs expansion and development* (Discussion Paper No. 2014-34). Philippine Institute for Development Studies. https://pidswebs.pids.gov.ph/CDN/PUBLICATIONS/pidsdps1434_rev2.pdf

Parker, M. (2024). A global database for energy consumer price indices. *Energy Economics, 136*, Article 107645. https://doi.org/10.1016/j.eneco.2024.107645

Philippine Statistics Authority. (2002). *2002 Philippine statistical yearbook*. https://psa.gov.ph/philippine-statistical-yearbook/year/2002

Philippine Statistics Authority. (2010). *2010 Philippine statistical yearbook*. https://psa.gov.ph/philippine-statistical-yearbook/year/2010

Philippine Statistics Authority. (2015). *2015 Philippine statistical yearbook*. https://psa.gov.ph/philippine-statistical-yearbook/year/2015

Philippine Statistics Authority. (2016). *2016 Philippine statistical yearbook*. https://psa.gov.ph/philippine-statistical-yearbook/year/2016

Philippine Statistics Authority. (2018). *Family income and expenditures survey*. Author.

Philippine Statistics Authority. (2022). *2022 updates to the 2012 Philippine standard occupational classification*. https://psa.gov.ph/classification/psoc/technical-notes

Philippine Statistics Authority. (2023a). *2023 annual provincial labor market statistics (Preliminary results)* [Data Table]. https://psa.gov.ph/system/files/iesd/Table%202.%20Total%20Employed%20Persons%20and%20Employment%20Rate%202022f%20and%202023p.xlsx

Philippine Statistics Authority. (2023b). *2023 Philippine statistical yearbook*. https://psa.gov.ph/philippine-statistical-yearbook/year/2023

Philippine Statistics Authority. (2024a, January 31). *2020 census-based population projections* [Data Table]. Retrieved March 2, 2024, from https://psa.gov.ph/sites/default/files/dhsd/Statistical%20Tables%20CBPP_0.pdf

Philippine Statistics Authority. (2024b, February 7). *Unemployment rate in December 2023 was estimated at 3.1 percent* [Data Table]. https://psa.gov.ph/system/files/iesd/TABLE%20B%20-%20Employment%20by%20Major%20Industry%20Group%20and%20Total%20Hours%20Worked%2C%20Philippines_2.xlsx

Philippine Statistics Authority. (2024c, July 22). *Percentage of Filipino families classified as poor declined to 10.9 percent in 2023* [Data Set]. https://www.psa.gov.ph/content/percentage-filipino-families-classified-poor-declined109-percent2023#:~:text=Based%20on%20the%20preliminary%20results,at%2010.9%20percent%20or%20equivalent

Philippine Statistics Authority. (2025a, May 19). *Clarification on the alleged 19 million functionally illiterate high school graduates and junior high school completers* (PSA Press Release No. 2025-185). https://psa.gov.ph/content/clarification-alleged-19-million-functionally-illiterate-high-school-graduates-and-junior

Philippine Statistics Authority. (2025b). *Unemployment rate in December 2024 was estimated at 3.1 percent* (Labor Force Survey Press Release No. 2025-41). https://psa.gov.ph/statistics/labor-force-survey/press-release/node/1684066682

Power, J. H., & Sicat, G. P. (1971). *The Philippines: Industrialization and trade policies*. Oxford University Press.

Prebisch, R. (1962). The economic development of Latin America and its principal problems. *Economic Bulletin for Latin America, 7*(1), 1–22. (Original work published 1950)

Presidential Communications Office. (2024, June 29). *PH Gov't unveils comprehensive framework for 10-year employment plan*. Presidential Communications Office. https://pco.gov.ph/other_releases/ph-govt-unveils-comprehensive-framework-for-10-year-employment-plan/

PricewaterhouseCoopers. (2017). *The world in 2050: The long view: How will the global economic order change by 2050?* [Data Table]. https://www.pwc.com/gx/en/research-insights/economy/the-world-in-2050.html?fbclid=IwY2xjawNj9rpleHRuA2FlbQIxMQABHu86KFLVicJPe8ePJL1n1aJk-_XWOhltstjJY7-ZtHVMu2T6quIRqZx4WyxT_aem_IM5P3OWIThJ3r8gW_Kvgqw

Pritchett, L. (2003). A toy collection, a socialist start, and democratic dud: Growth theory, Vietnam and the Philippines. In D. Rodrik (Ed.), *In search of prosperity: Analytic narratives on economic growth* (pp. 123–151). Princeton University Press.

Pritchett, L. (2022, June 23). *Economic growth in five figures (one with five variants).* https://lantpritchett.org/economic-growth-in-five-figures-one-with-five-variants/

Pritchett, L., & Lewis, A. (2022). *Economic growth is enough, and only economic growth is enough.* Manuscript. https://lantpritchett.org/wp-content/uploads/2022/05/Basics-legatum-paper_short.pdf

Pritchett, L., Sen, K., & Werker, E. (Eds.). (2018). *Deals and development: The political dynamics of growth episodes.* Oxford University Press.

Pritchett, L., & Summers, L. H. (2014). *Asiaphoria meets regression to the mean* (Working Paper No. 20573). National Bureau of Economic Research. https://doi.org/10.3386/w20573

Pritchett, L., & Werker, E. (2012). *Developing the guts of a GUT (Grand Unified Theory): Elite commitment and inclusive growth* (Working Paper No. 16). https://www.effective-states.org/working-paper-16/

Punongbayan, J. C., & De Dios, E. S. (2025). Debt, dictatorship, and decline: The enduring economic impact of the Philippines' 1980s crisis. *Review of Development Economics.* https://doi.org/10.1111/rode.70066

Quimpo, N. G. (2007). The Philippines: Political parties and corruption. *Southeast Asian Affairs, 2007*(1), 277–294.

Ramos, M. (2023, May 3). IMI of Ayala Group inks deal to produce zero e-motorcycles in PH. *Inquirer.Net.* https://business.inquirer.net/398908/imi-of-ayala-group-inks-deal-to-produce-zero-cycles-in-ph

Rasmussen, M. B., & Knutsen, C. H. (2021). Party institutionalization and welfare state development. *British Journal of Political Science, 51*(3), 1203–1229.

Ravago, M. L. (2022). *The nature and causes of high Philippine electricity price and potential remedies* (Working Paper No. 2023-01). Ateneo Center for Economic Research and Development. https://www.ateneo.edu/sites/default/files/2023-01/AdMU%20WP%202023-01_0.pdf

Ravago, M.-L. V., Brucal, A. Z., Roumasset, J., & Punongbayan, J. C. (2019). The role of power prices in structural transformation: Evidence from the Philippines. *Journal of Asian Economics, 61*, 20–33.

Recto, R. G. (2024, May 27). *Keynote speech: Philippine economic briefing* [Conference presentation]. Philippine Economic Briefing. Manila, Philippines.

Reinert, E. S. (2019). *How rich countries got rich . . . and why poor countries stay poor* (2nd ed.). PublicAffairs.

Remo, A. (2014, July 25). SMEs hobbled by high power cost. *Philippine Daily Inquirer.* https://business.inquirer.net/175276/smes-hobbled-by-high-power-cost

Reyes, M. A. L. L. (2021, August 28). MSMEs are key to Philippine growth. *Philstar Global.* https://www.philstar.com/business/2021/08/28/2123064/msmes-are-key-philippine-growth

Rimando, L., & Mercado, E. (2012, July 22). *Why electricity rates in Philippines are high.* Rappler. http://www.rappler.com/business/features/8985-rappler-animate-why-electricity-rates-in-philippines-are-high

Rodrik, D. (2013). Unconditional convergence in manufacturing. *Quarterly Journal of Economics, 128*(1), 165–204. https://doi.org/10.1093/qje/qjs047

Rodrik, D., Diao, X., & McMillan, M. (2017). The recent growth boom in developing economies: A structural-change perspective. In M. Nisanko & J. A. Ocampo (Eds.), *The Palgrave handbook of development economics* (pp. 281–334). Palgrave Macmillan. http://drodrik.scholar.harvard.edu/publications/recent-growth-boom-developing-economies-structural-change-perspective

Rosenstein-Rodan, P. N. (1943). Problems of industrialisation of Eastern and South-Eastern Europe. *The Economic Journal*, *53*(210–211), 202–211. https://doi.org/10.2307/2226317

Rosenstein-Rodan, P. N. (1961). International aid for underdeveloped countries. *The Review of Economics and Statistics*, *43*(2), 107–138.

Second Congressional Commission on Education. (2024). *Miseducation: The failed system of Philippine education, EDCOM II year one report*. Second Congressional Commission on Education. https://edcom2.gov.ph/media/2024/02/EDCOM-II-Year-One-Report-PDF-022924.pdf

Sen, K., & Tyce, M. (2019). The elusive quest for high income status—Malaysia and Thailand in the post-crisis years. *Structural Change and Economic Dynamics*, *48*, 117–135. https://doi.org/10.1016/j.strueco.2017.11.007

Serafica, R. (2024). Exploring the prospects of services-led development for the Philippines. *Philippine Review of Economics: Special Issue on Industrial Policy*, *61*(2), 114–138.

Severino, R. C., & Salazar, L. C. (Eds.). (2007). *Whither the Philippines in the 21st century?* ISEAS-Yusof Ishak Institute.

Shair-Rosenfield, S. (2016). The causes and effects of the local government code in the Philippines: Locked in a status quo of weakly decentralized authority? *Journal of Southeast Asian Economies*, *33*(2), 157–171.

Sicat, G. P. (1986). *A historical and current perspective of Philippine economic problems* (Monograph Series No. 86-11). Philippine Institute for Development Studies. https://pidswebs.pids.gov.ph/CDN/PUBLICATIONS/pidsms86-11.pdf

Sicat, G. P., & Abdula, R. D. (2003). Public finance. In A. Balisacan & H. Hill (Eds.), *The Philippine economy: Development policies, and challenges* (pp. 106–135). Oxford University Press.

Singer, H. W. (1950). U.S. foreign investment in underdeveloped areas: The distribution of gains between investing and borrowing countries. *American Economic Review*, *40*(2), 473–485.

Socialist Republic of Viet Nam. (n.d.). *Industrial development strategy through 2025, vision to 2035*. https://vietnam.gov.vn/period-20112020/industrial-development-strategy-through-2025-vision-to-2035-10054959

Solow, R. M. (1957). Technical change and the aggregate production function. *The Review of Economics and Statistics*, *39*(3), 312–320. https://www.jstor.org/stable/1926047

Statistics Netherlands. (2023, November 2). *Occupational skill level*. https://www.cbs.nl/en-gb/news/2023/44/young-technicians-four-times-as-often-male/occupational-skill-level#:~:text=Skill%20level%203%20%28ISCO%202008,procedures%20in%20a%20specific%20area

Studwell, J. (2013). *How Asia works: Success and failure in the world's most dynamic region*. Grove Press.

Szirmai, A. (2012). Industrialisation as an engine of growth in developing countries, 1950–2005. *Structural Change and Economic Dynamics*, *23*(4), 406–420.

Szirmai, A., & Verspagen, B. (2015). Manufacturing and economic growth in developing countries, 1950–2005. *Structural Change and Economic Dynamics*, *34*, 46–59.

Tadem, T. E. (2019). The emergence of Filipino technocrats as Cold War "pawns". *Journal of Contemporary Asia*, *50*(4), 530–550. https://doi.org/10.1080/00472336.2019.1694961

Takagi, Y. (2016). *Central banking as state building: Policymakers and their nationalism in the Philippines, 1933–1964*. Nus Press.

Tan, K. W. (1999). South Korea. In K. S. Jomo & T. K. Wah (Eds.), *Industrial policy in East Asia: Lessons for Malaysia* (pp.75–137). University of Malaya Press.

Tapales, P. D. (1992). Devolution and empowerment: LGC 1991 and local autonomy in the Philippines. *Philippine Journal of Public Administration*, *36*(2), 101–114.

Teodoro, E. S. (1967). *Industrialization in the Philippines: The ISI experience*. University of the Philippines School of Economics.

Thirlwall, A. P. (1969). Okun's law and the natural rate of growth. *Southern Economic Journal*, *36*(1), 87–89. https://doi.org/10.2307/1056813

Thirlwall, A. P. (1979). The balance of payments constraint as an explanation of the international growth rate differences. *PSL Quarterly Review*, *32*(128), 45–53. https://doi.org/10.13133/2037-3643/12804

Timmer, M., deVries, G. J., & DeVries, K. (2015). Patterns of structural change in developing countries. In *Routledge handbook of industry and development* (pp. 65–83). Routledge.

Torio, P., Feliciano, P., Manalo, M. S., & Jaminola, L. M. (2021). *Philippine conglomerates: Their role in promoting inclusive development* (ASOG Working Paper No. 21-025). http://dx.doi.org/10.2139/ssrn.3919558

Trabaho Para sa Bayan Act, Republic, Act No. 119621. (2023). (Phil.). https://lawphil.net/statutes/repacts/ra2023/pdf/ra_11962_2023.pdf

Ulep, V. G. T., Casas, L. D. D., Manuel, A. C. G., Mendoza, J. P. D., Bagas, J., & Dela Luna, K. L. G. (2024). *Behind the slow start: An assessment of early childhood care and development in the Philippines* (Discussion Paper Series No. 2024-04). Philippine Institute for Development Studies. https://doi.org/10.62986/dp2024.04

Ulep, V. G. T., Casas, L. D. D., & Taparan, S. M. (2023). *Starting strong: Why early childhood care and development matters in the Philippines* (Policy Notes No. 2023-13). Philippine Institute for Development Studies. https://doi.org/10.62986/pn2023.13

United Nations Industrial Development Organization. (2025). *National accounts* [Database]. https://stat.unido.org/data/table?dataset=national-accounts#data-browser

United States Energy Information Administration. (2023). *Annual energy outlook 2023: Table 1. Total energy supply, disposition, and price summary* [Data Table]. https://www.eia.gov/outlooks/aeo/data/browser/#/?id=1-AEO2023&region=0-0&cases=ref2023~highmacro~lowmacro~highprice~lowprice~highZTC~lowZTC&start=2021&end=2050&f=A&sourcekey=0

Universal Access to Quality Tertiary Education Act, Republic Act No. 10931. (2017, August 3). (Phil.). https://www.officialgazette.gov.ph/2017/08/03/republic-act-no-10931/

Vernengo, M., & Pérez Caldentey, E. (2020). Modern money theory (MMT) in the tropics: Functional finance in developing countries. *Challenge*, *63*(6), 332–348.

Viotti, E. B. (2002). National learning systems: A new approach on technological change in late industrializing economies and evidences from the cases of Brazil and South Korea. *Technological Forecasting and Social Change*, *69*(7), 653–680. https://doi.org/10.1016/S0040-1625(01)00167-6

Vos, R., & Yap, J. T. (1996). *The Philippine economy: East Asia's stray cat?* St. Martin's Press.

Wage Rationalization Act, Republic Act No. 6727. (1989, June 9). (Phil.). https://www.officialgazette.gov.ph/1989/06/09/republic-act-no-6727/

Werker, E., Mandviwala, Y., Motte-Muñoz, H., & Wit, A. (2014). *Ayala Corporation and the Philippines in a growing economy (A)*. Harvard Business School Case 713-093.

Wilcox, C., Weatherford, W., & Hunter, H. (1962). *Economies of the world today: Their organization, development and performance*. Harcourt, Brace, and World, Inc.

World Bank. (2020). *Getting electricity: Price of electricity (US cents per kWh) (DB16-20 methodology)* [Data File]. https://databank.worldbank.org/source/doing-business/Series/IC.ELC.PRI.KH.DB1619

World Bank. (2021). *Doing business data: Historical data (DB04-DB20)* [Data File]. https://archive.doingbusiness.org/content/dam/doingBusiness/excel/db-2021/Historical-Data--DB04-DB20-.xlsx

World Bank Group. (1976). *Philippines: A review of industrial development policy* (Report No. 1324-PH). World Bank.

World Bank Group. (1984). *The Philippines: Public expenditures and their financing.* (Report No. 4919–PH). https://documents1.worldbank.org/curated/en/374101468107644993/pdf/multi-page.pdf

World Bank Group. (1993). *The East Asian miracle: Economic growth and public policy.* Oxford University Press.

World Bank Group. (2022). *Philippine learning poverty brief.* https://documents1.worldbank.org/curated/en/099000207152223103/pdf/IDU002b5536c0db4104ec3087d809906ec2eae56.pdf

Yu, J. (2019). Introduction: Local governance in China—past, present, and future. In J. Yu & S. Guo (Eds.), *The Palgrave handbook of local governance in contemporary China* (pp. 1–21). Palgrave McMillan.

Zubairi, A., & Rose, P. (2017). *Bright and early: How financing pre-primary education gives every child a fair start in life: Moving towards quality early childhood development for all*. London: Theirworld. https://s3.amazonaws.com/theirworld-site-resources/Reports/Theirworld-Report-Bright-and-Early-June-2017.pdf

INDEX

Note: Numbers in **bold** indicate a table. Numbers in *italics* indicate a figure. Numbers followed by n indicate an endnote

4IR *see* Fourth Industrial Revolution

accommodation & food: description and subsectors **105–111**; forecasts *286, 288, 290, 291, 323–330*
Acemoglu, D. 7, 157, 245
ADB *see* Asian Development Bank
aerospace **136**, 180, 183, 198n15
Age of Diminished Expectations 353
aggregate production function 49, 8n6
Agricultural Land Reform Code 1963 148
agriculture: contribution to Real GDP growth *80*, 101, *150*, *288*, *288*; description and subsectors **105–111**; forecasts *286–291*, *303*, *304*, *306*, *307*; share in Real GDP 21, *80*, 150, 160n2, *286*, *288–289*; share in total employment 35, 39, 54, *77*
Aguinaldo 20
AI *see* artificial intelligence
Albert, J. R. G. 348n3
Aldaba, F. 206
Aldaba, R. M. 206
Aldeguer (Congressman) 32–33
Ambisyon Natin 2040 11, 122, 138, 282, 296, 332, 335–336
Ambisyon Natin 2040 program 11, 122, 138, 282, 296, 332, 334–336
Amsden, A. H. 154–155, 196n8
Amsden, Alice 154, 155–156, 196n8
An Act Amending Sections 197n11; and Adding New Sections 135-A, 295-A, 296-A, and 297-A of the National Internal Revenue Code of 1997, as Amended, and for Other Purposes, Republic Act No. 12066 (2024, November 8) (Phil.) 197n11; *see also* CREATE MORE Act (Republic Act 12066, 2024)
An Act Liberalizing the Importation, Exportation and Trading of Rice, Lifting for the Purpose the Quantitative Import Restriction on Rice, and for Other Purposes, Republic Act No. 11203 (2019, February 14) (Phil.) 151
An Act Making Mariveles, Province of Bataan, a Port of Entry by Amending Section Seven Hundred One of the Tariff and Customs Code of the Philippines, as Amended, Providing for the Establishment, Operation and Maintenance of a Foreign Trade Zone Therein; Creating a Foreign Trade Zone Authority; and Authorizing the Appropriation of the Necessary Funds Therefor, Republic Act No. 5490. (1969, June 21) (Phil.) 355, 358
An Act Providing for the Local Government Code of 1991, Republic Act No. 7160. (1991, October 10) (Phil.) 216
Anker methodology 335
Anker, M. 235
Anker, R., 235
Aquino family 148
Aquino, Benigno III 52
Aquino, Beningno Jr. 170, 172, 212n2
Aquino, C. 1, 36, 60, **61**, 131, 133, 146, 149, 171, 178, 216
Aragones, E. M. 76, 103n3, 141n5, 141n9

Araneta, S. 30–32, 265n6
artificial intelligence (AI) 55, 197n15, 245, 292–293
ASEAN *see* Association of Southeast Asian Nations
Asia's Green Revolution 153
Asian Development Bank (ADB) 74, 103n10, 138
Asian Drama 14n1, 22: Myrdal, Gunnar 14n1, 22; soft state 26
Asian Financial Crisis of 1997–1998 146, 155, 160n1, 165
Asiaphoria 7, 47; Pritchett, Lant 2, 6, 7, 10, 12, 45, 47, 57, 59; Summers, Lawrence H. , 45, 47
Association of Southeast Asian Nations (ASEAN) 138, 152, 184, 186
austerity 12, 30–33, 41n15, 168, 250, 265n9; American-imposed, in the Philippines 41n15; orthodox 8, 250; Tory (UK) 265n9
austerity measures 168
austerity programs: Cuaderno 31–32; Garcia 30
automation 197n15, 245
autoregressive distributed lag (ARDL) 144, 247n3

balance of payments crisis 52
balance of payments crisis of 1949 31, 35
Balance-of-Payments-constrained (BOPC) growth rate 49–53, 61n9, 69n10, 166, 284–285
Balisacan, A. 14n2, 125
Bangko Sentral ng Pilipinas (BSP) 129, 251, 254–260, 267n13, 269n22, **271**, **272**; bonds issuance and policy rates of 256, 257, 279; debt instruments issued by 254; how the Bangko Sentral ng Pilipinas and the Bureau of Treasury coordinated in March 2020 (COVID-19) 274–276; how does it operate 257–259; operations Involved in the PHP 20 billion advance dividend payment to the government by **277**; quantity of money not controlled by 254, 267n16, 269n22; sovereign credit issued by 267n13; what it does 187, 233, 287
Bangkok 69n15
Bangladesh **163**, 211
banknotes 265n7
Barabasi, A. L. 75
barangays 16, 18, 214, 217
Bardhan, P. 158
Basco y Vargas, J. 18
Bases Conversion and Development Authority (BCDA) 187
basic food and non-food needs 332, 340
Baumol's cost disease 55, 69n16; Baumol, W. J. 55
BCDA *see* Bases Conversion and Development Authority
behind-the-frontier catch-up 204–206, 228, 247
Bell Mission 1950 29, 35
Bell Trade Act of 1946 28, 29, 32, 33; stipulations of 33; sugar interests in 28; *see also* Trade Act
Bell, D. W. 29
Bell, Jasper 27
Bénétrix, A. S. 162, 164
Bernanke, Ben 249
big push xvii, 8, 40, 42n28, 134, 349; Nurkse, Ragnar 40; Rosenstein-Rodan, Paul N. 40
BIR *see* Bureau of Internal Revenue
BOI *see* Bureau of Investments
bonds 31, 254, 255–256, 257, 260, 262, 235nn14, 15
Booth, A. 22, 40n5
brain drain 15n4, 233
Bretton Woods system 202
Broad, R. 196n4
Brucal, A. Z. 191–192
Bureau of Internal Revenue (BIR) 217
Bureau of Investments (BOI) 203
Bureau of Treasury: how the Bangko Sentral ng Pilipinas and the Bureau of Treasury coordinated in March 2020 (COVID-19) 251, 260, 274–279

CAB *see* capital account balance
Canlas, D. B. 264n4
capabilities xiii, 13, 53, 59, 66, 69n12, 70n25, 71–72, 75–76, 89, 100, 102, 133, 140, 165, 172, 173, 179, 199–212, 263–264, 286, 292, 316, 352
capital account balance (CAB) 270, *272*, 279n1
Capital Market Efficiency Promotion Act 2025 (CMEPA) 187, 350
CARL *see* Comprehensive Agrarian Reform Law
CARPER *see* Comprehensive Agrarian Reform Program Extension with Reforms
CARS program (Executive Order 182, 2015) 179, 184–187
CBs 259
CBS channel 264n1
central banks 250, 257, 260, 265n7, 266n11, 267n16, 268n21, 274, 278, 279n5; 1980s lessons learned by 264n3; BSP (*see* BSP); gold standard and 265n7, 335; independent 268n21; interest rates raised by 268n20; interest rate targeting, corridor system for *258*, 278; power of 266n11; sterilizing central bank support of government in the corridor system *260*; TDF used by 276n5; what they do 266n11
Chang, H.-J. 40, 200, 212n4
Charles III 18

China xii, xv, xxi, xxii, xxiv, 1–9, 17, 19, 22, 34, 46, 48, 56, 67, 71, 77, 162, 163, 168, 189, 196n5, 206, 211, 214, 223–226, 268n19, 350; 1978 economic reform in 9; economic growth of **136**; economic planning in 34, **137**, 138; EDB China compared to EDB Malaysia 189; GNI *3*–5, **124–126**, 128, 135, 143, 283, 291–299, 350; growth-rate of labor force in 47, 48; industrial production growth in **135**, 162; labor force growth of 49, 204, 206, 283, 284, 298, 352; labor productivity in *77*, **78**; as middle-income country 48; Philippines economy compared to 357; Philippine's economy overtaken by 312; Philippines fragmentations compared to 213, –226, **225**; population growth in 1, 67, 353; shift of manufacturing jobs toward 56; silk trade 16; spatial fragmentation in 140, 213, 214, 223–226; super-rapid economic growth maintained in 46; WTO joined by 183, 196n5, 205, 212n4; year the economy entered 5% or higher annual industrial growth, and annual growth rates (%) xii, 67, **163**
China trade: US use of the Philippines as base for 19
Chua, Y. T. 40n6, 150, 158, 159
Cimoli, M. 211
Clarete, R. L. xxvii, 2, 5
Claudio, L. E. 41n15
Clemente, Tina S. 17
clerical and support 85, **115**, 319: clerks 85, 87, **115**, 230, 240, 248, 302–331; description, skill level, and subgroups **113–120**; forecasts 11, 12, 17, 122, 125–131, 133, 140, 141n1, 143, 144, 213, 281
clientelism 7, 63, 219, **222**; competitive **57**, **61**
CMEPA *see* Capital Market Efficiency Promotion Act 2025
Cold War 22, 34, 202
Committee on Sustainability Assessment & KIT Royal Tropical Institute 335
Compañia General de Tabaco de Filipinas 18
competitive asset 156, 157
complexity concept 75, 103n2
Comprehensive Agrarian Reform Law (CARL) 149–150
Comprehensive Agrarian Reform Program Extension with Reforms (CARPER) 149
Comprehensive Automotive Resurgence Strategy (CARS) Program 179, 184–187, 197n11
conglomerates 61, 63–67, 70n23, 89, 92, 93, 102, 160, 172, 201, 352
construction xii, 15n4, 63, 70, 78, 79, 81, 82–84, 87, 101, 103n3, 105, 112, 113, 117, 119, 120, 135, 137, 142, 143, 163, 184, 185, 188, 189, 198n21, 201, 206, 229, 231, 234, 235, 285–291, 302, 305, 306, 308, 313, 314, 330; description and subsectors **105–111,** 135, 175, 231; forecasts 11, 12, 17, 122, 125–131, 133, 140, 141n1, 143, 144, 213, 281; share in total employment *87, 112, 290*
Consultative Group for the Philippines 203
consumption 10, 53, 128, 141n5, 143, 144, 161n9, 266n10, 269n27, 335–337, **338**, 347, 352
Coronel, S. 40n6, 150, 158, 159
Corporate Recovery and Tax Incentives for Enterprises (CREATE) Act 160, 179, 180
Corporate Recovery and Tax Incentives for Enterprises to Maximize Opportunities for Reinvigorating the Economy (CREATE MORE Act) (RA 12066, 2024) 136, 160, 180; EOEs certified under 198n16
corridor system 256–258, *258*, *260*, 262, 262
corruption (Philippines): 19th century 15; 2020s scandal 354n1; anti-dictatorship movement fuled by backlash against 212n2; Basco y Vargas' task to reform 18; Bell Mission in response to 29, 35; crony capitalism and (*see* crony capitalism); economic growth stunted by 63, 169, 203, 250; high tariffs as factor in 166, 197n9289; kickbacks 166, **222**; Macapagal administration's attempt to address 269n24; Magsaysay's reduction of 29–31, 41n11, 61, 265n6; political 2, 18, 26, 29, 30, 38, 59, 60, 67, 168, 212n2, 218, 221, 226, 350; PPPS as factor in 136, 263, 264; public works corruption scandal (present-day) 354n1; regulatory rents as being prone to 58, 63–67, 352; "soft state" 26; stagnation of the economy and 46, 57, 67, 346, 350, 353
COVID-19 5, 62, 69n11, 251, 260, 274, 276; how the Bangko Sentral ng Pilipinas and the Bureau of Treasury coordinated in March 2020 (COVID-19) 274
crafts and trade workers 238; description, skill level, and subgroups **101–106**; forecasts *284, 286, 288, 289, 290, 296*; plumbers 246; welders 246
CREATE Act *see* Corporate Recovery and Tax Incentives for Enterprises (CREATE) Act
CREATE MORE Act (Republic Act 12066, 2024) see Corporate Recovery and Tax Incentives for Enterprises to Maximize Opportunities for Reinvigorating the Economy, or CREATE MORE (RA 12066, 2024)
Creating the Export Processing Zone Authority and Revising Republic Act No.

5490, Presidential Decree No. 66 (1972, November 20) (Phil.) 149, 167, 216
crisis xv, xvi, 1, 29, 31, 35, 52,146, 150, 160, 165, 170, 195, 227, 229, 243, 246, 250, 264n3, 269n24, 278, 296, 298, 315, 333, 351
crony capitalism 63, 169, 203, 250
crowding out 256
Cruz, B. B. 40n6, 150, 158, 159
Cuaderno, Miguel 30–33, 265n6
current account balance (CAB) 51, 254–255, 270–273
Cushner, N. P. 40n3

DA *see* Department of Agriculture
De Dios, E. S. 6, 21, 52, 70n21, 162, 165, 169–170, 250, 264n3, 350
De La Salle University ANIMO econometric model (DLSU ANIMO econometric model) 11–13, 76, 81–84, 88, 99, 103n3, 122, 126–133, 141n2, 142, 145, 236, 281, 284, 286, 287, 289, 291, 293, 294, 295–299, 317n4, 333, 334, 351; database 103n3; forecasting with, data required for 282; forecasts for the PDP 2023–2028 **126**; overview of main features of 126, 142, 179 (Appendix); schematic diagram of *128*
De Mesquita, B. B. 221
deals (business) 10, 57–60; closed 59, **61**, 63; dualistic 63–64; exclusive 63; for growth 64–68; open 59, **61**; ordered **61**; transactional 63
deals space 57, 58, **59**, 59, **61**, 64, 66, 68; *see also* KPSW framework
debt-to-GDP ratio 129, *130*, 139, 260, 261
decent basket 11, 14, 332–347, 353; standard of living 247, 234–337, 339–340, 344–347
decent work, jobs 229, *231*, 231, 247, 308, 317
decentralization 215, 220, 289
decolonization 12, 16, 22, 35, 39
deficit-to-GDP ratio 122, 125, 130, *130*, 139
Deng, K. 21, 40n5
Department of Agriculture (DA): Farm to Market Road Programs 217; prices of food commodities from 336
Department of Budget and Management 10
Department of Economy, Planning, and Development (DEPDev) 36, 300n3, 335; 2024 Philippine Development Report 125; National Economic Development Authority (NEDA) xvi, 125, 334, 300n3; *see also* Philippine development plan 2023–2028
Department of Finance (DoF) 10, 249, 260, 262
Department of Science and Technology (DOST) 200, 201
Department of Trade and Industry (DTI): CREATE MORE law and 198n16; prices of food commodities from 336; sari-sari stores to be boosted by 291–292
DEPDev *see* Department of Economy, Planning, and Development
development plans 12, 121–141, 353; comparison Philippines, Malaysia, Vietnam **135–139**
development progeria 5, 55; Fabella, Raul xxvi, 4, 55
developmental state 39, 154, 173
devolution 213, 214, 217, 223
displacement and replacement 245
DLSU ANIMO econometric model *see* De La Salle University ANIMO econometric model
DLSU High-Frequency Model 144
DOF *see* Department of Finance
DOST *see* Department of Science and Technology
drivers of growth 101, 262; exports 8, 10, 12, 27, 28, 32, 50–55, 58, 64, 67, 68n9, 72, 75, 95–99, 102, 133, 135, 139, 140, 143, 144, 153, 164, 166–168, 174–183, 194n16, 201, 227, 284, 285; manufacturing 50, *71*, *74*, 137–138, 150; structural transformation xxiv, 8, 13, 35, 52, 53, 56, 60, 64, 65, 67, 69n12, 70–74, 83, 84, 88, 99, 101, 103n6, 122, 133, 147, 171, 213, 223, 226–228, 234, 235, 239, 247, 316
DTI *see* Department of Trade and Industry
Duterte, R. 52, **61**, 62, 172

early childhood 232; missing the critical window in early childhood and basic education 243–247
early childhood care and development (ECCD) 315
early childhood education (ECE) 243, 244, 315
Ease of Doing Business (EDB) indicators of the World Bank 188, **189**, 190, **191**, 192; distribution of EDB scores *188*; indicators *192*
Ease of Paying Taxes Act, Republic Act No. 11976. (2024, January 5)(Phil.) 312
East Asian Miracle Report 5
Easterly, W. 138, 140; planners 138, 175, 200; searchers 138
ECCD *see* early childhood care and development
Eccles, M. S. 256
ECE *see* early childhood education
economic functions of local government units (LGU) 216–218
Economic Planning Unit of Malaysia's Prime Minister's Department 138
economic stratification 342

EDB *see* Ease of Doing Business (EDB) indicators
education system 26, 228, 237, 242, 316; Australia 246; basic education system 70n25, 227, 228, 236, 241, 243, 245, 246, 247n4, 263, 301, 315, 316; higher education system 242
education: basic 70n25, 227–228, 236, 241, 243–246, 247n4, 263, 265n6, 301, 315; description and subsectors **105–111,** 135, 175, 231; early childhood 232, 243, 244, 246, 315, 28; forecasts 11, 13, 72, 144, 213, 281, *284, 286, 287, 290,* 301–311*, 314,* 318–323; local universities and colleges 201; postgraduate 228, 237, 247n4, 307, 309, 313–319, 327–329; primary 40n5, 87, 115–119, 227–244, 247n4; public higher education 242, 309, 315; secondary40, 87, 101, 108, 114, 227, 233, **234**, 238, 240, 242, 247n4, 259, 275, 306; state universities and colleges 238; tertiary40n5, 85, 87, 227, 228, 232, **233**, 234–246, 247n4, 306–314; tertiary graduates 227, 234, 238, 246, 247, 308, 310, 313
educational degrees 87
education-to-occupation transition 317n2, 319–320
Edwards, S. 176, 196n8
elasticity 45, 50–53, 64, 144, 190; income elasticity of the demand for exports 51, 69n9, 284, 285; income elasticity of the demand for imports 69n16, 284, 285
electricity 68, 89, 93, 106, 107, 156, 173, 188–195, 197n13, 293, 336–338, 340; cost of electricity 68, 190; distribution of electricity prices *192*
electricity rates and prices (eprice) 190, 192; 2005–214 distribution of (selected Southeast Asian countries) 45, 57, 62, 89, 90, 108, 188, 192, 211, 230, 238, 239, 302, 305, 318, 340–347; 2014 distribution of (Philippines) *188*; eprice 194, **194**; industrialization indicators and **194**
electronics industries 70n24, 155
elementary occupations 85, 119, 238, 248n5, 309, 319; description, skill level, and subgroups 34, 103, **105–120, 126,** 141n9, 215, 266, 281; forecasts, laborers 84–86, **119**, 238, 248n5, 302–319
employment 227, 229, 231–235, **236**, 240, 250, 252, 261, 262, 309, 313, 316, 318–348, 350, 352; share in total employment 227, 229, 231–235, 240, 250, 252, 261, 262, 309, 313, 316, 318–348, 350, 352
employment and education 11, 13, 227, 229, 231, 233–247; early childhood education (*see* early childhood education (ECE)); employment and decent work score by sector *231*; employment share (%) by occupation 84–86, *238*; employment share (%) and labor productivity by sector (2010 and 2023) *79*; labor market policies and 280–286; mean years of schooling (various countries, 1970–2020) *239*; monthly wage rates *230*; misconceptions about 227–250; overeducation (*see* overeducation, problem of); tertiary degrees and sectoral wage growth **235, 236**; tertiary education and differential returns per sector (agriculture, mining, etc.) **234**; tertiary graduates by occupation *238*; tertiary gross enrollment rates (various Asian countries, 1980–2020) *241*
enclosure movement 150
endogenous money creation 266n12
endogenous money theory 266n12
Enhanced Net Operating Loss Carry Over (NOLCO) 197n13
enrollment rates 240, 244
Estrada, G. 68n5
Estrada, J. 1, 60, **61**, 172
Export Incentives Act of 1970, Republic Act No. 6135 (1970, August 31)(Phil.) 147
Export Marketing Bureau (DTI) 182
export processing zones (EPZ) 167; Bataan 167
export structure: Philippines 56, 65, *72*; South Korea 71, *73*; Taiwan 71, *73*
export-oriented enterprises (EOEs) 182, 198n16
Export-Oriented Industrialization 202
export-oriented regime 9, 166
extractive institutions 156, 214

Fabella, R. xxvi, 4–5, 55; *see also* development progeria
failed industrialization programs 13, 147, 162–173
failed land reform 147–154
Family Income and Expenditures Survey 337, 348n1
farm consolidation 151
farming **120**, 150–151, 152, 161; smart **136**
Felipe, J. iii, 1, 5, 48, 52, 56, 60, 68n5, 69n12, 70n25, 71–72, 76, 82, 89, **90–92**, 93, **94–96**, 97, **98–99**, 100, 104n11, 168, 173, 179, 211, 228, 235, 247n1, 268n18, 274n1, 279–280, 285
fiat money 10, 251, 255, 265n7; *see also* money
"Filipino First" policy (Garcia administration) 12, 30–35, 37, 159
finance & insurance 79, 83, 84, 231, 286, 287, 290, 291, 324, 327; description and subsectors **105–111**, 135, 175, 231; forecasts *72, 286, 287, 290, 293, 298–301*
fiscal balance 255, 266n10, 271; fiscal deficit 11, 13, 249–253, 261, 266n10, 269n23, *272, 273*; fiscal surplus 254, 266n10, 272, 273

fishing and aquaculture sector *80*, **105**, **111**, *288*
Food and Nutrition Research Institute 236
food expenditures 336, **336**, 347; threshold 347n1
food security **136**, 151
food service 63, **111**, 308, 313
foodstuffs 17, **117**, **118**
forecasts: contribution to real GDP growth *284*, 286; debt-to-GDP ratio 129, 130, 139, 261; deficit-to-GDP ratio **124–130**, 139; educational requirements for workers *306*, *308*, 313, 320, *326*; employment share *256*; GDP growth *44, 60, 79, 80,*, **124–126,** 131, 132, 135, 143, 281, 284, 296, 333; GNI per capita 3, 4, **124–126**, 128, 135, 143, 283, *291, 296, 297, 299, 350*; headline indicators 123**, 124–126,** 140; headline inflation *124, 126, 129*; investment-to-GDP *298*; labor force *298*; labor force participation 128, 141n6, *142, 229, 294, 295*; labor productivity 47–49, 54, 68, 76–83, 95, 100, 135, 139, 156, 177, 204, 206, 235, 280, 283, 285; occupational structure 301, 302, 317n1; output share 79, 80, 96, 168, 286, *287, 288,* 309; Overseas Filipino Workers (OFW) *88,* 141n6, 143, 283, *293*; population *293*; potential growth *284*; poverty *131*, *133*, **135–**, **137**; real wage rate 84, 86, *291*; share of graduates by occupation *310;*simulations 142*, 298*; supply and demand imbalances *311, 314*; unemployment rate **48, 124, 126**, 128, 129, 142, 229
foreign exchange allocation 33, 166, 166
foreign exchange controls 28, 31, 33–36, 37, 42n22, 164
Foreign Investments Act (FIA) Amendatory Law 160
forest products 17, **105**
forests and farming 151
Four-Point Program 37; Truman, Harry S. 29, 37
Fourth Industrial Revolution (4IR) 100, 104n15, 197n15, 206, 285, 292
fragmentation 10, 13, 140, 213, 214, 218, 223–226; spatial fragmentation 140, 213, 214, 223–226; temporal fragmentation 10, 13, 213, 214, 218, 223–226
fraud 166; bank 292
free enterprise 9, 38, 42n22
Free Enterprise Society of the Philippines: founding in 1955 of 38; Roxas not a member of 42n23
Fukuyama, F. 7
Fullwiler, S. 274
functional finance 250, 252; Lerner, Abba 250, 252

Garcia, C. xxvi, 9, 30–34, 35, 37, **61**; *see also* "Filipino First" policy
general-purpose technology (GPT) 292–293
Gerchenkron's latecomer model 76, 154–157
Gerschenkron, A. xvii, 41n9, 76, 154–157; *see also* latecomer model
global value chains (GVCs) 72, 76, 88–89, 100–102, 138, 180, 182, 184, 205, 208
Gochoco-Bautista, M. S. 264n4
gold standard (monetary) 265n7
government: central government xxii, 26, 202, 223, 250; local government units (LGU) 140, 181, 213, 215, 216, 224, 226, 289; Local Government Code 214–216; national government 78, 152, 165, 214–218, 220, 223, 225, 265n4, 276–277
graft 30, 38
Green Revolution 153
gross national product (GNP) per capita 1961 (various countries) **23–25**
growth: acceleration 46, 59; balance-of-payments-constrained 364 (*see also* Balance-of-Payments-constrained growth); constraint 153; decomposition53, 74, 79, 84, 99; driver of 12, 102, 207 (*see also* driver of growth); engine of xxiii, 12, 49, 54, 75, 101, 160, 207, 227, 237; export-led 5, 7, 53, 147, 172, 173; natural 47 (*see also* natural growth rate); non-persistent 46, 47; potential 12, 43, 48, 49, 51, 52, 59, 66, 68, 122, 123, 131–141, 180, 204,–206, 211, 243, 280–296, 298 (*see also* potential growth rate); stylized facts 43, 45
growth diagnostics framework: Hausmann, Rodrik, and Velasco growth diagnostics framework 227

Hall, D. G. E. 26–26, 36n14
halo-halo of reforms 350
Hares-Hawes-Cutting Act 20
Harrod, R. 47, 68n6; *see also* natural growth rate
Hausmann, R. 9, 75, 103n2, 227, 353
Hayashi, Takeshi 177
HCI *see* Heavy and Chemical Industries
headline indicators 123, **124**, 125, **125**, 126, 131, 140
health & social work 142, 233, 302, 308; description and subsectors **105–111**; forecasts *286–287, 290, 291, 323–326*
Heavy and Chemical Industries (HCI) program 174; *see also* South Korea
heavy industry 169
Heckman, J. 244

Henares Jr., H. ("Larry") 42n21
Hidalgo, C. A. 75
Hill, H. 2
Hirschman, A. O. 35, 166
Hobday, M. 154
Hodrick-Prescott (HP) filter 48, 68n4, 283, *284*, 320
Hong Kong 1, 41n10, 71, 156, 198n16
Hooley, R. 42n27
Huk Communist guerilla movement 21, 27–28, 41n7, 41n11, 146–148
Huntington, S. P. 220
Hutchcroft, P. D. 217, 220–121
hyperinflation 269n24

i3S *see* Inclusive Innovation Industrial Strategy
ideology xv, 37, 202–204, 219, 223
ILO *see* International Labour Organization
import substitution industrialization (ISI) policy 9, 30, 33–30, 33–34, 164–166, 202
Inclusive Innovation Industrial Strategy (i3S) 179
income: distribution of 45, 57, 62, 63, 89, 90, 107–110, 148, 149, 152, 161n6, 182, 198n23, 206, 211,, 217, 224, 230, 234, 238, 302, 305, 317n1, 340, 342, 347; high income 8, 9, 14, 55, 56, 67, 78, 82, 121, 125, 168, 195, 235, 242, 283, 291, 293, 296, 298, 342–353; income per capita 1, 2, 5, 7, 11, 14, 22, 43, 45, 56, 68n1, 100, 102, 142, 173, 189, 193, 198n22, 207, 240, 282, 290, 337, 340, 350; shortfall 345
India: 1980s economic reform in 39; damage to central bank credibility in 278; economic example of 10, 305; economic growth of **136**; GNP 1961 3, **22**; industrial production growth in **135, 162**; year the economy entered 5% or higher annual industrial growth, and annual growth rates (%) **163**
Indonesia 1, 2, 5, 6, 16, 17, 22, 25, 41n7, 44, 75, 77, 80, 82, 155, 156, 160n2, 163, 190, 193, 195, 239, *241*, 278, 280, 350, 353; decolonization of 12, 16, 22, 35, 39; GDP growth rate *126, 127,* 285; GNP 1961 **3, 22**; gross tertiary school enrollment rates *240*; industrialization pursued by 289; industrial production growth in **135,** 162; labor productivity in *77*, **78**; share of manufacturing in GDP% in *80*; share of manufacturing in total employment% in *80*; year the economy entered 5% or higher annual industrial growth, and annual growth rates (%) **163**; years of schooling in *239*, 232, 240, 242
industrial policy xvi, 8–10, 13, 35–36, 42n19, 72, 102, 140, 154, 156, 157, 167, 169, 170, 173, 174, 177–181, 199–211, **225**, 228, 265n6, 316, 351; modern industrial policy 8, 13, 102, 199–212
Industrial Revolution(s) 18, 100, 103, 104n15, 156, 197n15, 206, 285, 292; Fourth (*see* Fourth Industrial Revolution) (4IR))
industrialization 173–178, 188–195; industrial programs 162–196; proto-industrialization 21; Mendels, Franklin F. 21; premature deindustrialization 168
inflation (economic) 5, 22, 30, 31, 32, 38, 48, 124–128, **135**, 139, 151, 250, 256, 261, 264n4, 265n6, 267n16, 268n21, 269n24, 278, 279, 340, 349; Philippines 348n4; budget deficits and 6, 140, 250, 264n4, 265n4; fiscal policy as source of 30, 250, 252, 254, 261, 278, 279; food security issues and 151; PDP 2023–2028 headline indicator **131**, spike 33; stable 48; tax as solution to 31, 68n6, 141n5, 144, 151, 210, 226, 242, 243, 261, 264, 282, 288
inflation rate 128
inflationary government spending 252, 255
information & communication 79, 83, 84, 231, 286, 287, 289, 291, *304, 307, 331*; description and subsectors **105–111,** 135, 175, 231; forecasts *72, 286, 287, 290, 293, 298–301*
information and communication technology (ICT) sector 55
innovation 13, 42n17, 54, 123, **124**, 136, 138, 177, 179, 197n15, 199, 201, 203, 206, 211, 28, 247n4, 264
Internal Revenue Allotment (IRA) 216
International Labour Organization (ILO) 103n3; International Standard Classification of Occupations (ISCO) of (*see* ISCO)
International Monetary Fund (IMF) 6, 31, 34–38, 42n24, 166, 170, 202, 203; Bretton Woods system and 202; failures of 203; IMF-WB policy 34–36; Marcos Sr. and 202, 203; MIPS and 169, 170; Philippine economic reform 1970s and 1980s and 157; technocrats access to and support from 40n24, 202; world GPD growth forecasts from 258
International Rice Research Institute (IRRI) 153
International Standard Classification of Occupations (ISCO)(ILO) 86, **113–114**, **120**
investment 9, 26, 36, 37, 48, 53, 60, 62, 64, 123, **136–143,** 144, 160, 167–170, 175, 181, 185, 190, 195, 196n5, 197n13, 197n15;203, 205, 212; investment-to-GDP ratio 298

Investment Incentives Act, Republic Act No. 5186. (1967, September 16)(Phil.) 167
IRA *see* Internal Revenue Allotment
ISCO *see* International Standard Classification of Occupations
ISI *see* import substitution industrialization
islands of competence 200, 202
IT-BPO sector 8, 55, 70n17, 245

Japan 1, 15, 18, 19, 27, 63, 103n1, 137, 147, 153, 154–163, 169, 171, 173, 175, 201, 105, 241; agricultural sector employment 100n1; agriculture and development in 144; debt-to-GDP ratios in 129, 130, 131, 139, 261; diesel engine manufacturing 170; economic success of 70; exchange rates compared to Philippines 27; GNP **22**; gross tertiary school enrollment rates *240*; Huk movement formed to fight 40n7, 138; innovation 184; investment in Thailand by 4; keiretsu system 66; Korea colonized by 160; Korean industrial policy modeled after 160–162; lacquerware 17; land reform in 148, 149; latecomer industrialization model applied to 155; Marubeni smelter 169; MIPS and 169, 170; NASSCO anticipated by 165; Park (S. Korea)'s normalization of relations with 165; Philippines attacked by 20; Philippine's 1970s acquisition of secondhand vessels from 161; Plaza Accord and 2; post-WWII industrialization of 175–182; post-WWII per capita income of 41, 60, 163, 195; "superstar" firm system in 241; year the economy entered 5% or higher annual industrial growth, and annual growth rates (%) **163**; years of schooling in *239,* 242
Joaquin, N. 134
Jon, Y. 165
Jung, K.-H. 174

K-12 program 241, 242, 315
Kaldor, Nicholas 12, 69n13
Kaldor's engine of growth 12
Kaldor's laws of growth 69n13
Kaldor-Verdoorn features 142
Keynesian proposal 30; post-Keynesian endogenous money theory 266n12
Khan, M. H. 10, 57, 76; political settlement theory of 10
Khan-Pritchett-Sen-Werker (KPSW) political economy framework 10, 57, 60, 157; application to the Phillippines of 63–70; closed deals 59, 63; deals space 57–68; disordered deals 59; open deals 59; ordered deals 59, 60; political settlement 10, 57–65; regulatory rents 58, 63, 65, 67, 352; rents space 57–65
kickbacks 166, 222
Klinger, B. 75
Korea *see* South Korea
Kremer, M. 207; *see also* O-ring theory
Krugman, P. R. 353
Kuznets, Simon 42n17

Labor Force Survey 86, 103nn3, 8–9, 229, 301, 318, 319
land reform: Agricultural Land Reform Code of 1963 148; Comprehensive Agrarian Reform Law (CARL) 149–150, 161n6; Comprehensive Agrarian Reform Program Extension with Reforms (CARPER) 149; Department of Agrarian Reform 29, 149, 151, 289; emancipation patents 149; New Agrarian Emancipation Act 149; Philippine Rural Reconstruction Movement 148; stock distribution option 161n6
landed gentry and elites 26, 28, 37, 158, 161n4
Lane, N. 177
largest firms 89–93, **91–92**
latecomer model 41n9, 76, 154–157; Gerschenkron, Alexander xvi, 41n9, 76, 154–157
Laurel, J. 21
Laurel-Langley Agreement 28, 32, 33, 166
League of Provinces of the Philippines (LPP) 214–216
learning-by-doing (LBD) 76, 209, 228
Leon-Ledesma, M. A. 48
Lerner, A. 250, 252; *see also* functional finance
Lewis turning point 147
Lewis, A. 45
LGUs *see* local government units
Liddle, B. *192*, 192–193
Liga ng mga Barangay 216
living income 14, 235–341; below living income 342, 344, *345*
loanable funds 255, 256, 267n14
local government units (LGUs) 213–226; devolution of national power to 214; earliest attempts to establish 215; economic functions and political impact of 216–220; enactment into law of 189; hindrances to functioning of 147, 257; justification for 139, 215
low human capital 227
LPP *see* League of Provinces of the Philippines

Macapagal, D. 9, 30, 34, 36–39, 42n21, 60, 61, 142, 159, 165; economic liberalization under 36, 37, 39, 42n24, 136, 159, 172, 176, 202, 203; end of 'Filipino First' policy under 12, 30, 31–37, 159; Free Enterprise Society of the Philippines co-founded by 33;

industrialization efforts by 9, 38, 42n22; ISI regime of 36; land reform undertaken by 148; protectionist stance of 42n21; Roxas resignation involving Macapagal administration 42n21; sugar industry opposed to 30, 40n6, 42n22, 157
Macapagal-Arroyo, G. 60, **61**, 172
Marcos Sr. regime 350
Maddison, A. 16
Magellan 16
Magsaysay, R. 9, 29–31, 41n11, 265n6
Maharlika Investment Corporation (MIC) 187, 351
Maharlika Investment Fund (MIF) 187, 198n17
Major Industrial Projects (MIPS) program 169–170
Malay population 16
Malaysia 1–5, 16, 17, 22, 25, 44, 77, 80, 82, 122, 134, 135–139, 141, 155, 156, 160, 163, 168, 169, 189, 190, 193, 201, 239, 241, 243, 289, 353; decolonization of 12, 16, 22, 35, 39; economic growth of 1; EDB China compared to EDB Malaysia 188; GDP growth rate 38, *44*; GNI per capita *3*, 4; GNP 1961 **22**; gross tertiary school enrollment rates *240*; industrialization pursued by 350; IT industry in 4; Islam 17; labor productivity in *78, 79*; lessons for the Philippines from 121–141; TP Act compared to similar legislation in 139, 148, 149, 151, 200, 222 (*see also* TP Act); Twelfth Malaysia Plan 2021–2025 compared to other countries' development plans of 11, 108, **120–122**; Malay from 16, 18; overall development vision of, Philippines compared to 124–126; share of manufacturing in GDP% in *82*; share of manufacturing in total employment% in *85*; years of schooling in *239*–242
malnutrition xiii, xxv, 244, 250, 252, 263, 315, 351
managers and supervisors 113, 319; description, skill level, and subgroups **101–106**; forecasts *141n2, 143, 144, 281, 284, 286–298*; managers 55, 85, 86, 113, 159, 208, 210, 239
Mandanas-Garcia ruling 217–218
Manila Bay 17
Manila–Acapulco galleon 17
manufacturing: decomposition of productivity growth *85*; description and subsectors **105–111**; forecasts *141n2, 143, 144, 281, 284, 286–298*; perfect deindustrialization storm 168; share in Real GDP 80, 288; share in total employment *87, 112, 290*; unconditional convergence in 235
Marcos family 62
Marcos Jr., F. R. "Bongbong" 62; administration 62–64; CREATE MORE Act signed by 160 (*see also* CREATE MORE); dualistic deals approach of 63; election of 60, 177; New Agrarian Emancipation Act signed by 149; PSAC created by 178; TP Act approved by 182–184 (*see also* TP Act)
Marcos Sr., F. xi, xv, xxii, 1, 2, 9, 32, 34, 36, 38, 40, 42n24, 61, 62, 70n21, 134, 146–149, 164–168, 172, 178, 196, 202, 215, 218–220, 250, 350; economic and political mismanagement of 2; fall of 62; industrialization efforts undertaken by 9, 72, 165, 172; martial law years of 61, 70n22; Snap Elections orchestrated by 62; technocrats under 40n21
Marcos, I. 212n1
"more of the same" (MOTS) xiii, xxiv, 14, 138, 141, 173, 247, 280, 281, 301, 351–353; can the Philippines' economy do better or is it just MOTS? 352; employment and education and 218; forecasting the Philippines' future regarding 12, 313, 315; MIC and industrial development and 165; PDP 2023–2028 and 267; possibly economic improvements in the Philippines but also possibly MOTS 249–262
martial law xvi, 1, 60, 70nn21, 22, 146, 148–149, 166, 171, 202–203, 219, 226
Masagana Rice Industry Development Program 153
Matatag Curriculum 243
McCombie, J. S. L. 71
McLeay, M. 266n12
Mendels, F. 21; *see also* proto-industrialization
Mendiola massacre 149
Mendoza, R. 63
Mincerian log-wage equation 247n2
mining & quarrying 142, 198n21, 233, 308; description and subsectors **105–111**; forecasts *286–287, 290–291, 323–329*
MIPS *see* Major Industrial Projects (MIPS) program
mismatch xvi, 235, 243, 290, 302, 311–235; supply-demand imbalance *311–312*
model diet 336
modern industrial policy 8, 102, 199–212; *see also* industrial policy
monetary reality xiii, xxii, 10, 11, 139, 249–264, 264n2, 281, 349, 351
monetization 259, 262, 268n18, 274, 278
money xii, xxiii, 10–11, 249–257, 259–264, 265n7, 266n12, 266n13, 267n16, 269n22, 24, 274, 278, 282; fiat 10–11, 251, 255, 265n7
monopolization 66
monopoly rents 168

monopoly(ies) 151, 153, 232
Montes, M. F. 134, 158–159, 160n2, 171, 179
Morduch, J. 334
MOTS *see* more of the same
Myanmar: GNI per capita *3*; year the economy entered 5% or higher annual industrial growth, and annual growth rates (%) **163**
Myrdal, G. xxv, 14n1, 22, 26; *Asian Drama* 22; "soft state" of 26

NASSCO *see* National Shipyards and Steel Corporation
national debt xiii, 11, 13, 249–264, 266n9, 278
National Economic and Development Authority (NEDA) 36, *123*, 300n3, 334; *see also* Department of Economy, Planning and Development; DEPDev
National Economic Council (NEC) 32
National Food Authority (NFA) 151–153, 161n8
National Shipyards and Steel Corporation (NASSCO) 165
natural growth rate 47–52, 68n6, 283; Harrod, Roy 47, 68n6
NEC *see* National Economic Council
NEDA *see* National Economic and Development Authority
Nepal **25**, **163**
New Agrarian Emancipation Act (Republic Act No. 11953) 149
New Deal 30, 31
new money 254, 264, 266n12
New People's Army (NPA) 148
Noble, L. W. T. 278
non-food expenditures 337
NPA *see* New People's Army
Nurkse, Ragnar xvii; *see also* big push
nurses 246

occupational sorting 233, 235, 247n4
occupations: description and subgroups **101–106**; forecasts 303–304, 306–307, 310, 310–312; occupational structure 301–303, 321, 323, 330; number of workers by occupation *85*; share of graduates by occupation *238, 303*
OECD *see* Organisation of Economic Co-operation and Development
Office of the President, Constituting Green Lanes for Strategic Investments, Exec. Ord. No. 18. (2023, February 23) (Phil.) 102, 182, 350
oil prices **143**, 175, 281
Okun's law 48, 68n4, 283; Okun, Arthur 48
Okun's regression 48
oligarchs and oligarchy **222**; business 63, 159; landed 146, 158; local 19
ordinary least square (OLS) 247n3
Organisation of Economic Co-operation and Development (OECD) countries 46, 191
organizational capabilities 42n17, 66, 70n25, 89, 100, 102, 133, 140, 173, 199, 204, 206–212, 247, 286, 308–309, 315, 316, 352; *see also* capabilities
O-ring theory 207; Kremer, Michael 207
other services 212, 247n2, 301; description and subsectors **107–111**; forecasts 323, 326, 332–334; share in total employment *87*, 112, 290
overdraft, government 265n8, 267n14, 267n15
overeducation, problem of 228, 235, 238, 242, 246, 301, 308, 309, 315; among tertiary graduates 227–247
overnight reverse repurchase 257
overseas filipino workers (OFWs) 15, 88, 283, 293; temporary labor migrants 280
overworking of students 243, 246

pandemic *see* COVID-19
parity clause 28, 33
Park, C.-H. 172, 178; *see also* South Korea
PDP 2023–2028 *see* Philippine Development Plan 2023–2028
Pérez Caldentey, Esteban 252
PEZA *see* Philippine Export Zone Authority
Philippine Development Plan (PDP): development misunderstandings 117–135; a heritage of smallness in 116–119; learning from neighbors (Malaysia and Vietnam, i.e. comparison of each country's development plans) regarding 129–134; PDP 2023–2028 (*see* PDP 2023–2028); from plans to prosects **126**
Philippine Development Plan 2023–2028 (PDP 2023–2028) 43, 45, 56, 122, 135–137, 229, 334; headline indicators in **124**, 125, 126, 140; comparison with other development plans 132–140; creation of 107–108; decent jobs promised by 292; heritage of smallness 131, 134; issues not addressed by 229; objectives of 84, 223, 229; plan for economic and social transformation 121, 122, **135**; weakness of 213–218, 224, 226; will its targets be met? 122
Philippine economy towards 2050: actual and potential growth *280*; agriculture and employment shares 288; aspirations and reality of 280–299; can the Philippines do better or is it MOTS? 14–187, 247, 301, 352; demographics 49, 232, 283, 294, 302, 321, 321; DLSU ANIMO model applied to (*see* DLSU ANIMO model); employment share by sector 81, *290*; labour productivity *286*; output shares and contribution to output growth *286,–288*; possible scenarios for economic growth

296; possibly improvements but also MOTS 14, 187, 247, 301, 352; poverty and OFWs 283, *293*; wages and income per capita *290*
Philippine economy until 2040 282–283
Philippine Export Zone Authority (PEZA) 200–201
Philippine Private Sector Advisory Council (PSAC) 178
Philippine Qualifications Framework 229
Philippine Rehabilitation Act 27, 41n12; Tydings Act 27
Philippine Rice Tariffication Law (Republic Act No. 11203) 151
Philippine Rural Reconstruction Movement 148
Philippine Statistics Authority 42n27, *112*, 132, 143, 229; microdata from 301, 319
Philippines: Agricultural Land Reform Code 1963 148; American (US) colonial period of 12, 17, 19, 21, 147, 159, 215; American influence on development thinking in 16, 34; Bell Act (*see* Bell Act); ceded to the US 16; BSP (*see* BSP): colonization by Spain and the US of 16; comparison with other development plans of 108, **121–145**; decolonization and political independence of 12, 16, 22, 35, 39; DOST 200, 201; the economy until 2040 282; the economy towards 2050 248 (*see also* Philippine economy towards 2050); employment and education in 11, 13, 227, 229, 231, 237, 239–247; employment share (%) and labor productivity by sector (2010 and 2023) *79, 286*; employment share by occupation (%)(2001–2022) *240*; fiscal debt and monetary reality in 249–279; fiscal deficit and national debt in, fallacies and realities about 252; four important issues that help explain why the Philippines did not join East Asia's fast-growth club 147; GDP growth rate *44*; Gerschenkron's latecomer model and the role of the State in 154; GNI per capita *3*; government finances in 261–262; Great Depression's impact on 30; Great Policy debate in 30–33; Huk problem (*see* Huk guerilla movement); ideology and the American influence in 16, 34, 202; industrialization programs (failed) in 13, 134, 147, 162, 170; industrial policy levers for 200; industrial policy today in 178; innovation in 199–212; innovation/firms/capabilities in 199–212; Japanese attack of 147, 156, 165, 173, 177, 205; labor market policies in 212–216; lack of industrialization and poor business environment in175–182; labor productivity in *78*, **79**; labor productivity by province and highly-urbanized city in *78*; land reform (failed) in 147–151; largest firms by subgroup in **91, 92**; Laurel as puppet president of 21, 28, 32, 33, 166; learning from its neighbors (Malaysia and Vietnam) 122–138, 201, 289; liberalized foreign investment in, legislation related to 139, 148, 149, 151, 200, 222; misconceptions about employment and education in 229; modern industrial policy in 8, 13, 102, 109–111; New People's Army (NPA) 148; overview of economic history of 16–39; political parties in, brief history of 214, 215, 219 (*see also* political parties); poverty in 47, 82, 132 (*see also* poverty); PPPS 139, 263, 264; Reforms Type I and Type II in 89, 91, 92, 172, 350; sales/assets/profit rates of companies in 93, **94**; sector finance balances (SFB) 253; sectoral structure of conglomerates in **92**; share of manufacturing in GDP% in *77*; share of manufacturing in total employment% in *82*; Spanish colonial period of 159; the state and the private sector in 147, 157; technocrats and the new policy regime since 1960 36; TP Act (*see* TP Act); "tutelage colonialism" in 19; Tydings Act 1946 24; Tydings–McDuffie Act 1934 18; who can afford a decent life in the Philippines? 335–341; why is the Philippines a state weak? 213–225; why progress in the Philippines has been slow (incomplete land reform and weak state with rent-seeking) 130–143 (*see also* rent-seeking); why progress in the Philippines has been slow (failed industrialization) 142–173; year the economy entered 5% or higher annual industrial growth, and annual growth rates (%) in **163**; years of schooling in *239*, 240, 242
PIA *see* Program Implementation Agency
PISA 2022 243, 246
planners 138, 175, 200; *see also* Easterly, William
plant machinery operators and assemblers 115, 119, 238, 319; assembly line workers 213; description, skill level, and subgroups **101–106**; forecasts *141n2, 143, 144, 281, 284, 286–298*; plant workers 85, 86, 238, 240, 248n5, 312–323
Plaza Accord 1985 5
political parties: brief history in the Philippines of 214, 215, 219; China and Thailand political parties compared to the Philippines 219–239; economic functions and political impact of 212, 220; patronage and personality politics in 62; role of 146–156; role in the economy of 40; Thailand

189–198; weak and strong 220; temporal fragmentation and 10, 13, 213, 214, 223–226
political settlement 57–60; defining 57; *see also* KPSW framework
political settlement theory 10
political settlement/rents space/deals space 57, **61**
post-Keynesian endogenous money theory 266n12
potential growth rate 43, 48, 51, 68n5, 122; *see also* natural growth rate
poverty: definition 32; forecasts *297*; incidence 122, 124–126, 131–139, 141n8, 280, 282, 296, 332–334, 341; living income and 335–339; recent trends and forecasts 332; reduction targets 334; rural 7, 21, 26, 29, 37, 40n5, 108, 137, 147, 148, 150, 158, 159, 170, 179, 224, 225, 293, 337; threshold 282, 293, 332, 334–347, 348n3; who can afford a decent life in the Philippines? *304–309*
poverty threshold: comparing living income to 340–341
Power, J. H. 165
PPPS *see* public-private partnerships
Presidential Decree 27 149
Presidential Decree 66 (1972) 167
Presidential Decree 144 (1973) 216
printing money 259, 268n18, 278, 259
Pritchett, L. 2, 6, 10, 45; *see also* Khan–Pritchett–Sen–Werker framework
productivity: decomposition 53, 74, *79, 84, 99*; labor productivity 47–49, 54, 68n4, 76–79, 83, 95, 100, 135, 139, 156, 177, 204, 206, 208, 280
products that make a nation 139, 349
professional & business services 231, 234, 286; description and subsectors 76, 93, 95, 99, 101, **105–111**, 135, 175; forecasts *141n2, 143, 144, 281, 284, 286–298*
professionals 85–87, 113, 114, 233, 235, 238, 240, 242, 244, 248n5, 302–309; description, skill level, and subgroups **101–106**; forecasts *141n2, 143, 144, 281, 284, 286–298*
Program Implementation Agency (PIA) 36
programmatic and particularistic politics **222**; meso-particularistic 221, 222; micro-particularistic 221, **222**; private goods 191–195, 197–199; public goods xxiii, 10, 66, 139, 140, 157, 173, 200, 213, 218, 220, 221, 225, 250, 252, 263
proto-industrialization 21
PSA *see* Public Service Act (PSA) Amendatory Law
PSAC *see* Philippine Private Sector Advisory Council (PSAC)
public administration 142, 176, 231, 233, 302, 308; description and subsectors **105–111**; forecasts *286–287, 290–291, 303–329*
public procurement 201
Public Service Act (PSA) Amendatory Law 160
public-private partnerships (PPPS) 139, 251, 263–264
Punongbayan, J. C. 6, 42n24, 54, 70n21, 162, 165, 166, 196n6, 250, 264n3, 269n27, 350

Quezon, M. 40n4
Quimpo, N. G. 219–220
Quirino, E. 9, 28–30, **61**, 265n6

RACE program *see* Revitalizing the Automotive Industry for Competitiveness Enhancement (RACE) program
race, social divisions by 19
Radia, A. 266n12
Ramos, F. 1, 60, **61**, 165, 172
Ravago, M. L. 190–192
RBs *see* reserve balances
real estate 63, 64, 78, 79, 43, 84, 89, 92–94, 110, 142, 158, 172, 231, 234, 285–291, 308, 313, 324, 327, 328; description and subsectors **105–126**; forecasts *141n2, 143, 144, 281, 284, 286–298*
Recto, R. G. 249, 299
reforms 5, 7, 9–10, 13, 15, 18, 20, 29, 36, 41n11, 57, 62–64, 68, 102, 141, 146, 147, 159, 166; Type I 89, 91, 92, 172, 350; Type II 91, 92, 172, 350
Regional Tripartite Wages and Productivity Boards 232
regression 48, 68n2, 3, 7, 69n12, 190, 194, 195, 247n3; autoregressive distributed lag 144, 247n3; Mincerian log-wage equation 247n2; returns to higher education 228, 235
regulated market economy 174
regulatory rents **58**, 63, 64, 67
Reinert, E. S. 35
rents 57–68; excessive 27; KPSW framework for 57–60
rents space 57–59, **61**, 65; *see also* KPSW framework
rent-seeking 13, 64, 146, 155, 200, 218, 221, 223
repurchase agreement 251, 260, 274–277
reserve balances (RBs) 257–258, *259*, 275–277, **277**
resources 250, 261, 263
revealed technology advantage 100, 104n15
Revitalizing the Automotive Industry for Competitiveness Enhancement (RACE) program 186
Reynolds Metal (US) 169
Rhee, S. 173

Rice Competitiveness Enhancement Fund (RCEF) 152
Rice Tariffication Law (RTL) 151–153
Rimban, L. 40n6, 150, 158, 159
Robinson, J. A. 157
Rodrik, D. 74
Roosevelt, T. 19
Rosenstein-Rodan, Paul N. xvii; *see also* big push
Roumasset, J. 191
Roxas, M. 9, 21, 26, 28, 30, **61**
Roxas, S. 38–39, 42n23
RTL *see* Rice Tariffication Law
ruling elites 59, 62

Salazar, L. C. 2, 6
sales and service workers 84–87, 115, 302, 305, 313; description, skill level, and subgroups **101–106,** 135; forecasts *141n2, 143, 144, 281, 284, 286–298*; salespersons 245, 302, 305, 318; sales workers 84–87, 115, 302; waiters 316, 305, 313; sari-sari stores 110, 291, 292
sari-sari stores **110**, 134, 231, 291–292
Saudi Arabia: GNI per capita growth of *3*, **143**
saving 152, 159, 252–253, 257, 261, 266n10, 267n16, 269n27
SBTC *see* skill-biased technical change
searchers 138; *see also* Easterly, William
Second Congressional Commission on Education (EDCOM2) 244
sector financial balances (SFB) 261, 269n27, 270–279, *272, 273*; sector financial balances map *272*; sectoral financial balances, Philippines, Q1 2018–Q3 2024 *272*; sectoral financial balances, map, Philippines, Q1 2018–Q3 2024 *272*; three sectoral balances (% of GDP), Q1 2018–Q3 2024 **271**
sectors (Agricultural, Construction, Mining etc.) and definitions **105–111**
semiconductor industries 5, 70n24, 167, 176, 180
Sen, K. 10, 45, 57; *see also* Khan–Pritchett–Sen–Werker framework
Serafica, R. 56
service sector 56, 66, 67, 103, 172, 233, 235, 308
Severino, R. C. 2, 6
SEZs *see* special economic zones
Shair-Rosenfield, S. 218, 226
Sicat, G. P. 165, 265n4
Singapore xiii, xvi, 1, 5, 22, 24, 41n10, 43, 68n1, 70n25, 134, 155, 163, 169, 193, 212n4; big push industrialization programs in 134; Economic Development Board 155; Gerschenkron's principle applied to 139–141; industrialization pursued by 353; manufacturing exports and government policy/incentives for 156–157; Singapore Economic Development Board 155; very fast economic transformation of 71
SIPP *see* Strategic Investment Priority Plan
skill-biased technical change (SBTC) 234
skilled agriculture, forestry, and fishery workers; agricultural workers 85, 86, 88, 116, 238, 239, 248n5, 311, 312, 319; description, skill level, and subgroups **89**; farmers 28, 29, 41n7, 148–150, 161n7, 231, 240, 269n24; forecasts *128–133, 141n2, 143, 144, 281, 284, 286–298*
Socialist Republic of Viet Nam 138
soft state xxv, 26; *see also* Asian Drama
Solow, R. M. 49, 68n6, 293
South Korea 2, 4, 5, 22, 25, 46, 56, 70n25, 71, 73, *77*, 82, 99, 101, 147, 153, 155, 162, **163**, 168–170, 190, 196, 202, 210, 239, **241**; agriculture and development in 141n8; agricultural employment decline in 8, 35, 39, 53, *72*, 213; big push industrialization programs in 8, 40, 42n28, 134, 349; chaebols 155, 175, 177, 178, 197n9, 154–156, 173nn8–10; decolonization of 35; Export-Oriented Industrialization in 39, 202; export structures (1962 and 2023) *71*, 73; Gerschenkron's principle applied to 41, 76, 154–157; GNP 1961 **23**; gross tertiary school enrollment rates *240*; heavy industry encouraged by 139, 169; HCI industries in 176–177; as hub of electronic and semiconductor production 5; Industrial Development Law 174; "industrialization miracle" of 174–179; industrialization pursued by 350, 353; industrial policy 72, 156, 169, 170, 173, 174, 177; industrial production growth in **135,** 162; labor productivity in *77*, **78**; land reform in 149, 173; manufacturing exports and government policy/incentives for 10, 97, 175, 177, 351; original equipment manufacturing (OEM) 174, 184, 185; Park Chung-Hee xvi, 172, 173; regulated market economy 174; Rhee, Syngman xvi, 173; strategic industrial policy in 101; super-rapid growth in 46; "superstar" firm system in 241; year the economy entered 5% or higher annual industrial growth, and annual growth rates (%) 67, **163**; years of schooling in *239*, 240
Spain 16, 69n15, 147, 169, 302, 305, 309, 316, *330*; colonization 16–19, 26, 40n4; occupational structure *330*
spatial fragmentation (China) 224

spatial fragmentation (Philippines) 140; defining 213; national vs. local government 214–215, 126
spatial fragmentation (Thailand) 223
special economic zones (SEZ) 201
Strategic Investment Priority Plan (SIPP) 180, 180, 181, 183
structural transformation xxvi, 8, 35, 52–57, 60, 64, 65, 67, 69n12, 70n24, 71–72, 74, 83, 88, 99, 101, 103n6, 122, 133, 147, 171, 213, 223, 225–228, 234, 235, 239, 247, 316
Studwell, J. 155, 161n3
stunting 244
sugar barons 20
sugar industry (South Korea) 174
sugar industry and interests (Philippines) 19, 27, 30; Bell Act of 1946 and 157; change resistance in 40n6; duty-free American market for 166–167; Macapagal opposed by 42n22; planting at scale by 153
sugar landlords 202
sugar production 21
Summers, L. H. 45; *see also* Asiaphoria
supply-demand imbalances: in education *314*; in occupations *311*
Szirmai, A. 74

T-accounts 251, **259**
Tadem, T. E. 37, 42n21
Taft, W. H. 220
Taiwan: agriculture and development in 147; agricultural employment decline in 8, 35, 39, 72; big push industrialization programs in 134; decolonization of 12, 16, 22, 35, 39; economic success of 71, 74, 76, 154, 165, 200, 244, 300; Export-Oriented Industrialization in 39, 202; export structures (1962 and 2023) *71, 73*; farm consolidation and rice yield in 151; Gerschenkron's principle applied to 41n9, 76, 154, 156, 157; heavy industry encouraged by 139, 169; as hub of electronic and semiconductor production 5; industrialization pursued by 350; Industrial Technology Research Institute 155; land reform in 39, 147, 153; manufacturing exports and government policy/incentives for 10, 9, 175, 177, 351; MIPS and 169, 170; strategic industrial policy in 101; structural transformation and upgrading in 72; super-rapid growth in 42; Taiwan's Industrial Technology Research Institute 155; TP Act compared to similar legislation in 182–184 (*see also* TP Act); year the economy entered 5% or higher annual industrial growth, and annual growth rates (%) **163**
Takagi, Y. 30, 32–35, 38, 42n22
Tatak Pinoy Act (TP Act) (Republic Act 11981, 2024) 102, 179, 182–184, 200, 207
Tatak Pinoy Strategy (TPS) 183
tax reforms 62, 180, 350
tax revenues 29, 144, 159, 217, 255, 258, 262; government overdraft and 267n14, 267n15; SFBs and 270
taxes: household *254*
TDF *see* term deposit facility
technicians and associate professionals 85, 114, 319; associate professionals 85, 114, 319; description, skill level, and subgroups **113–120**; forecasts *141n2, 143, 144, 281, 284, 286–298*; technicians 85, 86, 114, 156, 176, 238, 240, 246, 248n5, 302–305, 309–331,
technocrats 36–39, 42n21, 42n24, 170; American-trained 202–203; Marcos-administration 203; obstacles facing 212n2; reformist 174; World Bank foreign development funds accessed by 203
technology adoption 210
temporal fragmentation (Philippines) 10, 13, 213–214; defining 213–214; solutions in the context of 226; weak and uninstitutionalized political parties and 218–221
temporal fragmentation (Thailand) 213
term deposit facility (TDF) 275–277, **277**, 279n5
Thailand: economy of 1–2; GDP growth *44*; GNP 1961 3, **22**; gross tertiary school enrollment rates *240*; growth rate 6, 7, 10, 25, 44, 48, 69, 77; industrialization pursued by 350; industrial production growth in **135**; labor productivity in *48*, **77**; as middle income country 127, 264, 301, 350; per capita income in 5, 22; share of manufacturing in GDP% in *80, 82,* 92, **93**, 168, 170,190, 193, 235, 290, 350; share of manufacturing in total employment% in *77*; spatial fragmentation in 140, 213, 214, 223–226; temporal fragmentation in 10, 13, 213, 218, 223–226; tourism in the Philippines competing with 69n15, 206, 256; years of schooling in 239, 240, 242
Thirlwall, A. P. 48
Thomas, R. 266n12
Torio, P. 70n23
tourism 8, 55, 69n15, 139, 178, 180, 196n2, 291
TP Act *see* Tatak Pinoy Act
Trabaho para sa Bayan Act (Republic, Act No. 119621) 229
Trade Act 27; Bell Act 27, 29, 32, 33

trainability 70n25, 237, 242, 243, 244, 246
transport & storage: description and subsectors **105–111**; forecasts *286–287, 290–291, 303–304, 306–307*; share in total employment *81*, *83*, 290, *290*
treasury xii, xxvi, 10, 13, 32, 144, 255, 256–257, 274
Truman, H. S. 29
turncoatism 219, 226
Twelfth Malaysia Plan 2021–2025: comparison with other development plans **135–137**
Tyce, M. 10
Tydings Act 1946 27; *see also* Philippine Rehabilitation Act
Tydings–McDuffie Act 1934 20

unemployment 29, 47, 48, 129, 142, 229, 232, 241, 265n6
UNICEF 315
United Nations Industrial Development Organization 198n21
United States 6, 9, 16, 19, 20, 22, 23, **25**, 26, 34, 37, 39, 40n4, 41n9, 103n1, **143**, 147, 148, 156, 163, 167, 169, 176, 198n16, 202, 211, 215, 219, 252, 260, 354n1; American 6, 16, 19, 20, 22, 26, 27, 34, 35, 37, 40n15, 166, 202, 215, 353; colonization 8, 16–19, 40n4, 157; independence 8, 16, 18, 19, 20, 22, 26, 27, 34, 37, 39, 147, 156, 162, 215, 219
Universal Access to Quality Tertiary Education Act, Republic Act No. 10931 (2017, August 3) (Phil.) 237
unpaid farm workers 229, 231
upgrading 9, 64, 72, 76, 100, 133, 139, 147, 166, 173, 174, 180, 195, 199–201, 239
urban-rural disparity 344
utilities 28, 78, 93, 142, 160, 166, 167, 198n21, 233, 285, 308; description and subsectors **105–111**; forecasts *286–287, 290–291, 323–329*

Verdoorn's law 54
Vernengo, Matías 252
Verspagen, B. 75
Vietnam 189; GDP growth rate *126,* 127, 285; gross tertiary school enrollment rates *240*; labor productivity in **77,** 78, 139, 280, 285, 286; lessons for the Philippines from 47; TP Act compared to similar legislation in 182–184 (*see also* TP Act); share of manufacturing in GDP% in *77*; share of manufacturing in total employment% in *82*
Vietnam Industrial Development Strategy 2025 Vision to 2035: comparison with other development plans **135–137**; overall development vision of, Philippines compared to 122, 138–141
VinFast e-car 211
vote-buying 213, 219–220, 224–226

Wage Rationalization Act, Republic Act No. 6727. (1989, June 9) (Phil.) 232
wages 2, 8, 10, 11, 13, 47, 55, 69n16, 72, 76, 80–88, 95, 101–103, 142, 147, 150, 156, 179, 196, 201, 204, 208, 228, 230–245, 247n3, 261, 268, 281, 290, 291–296, 305, 308, 312, 316, 347, 352, 353; cumulative distribution of *230*; nominal wage 142; real wage 84, 86, 290, 291
War Production Board (WPB) 42n17
wasting 244
weak state 13, 158, 200–202, 349
Werker, E. 10, 70n24; *see also* Khan–Pritchett–Sen–Werker framework
WGFE *see* within-group fixed effects (WGFE) estimator
wholesale & retail trade: description and subsectors **105–111**; forecasts *286–287, 290–291, 303–304, 306–307*; share in total employment *81*, *83*, 286, 290, *290*
Williamson, J. 21, 54, 162, 172
within-group fixed effects (WGFE) estimator 247n3
World Bank 3–5, 14n2, 34–38, 42n24, *44, 77*, 128, 143, 146, 166, 170, 188–194, 196n4, 202, 203, 241, 243, 280, 350; 2024 income thresholds for upper-middle-income category 8, 14n2, 127, 128, 280, 301, 332; data 3–5, *44, 77*, 128, 143, 188, 192, 198n21, 241; development assistance to the Philippines by 27; 'Doing Business' methodology 198n20; EDB indicators (*see* EDB); electricity database 188; IMF–World Bank policy prescriptions for developing countries 36; jobs projections by 334; MIPS program and 169, 170; tariff reductions supported by 166, 175
World Bank Group 5, 196n7; *East Asian Miracle* 146
World Bank World Development Indicators (WDI) 42n27, 198n22, 198n24
World Trade Organization (WTO) 151, 196n5, 205, 211, 212n3

years of schooling 239–240; France *239*, 242

Zimbabwe **25**; hyperinflation in the 2000s 269n24

For Product Safety Concerns and Information please contact our EU representative GPSR@taylorandfrancis.com Taylor & Francis Verlag GmbH, Kaufingerstraße 24, 80331 München, Germany